POMPEY

The F.A. Cup triumph of 1939

POMPEY

The History of Portsmouth Football Club

Mike Neasom, Mick Cooper & Doug Robinson

Published by Milestone Publications
62 Murray Road, Horndean,
Portsmouth, Hants. PO8 9JL

Design Brian Iles

Typeset by Grosvenor Press, Portsmouth

Printed and Bound in Great Britain by
R. J. Acford, Industrial Estate, Chichester, Sussex

British Library Cataloguing in Publication Data
Neasom, Mike
Pompey.
1. Portsmouth Football Club—History
I. Title   II. Cooper, Mick
III. Robinson, Doug
796.334'63'09422792   GV943.6.P/

ISBN 0-903852-50-0

Captions for Bookjacket Illustrations
from l. to r.
1939 Final, Pompey meet King George VI.
Albert Thorogood Buick.
Pompey with Div. 3 Shield 1924-25.
Flewin and team with Championship Trophy.
Alan Biley in action.
Jimmy Guthrie with FA Cup 1939.
Duggie 'Thunderboots' Reid.
Jimmy Dickinson, Portsmouth and England.
John Deacon and his Championship team
celebrate their return to Division 2.

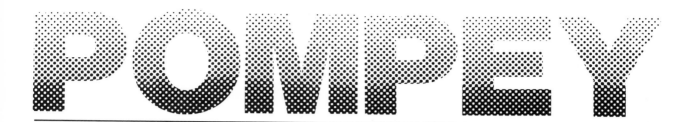

Contents

Acknowledgements

No book such as this is possible without the assistance of many people. To all of them my heart-felt thanks. To John Deacon, chairman of Portsmouth Football Club, and to club secretary Bill Davis for their assistance, to the General Manager of The News and Executive Editor for their backing and generosity in allowing the use of the paper's files and photographic records. To The News Librarian Maurice Hulbert for his willing co-operation and The News photographic department for their uncomplaining response to many demands.

Thanks are also owed to Ron Brown, whose research provided material for references to early pre-Pompey days. To the many people who willingly rummaged to find old photographs, among them Richard Owen, Ted Burridge, Barry 'Dinks' Thomas, Mr. and Mrs. Bryn Mills, Bob Moffatt, Len Worth and Mrs. Pat Lewsley. Thanks to 'Plum' of The Evening News for the right to reproduce his excellent cartoons and my old friend Ron Davies for his superb caricatures. Without the support of these and others, 'Pompey – the History of Portsmouth Football Club' would have been stillborn.

And finally and most importantly, my lasting thanks go to my long-suffering wife Gill. Without her support and encouragement at times when enthusiasm waned, there would have been no book; without her hard work in clean-typing my typical two-fingered journalist's first manuscript, type-setting would have been no fun.

Mike Neasom, June 1984

I, in my turn, also have many people to thank, firstly Stephen Cribb, a former Chairman of Pompey F.C., and a photographer by profession, he left us so many fine examples of his work, and thankfully many of his photographs were of the Pompey team.

Mr. Alan King and the staff of the Portsmouth Central Library, who "put up with me" on so many occasions as I waded through many old newspapers. The late Jimmy Dickinson M.B.E. for his help and encouragement, Tracy Hoile for her persistance in typing my almost unreadable notes. Leslie Bern, John Thorpe, Sue Saunders, David Barber of the Football Association, Frank Nobes, Roger Holmes, Robin Wyatt, and so many former Pompey players for providing information and assistance.

The help of all those above was so vital in the completion of this volume, regretably I was never good enough to play for Pompey so this book is my next best offering.

Mick Cooper, June 1984

I would like to thank the following people for their help: Bill Phipps, ex-Pompey player Derek Dimmer, Roger Holmes, Mr. Alan King and the staff of the Central Library for also putting up with me on numerous occasions, the late Jimmy Dickinson for his help, David Barber of the Football Association, and finally my wife Yvonne, another football widow, for putting up with me for the last four years while the researching has been going on.

Doug Robinson, June 1984

Photographs and illustrations on pages 2, 40, 46, 47, 50, 54-63, 65, 66, 67, 69, 79, 82, 83, 86, 87, 89, 90, 91, 93, 96, 97, 99, 100-113, 115-124 are by courtesy of 'The News', Portsmouth.

Photographs on pages 34, 68, 114 by courtesy of M. C. Photographic.

1. Military Roots

Why Pompey? That is possibly the greatest mystery in the story of Portsmouth Football Club. The origins of the club itself are firmly documented; more obscure though are the origins of a nickname which is perhaps the most instantly recognised in the English game. What is not disputed is that Pompey is Naval in origin – but about the origins of that nickname are numerous theories.

Some claim it lies in an 80-gun French warship Le Pompee captured in 1793 which later fought with distinction in the battle of Algeciras in 1801 and then became guardship of Portsmouth Harbour. Others maintain it was the product of a far from sober sailor's interruption of a talk by Agnes Weston, the naval temperance worker. He surfaced from a beery slumber during her lecture on the Roman Empire to hear that the general Pompey had been killed. 'Poor old Pompey' he is said to have shouted . . . . such are the roots of legend. But there is another more authenticated potential root in Naval folk-lore. In 1781 some Portsmouth-based English sailors scaled Pompey's Pillar near Alexandria and, 98 feet up above Egypt, toasted their ascent in punch. Their feat earned them the Fleet's tribute as 'The Pompey Boys'. . . . What-ever the truth, there is no doubt that Portsmouth Football Club is the Royal Navy's Club. Fratton Park's terraces have been a magnet for countless off duty sailors for 80 years and more and the memories of hours spent there have gone with them around the world and Pompey's successes or failures still strike chords in almost every corner of the globe.

Yet curiously the Service root on which Portsmouth Football Club has grown is military rather than Naval. For it was the Army, in the guise of the Royal Artillery which first exploded interest in soccer and ultimately led to the meeting on April 5, 1898 at which the decision to establish a professional club in the City was taken. Until then Portsmouth had lagged behind other areas in Hampshire in adopting the still infant game. While clubs had been established in Southampton, Bournemouth,

Ringwood, Fordingbridge and Basingstoke in the '70's, Portsea Island had none.

In Portsmouth soccer was a haphazard affair until the Cambridge Graduate son of a local Justice of the Peace took a hand. Norman Pares, one of four sons of the JP, had caught the football 'bug' while at Eton and it stayed with him. On his vacations from Cambridge, he organised matches; when he returned to Portsmouth to become a curate at St. Jude's and master at Portsmouth Grammar School, his enthusiasm found a ready response. By the mid-1880's, the seeds he had sown began to grow. Clubs began to spring up – they included the Portsmouth Football Association Club, whose regular members included a certain Dr. Arthur Conan Doyle, also the Hilsea Ramblers, Havant, Southsea Rivals and the Sunflowers. The inaugural Portsmouth Cup competition in 1887, saw the Portsmouth Club beat the powerful Woolston Works side 1-0, and they successfully defended their trophy the following year against Portsmouth Grammar School.

The game snowballed. Clubs were launched throughout the area and in 1890 the Portsmouth District Football Association was formed. But despite that, the true strength of the game locally lay in the many Service establishments. Naval pioneers were HMS Excellent, thanks largely to the 'missionary' zeal of a Petty Officer George Wroe, who took a Football with him where-ever he served. But, without the handicap of 'sea-time', the Army inevitably had the edge on opportunity and every establishment had its team. Two though dominated. At Fareham, the 15th Company Royal Artillery; in Portsmouth, the Depot R.A. Initially rivalry was intense. But in 1894 they amalgamated and the springboard was built which was to ultimately result in Pompey's formation four years later.

That military marriage created The Royal Artillery, a club which was to sweep all before it locally for five spectacular years – a shooting star of success which ultimately met a cruel, and from this distance, almost trivial

Portsmouth 1891 (which one is Conan Doyle?)

end. Under the leadership of Sgt. Major Windrum and Sgt. R. Bonney, the Royal Artillery won the Army Cup in 1895 and 1897, the Hampshire Cup in 1896 and the Portsmouth Cup in 1897. But it was in the English Amateur Cup in 1896 that they became nationally known. They reached the final where they eventually lost by the only goal to Bishop Auckland. Three years later, they seemed about to repeat their success – and it was to undo them. Favourites to beat Harwich and Parkstone, they instead found themselves drummed out of the competition in disgrace for breaching the strict rules relating to amateurism. Their approach to the 1899 final was too professional. They withdrew to the East Coast for seven days special preparation. Inevitably there were expenses – and those were their downfall. The R.A. were judged to have breached the amateur regulations and were disqualified. Their appeal was heard in Birmingham, but was in vain. Their cause was undone by these items among their East Coast expenses:- carriages £6.6s; wines £2.19s; billiards £2.4s; cigars £1.11s.3d. It was too much for the Emergency Committee of the Football Association; this was the lifestyle of professionals. So the career of the R.A. was over and although the suspensions were later rescinded, their era was done.

But the seeds they had scattered locally were germinating. The R.A. had not only rippled the waters of Cup football, they had also entered the Southern League in 1897-8, winning the Second Division with an impressive 19 victories in 22 matches and a 75-22 goal aggregate. Promotion to Division 1 saw them out of their depth and in 1898-9 they won only four of their 24 matches. They had, though, whetted the appetites of the people of Portsmouth for something more than local football. At the same time, events along the Solent were eyed with some envy. Southampton St. Mary's had been formed in 1885 and nine years later they had turned professional – a gamble which had paid attractive dividends.

It was a smaller town than Portsmouth, yet the public had responded to the change in status. In the year before the change, Southampton's revenue had been £800; in 1897 it had risen to £3,300 – and by April 1898 when a series of public meetings and considerable debate ended in the decision to form a professional club in Portsmouth, it was being estimated that Saints' income for the year would top £6,000.

Royal Artillery (Portsmouth) Football Team 1894–5   *Winners of Army Cup 1894–5*

Sergt. BONNEY (Secretary)   Lieut. HAYNES (Treasurer)   Regt. S·Major WINDRUM (Trainer)

Gunner REILLY (Goal)   Gunner HOGG (Centre Half)   Gunner PATTERSON (Left Half)   Gunner KINMAN (Right Half)

Sergt. WILLIAMS (Outside Right)   Gunner MAXWELL (Inside Right)   Bombardier ALLEN (Inside left)   Gunner JARDINE (Outside left)

Bombardier HARMS (Right Back)   Bombardier HANNA (Captain-Centre)   Gunner PHILLIPS (Left Back)

So on April 5, six businessmen and sportsmen met at 12, High Street, Portsmouth, formed themselves into a syndicate and decided to buy almost five acres of agricultural land close to Goldsmith Avenue for £4,950. The six who took that momentous decision were: John Brickwood, later Sir John, head of Brickwood's Brewery, who became the club's first chairman. Alfred H. Bone, an architect and surveyor, whose professional qualities, were to prove invaluable to the initial development of Fratton Park. John Wyatt Peters, a local wine importer. William Wiggington, a successful Government contractor. George Lewin Oliver, founder of one of Portsmouth's best known private schools. The sixth man at the meeting was solicitor John Edward Pink, who was initially company solicitor and later joined the Board.

Events moved quickly from that first meeting. In a matter of weeks, the Football Association's representative Mr. W. Pickford joined Mr. Oliver to gaze over a five-barred gate to see cows grazing on the five acres of land which the company had bought – an improbable prospect now for Fratton Park. The ground was quickly levelled, drained and turfed; a 100 foot stand with seven rows of seats was constructed on the South side of the ground and to the north another 240 foot long stand and terracing was built. The Founding Fathers were thinking big; and they thought big again when they looked for the man to turn their dream into on-field reality. Frank J. Brettell was one of the most respected men in football. He had started as secretary-player with St. Domingo Club in Liverpool, helping to create the organization which became Everton. He then transferred to Liverpool and played a major part in their development, then moved to become secretary of Bolton Wanderers and finally in 1897 came south to manage Tottenham Hotspur . . . . 22 years of rich experience which was now lured to the new stadium of Fratton Park.

Pompey had acquired a manager respected universally for his player-judgement and a man with a simple but effective philosophy – give the public good players and value for money. He took local advice about his first recruit – Matt Reilly, the Royal Artillery's 25 year-old

Irish goalkeeper, who was already established as a favourite with the Portsmouth public. Brettell also signed Harry Turner, one of the R.A.'s full backs, but generally he exploited his Northern contacts and a string of men from Lancashire made the trip to the South Coast. Tom Wilkie (Hearts and Liverpool), wing-half Bob Blyth and centre-forward Alex Brown were drawn away from Preston North End, Everton yielded Edward Turner, Harold Clarke and Harold Stringfellow and Liverpool, Tommy Cleghorn, Bob Marshall and Danny Cunliffe.

So Brettell built his team from scratch, and while he did so his directors worked to find a competition for it to play in. They proved as persuasive with the Southern League as their manager had with his players – Pompey gained admission to Division I for the 1899-1900 season without a proving run in Division II. The League committee's faith was well founded; Pompey were to spend 16 seasons with them. On their debut they finished second to Brettell's old employers from White Hart Lane, and to the delight of everyone six points better off than Southampton. They were rarely to be out of the top group during their membership although they once knew the bitter taste of relegation.

The Original Record of the Formation of the PORTSMOUTH FOOTBALL CLUB
5TH APRIL 1898.

The first minutes of the first meeting

2. Southern League Days

The league they had entered had a quality look about it - Spurs, Southampton, Bristol City and Rovers, Brighton, QPR, Reading, Swindon, Millwall, plus clubs like Thames Ironworks, Sheppey, Chatham and New Brompton. Eventually 15 months after that April meeting had set the ball rolling, Pompey took the field for their first League match at Chatham on September 2, 1899, where 24-year-old winger Harold 'Nobby' Clarke made history by scoring the goal which earned their first-day victory. The team was: Reilly, Harold Turner, Wilkie, Blyth, Stringfellow, Cleghorn, Marshall, Cunliffe, Alex Brown, Bill Smith, Clarke. They wore salmon pink shirts with maroon collars and cuffs and were quickly dubbed 'The Shrimps'. Three days later Fratton Park was 'christened' by a friendly against Southampton which was won by goals from Cunliffe and Clarke in front of a gate who paid £125. The following Saturday Reading were the visitors for the first home League match, again Clarke and Cunliffe scored and this time receipts totalled the princely sum of £263.

So things had started well and were to continue so. In the end Pompey won 20 of the 28 matches to finish 2nd. three points behind Spurs. In addition they also competed in the Southern District Combination, winning eight and drawing two of their 16 matches, and proved equally powerful in their first involvement in the English Cup. Their run was eventually ended by Blackburn Rovers in a second replay at Aston Villa – the teams had drawn 0-0 at Blackburn and 1-1 at Fratton. Blackburn, who had already won the Cup five times, triumphed 5-0 . . . . a score some put down to Reilly's shock at being capped for the first time against England. The telegram informing him of his selection arrived shortly before the kick off! Disappointment though was short-lived; a first season which ended with a record of 42 wins in 63 competitive matches and a 140-70 goal aggregate could only be satisfactory. Less satisfactory though was the public response to the venture. A total of almost 161,000 watched the home matches, but after visiting clubs had

been paid their share, gate receipts totalled £4,596, and the operating loss was £875.

By the time the next season arrived there had been two major changes at the Park. Sandy Brown, who had scored 29 of those first season goals, had moved to Spurs where he was to help them win the English Cup in 1900-01 and Brettell had immediately replaced him with QPR's highly rated Frank Bedingfield. At the annual meeting during the summer, the directors were able to report that Fratton Park had been completed at a cost of £6,538, with the stands, dressing rooms, committee room and turnstiles costing another £9,372. They also reported that players' wages were to be £4 a week without bonuses.

Pompey's second season was to be one of no great excitement – on the field at least. Off it, January 27 produced a storm which ripped off the roof of the South stand, damage which cost the club £120 it could ill afford. The up-shot of the lack of success was a drop in attendance to 126,000 and a rise in overall loss to £1,530. Bedingfield repaid Brettell's judgement by top scoring with 30 goals in what, tragically, was to prove his only full season.

The summer of 1901 saw the first managerial change at Fratton Park. Frank Brettell moved to Plymouth Argyle to begin the job of starting another club off towards ultimate membership of the Football League. The directors looked no further than Bob Blyth for his replacement and the change was marked by the club's first major success. Brettell had bequeathed his successor a powerful playing staff with Bedingfield very much one of its stars.

Tragically his full potential was never to be realised. By early February Bedingfield had scored another 25 goals to help Pompey into a strong position in the League and into the second round of the English Cup at Reading. That match, on February 8, was to prove his final triumph. He had been forced to miss the week's pre-match training at Singleton because of a heavy cold

PORTSMOUTH F.C.
1899 – 1900

Presented to Pompey F.C. + Players by 'Old Supporter'

	Turner		Reilly		Wilkie	
Marshall	Blyth		Stringfellow		Cleghorn	Clark
	Cunliffe		Brown		Smith	

D. Cunliffe

S. Smith

E. McDonald

W. Lee

G. Harris

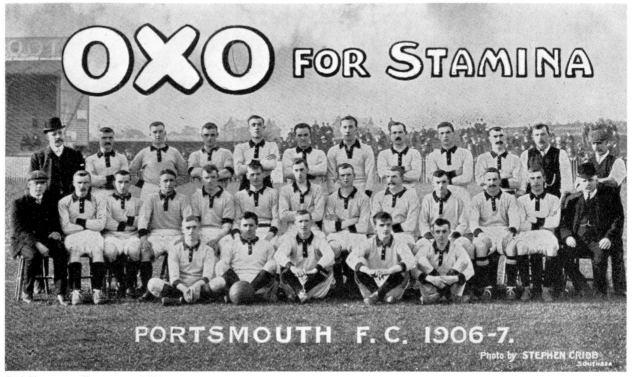

Did Pompey really train on OXO?

but played and scored the only goal after a run from the halfway line. After the match, celebrations were cut short as Bedingfield collapsed in the dressing room, consumption was diagnosed and, although a public subscription raised the money to send him to the sun of South Africa, it was too late to avert a premature death in November 1904.

One of Blyth's first acts as manager had been to recruit England international centre-half Arthur Chadwick from Southampton and he had also brought in another international, Steve Smith from Aston Villa. Smith, whose brother Billy had been one of Brettell's first signings, gave the side extra pace on the wing, and this reinforced side stormed to the Southern League championship, dropping only 13 points in 30 matches. They won 20 and finished with 69-32 goal aggregate. On top of that they also won the Western League for the third time, a feat marked by the presentation of a special banner. Inevitably this success was reflected at the turnstiles; total attendances rose to 224,304 and for the first time a season ended in profit – £1,939.

Blyth set about strengthening his side for the defence of the title. He signed former England international inside forward Fred Wheldon, giving Pompey the first of several footballing cricketers. Wheldon in fact was unable to join his new team mates until September when he had completed his duties as a batsman with Worcestershire. When he was available he found himself back with Steve Smith, a partnership which had been highly successful at Aston Villa, where Wheldon had been part of the League and Cup winning side of 1896-7. Blyth had also brought Sandy Brown back from Spurs to replace Bedingfield, and Brown once more proved his effectiveness by scoring 32 goals. But it was not enough to defend the title and in the end Pompey finished third.

The season also saw the end of their proud record of Fratton Park invincibility – on October 18, 1902, Northampton became the first side to visit Pompey and win. It was a match memorable for the goalkeeping of Northampton's Fred Cook – a performance which had much to do with Pompey signing him three years later. A notable addition to Pompey's playing staff this season was the legendary C. B. Fry, but he was to play only three matches – the third in the first round of the Cup ended his career. Playing at right back, Fry was badly injured early in the match and Pompey were eventually thrashed 5-0. This was one of the most powerful Pompey playing squads ever – during the season nine internationals played for the club. One was Fry, who had made one appearance for England, the others were Matt Reilly (Ireland), Arthur Chadwick (England), Robert Marshall (Scotland), 'Sandy' Brown (Scotland), Steven Smith (England), Albert Houlker (England), Daniel Cunliffe (England), and Fred Wheldon (England).

Despite the failure to defend their championship, it had been a good season financially, with attendances rising to a total of 260,000, and the directors happy to declare a five per cent dividend to shareholders after a profit of £2,045. Unhappily, it was to be followed by a summer of controversy, with an F.A. commission set up to investigate the transfer of three players – S. Raybould, W. Goldie and J. Glover from Liverpool. The Commission found against Pompey. Player-manager Blyth was suspended until New Year's Day without wages, Harry Stringfellow, who had been involved in the negotiations, was suspended for three months, and the club fined £100. The season which followed was also anything but happy with it hitting a low spot on January 30th 1904 at Swindon. The match was interrupted by crowd trouble and Matt Reilly, incensed by being bombarded with clinker by the Swindon supporters, took matters into his Irish hands and hit one of them – an incident which earned him a two week suspension.

Still F.A. Cup success continued to elude the club. Drawn at home to Derby County in the first round, Pompey once more went into 'retreat' for the week at Singleton but were eventually beaten 5-2 by their First Division visitors. In the end though there was slight local interest for Portsmouth folk when the final was played at Crystal Palace – Robert Struthers, one of Pompey's earliest signings, was left back in the Bolton side beaten 1-0 by Manchester City.

The comparative lack of success – fourth in both Southern and Western Leagues – was reflected financially with the profit for the season down to £593. Before the 1904-5 season began, Blyth's term as manager officially ended, and Richard Bonney relinquished his seat on the Board to take charge of playing matters. There were also major departures from the dressing room. In particular, Matt Reilly moved on, joining Dundee, while Wheldon moved to Worcester City and Chadwick to Northampton.

The season which followed was not a happy one – except that it at last produced some of the Cup excitement the public had craved. Initially there was frustration when in the final qualifying round, Pompey were drawn away to Chesterfield. But for a £400 'consideration' the Second Division club agreed to play the match at Fratton Park. It ended in a draw; the replay was also at Fratton and Pompey won 2-0. That earned them a meeting with Birmingham side Small Heath who were well placed in the First Division and Pompey created a major shock by winning 2-0 away from home. The reward was another draw against First Division opposition – The Wednesday – and an end to the dream of a visit to Crystal Palace with a 2-1 defeat, the winning goal coming in the last minute. All this offset the disappointments of the League season – seventh in the Southern League and fourth in the Western. And it helped the club show a useful profit of £1,032.

During the summer of 1905 Fratton Park had something of a facelift. The enclosures were terraced and a pavilion built at the Frogmore Road entrance to the ground, topped by a clock tower, the gift of Sir John Brickwood. Manager Bonney worked hard to strengthen his staff; goalkeeper Cook who had played such a key part in Northampton ending Pompey's unbeaten home record, was brought in from West Brom-

Portsmouth Football Club, 1902-3.

P. G. Whitmy W. Wigginton B. Murtough G. L. Oliver

J. Brickwood A. E. Houlket J. Hodge D. Gair E. Turner C. Burgess H. Turner M. Reilly G. Harris A. Brown D. Halliday G. F. Wheldon R. Bonney A. Chadwick

R. G. Marshall A. McDonald S. Smith D. Cunliffe R. Blyth H. Stringfellow T. Corrin W. Smith T. Wilkie J. R. Clayton

STEPHEN CRIBB,   SOUTHSEA.

Champions Southern and Western Leagues and Portsmouth Cup, 1902-3.

wich Albion, full back George Molyneux from Southampton and inside forward John 'Sailor' Hunter from Liverpool. But it was a lean season, and the club slipped back into loss – £263. In January they feared they had lost goalkeeper George Harris who was playing in place of Cook against Q.P.R. Making a brave save, Harris was kicked over the eye, and then crashed into a post. He was carried to the dressing room where at one stage the doctor feared he might die, but he made a dramatic recovery and by the end of the match was up and about.

Bonney once again spent a busy summer reinforcing his team, making a major signing when he persuaded

Saints to allow defender Jack Warner to move after four successful seasons at the Dell. He also brought in Scottish full back Jimmy Thomson, who was to form a highly effective partnership with fellow Scot Roderick Walker. Irish international winger Harry Buckle was also signed from Sunderland. It made for a better season, eventually finishing second in the Southern League – but it was memorable for the Cup.

The first round saw them at home to Manchester United, already one of the country's major clubs. It was a prospect which caught the imagination of the Public; 24,329 were crammed into Fratton Park, paying the first four figure gate in the club's history – £1,101.10s. – to see a 2-2 draw. The replay saw Pompey gain a famous 2-1 success. But still there was to be no Crystal Palace glory; the second round ended in a single goal defeat at Barnsley. The return of playing success brought Pompey back into profit with the year ending £287 to the good. They also attracted attention from overseas and in May 1907 made a highly successful tour of Germany and Austria. In the first match against Leipzig, centre forward Bill Kirby, who had scored one of the goals which beat Manchester United, scored four in a 6-1 success, and in the third – another 6-1 triumph this time against Dresden – new signing Randall scored a hat trick. But the party had left for the Continent saddened by the death from typhoid of club secretary Percy Whitney who had recorded the minutes of that inaugural meeting back in 1898.

Pompey were now heading for a spell of comparative mediocrity, and increasing financial difficulties, as gates fell and losses mounted. Pompey were still playing in their Salmon Pink, but in 1909 changed to white shirts with dark blue shorts. Kirby, who had signed from Swindon in 1905, was granted a benefit in October 1910 after scoring his 100th goal for the club . . . . the match eventually produced £200 for the centre-forward. The first transfer fees were also being reported – Pompey had sold Joe Dix to Clapton Orient for £100, Fred Clipstone to Northampton for £150 and Bill Beaumont to Southampton for £75. One of the few bright spots for Pompey's supporters at this stage was the emergence of Arthur Egerton Knight. An amateur from Godalming he was to become a legendary character with the club in his 13 years on their books. Another of their cricketing footballers – he spent ten years on Hampshire's staff – Knight played many times for the England amateur international side and made his sole appearance for the full England side against Northern Ireland in October 1919, although playing in a 'Victory' match against Wales the same month. But Knight was in a team and a club approaching its first major crisis after ten years when fate had smiled with comparative kindness on the new venture.

Arthur Egerton Knight, Pompey's forgotten international

OGDEN'S CIGARETTES.

PORTSMOUTH.

GALLAHER'S CIGARETTES.

J. WARNER,
PORTSMOUTH, 1909-10.

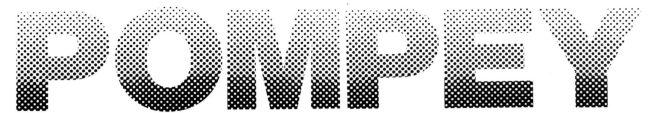

3. Crisis Time

The financial year 1909-10 had seen the loss escalate to £1,557 and the following season the crisis broke. On the field little went right; Pompey managed only eight wins - none after the turn of the year – and they finished the season bottom and relegated. Inevitably, difficulties on the field mirrored those off it. Manager Bonney resigned and in May was replaced by Robert Brown from Sheffield Wednesday. But it was the financial crisis which was the major concern. Gate receipts had tumbled to a mere £4,332 and the club's overall debts had reached £4,215. So in May, presaging events which were to be repeated more than 50 years later, the club appealed to the public for money to see it through its difficult period. Within less than a week £247.7s.6d. had been raised, including £5 from former manager Bob Blyth who had been re-instated as an amateur.

But the inspiration at this difficult time was founder director Mr. George Lewin Oliver who told a stormy shareholders meeting that he would carry on the club single handed if necessary. It helped turn the tide; in mid summer there was sufficient confidence in their future for Portsmouth to be one of the clubs to back an unsuccessful move to form a Third Division of the Football League. So Pompey had to face the prospect of one season at least in the Second Division of the Southern League, which in those days was little short of being the Welsh League. Their new itineraries included jaunts to places such as Merthyr Tydfil, Cardiff, Treharris, Aberdare, Ton Pentre, Pontypridd and Mardy. Difficult journeys and matches which were unlikely to prove too attractive financially – a key matter for a club in Pompey's predicament. Manager Brown had completely re-structured his playing staff to meet the challenge of all those trips along the branch lines of the railway system in South Wales.

Jack Warner was still at Fratton as team captain, but Brown brought in two men who had served him well at Sheffield Wednesday – Frank Stringfellow and Michael Dowling to make up the new right side of his attack. He also added a strong Scottish contingent – winger Duncan from Cambuslang, goalkeeper Dan Sanderson from Albion Rovers, and half-backs Sandy Wardrop, (Airdrie and Middlesborough), 'Jemmy' Menzies (Albion Rovers) and Robert Reid. But Brown also pulled off a master-stroke in planning Pompey's season. Not relishing too many trips to the Valley grounds of South Wales with their spartan and often primitive facilities of the depth of winter, he arranged the bulk of their away matches for the first half of the season.

But it was in January that he achieved his greatest coup with the aid of a Northern scout. Pompey were handily placed but in need of extra scoring power if they were to seriously challenge for promotion. The scout answered the manager's demand for a centre-forward with a former Barnsley player named Harry Taylor. He was to prove a sensation; he made his debut in mid February against Cardiff and from then until the end of the season scored in every match. Against Chesham he scored six and by the time Pompey had clinched second place behind Merthyr with 41 points from their 26 matches – 19 wins and three draws – Taylor had scored 17 of their 73 goals. But though there was success on the playing field, relegation had inevitably had its financial effect. Gate receipts at £4,709 little more than covered running expenses – and the £2,716 wage bill still had to be met.

By May things had reached crisis point. The club's liabilities now totalled in the region of £10,000 and Pompey's fate was the subject of constant debate – the possibilities including an end of professional soccer in the City. So on May 8, 1912, Mr. Oliver presided over another shareholders' meeting. The alternatives, he told them, were for the original Company to be wound up and re-constituted on more business-like lines, or for some compulsory scheme to be introduced. Fears were expressed at the meeting that failure to take the re-construction course would lead to Fratton Park falling into the hands of property speculators . . . . an ultimately groundless alarm which was to have its echoes some 60

PORTSMOUTH FOOTBALL CLUB===Season, 1910=11.
OFFICIALS & PLAYERS.

-STEPHEN CRIBB]   R. W. Turner   F. Sparrow   F. Count   T. Cope   J. Cameron   H. V. Ellery   G. Wiggins   [SOUTHSEA
A. Hall   J. Jacobs   F. Cook   W. Kirby   J. Shufflebotham   J. Thompson   A. Turner   E. Long
H. Wood,   C. F. Preston,   Rev. E. Bruce Cornford   R. Blyth, Esq.   J. Poole, Esq   W. Wigginton, Esq. B. Murtough, Esq., T.C. H. W. Hulme, Esq.   J. H. Slater, Esq.   D. Halliday,
Trainer.   Secretary.   Manager Reserves.
A. Buick   E. McMahon   W. Yates, Vice-Capt.   J. Warner, Capt.   T. Worthington   A. E. Knight   R. Noble   J. Trice, Asst. Trainer

S. CRIBB]   **PORTSMOUTH FOOTBALL CLUB.   Season, 1911=12.**   [PHOTO

R. Croft   F. Langford   J. Hogg   V. Fisher   D. Sanderson   J. W. Baker   W. Parker   H. Salter
G. F. Preston,   J. Poole, Esq.   R. Blyth, Esq.   H. W. Hume, Esq.   Rev. E. Bruce Cornford   B. Murtough, Esq., J.P.   J. H. Slater, Esq.   W. A. Halliday   A. Farlam
(Fin. Sec.)   (Directors)   (A Team Manager) (B Team Manager)
J. D. Cooper (Trainer)   A. J. Knight   J. Menzies   M. Dowling   F. Stringfellow   J. Warner (Capt.)   J. Hunt   J. L. Jones   A. E. Knight   R. Brown (Sec.-Manager)
J. Jacobs   J. Cullen   W. J. Probert   A. Wardrope (Vice-Capt.)   A. Duncan   R. Reid

years on . . . . In the end shareholders backed re-constitution and Portsmouth Football Company Limited was eventually formed on July 27.

The change in status also brought another change in club colours – when Jack Warner led them out for their first match back in the First Division of the Southern League, Pompey were wearing royal blue shirts with white shorts. It was a team defensively re-inforced by the signing of centre-half Jack Harwood from Southend with a new wing-half in Scotsman Jimmy Walls. Overall the return was satisfactory with Pompey ultimately finishing in 11th place with the major disappointment their first round F.A. Cup exit against Brighton at Fratton Park. Elsewhere some indication of the way the game was moving came when Burnley paid £1,000 for Motherwell winger Jimmy Bellamy . . . a player Pompey had released after the 1907 season.

The one constant factor about the Fratton Park team remained Arthur Knight. Now a fixture in the England amateur team, Knight was also selected for the England party at the Stockholm Olympics in 1912. His outstanding contribution to Pompey's performances over the years was marked in November, 1912, when he was presented with a silver mounted walking stick at a dinner at the Wiltshire Lamb. Not so lucky was Harry Taylor who had made that sensational entry into Pompey's affairs to power them out of their Welsh torment. Before the 1913-14 season started he returned home to the North because of failing health. His replacement was a 22 year-old from Middlesbrough, Billy James, who cost Pompey an undisclosed 'record fee'. He repaid this by

scoring 22 goals in a season played out against the rising tide of rumours of war. Before the season ended, full-back Charlie Dexter had made his own little bit of Pompey history – he became the second player to be sent off playing for the club. The first was also a full-back, Roderick Walker in 1905 against Bristol Rovers at Fratton. Dexter got his marching orders against Northampton and was eventually suspended for seven days. Pompey also collected one of their biggest transfer fees so far – £250 for reserve goalkeeper Bill Bradley when he joined Newcastle.

Despite the outbreak of war in August 1914, there was a full Southern League programme in 14-15, with Pompey eventually finishing seventh in the table. But it was a time of uncertainty with rapid turn-over in playing staff as more and more men volunteered for the armed forces. Arthur Knight, in fact, missed the start of the season because of his duties with the 6th Hampshire Territorials. It was a costly season, too, with Pompey finishing with a loss of £865 and an overall deficit of £1,474. After that, league soccer was suspended for the duration of hostilities although like most clubs Pompey continued to play friendlies, providing relaxation for servicemen home on leave. By this time Fratton Park was a well appointed stadium which had seen 27,825 crowd in for a Cup match against Sheffield Wednesday and 20,447 for a derby Southern League match against Southampton. The South Stand could seat 1,028 – but in mid 1916 was again in need of major repairs after a whirlwind, for the second time, ripped off the roof. Predictably life was an uncertain affair; teams often arrived for matches short

PORTSMOUTH F.C. 1912-13.   S. CRIBB. S'SEA

of players and in 1917, London clubs suddenly vetoed travelling to either Portsmouth or Southampton. The war also produced one unique entry into the record of Fratton Park – baseball. On June 6, 1918 the United States Army beat the Canadians 4-3 in front of a bemused Portsmouth audience . . . . the beneficiaries were the British Red Cross.

It was to be another year before normality returned. Season 1918-19 was another when clubs found it hard to produce teams and what friendly matches there were generally attracted few people. One match in which Pompey were involved, however, proved anything but friendly. In March 1919 they met Harland and Wolfe at the Dell and after a stormy contest, the final whistle was greeted by a fierce outbreak of fighting between spectators with the referee chased to the safety of the dressing room by an angry crowd. A month later Pompey provided four players – William Probert, George Arnold, James Hogg and Frank Stringfellow – for the Provincial Southern League Clubs against the London Southern League Clubs. The match was played at Fratton Park, drawing a crowd of 8,000, to see the Provincials win 3-0.

So in August 1919 football picked up the threads which the Kaiser had severed five years earlier. Pompey were in the First Division of the Southern League, and a doubly significant season began. It was significant because it was to bring their second championship; and significant because it was to be their last before election to the new Third Division for which they had been such long-standing advocates. Pompey were to make the running all season, but in the end they took the title only on goal average. With only two matches left, they were three points ahead of Watford and their supporters were ready to celebrate. Pompey's last two matches were away but a draw at Millwall while Watford were beating Reading 2-1 seemed to have wrapped up the trophy's destination. Pompey's final fixture was across the River Severn, a journey they had never really enjoyed. Newport were the opposition and not expected to provide too much of an obstacle to Pompey gaining the point which would give them the undisputed championship. But chicken-counting proved fatal; in the end in front of 12,000 people, Pompey were beaten 1-0 – and at the same time Watford beat Saints 3-0. So both finished with 58 points from 42 matches but the trophy finished up in Pompey's clubroom on the strength of a vastly superior goal average. They scored 73 goals and conceded 27 while Watford's tally was 69-42.

The championship sweetened things for supporters after one of the bitterest disappointments in the Cup dream. Drawn away to First Division Bradford City, Pompey had outplayed their hosts on a waterlogged pitch and goals by Stringfellow and Turner in a minute gave them the lead at half time. But in the second half with conditions worsening, Bradford scored a disputed equaliser and the referee, unable to find the now submerged centre spot to resume the match, abandoned it. The prize at stake the following Saturday was a home tie against Sheffield United and this time Bradford won 2-0.

While the first match was being played, Fratton Park was the stage for another first round match of epic proportions – Hampshire League Thornycroft holding Burnley, who were to finish runners up in the First Division, to a goal-less draw! Burnley won the replay 5-0. Two players appeared in all Pompey's 44 matches that season – Stringfellow who was top scorer with 21 goals and long-serving defender Probert – and at the celebration dinner each received cheques for £400 to mark their achievements. The success of the side and the resurgence of interest in the game after the bleak days of war, was marked at the turnstiles for some 420,000 watched matches at Fratton with a top attendance of 24,606 for the match against Cardiff.

The final throes of the championship battle were fought out against an unhappy domestic background with chairman Mr. George Lewin Oliver and manager Robert Brown resigning after a difference over future policy. Mr. Oliver remained on the board and was to give the club he had helped to form another 14 years invaluable service. But Brown left, and after a spell acting as adviser to Gillingham, returned to Sheffield Wednesday. The new chairman was the Rev. E. Bruce Cornford who had been on the board for more than ten years; the new manager was John McCartney who moved south from Scotland in May. He was a man with vast experience – he had managed Heart of Midlothian for ten years, Barnsley (four) and St. Mirren Paisley (six). As a player he had captained Newton Heath, who were the forerunners of Manchester United, Glasgow Rangers and Barnsley. Throughout the season pressure had been growing for the introduction of the long debated Third Division and this time it paid off. Pompey's new chairman, an eloquent speaker, was often the Southern League's main advocate and produced a particularly persuasive performance at what was to prove the decisive conference.

The Rev. Edward Bruce Cornford
Director and Chairman 1909-1927

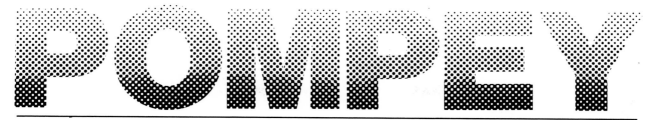

4. Football League at Last

So the Third Division of the Football League came into being and the Southern League's days as a first class competition were over. The new section was southern dominated – Northampton was its most northerly outpost. New manager McCartney inherited the team which had won the championship – and some problems. It took him time to smooth out difficulties over bonus payments with some of the more senior players.

But those who expected Pompey to pick up where they had left off the previous season were disappointed. That first season in Football League saw them finish an unflattering 12th with 39 points. The title went to Crystal Palace who had ended their Southern League career in third place behind Pompey and Watford. The season had its minor controversy when in a match against Southend in November, Pompey's right-half – Ernie Thompson was sent off, then recalled after players of both sides appealed to the referee. In the end both clubs were cautioned by the League over the incident. Thompson, the central figure in this, was to leave Pompey at the end of the season. He rejoined manager Brown at Sheffield Wednesday and received the entire transfer fee in lieu of the benefit he was due. The change of competition did nothing to change Pompey's F.A. Cup luck and they went out in the first round again, this time beaten 3-0 at South Shields, then a moderately successful Second Division side.

So manager McCartney decided to re-shape his playing resources. Money was not available to allow him to compete in the market where transfer fees were beginning to escalate. But he operated shrewdly, exploiting his Scottish contacts and bringing in young local players as well. One of those was centre-forward Percy Cherrett from Bournemouth who was to prove a particularly shrewd signing, scoring 21 goals in his first full season, which had not started too well for him for he was still in the Army and was unable to get leave for some of the season's early matches.

McCartney gradually developed what was to become universally known as the 'Pompey Style' – solid team work as opposed to brilliant individualism. At one stage it looked like paying immediate dividends with Pompey looking capable of achieving promotion. But in the end they faltered although their final placing – third – was a marked improvement. The title eventually went to neighbours Southampton on goal average from Plymouth. Again the first round of the Cup proved an insurmountable hurdle – Stringfellow's goal earned a replay with Luton but although he scored again at Luton, Pompey went out 2-1. Stringfellow, who at 5ft 5in was one of the smallest players ever to be a regular in Pompey's side, finished the season with 14 goals – and then moved to Heart of Midlothian, now managed by John McCartney's son Willie.

This was also to be the final season when the legendary amateur Arthur Knight was a regular after more than a decade of loyal service and Probert and Shirley Abbott became the first choice full backs. Pompey also lost their dependable goalkeeper Ned Robson. Signed from Watford after the war, Robson suffered a serious hand injury in a match at Southampton on March 25 1922 and was not to play for them again – in the summer he joined Sunderland for £150. Abbott was the hero that day; for 75 minutes in goal he took everything the eventual champions could fire at him to earn Pompey a goalless draw.

So Pompey prepared for their third season as a Football League club with manager McCartney sending the following epistle to his players in mid-July. 'Kindly take notice that training commences on Thursday, 3rd August, at 10 a.m. The Directors desire, in view of the strenuous work before you, that prompt and ready compliance with the requirements of this letter will be given. I have to convey to you the heartiest good wishes of the Board that a large measure of success may be yours. Triumphs are bound to follow diligent work at training and whole-hearted effort on the field.'

Unfortunately the homily did not, apparently, find responsive readers. Hopes that Pompey might be able to build on the promise of the previous season proved false. In the end they were to finish sixth with 46 points and again they were to fall at the first hurdle in the Cup. This time their opponents were Leeds United from the Second Division – and Pompey prepared with a week's training at Grayshott. The match at Fratton ended in a goal-less draw and they lost the replay 3-1 with their goal scored by winger Angus Meikle, who had moved from Hearts as Stringfellow had gone North. The season was notable largely for the creation of a new club scoring record. Alf Strange, a powerfully built youngster from Ripley, had impressed in the reserves, once scoring seven times in an 8-0 win over Reading. With Cherrett finding the form of the previous season elusive, Strange was given his chance in December, and within a month had set the record by scoring five goals against Gillingham.

But in the long term the day Strange made his debut was more significant for a name which appeared on the reserves team sheet. A certain William Wyndham Pretoria Haines played at centre-forward; the legend had arrived. Haines, from Frome, had been recommended to Pompey by a supporter, Mr. Fred Prescott. Manager McCartney watched him play once for Somerset and immediately offered him terms. His first appearance as a professional was for the reserves on February 10, 1923, and 'The Farmer's Boy' celebrated by scoring a hat trick. By the end of the season this powerfully built centre-forward had forced his way into the first team and in eight matches scored four times.

Pompey's League adventure was proving no enormous financial success; the third season ended with a profit of £166.15s.6d. on gate receipts of £15,603. During the summer of 1923, McCartney once more made the transfer market a family affair, signing goalkeeper Alex Kane from Hearts where his son was still manager. He also bought Joe Davison from Middlesbrough but another Fratton stalwart, Shirley Abbott, who had first joined from Derby County in 1914 and who had been first team captain the previous season, moved on to Queen's Park Rangers – and in mid-summer his steps were followed by Pompey's reserve team skipper Charlie Cooper. The fast developing transfer market was highlighted in June when Pompey's old favourite Frank Stringfellow moved from Hearts to new Southern League club Weymouth for £1,000.

So Pompey approached their fourth season in the League – and this time they were to sample success. Thanks largely to 'Windy' Haines' power, Pompey's attack was the deadliest in the League. Eventually they won the title by four points from Plymouth, scoring 87 goals and conceding only 30. Haines missed 11 matches through injury towards the end of the season, but finished with 28 League goals.

It was also the season which saw Pompey sample reasonable F.A. Cup success for the first time. They began with a comfortable 5-1 win over non-league opposition London Caledonians – inevitably Haines scored twice. The second round though proved a difficult hurdle with Brentford, who were to finish low down the Third Division table, holding them to a 1-1 draw at Griffin Park – again Haines was the scorer. In the replay Pompey had to go to extra time before Jimmy Martin got the only goal. So they paired with mighty Newcastle in the third round and the Geordies powered through on their way to their second winning final, 4-2.

Stringfellow had also sampled his bit of Cup glory that same season. He helped Weymouth beat the Portsea Gas Co., in a preliminary round tie at Tipnor and then scored the goal in a replay at Gosport and another when the Dorset club won the second replay 3-0. The season was also tinged with sadness for Pompey and their supporters. In April their young Scottish reserve winger Duncan Gilchrist collapsed and died after heading a ball in a match against Gosport. But despite the League success and the mini-Cup run the season was one of some financial concern for the board, ending in a loss of £1,216. The players' reward for promotion was to make a three-match tour of Denmark.

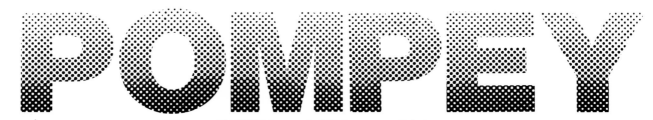

5. Going Up

As the new season and the Second Division approached Pompey went into intense training. It was so severe that on August 14 1924, manager McCartney took a party of 80 players, officials and their families on an afternoon excursion to Portchester Castle. As it started the Rev. Bruce Cornford, chairman for four years, resigned and the way was open for Robert Blyth to complete a unique progress. The one time player and manager who had been suspended by the Football Association in 1904 for irregularities over the signing of three Liverpool players – had remained with the club and had been on the board since 1909. So his election to the chair had seen him serve the club he had joined as a player for the initial Southern League season before the turn of the century, in every position.

1924-25 Pickford Cup. 3rd Div. Shield. Rowlands Cup from l to r. J. McCartney, H. Foxall, A. Kane, J. Davison, W. H. Probert, J. Parker, W. Beedie, J. McColgan, R. Davies, J. Mackie, J. Martin, W. Haines, D. Watson, A. Miekle, J. Warner.

McCartney made a few additions to his playing staff for the challenge of the Second Division. Wing-half Arthur Foxall, whose brother Harry had been signed from Merthyr early in the year to play his part in clinching promotion, came from Watford. But generally Pompey relied on the players who had taken them up – and for much of the season it seemed they might go straight through. It was not to be, although 'Windy' Haines scored another 17 league goals, Pompey eventually did well to finish in fourth place with 48 points, 11 fewer than champions Leicester City. The F.A. Cup provided a marathon second round tie against First Division Blackburn Rovers – a goal-less draw in Lancashire followed by another at Fratton and a second replay at Highbury which ended in a 1-0 defeat. It was also the season when Fratton Park staged Rugby Union. In December 1924, Hampshire were hosts to the touring All Blacks and Fratton offered the biggest and best facilities in the County. The match ended in a 22-0 win for the New Zealanders.

But if Fratton Park was Hampshire's best stadium, it was not good enough for a board of directors determined to bring First Division football to the South Coast. So, when the season ended, the builders moved in. The old South Stand was demolished and work started on a new £20,000 stand. The new stand was 360 feet long, twice as long as its predecessor. It provided seating for almost 4,000 people and covered accommodation for around 8,000 on the new terracing beneath it. For the logistically minded, the new stand used 104,425 bricks, 300 tons of steel, 13 tons of asbestos roofing, 20,000 linear feet of 9in x 3in decking and 3,600ft of roof glazing. Its construction employed 100 men during the summer. It also meant a slightly smaller playing surface. The goals were moved two yards to the north and the pitch was narrowed from 77 yards to 73.

The new pride of Pompey even meant a 15-minute delay to the start of the new season. Football League President Mr. John McKenna declared it open at 3 p.m., on August 29, 1925 – and the match kick off was put back to 3.15 p.m. Mr. McKenna congratulated the directors on their courage in guaranteeing a bank overdraft of £24,000 in the cause of customer comfort.

The summer had seen the departure of one of Pompey's longest serving players Bill Probert who had been with them since he was 16. He moved to Fulham although his debut for them was delayed by an appendicitis operation. As the season started Alex Kane, the former Black Watch sergeant, who had been regular first choice goalkeeper, was transfer listed after losing his place to Dan McPhail and quickly moved to West Ham after making 135 appearances for the club. Overall it was a disappointing season and from that promising fourth, Pompey slipped to 11th, winning only 17 matches. There was also trouble for Haines; playing for the reserves against Nuneaton in the Southern League, he struck an opponent and was suspended for a month. The F.A. Cup brought another marathon – and another disappointment. Their third round tie against Derby ended in a 2-0 success for the Midlands club in a second

replay at Leicester. Shortly before the season ended McCartney made one of his shrewdest signings – Newport's Welsh international winger Freddie Cook.

Having created the stage for top level football with their far-sighted gamble on the new stand, Pompey's directors were to be rewarded in its second year. The climb from Third to First was to have taken only seven seasons – but in the end it turned on one of the most dramatic finishes the Football League had yet seen. Pompey – and in particular – Haines had warmed up for the 1926-27 season in some style. In mid-August the first club trial saw the Reds beat the Blues 8-1 with Haines scoring four; three days later Haines got another six as the Reds won 8-0. A week later the season opened with the 101st meeting between Pompey and their neighbours Southampton. To the delight of a crowd of 28,200, Pompey won 3-1 to go 46-42 up in the series. Four days later Pompey made their first-ever visit to Manchester City's Maine Road ground and were soundly beaten 4-0 by a side who had been relegated the previous Spring. A break from the chase for League points came in mid-September when Hearts, still managed by John McCartney's son Willie, became the first Scottish side to visit Fratton. Some 6,000 watched a 1-1 draw in a benefit match for Pompey's Scots inside-forwards Jimmy Martin and David Watson.

November brought its minor addition to the Pompey record-book. On Saturday the 13th the match against Clapton Orient at Fratton Park was postponed because the pitch was waterlogged . . . the first time a Football League match had suffered that fate there and only the fourth time in the club's history. The F.A. Cup was not to interfere with Pompey's bid to reach the First Division. In the third round they needed a replay with Bristol Rovers after a 3-3 draw in Bristol. They cruised through that 4-0 to be drawn away to Reading and lost 3-1. Early in the New Year, a double signing from Newport strengthened the playing staff – Ted Smith and Freddie Forward.

Steadily the race for promotion gained in momentum; Middlesbrough were always in the lead but Pompey and the side who had given them such a beating early in the season – Manchester City – reached the final match locked together on 52 points. Manchester, like Middlesbrough had scored 100 goals, but Pompey, thanks to the soundest defence in the top two divisions, had a marginal advantage on goal average. By a quirk of fate the kick off times of the two matches were staggered – Manchester, at home to already relegated Bradford, started at 3 p.m., Pompey's Fratton meeting with sixth placed Preston at 3.15 p.m. Things went well enough for the crowd with a hat trick by Haines and a goal by Forward building a 4-1 lead. But then came the awful news from Maine Road – Manchester had won 8-0 and the crowd was already celebrating their return to the First Division. Rapid calculations showed that City were promoted by 0.15 of a goal if the Fratton score remained unchanged. So the message was passed to the Farmer's Boy – 'we need another goal' – and in a dramatic finish he obliged. It meant Pompey were promoted with a goal average of 1.7755 to Manchester City's 1.77049!!

Pompey Players Season 1925-26.

TOP ROW: H. HAYWARD.   E. J. BRENT,   J. McCOLGAN,   D. McPHAIL,   J. MARTIN,   A. KANE,   G. CLIFFORD,   J. DAVISON,   H. P. GOODWIN.   [Stephen Cribb, Southse
MIDDLE ROW: J. WARNER (Trainer),   S. DEARN,   J. FORSYTH,   H. FOXALL,   G. BARLOW,   W. MOFFAT,   R. DAVIES,   J. RUSSELL   A. WARDROPE (Assis. Train
BOTTOM ROW: J. McKECHNIE,   A. MEIKLE,   J. MACKIE,   A. MERRY,   MR. J. McCARTNEY   W. HAINES,   D. WATSON,   W. BEEDIE,   W. WILLIAMSON,   F. TONER.
                                                                          (Secretary-Manager).

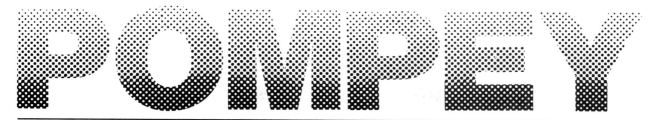

POMPEY

6. Promised Land

So in 1927 the South had its first-ever club in the First Division and Pompey were the first to make the climb from the Southern League. But again celebrations were blighted; the strain of guiding Pompey from Third to First had impaired manager McCartney's health and a week after that nerve-wracking win over Preston he resigned. But he left his successor John W. Tinn from South Shields with a solidly based team and a club on a sound financial footing. The promotion year saw Pompey make a profit of £4,520 – £1,000 more than the previous year. In mid-summer the club had further cause for celebration when their President, Mr. John Brickwood, who

had been their first chairman, was knighted in the Birthday Honours List. Promotion had been achieved, as so often, by a largely settled side. Seven players did not miss a match – right back George Clifford, right-half Reg Davies, skipper and centre-half Harry Foxall, left half Billy Moffatt, left-winger Freddie Cook, centre-forward Billy Haines and Jimmy Mackie. Haines finished the season with 40 goals, a record which still stands, since his debut in February 1923 the powerfully built man from Frome had scored 109 competitive goals. But an equally decisive part in promotion was played by goalkeeper McPhail. The 6ft Scot who had displaced

PORTSMOUTH. 1927-28.

Stephen Cribb. Warner (Trainer) — McIlwaine. — Clifford — McPhail. — McColgan. — Irvine. — J. W. Tinn (Sec. Manager) South.
Nichol. — Mackie. — Davies. — Foxall. — Moffat. — Watson. — Weddle.
Smith. — Forward. — Haines. — Cook.

Kane, saved four of the five penalties awarded against Pompey. During the summer Pompey cut their last ties with the Southern League, their reserves withdrawing to concentrate on the London Combination League.

They approached the 1927-28 season without major signings and to relax the atmosphere, manager Tinn took 50 players, wives and children on an afternoon outing on the motor-launch Skylark to Portchester Castle in mid-August. He followed that by an outing to Hayling - and missed the bus himself and had to catch up with his players by horse and carriage. Times change! As the season approached the first new players began to arrive with Mr. Tinn exploiting his knowledge of the North East. One of the first was 20-year-old Sep Rutherford, an outside left and brother of Leicester's Jack, then in late August 19-year-old John Weddle, a miner from Fatfield Albion, near Sunderland, also came down for trials. Both quickly signed as professionals and in time were to make their niches in the fabric of the club's history.

Pompey began their great adventure away to Sunderland, who the previous season had finished third to Newcastle and Huddersfield. And, when they returned with a 3-3 draw, their supporters felt that fears about the side's ability to bridge the gap between Divisions were unfounded. Confidence quickly turned to disillusion and when December arrived without a win, it had been replaced by near despondency. So Mr. Tinn was given the authority to re-build; Jimmy Nicholl was bought in from Gillingham, inside-forward Jack Smith arrived from South Shields, and on his debut brought a smile to worried faces with both goals in a 2-1 home win over West Ham. February saw centre-half John McIlwaine bought from Falkirk for £4,500 with the Scots club due to visit Fratton to play a charity match as an extension of the deal – but that never materialized. Finally Mr. Tinn completed his re-build by paying another sizeable fee for Everton's Irish international inside forward Bobby Irvine, and strengthening his defence with Southend's skipper and left-back Tommy Bell.

Tinn's re-shuffle worked; a run of seven unbeaten matches brought 13 life-saving points and at the end of the season Pompey finished third from bottom with 39 points – Spurs and Middlesbrough, the runaway Division two champions of the previous campaign, were relegated. Tinn's transfer activity had cost Pompey around £11,000 and meant a loss of £715 in their first season in the First Division, when almost half a million people (477,774) watched the 21 home matches. But that season was the last for Billy Haines, in May he followed Jerry Mackie and moved to Southampton, after scoring 128 goals in some 180 League and Cup matches. As he moved wing half Bob Kearney arrived from Dundee to become a great favourite with the Fratton Public until his untimely death in 1931 from pneumonia.

The summer was again a busy one at Fratton Park with the board approving a scheme to re-terrace the Milton End of the ground and when the 1928-29 season arrived the work was complete and Fratton's capacity had risen by some 3,000 to 40,000. When it began, Pompey were without centre-half McIlwaine who was suspended for the first four weeks after being sent off at Middlesbrough in April. But their playing strength had been reinforced by the signing of David Thackeray from Motherwell and Arsenal full-back Alex Mackie. The going was still very, very hard and in October they were humiliated 10-0 at Leicester . . . . the day ten swans flew over the ground as the match was on. In December Pompey forged yet another link with Heart of Midlothian as they signed goalkeeper John Gilfillan – and the next day added another Hearts player in centre-forward John McNeil. Interestingly the legendary Arthur E. Knight was still playing; on December 15 he played for Corinthians against the Royal Navy at the United Services ground.

For once though the F.A. Cup was to provide a welcome relief and Pompey were able to push all their relegation worries aside, to reach Wembley for the first time. The run began on January 12, 1929 with a 2-1 win over Charlton Athletic with goals by new signing McNeil and Jack Smith. McNeil scored again in the fourth round when another from Irvine saw them beat Bradford City 2-1 at Fratton. Then Weddle, already proving an admirable successor to Haines, scored his first Cup goals – earning a 1-1 draw at Chelsea in the fifth round and seeing them through with the only goal of the replay. Weddle got his third goal to decide the sixth round meeting with West Ham at Fratton, clinching a 3-2 win after Smith and Freddy Cook had squared things at 2-2. So Pompey were through to the semi finals . . . . no mean feat for a side bottom of the First Division with only ten wins in 31 matches and a wretched 42-70 goal record.

Pompey had prepared for this historic run by making regular trips to the Isle of Wight and that was where they went again to build up for their Highbury semi-final meeting with high-flying Aston Villa. On March 23 Jack Smith's third goal of the run clinched a 1-0 win and a place at Wembley against Bolton Wanderers, another side not enjoying the best of League seasons. Cup fever swept Portsmouth. The club's allocation of tickets was just 3,750 – applications to Fratton Park totalled 15,000. Forged tickets now appeared in the City and the police investigated although no one was charged. An application for the BBC to broadcast the match was turned down by the F.A. but Pompey overcame the problems of supply and demand by arranging for the final to be broadcast to the crowd at a reserve match at Fratton Park.

In the end it was a case of valiant but . . . . Pompey battled bravely but were disorganised by the loss of Bell and eventually lost 2-0 in front of 92,570. The stimulus of reaching the final carried through to the more mundane world of the league and Pompey eventually scrambled to safety for the second year running this time finishing five points clear of relegation. The Wembley adventure was obviously reflected in the balance sheet and turned the previous year's £700 loss into a welcome profit of £6,377. The players were entertained at a Civic

Aerial view of Wembley Stadium taken during the Bolton W. v Pompey Final Tie on April 27, 1929

reception after the final and later to a celebration dinner by the Lord Mayor Cllr. J. E. Smith at which long serving full-back John McColgan was presented with a benefit cheque for £400.

By the time the players reported back for pre-season training in early August, 1929 they had been joined by four young hopefuls, including a certain Eddie Lever from north eastern league club White-le-Head. Lever, of course, was to feature significantly in Pompey's story 20 years on. The disappointment of Wembley looked to have bitten deep as Pompey started the next season disastrously with two months elapsing before they managed their first win 1-0 against West Ham. That success

coincided with the formation of Portsmouth Football Supporters Club by Mr. Percy Mabb and Colour Sgt. F. Brimer. Despite their perilous position near the bottom of the table, Pompey's directors released Freddy Cook at the end of the month to earn his fifth Welsh cap – his third as a Pompey player – against Scotland. Not with happy results as the Scots won 4-2. Cook's sixth cap came a month later, but, with the rest of his team mates watching, Wales were thrashed 6-2 by England at Stamford Bridge. Gradually though things perked up on the field, although there was to be no repeat of the previous season's Cup excitement.

BOLTON WANDERERS

Colours: White Shirts, Blue Knickers

Goalkeeper
1. R. H. PYM

Right Back
2. R. HAWORTH

Left Back
3. A. FINNEY

Right Half-Back
4. F. M. KEAN

Centre Half-Back
5. J. SEDDON

Left Half-Back
6. H. NUTTALL

Outside Right
7. W. BUTLER

Inside Right
8. J. McCLELLAND

Centre Forward
9. H. A. BLACKMORE

Inside Left
10. G. B. GIBSON

Outside Left
11. W. COOK

Referee
A. JOSEPHS (Durham)

Linesmen—
C. E. LINES (Birmingham)
C. F. MOON (Gloucestershire)

Daily News BEST FOR ALL SPORT

Outside Left
12. F. COOK

Inside Left
13. D. WATSON

Centre Forward
14. J. WEDDLE

Inside Right
15. J. W. SMITH

Outside Right
16. F. FORWARD

Left Half-Back
17. D. THACKERAY

Centre Half-Back
18. J. McILWAINE

Right Half-Back
19. J. NICHOL

Left Back
20. T. BELL

Right Back
22. J. A. MACKIE

Goalkeeper
22. J. GILFILLAN

PORTSMOUTH

Colours: Royal Blue Shirts, White Knickers

If the result is still a draw, the Match will be replayed on the ground of the West Bromwich Albion Football Club on Wednesday, 1st May, Kick-off at 3 p.m.

... of **Daily News** SPORTS WRITERS
LONDON & MANCHESTER

SPECI... REPO... OF TH... MATC... ON MOND...

BUCHAN   FRANK THOROGOOD   FRED DARTNELL   J. N. SHERWOOD   S. W. BAYLEY   FRANK POXON   ALAN PAGE   "THE PICQUET"

Centrefold of 1929 Final Programme, and ticket. Note the price.

PORTSMOUTH. F.C.

SEASON 1928-29

F. Forward.
J. Nichol.
J. M'Kirr.
G. Haslam.
W. Moffat.
J. Charlton.
H. Foxall.

J. Weddle.
Geo. Clifford.
S. Parker.
J. Forsyth.
F. Cook.
H. Davey.
J. Jervis

W. Haines.
T. Birks.
E. Smith.
J. J. Scott.
B. Thomas
S. Rutherford
J. Callaghan

A. Wardrope (Trainer)
J. Mackie
R. Davies
D. Watson
F. Watts
R. Ronald
J. Jeffrey

Pompey team receive their losers medals after the 1929 Final

Preston North End were beaten 2-0 in the third round but neighbours Brighton caused one of the upsets of the competition by winning 1-0 at Fratton in the fourth. Once again the glamour of the Cup was shown; some 10,000 made the trip from Sussex and the gates were shut on a packed ground almost an hour before the kick off. But the defeat was not allowed to erode their increased confidence and by the end of the season Pompey had clawed their way up to 13th place. Once again Weddle did not miss a match and top-scored with 21 goals. Their most outstanding performance was produced at Leicester, where despite being reduced to ten men by injury to Bell, they avenged the Day of the Swans, with five goals.

Late in the season the crowd at a reserve match saw the debut of another man who was shortly to become a giant at Fratton – and elsewhere. Jimmy Allen, a 6ft 20-year-old centre-half from Poole, made a big enough impression in that first match to be signed. Up country though it is a former Pompey player who was making the news – Alf Strange. The centre-forward who had lost his place to Haines after his record-breaking entry into Pompey' side, was now a powerful wing-half with pace-setting Sheffield Wednesday. In March 1930 Strange played for 'The Rest' in a trial against England at Liverpool – Pompey's Jack Smith was an England reserve – and when England met Scotland Strange earned the first of his 20 caps.

Later still in the season Pompey had lost their now famous Royal blue kit in a fire in the Fratton drying room, with major damage averted by manager Tinn and others. But it meant the old Salmon pink shirts had to be found for a friendly match at Bournemouth – Pompey won, but to convince them that it was not their day, the charabanc ran out of petrol on the way home. Former Pompey manager John McCartney, who had been forced to retire after achieving his ambition of bringing First Division football to Fratton, had for some time been in charge at Luton, but during the winter his health had failed again forcing a second and final retirement. But the affection for this hard working Scot in Portsmouth prompted the launching of a testimonial fund which quickly reached £300.

During the summer of 1930, the Fratton pitch was completely re-turfed and the public heard of the surprise departure of John McIlwaine. Pompey's costliest signing at £5,000 moved to Southampton for another record fee. The summer passed without major additions to the playing staff, but as the 30-31 season got underway and Pompey hit the most consistent form they had so far produced. Jimmy Easson another recruit from Scotland was now challenging Weddle for the title of marks-man supreme and the competition made Pompey formidable opposition. Their early season surge included a 7-4 win at Newcastle and, unbeaten at home for the first three months of the season, they were second at the end of November and people were beginning to talk championship talk. And come the early weeks of 1931 and dreams of the double even started to take root.

In the third round of the Cup they were drawn away to Fulham and won 2-0, then returned to London for the fourth round and thanks to a Jack Smith goal beat Brentford. The Bees were skippered by former Pompey player Reg Davies and their goalkeeper and trainer was another former Fratton man Bob Kane. That brought a home draw with Second Division West Bromwich; enthusiasm was enormous, seat tickets sold out and by the time the match arrived could have been sold three times over. But Valentine's Day held no joy; the Midlanders won by the only goal.

Less than a week later Pompey's supporters learned that centre-half Bob Kearney was ill with pneumonia. Two days later a medical report described his condition as 'fairly satisfactory' but by the final edition of the Evening News that day, the doctor's bulletin was 'pretty grave'. Unhappily that was to prove correct for on February 24, 1931 after a five day illness, the 27-year-old defender died leaving a widow and child. He was buried at Milton Cemetery on February 26, and the following day a relief fund was launched for his dependants. Helped by a testimonial match in which a combined Pompey-Saints side met a London Representative team which produced receipts of £368.2s.6d.,the fund closed after two months at almost £1,700.

Robert Kearney's gravestone – courtesy of the Pompey directors

Eventually Pompey's season finished with them in fourth place, their highest position, with 49 points and for the first time since he had come into the side Weddle was not top scorer. Easson pipped him by four with 29. Both did not miss a match, neither did Mackie, Gilfillan, Willie Smith or Forward. As the season ended Pompey should have played Saints in the Pickford Benevolent Fund Cup, but their rivals were riven by disagreement over terms for the next season. Only six Southampton players had accepted the Club's offer and so eventually Pompey played and beat a side consisting of the six non-rebels and five Hampshire County players. The side's success resulted in a healthy £7,729 profit and the overdraft which had been incurred to build the new South stand was down to £13,388.

Easson's goal scoring success had earned him his first Scotland cap against Austria early in May, and he made his second appearance and scored his only international goal as Switzerland were beaten 3-2 at the end of the month. Oddly, he was to play only once more - in a 3-2 defeat by Wales in 1933. Jack Smith in the meantime spent some of the summer of 1931 touring Canada with England – a trip which meant him missing the start of pre-season training. By then Dan McPhail had moved to Lincoln City and Pompey's list of recruits included amateur defender Bill Rochford who was to become a familiar character along the South Coast in the years to come.

But the 1931-32 season arrived amid rare controversy. In August Pompey announced the signing of John Walker Cameron from Scottish junior club The Vale of Clyde. But at the last moment Arsenal stepped in and signed Cameron. On August 21 the Football Association staged an inquiry – and both clubs lost out. The F.A. ruled that neither could sign Cameron and legendary Arsenal manager Herbert Chapman was censured for signing him when he had already been registered by Portsmouth. In the end it was Spurs who had last laugh for on August 26 they announced they had signed Cameron. Arthur Knight continued on the scene; in the summer he had played cricket for Hampshire Club and Ground; on September 2 he was found to be running the line for the First Division match between Pompey and Everton when the referee failed to arrive. The next week the improved North stand which offered extra covered standing accommodation was opened to the public and Pompey soon announced that charges for watching the reserves in action were to be increased – by one penny to 7d (approx. 3p). Jack Smith was now a regular member of the England side – he scored against a Wales side which included Freddy Cook in November and twice as Spain were beaten 7-1 in December.

On the League scene hopes that the previous season's success might herald the long awaited first title were quickly shattered. Everton who had been relegated in 1930 and had bounced straight back as Second Division champions inflicted the first damage – winning that home match which Arthur Knight had 'lined' 3-0. By the

end of September Pompey had lost five of their seven matches and gloom was fast descending . . . . deepening in November as they hit bottom place. By that time manager Tinn had made his first major signing of the season, recruiting Freddie Worrall from Oldham Athletic for a moderate fee. The year turned with Pompey having helped Newcastle make League history – the first match without a single corner kick being endured by a patient crowd at St. James's Park on December 5 – predictably a goal-less draw. Again the turn of the year brought an improvement and by the end of the season Pompey had climbed to a highly respectable eighth place. Once again their dependable goalkeeper Gilfillan played in every match while Weddle had regained his top-scoring role, pipping Easson 22-21. They had rounded the season off with a journey to championship celebrating Everton and had returned to celebrate themselves having avenged their defeat of the opening match by a single goal.

The F.A. Cup had seen them bow to eventual finalists Arsenal in the fifth round. In the third they had beaten Middlesbrough 3-0 with two goals by Easson and one by Worrall to be drawn at home to mighty Aston Villa. That was drawn 1-1 with David Thackeray scoring and the replay saw them shock a massive Villa Park crowd by winning with a goal by Easson. So Arsenal came to Fratton on February 13, 1932 – the day after Pompey's founder chairman Sir John Brickwood had died at the age of 79. Centre-section seats in the South Stand cost 6s.5d. (32½p) for the match but there was disappointment with the Gunners winning 2-0.

Before the end of the season Pompey had paid out two more four figure fees – James C. Nicol a centre-forward joining from Leith Athletic, and winger Friar from Hibernian. The season ended with Pompey losing the Rowlands Cup on the toss of a coin after a 2-2 draw at the Dell . . . . and on the way home the players stopped off at the Dolphin Hotel at Botley for their traditional end of season supper and sing-song . . . . Interestingly even at that time there was debate about whether football should have a mid-winter break . . . . and manager Tinn was a strong opponent of the suggestion. At the annual meeting in the summer a drop in profits from £7,700 to £1,065 was reported with some £6,500 having been spent in the transfer market. Chairman Robert Blyth was re-elected – so too was G. Lewin Oliver for his 34th year on the board.

Season 1932-33 was to be another of great early promise. They started in great style, going to the top of the table with a 2-0 win over Wolves, and remaining unbeaten until the end of September when they lost 5-4 at Middlesbrough. But again although Weddle, encouraged by the announcement of a richly earned benefit, topped 20 goals, Pompey were unable to sustain the pace and eventually finished ninth with a no more than average 43 points from 42 matches. An oddity of the season was that in two matches Pompey had to use untried amateur goalkeepers. In January flu ruled out both Gilfillan and reserve John McHugh so Salisbury F.C.'s 'Jessie' Weekes was hustled into the side and performed heroically. Happily Gilfillan had recovered by the time Pompey travelled to Grimsby with only 12 fit players for the third round of the Cup but the journey ended in a 3-2 defeat. Then in the final match of the season it was Hampshire County goalkeeper Cyril Jolliffe who had just signed as an amateur who found himself making his debut at Roker Park as Sunderland were beaten 3-0. Jimmy Allen had by now firmly established himself as one of the outstanding defenders in the country and appeared in every match.

But generally there was a feeling of gloom throughout the country as gates fell away with Pompey among the luckier clubs as their average held at around 15,000. In fact only that average turned up when England played and lost 5-1 to the Rest at Fratton Park on March 22. Alf Strange played for the Rest in a match notable as the first in which players wore numbered shirts. In January 1933 John McCartney had died aged 67 in Edinburgh and had been buried a short distance from the Heart of Midlothian ground where both he and his son Willie had been successful managers. Before the annual meeting when a profit of just £243 and transfer expenditure of £115 were reported, Pompey had signed outside left William Bagley, a 23-year-old from Newport County. During the summer two players moved on – reserve goalkeeper McHugh to Watford and James C. Nicol, who had cost £1,000 to Aldershot . . . . both had made only three first team league appearances.

Pompey players enjoying a game of snooker from l to r
S. Rutherford, A. Smith, D. Thackeray, W. Bagley, W. Smith, F. Worrall, J. Allen, J. Gilfillan, J. Nichol, J. Weddle

'HMS POMPEY'
Recommissioned
1933-4 1st division
squadron

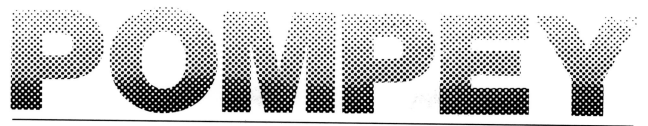

7. Return to Wembley

Season 1933/4 was, of course, to be another dominated by the F.A. Cup. It began with Pompey wearing shirts of a slightly darker shade of blue and until the third round of the Cup arrived in January, promised to be no more than ordinary.

But the Cup changed everything. The third round had them at Old Trafford where Bagley who had replaced Easson put them ahead but United equalized five minutes from time after Worrall had missed a penalty. The replay, watched by 18,748, saw Pompey romp home 4-1 with goals by Weddle (2), McCarthy, and Jack Smith to earn a home tie with Grimsby decided with some comfort by goals by Weddle and Jack Smith to the delight of 34,565. So Pompey had to travel to Swansea, leaving on Thursday lunchtime, for a match which was to prove more eventful off the pitch than on it. With Pompey leading by a Worrall goal, the referee enraged the Swansea crowd by turning down a penalty – and had to call in extra police to cut off a bombardment of oranges. The crowd of 29,700 was a record but put too much strain on some of the facilities and the afternoon's second hold-up came after crash barriers collapsed and a number of people were injured. It brought a match Pompey had long awaited – a meeting with Bolton and a chance to avenge the disappointment of the '29 final. Revenge was totally satisfying; – Pompey stormed through to the semi-finals 3-0 with two goals by Sep Rutherford and one from Weddle. The match was watched by 52,181 who had paid £3,778.

And so the Smith brothers were in opposition again, for Pompey were drawn against Leicester City. They had already lost 5-3 to them in the League, with four goals scored by Archie Gardner on a spectacular debut for the Midlands club. Pompey had included Jack and Willie Smith, and Leicester brother Sep. Again there was to be revenge; Pompey, thanks to a hat trick by Weddle and one goal from Rutherford, marched into the final 4-1 in front of 55,000 at St. Andrew's, Birmingham.

Their opposition at Wembley was to be Manchester City who had thrashed Aston Villa 6-1 with Tilson scoring four times. Interest in this final was ever greater than for the first as far as Pompey fans were concerned. The club's allocation of tickets was 7,500 – more than 30,000 applications were received. Pompey prepared for the match by staying at Harrow, a tour of the famous old public school being included in their build up programme. Eight special trains eventually travelled from Portsmouth to Wembley where one of Pompey's guests was their first-ever goalkeeper Matt Reilly. Interest was enormous – to the delight of the spivs – 2s.6d. tickets were selling at 16 shillings (80p) and 7s.6d. seats at £2.

Again injury was to turn the match against a Pompey side wearing white shirts and black shorts. This time Allen, their outstanding centre-half, suffered a severe head injury with Pompey leading by Rutherford's goal and Manchester snatched victory with two goals by Tilson. Pompey withdrew to lick their wounds at a banquet at the Trocadero – and in Portsmouth rumours spread that Jimmy Allen had died from his injuries. They, happily proved false; but a month or so later further rumours ran through the City – Allen was to be sold to Aston Villa. But on June 18 they seemed scotched when Allen re-signed for another season . . . . the next evening those rumours were seen to be accurate. The British transfer record was shattered as Allen moved to Villa for £10,775. The cause of turn-around was £200. Allen was due a benefit, most clubs paid £650, Pompey were offering their centre-half, who was shortly to receive the Freedom of his home town Poole, only £400. Allen had made his only appearances for England that season against Northern Ireland and Wales.

He was one of two senior players to move on for in November Freddy Forward had been transferred to Hull City. Shortly before Allen left, Eddie Lever had been transferred to Aldershot. He was already working fairly close to the North Hampshire town – at Alton where, of course, he was later to play such an important

SEMI-FINAL AT BIRMINGHAM.   V. LEICESTER CITY. 1934.

FINAL. WEMBLEY.   V. MANCHESTER CITY. 1934.

Pompey's share of the 1934 semi and final spoils

Presented by the P.F.C. Directors as a Memento of
the Cup Final v Manchester City. April 28th 1934.

Stephen Cribb

Southsea.

A.Mackie.   J.Gilfillan(coach)   W.Smith.
J.Nichol.   J.Allen.   D.Thackeray.
F.Worrall. J.Smith.   J.Weddle. J.Easson. S.Rutherford.

Players meet King George V before the 1934 Final
l to r. A. Mackie, J. Easson, J. Weddle, B. Smith, J. Allen, J. Smith, King George V, D. Thackeray, unknown

role in shaping the Jimmy Dickinson legend. Halfway through the season, 20-year-old winger Cliff Parker signed from Doncaster Rovers for a 'substantial' fee. In the reserves he joined another youngster who was beginning to push for recognition with his goal-scoring – Jock Anderson. The Cup final appearance meant a profit of £10,592 on the year – but with the old North Stand demolished, there was work to be done. Although it was not until Christmas 1934 that the board revealed their plans. The new North Terrace was to be covered, increasing the ground's capacity to more than 58,000 with some 30,000 under cover – work financed by Allen's sale which earned the title of 'The Jimmy Allen Stand'. No sooner had one distinguished product of Poole football moved on than another arrived. Twenty-year-old Tommy Rowe, like Allen a centre-half, signed amateur forms during the summer of 34 and in August joined the professional staff. Freddie Cook had been released at the end of 1933 season and now appeared in Ireland, playing for Waterford.

Season 34-35 was to be another of those ordinary affairs with Pompey never looking like making a challenge for honours, but never in any real danger. Early on a landmark was passed as Jack Smith made his 500th League appearance – but at the end of the season he too moved on, joining Bournemouth. Smith was a remarka-

ble player – he made the first of his three appearances for England when he was 33! Meanwhile Anderson was keeping up his pressure on the seniors with three hat tricks in the first months of the season to power the reserves to the top of the London Combination. His fourth came in late October giving him a total of 20 goals in 13 reserve appearances. December was again a time of sadness for the club with the death at the age of 80 of Mr. Oliver.

There was always the Cup to stimulate and save the season – but not this time. After a third round replay win at Huddersfield, thanks to two more goals by the dependable Weddle, Pompey were drawn at home to Third Division Bristol City and were surprisingly held to a goal-less draw. The replay ended disastrously for them – and almost tragically for their hosts. The recorded attendance was 42,800 but a large number of people climbed into the ground without paying, barriers and walls collapsed and the crowd spilled on to the playing area. Mercifully no one was seriously injured and when the pitch was eventually cleared, City went on to a major upset with a 2-0 win. As the season ended another name of the future began to appear for the first time – Reg Flewin was at centre-half for the Portsmouth Boys team against Bournemouth at Fratton Park.

The summer was a quiet affair and it was not until the players had reported back for training for the 35-36 season that Mr. Tinn made his two major signings – John Scott Symon, Dundee's captain and centre-half, and Lew Morgan, also from Dundee. The season had opened in some style – Football League President John McKenna repeating the journey of ten years earlier, this time to officially open the new North Stand. But once again it was to be a season when the first team failed to make any real impact. Weddle started off sensationally, scoring ten goals in the first nine matches, but then endured a wretched spell and in the remainder of the season scored only six more. Again the Cup failed to cheer – although there was one lucky side to it for Pompey. On their way to meet Manchester City in the third round, their train ran into a fallen tree just outside Stoke but fortunately was not de-railed and no one was injured. The match itself was not a happy affair with Pompey beaten 3-1 and Pompey needing a penalty by Worrall to score.

The bright spot was provided by the reserves where Anderson and Parker in particular were mounting a powerfully developing challenge to the older established players. By mid-March they had won the race to one hundred Combination League goals, with Anderson taking his total to 24 with all five in a 5-2 win over Millwall and they duly became the first provincial winners of the Combination in 20 years when they beat Southend 2-1 in early May. The reserves pulling power was proved over Christmas when 12,519 watched them play Charlton Reserves at Fratton on Boxing Day. The season saw the departure of Alex Mackie to Northampton after eight good years at Fratton and also saw Pompey fined for failing to make Brentford in time for a match – they were delayed in a London pea-soup fog and were still stuck when it was postponed 15 minutes before kick off. The indifferent League form and the first hurdle exit in the Cup, coupled with spending £10,623 in the transfer market (Scott Symon, Morgan and Arthur Groves from Derby) meant the first loss since 1927-28 – £5,163. The accounts also revealed that £7,072 had been spent on covering and terracing the North side of the ground. By the time the players reported back, Dave Thackeray, who had been such a great servant to the club, announced his retirement from football after being released.

The 1936-37 season arrived with strong rumours that Pompey were to sign Dundee's Jimmy Guthrie, and with the disbanding of the Supporters Club after seven years – their membership had slipped from a peak of 1,700 to a mere 143; but within a month they had re-formed. It was a campaign which held great, though eventually unfulfilled, promise. In September they actually led the table for a brief spell and by Easter were still in third place – but they managed only three points from their holiday programme and slipped away to ultimately finish ninth. The season marked the end of Jock Gilfillan's reign as undisputed first choice goalkeeper – after Arsenal had won 5-1 at Fratton Park he lost his place to George Strong.

Arsenal in fact did an impressive double over them that season – although the second 'leg' was a curious affair. Both Morgan and Bob Salmond were injured and both were later found to have fractured collar bones. The 'fly' in Pompey's ointment that day was reported to be a certain young outside left who scored two goals – Denis Compton. The bonus, though, was the breakthrough of Cliff Parker who was the only ever-present in the side and finished top scorer with 12, one more than Weddle and two up on Anderson. Salmond's injury was particularly ill-timed, for two days earlier he had been named as reserve centre-half for Scotland – and he was never to get another chance! Relative League success was again accompanied by Cup disaster – Spurs romped to a 5-0 win at Fratton to make a mockery of the Division difference in status.

The rumours relating to Guthrie continued but it was another Scot who eventually came South – after some problems. Pompey attempted to sign St. Johnstone centre-forward Jimmy Beattie in January but negotiations broke down when four of the Scottish club's directors went down with flu and others were unwilling to sell. Eventually though after a month's delay, Beattie was signed for £3,000. At the end of the season, trainer Jack Warner retired and both Jock Gilfillan and Jimmy Nichol were placed on the transfer list.

And down in the West Country another famous Pompey character finally said 'Enough'. Farmer Haines, now 38, climaxed his five year stay with Weymouth by helping them to the Western League Division II title. He scored 62 goals to take his aggregate in his time with the Dorset club to a staggering 279. It was a summer of change. In May Nichol returned to Gillingham, from whom Pompey had signed him nine years earlier, then Gilfillan moved to QPR. He took with him a unique record of playing in both Scottish and English Cup finals – and being three times a loser; with East Fife in 1927, and Portsmouth in '29 and '34. Pompey had replaced trainer Warner with Dundee's Jimmy Stewart, but before he had moved South, chairman Mr. Albert Hooper had died after a lengthy illness, and in August was succeeded by Mr. William Kiln.

As the players reported back for the 1937-38 season, one of the young hopefuls was Reg Flewin and before the kick-off started a year of rumour and speculation came true when Jimmy Guthrie eventually signed from Dundee for a 'large' fee – £4,000. Guthrie went straight into the team, but the start was scarcely promising for the club and by mid-September they were bottom of the First Division. Further reinforcements came in November when Guy Wharton and Eric Jones were signed from Wolves and a month later Flewin, having proved his potential in the A team, signed as a professional. Still little went right and they arrived in 1938 as favourites for relegation.

But towards the end of January a draw with Middlesbrough lifted them off the bottom of the table and they set off on a run which was to see them eventually kill off the threat in their final home match. Some 30,000 were drawn to Fratton Park to watch the decisive clash with comfortably placed Leeds. They were rewarded by a 4-0 win with two goals from Beattie, and one each from Groves and Worrall. The statistics of that saving sequence were impressive – only champions Arsenal bettered their record of 33 points from their last 27 matches. The F.A. Cup held a 2-1 third round win over Third Division Tranmere Rovers but a 2-1 defeat at Brentford in the next match.

Jack Tinn though was building for the future; in the second half of the season he signed goalkeepers Harry Walker (21) from Darlington and Ernie Butler (18) from Bath plus 18-year-old Bradford City full back Phil Rookes. But eras were also ending; Gilfillan announced his retirement and the legendary Weddle was allowed to move to Blackburn Rovers without a fee. He had made 369 League appearances for the club and scored a record 173 goals, with another 13 in 28 Cup-ties. Also on the move was William Smith after 311 League appearances at full-back, and another 24 Cup-ties.

It was also the season when Pompey almost played 'an international' match. In March, 1938 France were on the look out for opposition after their match with Austria had collapsed following Hitler's annexation of that country. For some time Pompey looked like travelling to Paris; in the end Belgium took the fixture.

In the summer of '38, the ranks of Pompey's cricketing footballers gained another name. Reserve wing-half Abe Duffield made his debut for Sussex against Glamorgan in Swansea, taking four wickets for only 27 runs in the second innings. The year cost the club £6,289 and the accounts also showed they had spent £13,840 in the transfer market. A second player was also to make the cricketing headlines before he reported back; Scot Symon, who had had unsuccessful trials with Hampshire, took five Australian wickets for only 33 as he played for Scotland at Dundee. Scot Symon was in fact to be back in Scotland before the 1938-39 season started, with Glasgow Rangers. The season he missed was, of course, to be the epic of Wembley triumph.

The City trams show their support for Pompey

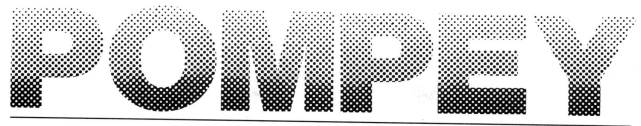

8. Third Time Lucky

The new season arrived, though, against the backcloth of another fight to preserve First Division status which was not won until Stoke were beaten in the 40th match. In the first half of the season there was little to suggest the drama which was to later unfold. Pompey struggled to make any impact in the League and in December, Jack Tinn paid a club record £6,000 for Belfast Celtic's 20-year-old Irish international inside forward Jimmy McAlinden. But the Second Division began to loom ever nearer; in February as the Cup run was beginning to gain momentum, Pompey went six League matches without a single goal and when they beat Leeds 2-0 on March 8 1939, it was the first win since Christmas!

The contrast between League and Cup was stark. In the third round Pompey were drawn at home to Lincoln who had old Pompey goalkeeper Dan McPhail in their side, and goals by Anderson (2), Parker and Worrall saw them comfortably through. The reward was another home draw, against West Bromwich Albion, and Anderson obliged with another two goals – training at Bognor Regis was paying off. They had seven days there again early in February to prepare for their fifth round home meeting with West Ham. This match saw Fratton bulge with a record attendance of 47,614 who saw Pompey ease through 2-0 with goals by Parker and Worrall.

What a contrast to the league; this was in the middle of that dreadful six match goal-less run! Again fate smiled, for the fourth time Pompey were drawn at home for the sixth round and a goal by Anderson saw them through against Preston. Pompey had by then strengthened their staff by signing Bert Barlow from Wolverhampton – a curious twist as it was to turn out. They were paired with Huddersfield in the semi final; the match to be played at Highbury on March 25. Interest was enormous; some 6,000 travelled from Portsmouth by train, another 1,000 on a fleet of 30 buses. Both teams wore 'second' colours; Pompey were in white shirts and black shorts, Huddersfield, who shared their League problems, were in Red shirts and

white shorts. The match, watched by 55,000, made its own little bit of history – it was the first time shirts had been numbered for a club match. For much of the afternoon it looked as though the dream would end with Huddersfield leading by a single goal by Bobby Barclay, but in the last 12 minutes, Barlow and Anderson saw Pompey to their third final.

It looked likely to be a lost cause though; Barlow's old club Wolves were riding high in the First Division and had stormed through to Wembley in devastating style. They had beaten Bradford (3-1), Leicester (5-1), Liverpool (4-1), Everton (2-0) and Grimsby (5-0) – an aggregate of 19-3 to Pompey's 11-1. But Pompey's path through the weeks to their Wembley appearance was not smooth. On April 1, Wharton, their powerful left-half, was sent off in a match against Birmingham – how long would the suspension be? In the end it was seven days. It meant him missing two matches, but, happily, not the final. Off the field there was anything but harmony. The Supporters' Club were far from happy over ticket allocation arrangements. There was talk of a boycott of the match against Stoke which was ultimately to see the relegation bogey laid, but that did not materialize. However, on April 17, some 3,000 attended a protest meeting at the Methodist Central Hall in Fratton. In the end some 13,000-14,000 Pompey fans eventually got tickets for the match. Pompey were on a bonus of £12 to win, and a local tailor offered a suit for every goal scored.

Freddie Worrall was the only survivor of Pompey's 1934 final. Wolves were 5-2 favourites and in the opinion of most, their international-studded team had merely to attend to pick up the Cup. But favourites had fallen before and were to do so again.

Pompey responded to the occasion by playing some calm and composed football and took the lead in the 31st minute, with Barlow beating his old team mate Bob Scott with a rising shot after fine build up between Guthrie and Anderson. Two minutes from the interval Stan Cul-

PLAN OF THE FIELD OF PLAY

PORTSMOUTH
COLOURS : Royal Blue Shirts, White Knickers

1
Goalkeeper
WALKER

2
Right Back
MORGAN

3
Left Back
ROCHFORD

4
Right Half-Back
GUTHRIE (Capt.)

5
Centre Half-Back
ROWE

6
Left Half-Back
WHARTON

7
Outside Right
WORRALL

8
Inside Right
McALINDEN

9
Centre Forward
ANDERSON

10
Inside Left
BARLOW

11
Outside Left
PARKER

Outside Left
MAGUIRE
11

Inside Left
DORSETT
10

Centre Forward
WESTCOTT
9

Inside Right
McINTOSH
8

Outside Right
BURTON
7

Left Half-Back
GARDINER
6

Centre Half-Back
CULLIS (Capt.)
5

Right Half-Back
GALLEY
4

Left Back
TAYLOR
3

Right Back
MORRIS
2

Goalkeeper
SCOTT
1

WOLVERHAMPTON WANDERERS
COLOURS : Old Gold Shirts, White Knickers
KICK-OFF 3 P.M.

Should the Match result in a draw after ninety minutes' play an extra half-hour will be played

Referee :
T. THOMPSON (Northumberland)
Linesmen :
P. SNAPE (Manchester)
S. A. DONALDSON (Essex)

From the 1939 Final Programme.

FINAL TIE

OF THE FOOTBALL
ASSOCIATION CHALLENGE
CUP COMPETITION

SATURDAY,
APRIL 29th,
1939

PORTSMOUTH
v.
WOLVERHAMPTON WANDERERS
OFFICIAL PROGRAMME SIXPENCE

NATIONAL SERVIC

A Message to All

THE world is in a very disturbed state and nobody can b sure what will happen. One thing is certain, this state affairs means possible danger of war. If this should happe you should understand that the danger and horror of moder warfare may be brought to your own door.

These dangers can be met and defeated if everybody knows right away what to do and how to do it. There is only one way to find out. Put your name down at once for some form of National Service and get yourself trained in the job you can do best. It is an appeal to your own common-sense to protect your home and your family. It is your duty to do so. It is absolutely necessary for your future.

There are serious deficiencies in the ranks of the Defence Services. In particular, the Air Raid Precaution Services need more Wardens, Stretcher Bearers, Rescue Workers, Decontamination Squads, and Auxiliary Firemen. The Territorial Army needs additional volunteers to bring its strength up to the standard recently agreed upon. Do not think that because your occupation is included in the Schedule of Reserved Occupations that you are debarred from enrolling for National Service. Everyone can undertake some form of National Service. If you are in doubt you can obtain advice from the nearest National Service Office.

It is imperative that you should volunteer at once if you have not already done so. Please, therefore, complete an enrolment form as soon as possible. You can obtain one from any Post Office or National Service Office.

This urgent appeal is made to you in the fu' knowledge that it will not go unheeded.

The goal that started it all. Scott, the Wolves' 'keeper, is well beaten by a shot from Pompey inside-left Bert Barlow, who is out of the picture. This was after 31 minutes and from then on Pompey never looked back.

DAY OF POMPEY'S GREAT GLORY

☆

(By LINESMAN)

In those nervous days in the shadow of World War II, the 1939 Cup final between the fancied young thoroughbreds of Wolverhampton, and Mr. Jack Tinn's unfashionable Pompey was preceded by the biggest ballyhoo of any Wembley clash.

Worrall's mascots

Was there ever such a superstitious player as Freddie Worrall, Pompey's outside-right?

He never went away for a match without three or four mascots — and he took them out with him at Wembley.

In his pocket, he had a small horse-shoe. Down each stocking he pushed a sprig of white heather, and he tied a small white elephant to one of his garters.

Worrall also "officiated" when Mr. Jack Tinn, the Manager, put on his famous spats.

Worrall's wife, by the way, had dreamt that Pompey would win 2—0 at Wembley. "She must have woken up at half-time," quipped Worrall.

A Portsmouth tailor had offered to give a suit for every goal scored by Pompey. Parker won two, but afterwards said he wanted the value of the extra suit to be divided by the two reserves, Bill Bagley and Abe Smith.

☆

The soccer world thrilled all the more as Pompey, the underdogs, who were near the bottom of the First Division table, gave one of the best performances ever seen at Wembley to win 4—1.

When Pompey brought the Cup back that night, the whole city and the surrounding area seemed to be present to watch their triumphant procession. There was not a spare space in the Guildhall Square as thousands packed to honour the men who had made it all possible.

Pompey held the trophy right through the war years. Even during those dark days, when the fight for survival was on, men still marvelled at the tales of Pompey's third-time-lucky visit to Wembley.

How those tremendous Pompey Chimes rang out, through the community singing before the match, right through the 90 minutes of glory, all over London after the match, and again amid the cheering thousands waiting at home.

The gland treatment received by both teams was one of the main issues as the teams "warmed up" for Wembley. There was no point talking about the result. Everyone except

Pompey and their supporters thought it a foregone conclusion.

Ever since 1939, it has been said that Pompey took heart from the fact that autographs of the Wolves' players were so shaky in the books which were

LINE-UP

PORTSMOUTH
Walker
Morgan   Rochford
Guthrie   Rowe   Wharton
Worrall McAlinden   Barlow Parker
Anderson

Westcott
Maguire Dorsett   McIntosh Burton
Gardiner   Cullis   Galley
Taylor   Morris
Scott

WOLVERHAMPTON

later brought into the Fratton Park men's dressing-room.

My former colleague, Ranger, wrote from Wembley: "Portsmouth were always the better side and five minutes after the start, the issue never seemed in doubt.

"The whole football world must stand up and salute Portsmouth on their magnificent triumph. They started the match with the odds against them, but they rose to the occa-

sion splendidly and won on their merits.

"Portsmouth's two goals in the first-half were really perfect efforts and the result of excellent team work and understanding, finished off in the coolest of fashions. During the first 45 minutes, Pompey made the Wolves look a second-rate team."

Cullis spun the coin, but his old adversary, Jimmy Guthrie, called correctly.

It was in the 31st minute that Pompey took the lead and the honour of the first break-through went to Bert Barlow, the inside-left bought from Wolverhampton (on the never-never, too).

Jock Anderson, the Pompey centre-forward, now the licensee of a public-house on the way to Fratton Park, moved to the inside-right position, nodded the ball into the midde. Barlow got it under control, steadied himself, and beat Scott with a great, floated shot.

A minute from half-time, Guthrie provided the opening for Anderson to get a fine second goal.

More sensation at the start of the second-half. Cliff Parker, Pompey's great outside-left, scored within a minute.

He beat Morris and turned the ball back to Barlow, who advanced a few yards and drove in a terrific shot. Scott saved by throwing himself full length and holding the ball on the line. But Parker was following up, and with Scott on the ground, got it over the line.

It transpired afterwards that Parker had shouted: "That's my first, Scotty. I'm coming back for another."

Linesman reflects on Pompey's Greatest Day.

1939 Final l to r. Scott, Morris, J. Anderson, F. Worrall
Jimmy Guthrie receives the F.A. Cup from King George VI.

Supporters welcome back the cup on coach in Guildhall Square

lis was beaten by the bounce of Worrall's centre and Anderson grabbed his share of the glory. Thirty seconds into the second half Parker raced away, pushed a pass to Barlow and when Scott beat out the shot, the little outside left was there to make it 3-0. As he passed the fallen giant Scott – at 6ft 3in he was the tallest keeper in the game – Parker promised to be back for a second. And he was; Dorsett made it 3-1 with a fine shot which gave Harry Walker no chance, but then Worrall floated over another accurate centre and Parker timed his run to perfection to beat Scott with a powerful header. So Pompey had won the Cup at the third attempt – and, through the efforts of Hitler, were to hold it until normality returned after World War II. Pompey's team was: Walker, Morgan, Rochford, Guthrie, Rowe, Wharton, Worrall, McAlinden, Anderson, Barlow and Parker.

The players returned to Portsmouth to a tumultuous reception from an enormous crowd and among the first people to get a close up view of the fabled trophy were the people of Bognor Regis who had hosted Pompey throughout their preparations. Pompey's share of the Wembley gate was £5,380 – and the players total bonus for the run to their triumph was £42!

It was during this season that Robert Blyth, that man of unique service to the club, resigned from the Board because of ill health. In November Salmond had been transferred to Chelsea, and a certain Peter Harris scored a hat trick as Portsmouth Schools beat Eastleigh 13-0.

December saw Scot Symon win his only Scottish cap against Hungary. Shortly before the semi final, Jimmy Easson's long service to the club ended with his transfer to Fulham, while in April the Barnes brothers from Gosport signed as amateurs. Wally, then an inside-forward, was later to 'make the grade' as a full back with Arsenal and Wales. In April, Flewin made his first team debut for Pompey as Grimsby were beaten 2-1 at Fratton and three days later they signed right back Bill Hindmarsh, who had played for Willington in the Amateur Cup final a short while earlier.

Pompey actually finished the season in 17th place, five points better off than relegated Birmingham. As they did so Beattie moved on to Millwall after scoring 28 goals in his 58 league appearances and during the summer the departures included Arthur Groves. The Cup run meant Pompey were able to show a credit balance of £9,075 after clearing off the previous year's loss of £6,289.

But the clouds of war were building up. In July Pompey's fans held their breath as their Cup final captain Jimmy Guthrie fought for his life in a Yorkshire hospital. Guthrie and Everton players Bill Cook and John Thomson had been involved in a car crash during an ARP blackout practice. Manager Tinn revealed that Guthrie had been defying a ban on players driving cars which had been imposed a fortnight previously. Happily after some time critically ill, Guthrie recovered and was able to watch the initial practice matches for 1939-40

Pompey manager Jack Tinn puts his spats and the Cup in a safe place.

season which was never to take place. It opened on August 26 against a Blackburn team which included John 'Dixie' Weddle and for the first time Pompey wore numbered shirts in a League match. But on September 3 war was declared and four days later League football was suspended for the duration. Later the F.A. sanctioned two regional competitions but there was little real interest. Fratton Park's attendance was limited to 8,000 and soccer became a somewhat haphazard affair, with players guesting for clubs, travel often difficult and the intervention of the Germans always possible.

In 1941 Pompey's scheduled home match with Brighton was a victim of enemy action but when matches were possible there were plenty of goals. Wilkes, the West Bromwich Albion centre-forward, who guested, was Pompey's top scorer in 1940-41 with 26 while centre-forward Andy Black, of Hearts and Scotland scored 16. Significantly in March 1941, Jack Froggatt made his debut for the reserves against Bitterne Nomads. A month earlier, Robert Blyth – a former player, captain, manager, director and chairman – died at the age of 71.

In 1942, Pompey reached the final of the War Cup and were beaten 2-1 by Brentford, but with a constant ebb and flow of players consistent competition was difficult. Pompey's reserve goalkeeper Ernie Butler returned from three years at sea in 1942 to play for Bath City – but a public appeal had to be made to find him a pair of boots. By then the name James William Dickinson appeared on the Fratton playing staff for the first time.

In 1943 another phenomenon developed; seven a side matches during factory dinner breaks to raise money for various funds. The first was in February and the players involved included Pompey's Guthrie, Barlow, Parker, Anderson, and Summerbee (actually a Preston North End player), Jimmy Allen (Aston Villa) and Buchanan and Foss of Chelsea. Admission was 6d. (2½p) and the match raised almost £40 for the London Bomb Children. Another seven-a-side match against Southampton raised money for the Aid to China Fund and goals by Barlow and Anderson earned a 2-2 draw.

In May 1943 Eddie Lever's discovery, Jimmy Dickinson 'gave a good account of himself' against Reading; on Jan 8 1944 Dickinson signed as a professional. November saw Pompey beat Aldershot 4-1 – the Shots included six internationals, Cullis, Britton, Mercer, Hagan, McCullock and Cunliffe, and repatriated prisoners of war were admitted free. Tommy Rowe, Pompey's Cup winning centre-half, had already been reported missing once when, in December 1943, he was awarded the Distinguished Flying Cross. Unhappily by the next March, Rowe who had been promoted Squadron Leader, was a prisoner of war having been shot down on a mission.

In March 1944, General Montgomery was elected Pompey's President and that same month Jack Tinn completed 25 years in management – 17 of them at Fratton Park. Later that year another name, shortly to become an integral part of the Fratton Park story, was heard for the first time. In October the Royal Navy beat a Royal Marines side which included Reg Flewin and Bill Pointon. The Navy side included an unknown sailor from H.M.S. Dolphin – right-half Jimmy Scoular. The match meant that several players, notably Flewin, were unable to play for Pompey against Watford, and so 18-year-old local winger Peter Harris made his debut. A month later, after scoring twice against an international-laden Aldershot side, Harris signed professional forms for the club. As the war entered its final throes, Tommy Rowe was welcomed back to Portsmouth in May 1945 after two years in a prisoner of war camp.

But players were still scattered and it was some time before any hint of normality would be seen. Goalkeeper Butler was still based in the North West and Pompey agreed to him helping Tranmere for a second season while Guy Wharton was to continue as captain of Darlington. In August 1945 Fratton Park was the stage for a major boxing tournament with 10,000 there to see Jock McAvoy knock out Johnny Clements in the sixth round. At the same time Pompey announced that for the first time since 1939, they would run a reserve team. Jack Froggatt, who had made intermittent appearances for the club during the war, eventually signed in September 1945. Two months later Tranmere's attempt to make Butler's signing permanent was refused and he returned to Pompey – and as he did so sailor Jimmy Scoular played for Pompey Reserves as they beat Aldershot 3-1.

But the boom days were approaching, with the public released from the constraints of the wartime situation desperate for entertainment. That was amply proved in December 1945 when a crowd of 30,000 watched the Combined Services beat an F.A. XI including Peter Harris 4-1 at Fratton Park. A few days before that match, an almost unknown inside-forward who had impressed with his performances for the Royal Marines, led Pompey Reserves attack as QPR were beaten 3-1. Len Phillips had arrived.

In January 1946 the F.A. Cup's long sojourn with Pompey ended. The emergency competition was played over two legs and Pompey's hold on their cherished trophy was broken by Birmingham City by the only goal of the two matches – and that cruelly was an own goal by Flewin. Gradually though the team for the future took shape. In March Duggie Reid was bought from Stockport County and Harry Ferrier came South to guest from Barnsley and quickly made the move permanent. In April McAlinden who had returned to Ireland on the outbreak of war, rejoined Pompey but as the last season of war-time stringency ended Pompey gave free transfers to such men as Lew Morgan, Tommy Rowe and Freddie Worrall while Jimmy Guthrie, Jock Anderson and Bill Rochford were transfer listed. Anderson was quickly snapped up by Aldershot after scoring 36 goals in 80 league appearances for Pompey while Rochford moved to Southampton and Morgan to Watford. As they went, Jasper Yeuell, a 22-year-old soldier arrived.

But times were hard. The war years had taken their toll on Pompey's kit and before they could pick up the threads of their First Division adventure, had to be re-placed. Rationing was still in force, so the club appealed for 500 clothing coupons to allow the shirts to be acquired. Eventually enough came in and so the Football League resumed for the 1946-47 season – but without spectacular success for Pompey.

It began with Dickinson playing his first League match on August 31, the day that Guthrie was elected the fifth chairman of the Professional Footballers' Association – Guthrie in fact was to join Crystal Palace in the November as player-coach. But although Reid, whose signing had been treated with some scepticism by a public deceived by his leggy appearance, had quickly won them over with the power of his shooting, Pompey found the going hard. By Christmas they were at the bottom of the table and by the halfway mark in the programme had collected only 15 points.

The turn of the year brought a dramatic turn-around and from New Years' Day until March 15 they were unbeaten and gradually killed off the talk of relegation to finish in a respectable 12th place with 41 points from 42 matches. Reid was the side's only ever-present and his 29 goals were the best since Easson hit 29 in 1930-31. Their attempt to re-gain the F.A. Cup was short-lived. Doncaster were beaten 3-2 away from home in the third round and in the fourth Birmingham repeated their single goal win of the previous season. But as the season drew to a close with gates averaging 30,000 few realised that an era was ending. As the last match was played, Jack Tinn announced that he was retiring after 20 dramatic years in which he had steered Pompey to three Wembley finals, culminating in the triumph of 1939. At the same time his reserve team in 1936 had been the only

provincial side to take the London Combination title out of the capital.

Pompey's Board did not have far to look for the successor to Jack Tinn. Bob Jackson had been their chief scout for some time and had massive experience as a player in his native North West, as a scout and then coach with Bolton Wanderers and as manager of Southern League Worcester City. The massive gates were reflected in the financial statistics of that first 'normal' season – a profit of £20,350. McAlinden was, in fact, to play only one League match of the '47-48 season which ended in a 1-0 win for Burnley at Fratton Park. Then the Irishman, who was later to figure in one of the most dramatic and controversial phases in the Fratton story, was transferred to Stoke City for £7,000.

Jackson quickly made his first major signing – and a significant one it was to prove. He signed Ike Clarke, a powerfully built centre-forward, from West Bromwich Albion . . . . the last link in the chain which was to carry Pompey to the pinnacle had been forged. By then Dickinson had finally completed his Royal Navy service. But there was no consistency about the side's performance and eventually they finished in eighth place in spring 1948. Again Cup success eluded them. Brighton were soundly beaten 4-1 in the third round but Preston North End ended their crowd's dreams 3-1 at Fratton Park. Late in the season Pompey paid a fee of £10,500 for Dundee's centre-forward Albert Juliussen but it was to prove a brief stay on the South Coast for the former Huddersfield player. Within six months he had been sold to Everton. There was no loss; the fee was the same £10,500 and Juliussen left with a record of scoring four goals in seven appearances.

Duggie 'Thunderboots' Reid

Sir Harry Lauder, Manager Tinn and Trainer Jack Warner with the Pompey squad in training kit.

Pompey season 1946/47

Back row: A. Stott, E. Butler, R. Humpston, H. Walker, J. Foxton
Centre row: J. Easson (Asst. Trainer), R. Flewin, L. Phillips, P. Rookes, F. Evans, D. Reid, H. Ferrier, T. Hedworth, W. Thompson, D. J. Clarke (Asst. Sec.-Manager)
Front row: Mr. J. W. Tinn (Sec.-Manager), R. Nutley, P. Harris, W. Hindmarsh, J. Froggatt, G. Wharton (Captain), H. Barlow, J. McAlinden, C. Parker, J. Stewart (Trainer, Coach)

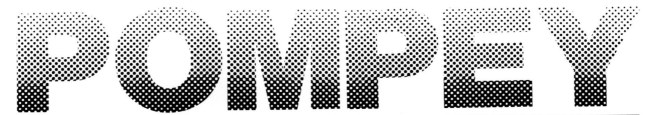

9. Golden Glory

So Pompey approached 1948-49, their Golden Jubilee Year – with this challenge from chairman Vernon Stokes. "Win the championship for the Jubilee!" was his message to the players as the season approached. This was to be the first full season for Pompey's famous red-socks; the change had been made the previous Christmas. The players' response must have surprised even the optimistic Mr. Stokes.

Pompey had traditionally been slow starters – not this time. They opened by drawing 2-2 at Preston but then strung together six wins to be top of the table by mid-September. It was a run in which they conceded only one goal – at home to Charlton – while they scored 15. Indeed it was not until mid-October that they lost their first match – 22 points from a possible 36. Significantly a settled side was paying off – Gerry Bowler had twice stood in for Flewin, otherwise manager Jackson had been able to say 'same again' every time. And, inevitably, their success was an enormous magnet to the public. On October 10 Newcastle were visitors. The first queues began to form at 9.30 a.m., by 1 p.m. the South Stand was completely full. In the end Fratton bulged with a then record 46,327 crowd who were rewarded by a Phillips goal which gave them victory and a three point lead at the top.

Pompey's birthday though was planned for November 27 when Arsenal were the visitors. Again there was another enormous crowd, including many players who had been with Pompey from their Southern League days. They and the entire 1939 F.A. Cup winning team, were the guests of honour. They were introduced to the crowd by Pompey's President Lord Montgomery and before the kick off Monty and team captain Reg Flewin cut a large birthday cake. By this time Reid was out of the side and Clarke had come in and the team rose to an electrifying atmosphere of the day by producing a superlative display of football to beat Arsenal 4-1 with a goal each from Froggatt, Phillips, Barlow and Clarke. And so the triumphal progress continued until April 23

when they clinched the title in their 39th match.

They did so away from home and the win was doubly historic – for it was also the first time that Pompey had managed to win at Bolton. The championship trophy was presented a week later at the final home match when Huddersfield were beaten 2-0 to preserve a proud un-beaten Fratton Park record – 18 wins and three draws. But, perhaps, in anti climax the champions were to end the season with two defeats – at Highbury and Old Trafford where Arsenal and Manchester United both won 3-2. That win clinched second place for United – and this was the only occasion that Pompey lost two matches in a row all season. Pompey actually used 18 players to achieve their success – but effectively only 12 for Hindmarsh, Yeuell, Parker, Bill Thompson, Bowler and Lindy Delapenha made ten or fewer appearances.

Butler and Scoular were the only players to appear in every match, Dickinson and Froggatt each missed one, Ferrier, Harris and Phillips two. Harris and Reid finished joint top scorers with 17 goals – Reid's coming in 29 matches – with Froggatt, Clarke and Phillips also in double figures. Oddly though Pompey's enormous success did not attract the international selectors – not one player was called up by his country that season.

The response of the public to these events was staggering; Pompey's 21 home matches were watched by a total of 762,398, an average of some 36,000, not including the 1,000 shareholders and season ticket holders. And for much of the season there was also a prospect of Pompey emulating Preston North End and Aston Villa by becoming the first side to achieve the League and F.A. Cup double in the 20th Century. Hapless Stockport County from the Third Division North were overwhelmed 7-0 in the third round. Harris hit the first of his senior hat tricks with Clarke and Phillips each getting two. The fourth round brought Sheffield Wednesday to Fratton and a massive 47,188 watched Pompey win 2-1 with goals by Harris and Phillips; then Newport County were eased out of the way 3-2 (Phillips two more

PORTSMOUTH FOOTBALL CLUB
Football League Division 1. Champions 1948–49.

Sons

(signatures) Jackson.   D. Reid   McCumm.   E. Butler   H. Ferrier   J. Dickinson   J. M. Stew

Francl.   J. Scoular   L. Flewin   J. Clarke   S. Phillips   Froggat

Montgomery of Alamein.

and Froggatt) to bring Derby County to Fratton for the sixth round.

This was a meeting of collosus, Derby had become the second team to arrest Pompey's march towards the title with a single goal win at the Baseball Ground in November, and everyone wanted to see it. In the end the gates were forced shut on a staggering 51,385 – a record which will never be beaten – and they were rewarded by two goals from Clarke which clinched a 2-1 win. Now the twin towers of Wembley were beckoning; only Second Division strugglers Leicester City stood between Pompey and a fourth final appearance. The semi-final at Highbury lured almost 25,000 Pompey fans to London – to be bitterly disappointed. Pompey chose this occasion to produce their poorest form of the season and Leicester won 3-1 preventing a repeat of that 1939 final against Wolves.

It was to be a busy summer for Pompey. Their success brought an invitation to tour Sweden and Denmark. In Sweden they did much to repair the image of English football which had been dented by Sweden's 3-1 victory over England. The repair job was done by becoming the first side to beat Gothenburg in Gothenburg since 1939, winning 4-2 in front of 27,900. Four matches were played in Denmark, three won and the other drawn. Dickinson missed most of the matches as he was with the England party touring Scandinavia; playing for the 'B' side in Finland and the 'A' in Norway – the start of his illustrious international career. Pompey retained 40 professionals, including 17-year-old Johnny Gordon, transfer listing only two – Tommy Brown, one of manager Jackson's first signing's on succeeding Jack Tinn – and Gordon Neave.

By the time the players reported back to begin preparations for the defence of their title, Fratton Park had had a facelift with the Milton End re-terraced. This was to be Cliff Parker's 18th season at Fratton – and Phil Gunter's first. It was also preceded by Bowler's transfer to Hull City. The defence opened encouragingly with a 3-1 win at Newcastle but the first home match was drawn, the second lost! Blackpool visited on August 27, 1949 and won 3-2 – the first side to leave Fratton smiling since Boxing Day 1947.

So began a season which ultimately had a climax as tight and tense as that epic of '26-27 and the goal average promotion to the First Division. In the first six matches Pompey suffered three defeats and by the end of September had only 12 points from ten matches. The consis-

Keenly watching the players training are (left to right) Mr. R. Vernon Stokes (Chairman), Mr. S. B. Leverett (Director), Mr. Bob Jackson (Manager), Messrs. Jimmy Easson and Billy Wright (Trainers) and Mr. Jimmy Stewart (Chief Trainer and Coach)

A narrow squeak for Elvy the Bolton goalkeeper with Peter Harris attacking strongly in the first half.

Newlands, the Preston 'keeper received attention for injury after this goalmouth tussle with Jack Froggatt. Peter Harris can be seen in the centre and Ike Clarke on the right.

Peter Harris jumps high to head the ball goalwards. No. 5 is Charlton's centre-half Phipps. Doug Reid is on the right.

Len Phillips Pompey's clever inside-left displays perfect balance and ball control watched by Jack Froggatt and Preston defender.

Harry Ferrier (No. 3) Pompey's left back, starts an attack, with Bert Barlow and Jim Dickinson on the left. Taken on the south side, near players' entrance, looking towards Fratton End and Villa goal.

Reg Flewin (No. 5) Pompey captain and centre-half heads away. Watched by from the left Ernie Butler, Jim Dickinson (3rd from left), Phil Rookes, Jasper Yeuell (behind Flewin) and Stanley Mortensen on extreme right. Fog persisted throughout the game.

Robertson, Chelsea's goalkeeper, clearing an attack by Jack Froggatt, who is obscured by a Chelsea defender. Jim McAlinden and Doug Reid are on the left. Taken at the Milton End looking towards North End.

Robinson (R), Sunderland goalkeeper, holds a shot from Peter Harris (No. 7). Sunderland centre-half Hall is obstructing Doug Reid. Taken at Milton End.

tency of the previous season continued to elude them and early on the defence was disrupted by the loss of Flewin who had an appendicitis operation which kept him out for almost three months. In the autumn, Jackson worried by injuries to his full-backs, signed Bradford Scottish international Jimmy Stephen for £10,500 and in November he made his debut against Sunderland – his only appearance that season – and so too did Danish international centre-forward Dan Ekner, the first Continental to pull on a Pompey jersey. Ekner was to play just four times without scoring and then returned to Scandinavia in March.

In March at Derby, Scoular and England's Johnny Morris were both sent off after an angry clash – and almost two months later that was to be the cause of angry recrimination by Pompey and their supporters. For it was not until the end of April, with the championship battle delicately poised – Pompey, Wolves, Sunderland and Manchester United were all very interested – that the F.A. announced that Scoular would be suspended for 14 days from May 1. Horrified, Pompey realized that their tough tackling Scot would miss the last two matches at Arsenal and at home to Aston Villa. Without Scoular Pompey were to lose 2-0 at Highbury and so everything rested on the last match.

Pompey had to win. But if they dropped a point to Villa and Wolves beat already relegated Birmingham, then the Midlanders would snatch the title by a point. It was a nail-biting afternoon for another huge Fratton crowd. Bill Thompson, deputizing for Clarke, got things off to a sensational start with a goal inside a minute – almost immediately the news came through that Pye had scored for Wolves. By half time Pompey were 2-0 up, Wolves 5-0. Pompey added three more in the second half to win 5-1 while Wolves finished 6-1 winners. It left both with 53 points, and Pompey the first club since Huddersfield in 1923-24 to win on goal average and the first since Sheffield Wednesday in '28-29, 29-30 to successfully defend the title. In the end their superb defensive record – only 38 goals conceded in 42 matches - saw them home. Pompey's average was 1.947, Wolves 1.551. Butler again appeared in every match, so too did Ferrier, with Dickinson missing two, Harris and Froggatt three. Clarke, who missed the two last matches, was the top scorer with 17 goals with Harris, Froggatt and Reid all in double figures.

The F.A. Cup held another 'mini' run. Norwich were beaten in the third round, although it needed a replay after the Third Division side had surprisingly drawn 1-1 at Fratton Park. Delapenha scored the goal which prevented a giant killing in what was to be his penultimate appearance for the club. For in the last week of the season the Jamaican was sold to Middlesbrough. In the replay at Carrow Road Reid scored both goals and in the fourth round Grimsby were thrashed 5-0, before the fifth round produced an away meeting with Manchester United. That saw an epic battle and a 3-3 draw, goals by Clarke, Parker and a Ferrier penalty. But the replay at Fratton went wrong and Manchester won 3-1. De-

lapenha was one of two notable departures during the season – Bert Barlow, of Wembley glory, also moved to Leicester City. Pompey's success finally caught the selectorial eye for Dickinson, Harris and Froggatt were all capped, although at the end of the season only Dickinson made the England party for a Continental tour which was to be a 'shake down' trip for the World Cup in Rio.

In late May though Pompey's supporters were stunned by the shock news that the club's chairman Vernon Stokes and another director Harry Wain had been suspended sine die for irregularities over the return of McAlinden to Fratton from Ireland. There was an alleged illegal payment of £750 to the Irishman who was suspended from playing until October 1 while manager Jack Tinn was censured and Pompey were fined £750. It stirred up a furore and in February 1951 after a re-consideration of the evidence and after receiving a 25,000 signature petition from the Supporters' Club the F.A. lifted the ban and Messrs. Stokes and Wain were reinstated. So in Portsmouth, at least, the news of England – Dickinson included – losing 1-0 to the United States in the World Cup in late June was almost insignificant against the McAlinden affair. While Dickinson was in South America, Reg Flewin toured Canada with the F.A.

It was a summer without major changes of playing staff, Cliff Parker was there for a 19th season, so were all the men who had played the major roles in the championship. Now the question was whether Pompey could achieve a hat trick as Arsenal had in the early years of the 1930's. Before a ball had been kicked the first disappointment hit – Butler, who had stretched out a run of 113 consecutive appearances, damaged a finger in a practice match and was ruled out of the opening match of the 50-51 season against Middlesbrough. So Ron Humpston, who had waited patiently since January 1948 when he had made two League appearances, was in goal against a Boro side which included Delapenha. It took four matches for them to record their first win – 4-1 against Sheffield Wednesday – and in between Reid had scored his 100th League goal. Early in the season National Service claimed Pompey's 18-year-old Scottish centre-forward Jackie Henderson who had already begun to make a name for himself in the reserves. Humpston kept his place for seven matches but then Butler returned although he too had to settle for a spell in the reserves in mid-season as Maurice Leather took over. Consistency though was missing and it was quickly obvious that the title was not to be their's for a third time.

Significantly early in the New Year, Froggatt made the switch from attack to centre-half to take over from Flewin and Belgian-born Marcel Gaillard, who had been signed from Crystal Palace, replaced him in the number 11 shirt. His second match was a milestone in Pompey's history – their 700th League match, although it ended in a 2-1 defeat at Liverpool. It was also a milestone for both Dickinson and Froggatt – Dickinson's

Pompey claim their second successive League Championship.

Jimmy Scoular

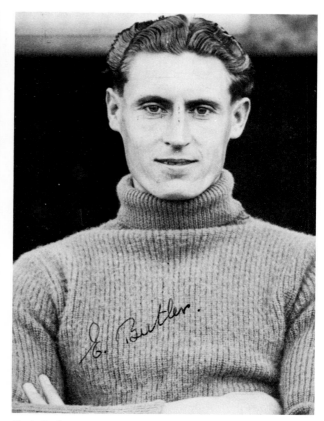

Ernie Butler

190th appearance for the club and Froggatt's 180th. Butler eventually reclaimed his place in late February and it coincided with Pompey's first consistent run of the season. They lost only one of their final 14 matches and eventually fought their way up to finish in seventh place. That run also saw the start of Albert Mundy's career, having signed from Gosport in February. By the end of the season, Mundy had scored five goals in 12 matches. Reid was once again Pompey's top League scorer with 21 goals in 38 appearances.

The F.A. Cup held the biggest disappointment for years – a fall at the first hurdle, beaten 2-0 at Luton. At the end of the season, the club announced that the North Stand was to be improved during the summer, with the installation of 4,226 seats. Season tickets there would cost £6.10s., the same as those in the centre section of the South Stand with those in the Milton wing of the South Stand £1 cheaper. They also announced that they would be retaining 50 players, but transfer listed fullbacks Bill Hindmarsh and Phil Rookes.

As soon as the season ended, Pompey embarked on their biggest overseas adventure – a three week tour of South America. It was to produce no great glory but many new experiences. The first match produced an incident which cast a shadow over the rest of the trip. Jimmy Scoular was sent off against Fluminese and eventually Pompey lost 2-1 in front of a crowd estimated at almost 200,000. Eventually Scoular returned home on his own and Pompey stayed on to lose two more matches and draw two. They lost 3-2 to Brazil's leading club America and 4-0 to Santos but drew 1-1 with Sao Paolo and 0-0 with Palmeiras who were on their way to the Brazilian championship. The party returned to Hampshire with tales of matches played behind security fences and moats – a taste of English things to come – of crowd's throwing firecrackers and of poor hospitality.

During the summer Pompey paid out their biggest ever fee – £20,000 – to sign Chesterfield outside left Gordon Dale. They also allowed amateur John Atyeo who had made two League appearances in the 1950-51 season, to join Bristol City as a part-time professional – a move which was to be spectacularly successful for him. Atyeo went on to make more than 600 senior appearances for the West Country club and score 315 League goals.

As the 1951-52 season started, Vernon Stokes was re-elected chairman, some six months after being re-instated, and at the annual meeting it was reported that the club had paid a massive £25,506 in tax and entertainment tax the previous season. Injuries made things difficult at the start and manager Jackson was forced to give 18-year-old Johnny Gordon his debut in the second match of the season – a 3-1 home defeat by Blackpool. Gordon, who was doing his National Service stationed

Harry Ferrier

Peter Harris

conveniently at Hilsea – as was Henderson – played the next match but then had to wait until the final fixture of the season for his third. Despite the injuries, Pompey still made a solid start – five wins and a draw in the first seven matches – and hopes began to run high again. But they were unable to field a settled side and results were inconsistent. Henderson got his chance in mid-autumn and his emergence signalled the beginning of the end for Clarke.

But they were still well placed as the run-in to the season began, only to hit a disastrous spell, winning only three of their last 11 matches. The last four were all lost and in the end Pompey finished fourth to Manchester United, but only six points short of second place. It was a season of personal milestones – Ferrier, Butler, Scoular and Harris all made their 200th League appearances, while Alec Wilson, Phil Gunter and Charlie Dore all made their debuts. In the end Pompey used 28 players in League matches with Dickinson and Harris each missing only two and Reid again top scoring with 16 goals in 30 appearances. Almost 700,000 saw the home matches – an average of 32,500.

The Cup had its moments. In the third round they beat Lincoln City 4-0, then Notts County were visited and beaten 3-1, in the fifth round Doncaster were the Fratton Park victims of a 4-0 defeat to bring Pompey up against Joe Harvey's Newcastle in the sixth round. Tick-

ets for that match were put on sale a week previously at the Reserve match at Fratton Park – the result was a crowd of 30,289. Not so happy was the result when Newcastle arrived; they won 4-2 and were ultimately to go on to lift the trophy, making up for their defeat at Wembley the previous season. Gaillard who had not previously played a Cup match, scored in every round, two against Lincoln.

It was the season when Pompey played their first floodlight match – a friendly against Saints at the Dell on October 22 – and the same month hospital broadcasting started from Fratton Park. In November Len Phillips won his first England cap against Ireland, with Dickinson also in the team, and shortly before Christmas Humpston, who had so long and patiently understudied Butler, moved to Huddersfield. Phillips went on the transfer list in January 1952 and Pompey were reported to be seeking £30,000, but before anything came of it, differences were patched up and Phillips came off the list.

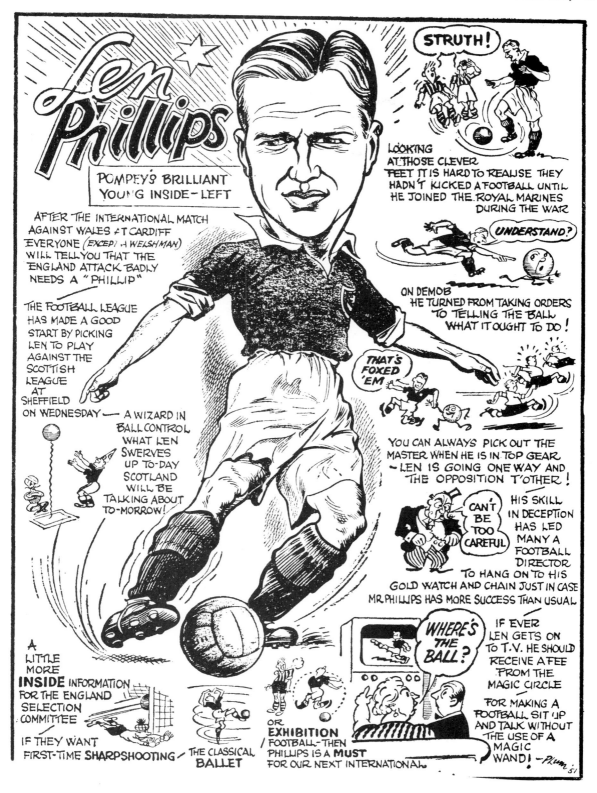

An Evening News tribute by 'Plum' in 1951.

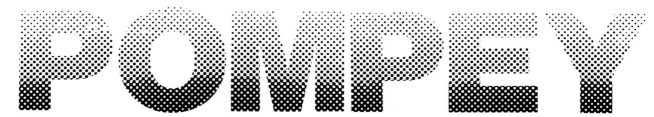

10. End of an Era

The summer was to hold a major shock with the announcement that manager Bob Jackson was leaving the club. Jackson, who had steered Pompey to their twin championships, had been offered a five year contract by ambitious Hull City and moved to the East Coast. Unhappily, the change did not pay off for the man who had given Pompey such loyal and successful service and four years later he was back in the headlines, suing Hull for wrongful dismissal. Again, as in the summer of '47 when Jack Tinn retired, Pompey's board went for a man they knew. Eddie Lever, who had first moved to Fratton in 1929, had always retained some links with the club although he had been released and was teaching in Alton. He had for some time been working with the reserves and it was he who took over in August 1952 as the eighth manager in Pompey's history. During the summer Jasper Yeuell, who had played a supporting role in both championships moved to Barnsley.

Lever's reign scarcely started propitiously, with Blackpool winning 2-0 at Fratton in the opening match and he had to wait until the fifth to celebrate his first victory – a 2-0 success over Manchester United. The next match saw Lever's Alton protege Dickinson reach a club milestone – the first player to play 250 League matches. The previous best was Cliff Parker's 244, but Parker, the last survivor of the '39 Wembley team was now a permanent member of the reserves and not in the first team reckoning. Lever's first move into the transfer market came in early November when he signed goalkeeper Norman Uprichard from Swindon, and the Irishman marked his debut with an own goal against Spurs – but had the last laugh with Pompey gaining a welcome 2-1 win. His arrival put a major question mark over the future of Butler – and then in early December the goalkeeping stalwart of the championships fractured a wrist in a reserve match – and that was to finish his distinguished career. The bone failed to knit properly, the wrist was still in plaster at the end of the season and during the summer of 1953 he retired from the game.

Butler's injury came a week before another step in the break up of the championship team. Scoular, that tough and uncompromising character who had fought so many battles for the club, was placed on the transfer list at his own request after being dropped. His absence was brief, but even when he regained a regular place, he remained eager to move and that wish was granted during the summer when he joined Newcastle. But on the playing field, Lever's side found a consistent level of performance elusive and Pompey had their hardest time for some years. Again Lever went into the transfer market in March signing 31-year-old centre-forward Charlie Vaughan, an England 'B' player, from Charlton – the first player signed from a fellow First Division club since Barlow in 1939. He scored on his debut, in a 2-1 home win over Burnley.

But results remained patchy, although the later stages of the season held one of the highlights. Pompey had to face Newcastle without either Dickinson or Froggatt who were in the England side which drew 2-2 with Scotland at Wembley. Duggie Reid deputized for Froggatt in the middle of the defence, Reg Pickett for Dickinson, and Pompey romped to a 5-1 success, helped by Vaughan's second goal. But that was their last success of the season, the final two matches were lost, and Pompey finished in 15th place, only four points ahead of relegated Stoke City.

The one consistent factor during the season had again been Harris. Although still overlooked by England the flying winger missed only one League match and scored 23 goals. The F.A. Cup held similar disappointment to the League; Burnley fought a tough 1-1 draw in the third round at Fratton and then won the replay 3-1. A major development though was the installation of Fratton's first floodlights and on March 2 neighbours Saints repaid the visit Pompey had made to the Dell the previous season, to open the era of night football with a 1-1 draw. That same month a young man who was shortly to make an exciting entry into Pompey's world, Pat Neil of

Froggatt for England!   —By Plum

'Plum' – Alexander Plummer – pays another tribute.

Portsmouth Northern Grammar School, played for England Schools against Wales at Wembley. And a month later he helped England beat Eire 8-0 at Fratton.

The season had opened with a massive gate of 43,072 to watch the first match against Blackpool, but the last - a crushing 4-1 defeat by Middlesbrough – was seen by only 18,765. Despite that the average was still a very healthy 31,270. There followed a summer of departures. Ernie Butler, of course, retired; so too did the veteran Parker while Scoular finally got his move and took over as captain of Newcastle.

But there were no major recruitments and 1953-54 season got underway disastrously. The first four matches were lost and 16 goals were conceded. To add to the problems, Uprichard sustained an injury which was to prevent him playing from August 25 until the first match of the following season. So Lever quickly brought in Ted Platt from Arsenal while the defence was restructured with Duggie Reid switching to centre-half, a role he had carried out occasionally, and Phil Gunter and Barry Mansell getting the full-back berths. But it was in early November that the decisive changes were made which were to transform the season. A second Mansell was added to the wage bill – Jack from Cardiff – and Lever paired him with young Scotsman Alex Wilson who had been awaiting his chance for some time. Len Phillips also switched to right half and from the middle of November Pompey suddenly became invincible in front of their own fans. From then until the end of the season they were unbeaten in 12 matches – nine wins and three draws. So in the end Pompey, though not the old force, finished in 14th place.

The second half of the season was also illuminated by tremendous F.A. Cup excitement. Pompey were drawn at home to Charlton Athletic in the third round and were held to a 3-3 draw but snatched a dramatic 3-2 replay victory with an extra time winner by the dependable Harris. It was a match which saw local boy Mike Barnard score his first goal and veteran Flewin make his first senior appearance for more than 12 months. Their opponents in the fourth round were Third Division North promotion dreamers Scunthorpe United. The match at the Old Show Ground was a dramatic affair.

After 14 minutes Platt was injured and Duggie Reid went into goal; but the ten men held out to earn a 1-1 draw. Scunthorpe were unimpressed by Pompey's growing reputation for home invincibility and earned a 2-2 draw in the replay in front of more than 30,000. Pompey now had both senior goalkeepers injured and R.A.F. amateur Mervyn Gill played in that match and in the second replay at Highbury where class eventually told and Pompey won 4-0 helped by two goals by Froggatt who had been recalled from the reserves to his old role at outside left. Bolton Wanderers were awaiting the winners, and Pompey, with Gill still in goal, battled to force a 0-0 draw in Lancashire. The replay lured 45,806 through the Fratton turnstiles, but Bolton eventually won 2-1. The seven Cup ties were watched by a total of 247,222 people with total receipts of £32,554.

Jack Froggatt

Froggatt also played in the two Bolton matches and then in the 3-2 League win over Burnley at Fratton on February 27 – and was then sold to Leicester City; another link gone. The season contained yet another milestone for the mercurial Harris – his 100th League goal coming in his 268th appearance. Again he finished top scorer with 20 goals in 40 matches but he was hard pressed by Johnny Gordon who scored 18 in the same 40 matches. By the time the season ended Dickinson had stretched his run of League appearances to 324. In all Gill played seven matches as stand-in for Platt – yet it was not to be the start of a dramatic success story for the young airman. The following season with Uprichard fit once more both he and Platt played only once – and Gill's appearance was in a friendly.

As the season ended Tommy McGhee, who had been spotted playing Naval football and had made a big impression in the reserves, signed on – and championship team full-back Harry Ferrier moved to manage Gloucester City after more than 240 appearances. Two ambitious inside-forwards – Ron Rafferty and Derek Rees – signed from amateur football during the summer but Charlie Vaughan, after a season of injuries, stepped down into non-league football with Bexley Heath. The problems Lever had faced in that second season in charge were probably best summed up by this statistic – in all matches, friendlies included, Pompey used 37 players!

The contrast was to be seen in season 1954-55. Pompey had still not made any major signings but Lever was able to call on a largely settled side – with one major exception. For this was to be the season when they had to make do for long periods without Mr. Unflappable – Jimmy Dickinson. He missed the first six matches through injury, then came back but in November broke an ankle playing at Cardiff and was absent for four months, giving a rare chance of regular work to Pickett. Uprichard was now fit and to miss only one match all season – on October 2 he was playing for Northern Ireland and was beaten by shots by Johnny Haynes and Don Revie as England won 2-0 in Belfast. In his absence Pompey drew 1-1 against Preston. At home Pompey picked up where they had left off the previous season and stretched their unbeaten run a further eight matches before Cardiff won 3-1 on November 20 – a span of 53 weeks.

But although the side was largely settled, they were still capable of wildly fluctuating performances and in the end it was to cost them the chance of a third championship. They reached Easter handily placed for the title and facing a West Bromwich side already thrashed 6-1 at Fratton and Charlton who had also been comfortably beaten. But at the Hawthorns they lost 3-1 and then their failure to do more than get a point at the Valley effectively spelled the end of their challenge. Just to underline their unpredictability, they rounded off the season by losing 5-2 to a Sheffield United side beaten 6-2 earlier. So they eventually finished in third place behind Chelsea and Wolves. In the end nine players played 30 or more matches with Mansell the only ever present and Harris and Jackie Henderson missing only one each. Harris who took his appearance record to 323, once more top scored with 23 goals – four of them in the 6-2 win over Sheffield United – while Henderson, always a figure of controversy with the Fratton public, hit 13.

Dickinson had recovered from his broken ankle to resume his place for the later stages of the season and was a member of the England party which played three matches on the Continent in May – a none too successful expedition which ended in defeats against France and Portugal and a draw in Madrid. But his return had virtually coincided with the loss of Len Phillips with knee trouble – an injury which effectively finished a brilliant career. To further underline their unpredictability Pompey had also contrived to lose 2-1 away to Bristol Rovers from Division II in the third round of the F.A. Cup. The season had seen another full-back partnership forged; Mansell had begun with Wilson at right-back, but National Service removed the Scot and McGhee moved in. In the Spring the Army also claimed local boy Ray Crawford who had stepped up to full professional status during the season. Plans for covering the Fratton End were announced during the season and the development was also to include a small gym. Three prominent figures in the club's history died during the season – vice chairman Mr. Harry Wain, trainer and former player Jimmy Nichol and Pompey's first goalkeeper Matt Reilly.

Reilly 'a fine-looking, moustached Irishman', died at his home in Donnybrook, Dublin, in December.

The notable change in the team when season 1955-56 began was the inclusion of schools international Pat Neil as deputy for the injured Harris in the opening match at Huddersfield. Harris was back for the first home match at the expense of the youngster, but Neil replaced Dale for the third match and by mid-October had played nine times and fitted in two amateur international appearances as well. Neil marked his home debut against Blackpool on August 27 with his first goal and with Henderson and, inevitably, Harris also scoring, Pompey drew 3-3. Their start was solid, five wins and two draws in the first nine matches, and hopes ran high. But again they were unable to sustain their consistency and although they put together a six match unbeaten run around Christmas, they eventually did well to finish in mid-table.

The season saw the end of Duggie Reid's great service to Pompey. He was at centre-half for the first 18 matches, then lost his place to Phil Gunter and although he played the last match of the season in attack, it was his 309th and last. In that time the big, raw-boned Scot had repaid a paltry fee by scoring 128 League goals. Three players missed only one League match – Uprichard, Harris and Mansell. Uprichard's only absence came when he helped Northern Ireland to a 2-1 win over

Jimmy Dickinson

Scotland to provide Alan Barnett, who had signed from Croydon in September, with an early debut. Harris took his total League appearances to 364 – just 22 fewer than Dickinson – and late in the season he scored his 150th League Goal. The F.A. Cup held a double disappointment – early defeat and the end for Phillips. He had made a tentative return in the reserves in December and by the time Grimsby came to Fratton in early January in the third round, was ready for a major test. But his injury recurred and it was to be his last appearance in Pompey's colours. Happily at least, the match ended in a 3-1 win but they were beaten 2-0 by West Bromwich Albion at the Hawthorns in the next round.

February 22 1956 was to be a significant day for football as a whole. Newcastle were the visitors and won 2-0 in the first Football League match to be played under floodlights. In March Arthur Egerton Knight, that legend of Pompey's early days, died at the age of 68. During the summer, Harris who had had the mis-fortune to be in the prime at the same time as Tom Finney and Stanley Matthews, earned a little more recognition. In addition to his two England caps – one in 1950 and the other four years later – he was now invited to tour South Africa with the F.A. Jack Mansell was also in the party. It was to be a costly trip for Mansell. He damaged a cartilage and was to miss the first three months of the 1956-57 season.

That season opened with the new £40,000 Fratton End Stand in use and with the appointment of Stephen Cribb as Pompey's first Vice President in recognition of 38 years' service to the board. The unfortunate Phillips had joined Poole Town and Duggie Reid had taken over as player-manager of Tonbridge . . . . the championship connection was slimming down, only Dickinson and Harris survived of players who had won the title. They were both to pass the 400-match milestone during the season.

But Pompey were headed for their most difficult campaign for 30 years. They endured a dreadful September, winning only one of their first ten matches, and from then until the end of the season were never higher than fifth from bottom. Once again injury played its part. This time Mike Barnard, their locally raised Hampshire cricketing inside-forward, damaged a cartilage in October after showing his most consistent and promising form, and was not to play again all season. By the time March arrived, the public were beginning to resign themselves to the end of the First Division adventure. They slumped to second from bottom and when a run of nine matches into early April brought a return of only five points, it seemed their fears would be borne out. But at Bolton, the scene of some of their leanest returns, Pompey battled to a 1-1 draw on April 13 and they followed that with three wins in a row. Cardiff were beaten 1-0 at Fratton, Wolves 1-0 – avenging a 6-0 humiliation at Molyneux in Dickinson's 400th match – and then they won 2-0 at Ninian Park. It was a mini-run which was just enough to steer them clear of relegation, the fate reserved for Charlton and Cardiff.

Arthur Egerton Knight – no mention on the stone of football

Dickinson played in every match, for some of the season switching to the problem position of centre-half, even though that effectively brought a premature end to his international lifespan . . . . Pompey came first. Harris missed only three matches but for once was not top scorer. That honour went to Gordon with 13, Harris and Henderson each got 11. The goal Harris remembered most was the ninth on April 19 – that beat Cardiff at Fratton and came in his 400th appearance. It had not been Harris's best season, for once much of his sparkle had been missing, but he was his old self in early January as he scored twice to see Pompey to a 3-1 F.A. Cup third round win over Bury at Gigg Lane. They managed that victory with some comfort although Dickinson was injured, but in the fourth round went out 3-1 at home to Nottingham Forest. Pompey had struggled although Lever had been busy in the lower reaches of the transfer market bringing in Derek Weddle from Sunderland for £6,500 and Jimmy Clugston from Glentoran – both in January – and then Alec Stenhouse from Dundee the following month.

On The Honours List! —By Plum

Evening News artist 'Plum' pays homage again.

But none were really ready for the demands of the battle, although Weddle, a centre-forward like his namesake of the 30's, was to score six goals in 17 appearances. More significantly, Crawford had returned from Army Service in Malaya with the nickname Jungle Boy and a thirst for goals. Over Easter while the seniors were battling for survival, the reserves were stating their case for consideration with 15 goals in three matches . . . . nine of them by Crawford. The end of the season brought an exodus of fringe players – Pickett, who had so often deputized with distinction at wing-half, joined Ipswich, so too did Derek Rees, Harry Penk went to Plymouth, Les McDonald to Exeter and David Griffiths to Aldershot. But there were no significant additions to a playing staff who had almost found the demands beyond them the previous season. By the time they reported back the biggest change was that Doug Davidson, the former East Fife and Blackpool player, had joined the training staff. Then in late August 1957 Eddie Lever's pursuit of a 19-year-old Belfast born centre-forward paid off and Derek Dougan arrived from Distillery. But when the season opened it was Crawford who led the attack and two crushing wins over Spurs in the first four matches raised public hopes. Crawford scored his first League goals in the 5-0 win over the Londoners at Fratton with Harris getting a hat trick, but in his fifth match Crawford chipped a bone in an ankle and that opened up the way for Dougan to be quickly promoted to the first team. His entry coincided with the re-entry of Uprichard as first choice goalkeeper. Dougan's first goal came in his fourth match – interestingly against Wolves the club he was later to serve with such distinction – and then 25 years on to re-join as Chief Executive. But performances and results were still inconsistent although as Easter approached there seemed no great danger. Any feeling of comfort among supporters quickly evaporated as Pompey suddenly hit their worst run of the season, taking only one point in their last six matches. That point, from a 3-3 home draw with Manchester United was, however, to prove priceless. For in the end, although they lost the final match at home to Sunderland, it was their conquerors who were relegated with Pompey escaping on goal average.

There had been two major changes in the later stages of the season. Henderson had joined Wolves after making more than 214 League appearances for the club which discovered him as a schoolboy, while Mansell who had lost his place to Wilson, had joined Eastbourne United as manager-coach. In addition, Dale who had slipped out of the first team reckoning, had also moved to Exeter. Henderson had played most of his 24 matches before his sale at outside left and was replaced by Alex Govan, who cost £8,000 from Birmingham, while Lever also spent another £8,000 on Belfast-born inside forward Sammy Chapman from Mansfield. The F.A. Cup had held another disappointment; neighbours Aldershot were duly thrashed 5-1 in the third round but Wolverhampton, on course to the First Division title, in turn thrashed them 5-0. Once again the old faithfuls were the

men of the season. Dickinson yet again appeared in every match while Harris missed only two and top scored with 18. Crawford finished with eight in 16 and Dougan eight in 26.

But there were significant developments off field during the season. The most ambitious was the launching of the youth scheme by chairman Jack Sparshatt which was designed to provide the players of the future and school them into Pompey's ways. The scheme's first recruit was a 15-year-old centre-half from Esher, Bill Williams. The season had also seen the return of Duggie Reid from Tonbridge to become groundsman at the club's new Tamworth Road training ground – all part of the Sparshatt Plan.

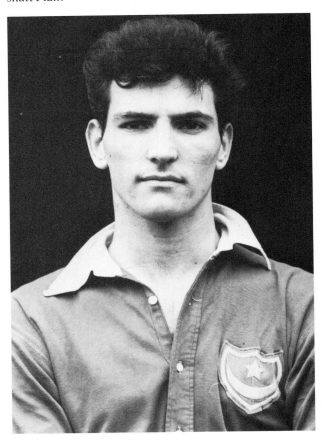

Derek Dougan

11. Exit Eddie - Enter Freddie

The hairsbreadth escape from relegation after the previous season's near miss had its inevitable result in May 1958 with Pompey and Eddie Lever parting company – the ending of a link which was almost 30 years old. This time there was no natural successor with Fratton connections as there had been when Jack Tinn retired or Bob Jackson moved. But along the Coast former Arsenal winger Freddie Cox had hit the headlines the previous season by steering Third Division Bournemouth to the sixth round of the F.A. Cup with giant-killings over Wolves and Spurs on the way, and he took over.

It was the start of an era of controversy and of hectic comings and goings. Three players came in during the summer – wing-half Tommy Casey from Newcastle, Harry Harris from Newport for £10,000 and centre-half Basil Hayward from Port Vale. But as the 58-59 season started with three defeats, centre-forward Ron Saunders was brought in from Gillingham and Reg Cutler from Bournemouth. Then the outgoings started; Crawford, after playing two matches, was sold to Ipswich for £6,500 and Govan to Plymouth after only 11 appearances. Next to go was Gordon to Birmingham for £15,000 after 210 League appearances and 70 goals. As discord grew, Rutter, Weddle, Chapman, Stenhouse and Barnett were all transfer-listed and Gunter and Dougan asked to join them – Barnett was the first to move on, joining Grimsby in December.

But on the field there was little cause for optimism with only six wins in the first 18 matches. The sixth of those was against Burnley on November 22. Two goals by Saunders, who was already proving a shrewd signing, and one each from Harry Harris and Ron Newman, earned a 4-2 success. The full significance of that occasion was not to be appreciated until August 26, 1959 when Pompey won at Lincoln . . . . In between they did not win a single League match – a disastrous run of 20 defeats in 24 matches which made the end of their 32 years in Division I inevitable. They ultimately finished with a wretched 21 points – the lowest since Leeds' 18 in the first season after the war.

By that time there had been still more changes. Ron Howells, a Welsh under 23 international wing-half, was signed from Wolves while Dougan, who had played only seven times that season, was sold to Blackburn Rovers and Casey to Bristol City. Only the F.A. Cup held any encouragement with wins over Swansea and Accrington Stanley – before Burnley ended their run with a single goal. During the season Dickinson passed another career landmark – his 500th appearance – in a match at White Hart Lane in February where Pompey led 4-3 until the minute when Spurs equalized. The saving grace, if there could be one in a season of such frustration, was that Harry Harris and Saunders at least had shown they could bridge the gap from Third and Fourth Divisions. Saunders scored 21 goals in 36 matches, Harris 13 while his namesake Peter after a season when injury restricted him to 26 appearances, also got 13 to take his career tally to 192. In March 1959 16-year-old youth team forward Jimmy White had been pitched into history by becoming Pompey's youngest First Division player – and he scored on his debut to earn a point against Birmingham. The youth team, in fact, held out promise for the future, enjoying a successful season in the South East Counties League, reaching the quarter final of the F.A. Youth Cup before losing 1-0 at Blackburn in front of a crowd of 16,700 and then representing England in a prestige international tournament in Hanover. Eventually they were to finish second of 12. Sadly one of the promising youngsters died during the season. Seventeen year old Jackie Ambler suffered severe stomach injuries during a match in October when he was hit by the ball from close range, and in January died after an operation.

Relegation had its inevitable results – the staff was trimmed. Uprichard moved to Southend, McGhee to Reading Weddle to Wisbech while Mike Barnard and another local player Bill Albury who had made 23 league appearances were also released – so too was Barnard's brother Sam who had been Pompey's physiotherapist since 1952. Inevitably, the season's story was reflected financially – a loss of £8,383. But Cox's wheeling and dealing made a £1,155 profit – he spent £42,600 but the sale of players like Dougan, Crawford, Gordon and Casey brought in £43,755. For the members of the Supporters' Club though there was one slight consolation – although they had been in existence since 1929, it was only during the 1958-59 season that Pompey officially recognized them! Cox's summer reinforcements included winger Jimmy Campbell from West Bromwich and Celtic goalkeeper Dick Beattie.

The additions to their squad of young hopefuls included goalkeeper John Milkins, inside-forward Brian Yeo, and schoolboy international Brian Caple. As an extension of the youth scheme, the club opened a hostel for the players. Duggie Reid and his wife Mary were to run it and it was called Leverett House in memory of Mr. Sidney Leverett, chairman during World War II and a director for 47 years until his death earlier in the year. The 1959-60 season began encouragingly enough with a goal-less draw at Middlesbrough and then the win at Lincoln which ended the dreadful sequence which had

John Milkins

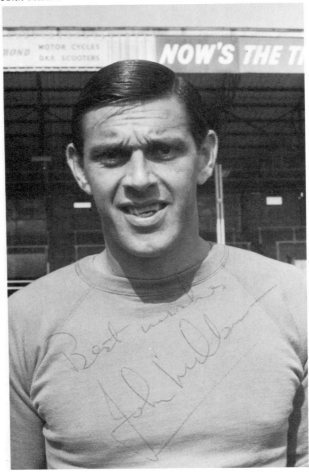

begun the previous November. But premature complacency was ended by a run of nine successive defeats which brought home to everyone that another season of struggle had begun. Worried by defensive problems, Cox paid £12,000 for Blackpool centre-half Brian Snowdon in October, immediately appointing him team captain. But within a month, Pompey's fans were stunned to learn that Peter Harris had a serious chest ailment and faced a lengthy stay in a sanatorium. He played 11 matches, making what was to be his final appearance of a magnificent if internationally over-looked career, on November 21 1959 in a 2-1 defeat at Rotherham. Snowdon's move was scarcely too happy for he was hit by recurrent shoulder dislocations and ultimately needed surgery to correct the problem.

Pompey recovered slightly from that disastrous early run but could never strike truly consistent form and in the end were spared the ignominy of immediate relegation to the Third by a mini-run in March when they collected seven points in four matches. In the end those points made the difference and Pompey were one place and two points ahead of relegated Hull. The sombre mood of the season was reflected in the Cup, with a third round defeat at Bramall Lane by fellow Second Division side Sheffield United depriving Pompey's fans of a taste of 'fever'. Dickinson was again the one ever present while, for the second season running, Saunders topped the scoring list with 17 goals. Still the juniors held out hopes of better things to come – with time. Williams, the Sparshatt plan's first recruit, appeared for the England Youth team against Scotland in Newcastle in February and then in April Milkins earned rave notices for his debut in the reserves. But they were doing so against a bleak background – warnings in the club match-day programme of austerity and an end to big spending and then at the end of the season of further playing-staff contraction.

Pompey were to approach 1960-61 with only 16 senior professionals plus 12 juniors. Among the casualties were John Phillips who had once looked like emulating his more famous namesake at wing-half and reserve goalkeeper Fred Brown. The financial strictures – the season had brought a loss of £30,000 – meant Cox was unable to reinforce his playing staff. Lincoln again provided encouragement – Pompey beat them 3-0 in the opening match of 1960-61 with Saunders taking his goal tally to 40 in 75 matches – but then came successive away defeats. The first was a single goal affair at Luton, the next a chastening experience for players and supporters. Saints had won the Third Division – and so the Hampshire neighbours were paired together for the first time in 33 years . . . . and at the Dell Saints romped home 5-1. Hard on the heels of that came an emotional occasion – a testimonial match for Peter Harris. It brought men like Reid, Butler, Ferrier, Clarke, Phillips and Froggatt back to the ground on which they had thrilled, and receipts of £1,927 swelled Harris's fund to £2,800. That was followed swiftly by another break in the now slender links with the past – Flewin, centre-half, captain, and latterly assistant manager, left after after 23 years to become his own boss with Stockport County.

But at Fratton Park at least, Pompey were a tough proposition, winning their first five matches, until Rotherham broke the sequence with a 2-2 draw on a rain-lashed afternoon watched by only 7,759 people – one of the worst gates for many years. Pompey were never to pick up the momentum after that draw and won only one of their next nine home matches – a run mirrored by away form to send them sliding back into trouble. But in the middle of that awful sequence the Cox era ended in February and Bill Thompson took temporary control. While Pompey were pondering over Cox's successor, Thompson bought Gordon back from Birmingham for £9,000 and spent a further £4,000 on 34-year-old Allan Brown, the former Scottish international inside-forward. Both made their first appearances in the same match – a desperately needed 3-1 win over Leeds on March 18.

But it was too late and when George Smith was appointed manager in April, he warned his new employers that the Third Division was a near inevitability. His first three matches saw Pompey unbeaten – draws with Ipswich and Scunthorpe and a 3-0 win over Bristol Rovers – but they then lost at Middlesbrough and victory over Derby County in the final match could not prevent a return to the Third Division after 37 years. Dickinson yet again made most appearances – 40 this time mostly

in the number three shirt to get within sight of his 600th League match – while Saunders with 20 goals was the only man in double figures. In November Milkins played his first two League matches.

Season 1960-61 saw the introduction of the Football League Cup and the new competition provided a rare avenue of comparative pleasure for Pompey. After a bye in the first round, 4,523 watched them beat Coventry 2-0, that had swollen to 10,386 as Manchester City were defeated 2-0 in the third and to 13,054 for the fourth when Chelsea were beaten by a Jimmy White goal. The quarter final saw them drawn away to Rotherham, the eventual runners up to Aston Villa, who progressed 3-0. It was in marked contrast to the F.A. Cup where giant killers Peterborough had the temerity to win 2-1 in the third round at Fratton.

The summer was a quiet one as Pompey prepared to make sure that their stay in Division III was as brief as possible. Milkins, who had shown outstanding form for the youth team, signed as a professional and before the players reported back, Smith made his first senior recruitments. Goalkeeper Peter Shearing came from West Ham as understudy to Beattie and on the eve of the season inside-forward Harry Middleton from Scunthorpe. There were also departures – Brian Carter joined Bristol Rovers, Rees Thomas, Aldershot, while Bill Williams, the first graduate of the Sparshatt plan, moved on to Queen's Park Rangers.

Back row: S. Chapman, B. Carter,   R. Smith, W. Williams, G. Hodgkins,   . Evans, B. Ridley, K. Blackburn
Middle row: R. Edmunds, B. Watts, J. Campbell, R. Howells, R. Newman, J. White, O. Dawson, A. Wilson
Front row: A. Priscott, J. Fraser, C. Rutter, R. Cutler, B. Snowdon, P. Gunter, H. Harris, R. Saunders, R. Beattie, J. Dickinson, R. Summersby
July 1960

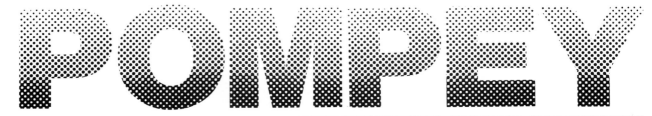

12. Straight Back

When the season 61-62 eventually arrived, Pompey took it firmly in their stride, and stretched out their best start to a season since the championship year of '48. It was October 7 before they were beaten 2-1 at Notts County in their 13th match. A 19-point lift off to the dream of instant promotion. It was a run which included yet another Dickinsonian milestone – his 600th League appearance on September 9 against Barnsley. The occasion was marked by the presentation of a gold-watch from the Supporters Club, – and a 3-2 win. It also brought fresh confirmation that the public interest was there – provided the team were winning. The final match of that unbeaten start saw Bournemouth, also unbeaten, at Fratton and the 1-1 draw was watched by 25,600 – the best gate outside the First Division.

But the defeat at Meadow Lane did not throw the campaign off course and in December Smith moved to add fresh impetus by signing two wingers – Tony Barton from Nottingham Forest and Dave Dodson from Swansea. They made their debut in a 2-2 draw against Swindon with Dodson making the start of which dreams are made – a goal in 20 seconds. By Christmas they were top and from that point it was always more a question of whether they would win the title than go up. They were unbeaten for three months until losing to Bournemouth in mid-February – a run which included a 5-0 win at Newport, the club's best away result for ten years. But in mid-March, after a crushing five goal win over Bristol City at Fratton, the general mood of complacency was suddenly destroyed. In five matches they picked up only a point from a goal-less draw at Watford, and everyone held their breath. But on April 23 in the 44th match Watford were beaten 2-1 at Fratton and the championship was Pompey's. That decisive match saw the end of Shearing's patient wait for a chance, and he was in goal for the final three matches – a change which precipitated Beattie's departure to Peterborough in May. Again the incredible and seemingly ageless Dickinson did not miss a match with Brown and Gordon ab-

Tony Barton

sent only twice. Saunders missed four but still managed 26 goals.

There was, however, little Cup joy. Relegation of course meant a place in the first round of the F.A. Cup - and that was that; Crystal Palace won 3-0 at Selhurst. The League Cup held a little more pleasure. Barrow were beaten 2-0 in the first round, to earn a home pairing with Derby County. That match ended in a 1-1 draw and on November 1 Middleton staged a one-man spectacular as he scored all the goals in a dramatic 4-2 win to shock a Baseball Ground crowd of 13,984. But that was that. Pompey then had to travel to meet Sheffield United and were beaten by the only goal. There was also heartening evidence that the future of the club was being built on solid foundations with the youth team through to the semi-final of the F.A. Youth Cup against Newcastle. They won the first leg 1-0 at Fratton but went down 4-2 in the return at St. James's Park. Their team in the first match was: Milkins, Moffatt, Wanklin, Prismall, Radcliffe, Taylor, Pound, Rencourt, Figgins, Yeo and Caple.

So Pompey were back in Division II, but there was no major transfer activity to prepare for 1962-63 season. The only addition to the staff was the return of Pat Neill from Wolves – this time as a professional. But there were changes on the Fratton 'landscape' and during the summer new 120ft high floodlight towers were built at a cost of £14,000 to be officially opened in October by a friendly against Burnley. By then the season had got away to an encouraging start with three wins and two draws in the first five matches. The final match of that run saw Derby beaten 1-0 as Albert McCann made his debut after a £6,000 move from Coventry City . . . . the start of a long career with the club. Dickinson quickly passed his 650th appearance and then in mid-October the visit of Southampton drew a gate of 32,407 – the best since 1958.

But the signs were good; by Christmas Pompey were comfortably placed and had lost only four matches – but then came some of the worst weather in living memory and from Boxing Day until February 23 only one match was played – an F.A. Cup third round tie with Scunthorpe. That ended in a 1-1 draw and it was almost six weeks before the replay was possible. The weather interrupted Milkins' first run in the side and by the time normality resumed, Smith had paid £5,000 for Nottingham Forest's reserve keeper John Armstrong. He had also replaced Dodson with Mickey Lill from Wolves for £12,500. The break did little for Pompey. Although the resumption of the League programme on February 23 saw Luton beaten 3-1, they then lost nine matches in a row to slip down the table. The slide was arrested – just - but in the end Pompey finished 16th with the curtain crashing down on the season as Chelsea blasted their way back into the First Division by thrashing them 7-0 at Stamford Bridge in front of 54,558! Yet again Dickinson did not miss a match, neither did Barton, while Gordon, who passed 300 appearances, was absent only once and Saunders twice. Saunders was again top scorer with 19, to top 100 League goals in fewer than 200 matches.

Pompey's Cup luck survived the icy break better than their League form, after ten postponements they eventually got their second crack at Scunthorpe. The Lincolnshire club were riding high in the Second Division after getting within six points of the First Division the previous season, and Pompey won 2-1 thanks to two goals from the ultra-sharp Saunders. The fourth round

Albert McCann

turned into a three match marathon against Third Division Coventry. The first meeting at Fratton ended 1-1, the second at Highfield Road 2-2 with McCann getting his first Cup goal against his old club, but Coventry won the second replay at White Hart Lane 2-1. The first two ties against Coventry saw Worthing-born Brian Yeo make his only senior appearances before being released to join Gillingham where he became a record-breaking goal scorer. That F.A. Cup exit against Coventry was in sharp contrast to the meeting between them in the League Cup. Pompey had thrashed Brighton 5-1 in the second round and repeated that scoreline when they entertained Coventry in the third. Sunderland then drew 0-0 at Fratton and won the replay at Roker 2-1. Yeo was one of two players who had appeared in the first team to be released at the end of the season – the other was Neil who had made a solitary appearance on his return to his home town club.

The difficulties were reflected in the balance sheet for there was a loss of £3,437 on the year, but despite that 1963 was Smith's busiest transfer-market summer. Winger John McClelland cost £10,000 from Q.P.R. and Brian Lewis £8,000 from Crystal Palace while full back

Roy Lunniss, who had been an amateur with Palace, also signed. But, after the encouragement of a first-day win away at Manchester City, Pompey again found the going tough and by the end of September 1963 had managed only two other victories – at Cardiff and at home to Southampton in front of almost 30,000, although Saints had wing half Cliff Huxford in goal for most of the match, after injury to Ron Reynolds. Snowdon had started the season at centre-half with Dickinson alongside him, but after three matches Dickinson took over and Snowdon was sold to Millwall for £5,000 after more than 114 league appearances. Dickinson remained one constant factor – the other was Saunders. He grabbed hat tricks in successive matches against Newcastle and Leyton Orient in October and by mid-March had scored 30 League goals – a postwar club record. That 30th goal came against Plymouth Argyle but was not enough to avert a 2-1 home defeat by a side which contained two men who were shortly to become familiar around Fratton – Nick Jennings and Mike Trebilcock. Eventually Saunders, who like Dickinson, was not to miss a match finished with 33 goals to take his League

tally to 136 in 231 appearances! Only one other player got into double figures – winger McClelland who scored 10 and whose exciting pace had brought a rejected £30,000 offer from Aston Villa in the Spring. But Pompey ultimately finished in the top half of the table with 43 points.

Again Cup success was comparative and confined to the still infant and far from thriving League Cup. Derby were beaten in the first round 3-2 on September 25, the first home success of the season. They then won 5-3 at Wrexham but hopes of further success were dashed by a 3-2 defeat away to Notts County. Still it was more than the F.A. Cup was to provide – the third round was their last round; First Division Stoke City brushed them aside 4-1 in the Potteries. As the season drew to a close there was money and talk of money in the air – the Supporters' Club, who for so long had been unrecognised, handed over £22,000 to the club while the Board announced a £17,000 facelift for the North Stand. On the player front, veteran Allan Brown was released in April to become player-manager of non-league Wigan Athletic and at the other end of the scale a certain Mick Mills, a 15-year-old

Nicky Jennings

Mike Trebilcock

winger from Godalming was added to the apprentice ranks . . . . During the summer the magnificent Dickinson received that stamp of 'Royal' approval – the M.B.E. "for services to Association Football" and he announced that 1964-65 would be his last season.

Before the players reported back for pre-season training, two new names had been added to the payroll and one familiar one had gone. The in-comers were Cliff Portwood, bought for £6,000 from Grimsby, and Ray Hiron, who had been breaking Hampshire League scoring records with Fareham Town, had taken his first step towards a successful League career. They had been passed in the doorway by long-serving Phil Gunter who moved to Aldershot after more than 350 appearances for Pompey – 319 league.

But as the season started there was a bitter blow to Pompey's fans as Saunders went on the transfer list and was sold to Watford for £15,000. It was a bad start to a season which, in its way, was to be as dramatic as any the club had experienced. Saunders' departure was reflected on the pitch; Pompey lost their opening match 5-2 away to Leyton Orient and won only twice in the first nine matches to be 20th in the table at the end of September. By that time Ron Tindall had signed to fill the gap left by Saunders. Christmas, though, arrived with deep gloom over Fratton.

They had been slumped in last place for two months and the Third Division beckoned. Then they were drawn at home to First Division strugglers Wolves in the third round of the F.A. Cup – and that seemed briefly to perk them up. Wolves were held to a goal-less draw at Fratton and won only 3-2 at Molyneux. It stimulated Pompey into their best run of the season – draws against Saints and Swindon, a win over Derby, a draw at Swansea and then victories over Huddersfield and Coventry. Suddenly Pompey were 16th in the table and there was a silver lining to the clouds. But it was too good to last. The next four matches were lost, including a 6-1 thrashing at Preston, and they slid back to 21st place.

Ron Tindall

29.4.13

Ray Hiron, nicknamed Twiggy by so many.

So Easter arrived and Pompey rallied, beating Norwich 4-0 in their final home match – an historic occasion for it was Dickinson's farewell Fratton appearance and his 763rd. Manager Smith stoked up a storm of controversy though by resting the legend the following day when Pompey made the return trip to Carrow Road to be beaten 2-1. So there was one match left and one relegation place still open. Pompey had to visit Northampton on April 24, Dickinson's 40th birthday, while Swindon also on 33 points, but with a better goal average, were at the Dell. That match kicked off at 3 p.m.; Pompey's at 7.30 p.m. Saints did their best to ensure that Pompey survived, winning 2-1 with a late goal by Terry Paine, leaving Swindon to wait and hope that Northampton, who were already assured of their first-ever elevation to the First Division, would go up in winning style. Thousands made the trip from the South Coast to the headquarters of Northampton County Cricket Club for this final drama as Pompey chased a draw and survival. And for a long time it looked as if they would get it, then in the 77th minute long serving local boy Gordon headed into his own net . . . . the Third Division beckoned cruelly. But with six minutes left, Wilson, who had scored only one League goal in more than 250 appearances, equalized and Pompey were safe – a dramatic end to Dickinson's magnificent career. Dickinson had played 764 League matches scoring nine goals, plus 58 Cup ties and a single goal, had never been cautioned by a referee . . . . and was to stay on with HIS club as Public Relations Officer.

This final drama was played out against an equally dramatic off-field scene. For Pompey, beset by increasing financial worries, had decided on a revolutionary course. Earlier in the month, the board had accepted manager Smith's radical solution to the problem of running more viably. They had agreed to reduce the playing staff from the mid-30's to just16; to scrap their reserve, A and youth teams and operate with a single side in the Football League. It was a contentious decision, but one planned to save £20,000 a year – and against a background of a mounting overdraft that was urgently needed. The move also meant that Pompey could realize the assets of their Tamworth Road training ground which ultimately went for around £15,000.

So, as the decisive match which kept them in Division II was played, the players knew their fate. The 16 to stay were John Armstrong, John Milkins, Alex Wilson, Ron Tindall, Roy Lunniss, Bobby Campbell, Johnny Gordon, Vince Radcliffe, Harry Harris, John McClelland, Brian Lewis, Cliff Portwood, Dennis Edwards, a mid season £15,000 signing from Charlton, Ray Hiron, Albert McCann and Tony Barton. The casualties included young Mills – a fact which was to return to haunt Pompey over the next 20 years as the little winger turned into one of the most consistent and respected full-backs in England with Ipswich.

Ron Tindall, Player & Manager

Derek "Harry" Harris

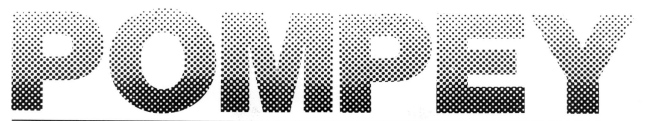

13. Revolutionaries

So Pompey passed their quietest ever summer waiting for season 1965-66 which would see them become trend setters. When it arrived, optimism was punctured in the second match when, after a solid opening win against Plymouth, they were heavily beaten at Preston. Then in the third match their plans which depended on freedom from injury, were sabotaged at the Dell when Radcliffe, their teenage centre-half, was carried off with a broken leg, an injury which effectively ended a promising career. Smith soldiered on until December but both Harris and Campbell were handicapped by injury and after a depressing run of eight matches without a win, which included an 8-2 thrashing by Wolves, bought centre-half Frank Haydock from Charlton for £20,000. Another poor run early in the New Year saw them slip down to 18th place to revive fears of another fight to survive.

Alarmed at this, the board sanctioned another £15,000 transfer expenditure to bring in Ipswich's fierce little mid-field player Bobby Kellard. Suddenly things took an upturn, Pompey won six of their last nine matches and lost only two to climb to mid-table. So the one-team scheme had been partially vindicated – and further vindication came from attendances with the average up by 1,500 to 14,644. The best gate of the season had been 25,860 for the visit of Southampton to Fratton. No player appeared in every match; Lewis missed one and Gordon two while McCann top scored with twelve goals with four players on ten – Lewis, Edwards, Hiron and McClelland.

The two Cup competitions held no joy – in the League Cup, after winning 2-1 at Oldham, Pompey went out 2-0 at Cardiff while the F.A. Cup held even greater disappointment. They were drawn away to Third Division Grimsby and worked hard for a goal-less draw – then crashed 3-1 in the replay in front of 23,735 disillusioned fans.

The autumn had held one very sentimental occasion, a farewell to Jimmy Dickinson. Almost 20,000 crowded into Fratton Park to pay their tribute to this unique club

Bobby Kellard, built like a pocket battleship and sporting a neatly-trimmed beard, is always in the thick of the battle in mid-field

servant. The evening's curtain raiser was a match between the ex-champions side, including such men as Phillips, Froggatt, Harris, Reid, and Clarke, and Old England – Matthews, Finney, Wright and Lofthouse. Then Pompey played West Ham – but the Londoners showed the class gap by winning 4-1.

The final verdict on the Smith Revolution's first year had to be financial – and that was disappointing. Although gates and receipts were up, when the accounts were finally released there had been an overall loss of £8,441 – despite the savings from the reduction in playing staff. So, inevitably, the summer was another of little transfer activity and when the 1966-67 campaign began with a goal-less draw at Norwich followed by a 5-4 home defeat by Birmingham, the only newcomer was full back Roy Pack on a free transfer from Arsenal. The signs were ominous. By the end of September Pompey had won only three times and had been hounded out of the League Cup at Swindon – and to rub it in former Pompey old boy Keith East scored two of the goals in a 4-1 win for the Third Division side whose captain was another former Fratton junior Owen Dawson. But gradually they pulled round, stringing together a run of six matches without defeat into November and they turned the year in mid-table.

Pompey's squad strength had been reduced from early season when Barton injured a knee then McClelland injured his back, and so shortly after Christmas Smith paid £25,000 for Plymouth's outside-left Nicky Jennings. Jennings made his debut on his 21st birthday and celebrated with a goal in a 3-2 win over Rotherham. Later in the month Pompey's attack was reinforced by former England centre-forward Ray Pointer – the cost this time was £15,500, plus the versatile and popular Lewis.

But luck turned savagely against them early in the New Year. Milkins, now regular first choice goalkeeper, broke an arm in late February and was out for the rest of the season and at the same time Haydock entered hospital for a cartilage operation. But there was no more money to spend and Pompey had to soldier on, clinging gamely to a mid-table position. Then in the last week of the season Smith moved once more, signing Exeter's 21-year-old left-back George Ley for £8,000. Jennings had arrived just in time to play his full part in a mini-F.A. Cup run which set the fans' blood pulsing. Drawn against Hull in the third round, Pompey grafted to a 1-1 draw at Boothferry Park, and Fratton enjoyed its biggest crowd since 1958 – 33,107 for the replay which ended 2-2. The second replay was at Coventry's Highfield Road and the return to his old surroundings inspired McCann who scored two in a 3-1 win. It earned the dubious privilege of a visit to White Hart Lane to face a Spurs side actively pursuing a League and Cup which was ultimately to elude them. But on February 18 1967, Greaves, Gilzean and Co took a step towards winning the Cup by beating a battling Pompey 3-1 in front of 57,910.

But financially Smith's revolution was some way short

Ray Pointer

of its target. It was a season which saw the departure of the last two playing links with the First Division – Gordon and Wilson. Gordon had made 445 league appearances for his home town club, broken by his brief spell with Birmingham, scoring more than 100 goals, plus 38 Cup ties, while Scotsman Wilson had topped 350 games in all. The other players released were the unfortunate Radcliffe who had played ten league matches but who was still a victim of that broken leg, and Armstrong. Armstrong's replacement was Ray Potter on a free transfer from West Bromwich, while Smith paid his fourth fee of the year in early May when he spent £20,000 on another battling midfield competitor – his name-sake George Smith from Barrow. Everything was up; gate receipts to £82,984, wages to £45,666 – an increase of £9,000 – and general running costs to £100,983 from £76,000. Also Pompey had spent more than £50,000 in the transfer market and the overall loss was £11,298. Armstrong eventually moved to Southport during the summer while Smith made one other signing – utility player Micky Travers from Reading on a free transfer.

George Ley

So it was a largely reconstructed team which faced Queen's Park Rangers on August 19 for the first match of season 1967-68. And what a season that was to prove for success starved supporters. Pompey were unbeaten for nine matches – six wins – and even when Charlton ended the run at the Valley, the 4-1 defeat was not enough to halt the momentum. November 4 brought a 3-0 win over Hull at Fratton, and 17,602 celebrated as Pompey hit top spot. They were still there at Christmas and when January ended with them in second place and promotion beckoning, Smith persuaded his board to invest a record £40,000 on Cornishman Mike Trebilcock whose two goals had won the F.A. Cup for Everton 18 months earlier. But the goal-touch had deserted him and Trebilcock was to score only one League goal in 13 appearances.

Pompey were still in the promotion 'frame' at the end of February but then ran out of steam and the last 12 matches brought a minimal eight point return. So when the dust and excitement had settled, Pompey had finished in fifth place with Queen's Park Rangers ultimately pipping Blackpool on goal average for second place and promotion with Ipswich. The success though mirrored the value of a settled team. Ley and Kellard played every match while Milkins, Tindall and Smith missed only one and Harris two. But Pompey were short on firepower with McCann's 14 in 28 appearances the best followed by Pointer and Jennings as the only others in double figures – both on ten.

Excitement was not confined to the League – the F.A. Cup provided its share. In the third round Pompey had had to work hard to beat Peterborough 1-0 away from home. They then went to Craven Cottage and brought Fulham back to Fratton Park with a 0-0 draw. The replay fired everyone's imagination and a ground-bulging crowd of 44,050 – the best for 16-years – saw Pompey through by a single Trebilcock goal. So they were in the fifth round for the first time since 1959 and were drawn at home to West Bromwich Albion eventually losing 2-1 watched by 42,642 paying record receipts of £11,976. All that contrasted sharply with the League Cup where Pompey had beaten Port Vale 3-1 in the first round and then crashed 4-1 away to Fourth Division strugglers Darlington. During the season Barton had conceded defeat in his struggle against injury and had joined Pompey's scouting staff while Edwards, after 69 appearances and 14 goals, had moved to Aldershot for £5,000.

Inevitably the events of the season were reflected when the accounts were published – the previous year's five figure loss had been replaced by a profit of £2,387 – and the average gate had jumped to 22,000. The summer held one major shock for Pompey's fans as they dreamed about their club going one better and returning to the First Division at the end of the 1968-69 season. In July Pompey announced that Kellard, who had made himself a firm favourite with the crowd with his bustling aggression, had joined Bristol City for £35,000. So when the players reported back the only new faces were those of 18-year-old defender Tommy Youlden, who had been released by Arsenal, and centre-forward Bill Brown, another free signing from Gillingham. Another familiar face missing was that of McClelland who had joined Newport County.

Before the 68-69 season was a fortnight old, Pompey had turned down a record £65,000 offer from Aston Villa for Smith. But the season was in sharp contrast to its predecessor. Although Pompey were unbeaten for the first three matches – two away goal-less draws followed by a 3-0 win over Middlesbrough – they had to wait until late September for their second victory and by the end of the month were down in 18th place. There was to be no dramatic recovery from that difficult start and Pompey were never to climb into the top half of the table, although there was never any risk of a survival battle. In late October Smith added the grafting qualities of Eire international Eoin Hand to his defence for £7,500 and a fortnight later spent £25,000 on Bolton's former England youth international Brian Bromley. But manager Smith and player Smith were having problems and in December, the powerful midfield player was transfer-listed and a month later sold to Middlesbrough for £50,000 – a Pompey record. Ten days later Haydock

Pompey Season 1967/68
Back l to r R. Kellard, C. Portwood, G. Ley, R. Pack, D. Edwards, J. Milkins,
R. Potter, R. Hiron, F. Haydock, M. Travers, A. Barton, G. Smith
Front N. Jennings, J. McClelland, A. McCann, G. Neave, R. Mulcock, G. Smith,
J. Dickinson, R. Campbell, R. Tindall, D. H. Harris, R. Pointer

Tommy Youlden

Eoin Hand

joined Southend for a nominal fee after a handful of appearances. Pompey's main problem all season was in finding goal-scoring support for Hiron, the lanky Fareham lad who was beginning to live up to the reputation which had persuaded Smith to recruit him from his Dockyard job. Bill Atkins was bought for £10,000 late in the season to partner him, but when the last match was played, Hiron was the only player in double figures – his 17 including a remarkable four in a 5-2 win over Norwich in the final home match.

The contrast between the two seasons was as sharp in the Cup competitions, too. Coventry bundled them out in the League Cup at the beginning of September, and in the F.A. Cup, after beating Chesterfield 3-0 in the third round, they themselves were defeated 4-0 at Blackburn in the fourth. Late in the season, Smith had failed in an attempt to persuade Bristol City to sell Kellard back to him for £25,000, and so during the summer, he signed Sheffield United utility player Dave Munks for £20,000 – after first insisting Munks got his hair cut! Two free transfer signings – Brian Turner (Chelsea) a New Zealand international and Roger Davidson (Arsenal) – brought the squad up to 18, two above the Smith plan's limit, by the time training started. Despite the difficulties, Smith's transfer dealings had enabled the club to show a profit of £32,000 on the year.

Season 1969-70 was one of the less memorable in Pompey's long history. It opened with a defeat at Blackpool, the first midweek match saw Brighton bounce them out of the League Cup, and the first home match ended in a crushing 5-1 defeat by Sheffield United. In mid-September Youlden broke his leg playing against Hull and was not to return until February, while Milkins damaged a cheekbone at Watford in mid-October, and that forced Smith into borrowing Bob Widdowson from York City as deputy to Potter, who played only twice in two seasons as Milkins' understudy. Potter managed only two matches before damaging a finger, to give Widdowson a run of four matches before Milkins was back. As Widdowson arrived, so Atkins left, sold to Halifax for £9,000, after failing to make any impact. Pompey now recruited former Leeds striker Jim Storrie from Rotherham for £5,000 as Hiron's partner, but they were still perilously close to the bottom reaches of the table when 1970 arrived. It came with fresh disappointment – a stunning 2-1 Fratton defeat in the third round of the F.A. Cup by Third Division Tranmere Rovers. Pompey responded to Smith's demand for atonement by being unbeaten for the rest of January – a draw against Bolton and wins over Aston Villa, Oxford and Charlton – which lifted them to 12th place and probably staved off a fight against relegation. For in the remainder of the season they remained inconsistent but gathered just enough points to finish in 17th place.

It was a sad end to the Smith era as manager. In late April he became general manager and handed over team matters to Tindall. Tindall's assumption of control was marked by a flurry of transfer activity. His first signing was Norman Piper from Plymouth for £40,000 and

Jim Storrie

Norman Piper

he followed that by recruiting two Burnley defenders – full-back Fred Smith for £10,000 and burly centre-half Colin Blant. Tindall rounded off his first campaign by signing Jim Standen, like him a County Cricketer, as goalkeeping cover since Potter's broken finger had forced his retirement. The signing of Smith and Blant coincided with the latest round of admission price increases – the ground was to cost 6s (30p) and the South Stand 14s (70p) for 1970-71. The signings contributed to a lean financial result – an overall loss of £57,985. But off-field events were beginning to be increasingly heard.

In November 1969, the City Council had unveiled its plans for an East-West relief road – straight through the middle of Fratton Park. There was talk that Pompey would be re-located at the Airport in a multi-purpose stadium which would cost some £2,5 million . . . . a plan which was to rear its head periodically over the years until the opportunity was finally lost when houses and factories went on to the ideally situated site. And at the same time Pompey also began to seek extra avenues of finance to bridge the gap between income and their dreams. In December the club launched a £100,000 loan scheme in the vain hope that it might provide the finance for promotion. Then in May 1970 there was talk of an injection of American capital – another unfulfilled hope.

The new regime's start could scarcely had been more promising – a five match unbeaten start in the League plus wins in the League Cup over Plymouth and Walsall. The League run ended at Swindon; the League cup at Old Trafford to a single goal: and from that point inconsistency became the hallmark of results. But for the first time Trebilcock looked like living up to his scoring reputation – even though his appearances were intermittent. He scored a hat trick in a 5-0 win over Watford – a result which highlighted Pompey's inconsistence as it followed another 5-1 home defeat by Sheffield United. The Watford result was followed by four successive defeats which dumped Pompey down to 18th place, and then Trebilcock got another three in a 4-1 win over Blackburn to check the slide. But he was to carve his niche in Pompey's history once the F.A. Cup arrived in January. Pompey were drawn at home to Sheffield United, who started hot favourites to win after their runaway league win in the autumn. But goals by Hiron and Trebs saw Pompey through 2-0 – a week later Sheffield completed a League double at Bramall Lane by the same score! Pompey's reward was a home meeting with mighty Arsenal and on January 23, to the delight of most of the 39,659, Trebilcock scored again to earn a 1-1 draw – but he was unable to get on target as Pompey went down 3-2 in the replay after a tremendous battle watched by 47,885. After that peak, the season drifted into anticlimax. There were 17 matches left after the replay – in only two did Pompey manage to score twice – and failure to win any of the last ten left them to finish in an unhealthy 16th with their worst scoring record since the war, only 46 goals in 42 matches . . . . 14 of them to the now dependable Hiron.

Again there were significant off-field events with the club debating the resumption of the normal format of a reserve and youth side. Eventually it was decided that the most practicable step was for Pompey to use a neighbouring Southern League club as the development ground for their second team players. Initially there was talk of either Waterlooville or Winchester becoming the 'nursery'. Waterlooville's chairman Peter Faulkner joined Pompey's board to strengthen the link and Pompey's assistant coach Bobby Campbell, whose playing career with the club had been prematurely ended by injury, was to become manager at Jubilee Park. As this was being decided, Pompey and George Smith, the architect of the one-team revolution which was now under threat, parted company on an amicable basis at the end of March.

The response to the idea was overwhelming as far as hopeful youngsters in the area were concerned. 100 turned up for the first trials and by the end of the summer that number had doubled as Pompey held further coaching sessions. But the official 'marriage' between the clubs was never sanctioned and although there were links, the grand-design did not materialize. Finance decreed that Tindall had little room to strengthen his squad and his only close-season signings were former Welsh Schools captain John Collins who cost £20,000 from Spurs, and Richard Reynolds from Plymouth on a free transfer.

The start to '71-72 though was comparatively encouraging and by mid-September Pompey were to be found in sixth place; . . . . an elevation which promised to deceive. They were short on firepower and consistency – only once during the season did they manage consecutive victories and that in the early period of false promise. So by mid-season they were below half way and were never to climb above 12th place. In January Bromley was sold to Brighton, where he had been on extended loan, for £15,000 and the money, plus another £10,000, was promptly invested in Blackburn full-back Billy Wilson. As the season drew to a close, Pompey found £8,500 to bring Brian Lewis back from Colchester. The cup competitions had once more offered little relief; in the League Cup Pompey crashed out to ambitious South Coast rivals Bournemouth while in the F.A. Cup they had to work hard to beat non-league Boston United 1-0 in the third round, had less trouble against Swansea from the Third who were beaten 2-0 but then lost 3-1 at Birmingham in the fifth.

The pressures though were mounting. The overdraft had pushed up to around £70,000 and the years of mediocrity were being reflected at the turnstiles. Fratton's attendance graph charted four-figure gates for the last three matches of the season – with a wretched 5,885 there to see Burnley bring the curtain down with a 2-1 win. During the season, too, one of the legends of their past – Jack Tinn of the lucky spats, died at the age of 93. There was one glimmer of hope, however. The youth scheme had gradually gained in momentum, starting to play matches in the South West Counties League from

Richard Reynolds receives The Bobby Tambling Player of the Year Award, May 72.

November. Their team for the initial match against Basingstoke included goalkeeper Phil Figgins, who was later to come through to play occasional matches for the first team before emigrating to Australia. But the hopes of the nursery link with Waterlooville were never to be fulfilled. Campbell left to further his coaching career in London and the official liaison was frowned upon by the Southern League.

So Pompey prepared for season 1972-73. Tindall released Storrie, Standen and Travers while Ray Pointer had officially retired – prematurely it was to prove – after a distinguished career and had joined the Fratton staff with special responsibilities towards developing the youth scheme. Despite the worsening financial situation - the accounts later were to show Pompey had lost £92,892 on the year – Tindall was allowed to add to his squad. Centre half Alan Stephenson was bought from West Ham for £32,000 and Welsh under 23 striker Peter Price from Peterborough for £27,000 while Standen's departure was covered by the loan of 17-year-old Graham Horn from Arsenal. There were other departures, too. Trebilcock, that figure of controversy, joined Torquay on a free transfer, Blant returned north to Rochdale and Youlden moved to Reading. So, when the 1972-73 programme began, Pompey had 16 senior professionals with the same number of hopeful youngsters in the youth squad, including Southern Grammar School pupil Peter Ellis.

The season began well enough – five points from the first three matches – saw Pompey in second place when the first tables appeared. But by then Price had already been hit by the back injury which was to turn his spell with the club into a nightmare and ultimately bring early retirement. Less than a month after it had begun, Ley had moved to Brighton for £28,000 and it quickly became clear that the club were heading for another season of hardship and struggle. September produced two wins, October only a single point to see them nosedive to 20th place and send gates once more tumbling alarmingly. But, unknown to everyone, Pompey were approaching one of the most significant moments in their long history.

As Christmas neared, the visit of Middlesbrough to Fratton Park on December 16 was to be a landmark . . . . for events in directors box and board room more than anything else. For as Pompey struggled to a 0-0 draw which left them in 21st place in front of a wretched 4,688 - the smallest league gate in Fratton's existence – the directors' guests included Bramwell John Deacon. The 60-year-old Southampton property magnate had been introduced by his solicitor, Sir Alfred Blake, Pompey's Life Vice President, and after so many false hopes, it seemed the search for financial security for the club had been rewarded. Negotiations lasted until after Christmas then on December 27 Pompey announced that Mr. Deacon would be joining the board and investing a considerable amount of capital.

So a new era dawned with the proud old club staring the Third Division in the face. The first playing reinforcements quickly arrived; Kellard returned to Fratton from Crystal Palace two days after John Deacon's appointment was announced, then winger Ken Foggo was signed from Norwich for £25,000. The players themselves responded to the changes with a seven match unbeaten run which effectively lifted the threat of relegation and gates improved marginally although still rarely into five figures. As the improved run ended at Middlesbrough, Pompey lost Horn who was recalled by Arsenal and then sold to Luton despite Pompey's attempt to buy him. Arsenal compensated by loaning them Ron Tilsed. Pompey eventually finished the season in 17th place and could look back on a campaign which held little on-field joy. In the League Cup they had managed to win at Torquay but had lost in the second round at home to Third Division Chesterfield while in the F.A. Cup, after a 1-1 draw at home to Bristol City, had been soundly beaten 4-1 at Ashton Gate.

Bill and Ben (alias Ken Foggo and Bobby Kellard) with Manager John Mortimer as the littleweed.

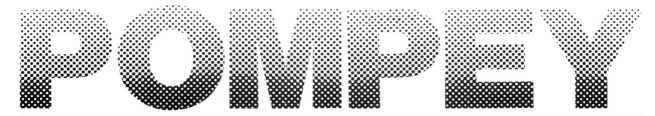

14. Action Man

But the events behind the scene were momentous. Pompey were approaching their 75th anniversary and John Deacon was determined to make that landmark memorable. As the season ended, Pompey went on the biggest shopping spree in their history. In a few days they spent almost £200,000 on Ron Davies, Saints veteran Welsh international centre-forward, Peter Marinello, Arsenal's charismatic if controversial Scottish winger, and Phil Roberts, Bristol Rover's Welsh under 23 full-back. Interest was enormous; the three newcomers were on parade as Pompey met West Ham in McCann's testimonial match and more than 20,000 were there to watch Pompey win. In the midst of that whirlwind of transfer activity the revolution continued below stairs. Dennis Collett stood down to allow John Deacon to become chairman and a new management structure was announced. Tindall was to become general manager and John Mortimore, who had impressed the new chairman with his coaching success at Southampton, was to return from management in Greece to take over from his old Chelsea friend Tindall.

So when the 1973-4 anniversary season began hopes were running high with the new chairman pledged to guiding Pompey back into the First Division in three years. The public's imagination was captured. There were almost 20,000 inside Fratton as the season began - to watch Jack Charlton's Middlesbrough spoil the party by counter-punching their way to the first of 27 wins which were to take the title to Ayresome Park. Indeed events quickly proved how far reality and dream were apart. By the end of September Pompey had won only once – and that away from home – and were in 21st place. Two goals by Hand eventually gave them a home win against Carlisle on October 2, but they were obviously a long way short of fulfilling their new chairman's ambitions and as the end of the year drew near there was further frantic activity. In two days in early December Pompey spent another £200,000 on a new central defensive partnership – Malcolm Manley from Leicester and Paul Went from Fulham for a record £155,000.

But the cost of chasing dreams was brought home at the December annual meeting. The accounts for the year to the end of June showed Pompey had spent £162,382 in the transfer market and had lost £167,239 with the overall debt £287,000. The meeting also saw a change in the club's financial base. Chairman Deacon took up all of a new 150,000 share issue, giving him and his company 69 per cent of the total share capital, and also announced another £100,000 loan. But all was not happy and before Christmas Pompey had made 11 players available for transfer, including Wilson, Hand, Stephenson, Munks, Smith, Jennings, Foggo, Hiron and McCann. One moved immediately – Munks joining Swindon after 132 league appearances.

The Went-Manley partnership was an instant success - but tragically was to be a short-lived affair. Went and Manley were together for the first time when Bristol City were beaten at Fratton on December 8, the next two matches were won and the fourth drawn, and although the year ended with a solid defeat at Bolton, Pompey's star was rising. They began 1974 with a New Year's Day win over Cardiff which lifted them to tenth place and that position was sustained into February while Cup fever took over. Pompey were drawn at home to Swindon in the third round and battled to a memorable 3-3 draw in front of 16,682 and won the replay by a single Kellard goal. It brought a home tie with the Orient and for the first time Fratton saw Sunday soccer as the Country battled to face the problems of a national power dispute. The event and the novelty brought Fratton's first 30,000 plus gate for years, and a 0-0 draw. The replay ended 1-1 and the second at Crystal Palace was won 2-0 to take Pompey to Nottingham Forest in the fourth round. A massive invasion force of Pompey fans swelled the City Ground gate to 38,589 but the match was lost by a single goal. But by then sadly the Went-Manley combination, which older fans were already rating one of the best in the club's history, had been broken. Manley had injured a knee at Notts County in early

Rising to the occasion again is Pompey chairman Mr. John Deacon,
who is prepared to spend even more to strengthen the Fratton Park Squad.
The vision of Ron Davies, caricaturist centre forward.

Peter Marinello

Paul Went

February and was to play only once more – and that after a year of operations and disappointments. Pompey had also lost Tilsed earlier in the season with a broken arm and in March, although he had recovered, they spent a further £22,500 on Ipswich Town's keeper David Best.

But as the season ended with Pompey in 15th place – a poor return on a massive outlay – the first fruits of the re-born youth team were seen. The youngsters were now being coached and groomed by Pompey old boy Ray Crawford. In April 17-year-old apprentice striker Andy Stewart made his senior debut – and in four matches scored twice to raise ultimately unfulfilled hopes. And in the last match at home to Forest, local boy Ellis made his first appearance. McCann had left the club late in the season for a new career in South Africa and as the programme ended Jennings, too, moved on to Exeter. Jennings like Smith and Tilsed had been given a free transfer. McCann had played 331 league matches scoring 83 goals with another 13 in his 40 Cup appearances. The season ended with Davies the only player to appear in all 50 competitive matches, top scoring with 16 goals, followed by Piper on 12 – and then no one with more than six. During the summer, three other players moved on. Tilsed to Hereford, Milkins, the one success of that George Smith – terminated youth policy, left for Oxford after more than a decade and 343 League appearances, and Collins was sold to Halifax for £8,000.

Season 74-75 arrived without fresh recruits and was only six matches old when sensation flared. It had begun badly. Pompey were minus the suspended Went, Kellard and Marinello, as they lost the opening match at Bolton and by early September, although they had beaten Swindon 1-0 in the League Cup, they had managed only three points from four matches. On the morning before West Bromwich Albion were to visit Fratton, chairman Deacon shocked everyone with a terse statement announcing that manager Mortimore had been suspended by the club for 'lack of success'. Tindall was appointed on a caretaker basis – a ten day three match inter-regnum in which Pompey were beaten three times, including a 5-1 humiliation by First Division championship-headed Derby County in theLeague Cup. On September 13 Mr. Deacon announced the appointment of Motherwell manager Ian St. John, the former Liverpool and Scotland forward, and promised additional money for transfer activity. The players responded to meeting St. John for the first time by winning at Nottingham Forest and picked up points from the first two home matches under his management. But his arrival was not the panacea to Pompey's ills; the players were not good enough despite their cost and enormous wagebill and by early November had sunk to bottom place. St. John now found he had no money to buy but was expected to finance any transfer activity by selling players.

The seriousness of the situation was brought home in December by accounts which showed that the chairman was finding between £1,000-£2,000 a week to keep the club running, that the overdraft was more than £300,000 and Mr. Deacon's stake some half a million pounds. The overall loss on the year had been £415,684. Pompey increased the prices; terrace admission went up to 60p, a seat to £1.50. Late in November, St. John made his first signing, swapping Davies for Manchester United's veteren Scottish international George Graham. And that, apart from recruiting Paul Cahill on loan from Coventry, and young Scot Alan Kane was to be St. John's only signing that troubled season. He did, though, allow Price, still struggling to overcome his constantly recurring back trouble, to move to Barnsley.

It was a time of largely unrelieved gloom although young Stewart still promised excitement as he twice caught the eye of Scottish youth selectors. Pompey crashed out of the F.A. Cup at Notts County in the third round but followed that with their best run of season – three successive victories – which dragged them up to 17th place where they were ultimately to finish. As the season ended, St. John 'cleared the decks'. He allowed Reynolds to cross the Atlantic to summer with Dallas Tornados while Kellard had followed McCann to South Africa – and Manley too was sent there in the hope that his knee might respond to prolonged warmth and rest. The real clearance though came with the retained list – Hiron, Stephenson, Foggo, Best, and Lewis, all players aged 31 or more, were released – so too was 19-year-old Gordon Bartlett, the first apprentice signed when Tindall had revived the youth team. Bartlett had made infrequent appearances but had never looked like becoming a regular.

Pompey desperately tried to stimulate fresh avenues of finance. They announced ten year season tickets at £220 and four year tickets at £100 – but the response was poor. Increasingly though it became clear that all was not harmonious behind the scenes.In April 1975 Vice Chairman David Sparshatt resigned after six years on the board – the first of six directors to quit in nine months. A month later Tindall, too, was gone after ten years with the club. The other directors who left were John Brogden in May, Guy Sprigings and Arthur Oliver, son of George Lewin Oliver, in November after both had served for 25 years or more, Edwin Reeves in December and Peter Faulkner in January after a brief spell as Vice Chairman. Pompey's summer was quiet. St. John's only recruiting avenue was the free transfer market. He brought in goalkeeper Graham Lloyd from Liverpool and forward Bobby McGuinness from Motherwell.

Pompey's playing resources still looked painfully thin and when the 1975-76 season opened in mid-August people's fears were quickly substantiated. By the end of September Pompey had a solitary League win to their name – at the Orient – and were already in bottom place. St. John had by then already pitched youth team players Steve Foster and Chris Kamara into the League side while another Billy Eames had come on as substitute to earn his little bit of instant fame by scoring the goal which earned a League Cup second round draw with First Division Leicester City; but the replay was to end in a harsh extra time defeat at Filbert Street. On the

Steve Foster

League front though it was unrelieved gloom. Unable to buy, St. John had to try to recruit extra strength through the loan system but with little success. He did sign his old team mate Chris Lawler on a free transfer but the full-back who had been such a calm influence with Liverpool, failed to contribute to Pompey's cause. Midfield player John McLaughlin was borrowed from Liverpool but, perhaps to underline the low pitch to which Pompey's luck had sunk, he damaged knee ligaments and limped back to Merseyside after only five appearances. Tony Macken, a busy little utility player from Derby made a bigger impact in two spells, but Jeff King and Martyn Busby, borrowed from Derby and Q.P.R. respectively, achieved little.

Pompey had to wait till mid-December for their second League win and although January offered short-lived excitement in the F.A. Cup, it was scant consolation. Then Pompey gained a creditable third round replay victory at Birmingham with a goal by McGuinness and then seemed to do the hard work by drawing at Charlton in the fourth. The replay lured 31,722 to Fratton – and Pompey failed miserably losing 3-0. Long before the end it was obvious that Pompey were headed for a return to the Third Division and in the last few matches, St. John gave experience to other products of the youth team Keith Viney, Peter Denyer, David Pullar and Figgins. Against this gloomy background, there were fears for Pompey's survival. The public's feelings for the club showed as more than a thousand crowded into the Guildhall to hear chairman Deacon explain the gravity of the situation. He told them he had put in between £400,000-£500,000 in cash and had also guaranteed a further £350,000 at the bank. The public dipped into their pockets and a collection raised £1,109.71 towards a £100,000 appeal target set by commercial manager Bill Davis. Marinello's inconsistent stay at Fratton ended in December when he was sold to Motherwell for around a quarter of his cost.

But now all was acrimony off the field with chairman Deacon and his predecessor Dennis Collett clashing at an angry annual meeting. There was still talk of moving Pompey to a new home at the airport but again it was only talk and in the Spring Pompey approached the City Council for a £50,000 loan but were rejected. So a desperately unhappy season ended with St. John instructed to cut his wagebill for the next season and with coach Pat Wright the first victim of the economies. The summer passed with Matt Pollock the only new face on a free transfer from Luton and when August 1976 arrived the start of Pompey's third stay in the Third Division was scarcely promising. They went out of the League Cup at the first attempt, beaten 3-2 on aggregate over two legs by Crystal Palace and struggled in the League. By the end of September they had won only one match and were slumped in 22nd place in the table and fears again mushroomed over their ability to stay the course financially. Eventually after considerable pressure Mr. Deacon admitted his concern and challenged the public to raise £35,000 in six weeks to avert the crisis. The News, Portsmouth, immediately launched SOS Pompey – under the chairmanship of local businessman Harry Garcia, – and the money began to roll in. As the clouds deepened another director, television man Peter Clark resigned, but in November two local men joined the board – Jim Sloan and Gordon Gauntlett, who was treasurer of the SOS Committee. As he joined the appeal fund reached £20,000 and some of the more immediate debts were cleared.

But on the field there was still little cheer. In October Went was sold to Cardiff for £30,000 after a long series of disputes with St. John, and, after Pompey had hit bottom place on October 16 by losing at Northampton, St. John took his biggest gamble. The team he sent out against Port Vale on October 23 was probably the youngest in Pompey's history – seven of the 12, Chris Kamara, Peter Ellis, Clive Green, Peter Denyer, Keith Viney, David Pullar and substitute Steve Foster, had graduated through the youth team. They responded by earning a 1-1 draw and three nights later gave a display of considerable character to take another point at Millmoor against a Rotherham side who were ultimately to miss promotion on goal average alone. St. John's shrewdest market move came in mid November when he swapped Graham, with whom he was at loggerheads, for Crystal Palace reserve striker David Kemp who quickly struck up a rapport with the fans and began to get the goals he had promised on signing. But the strain inevitably told on the youngsters around him who were carrying Pompey's salvation.

By the turn of the year they had dragged themselves up to 17th place and had earned a third round F.A. Cup visit to Birmingham thanks to a replay win over Aldershot and a hard earned second round victory over non-league Minehead. Again the Cup fired people's imagination and there were thousands of Pompey fans in the 31,598 crowd at St. Andrew's who watched Pompey edged out 1-0 after having Cahill sent off. But survival was never certain and in March, St. John, for the first time in his stay, experienced the luxury of signing a player for cash – Paul Gilchrist from Southampton for £5,000. By that time the SOS appeal had been wound up after raising some £35,000 in five months – a tremendous public response. But April arrived with Pompey in 20th place and even though they suddenly thrust all their worries behind them and thrashed promotion chasing Rotherham 5-1 with Kemp hitting their first league hat trick since Trebilcock's two in October 1971, the month ended with them in 21st place with four matches left. On May 2 they lost the first of that final four at Mansfield and two days later St. John, who had been under increasing pressure from the crowd, became the second manager in less than three years to be suspended.

This time the appointment of his successor was announced within minutes of his departure – Jimmy Dickinson, secretary during the black days of financial nightmare, answered the board's appeal for help. He had always maintained that he would never manage – but when Pompey needed him, he put their cause before himself. So on May 7, 1977 Dickinson sent out his first team as manager. He recalled experienced Roberts and Wilson to his defence and Pompey grafted to a goal-less draw at Preston; the following week already doomed York were beaten at Fratton and 14,288, the best league gate of the season with the exception of the massive 32,368 of Brighton's Christmas visit, celebrated safety. In the end it was close, – Pompey stayed up at Reading's expense by a point.

Paradoxically, the reserves had done well, winning the Midweek League title for the second time in four years, and the youngsters gathered fresh experience. Dickinson's right hand man was Crawford who had been so influential in bringing through the players on which

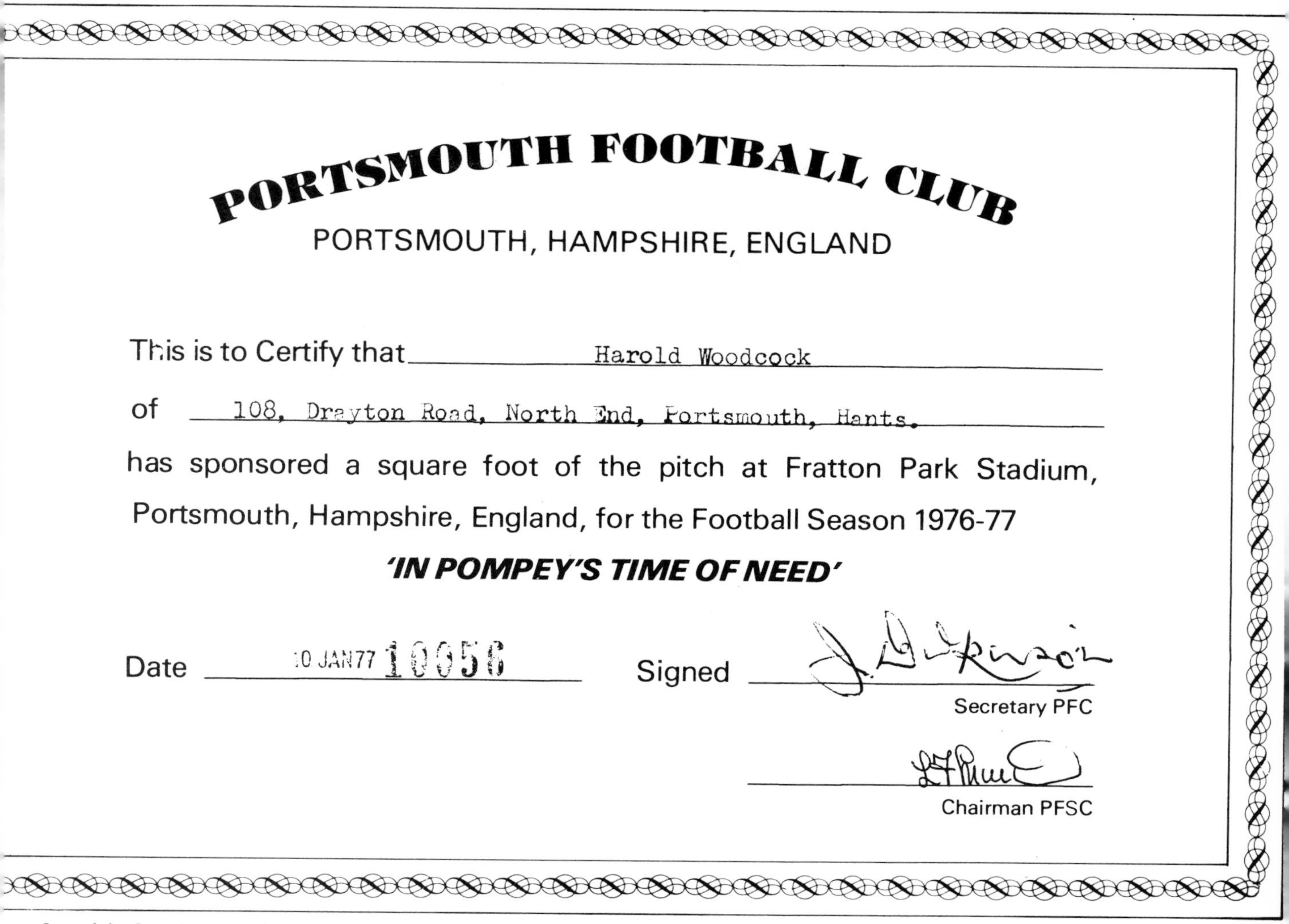

PORTSMOUTH FOOTBALL CLUB

PORTSMOUTH, HAMPSHIRE, ENGLAND

This is to Certify that _____ Harold Woodcock _____

of _____ 108, Drayton Road, North End, Portsmouth, Hants. _____

has sponsored a square foot of the pitch at Fratton Park Stadium,

Portsmouth, Hampshire, England, for the Football Season 1976-77

'IN POMPEY'S TIME OF NEED'

Date _____ 10 JAN 77 10056 _____   Signed _____

Secretary PFC

Chairman PFSC

One of the Save-Pompey ideas.

Pompey would largely have to rely in 1977-78. After St. John's departure, three of his recruits quickly followed – Lawler negotiated a settlement of his contract to play in America, McGuinness went to Australia and Lloyd back to Liverpool. But St. John had left one legacy – he had turned Foster, who had joined the club as a hopeful centre-forward after being released by Saints, into a centre-half of considerable promise – which was later to be realized when he became their first six figure sale and an England player.

The season also saw an end to the boardroom battles which had scarred the previous two years. The feud between Deacon and his predecessor Dennis Collett which had surfaced at the previous year's protracted annual meeting when Collett had called for his successor's resignation, summarily ended at the shareholders' meeting in December 1976. Three directors Collett, John Parkhouse and David Deacon offered themselves for re-election; two, the recently arrived Jim Sloan and Gordon Gauntlett, for election. At the start of the meeting Mr. Deacon revealed his strategy – one-share-one-vote poll rather than the traditional show of hands. His massive holding went against Collett, in favour of the other four. So Collett's 21 years on the board ended with his polling 19,296 votes – with 188,346 against.

Dickinson had no more buying power than St. John and when his first full season began he had made only two signings – goalkeeper Steve Middleton had joined from Saints on a free transfer and locally born striker Bobby Stokes, whose goal had won the F.A. Cup for Pompey's nearest neighbours only 18 months earlier. But he surprised people by selling Kamara to Swindon for £17,000 on the eve of the season. Pompey raised the curtain on the 1977-78 programme by beating Newport County 5-4 on aggregate in the League Cup, then, after taking only one point in their first two League matches, built hopes for the future by beating First Division Leicester City in the second round of the Cup 2-0. But

David Kemp

although the first home league match brought a welcome 3-0 win over Chesterfield, with Stokes getting the first of the only two League goals he was to score in an unhappy stay, Pompey had only bought a year by escaping relegation the previous spring. Their League Cup hopes were ended in the replay at Swindon, with Kamara delighting in helping his new club to a 4-3 win, and four days later a crushing 5-2 home defeat by Tranmere dumped them to the bottom of the table . . . . and from that point they were never to scramble clear of a relegation place.

Even the F.A. Cup held no respite; they struggled to beat Western League Bideford in the first round and then went out to Fourth Division Swansea in a replay. In December Dickinson borrowed midfield man John Ruggiero from Brighton and also re-signed Hand who had returned from playing in South Africa – Ruggiero stayed only a month and Hand's contribution to a doomed cause was limited by injury. Pompey and Crawford parted company in January and at the end of the month Frank Burrows arrived from Swindon to be Dickinson's coach. There followed a hectic spell of transfer market activity which re-vamped the squad – but did little to alter results. Veteran defender Tony Taylor, who had been interviewed with Burrows for the coach's job, instead signed as a player and in February Pompey paid

£25,000 for Brighton defender Steve Piper and £15,000 for Huddersfield winger Jim McCaffrey. But the controversial decision came on the eve of the transfer deadline in March when Kemp, such a favourite with the crowd, was sold to Carlisle in a deal which included midfield man John Latham moving to Fratton Park. Pompey took some of the sting out of the public's reaction by signing Colin Garwood from Colchester to replace Kemp. At the same time there was another notable departure from the scene – Norman Piper who had made more than 300 appearances and had brought Pompey their first international recognition for some time with his England under 23 appearances, was released to join Fort Lauderdale Strikers in Florida.

But amid the change the one thing which did not alter was Pompey's position; in the last two months of the season they won only three matches and were never out of last place in the table. The most significant event came in the final match at Rotherham where 16-year-old youth team goalkeeper Alan Knight made an encouraging debut in a 1-0 win. The casualties of Pompey's first-ever dip into the fourth Division included Stokes, Micky Mellows, Cahill and local products Figgins, Neil Hider and Clive Green.

Colin Garwood

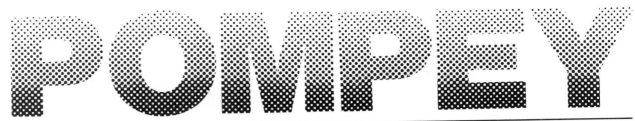

15. Into the Basement

So Pompey prepared for 1978-79 and the basement. They signed experience in goalkeeper Peter Mellor and centre-forward Steve Davey, both from fellow relegatees Hereford, and brought in Jeff Hemmerman from Port Vale and Jimmy McIlwraith from Bury. On the eve of the season, they added to their backroom staff by appointing Burrows' old Swindon defensive partner Stan Harland as youth coach. And when the season finally started there was an immediate further – unwelcome – Swindon link with the Wiltshire club bundling them out of the League Cup 4-2 on aggregate. There was no greater joy when the Fourth Division arrived; Bradford won by a single goal in the opening match, then the first away match ended in a disastrous 5-2 defeat at York and on the following Friday Pompey were trailing for a long time at Hartlepool until Davey's first goal earned a draw and averted bottom place residence.

But they then got their act together and a run of six matches in which they dropped only one point swept them into the upper reaches of the table. That run earned Mellor an entry in the record books – the first Pompey goalkeeper since World War II to stretch out six consecutive clean sheets. By mid-November they had climbed to second place and there was talk of promotion. But by then their settled defence had been disrupted by the loss of Steve Piper. He had damaged a knee against Darlington at the beginning of the month and was never to play again – a cruel blow to club and player. Davey enthusiastically filled in and to the turn of the year things looked good.

Even Reading's 1-0 F.A. Cup victory at Fratton in early December could not check confidence and Pompey welcomed in 1979 by climbing into first place and Dickinson, who had been voted November's Fourth Division manager of the month, looked like leading HIS club straight back into Division III. Optimism was high. England boosted it by calling up goalkeeper Knight and full back Keith James for the international youth team, and then Foster was included in the under 21 squad but was ruled out by injury. After a weather-interrupted start to the second half of the season, Pompey suddenly lost their rhythm. Dickinson tried to stimulate things by signing Bournemouth's former Welsh international forward Derek Showers and then Northampton's utility player Steve Bryant for £25,000 – but the earlier consistency had gone. Then on Friday March 30 they were devastated by the loss of Dickinson. The legendary character left his directors' box seat after a pulsating 1-1 draw at Barnsley but on reaching the dressing room collapsed with a massive heart attack and was rushed into intensive care. By then Pompey had slipped to eighth place in the table and were unable to make up the lost ground, eventually finishing seventh, nine points adrift of promotion. The 'escape' of promotion and the loss of Dickinson who in May formally resigned and was replaced by Burrows, were not the only blows the club suffered during the season. Financially there was also worry. In early 1978 Pompey had joined the army of clubs who were cashing in on the lottery boom and, linking with Ladbrokes, had launched a lottery aimed at making £4,000 a week. Initially the response had been good; but inside the year it had tailed off and in March Ladbrokes interest had cooled sufficiently for Pompey to decide to go it alone with the expertise of Crystal Palace lottery manager Les Allen to guide them.

The summer of 1979 with Burrows and chairman Deacon determined to make it second time lucky was one of the most active Pompey had ever known. The action was funded by the sale of Foster to Brighton for £150,000. Burrows cut off any possible criticism of this sale by immediately announcing that Swindon's experienced centre-half Steve Aizlewood would replace Foster in one of the first transfers to require the new Football League fee arbitration system. Within a few days Aizlewood's defensive team mate John McLaughlin and Plymouth winger Alan Rogers had come by the same method – ultimately Swindon collected a total of £90,000, considerably less than their valuation – and

Peter Mellor

Steve Davey

Jeff Hemmerman

Plymouth £25,000. Burrows also made three other significant signings – midfield men Joe Laidlaw from Doncaster for £15,000, Charlton's Terry Brisley and Peterborough full-back Archie Styles, both on free transfer. There were also other departures in addition to Foster. Peter Denyer and David Pullar, two more of the home produced youngsters who had provided that glimmer of hope for St. John at Rotherham back in October 1976, also moved on – Northampton signing the dependable Denyer and Exeter, Pullar. In addition McIlwraith, a temperamental and inconsistent character, returned to Bury. By an odd quirk of regionalization, the League Cup again paired Pompey with Swindon in the first round – and again the Wiltshire club came out on top, this time 3-1 on aggregate.

But when the League programme opened, they produced the best start any Pompey side had made since the war – five straight wins. That took them to the top and with Burrows driving hard and exploiting the transfer market hard, Pompey experienced their first taste of genuine success for years. In October Pompey signed Ken Todd from Port Vale for £25,000, in November Ian Purdie from Wigan for a similar amount although neither was to make an impact and striker Steve Perrin from Plymouth for £15,000, then in December David Gregory from Bury for £60,000. Pompey were averaging around 15,000 through the turnstiles with the visit of Bradford and Newport drawing 23,871 and 20,755 inside four days. By mid-programme, Pompey had not been lower than second, and then the F.A. Cup stoked up more fervour.

Newport, who had destroyed the unbeaten home record in October, were beaten 1-0, then a protracted second round with Wimbledon ended with Pompey win-

Terry Brisley and Joe Laidlaw

Steve Aizlewood

ning the second replay 1-0 after the first, on the night of Christmas eve, had ended 3-3. It brought talented First Division Middlesbrough to Fratton to escape with a 1-1 draw after an 89th minute 'winner' by Hemmerman had been disallowed to the frustration of 31,743. But Pompey slumped wretchedly at Ayresome and, almost without a whimper, were beaten 3-0. Burrows continued to work the market – in January former Aston Villa midfield man Jimmy Brown signed on a free transfer and then, after selling Garwood to Aldershot in a move which generated much public criticism, he paid £60,000 for Watford central defender Alan Garner. Garner and Aizlewood quickly showed signs of forging a powerful understanding – but before the promise could be fully fulfilled injury intervened with first Aizlewood and then

Garner ruled out for the rest of the season.

So Davey and Ellis were paired together over the decisive final matches. After 42 matches Pompey were still in fourth place and seemingly booked for promotion, but a draw at home to lowly Crewe saw them slip 'out of the frame' for the first time in the season. But even though they then beat Halifax and Peterborough, they went into the last match of the season still not complete masters of their destiny.

They had to win at Northampton, the scene of that dramatic last gasp escape from Division II relegation on Dickinson's 40th birthday but unless Peterborough and Walsall played their part by beating Bradford and Newport respectively, victory would not be enough. Thousands made the journey from Portsmouth to the

Peter Ellis

County Ground to be kept on tenter-hooks. Burrows' team did their bit winning 2-0 and then came the wait; Newport had gained a dramatic victory at Walsall but Peterborough had beaten Bradford by a single goal and Pompey were up by a wide goal-difference margin – plus 42 to the Yorkshire side's 27. So Pompey celebrated with a massive crowd in front of the Guildhall as the City honoured the club and players – the only discordant note provided by the public's unsuccessful attempt to prevent Brown, who had played in the final three matches, being released.

Players and Officials on Portsmouth Guildhall steps celebrating promotion from Div. 4

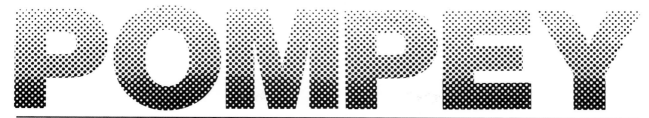

16. And out Again

Pompey made only one summer signing to prepare for the return to Division III – Mick Tait was bought from Hull City for £100,000. But they were short-priced to go straight through when the 1980-81 programme began. At the start public confidence looked well founded. They began with a 3-1 aggregate League Cup victory over Plymouth, then opened in the League itself with four wins. The fourth of those was away to Blackpool where Showers played and scored on his first match after winning a year-long battle to conquer a severe knee injury. Confidence ran high through September boosted by League Cup drama – Second Division Oldham were beaten in the second round on the away goals rule after the tie had finished 3-3 on aggregate, and then Bristol Rovers were defeated 2-0 in a replay. That brought the greatest prize in years – an away draw against Liverpool - and a demonstration of the special nature of Pompey's support. There were 32,000 in Anfield on October 28 – and almost half of them had travelled from the South Coast. Pompey eventually lost 4-1, with their goal scored by Liverpool's Alan Kennedy, but the occasion was one which has entered into Fratton's folk-lore.

But in the League, Pompey were beginning to find the going hard. Laidlaw and Brisley, whose midfield power and scoring ability, had been such crucial factors in the previous season's promotion chase, could no longer dominate and the attack needed a new cutting edge. The final proof came with an abject 3-0 F.A. Cup surrender at Colchester. John Deacon once more proved a willing spender; this time he found almost £200,000 to sign midfieldman Bobby Doyle from Blackpool and much travelled centre-forward Billy Rafferty from his sixth club Newcastle. Those deals bracketted the departure of Showers and Laidlaw to Hereford for a combined price of £28,000. The pair arrived shortly after Pompey had heeded their fans' feelings. Early in the season the board had been captivated by the apparent success of Fulham's decision to introduce Rugby League to Craven Cottage. So, after visiting London to sample the friendly atmos-

phere of a match against Leeds, Pompey proposed to follow their lead – to the fury of their supporters. Eventually John Deacon agreed to accept the findings of a referendum and when that came down almost 10-1 against the idea, it was dropped.

Mick Tait

No 9 Derek Showers claims the goal v Liverpool, but officially it was an own goal.

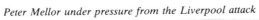
Peter Mellor under pressure from the Liverpool attack

Billy Rafferty

Bobby Doyle

The end of 1980 was particularly sterile with December's four matches failing to produce a single goal to peg them firmly in seventh place, and although they battled their way up to fourth by the end of February, they lacked a promotion side's consistency and ultimately finished in sixth place. Goal-scoring was the problem – 55 compared with the previous season's record-breaking 91. The second half of the season produced only 24 goals in 23 matches, five of those against Exeter when Tait scored a spectacular five-minute hat trick. The casualties of the season were Davey, who had played with cheerful professionalism in defence or attack, Perrin and Brisley. Just to underline, the ease with which mistakes could be made, as they were released, Graham Roberts, who had been allowed to slip away from Fratton less than four years earlier after breaking an ankle in the first few minutes of his senior debut in a pre-season friendly, starred in the centre of Spurs' F.A. Cup winning defence.

Rugby League was not the only issue on which Pompey's supporters 'voted' that season – they also decided the future policy on Sunday football. As clubs up and down the country experimented, Pompey who had seen a massive gate for their Sunday F.A. Cup tie against Orient in January 1974, decided to test public reaction to League soccer. So the visit of Oxford was switched to Sunday, March 29 – but the gate of 12,243 was no more than average and chairman Deacon promptly killed off further breaks with tradition.

The summer of 1981 was Burrows' quietest with only two additions to the staff before training started – Kamara returned from Swindon, preceded by his defensive team mate Andy Rollings. More significantly, when the season began Knight who had waited patiently for his chance, had displaced Mellor as first choice goalkeeper which was to hasten his departure from the club in December. As the second season back in the Third began, Pompey also signed former Scottish international midfield man Alex Cropley from America – a move which was to have an unhappy and untimely ending. League Cup victory over Southend – 4-1 – on aggregate – gave them their only success until late September when a run of three 2-0 wins over Oxford, Bristol City and Exeter held out promise. But they then had to wait until November for another win – a run which dropped them from eighth to 19th in the table – and saw them exit from the League Cup on the back of their painful introduction to the controversial Queen's Park Rangers' carpet. They were thrashed 5-0 at Loftus Road but gamely if vainly, drew the second leg 2-2 at Fratton.

In the heart of this run there was a further shock for the public with the sudden decision to swap Kamara for Brentford winger David Crown. Cropley's first goal checked the slide by beating Wimbledon on November 3, but there was no consistency about them and there was to be only one other victory before the New Year - 2-1 against Huddersfield. That bleak period also included an extra-time replay defeat at Millwall in the first round of the F.A. Cup and with gates slipping regularly into four figures, the prospects were gloomy. The pressure showed early in January when Burrows' aide Stan Harland was sacked and in early February, Bobby Campbell returned as first team coach. Since leaving Portsmouth when he had been on the point of becoming the first manager of the nursery link with Waterlooville, Campbell had coached Queen's Park Rangers and Arsenal and managed Fulham. As he arrived Pompey slipped to 21st place but results perked up and in ten matches only those at Swindon and Burnley were lost and there was a heartening 5-1 thrashing of Chesterfield – a match in which Cropley suffered the last of the many serious injuries which had always dogged him during a battling career.

Alan Rogers

Alan Knight

But that encouraging run which had eased Pompey back up to 15th was not enough to save Burrows and on March 31 he was sacked and Campbell took charge. His first match ended in defeat at Carlisle but Pompey were to lose only twice more in 11 matches and ultimately finished in 13th place. The run in was notable for two features – one good. That was the two goals which Trevor Senior scored against Reading, his first after a much ballyhooed arrival from Southern League Dorchester where his scoring feats had been legendary. Unfortunately they came two matches after 17-year-old former England Schools midfield player Paul Wimbleton's meteoric advance had been checked by a grave knee injury which was to need two major operations and kept him inactive for 19 months.

Off the field it was also significant for two changes – Portsmouth Football Club became a private company and came completely under the umbrella of John Deacon's Superior Properties. Ironically the shares which took him above the 75 per cent – holding needed to offset the club's losses against the holding company's profits came from the man who had fought him so bitterly – Dennis Collett. The benefits of this switch were to be revealed later in the year by the accounts – chairman Deacon had channelled £279,000 in to the club during the year; not the act of a man who at times still had to refute wild accusations of wanting Fratton Park merely to use as a housing site!

Campbell quickly set about re-vitalizing things; he released Hemmerman, and local products Viney and Leigh Barnard and in nine hectic days in early June 1982 signed former England winger Dave Thomas and Q.P.R. defender Ernie Howe on free transfers and 18-year-old England youth midfield player Neil Webb from Reading. Webb was ultimately to cost £87,500 on arbitration and then on the eve of the season, Pompey paid £100,000 for Everton striker Alan Biley. All this was enough to persuade more than 13,000 – the average the previous season had sunk to 8,550 – to Fratton for the opening League match against Sheffield United and a 4-1 win sent Pompey's promotion odds tumbling. Biley, Howe and Webb, the three newcomers on display, all scored on their debuts in a match marred by the sending off of Sheffield's Paul Garner for deliberate handball – early employment on the new clampdown by referees which was to cause such controversy. Although Crystal Palace blighted hopes by bundling them out of the League Cup 3-1 on aggregate, Pompey did not lose in the League until the sixth match when Newport won at Fratton. There was still an element of the inconsistent about them – in early November they showed their class by overwhelming pace-setting Lincoln 4-1 at Fratton with the help of Biley's first hat trick but two matches later slumped to a depressing 5-1 defeat at Bristol Rovers.

John McLaughlin

Ernie Howe

Neil Webb

Alan Biley

Those two matches bracketed the sudden death of Jimmy Dickinson at his Alton home. The legendary Pompey loyalist had gradually picked up some threads of his Fratton link, monitoring the books of the executive supporters' club which bore his name, but had suffered another heart attack in September. Again he seemed to be making progress when he died on November 8 1982 at the age of 57. His funeral took place at Aldershot Crematorium on November 16 and the following week St. Mary's Church, Portsea was crowded for a Memorial Service to Gentleman Jim attended by many who had played with him or had come to admire him over his 40 years service to HIS club.

Hopes of an F.A. Cup run to spice what was already developing into an interesting and potentially exciting season, did not survive the second round – Hereford were comfortably beaten in the first, but Fourth Division Aldershot then giant-killed their neighbours with some ease. But the setback proved a stimulant and Pompey entered 1983 in second place, then were beaten at Sheffield United and the Orient inside three days and again responded emphatically. They won their next seven matches – setting a new club Football League record with the 2-0 success at Bournemouth where the 13,406 crowd included some 10,000 from Fratton. The sequence was broken by a goal-less draw with Wigan – a match in which full back Colin Sullivan joined the players who had been hit by Pompey's penalty jinx. His miss was the eighth in 14 attempts, a catalogue comprising three misses by Doyle, and one each by Webb, Biley, Aizlewood and briefly loaned Everton defender Trevor Ross.

One minutes silence for Jimmy Dickinson. Pompey v Hereford 20/11/82.

Jimmy Dickinson

But by then Pompey were firmly in first place – put there by a 3-0 win at Lincoln – and Campbell had been honoured as the Division's top manager in March. The bandwagon was now rolling impressively forward with fresh reinforcements brought in on the eve of the mid-March transfer deadline when midfield man Kevin Dillon was signed from Birmingham for around £140,000 and striker Nicky Morgan from West Ham for £50,000. Pompey stayed in first place for six weeks, then were surprisingly beaten at home by Bradford – their first Fratton failure since mid-October – and for two weeks suffered the indignity of having someone above them. But a 2-0 win at Doncaster restored them to the top and although Orient surprisingly held them to a 2-2 draw at Fratton on May 2, promotion was clinched in front of 18,356 five days later and 1-0 wins over Walsall and at Plymouth in the final two matches crowned them champions by an emphatic five points. Dillon had proved the answer to Pompey's penalty problems – he had watched Aizelwood miss his second and the side's ninth at Brentford on Good Friday, and then the next day converted two to earn a point at home to Reading.

Pompey's return to the Second Division, completing a long and costly round trip for their chairman, hinged largely on the striking partnership of Biley and Rafferty. Biley eventually finished with a total of 26 goals – 23 in the League matches – to become the first player since Saunders to break the 20-barrier while Rafferty weighed in with 19 (17 League). Statistics also showed the benefits of a settled side – Knight, who gave Pompey their first England under 21 caps when he played at Fratton against Greece and Newcastle against Hungary, Sullivan and Biley played all 50 competitive matches. But another seven topped 40. Pompey's successful season was rounded off by the reserves winning the Midweek League championship thanks largely to the goal-scoring of Senior who ended the season on loan to Aldershot where he scored his first League hat trick in April. Campbell's reward for steering Pompey into the Second was a three year contract to go with his award as the Third Division's manager of the season.

Campbell celebrated that double in impressive style – in late May he caught his rivals on the hop by signing Coventry's England under 21 centre-forward Mark

At the Holiday Inn, Pompey players, Manager and Chairman receive Div 3 Championship medals from Ron Greenwood

Kevin Dillon

Guildhall Square celebrations 1983

Hateley.Several clubs, notably Queen's Park Rangers, hoped to sign him, but Pompey beat them to the punch – a move which ultimately cost them almost £220,000 after paying VAT on the arbitrated £180,000 fee. Apart from the achievements on the field, the season had been notable off it for one fact – Pompey appointed their first woman director. Mrs. Joan Deacon, who had enthusiastically backed her husband during his chairmanship, was appointed to the board at the December annual meeting. During the summer as club and city prepared themsleves for the return of Second Division football, the board took a decision which changed the face of Fratton Park more than anything since the construction of the new South Stand in the mid-20's – they approved the erection of perimeter fencing to prevent crowd invasions. That decision was taken in July – the month in which Percy Mabb, the Supporters' Club founder-secretary died at the age of 83, and in which Alan Ball, the England World Cup medal winner, was appointed youth coach. In early July, Senior was sold to Reading for £35,000, while Rafferty and Ellis had refused the offer of new contracts. Ellis, though, accepted his before the season started, leaving Rafferty in dispute – a wrangle which was ultimately not resolved until February when he joined Bournemouth.

Pompey made one other signing before the start of the 1983-84 season – Richard Money, a versatile defender Campbell once sold to Liverpool for £350,000 linked up with him again from Luton for around £50,000. But the welcome back to the Second Division was a chastening and controversial affair with Pompey beaten by a Middlesbrough goal scored while Knight was concussed in his goal-mouth. The final whistle proved that higher fences would be needed to contain determined troublemakers – and that prompted Mr. Deacon to declare war on them. He instituted life bans against people convicted of causing trouble at Fratton Park in a bid to halt escalating hooliganism. The injury also ended Knight's run of 54 consecutive appearances, giving understudy Andy Gosney his senior outing in the side beaten 3-2 at Hereford in the first leg of the Milk Cup first round – a defeat avenged a fortnight later as Pompey went through 5-4 on aggregate. That earned a meeting with Aston Villa, managed by former Pompey player and chief scout Tony Barton, which was to produce two epic matches before the Midlanders ultimately went through 5-4 on aggregate after extra time. The First Division side scored twice in the last few minutes at Fratton to escape with a 2-2 draw and won the second leg 3-2 – with Pompey reduced virtually to ten men by injuries to Aiz-

Mark Hateley

lewood and Money. Money's knee ligament injury was so severe he did not play again until appearing in the reserves in mid-March.

It was to prove a frustrating time for Pompey; their results did not match performances and they were never able to mount a genuine challenge for promotion. Hateley had quickly proved a bargain, in four days in November he scored hat tricks against Cambridge and Grimsby which took them to seventh – the highest placing they were to achieve. Home results more than performances were disappointing with the greatest disappointment of all reserved for late January and the F.A. Cup. After repeating their League success against Grimsby in the third round, Pompey were then paired against Southampton – the first sudden-death meeting between the neighbours since 1906. Nothing in recent years had so fired the imagination of the public, the 36,000 tickets were sold in hours more than days – but the occasion was to prove an anti-climax for Pompey's majority in the full house crowd. They had the best of what few chances there were until, with a replay seeming inevitable, Saints stole into the fifth round with an injury time goal. The disappointment seemed to eat deep; the next three league matches were lost – when all might easily have been won – and suddenly the events at the bottom of the table were of predominant interest.

Successive away wins at Cambridge, Grimsby and

Barnsley checked the flow of pessimism, but never completely obliterated it. For Pompey remained curiously vulnerable in front of their own increasingly worried supporters. The win at Grimsby was counter-balanced by a Fratton defeat against a dour Carlisle side making a lie of the need to spend big to succeed; that at Barnsley by a single goal reverse from a Crystal Palace side with an anxious eye on the rapidly developing relegation dogfight – the fourth successive home defeat. Suddenly Pompey made a nonsense of that awful run by scoring five goals in a devastating 13 minute second half burst to thrash neighbours Brighton, a match which saw Money dramatically return after five months injured. But it could not be sustained. April's five matches brought a return of a single point – from the second 2-2 draw of the season with ultimate champions Chelsea – and another home defeat. This was perhaps the most painful of the lot for Pompey led Blackburn by two Webb goals at half time only to concede four in the second half to suffer home a defeat for the tenth time.

So Pompey entered the last month of the season just above the relegation zone and, ominously, the wretched home results had taken an inevitable toll on public loyalty. Gates had generally been sustained close to the 13,000 economic level, but had forced a re-write of the year's financial forecasts. Chairman Deacon had written a gate money profit of £70,000 into his projections, but

Pompey 83/84 Back Row from l to r M. Tait, M. Hateley, E. Howe, K. Dillon
Middle Row P. Ellis, R. Doyle, S. Aizlewood, A. Knight, A. Gosney, N. Webb, N. Morgan, A. Ball (Youth team coach)
Front Row R. Campbell (Manager), C. Sullivan, J. McLaughlin, A. Biley, A. Rogers, D. Thomas, G. Neave (Physio)

Nicky Morgan

Bobby Campbell

they had long been abandoned. Only 8,915 saw the Blackburn match and that had sunk to 7,738 by the time an injury wracked Huddersfield gained a deserved 1-1 draw on May 5. The point, combined with other results, was enough to kill off the mathematical possibility of the ultimate disaster – immediate relegation – but the performance again disappointed and was compounded four days later at Derby County. The famous old Midlands club were doomed but bowed out at home in some style by inflicting Pompey's 21st defeat of the season to leave them just one place above the relegation plimsole line. But it was the overall performance which had again been the damning factor of the night – and ultimately it was to have fatal results for Campbell. Two days later he faced his chairman who was in search of reasons for the poor return on his latest considerable investment.

The result of that meeting was another managerial departure. Just a year and a day after they had stood at the front of the directors' box and taken the crowd's salute after the Third Division title had been put within their grasp, chairman Deacon and Campbell severed their connections. Campbell's reign at Fratton had lasted little more than two years and he went with two year's of his contract to run. He went, too, with one last match to play and it was Alan Ball, his youth team coach, who sent out the team to face long-doomed Swansea 24 hours later. Predictably Ball's caretakership began in style. The youthful Welsh side were outclassed by players with conscience their spur and the season of such promise and frustration ended with a five-goal salvo. Biley, whose season had been much like the team's, closed with his second hat trick for the club while Hateley hit the goal which took him to his father's pre-season target of 25. Reasons for Pompey difficulties were not hard to find. While they had scored a more than respectable 73 goals - one more in fact than promoted Sheffield Wednesday - they had also conceded 64. That was more the form of relegation – and their 32 at home was the worst in the Division save bottom club Cambridge.

In the wake of the final match Pompey parted company with Aizlewood and McLaughlin, stalwarts of the climb from Division IV, with Ellis, the first local boy to come through after the resumption of the youth team under Tindall, and with Howe whose impressive contribution to the club had been savagely disrupted by serious injury. There followed a month's hiatus while Pompey advertized for Campbell's successor and while Ball, with the willing co-operation of his chairman, began reconstructing the defence whose short-comings had torpedoed so many early season dreams. A new central partnership was forged by the signing of Mick Baxter from Middlesbrough and Billy Gilbert from Crystal Palace while Mick Kennedy, a hard-bitten and hard-tackling character from Middlesbrough, brought extra midfield bite at a cost of £100,000. Against that background it was no great surprise when on June 6, Mr. Deacon unveiled the sixth manager of his 12 years at Fratton – Alan Ball. And so the little red-haired ever-running legend of England's 1966 World Cup triumph accepted the challenge of turning the dream which had cost his chairman more than two million pounds into reality . . .

Pompey's fans were soon celebrating the club's first England caps for almost 30 years when Hateley played in all three matches of their South American tour, scoring in the win over Brazil, but within ten days of the tour's end he had been sold to A.C. Milan for £1 million. Forty eight hours after his sale, Pompey announced his successor – 21-year-old Scott McGarvey from Manchester United at a cost of £85,000.

Mr. Deacon with the new Manager Alan Ball

Oddities

23/8/1899
Brighton & Hove F.C. referred to as 'The Greenbacks' in the Portsmouth Times.

31/12/1903
Mr. A. L. Farrant, the well known Bristol referee, met with a bad accident after officiating in the game at West Ham yesterday. In the dressing room, while performing his ablutions, he stood in the wash bowl, which broke and caused such serious injuries that he was taken to hospital.

6/2/1905
The goalkeeper of a Berkshire football team is a man with a wooden leg, during the course of a game, he makes round holes in the ground.

21/11/1905
Two spectators of the cup tie at Fulham, last season, when the crowd broke into the ground, are suing Fulham Football Club Ltd. for compensation for damage to their bicycles, damage which they say was caused by the inrush of spectators.

17/9/1906
One of the players being somewhat 'sore', kicked the ball as hard as he could across the field and passed some very uncomlimentary remarks concerning Mr. Resien's prowess as a referee. However Mr. Resien persisted and thereupon the man struck him a heavy blow in the face. The referee left the field and the match was abandoned.

8/10/1917
The one legged members of the Cowen Training Home for Disabled Soldiers, Benwell Grange Newcastle, are forming a football team.

3/10/1928
During the Western League game between Bristol Rovers Reserves and Plymouth Argyle Reserves, the referee, Mr. A. J. Attwood, three times cautioned Pullen, the Argyle centre half, eventually he ordered him to the dressing room. Pullen immediately struck the ref twice giving him a cut lip and a swelling eye. Mr. Attwood's injuries were dressed, and he then continued with the game.

29/3/1931
The whole team of Elmsdale Wednesday and one player from their opponents Sutton Wednesday have been suspended by the Surrey F.A., as an outcome of rough play in the Croydon Midweek Charity Cup Semi final. Five players were ordered off, two were taken to hospital, the game was abandoned 10 minutes before time. 4 players have been suspended until the end of the year, and 8 are suspended until the end of the season.

22/6/1934
A 90 year old man played as goal keeper in a men v women football match in Maaland, Sweden. Eleven villages were represented, the mens team was composed of the head of each village.

22/9/1934
Joe Wilson, David Robinson and Bert Jones of Southend Utd. are in court accused of poaching on 16/9/1934. Police stopped their lorry and found 62 rabbits and four guns. Wilson was fined £1 and the others 10/-d, their guns were confiscated.

8/10/1934
Portsmouth Tram Boys beat Palmer Sports 40-0. (Forty goals to NIL). The goalscorers were; Boss, 10; Hunt, 5; Mitchell, 5; Eddy, 5; Miles, 4; Worth, 3; Lobb, 3; Aird, 2; Montague, 2; Hicks, 1. Every player except the goalkeeper scored.

20/11/1935
Diving headlong across the goal to make a spectacular save, a well known local keeper named Perez seriously injured his head during a match in Paris. He died on his way to hospital.

19/11/1943
Hartlepool Rovers have been presented with a quantity of disused flourbags. Their womenfolk have made a few alterations and now the entire team are wearing flourbag jerseys.

1/4/1950
For the second half of the game between Nottingham Forest and Bournemouth, an orange ball was used; but after an objection by Lewis, the Bournemouth captain, the original ball was re-introduced.

25/4/1953
In the final of the Portsmouth Inter Firms Cup Competition at the Airspeed ground, Bailey and Whites were leading 4-0 with five minutes to go. The winning team's goalkeeper jumped for a high ball, and grabbed the crossbar, – it snapped and the match was abandoned.

17/10/1953
Western Sports, in the Portsmouth League now have their complete team on the injured list.

24/3/1956
A Portsmouth Sunday league player named 'Crawley' who was married on a Saturday, played for Drayton the next day, scoring 11 goals out of a 14-0 win over 'Depot' in a div 1 match.

25/11/1983
Marconi reserves F.C. found that they were minus 11 pairs of shorts when they turned up to play Dunham Bush 80; in a Portsmouth Junior B Cup match. The referee Mr. Bernie Messum, made them start the match playing in their underpants, and after 10 minutes play their missing shorts were brought to the sideline and decency was restored. Marconi lost 2-1, after extra time.

Take cover lads! The Marconi team who had to start a match in their underpants

Full International Players

Date	Player	Position	For – Against	Venue	Score	Goals Scored
17.03.1900	D. Cunliffe	I.R.	England-v-N. Ireland	Dublin	2-0	
17.03.1900	J. "Matt" Reilly	Goal	N. Ireland-v-England	Dublin	0-2	
22.03.1902	J. "Matt" Reilly	Goal	N. Ireland-v-England	Belfast	0-1	
02.03.1903	A. E. Houlker	L.H.	England-v-Wales	Portsmouth	2-1	
04.04.1903	A. E. Houlker	L.H.	England-v-Scotland	Sheffield	1-2	
11.10.1919	A. E. Knight (Victory Game)	L.B.	England-v-Wales	Cardiff	1-2	
25.10.1919	A. E. Knight	L.B.	England-v-N. Ireland	Belfast	1-1	
29.10.1927	F. Cook	O.L.	Wales-v-Scotland	Wrexham	2-2	
28.11.1927	F. Cook	O.L.	Wales-v-England	Burnley	2-1	
04.02.1928	H. Davey	C.F.	N. Ireland-v-Wales	Belfast	1-2	
22.10.1928	R. Irvine	I.R.	N. Ireland-v-England	Liverpool	1-2	
26.10.1929	F. Cook	O.L.	Wales-v-Scotland	Cardiff	2-4	
20.11.1929	F. Cook	O.L.	Wales-v-England	London	0-6	
01.02.1930	F. Cook	O.L.	Wales-v-N. Ireland	Belfast	0-7	
22.02.1930	R. Irvine	I.R.	N. Ireland-v-Scotland	Glasgow	1-3	
16.05.1931	J. Easson	C.F.	Scotland-v-Austria	Vienna	0-5	
24.05.1931	J. Easson	I.L.	Scotland-v-Switzerland	Geneva	3-2	1
17.10.1931	J. Smith	I.R.	England-v-N. Ireland	Belfast	6-2	1
18.11.1931	F. Cook	O.L.	Wales-v-England	Liverpool	1-3	
18.11.1931	J. Smith	I.R.	England-v-Wales	Liverpool	3-1	1
09.12.1931	J. Smith	I.R.	England-v-Spain	Arsenal	7-1	2
04.10.1933	J. Easson	I.L.	Scotland-v-Wales	Cardiff	2-3	
14.10.1933	J. Allen	C.H.	England-v-N. Ireland	Belfast	3-0	
15.11.1933	J. Allen	C.H.	England-v-Wales	Newcastle	1-2	
20.10.1934	J. A. Mackie	R.B.	N. Ireland-v-Scotland	Belfast	2-1	
27.03.1935	J. A. Mackie	R.B.	N. Ireland-v-Wales	Wrexham	1-3	
18.05.1935	F. Worrall	O.R.	England-v-Holland	Amsterdam	1-0	1
18.11.1936	F. Worrall	O.R.	England-v-N. Ireland	Stoke	3-1	1
16.09.1944	R. Flewin	C.H.	England-v-Wales	Liverpool	2-2	
05.05.1945	R. Flewin	C.H.	England-v-Wales	Cardiff	3-2	
18.05.1945	J. W. Dickinson	L.H.	England-v-Norway	Oslo	4-1	
16.06.1946	J. McAlinden	I.L.	Eire-v-Portugal	Lisbon	1-3	
23.06.1946	J. McAlinden	I.L.	Eire-v-Spain	Madrid	1-0	
28.09.1946	J. McAlinden	I.R.	N. Ireland-v-England	Belfast	2-7	
22.05.1949	J. W. Dickinson	L.H.	England-v-France	Paris	3-1	
21.09.1949	J. W. Dickinson	L.H.	England-v-Eire	Everton	0-2	
21.09.1949	P. P. Harris	O.R.	England-v-Eire	Everton	0-2	
15.10.1949	J. W. Dickinson	L.H.	England-v-Wales	Cardiff	4-1	
16.11.1949	J. Froggatt	O.L.	England-v-N. Ireland	Maine Road	9-2	1
30.11.1949	J. Froggatt	O.L.	England-v-Italy	Tottenham	2-0	
15.04.1950	J. W. Dickinson	L.H.	England-v-Scotland	Glasgow	1-0	
14.05.1950	J. W. Dickinson	L.H.	England-v-Portugal	Lisbon	5-3	
18.05.1950	J. W. Dickinson	L.H.	England-v-Belgium	Brussels	4-1	
15.06.1950	J. W. Dickinson (World Cup)	L.H.	England-v-Chile	Rio de Janeiro	2-0	
29.06.1950	J. W. Dickinson (World Cup)	L.H.	England-v-U.S.A.	Belo Horizonte	0-1	
02.07.1950	J. W. Dickinson	L.H.	England-v-Spain	Rio de Janeiro	0-1	
07.10.1950	J. W. Dickinson	L.H.	England-v-N. Ireland	Belfast	4-1	

Date	Player	Position	For – Against	Venue	Score	Goals Scored
15.11.1950	J. W. Dickinson	L.H.	England-v-Wales	Sunderland	4-2	
22.11.1950	J. W. Dickinson	L.H.	England-v-Yugoslavia	Highbury	2-2	
14.04.1951	J. Froggatt	C.H.	England-v-Scotland	Wembley	2-3	
12.05.1951	J. Scoular	R.H.	Scotland-v-Denmark	Hampden Park	3-1	
16.05.1951	J. Scoular	R.H.	Scotland-v-France	Hampden Park	1-0	
27.05.1951	J. Scoular	R.H.	Scotland-v-Austria	Vienna	0-4	
20.10.1951	J. W. Dickinson	L.H.	England-v-Wales	Cardiff	1-1	
14.11.1951	J. W. Dickinson	L.H.	England-v-N. Ireland	Aston Villa	2-0	
	L. H. Phillips	I.L.	England-v-N. Ireland	Aston Villa	2-0	
28.11.1951	J. W. Dickinson	L.H.	England-v-Austria	Wembley	2-2	
	J. Froggatt	C.H.	England-v-Austria	Wembley	2-2	
05.04.1952	J. W. Dickinson	L.H.	England-v-Scotland	Hampden Park	2-1	
	J. Froggatt	C.H.	England-v-Scotland	Hampden Park	2-1	
	J. Scoular	R.H.	Scotland-v-England	Hampden Park	1-2	
30.04.1952	J. Scoular	R.H.	Scotland-v-U.S.A.	Hampden Park	6-0	
18.05.1952	J. W. Dickinson	L.H.	England-v-Italy	Florence	1-1	
	J. Froggatt	C.H.	England-v-Italy	Florence	1-1	
25.05.1952	J. W. Dickinson	L.H.	England-v-Austria	Vienna	3-2	
	J. Froggatt	C.H.	England-v-Austria	Vienna	3-2	
	J. Scoular	R.H.	Scotland-v-Denmark	Copenhagen	2-1	
28.05.1952	J. W. Dickinson	L.H.	England-v-Switzerland	Zurich	3-0	
	J. Froggatt	C.H.	England-v-Switzerland	Zurich	3-0	
30.05.1952	J. Scoular	R.H.	Scotland-v-Sweden	Stockholm	1-3	
04.10.1952	J. W. Dickinson	L.H.	England-v-N. Ireland	Belfast	2-2	
	J. Froggatt	C.H.	England-v-N. Ireland	Belfast	2-2	
15.10.1952	J. Scoular	R.H.	Scotland-v-Wales	Cardiff	2-1	
05.11.1952	J. Scoular	R.H.	Scotland-v-N. Ireland	Hampden Park	1-1	
11.11.1952	W. N. M. Uprichard	Goal	N. Ireland-v-France	Paris	1-3	
12.11.1952	J. Froggatt	C.H.	England-v-Wales	Wembley	5-2	1
	J. W. Dickinson	L.H.	England-v-Wales	Wembley	5-2	
26.11.1952	J. Froggatt	C.H.	England-v-Belgium	Wembley	5-0	
	J. W. Dickinson	L.H.	England-v-Belgium	Wembley	5-0	
15.04.1953	W. N. M. Uprichard	Goal	N. Ireland-v-Wales	Belfast	2-3	
18.04.1953	J. Froggatt	O.L.	England-v-Scotland	Wembley	2-2	
	J. W. Dickinson	L.H.	England-v-Scotland	Wembley	2-2	
06.05.1953	J. G. Henderson	O.R.	Scotland-v-Sweden	Hampden Park	1-2	
17.05.1953	J. W. Dickinson	L.H.	England-v-Argentina Abandoned after 23 mins	Buenos Aires	0-0	
24.05.1953	J. W. Dickinson	L.H.	England-v-Chile	Santiago	2-1	
31.05.1953	J. W. Dickinson	L.H.	England-v-Uruguay	Montivideo	1-2	
08.06.1953	J. Froggatt	O.L.	England-v-U.S.A.	New York	6-3	
	J. W. Dickinson	L.H.	England-v-U.S.A.	New York	6-3	
03.10.1953	J. G. Henderson	O.L.	Scotland-v-N. Ireland	Belfast	3-1	
10.10.1953	J. W. Dickinson	L.H.	England-v-Wales	Cardiff	4-1	
21.10.1953	J. W. Dickinson	L.H.	England-v-Rest of Europe	Wembley	4-4	
11.11.1953	J. W. Dickinson	L.H.	England-v-N. Ireland	Goodison Park	3-1	
25.11.1953	J. W. Dickinson	L.H.	England-v-Hungary	Wembley	3-6	
03.04.1954	J. W. Dickinson	L.H.	England-v-Scotland	Glasgow	4-2	
	J. G. Henderson	C.F.	Scotland-v-England	Hampden Park	2-4	
16.05.1954	J. W. Dickinson	L.H.	England-v-Yugoslavia	Belgrade	0-1	
19.05.1954	J. G. Henderson	C.F.	Scotland-v-Norway	Oslo	1-1	
23.05.1954	J. W. Dickinson	L.H.	England-v-Hungary	Budapest	1-7	
	P. P. Harris	O.R.	England-v-Hungary	Budapest	1-7	
25.05.1954	A. Wilson	R.B.	Scotland-v-Finland	Helsinki	2-1	
17.06.1954	J. W. Dickinson (World Cup)	L.H.	England-v-Belgium	Basle	4-4	og
29.06.1954	J. W. Dickinson (World Cup)	L.H.	England-v-Switzerland	Berne	2-0	
02.10.1954	W. N. M. Uprichard	Goal	N. Ireland-v-England	Belfast	0-2	
	J. W. Dickinson (World Cup)	L.H.	England-v-Uruguay	Basle	2-4	

Date	Player	Position	For – Against	Venue	Score	Goals Scored
03.11.1954	W. N. M. Uprichard	Goal	N. Ireland-v-Scotland	Hampden Park	2-2	
10.11.1954	L. H. Phillips	R.H.	England-v-Wales	Wembley	3-2	
01.12.1954	L. H. Phillips	R.H.	England-v-W. Germany	Wembley	3-1	
14.04.1955	J. W. Dickinson	R.H.	England-v-Scotland	Glasgow	1-1	
20.04.1955	W. N. M. Uprichard	Goal	N. Ireland-v-Wales	Belfast	2-3	
18.05.1955	J. W. Dickinson	R.H.	England-v-Spain	Madrid	1-1	
22.05.1955	J. W. Dickinson	R.H.	England-v-Portugal	Oporto	1-3	
02.10.1955	J. W. Dickinson	L.H.	England-v-Denmark	Copenhagen	5-1	
08.10.1955	W. N. M. Uprichard	Goal	N. Ireland-v-Scotland	Belfast	2-1	
22.10.1955	J. W. Dickinson	L.H.	England-v-Wales	Cardiff	1-1	
02.11.1955	J. W. Dickinson	L.H.	England-v-N. Ireland	Wembley	3-0	
	W. N. M. Uprichard	Goal	N. Ireland-v-England	Wembley	0-3	
09.11.1955	J. G. Henderson	O.L.	Scotland-v-Wales	Hampden Park	2-0	
30.11.1955	J. W. Dickinson	L.H.	England-v-Spain	Wembley	4-1	
11.04.1956	W. N. M. Uprichard	Goal	N. Ireland-v-Wales	Cardiff	1-1	
14.11.1956	J. W. Dickinson	L.H.	England-v-Wales	Wembley	3-1	
28.11.1956	J. W. Dickinson	L.H.	England-v-Yugoslavia	Wembley	3-0	
05.12.1956	J. W. Dickinson	L.H.	England-v-Denmark	Wolverhampton	5-2	
05.10.1957	W. N. M. Uprichard	Goal	N. Ireland-v-Scotland	Belfast	1-1	
15.01.1958	W. N. M. Uprichard	Goal	N. Ireland-v-Italy	Belfast	2-1	
08.06.1958	W. N. M. Uprichard (World Cup)	Goal	N. Ireland-v-Czechoslavakia	Halmstad	1-0	
	D. Dougan (World Cup)	C.F.	N. Ireland-v-Czechoslavakia	Halmstad	1-0	
17.06.1958	W. N. M. Uprichard (World Cup) Play Off	Goal	N. Ireland-v-Czechoslavakia	Malmo	2-1 a.e.t.	
04.10.1958	T. Casey	C.F.	N. Ireland-v-England	Belfast	3-3	1
15.10.1958	W. N. M. Uprichard	Goal	N. Ireland-v-Spain	Madrid	2-6	
	T. Casey	L.H.	N. Ireland-v-Spain	Madrid	2-6	
05.11.1958	W. N. M. Uprichard	Goal	N. Ireland-v-Scotland	Hampden Park	2-2	
04.05.1969	E. K. Hand (World Cup)	C.F. (Sub.)	Eire-v-Czechoslavakia	Dublin	1-2	
06.05.1970	E. K. Hand	R.H.	Eire-v-Poland	Dublin	1-2	
09.05.1970	E. K. Hand	R.H.	Eire-v-W. Germany	Berlin	1-2	
23.09.1970	E. K. Hand	R.H.	Eire-v-Poland	Dublin	0-2	
30.05.1971	E. K. Hand (Euro. Champ.)	R.H.	Eire-v-Austria	Dublin	1-4	
18.10.1972	E. K. Hand	R.H.	Eire-v-U.S.S.R.	Dublin	1-2	
15.11.1972	E. K. Hand (World Cup)	R.H.	Eire-v-France	Dublin	2-1	
13.05.1973	E. K. Hand (World Cup)	O.R.	Eire-v-U.S.S.R.	Moscow	0-1	
16.05.1973	E. K. Hand	O.R.	Eire-v-Poland	Wroclaw	0-2	
19.05.1973	E. K. Hand (World Cup)	O.R.	Eire-v-France	Paris	1-1	
21.10.1973	E. K. Hand	O.R.	Eire-v-Poland	Dublin	1-0	
05.05.1974	E. K. Hand	O.R.	Eire-v-Brazil	Rio de Janeiro	1-2	
08.05.1974	E. K. Hand	O.R.	Eire-v-Uruguay	Montevideo	1-2	
11.05.1974	P. S. Roberts	R.B.	Wales-v-England	Cardiff	0-2	
	R. T. Davies	C.F.	Wales-v-England	Cardiff	0-2	
12.05.1974	E. K. Hand	O.R.	Eire-v-Chile	Santiago	2-1	
04.09.1974	P. S. Roberts	R.B.	Wales-v-Austria	Vienna	1-2	
30.10.1974	P. S. Roberts	L.B.	Wales-v-Hungary	Cardiff	2-0	
20.11.1974	E. K. Hand (Euro. Ch.)	O.R.	Eire-v-Turkey	Izmir	1-1	
	P. S. Roberts	R.H.	Wales-v-Luxembourg	Swansea	5-0	1
10.05.1975	E. K. Hand (Euro. Ch.)	O.R.	Eire-v-Switzerland	Dublin	2-1	
18.05.1975	E. K. Hand (Euro. Ch.)	O.R.	Eire-v-U.S.S.R.	Kiev	1-2	1
21.05.1975	E. K. Hand (Euro. Ch.)	O.R.	Eire-v-Switzerland	Berne	0-1	
29.10.1975	E. K. Hand (Euro. Ch.)	O.R.	Eire-v-Turkey	Dublin	4-0	
02.06.1984	M. Hateley	C.F. (sub)	England-v-U.S.S.R.	Wembley	0-2	
10.06.1984	M. Hateley	C.F.	England-v-Brazil	Rio de Janeiro	2-0	1
13.06.1984	M. Hateley	C.F.	England-v-Uruguay	Montevideo	0-2	
17.06.1984	M. Hateley	C.F.	England-v-Chile	Santiago	0-0	

Amateur International Players

Date	Player	Position	For – Against	Venue	Score	Goals Scored
08.09.1908	L. A. Louch	C.F.	England-v-Sweden	Gothenburg	6-1	
20.11.1909	E. W. Williams	O.L.	England-v-N. Ireland	Leeds	4-4	
11.12.1909	E. W. Williams	O.L.	England-v-Holland	Chelsea	9-1	1
11.12.1909	A. E. Knight	L.B.	England-v-Holland	Chelsea	9-1	
19.02.1910	A. E. Knight	L.B.	England-v-Wales	Huddersfield	6-0	
16.04.1910	L. A. Louch	I.R.	England-v-France	Brighton	10-1	
18.02.1911	A. E. Knight	L.B.	England-v-Wales	Newtown	5-1	
04.03.1911	A. E. Knight	L.B.	England-v-Belgium	Crystal Palace	4-0	
23.03.1911	A. E. Knight	L.B.	England-v-France	Paris	3-1	
14.04.1911	A. E. Knight	L.B.	England-v-Germany	Berlin	2-2	
17.04.1911	A. E. Knight	L.B.	England-v-Holland	Amsterdam	1-0	
25.05.1911	A. E. Knight	L.B.	England-v-Switzerland	Berne	4-1	
21.10.1911	A. E. Knight	L.B.	England-v-Denmark	Park Royal	3-0	
18.11.1911	A. E. Knight	L.B.	England-v-N. Ireland	Huddersfield	2-0	
16.03.1912	A. E. Knight	L.B.	England-v-Holland	Hull	4-0	
08.04.1912	A. E. Knight	L.B.	England-v-Belgium	Brussels	2-1	

1912 OLYMPIC GAMES IN STOCKHOLM, SWEDEN

Date	Player	Position	For – Against	Venue	Score	Goals Scored
30.06.1912	A. E. Knight	L.B.	U.K.-v-Hungary		7-0	
02.07.1912	A. E. Knight	L.B.	U.K.-v-Finland	Semi-Final	4-0	
04.07.1912	A. E. Knight	L.B.	U.K.-v-Denmark	Final	4-2	
	1 CAP for 3 games					
08.10.1912	A. E. Knight	L.B.	England-v-N. Ireland	Belfast	2-3	
09.11.1912	A. E. Knight	L.B.	England-v-Belgium	Swindon	4-0	
08.02.1913	A. E. Knight	L.B.	England-v-Wales	Llandudno	3-1	
27.02.1915	A. E. Knight	L.B.	England-v-France	Paris	4-1	
21.03.1913	A. E. Knight	L.B.	England-v-Germany (Continental Tour)	Berlin	3-0	
24.03.1913	A. E. Knight	L.B.	England-v-Holland	The Hague	1-2	
08.11.1913	A. E. Knight	L.B.	England-v-N. Ireland	Belfast	2-0	
15.11.1913	A. E. Knight	L.B.	England-v-Holland	Hull	2-1	1
07.02.1914	A. E. Knight	L.B.	England-v-Wales	Plymouth	9-1	
24.02.1914	A. E. Knight	L.B.	England-v-Belgium	Brussels	8-1	
05.06.1914	A. E. Knight	L.B.	England-v-Denmark	Copenhagen	0-3	
10.06.1914	A. E. Knight	L.B.	England-v-Sweden	Stockholm	5-1	
12.06.1914	A. E. Knight	L.B.	England-v-Sweden	Stockholm	5-0	
18.11.1919	A. E. Knight (capt.)	L.B.	England-v-N. Ireland	Derby	5-0	
24.01.1920	A. E. Knight	L.B.	England-v-Wales (Victory International)	Merthyr	9-0	
05.04.1920	A. E. Knight (capt.)	L.B.	England-v-France	Rouen	5-0	
17.09.1955	P. T. Neil	O.L.	England-v-N. Ireland	Cliftonville	4-1	2
23.10.1955	P. T. Neil	O.L.	G.B.-v-Bulgaria	Sofia	0-2	
12.11.1955	P. T. Neil	O.L.	G.B.-v-W. Germany	Tottenham	2-3	

Statistics

Contents

Abbreviations used:

AET	– After Extra Time	RA	– Royal Artillery
ASC	– Army Service Corps	RAF (AAB)	– Royal Air Force Anti-Aircraft Brigade
BCD	– Behind Closed Doors	RAMC	– Royal Army Medical Corps
BFC	– Benevolent Fund Cup (Hants FA)	RFA	– Royal Field Artillery
EC	– English Cup	RFC	– Royal Flying Corps
F	– team selected from:	RMA	– Royal Marine Artillery
Fr	– Friendly	RNB	– Royal Naval Barracks
FA	– For and Against	RMLI	– Royal Marine Light Infantry
FAC	– Football Association Cup	RLSB/RLSC	– Regional League South 'B' or 'C'
FACSF	– Football Association Cup Semi Final	s	– Means the player was in the squad detailed in the preceding days Evening News
FACS	– Football Association Charity Shield		
FC	– Floodlight Cup	SA	– Southern Alliance
FLC	– Football League Cup	SARB	– Siege Artillery Reserve Brigade
FLJF	– Football League Jubilee Fund	SCC	– Southern Charity Cup
FLS or LS	– Football League South	SDC	– Southern District Combination
FT	– Full Time	SF	– Semi Final
HC	– Hospital Cup	SFCC	– Southern Floodlight Challenge Cup
HCC	– Hants Combination Cup	SHWL	– South Hants War League
HPC	– Hampshire Professional Cup	S or SL or SL1	– Southern League Division 1
HT	– Half Time	SL2	– Southern League Division 2
HVC	– Hants Victory Cup (1918/19)	Soton	– Southampton
KC	– Kent Cup	SRL	– Southern Regional League
LC	– London Combination	SWC	– South Western Combination
LWC	– London War Cup	v.	– Versus
LWL	– London War League	W	– Western League
MC	– Milk Cup	*	– means substituted
OG	– Own Goal		
p	– played, name mentioned in report, actual position unknown		
PBC	– Pickford Benevolent Cup		
PBC/HC	– Pickford Benevolent Cup/Hospital Cup		
R (after FAC)	– Replay		
(2)R (after FAC)	– 2nd Replay		

Superior figure by number (e.g. 8²) indicates goals scored.

While every effort has been made to ensure that these statistics are correct, mistakes do occur, and the authors will be pleased to hear from anyone with errors that have been seen.

Season 1899/1900 Southern League Division 1
Southern District Combination

Date	Venue	Team	Attendance	FA HT FT	Reilly M.	Turner H.	Wilkie T.	Blyth R.	Stringfellow H.	Cleghorn T.	Marshall R.G.	Cunliffe D.	Brown A.	Smith W.	Clarke H.	Turner E.	Brown J.	Hanna J.	Barnes G.	Hunter J.	Digweed H.	McKenzie	Struthers R.	Moore F.	Harms	Hill	Cotton	Cooke T.	Hall
Sept 2	A	Chatham S	4000	0-0 1-0	1	2	3	6	5	4	7	8	9	10	11¹	12*													
Sept 9	H	Reading S	9000	1-0 2-0	1	2	3	4	5	6	7	8¹	9		11¹	10													
Sept 16	A	Sheppey Utd. S		0-0 0-0	1	2	3	4	5	6	7	8	9		11	10													
Sept 18	A	Tottenham SDC		0-1 0-2	1	2	3	4	5	6	7		9	10	11	8													
Sept 23	H	Brighton Utd. S	6000	2-0 3-1	1	2	3	4	5	6	7	8¹	9¹	10¹	11														
Sept 27	H	Chatham SDC	3000	0-0 4-0	1	2	3	4	5	6	7	8			10¹			9²	11¹										
Sept 30	H	Ryde EC	4000	4-0 10-0	1	2	3	4	5		7²	8¹	9³	10³	11¹	6													
Oct 7	H	Bristol R. S	7000	3-0 8-2	1	2	3	4	5	6	7¹	8⁴	9²	10¹	11														
Oct 14	H	Cowes EC	6000	1-1 3-2	1	2	3	4	5		7	8¹	9	10²	11	6													
Oct 18	H	Southampton SDC	7000	2-0 5-1	1	2	3	4	5		7	8²	9¹	10²	11	6													
Oct 23	A	W'wich Arsenal SDC	small	1-0 2-0	1	p				p		8¹		10		p				p¹									
Oct 28	H	Swindon EC	10000	0-1 2-1	1		3	4	5	6	7	8¹	9	10¹	11	2													
Nov 1	H	Millwall SDC	good	0-1 1-3	1		3				7	8¹			11	2		9	4	5	6	10							
Nov 4	A	New Brompton S		0-1	1		3	4	5		7	8		10	11	2		9		6									
Nov 8	A	Reading SDC		0-1 0-2	1		3	4	5		7	8	9	10	11	2				6									
Nov 11	H	Gravesend S	4693	1-1 2-1	1		3	4	5		7	8	9²	10	11	2				6									
Nov 18	A	Bristol R. EC		0-1 1-1	1		3	6	5		7	8	9	10	11¹	2				4									
Nov 22	H	Bristol R. ECR	6000	2-0 4-0	1		3	6	5		7²	8	9¹	10	11¹	2				4									
Nov 25	H	Bristol C. S	6000	1-0 2-0	1		3	6	5		7	8	9¹	10	11	2				4									
Nov 29	A	Bristol C. SDC		1-0 3-1	1		3	6	5		7¹	8²	9	10	11	2				4									
Dec 2	A	Cowes S		2-0 4-0	1		3	4	5		7¹	8¹	9¹	10¹	11	2				6									
Dec 9	H	Bedminster EC	6000	1-1 2-1	1		3	4	5		7	8	9	10¹	11	2				6¹									
Dec 13	H	Reading SDC	1000	2-1 4-1	1		4¹		5		7	8	9	10¹		2			11²	6			3						
Dec 16	A	Millwall S		0-1 1-2	1		4		5		7	8	9¹	10	11	2				6			3						
Dec 23	H	Q.P.R. S		3-0 5-1	1			4	5	6	7²	8¹	9²	10	11	2							3						
Dec 25	A	Tottenham S	15000	0-3	1					p		p	p			p													
Dec 26	H	Bedminster S	11000	2-0	1			4	5	6	7	8¹		10¹	9	2			11				3						
Dec 30	H	Chatham S	3500	1-0 2-0	1			4	5	6	7	8¹	9¹	10		2			11				3						
Jan 6	A	Reading S		0-2 0-2	1			4	5	6	7		9	10	8	2							3		11				
Jan 13	H	Sheppey Utd. S	4000	1-0 3-0	1	2		4	5	6	7	8²		10¹	11	9							3						
Jan 17	H	Tottenham SDC	4000	2-1 2-2	1	2		4	5	6	7¹	8¹		10	11	9							3						
Jan 20	A	Brighton Utd. S		2-1 2-1	1		3	4	5	6	7	8		10	11¹	2				9¹									
Jan 27	H	Blackburn EC	16000	0-0 0-0	1		3	4	5	6	7	8	9	10	11	2													
Feb 1	A	Blackburn ECR		1-1 1-1	1		3	4	5		7	8¹	9	10	11				6				2						
Feb 3	A	Bedminster S	small	0-2	1	2		4	5			8	9	10	11			7	6				3						
Feb 5	†	Blackburn EC(2)R	7000	0-1 0-5	1	2		4	5	6	7	8		10	11					9			3						
Feb 7	H	W'wich Arsenal SDC	small	1-0 3-1	1		3		5	6	7	8¹		10¹	11	2				9¹	4								
Feb 10	A	Bristol R. S		0-1 0-4	1		3		5	6	7	8		10		2				9	4				11				
Feb 21	A	Q.P.R. SDC		1-0 2-0	1	2		4	5	6	7	8		10		9²			11				3						
Feb 24	H	Thames Ironwks S	3500	1-0 2-0	1	2		4	5	6	7¹	8¹		10		9			11				3						
Mar 3	H	Tottenham S	4000	1-0 1-0	1		3	4	5	6	7	8¹	9	10	11	2													
Mar 10	H	New Brompton S	5000	2-1 5-1	1		3	4	5	6	7¹	8¹	9²	10¹		2			11										
Mar 14	H	Q.P.R. SDC	1500	0-0 1-0	1		3	4	5	6	7	8¹	9	10	11	2													
Mar 17	A	Gravesend S		0-0 1-0	1		3	4	5	6	7		9¹	10	11	2				8		1							
Mar 24	H	Swindon S	4000	1-0 1-0	1		3	4	5	6	7		9	10	8¹	2			11										
Mar 28	H	Bristol C. SDC	small	0-0 0-0	1		3	4	5	6	7		9	10	8	2			11										
Mar 31	A	Bristol C. S	small	4-1 6-3	1		3	4	5	6	7	8²	9	10¹	11²	2													
Apr 2	A	Southampton SDC	1000	0-0 0-1	1		3	4		6	7	8		10	11	2		9				5							
Apr 5	A	Thames Ironwks S		2-1 4-2	1		3	4	5	6	7¹	8¹		10	9¹	2			11¹										
Apr 14	A	Southampton S	4000	1-0 2-0	1		3	4	5	6	7	8¹	9¹	10	11	2													
Apr 19	A	Millwall SDC		0-2	1	2										9			11	6	4		3			5	7	8	10
Apr 21	H	Millwall S	6000	1-0 2-0	1		3	4	5	6	7	8¹	9	10¹	11	2													
Apr 24	A	Chatham SDC		1-2								p¹																	
Apr 30	A	Swindon S		1-3 1-3	1				5	6	7	8	9	10¹	11	2			4				3						
May 7	A	Q.P.R. S		2-1 4-2	1	2		4	5		7	8¹	9³	10	11				6				3						
May 16	H	Southampton S	1000	2-0 2-0	1		3	4	5	6	7	8	9¹	10¹	11	2													
Southern League Appearances					30	6	23	29	28	25	30	28	23	27	28	24	6		8	9			9	2	1				
Southern League Goalscorers											7	21	19	10	7			1	1										
Southern District Combination Appearances					15	5	12	11	10	9	14	12	8	13	11	11	7	1	5	8	2	1	3			1	1	1	1
Southern District Combination Goalscorers												1	2	9	2	5	2		3	1									
English Cup Appearances					9	2	9	9	8	4	9	9	8	9	9	7				5			2						
English Cup Goalscorers											4	4	4	7	3				1									

Own goals: Bristol City (Nov 25), Bristol City (Mar 31)
† at Aston Villa
* substitute was allowed, and played

SDC Totals — P16 W 8 D 2 L 6 F 28 A 18 Pts 18 Posn 3rd
English Cup Totals — P 9 W 5 D 3 L 1 F 23 A 11
Southern League Totals — P 28 W 20 D 1 L 7 F 58 A 28 Pts 41 Posn 2nd

The Brighton Utd. and Cowes clubs were disbanded, therefore points did not count for these games.

Season 1900/01 Southern League Division 1
Western League

Date	Venue	Team	Attendance	FA HT	FA FT	Reilly M.	Turner E.	Wilkie T.	Blyth R.	Stringfellow H.	Cleghorn T.	Marshall R.G.	Smith W.	Joyce W.	Bedingfield F.	Clarke H.	Struthers R.	Hunter J.	Lewis J.	Goss W.	Miecznikowski W.L.	Digweed H.	"Louis"
Sept 1	A	Kettering S	3000	0-1	2-1	1	2	3	4	5	6	7	8^1	9^1	10	11							
Sept 8	A	Gravesend S		1-1	2-1	1	2	3	4	5	6	7^1	8	9^1	10	11							
Sept 15	H	Millwall S	10000	1-0	1-0	1	2	3	4	5	6	7	8	9	10^1	11							
Sept 22	H	Southampton S	12000	0-0	0-0	1	2	3	4	5	6	7	10	9		11							
Sept 29	H	Chatham S	7000	1-0	5-0	1	2	3	4	5	6	7	10^3	9		11^1	8						
Oct 6	A	Bristol C. S		1-3	2-3	1	2	3	4	5	6	7^2	10	9	8	11							
Oct 13	H	Swindon S	5000	1-0	2-0	1	2	3	4	5	6	7	10	9^1		11		8^1					
Oct 20	A	Watford S		2-2	4-2	1	2	3	4	5	6	7	10	9^3		11		8^1					
Oct 27	H	Luton S	5000	1-0	2-0	1	2	3	4^1	5	6	7	10	9		11^1		8					
Nov 10	H	West Ham S	4000	1-2	3-2	1		3	4	5	6	7	10^1	9^1		11^1	2		8				
Nov 17	A	Tottenham W		0-6	1-8	1		3		5	6	7^1	10	9		11	2	4	8				
Nov 24	A	New Brompton S	3000	0-2	0-2	1	3	2	4	5	6	7	10	9		11		8					
Nov 28	A	Swindon W	200	0-0	1-0	1	2	3	4		6	7	10	9		11			5	8			
Dec 1	H	Bristol R. S	4000	0-0	1-0	1	2	3	4		6	7	10	9		11			5	8^1			
Dec 5	H	Q.P.R. W	few	1-1	4-1	1	2	3	4	5	6	7	10^1	9^1				8^1		11^1			
Dec 19	A	Q.P.R. W			2-3	p	2		p			p	p^1	p^1				8^1		11^1			
Dec 22	H	Gravesend S	3000	2-0	5-1	1	2	3	4	5	6	7	10^1	8^1	9^3	11							
Dec 25	A	Tottenham S	12000	1-3	1-4	1	2	3	4	5	6	7	10^1	9	8							11	
Dec 26	H	Kettering S	10000	1-0	3-0	1	2	3	4	5	6	7	10^1	8^2	9	11							
Dec 29	A	Millwall S	7000	0-0	1-3	1	2	3	4	5	6	7	10^1	8	9	11							
Jan 5	A	Newton Heath EC	3000	0-0	0-3	1	2	3	4	5	6	7	10	8	9	11							
Jan 19	H	Bristol C. S		2-0	4-0	1	2	3	4		6	7	10^1	8^1	9^1	11^1	5						
Jan 16	A	Reading W		4-1	6-1	1						7^1	10^1	8^1	9^1	11^2							
Jan 26	A	Bristol C. W	small	2-0	2-2	1	2				6	7^1	10	9^1		11	8						
Feb 9	H	Watford S		0-0	2-0	1		3	4^1	5	6	7	10	8	9	11^1	2						
Feb 13	H	Bristol C. W	2000	0-0	3-0	1		3	4	5	6	7^1	10	9^1		11	2	8^1					
Feb 16	A	Luton S		4-1	4-2	1		3	4		6	7	10	9^3		11	2	5	8				
Feb 20	A	Bristol R. W		1-0	3-2	1		3	4	5		7^2	10	11	9^1		2	6	8				
Feb 23	A	Swindon S		2-0	3-0	1		3	4	5		7	10^2	8	9^1	11	2	6					
Feb 27	H	Reading W		0-1	2-1	1		3	4	5		7	10	8^1	9^1	11	2	6					
Mar 2	A	West Ham S		1-0	1-1	1		3	4	5		7	10	8	9	11	2	6					
Mar 6	A	Southampton W		1-0	4-0	1		3		5	6	7	10	8^2	9^2	11	2				4		
Mar 9	A	Q.P.R. S		0-2	2-3	1		3	6	5		7	10	8^1	9^1	11	2	4					
Mar 13	H	Millwall W	poor	1-1	1-1	1		3		5		7	10	8	9^1	11	2	4					
Mar 16	H	New Brompton S	6000	2-0	3-1	1		3		5		7	8^1	9^2		11	2	4	10	6			
Mar 20	H	Southampton W	1000	2-1	2-1	1		3		5		7	8^1	9		11^1	2	4	10	6			
Mar 23	A	Bristol R. S	4000	1-0	1-2	1		3	4			7		9^1		11	2	5	8	10	6		
Mar 27	A	Bristol R. W		2-0	2-0	1		3	4			7	8	9^2			2	5	10		6		11
Mar 30	H	Reading S	5000	1-0	2-1	1		3	4	5		7	10	9^2		11	2	6	8				
Apr 6	A	Southampton S	4000	0-1	0-2	1		3		5		7	10	9		11	2	4	8		6		
Apr 10	H	Swindon W	1000	0-0	1-0	1		3		5	6	7	10^1	9		11	2	4	8				
Apr 17	H	Tottenham W	3000	0-0	0-0	1		3	4	5	6	7	10	9			2		8^1			11	
Apr 20	A	Reading S		0-0	0-0	1		3	4	5	6	7	10	9			2		8			11	
Apr 22	A	Millwall W			1-3	1		3	4	5	6		10^1				2	p	8	p		11	
Apr 24	H	Tottenham Res. S	3000	1-0	4-0	1		3	4	5	6	7	10	9^1			2		8^2			11^1	
Apr 27	H	Q.P.R. S	large	1-1	1-1	1		3	4	5	6	7	10	9			2		8^1			11	
Southern League Appearances						29	17	28	27	25	22	29	27	21	21	26	13	15	11	1	4	3	
Southern League Goalscorers							2						3	12	13	16	6	2	5			1	
Western League Appearances						15	4	12	9	12	9	15	13	10	12	11	11	10	10	2	2	4	1
Western League Goalscorers												6	5	6	10	5	1		2			1	
English Cup Appearances						1	1	1	1	1	1	1	1	1	1	1							

Southern League Totals   P28 W17 D 4 L 7 F 56 A32 Pts 38 Posn 3rd
Western League Totals   P16 W11 D 2 L 3 F 36 A23 Pts 24 Posn 1st CHAMPIONS!

"Louis" may have been Miecznikowski on trial

Season 1901/02 Southern League Division 1
Western League

Date	Venue	Team	Attendance	HT	FT	Reilly M.	Turner H.	Wilkie T.	Blyth R.	Chadwick A.	Cleghorn T.	Marshall R.G.	Cunliffe D.	Bedingfield F.	Smith W.	Smith S.	Stringfellow H.	Burgess C.	McAuley W.	Corrin T.	Darling	Harris G.	Digweed H.	McDonald A.	Halliday D.A.	Lockyer A.	Langhorne	Miecznikowski W.L.
Sept 4	H	Southampton *W*	6000	0-0	1-0	1	2	3	4	5	6	7	8^1	9	10	11												
Sept 7	A	Kettering *S*	biggest	0-0	0-1	1	2	3	4		6	7	8	9	10	11	5											
Sept 11	A	Southampton *W*		0-0	3-1	1	2	3	4		6	7^1	8^1	9	10^1	11	5											
Sept 14	H	Luton *S*	9000	1-0	1-0	1	2	3	4		6	7	8^1	9	10	11	5											
Sept 21	A	Millwall *S*		2-1	3-2	1		3	4	5^1	6	7	8^2	9	10	11		2										
Sept 25	H	Reading *W*	4000	3-0	5-1	1		3		5	6	7	8^1	9^2	10^1	11	4	2										
Sept 28	H	Q.P.R. *S*	5000	1-0	1-0	1		3		5	6	7	8	9		11^1	4	2	10									
Oct 5	A	Reading *S*	5000	0-0	1-0	1		3		6	5	7	8	9^1	10	11	4	2										
Oct 9	H	Bristol Rovers *W*	1500	3-1	5-1	1		3		6	5	7	8^1	9^2	10^2	11	4	2										
Oct 12	H	Southampton *S*	10000	1-1	2-2	1		3		6	5	7	8	9^1	10	11^1	4	2										
Oct 19	A	Bristol Rovers *S*		0-1	1-1	1		3		6	5	7^1	8	9	10	11	4	2										
Oct 23	A	Reading *W*		1-2	4-2	1		3		6	5	7^1	8^1	9^2	10	11	4	2										
Oct 26	H	New Brompton *S*		1-0	3-0	1		3		5	6	7	8^1	9^2	10	11	4	2										
Oct 28	A	Q.P.R. *W*	3000	1-0	1-2	1		3	4	5	6	7	8		10^1			2	9	11								
Nov 2	A	Southampton *S*	14000	2-1	4-3			3		6	5	7	8	9^2	10	11^2	4	2			1							
Nov 9	H	Watford *S*	4000	1-0	2-0			3		5	6	7	8	9^2	10	11	4	2			1							
Nov 16	H	Tottenham *W*	10000	2-1	3-1			3		6^1	5	7	8	9^2	10	11	4	2				1						
Nov 23	A	Wellingborough *S*	4000	3-0	4-0	1		3		6	5^1	7^2	8		10	11	4	2		9^1								
Nov 25	A	West Ham *W*		1-0	4-2	1		3		5	6	7	8^2	9^1	10^1	11	4	2										
Nov 30	H	West Ham *W*	5000	2-0	3-2	1		3		5	6	7		9^2	10^1	11	4	2		8				1				
Dec 7	A	Swindon *S*	1000	2-1	2-1	1		3		6	5	7	8	9^1	10	11	4	2						1				
Dec 14	H	Small Heath *EC1*	10581	1-0	2-1	1		3		6	5	7	8^1	9^1	10	11	4	2										
Dec 21	H	Kettering *S*	3000	0-0	1-0	1		3		6	5^1	7	8	9	10	11	4	2										
Dec 25	A	Tottenham *S*	13000	1-1	2-1	1		3		6	5	7	8^1	9^1	10	11	4	2										
Dec 26	H	Swindon *W*	8000	2-1	5-1	1					6	p^1			p	p		9^4			4							
Jan 4	H	Millwall *S*	4000	0-1	1-1	1	3		4	5		7^1		9	10	11	2	8				6						
Jan 11	A	Q.P.R. *S*	5000	0-0	1-1	1	3			6	5	7	8	9^1	10		4	2	11									
Jan 13	A	Millwall *W*		1-0	2-0	1	3	11		5^1	6	7	8	9^1	10		4	2										
Jan 18	H	Reading *S*	9000	0-0	0-0	1	3		4		6	7	8		10		5	2	9	11								
Jan 25	A	Grimsby *EC2*	10000	0-1	1-1	1	3			6	5	7	8^1	9	10		4	2	11									
Jan 29	H	Grimsby *EC2R*	12000	2-0	2-0	1	3			6	5^1	7	8	9^1	10	11	4	2										
Feb 1	H	Bristol Rovers *S*	3-4000	3-0	3-0	1	3			6	5	7	8^1	9^1	10^1		4	2	11									
Feb 8	A	Reading *EC3*	8600	0-0	1-0	1	3			6	5	7	8	9^1	10		4	2	11									
Feb 15	H	Northampton *S*		2-0	5-1	1	6	3	9^1	5		7^1	8^1		10^2		4	2	11										
Feb 22	H	Derby *EC4*	22591	0-0	0-0	1	3			6	5	7	8		10	11	4	2	9									
Feb 27	A	Derby *EC4R*	25000	1-3	3-6	1	3	2		6	5^1	7	8^1				4		9	11								
Mar 5	H	Millwall *W*	2263	5-0	9-1	1	2	3		5^1	6	7^3	8^2		10^3		4		9	11								
Mar 8	A	Wellingborough *S*	1834	3-0	3-0	1	2			6	5	7	8^2		10		4	3	9^1	11								
Mar 15	H	West Ham *S*		0-0	0-0	1	3			6	5	7	8		10		4	2	9	11								
Mar 17	A	Tottenham *W*	5000	0-0	0-0	1	4	3	9		6				10	11	5	2	8	7								
Mar 19	A	Bristol Rovers *W*		0-0	1-2	1	4	3			6	7			10^1	11	5	2	8					9				
Mar 24	H	Swindon *S*	4000	1-0	4-0	1	4	3			6	7	8^1			11	5	2	10^1					9^2				
Mar 28	A	Watford *S*		2-0	5-0	1			4		6	7	8^4				11^1	5	2					9				
Mar 29	A	Brentford *S*		2-0	4-1	1			4		6	7	8^1				5^1	2	11^1					9^1				
Mar 31	H	Tottenham *S*	13408	1-0	1-0												p^1		11									
Apr 5	A	Northampton *S*		2-0	4-3	1	3		4		6	7	8^1				5	2	10^2	11^1				9				
Apr 7	H	W'wich Arsenal *SCC*	2522	1-0	1-2		2	3			6	7					8^1	11					1	4	9	5	10	
Apr 9	H	Q.P.R. *W*	1678	4-0	5-0	1	4	3			6	7	8^3			11	5^1	2	10^1					9				
Apr 12	A	West Ham *S*	6000	1-1	1-1	1	3				6	7	8		10		5	2	4	11^1				9				
Apr 16	A	New Brompton *W*	2000+	0-1	0-2	1	3				6	7	8		10		5	2	4	11				9				
Apr 19	H	Brentford *S*	4592	4-0	7-1	1	3				6	7	8^2		10^1		5	4		11				9^4	2			
Apr 23	A	Swindon *W*		2-0	2-0	1	3				6	7	8^1		10^1		5	2		11				9				
Apr 26	A	Luton *S*		0-1	1-2	1	3		4			7	8		10		5	2						9			6	11^1
Southern League Appearances						24	11	19	22	18	13	30	26	16	24	21	26	25	11	11	2	2	1	7	1	1	1	
Southern League Goalscorers								1	3			5	18	12	4	6	1		5	3				7				1
Western League Appearances						15	10	13	9	11	13	14	14	9	14	14	14	13	9	5	2	1		4				
Western League Goalscorers								1	2			5	13	12	11	1	1							6				
Total Cup Appearances						6	4	5	6	6	1	7	6	4	6	3	6	5	2	5			1	1	1	1	1	
Total Cup Goalscorers							2						3	3	1													

Southern League Totals   P30 W20 D 7 L 3 F 67 A24 Pts 47 Posn 1st CHAMPIONS
Western League Totals   P16 W13 D 1 L 2 F 53 A16 Pts 27 Posn 1st CHAMPIONS

Own goals: Reading (Sept 25), Swindon (Dec 7)

Season 1902/03 Southern League Division 1
Western League

Date	V	Team	Att	FA HT	FA FT	Reilly M.	Burgess C.	Wilkie T.	Blyth R.	Stringfellow H.	Houlker A.E.	Marshall R.G.	Cunliffe D.	Brown A.	Smith W.	Turner H.	Smith S.	Turner E.	Hodge J.	McDonald A.	Wheldon F.	Corrin T.	Chadwick A.	McIntyre P.	Burnett J.	Harris G.	Fry C.B.
Sept 1	A	Southampton W	6000	0-2	1-3	1		3	4	5	6	7	8^1	9	10	11											
Sept 6	H	Luton S	10000	3-0	3-0	1	2	3	4	5	6	7	8	9^1	10^1	11^1											
Sept 10	H	Southampton W	8000	3-0	4-1	1	2	3	4	5	6	7	8^2	9^2	10	11											
Sept 12	A	Reading S	5000	2-1	5-1	1	2	3	4	5	6	7	8^2	9^2	10^1	11											
Sept 20	H	Q.P.R. S	11000	1-0	2-1	1	2	3	4	5	6	7	8^1	9^1	10	11											
Sept 24	H	Reading W	3000	0-0	1-0	1	2	3	4	5	6	7	8	9^1					10	11							
Sept 27	A	Southampton S	16000	1-1	1-1	1	2	3	4	5	6	7	8	9^1	10		11										
Oct 1	H	Brentford W	8000	3-0	4-0	1			4		6	7		9^2	10^1			2	3		8	11	5^1				
Oct 4	H	Wellingborough S	6000	2-1	4-1	1		3	4		6	7	8^2	9	10^1			2				11	5				
Oct 8	A	Reading W	2000	0-0	1-0	1		3	4	5	6	7^1	8	9	10			2				11					
Oct 11	A	Bristol Rovers S		0-0	1-1	1		3	4	5	6	7		9^1	10			2		8		11					
Oct 18	H	Northampton S	6-7000	0-1	0-1	1			4	5		7	8	9	6			2		8		11	3				
Oct 20	A	Q.P.R. W		2-0	3-0			3	4		6	7	8^2	9^1				2		10				11			
Oct 25	A	Watford S	4000	3-1	4-1	1	2			5	6	7	8^2	9^2	4			3		10		11					
Oct 29	H	Bristol Rovers W	5000+	1-1	5-3	1	2			5	6	7	8^1	9^2	4			3		10^2		11					
Nov 3	A	Millwall W	2000	0-0	0-1	1	2			5	6	7	8	9	4			3		10		11					
Nov 8	A	Tottenham W	10000+	0-0	0-0	1	2				4	6	7	8	9	10		3				11		5			
Nov 15	H	West Ham W	7397	2-0	2-0	1	2				4	6	7	8^1	9	10^1		3				11		5			
Nov 17	A	Brentford W		0-2	2-2	1	2		4			6	7	8^1			10	3				11		5			
Nov 22	H	Millwall S	5000	2-0	3-0	1	2		4			6	7	8^2	9^1	10	3					11	5		9^1		
Nov 29	H	Tottenham W	8785	0-2	2-2	1	2		4			6	7	8	9		3			10^2		11	5				
Dec 3	H	Q.P.R. SCC	1816	1-1	4-2	1		3	4^1			6	7	8^1			2			10	11^1	5		9^1			
Dec 6	H	Swindon S	6000	2-2	3-2	1		3	4			6	7	8^2	9^1		2	11		10		5					
Dec 13	A	Kettering S	2000	1-0	2-1	1		3	6	4			7	8	9^1		2	11		10		5^1					
Dec 20	A	Luton S	3000	0-0	2-0	1		3		4	6	7	8	9^2	10		2	11				5					
Dec 25	A	Tottenham S	25000	0-1	2-2			3		4	6	7	8^1	9	10		2	11				5^1			1		
Dec 26	H	West Ham S	15746		2-0			3		4	6	7	8	9^1	10		2	11				5^1			1		
Dec 27	H	Reading S	14482	1-0	1-1			3		4	6	7	8	9^1	10		2			11		5			1		
Jan 3	A	Q.P.R. S	6000	1-2	3-4			3		4	6	7^1	8^1	9	10		2			11^1		5					
Jan 10	H	Southampton S	20447	0-0	0-3			3		4	6	7	8	9	10		2	11				5					
Jan 17	A	Wellingborough S		0-0	0-0			3		4	6	7	8	9	10		2	11				5					
Jan 21	H	Millwall W	3400	1-1	4-1			3		4	6	7		9^2	8^1					10^1	11	5			2		
Jan 24	H	Bristol Rovers S	7000	2-0	3-0	1		3	6	4		7	8^1	9^1						10^1	11	5			2		
Jan 31	A	Northampton S		5-0	5-2	1		3	4		6	7^1	8^2	9^1	10^1	2	11					5			2		
Feb 7	A	Everton EC1	32000	0-2	0-5	1		3		4	6	7	8	9		11				10		5			2		
Feb 14	A	Brentford S	3000	0-0	5-0	1	2	3	6	4		7	8^2	9						10^1	11	5^1					
Feb 28	A	West Ham W		1-0	2-0	1	2	3		4	6	7	8^1	9		11				10^1		5					
Mar 11	H	Q.P.R. W	3000	1-0	2-0	1	2			4	6	7	8^1	9^1	10	3	11					5					
Mar 14	H	New Brompton S	6000	2-0	4-0	1	2	3	4	5	6	7	8^1				11			10			9^3				
Mar 21	A	Swindon S	7000	0-0	1-2	1	2	3		4	6	7	8	9	10		11					5^1					
Mar 23	H	Reading SCC	4000	2-0	4-0	1	2	3		4	6	7	8^2				11			10^1		5	9^1				
Mar 28	H	Kettering S	500	1-1	4-2	1	2	3	6	4		7	8		10^2	11^1							5	9	7			
Apr 1	A	Bristol Rovers W		1-1	1-1	1	2	3	6	4		7	8	9	10^1	11						5					
Apr 4	A	New Brompton S	3000	0-1	0-1	1	2			3	4	7	8	9	6	11				10		5					
Apr 6	A	Millwall S		0-1	1-2	1	2			3	4	7	8^1		6	11				10		5	9				
Apr 10	A	West Ham S		1-1		1	2			3	4	6	7	8	9^1	11						5					
Apr 11	H	Brentford S	4000	2-0	4-1	1	2			3	4	6^1	7	8	9^1	10^1	11					5^1					
Apr 13	H	Tottenham S	11000	2-0	2-0	1	2	3			4	6	8^1		10	11					7	5	9^1				
Apr 18	H	Watford S	4000	0-0	1-1	1	2	3			4	6	7	8	9^1	11						5					
Apr 20	A	Millwall SCC		2-0	2-0	1	2	3			4	6	7	8^1		10	11					5	9^1				

	Reilly	Burgess	Wilkie	Blyth	Stringfellow	Houlker	Marshall	Cunliffe	Brown	Smith W.	Turner H.	Smith S.	Turner E.	Hodge	McDonald	Wheldon	Corrin	Chadwick	McIntyre	Burnett	Harris	Fry
Southern League Appearances	27	17	22	19	26	23	29	29	26	25	15	26	1		10	5	21	1	4	3	1	
Southern League Goalscorers			1		2		22	20	7		2					2	1	6	4			
Western League Appearances	15	12	7		13	15	16	14	15	13	11	12	1	1	1	7	3	6	3	1		1
Western League Goalscorers								10	11	4					6		1		1			
Total Cup Appearances	4	2	4	1	3	4	4	4	1	1	1	3			3	1	4	3				1
Total Cup Goalscorers								1							1		1	3				

Southern League Totals — P30 W17 D 7 L 6 F 69 A32 Pts 41 Posn 3rd

Western League Totals — P16 W10 D 4 L 2 F 34 A14 Pts 24 Posn 1st CHAMPIONS 3rd year in a row

Own goals: Wellingborough (Oct 4), Brentford (Feb 14)

Season 1903/04 Southern League Division 1
Western League

Date	Venue	Team	Attendance	FA HT	FA FT	Reilly M.	Hogg J.	Wilkie T.	Buck A.	Chadwick A.	Anderson J.	Marshall R.G.	Cunliffe D.	Burnett J.	Smith W.	Smith S.	Harris G.	Stringfellow H.	Rule A.	Wheldon F.	Blyth W.	Young G.	Murray T.	Holden A.	Platt J.	Brown T.	Halliday D.	Marshall A.G.	Blyth R.	Cooke R.	Taylor	Salter
Sept 2	H	Southampton W	11000+	1-2	1-2	1	2	3	4	5	6	7	8			11				10^1					9							
Sept 5	A	Reading S	6000	1-1	1-2		2		4	5	6	7	8			11	1			10		3			9^1							
Sept 7	A	Southampton W		2-1	2-5	1	2		4	5		7	8	6		11				10^1		3			9^1							
Sept 9	H	Plymouth W		0-0	1-2	1	2	3				7	8	6		11				4^1			10	9	5							
Sept 12	H	Wellingboro S	5000	3-1	3-1	1		3		5		7	8^1	6		11				10^1	4				9^1	2						
Sept 19	A	Bristol R. S		1-1	2-1	1	2	3		5		7	8^2	6		11	4			10					9							
Sept 23	H	QPR W	4000	1-0	3-0	1	2	3		5			8^1	6		11	4			10^2			7		9							
Sept 26	H	Brighton S		0-3	0-3		2	3		5		7	8	6		11	1		4	10			9								
Sept 30	A	Plymouth W	7400	1-3	1-3		2	3		5		7	8	9^1	6	11	1		4	10											
Oct 3	A	Swindon S	6000	1-0	1-0		2			5		7	8^1	9		11	1		4	10	6	3									
Oct 7	H	Reading W	5000	1-0	2-0		2			5	6	7	8^1			11	1		4	9^1		3	10								
Oct 10	A	Northampton S		1-0	3-0			3		5	6	7	8^1			11	1		4	9^2	10	2									
Oct 12	A	QPR W		1-1	1-1			3		5	6	7		9^1			1		4	10		2	11		8						
Oct 17	H	Brentford S	7233	0-1	3-1			3		5	6	7	8^1				1		4	9	10^2	2	11								
Oct 21	H	Southampton SCC	6000	4-3	4-5		2	3		5		7^1	8	6		11	1		4	9^2	10^1										
Oct 24	A	West Ham W		1-0	1-0			3		5		7	8			11	1		4	10^1	6	2			9						
Oct 31	H	Tottenham W	8000	0-3	0-3			3		5	6	7	8			11	1		4	9	10	2									
Nov 4	A	Reading W	1500	0-0	0-1	1		3		5		7	8				4					6	2	11	10	9						
Nov 7	A	Luton S	5000	0-1	1-1	1		3		5		7	8		10	11	4			9^1	6	2									
Nov 14	H	New Brompton S	6000	1-0	2-0	1		3		5		7	8		10	11	4			9^2	6	2									
Nov 21	H	Kettering S	2000	1-0	1-0	1		3		5		7	8		10	11^1	4			9	6	2									
Nov 28	H	Southampton S	12152	0-1	0-1	1	2	3		5		7	8		10	11	4			9	6										
Dec 12	H	Millwall S	5000	1-0	2-0	1	2	3		5			8		10	11	4			9^1	6		7^1								
Dec 19	A	QPR S	4000	1-2	1-6	1	2	3		5			8		10	11	4			9	6		7^1								
Dec 25	A	Tottenham S	26000	0-0	1-1	1	2			5			8^1		10	11	4			9	6	3	7								
Dec 26	H	West Ham S	12000+	2-0	2-1	1	2			5			8	9^1	10^1	11	4				6	3	7								
Dec 28	H	Plymouth S	8–9000	0-0	0-0	1	2			5		7	8		10	11	4			9	6	3									
Jan 2	H	Reading S	8000	1-0	1-0	1	2			5		7	8	9	10	11^1	4				6	3									
Jan 9	A	Wellingboro S		0-0	1-0	1	2			5		7	8		10	11	4			9^1	6	3									
Jan 16	H	Bristol R. S	8000	0-1	2-1	1	2			5^1			8	9	10	11	4				6	3	7^1								
Jan 18	A	Brentford W		1-0	2-1	1	2						8^1	9^1	10		5				6	3	7	11				4			
Jan 23	H	Brighton S	8000	1-0	1-1	1	2			5			8	9	10	11	4				6	3	7								
Jan 27	H	Brentford W	500	1-2	4-2	1				5	2	7	10				4			9^2	6	3			11^1	8^1					
Jan 30	A	Swindon S		1-0	1-0	1	2			5			8^1			11	4		9	10	6	3	7								
Feb 6	H	Derby EC1	20000	0-2	2-5	1	2		4	5			8		10	11				9^2	6	3	7								
Feb 13	A	Brentford S		0-1	0-4	1	2			5			8		10	11	4			9	6	3	7								
Feb 20	H	West Ham W	3000	1-0	3-0		2			5	6		8	9^3		11	1		4	10		3	7								
Feb 24	H	Bristol R. W	1500	0-0	1-0		2			5				9		11	1		4	10^1	6	3	7			8					
Feb 27	A	Tottenham W	14000	0-1	1-1		2			5			8	9^1		11	1		4	10	6	3	7								
Mar 5	H	Luton S	6000	2-0	3-0	1	2			5			8	9^1		11			4	10^1	6	3	7								
Mar 12	A	New Brompton S	5000+	1-1	2-1	1	2			5			8	9^2		11			4	10	6	3	7								
Mar 19	H	Kettering S	6000	3-0	3-2	1	2			5			8^1	9^1		11			4^1	10	6	3	7								
Mar 21	A	Bristol R. S		1-0	1-2	1	2			5			10						4		6	3	7	11	8^1	9					
Mar 26	A	Southampton S	15000	0-0	0-2		2			5			8	9	6	11			4	10		3	7								
Apr 1	A	West Ham S	8000		0-3	1	2			5			8		6	11			4			3	7								
Apr 2	A	Fulham S	8000	0-0	0-0	1	3		2	5			8		10				4			7		11	9				6		
Apr 4	H	Tottenham S	14000	0-0	1-0	1	3		2	5			8		10	11			4			7			9^1				6		
Apr 9	A	Millwall S	4000	0-0	0-1	1	2			5			8		10						6	3	7	11	9				4		
Apr 16	H	QPR S		0-0	0-0	1	2			5		7	8		10	11			4		6	3			9						
Apr 18	A	Fulham S		0-1	2-2	1	2			5		7	8		10^2	11			4		6	3			9						
Apr 23	A	Plymouth S			0-2	1	2			5		7	8		10	11					6	3			9					4	
Apr 30	H	Northampton S	4000	0-0	1-1	1	2			5		7	8^1			11		1			6	3			9					4	10

						Reilly M.	Hogg J.	Wilkie T.	Buck A.	Chadwick A.	Anderson J.	Marshall R.G.	Cunliffe D.	Burnett J.	Smith W.	Smith S.	Harris G.	Stringfellow H.	Rule A.	Wheldon F.	Blyth W.	Young G.	Murray T.	Holden A.	Platt J.	Brown T.	Halliday D.	Marshall A.G.	Blyth R.	Cooke R.	Taylor	Salter
Southern League Appearances						28	26	13	32	4	4	18	34	9	25	31	6	27	3	22	27	26	18	2	7	3	1		1		4	1
Southern League Goalscorers									1				10	5	3	2		1		2	9				4		1	2				
Western League Appearances						8	10	9	8	10	4	10	12	6	7	11	8	13	2	11	8	12	9	3	6	7	1		1			
Western League Goalscorers													3	7					1	8	1				1	2	1				
Cup Appearances						1	2		1	2		1	1	2			2	2	1	1	1	2	1	1	1						
Cup Goalscorers													1						2	3											

Southern League Totals P34 W17 D 8 L 9 F41 A38 Pts 42 Posn 4th
Western League Totals P16 W 7 D 2 L 7 F34 A23 Pts 16 Posn 4th

Own goal: Luton (Mar 5)

Season 1904/05   Southern League Division 1
Western League

Date	Venue	Team	Attendance	FA HT	FA FT	Thompson F.J.	Walker R.	Young G.	Bowman T.	Buck A.	McDonald E.	Porteous W.	Cunliffe D.	Axford D.	Smith W.	Smith S.	Harris G.	Campbell D.	Lee W.	Blyth W.	Digweed H.	Ford W.	Platt J.	Halliday D.	Holden A.	Salter H.	Hirst	Kirby W.	Didymus E.	Archbald	Taylor
Sept 1	A	Southampton *W*	6000	2-1	2-2	1	2	3	4	5	6	7	8^2	9	10	11															
Sept 3	H	Reading *S*	8–9000	1-2	3-5	1	2	3	4	5	6	7	8^1	9	10^2	11															
Sept 7	H	Southampton *W*	10000	0-2	0-2			3		5	6	7	8		10	11	1	2	9	4											
Sept 10	A	Bristol R. *S*			0-5		2	3	4	5	6	7	8	9	10	11	1	1													
Sept 14	H	Fulham *W*	5000	2-0	2-0	1		3	2	5	6		8^1		10	11		9^1	4			7									
Sept 17	H	Northampton *S*	8000	1-0	3-0	1		3	2	5	6^1		8		10^1	11		9^1	4			7									
Sept 19	A	Millwall *W*		1-0	2-1			3	2	5	6			9	10	11^1	1		4			7		8^1							
Sept 24	A	Brighton *S*	8000	1-0	1-0	1		3	2	5	6		8^1		10	11		9	4			7									
Sept 28	H	Millwall *W*	3000	0-1	1-1			3	2	5				9	10	11	6		4			7		8^1							
Oct 1	A	Brentford *S*		1-0	3-1			3	2	5	6	7^2	8^1		10	11	9		4												
Oct 5	H	Plymouth *W*	5000	1-1	2-1	1		3	2	5	6	7	8^2		10	11	9		4												
Oct 8	H	Q.P.R. *S*	12000	2-1	4-1	1		3	2	5	6	7	8^2		10^1	11^1	9		4												
Oct 10	A	West Ham *SCC*	4500	1-2	1-2	1		3	2	5	6	7	8	9	10^1	11			4												
Oct 15	A	Millwall *S*		1-2	2-4	1		3	2	5	6	7	8		10^1	11	9^1		4												
Oct 17	A	Fulham *W*		1-1	2-1	1		3	2	5	6		8^1		10	11	9^1		4			7									
Oct 22	H	Tottenham *W*	12000	0-0	1-0	1		3	2	5	6	7	8		10	11	9^1		4												
Oct 26	A	Plymouth *W*	6000	0-1	1-3	1		3	2	5	6	7	8		10^1	11	9		4												
Oct 29	A	Luton *S*		1-3	3-4	1		3	2	5	6	7	8^2		10^1	11	9		4												
Nov 5	H	Swindon *S*	6000	1-0	2-0	1		3	2	5	6	7^1	8		10^1	11	9^1		4												
Nov 9	H	Brentford *W*	2000	0-2	1-2	1		3	2		6	7	8	9^1	10	11			4	5											
Nov 14	A	Q.P.R. *W*	3000	0-2	1-6	1	2	3		5	6	7	8		10^1	11	9		4												
Nov 19	H	Wellingboro *S*	4000	3-0	5-1		2	3	4	5	6	7^1	8^1		10^1	11^1	9^1				1										
Nov 23	H	Bristol R. *W*	3500	3-0	3-2			3	2	5	6		8^3	9	10				4		1	7			11						
Nov 26	A	Southampton *S*	15000	0-0	0-1			3	2	5	6	7	8		10	11	9		4		1				11					
Nov 30	H	Reading *W*	2000	1-0	2-0			3	2	5	6^1	7	8	9	10				4		1				11					
Dec 3	A	Fulham *S*	7000	1-0	1-0			3^1	2	5	6	7	8		10	11	9		4		1									
Dec 17	H	Plymouth *S*	16000	1-1	3-2			3	2	5	6	7^1	8^1		10	11	9^1		4		1									
Dec 24	A	West Ham *W*		0-2	2-4			3	2	5	6	7^1	8		10	11	9^1		4		1									
Dec 26	H	West Ham *S*	15000	2-0	4-1		2	3	4^1	5	6	7^1	8^1		10^1	11	9				1									
Dec 27	A	Tottenham *S*		1-0	1-1		2	3	4	5	6	7	8		10	11	9^1				1									
Dec 31	A	Reading *S*	5000	0-4	0-5		2		4	5	6		8		10	11	9				1	7								
Jan 7	H	Bristol R. *S*	10000	1-2	1-2		2		4	5	6		8^1		10	11	9				1	7								
Jan 14	H	Chesterfield *EC1*	18000	0-0	0-0		2	3	4	5	6		8		10	11	9				1	7								
Jan 18	H	Chesterfield *EC1R*	10000	0-0	2-0		2	3	4	5	6		8		10^1	11	9^1				1	7								
Jan 21	H	Brighton *S*	5000	0-2	0-2		2	3	4	5	6		9		10	11			8		1	7								
Jan 28	H	Brentford *S*	5000	1-0	5-0		2	3		5^2	6^1				10	11	9^1		4		1	7					8^1				
Feb 4	A	Small Heath *EC2*	large	1-0	2-0		2	3	4	5	6		8		10	11^1	9^1				1	7									
Feb 11	H	Millwall *S*	8000	0-0	1-0			3	2		6		8		10	11	9^1		4		1	7				5					
Feb 18	A	Sheffield Utd. *EC3*	36413	1-1	1-2			3	2	5	6		8^1		10	11	9		4		1	7									
Feb 25	H	Luton *S*	7000	1-0	1-0			3	2	5	6		8		10	11	9		4		1									
Mar 4	A	Swindon *S*		0-2	1-3			3	2	5	6		8^1		10	11	9		4		1						7^1				
Mar 6	A	Brentford *W*		0-0	0-0	1	2	3	4	5	6		8		10		9		7								7				
Mar 11	H	New Brompton *S*	poor	1-1	1-1		2	3	4	5	6		8		10^1	11	9				1	7									
Mar 15	H	Q.P.R. *W*	2000	0-0	0-1		2	3		5			9						4	8	1	6			11		7	10			
Mar 16	A	Northampton *S*		1-1	1-1		2	3		5	6		8^1		10	11	9		4		1						7				
Mar 18	A	Wellingboro *S*	2000	0-0	4-1		2	3	4	5^1	6		8		10	11	9^3				1						7				
Mar 22	A	Watford *S*	2000	1-2	1-4		2^1	3	4	5	6		8		10	11	9				1						7				
Mar 25	A	Southampton *S*	12000	0-1	1-2		2	3		5	6		8		10	11	9^1				1						7				
Mar 29	A	Reading *W*	1000	0-3	0-3		2	3		5	6		8	9	10	11			4		1						7				
Apr 1	A	Fulham *S*		0-1	0-2		2	3		5	6		8		10	11	9		4		1						7				
Apr 5	A	Bristol R. *W*	1000	2-0	2-1			3	4				8	9^1	10	11^1		2			1	6				5	7				
Apr 8	H	Watford *W*	poor	0-0	1-0		2		4		6		8	9	10^1	11					1					5	7				
Apr 15	A	Plymouth *S*		0-1	1-2		2	3		5	6		8^1		10	11	9		4		1						7		3		
Apr 17	A	Tottenham *W*	3000	0-0	1-0		2	3	4						10	11	9^1				1	6	8			5	7				
Apr 21	A	West Ham *S*		0-1	1-1							p	p	p		1	p^1					6	8			5	p				
Apr 22	H	West Ham *W*	4000	2-0	4-0		2	3	4						10	11^1	9^2				1	6	8			5	7				
Apr 24	H	Tottenham *S*	10000	2-0	3-2		2	3	4	5^1			8^1		10^1	11^1	9				1	6					7^1				
Apr 25	A	Q.P.R. *S*		0-0	0-2		2	3	4	5					10	11	9				1	6	8				7				
Apr 29	A	New Brompton *S*	3000	1-0	3-0		2	3		5			8		10	11	9^2		4		1	6					7^1				4
Southern League Appearances						8	25	22	33	26	29	13	31	4	34	34	26	5	30	1	19	6	1	2	2	3	11	1	1		
Southern League Goalscorers							2		3		2	6	15		11	2		14	1				2				2		2		
Western League Appearances						10	12	13	19	14	15	10	15	8	19	17	10	8	10	8	7	5	5	4		1	5	1	1		1
Western League Goalscorers								1	1	9	3	2	3		5		7		5			2					2				
Cup Appearances						1	4	4	5	5	5	1	5	1	5	5	4	1	4		1	3		1		2					
Cup Goalscorers											1	2	1		2																

Own goal: West Ham (Apr 22)

Southern League Totals   P34 W16 D 4 L14 F 61 A56 Pts 36 Posn 8th
Western League Totals   P20 W10 D 3 L 7 F 29 A30 Pts 23 Posn 4th

Season 1905/06   Southern League Division 1
Western League

Date	Venue	Team	Attendance	FA HT-FT	Harris G.	Walker R.	Molyneux G.	Bowman T.	Buck A.	McDonald E.	Kirby W.	Cunliffe D.	Lee W.	Smith W.	Smith S.	Cook F.	Stewart T.W.	Archibald	Hughes	Salter H.	Holden A.	Hunter J.	Jackson R.W.	Digweed H.	Warrington J.	Wright E.G.D.	Hickleton W.	Harris S.S.	Bolitho V.	Dix J.	Foyle	Pa
Sept 2	A	Fulham *S*	3000	0-0 0-0	1	2	3	4	5	6											8		7									
Sept 4	A	Watford *S*		1-1 2-2	1	2	3		5	6	7	8^2		10							9	4										
Sept 6	H	Southampton *W*	6000	0-1 0-2		2	3		5	6			9	10		1				11	8		4	7								
Sept 9	H	Q.P.R. *S*	3000	0-0 0-0	1	2	3	4	5			8	9	10	11						6	7										
Sept 11	A	Southampton *W*		0-4 2-5	1	2^1	3	4	5		11	8	9^1	10							6	7										
Sept 16	A	Bristol R. *S*	7000	1-0 1-1	1	2	3	4	5	6		8	9^1	10							11	7										
Sept 20	H	Fulham *W*	5000	0-1 2-1	1	2		4	5	6^1		8	9^1	10					3		11	7										
Sept 23	H	New Brompton *S*	6000	3-0 4-0	1	2^1	3	4	5	6		8^3	9	10							11	7										
Sept 25	A	Fulham *W*		0-0 0-1	1	2	3	4	5	6			9	10						8	11	7										
Sept 30	H	Northampton *S*	10000	1-0 4-0		2	3	4	5	6		8	9^1	10^3		1					7				11							
Oct 4	A	Q.P.R. *W*	3000	2-1 2-1		2	3		5	6		8	9^2		11	1				10	7				4							
Oct 7	A	Swindon *S*		0-1 1-2	1	2^1	3	4	5	6		8	9	10	11						7											
Oct 11	H	Plymouth *W*	8000	0-0 0-0	1	2	3	4	5	6		8	9								7					11	10					
Oct 14	H	Millwall *S*	8000	1-0 2-1	1	2	3	4	5	6^1		8^1	9	10	11						7											
Oct 18	H	Q.P.R. *W*	3000	0-1 0-3	1		3	4		6	7	8	9				2			10	11						5					
Oct 21	A	Luton *S*		0-3 2-3	1	2	3		5	6		9	8	10^1	11						7	4^1										
Oct 28	H	Tottenham *W*	14000	0-0 0-0	1	2	3	4	5	6		8	9	10	11						7											
Nov 1	H	Southampton *HCC*	4000	1-0 1-0	1	2	3	4	5	6^1		8	9	10	11									7								
Nov 4	A	Brentford *S*		0-0 1-1	1	2	3	4	5	6		8	9^1											7		11	10					
Nov 8	H	Reading *W*	5000	1-0 3-0	1	2	3	4	5	6		8^1	9^1		11									7			10^1					
Nov 11	H	Norwich *S*	4000	1-1 2-1	1	2	3	4	5	6		8	9	10^1	11									7^1								
Nov 13	A	Southampton *SCC1*	1000	1-2 2-4	1		3		5	6		9^1		10	11^1		2			8				7	4							
Nov 18	A	Plymouth *S*		0-1 1-3	1	2	3	4	5	6		8^1	9	10	11									7								
Nov 25	H	Southampton *S*	16000	0-0 1-0	1	2	3	4	5	6	7	8	9^1	10	11																	
Dec 2	A	Reading *S*		1-1 1-1	1	2	2^1	3	4	5	6	7	8	9	11																	
Dec 6	A	Plymouth *W*	1000	0-2 2-2	1	2	3	4^1	5	6	7	8	9	10^1	11																	
Dec 16	A	Brighton *S*	7000	1-0 5-0	1	2	3	4	5	6	7	8^2	9													11	10^3					
Dec 23	A	West Ham *S*		0-1	1	2	3	4	5	6	7	8	9													10					
Dec 25	A	Tottenham *S*	30000	1-3 1-3	1	2	3	4	5	6	7	8	9	10	11																	
Dec 26	H	West Ham *W*	14000	2-2 3-3	1	2	3		5	6	7	8	9		11						10	4										
Dec 30	H	Fulham *S*	14000	0-0 1-0		2	3	4	5	6	7	8	9	10	11^1	1																
Jan 6	A	Q.P.R. *S*		0-1 0-2	1	2	3	4	5	6	9			10	11						8		7									
Jan 13	A	Southampton *EC1*	14000	0-2 1-5	1	2	3	4	5	6	7^1	8		10	11						9											
Jan 20	H	Bristol R. *S*		2-1 2-1	1	2	3	4	5	6	9	8		10^1	11								7^1									
Jan 24	H	Brentford *W*	1000	0-0 1-1	1		3	2	5			8^1		9						10	11		6	7	4							
Jan 27	A	New Brompton *S*		0-0 1-0	1		3	2	5	6	9^1	8		10							11		4	7								
Feb 3	A	Northampton *S*		1-0 1-0	1		3	2	5	6	9	8^1								11	10		4	7								
Feb 7	H	Bristol R. *W*		4-1 5-1	1		3	2	5	6	9^3			10	11						8^1		7^1	4								
Feb 10	H	Swindon *S*		1-1 1-2	1		3	2	5	6	9			10^1	11						8	4	7									
Feb 14	H	Millwall *W*	small	1-0 2-0	1		3	2	5			9^1		10	11						8	6	7	4								
Feb 17	A	Millwall *S*		0-3 2-3	1	2	3	4	5	6	9^1	8			11						10^1		7									
Feb 24	H	Luton *S*		2-0 2-0	1	3		2	5	6	9^1	8		10	11								4	7^1								
Mar 3	A	Tottenham *W*		0-1 1-1		2		5	6	9^1	8			11		1				10	3	4	7									
Mar 7	A	Reading *W*		0-1 1-2		3^1	2		6	7	8	9				1				10	5		4	11								
Mar 10	H	Brentford *S*	4000	2-0 5-0		3		2	5	6^1	7	8^2	9^1	10^1	11	1							4									
Mar 17	A	Norwich *S*		1-1		3		2	5	6	7	8	9	10	11	1							4									
Mar 19	H	Brentford *W*		1-0 1-0		3		2	6			9	10^1	11		1				8	5		7	4								
Mar 24	H	Plymouth *S*	8000	1-0 1-1		3		2	5	6	7	8	9			1							4			11	10^1					
Mar 31	A	Southampton *S*		2-1		3^1		2	5	6	7^1		9		11	1				8			4				10					
Apr 7	H	Reading *S*	8000	3-2 3-3		3		2	5^1	6	7		9^1	10^1	11	1				8			4									
Apr 13	A	West Ham *W*	8000	0-0 0-0		3		2		6	7	8		10		1						5	4							11	9	
Apr 14	A	Watford *S*	5000	2-0 4-2		3		2	5	6	9^1			10^2	11	1				8^1			4	7								
Apr 16	H	Tottenham *S*		0-0 1-0		3^1		2	5	6	7	8	9	10	11	1							4									
Apr 21	H	Brighton *S*		1-0 5-0		3^2		2	5	6	7		9	10^1	11^1	1				8^1			4									
Apr 25	A	Bristol R. *W*		0-1 1-2		3		2			8^1			10	7	1						6	4				11					
Apr 28	H	West Ham *S*		1-0 1-0		3			5	2		9		10	11	1				8^1	6	4					7					
Apr 30	A	Millwall *W*	500	0-1 0-4		2		3			8			6	11	1		4		10						5			7			

				Harris G.	Walker R.	Molyneux G.	Bowman T.	Buck A.	McDonald E.	Kirby W.	Cunliffe D.	Lee W.	Smith W.	Smith S.	Cook F.	Stewart T.W.	Archibald	Hughes	Salter H.	Holden A.	Hunter J.	Jackson R.W.	Digweed H.	Warrington J.	Wright E.G.D.	Hickleton W.	Harris S.S.	Bolitho V.	Dix J.	Foyle	Pa
Southern League Appearances				23	32	23	33	32	33	28	26	17	27	24	11					4	17	2	15	13	4		5			1		
Southern League Goalscorers					7		1	2	6	12	4	13	2							4		1	3			4					
Western League Appearances				12	15	13	18	12	16	11	15	10	13	11	8	1	1	1	4	5	13	6	7	9	1	8	2	1	3	1	
Western League Goalscorers					2		1		1	7	3	2	3							1			1			1					
Cup Appearances				3	2	3	2	3	3	2	2	1	3	3			1			1		1	1			1	2				
Cup Goalscorers									1	2										1											

Southern League Totals   P34 W17 D 9 L 8 F 61 A35 Pts 43 Posn 3rd
Western League Totals   P20 W 6 D 7 L 7 F 26 A29 Pts 19 Posn 7th

Season 1906/07   Southern League Division 1
Western League

Date	Venue	Team	Attendance	FA HT	FA FT	Hickleton W.	Hisbent J.	Didymus E.	Cookson W.	Dix J.	Phillip G.	Bowman T.	Walker R.	Digweed H.	Buick A.	McDonald E.	Tomlinson J.	Hunter J.	Parsons V.	Elston A.E.	Thomson J.H.	Warner J.	Bainbridge J.R.	Dalrymple R.	Kirby W.	Smith W.	Buckle H.	Jackson R.W.	Cook F.	Harris S.S.	McKenzie J.
Sept 1	H	Plymouth *S*	20000	2-0	4-0						1		4	5^1	6					2	3	7	8	9^2	10^1	11					
Sept 3	A	West Ham *W*		2-3	3-3	5			10		1		2	4	6		8		11		3	7^1		9^2						
Sept 8	A	Brighton *S*		1-1	1-1						1	2	3	4	5	6						7	8	9	10^1	11				
Sept 12	H	West Ham *W*	3000	1-2	2-3	5					1	2	3	4			7	8	9					10^2	11	6				
Sept 15	H	Reading *S*	8000	1-1	2-1						1		3	4	5	6	8				2	7^1		9	10^1	11				
Sept 19	A	Southampton *W*	3000	3-0	3-2			2			1		3	4	5	6^1	7	8		11				9^1	10^1					
Sept 22	A	Watford *S*		0-1	0-2						1	2	3	4	5	6						7	8	9	10	11				
Sept 26	H	Southampton *W*	5000	2-0	3-2								3	4	5	6	7			11	2		8	9^2	10^1					
Sept 29	H	Northampton *S*	10000	3-0	4-1								3	4	5	6^1	7	8		11	2			9^2	10^1		1			
Oct 3	A	Plymouth *W*		0-1	0-1	4							3		5	6	7	8		11	2		9		10		1			
Oct 6	A	Q.P.R. *S*		1-1	3-2								3	4	5	6	8			11^1	2		9^1	7	10^1		1			
Oct 13	H	Fulham *S*	8000	0-0	0-0						1			4	5	6	8			11	2	3	9^1	7				10		
Oct 20	A	Southampton *S*	12000	0-2	0-2						1	5	2		4	6	8					3	7	9	10	11				
Oct 24	H	Plymouth *W*	3000	1-0	1-0						1	5	2		4	6	8^1					3	7	9	10	11				
Oct 27	H	West Ham *S*	11000	3-1	4-3						1	5	3		4	6				11	2		7	8^2	9^1	10				
Nov 3	A	Tottenham *S*		1-1	1-1						1		3	4	5	6				11	2		7	8	9	10^1				
Nov 7	H	Tottenham *W*	2000	1-0	1-0	4			11		1		3^1		6	7	8				2		9	10		5				
Nov 10	H	Swindon *S*	9000	0-0	1-0						1		3	4	5	6				11^1	2		7	8	9	10				
Nov 14	A	Southampton *SCC*	3800	0-1	0-2						1		3	4	5	6	7	10			2		8	9		11				
Nov 17	A	Norwich *S*	8000	2-1	3-1						1		3	4	5	6				11	2		7	8^1	9^1	10^1				
Nov 24	H	Luton *S*	5000	1-0	1-0						1		3	4	5	6				11	2		7	8	9	10				
Nov 26	A	Tottenham *W*	2000	2-2	2-4	6	4				1					8				11	2	3	7	9^1	10^1		5			
Dec 1	A	Crystal Palace *S*		0-0	0-1						1		3	4	5	6				11	2		7	8	9	10				
Dec 8	H	Brentford *S*	6000	0-0	0-0			11			1		3	4	5	6	8				2		7	9	10					
Dec 15	A	Millwall *S*		1-0	1-0						1			4	5	6	7	10		11	2	3	8	9^1						
Dec 22	H	Leyton *S*	7000	2-0	5-0						1		3	4	5	6^1	7	10		11	2			8^3	9^1					
Dec 25	H	New Brompton *S*	15000	2-0	3-1						1			4	5	6	7	10		11^2	2	3	8	9						
Dec 26	H	Bristol Rovers *S*	16000	2-0	2-0						1		3	4	5	6	7	10^1		11	2		8^1	9						
Jan 5	H	Brighton *S*	8000	2-0	3-0						1	4	3		5	6	8			11^1	2		7	9	10^2					
Jan 12	H	Man. Utd. *EC1*	24329	0-1	2-2						1	4	3		5	6	10^1			11	2	7^1	8	9						
Jan 16	A	Man. Utd. *EC1R*	15000	0-1	2-1						1	4	3		5	6	8^1			11	2		7	9^1	10					
Jan 19	A	Reading *S*	4000	0-1	0-2						1	4	3		5	6				11	2		7	8	9	10				
Jan 26	H	Watford *S*	4000	1-0	1-0			11			1	4	3		5	6					2	7^1	8	9	10					
Feb 2	A	Barnsley *EC2*	10266	0-0	0-1						1	4	3		5	6	8			11	2		7	9	10					
Feb 9	H	Q.P.R. *S*		2-1	2-2			11			1		3	4	5	6					2		7	8	9^2	10				
Feb 16	A	Fulham *S*	25000	0-0	0-2			11			1		3	4	5	6	8				2			7	10					9
Feb 23	H	Southampton *S*	12000	0-1	1-2						1		3	4	5	6	10^1			11	2			8	7					9
Mar 2	A	West Ham *S*		0-1	0-3						1	5	3	4		6	10			11	2			8	7					9
Mar 6	H	Millwall *W*	2000	1-0	1-1	7	9				1	4^1		6		10				11	2	3		8				5		
Mar 9	H	Tottenham *S*	12000	2-1	3-1						1		3	4	5	6	10^1				2		7	8	9		11^2			
Mar 11	A	Millwall *W*		0-2	0-3		9	10			1	4	3		6					11	2		7		8			5		
Mar 16	A	Swindon *S*	5000	0-0	0-0							5	3	4		6					2		7	8	9	10	11	1		
Mar 20	A	Plymouth *S*	4000	1-0	1-0								3	4	5	6					2		7	8		10	11	1		9^1
Mar 23	H	Norwich *S*	12000	0-0	1-0								3	4	5	6					2		7	8	10^1		11	1		9
Mar 29	A	Bristol Rovers *S*		0-2	3-2								3	4	5	6	8				2		7^1		9^1	10^1	11	1		
Mar 30	A	Luton *S*	6000	0-2	1-3								3	4	5	6	10				2		7	8	9^1		11	1		
Apr 1	A	New Brompton *S*	6000	0-1	0-2					5			3	4		6					2		8	7	10	11		1		9
Apr 6	H	Crystal Palace *S*		2-0	6-0						1		3	4	5	6	8^1				2	7^1		9^3	10	11^1				
Apr 8	A	Southampton *HCC*	1500	1-0	1-0						1		3	4	5	6					2	7		9	10	11^1				
Apr 13	A	Brentford *S*		1-1	1-1						1		3	4	5	6					2	7		9^1	10	11				
Apr 17	A	Northampton *S*	moderate	2-0	2-0			11			1			4	5	6	8^1				2^1	3	7		9	10				
Apr 20	H	Millwall *S*	10000	2-0	2-0						1			4	5	6					2	3	7	8	9^2	10	11			
Apr 27	A	Leyton *S*		1-0	2-0						1		3	4	5	6	11				2		7	8	9^1	10^1				
Southern League Appearances						5					30	10	32	35	33	38	5	20		17	35	7	25	31	36	28	15		8	1	6
Southern League Goalscorers												1	2		6				5	1		4	8	21	11	3				1
Western League Appearances						3	4	1	2	3	8	6	6	7	3	6	5	8	1	7	6	4	4	6	7	2	5	2			
Western League Goalscorers												1	1		1			1				1	6	5					
Cup Appearances											5	3	5	2	5	5	1	4		3	4	1	2	5	5	3	2			
Cup Goalscorers																2								1	1	1				

Own goal: West Ham (Oct 27)

Southern League Totals	P38 W22 D 7 L 9 F 64 A36 Pts 51 Posn 2nd
Western League Totals	P10 W 4 D 2 L 4 F 16 A19 Pts 10 Posn 3rd

Season 1907/08 Southern League Division 1
Western League

Date	Venue	Team	Attendance	FA HT	FA FT	Phillip G.	Thomson J.H.	Walker R.	Digweed H.	Buick A.	Beaumont W.	Birtles T.	Knight A.J.	Wilson D.	Dix J.	Cook F.	Warner J.	Clipstone F.	McDonald E.	Bellamy J.	Glen A.	Kirby W.	Cooper W.	Smith W.	Elston A.	Allman M.	Williams E.W.	Hisbent J.	Bowman T.	Cameron J.	Louch L.A.	Randall
Sept 2	A	Norwich S	9000	0-2	0-4	1	2	3	4	5	6									7	8	9	10	11								
Sept 7	A	Watford S	6000	0-1	0-1	1	2		4	5							3		6	7	8	9	10	11								
Sept 11	H	Q.P.R. W	5000	2-2	3-4	1	2¹		4	5	6	7		10			3				9¹						8	11¹					
Sept 14	H	Norwich S	12000	0-0	1-1		2¹		4	5		7		10		1	3		6		9						8	11					
Sept 18	H	Brighton W	4000	1-0	3-1			2	4		5		8	11¹		1	3¹		6	7	9¹		10										
Sept 21	A	Northampton S		0-1	2-3		2		4	5			8				1	3	6	7¹	9		10				11¹						
Sept 28	H	Southampton S	18000	0-0	3-0		2	3	4	5			8				1		6¹	7	9¹		10¹				11						
Sept 30	A	Q.P.R. W	3000	3-0	5-3					5	7			11	1		3	6		8²	9³		10							4	2		
Oct 5	A	Plymouth S		0-1	1-2		2		4	5		7	8¹			1	3		6		9		10				11						
Oct 9	H	Leyton W	1600	1-1	1-1			2	4	5	7		8¹	11	1		3		6		10	9											
Oct 12	H	West Ham S	12000	0-2	0-2		2		4	5			8	11	1		3		6	7	9		10										
Oct 19	A	Q.P.R. S		2-2	2-3	1	2	3	4				8	11					6¹	7¹	9		10										
Oct 23	A	Brighton W	1500	0-2	1-3	1	2	3				7		9	11¹				6		8					10	4	5					
Oct 26	H	Tottenham S	10000	1-0	1-2	1	2	3	4			5	7						6¹		8	9	10				11						
Oct 28	A	Brentford W	2000	1-0	4-0		2	3	4				8¹					10		7	9³	11		5		6			1				
Nov 1	A	Swindon S	6000	0-0	0-0		2	3	4				8					10	6	7	9					11			5		1		
Nov 6	H	Brentford W	1000	1-1	3-1		2	3	6				8					11		7¹			10	9²		4	5			1			
Nov 9	H	Crystal Palace S	7000	0-0	0-1		2	3	4		5	8						6	7	9		10				11			5		1		
Nov 13	H	Plymouth W	1000	0-0	2-1				4		5	7	8	11¹			3		6¹	7			10						2	1			
Nov 16	A	Luton S	3000	0-0	0-2		2		4			7		10	11		3		6	8	9						5						
Nov 23	H	Brighton S	6000	2-0	3-0	1	2	3	4	5		7		11					6		8¹		10¹							9¹			
Nov 25	H	Chelsea SCC	2000	1-1	2-1		2	3	4		5¹	7	8¹	11					6		9			10						1			
Nov 30	H	New Brompton S	7000	2-2	5-2		2	3	4	5¹		7		11					6¹	8	10¹									1	9²		
Dec 4	H	Southampton S	1200	0-1	0-2		2	3	4		6	7	8	11						10	9						5	1				
Dec 7	A	Bradford P.A. S		2-1	2-3		2	3		5	4	7		11					6	8	10								1	9²		
Dec 9	A	Leyton W	small	0-0	1-0	1				4	7		8	11¹	2	3	6				10						5				9	
Dec 14	H	Millwall S	7000	0-0	2-0		2	3	4	5		7		11					6	8¹	10								1	9¹		
Dec 16	H	Southampton W	1500	0-0	1-0		2		4	5	6		10	11	3				7		9¹						1					
Dec 21	A	Brentford S	4000	1-0	1-1		2	3	4	5	6	7		11						8		10						1	9¹		
Dec 25	A	Leyton S		2-0	3-0	1	2	3	4	5¹				11					6	7	8		10¹							9¹		
Dec 26	H	Reading S		4-3		1	2	3	4	5		7		11¹					6¹	8¹	9¹		10									
Dec 28	H	Bristol R. S	10000	1-0	5-2		2	3	4		5	7¹		11					6	8¹	10²								1	9¹		
Jan 1	A	Plymouth W	3000	0-1	1-2				4	5	7				3	6				8¹	9					11		2	1			
Jan 4	H	Watford S	8000	1-0	2-0		2		4	5				11	3			6		7¹	10¹								1	9		8
Jan 11	A	Hastings & St.L. EC1	4000	1-0	1-0		2		4	5		7		11	3			6	8¹	9	10								1			
Jan 18	H	Northampton S	10000	1-0	†		2		4	5	6			11¹	3				7	10								1	9		8
Jan 25	A	Southampton S	6000	0-1	0-1		2		4	5				11	3			6	7	9	10							1			8
Feb 1	H	Leicester Fosse EC2	20000	0-0	0-0		2		4	5				11	3			6¹	7	9	10							1			8
Feb 8	A	West Ham S		1-1	1-2			2		4		5	7	11¹	3			6		10									1	9		8
Feb 12	H	Northampton S	4000	0-1	0-1		2		4	5		7		11	1	3		6		10											8
Feb 15	H	Q.P.R. S	4000	1-0	1-0		2			5	4			11	1	3		6	7	8	10										
Feb 22	H	Stoke EC3	20000	0-1	0-1		2		4	5				11	1	3		6	7	8	10										
Feb 29	H	Swindon S	6–7000	0-0	2-0		2		4	5				11²		3		6		8								1	9		
Mar 7	A	Crystal Palace S	8000	2-1	2-2		3		4	5	6	7		11¹		2				8								1	9		
Mar 14	H	Luton S	5–6000	0-0	1-0		2		4	5		7		11	1	3		6		8									9		
Mar 21	H	Brighton S	5000	0-0	0-0		3		4	5		7		11	1	2		6		8									9		
Mar 25	H	Plymouth S	2000	1-0	3-0		2	3	4	5		7		11				6		8¹							1			10
Mar 28	A	New Brompton S	5000	1-1	3-1		2		4	5		7¹		11¹	1			6		8							3	9		
Apr 4	H	Bradford P.A. S	8000	1-2	4-2		2	3	4	5		7		11¹	1			6¹		8¹								9		
Apr 6	A	Tottenham S	5000	2-2	3-2	1	2	3	4	5¹	6	7		11¹						8								9¹		
Apr 8	H	Millwall SCC SF	4000	1-1	1-1		2		4	5		7		11¹	1	3		6		8										10
Apr 11	A	Millwall S		0-1	1-1		2		4		5	7		11	1	3		6		8¹								9		
Apr 17	H	Leyton S	12000	2-0	3-1		2		4	5		7		11	1	3		6		8¹								9²		
Apr 18	H	Brentford S	7000	2-0	3-2		2		4	5	6	7		11²	3					8¹								9		
Apr 20	A	Reading S		0-0	0-2		2	3	4		5	7		11				6		8								9		10
Apr 25	A	Bristol R. S		0-2	0-3		2	3	4		5	7		11				6		8								9		10
Apr 27	A	Millwall SCC SFR		1-1	2-2															p¹										p
Apr 28	H	Millwall SCC SF(2)R		1-1	1-1		2		4		5	7	8	11				6		9							3	1		10
Southern League Appearances						9	38	20	37	26	18	28		7	31	12	19		33	17	7	36	16	2	1	7		4	14	22	8
Southern League Goalscorers						1			3		2		1	11					6	5	1	11	4		1				12	1
Western League Appearances						3	6	6	9	2	9	10	1	7	10	3	6	3	7	5	6	8	1	4		4	2	4	7	6	1
Western League Goalscorers						1				1		1	4	1				1	1	7	5			2	1
Cup Appearances						6	1	6	4	2	4	1	1	6	2	4		6	3		7		3	1		1	4		4
Cup Goalscorers						1				1				1				1	1	1								2

Southern League Totals P38 W17 D 6 L15 F64 A52 Pts 40 Posn 9th   † game abandoned at half-time, fog, first ever at Fratton Park
Western League Totals P12 W 7 D 1 L 4 F25 A18 Pts 15 Posn 2nd

Nicholson N.	McCafferty W.	Brown A. C.
10		
9		
9^1		
9		
10		
10^1		
10^1		
10		
9^1		
10^1		
10^1		
10		
9		
10		
10	1	
10	1	
	1	
	1	
13	4	
6		
1		
2		

Season 1908/09   Southern League Division 1
Western League

Date	Venue	Team	Attendance	HT	FT	Brown A.C.	Clipstone F.	Bowman T.	Churchill G.	Birtles T.	Kirby W.	Louch L.A.	McCafferty W.	Dix J.	McDonald T.	Warner J.	Digweed H.	Beaumont W.E.	McDonald E.	Reid W.	Buick A.	Thomson J.H.	Yates W.	Williams E.W.	Cameron J.	Smith J.	Halliday D.A.	Knight A.J.	Long E.	McMahon E.	Brawn C.E.	Pyne	Co.
Sept 2	H	Leyton S	5000	2-0	2-2	3				7	8		10^1		11	1	2	4	5	6	9^1													
Sept 5	H	Watford S	10000	2-0	2-0	3				7	8^1		10		11	1	2	4		6	9^1	5												
Sept 7	A	Bristol R. S		1-2	2-3	3				7	8					1	2	4		6	9^1	5	10	11									
Sept 12	A	Norwich S	7000	0-0	0-0					7	8				11	1	3	4		6	9	5	2	10									
Sept 14	A	QPR S		0-0	0-0					7		9	8		11	1	2	4		6	9	5		10									
Sept 19	H	Reading S	10000	1-0	1-1	3				7	8^1		10		11	1	2	4		6	9	5											
Sept 26	A	Southampton S	16000	0-2	0-2	3				7	8	9	10		11	1	2	4		6		5											
Sept 30	H	Southampton W	5000	1-0	4-2	3	4			7	8		10			1	2			6	9^3	5		11^1									
Oct 2	H	QPR S	10000	2-0	3-1	3	4			7	8^1		10^1			1	2	6			9^1	5		11									
Oct 7	H	Bristol R. S	3000	2-0	2-0		2			7	8						3	4		6	9^2	5	10	11	1								
Oct 10	A	West Ham S		0-0	1-3					7	8	10				1	3	4		6^1	9	5	2	11									
Oct 14	A	Plymouth W	3000	0-1	0-1		2			7	11	10				1	3	4		6	9	5	8										
Oct 17	H	Brighton S	7000	2-0	2-1	3				7^1	11	8	10			1		4		6^1	9	5	2										
Oct 21	H	Plymouth W	2000	1-0	3-0		4			7^1	11	10^1				1				6	9^1		8			2	5					3		
Oct 24	A	C. Palace S		1-3	2-3	3				7	11	8^1	10			1	2	4		6	9^1	5											
Oct 28	A	Southampton W	2000	0-3	1-4		4	6		7			10				3				9^1	5			1	2			8	11			
Oct 31	H	Brentford S	5000	2-3	2-3	3				7	11	10^1				1	2	4		6	9^1	5	8										
Nov 2	A	Bristol R. W	1000	2-1	2-2			3	6	7	8					1		4	5		9		2							11	10^1		
Nov 7	A	Luton S	6000	1-3	1-5	1	3			7	8	10						4		6	9^1	5		11	2								
Nov 14	A	Swindon S	5000	1-1	3-1					7	8	10				1	3	4		6	9^3	5	2	11									
Nov 18	H	Millwall W	poor	1-2	4-2	3	5			7		9^2	11^1					4		6				10^1	1	2				8			
Nov 21	A	Plymouth S	7000	1-0	2-1	1				7		10					3	4		6	9^2	5		11	2						8		
Nov 25	H	West Ham W	1500	2-2	2-3		5	4					11			1	3			6	9^2		8		2					10		7	
Nov 28	A	Exeter S	5000	0-2	1-4	1				7		10					3	4		6	9^1	5		11	2						8		
Dec 2	H	Bristol R. W		1-0	1-0	3	2	4		7		9^1	11			1		6				5	8								10		
Dec 5	H	Northampton S	5000	1-1	3-4	1	3			7	8^1	9	10^1					4	6^1			5		11									
Dec 9	H	Brentford W	poor	0-0	0-0	3				7	9		11					4			5	6						8		10			2
Dec 12	A	New Brompton S	6000	1-1	3-2	3	2			7	8^1							4			9^2	5	6	11									
Dec 14	A	West Ham W	moderate	1-1	4-2	3				7	8^2		10^1			1				6	9^1	5								11			2
Dec 19	H	Millwall S	6000	1-0	2-0	3				7	8					1	2^1			6	9^1	5		11									
Dec 25	S	Southend S		3-1	6-2	3				7^1	8		11^1			1	2			6	9^3	5								10			
Dec 26	H	Coventry S	15000	1-0	3-0	3				7^2	8		11^1			1	2			6	9	5							10			
Jan 2	A	Watford S		1-0	1-1	3				7	8		11			1	2	4		6	9^1	5							10			
Jan 4	A	Millwall W		0-1	0-1	2				7		9				1		4		6		5						8	11	10		3
Jan 9	H	Norwich S	8000	0-0	1-1	3				7	10		11			1	2	4		6	9	5							8^1			
Jan 16	A	Birmingham FAC1		3-1	5-2	3				7^1	8		11			1	2	4		6	9^3	5							10^1			
Jan 23	A	Reading S	3000	0-1	0-1	3	5			7	8		11			1	2	4		6	9								10			
Jan 25	A	Brentford W	small	0-2	0-4	3	5			7	8					1				6	9							10	11	4		2
Jan 30	H	Southampton S	12000	1-0	3-0	3				7	8^1		11			1	2	4	5	6	9^2								10			
Feb 6	H	Sheffield W. FAC2	27853	1-0	2-2	3				7^1	8		11^1			1	2	4		6	9	5							10			
Feb 11	A	Sheffield W. FAC2R	26066	0-2	0-3	3				7	8		11			1	2	4		6	9	5							10			
Feb 13	H	West Ham S	5000	3-1	4-1	3				7^1	8^1		11			1	2	4		6	9^2	5	2						10			
Feb 20	A	Brighton S		0-0	0-0	3				7	8		11			1	4	5		6	9		2						10			
Feb 22	A	Southampton §SCC	4000	0-0	0-1					7	8	9	11				3	4	5	6			2	10	1							
Feb 27	H	C. Palace S		0-1	1-1	3				7	8	9^1	11			1		4		6		5	2						10			
Mar 3	A	Leyton S	500	0-2	0-4								1			p	p	p														
Mar 6	A	Brentford S		†						7	8		11			1	3	4	5	6	9		2							10		
Mar 10	H	Southampton BFC	3000	1-0	1-1					7	8	10	11			1	3	4		6	9^1	5	2										
Mar 13	H	Luton S		1-0	1-0					7	8^1	10	11			1	3	4		6	9	5	2										
Mar 16	A	Southampton SCC1		2-1	2-1	3				7	8		11			1	3	4		6	9^1	5	2					10^1					
Mar 20	A	Swindon S		0-4	0-5					7	8	9	11			1	3	4		6		5	2						10			
Mar 27	H	Plymouth S	8000	1-0	2-0					7^1	11	8					3			6	9^1	5	2		1				10			
Mar 29	A	Brentford S		1-1	2-1					7	8^1		11				3			6	9^1	5	2		1				10			
Mar 31	H	Brighton SCC2	poor	0-1	1-2	2					8	9					3	5	6					10^1	1			11	7			
Apr 3	H	Exeter S		2-0	2-0	3				7	8^1		11				2			6	9	5			1				10^1			
Apr 9	H	Southend S	12000	0-0	2-0	3				7	10		8	11^2			2	4		6	9	5			1				10			
Apr 10	A	Northampton S	12000	1-0	1-0	3				7	10		8	11^1			2	4		6	9	5			1				10			
Apr 13	A	Coventry C. S	3000	2-0	3-5	3				7	8^3		9				2	4		6		5		10	1							
Apr 17	H	New Brompton S		1-1	1-1	1				7	8^1	9	10				3	4		6		5	2									
Apr 24	A	Millwall S		1-1	1-1					7	9		11				3	4		6		5	8		1				10			
Southern League Appearances						5	27	5		33	38	7	27	24	28	34	29	16	14	32	35	14	26	11	8	3		1			18		
Southern League Goalscorers										6	11	2	7	5	1			2	1		27										2		
Western League Appearances						7	9	4	6	11	1	7	5	10	4	3	6	4	8	7	8	1	2	5	1	5	5	5	1	2	4		
Western League Goalscorers							1	2		4	2								8				1	1							1		
Cup Appearances						5				2	7		7	6	5	6	4	3	2	5	5	3	7		2						1	4	1
Cup Goalscorers										2	1										5			1							2		

Southern League Totals   P40 W18 D10 L12 F68 A60 Pts 46 Posn 4th

Western League Totals   P12 W 5 D 2 L 5 F21 A21 Pts 12 Posn 4th

† abandoned 4 minutes before HT, score 0-0, quagmire pitch

§ 1907/08 Final

Banks	Grier	Thomson A.	
4			
4			
4[1]			
4			
4			
4			
4			
4			
4			
4			
	11		
	11		
		2[1]	
5	2	1	
1			
3			

Season 1909/10   Southern League Division 1

Date	Venue	Team	Attendance	FA HT	FA FT	Cope T.	Smith J.	Count F.	Worthington T.	Shufflebotham J.	McIntyre E.	Birtles T.	Kirby W.	McCafferty W.	McMahon E.	Dix J.	Knight A.E.	Guy R.	Hakin T.	Haycock G.	Long E.	Williams E.W.	Warner J.	Clipstone F.	Buick A.	Yates W.	Beaumont W.	Bowman A.	Thomson J.H.	Sparrow H.
Sept 1	H	Brighton S	6000	0-0	0-0	1			4			10	9		11		7		8				2	3	5	6				
Sept 4	A	Bristol City S		0-1	0-4	1			4			10	9		11		7		8				2	3	5		6			
Sept 8	A	Brighton S		1-2	1-4	1				6	5	7	10		11				9¹	8			2	3	5		4			
Sept 11	H	Norwich S		1-1	2-1	1				6	5	7¹	8¹	9	11				10				2	3	5		4			
Sept 13	A	West Ham S	3000	2-0	2-0	1				6	5	7	9¹		11				10¹	8			2	3	5		4			
Sept 18	A	Brentford S		0-0	0-2	1				6	5	7	9		11				8	10			2	3			4			
Sept 20	A	Southampton SCC1		1-1	2-3	1	2			6	5	7	9¹		11				10	8¹				3			4			
Sept 25	H	Coventry S		0-0	0-0	1				5		7	9		11				10	8			2	3		6	4			
Sept 29	H	West Ham S	1000	1-0	1-1	1				5		7	9¹		11				10	8			2	3		6	4			
Oct 2	A	Watford S		0-2	3-3	1	2			5		7	9¹		11				10¹	8				3		6¹	4			
Oct 9	H	Reading S		1-1	3-1	1				5		7	9¹			11²			10	8			2	3		6	4			
Oct 16	A	Southend S		0-0	0-0	1				5		7	9			11			10	8			2	3		6	4			
Oct 20	H	Exeter S		4-0	4-1	1				5		7	9²			11			10	8²			2	3		6	4			
Oct 23	H	Leyton S	7000	1-0	2-0	1						7	9			11¹			10	8			2¹	3	5	6	4			
Oct 30	A	Plymouth S		0-0	0-2	1						7	9			11			10	8			2	3	5	6	4			
Nov 6	H	Southampton S	12000	1-1	1-1	1						7	8¹			11			10				2	3	5	6	4	9		
Nov 10	A	Exeter S			0-5	1		3				7				11			10	8			2		5	6	4	9		
Nov 13	A	Croydon Common S		3-2	4-3	1	2			5¹		7				11²		3	10	8¹						6	4	9		
Nov 17	H	Crystal Palace S	4000	2-0	2-0	1				5		7				11		3	10	8						6	4	9²	2	
Nov 20	H	Millwall S		0-1	0-1	1				5		7				11		3	10	8						6	4	9	2	
Nov 27	A	New Brompton S		0-2	0-2	1				5			8			11			10	7			3			6	4	9	2	
Nov 29	A	Southampton BFC	very poor	3-2	3-2	1	2		4	5			8²			11		3	10¹	7						6		9		
Dec 4	H	Northampton S	4000	1-1	2-1	1				5			8			11			10	7²			3			6	4	9	2	
Dec 11	A	Q.P.R. S		4-2	5-3	1				5			8²			11			10	7			3			6	4	9³	2	
Dec 18	H	Luton S		1-0	3-2	1				5			8¹			11¹			10	7			3			6	4	9¹	2	
Dec 25	A	Swindon S		0-1	1-3	1				6			8			11			10	7¹			3		5		4	9	2	
Dec 27	H	Swindon S	15000	1-1	3-1	1							8			11				7¹			3		5¹	6	4	9¹	2	10
Jan 8	H	Bristol Rovers S		1-0	2-0	1				5			8			11¹			10	7¹			3			6	4	9	2	
Jan 15	H	Shrewsbury FAC1		2-0	3-0	1				5			8			11			10	7¹			3			6	4	9²	2	
Jan 29	A	Brentford S		0-1	0-2	1				5			8			11			10	7			3			6	4	9	2	
Feb 5	H	Coventry FAC2	12000	0-0	0-1	1			4	5			8			11			10	7			3			6		9	2	
Feb 12	H	Watford S	5000	1-0	5-0	1							8¹			11			10¹	7³	3	5				6	4		2	9
Feb 19	A	Reading S	1500	0-3	1-4	1							8			11				7		5	3			6	4	9¹	2	10
Feb 26	H	Southend S		1-0	1-1	1							8			11¹			10	7		5	3			6	4		2	9
Mar 5	A	Leyton S		0-0	0-1	1							8			11			10	7		5	3			6	4		2	9
Mar 9	A	Crystal Palace S	2000	1-2	2-4	1							8¹			11	7		10			5¹	3			6	4	9	2	
Mar 12	H	Plymouth S		2-0	4-0	1							8³			11			10	7		5¹	3			6	4	9	2	
Mar 19	A	Southampton S		0-0	2-1	1							8¹			11			10¹	7		5	3			6	4	9	2	
Mar 25	A	Norwich S		1-2	1-2	1							8			11			10	7		5	3			6	4	9¹	2	
Mar 26	H	Croydon Common S	6000	0-1	0-1	1			4				8			11			10	7			3		5	6		9	2	
Apr 2	A	Millwall S	meagre	0-0	1-0	1		2		7			9¹			11			8	10			3		5	6	4			
Apr 9	H	New Brompton S	5000	1-3	4-3	1				7			9¹			11			8¹	10			3²		5	6	4		2	
Apr 16	A	Northampton S		0-2	0-2	1			4	7			9			11			8	10			3		5	6			2	
Apr 18	A	Coventry S		0-1	3-1	1			4	7¹			9¹			11			8¹	10			3		5	6			2	
Apr 23	H	Q.P.R. S		1-0	4-0	1			4	7			9¹			11			8²	10¹			3		5	6			2	
Apr 30	A	Luton S		1-0	1-0	1			4	7			9			11			8	10¹			3		5	6			2	

						Cope T.	Smith J.	Count F.	Worthington T.	Shufflebotham J.	McIntyre E.	Birtles T.	Kirby W.	McCafferty W.	McMahon E.	Dix J.	Knight A.E.	Guy R.	Hakin T.	Haycock G.	Long E.	Williams E.W.	Warner J.	Clipstone F.	Buick A.	Yates W.	Beaumont W.	Bowman A.	Thomson J.H.	Sparrow H.
Southern League Appearances						42	3	1	9	18	4	19	41	5	12	31	10	3	19	28	18	10	28	18	23	35	37	19	24	5
Southern League Goalscorers										2		2	21			6			7	7	8		2		3	2	1	9		
Cup Appearances						4	1	1	3	4		3	3	4	3	1	1		2	3		1			3	2	3	2		
Cup Goalscorers										2			1			1	1		1								2		

Southern League Totals   P42 W20 D 7 L15 F 70 A63 Pts 47 Posn 6th

Season 1910/11   Southern League Division 1

Date	Venue	Team	Attendance	FA HT	FA FT	Cope T.	Buick A.	Thomson J.H.	Warner J.	Worthington T.	Yates W.	Noble R.	Kirby W.	Hall A.N.	McMahon E.	Long E.	Turner R.	Knight A.E.	Sparrow H.	Louch L.A.	Williams E.W.	Turner A.	Gittins A.	Shufflebotham J.	Reeves V.	Hunt J.	Nurthen W.	Count F.	Bell E.	Wiggins G.
Sept 3	H	Plymouth *S*	10000	0-0	0-0	1	5	2	3	4	6	7	8	9		11	10													
Sept 10	A	Southampton *S*		0-2	0-3	1	5	2	3	4	6	7	9		8	11	10													
Sept 14	H	Brighton *SCC1*	2000	0-1	0-1	1	5	2	3	4		7			8	11	10	6	9											
Sept 17	H	Southend *S*		2-1	3-2	1	5	2		4	6	7¹	8				10¹	3	9¹	11										
Sept 24	A	Coventry *S*		0-0	0-0	1	5	2		4	6	7	8				10	3	9	11										
Oct 1	H	New Brompton *S*	8000	1-0	2-0	1	5	2	3	4		7	8¹				10¹	6	9	11										
Oct 5	A	Crystal Palace *S*	4000	0-0	1-0	1	5	2	3	4		7¹	8				10	6	9	11										
Oct 8	A	Millwall *S*		0-2	1-3	1	5	2	3	4		7	8				10¹	6	9	11										
Oct 15	H	Q.P.R. *S*	9000	1-0	1-1	1	5	2	3	4		7	8				10	6	9¹	11										
Oct 22	A	West Ham *S*		0-0	1-3	1	5	2	3	4		7¹	8	9			10	6		11										
Oct 29	H	Luton *S*		1-0	2-1	1	5	2	3	4		7	8		10			6	9²	11										
Nov 5	A	Norwich *S*		0-2	0-2	1	5	2	3	4		7	8		10			6	9	11										
Nov 12	A	Northampton *S*		0-1	0-1	1		2	3	5	4	7	8		10	11	9	6												
Nov 19	H	Brighton *S*		1-0	1-0	1		2	3	5	4	7	8¹			11	10	6	9											
Nov 26	A	Exeter *S*		1-0	2-0	1		2	3	5	4	7	8¹	9¹		11	10	6												
Nov 30	H	Southampton *PBC*	1000	2-1	2-1	1		2	3	5	4	7	8	9¹		11¹	10	6												
Dec 3	H	Swindon *S*		0-0	1-2	1		2	3	5	4	7	8¹	9		11	10	6												
Dec 10	A	Bristol Rovers *S*		1-2	2-3	1		2	3¹	5	4	7	8	9¹		11	10	6												
Dec 17	H	Crystal Palace *S*	7000	0-0	0-0	1		2	3	5	4	7	8	9		11	10	6												
Dec 24	H	Brentford *S*		0-1	0-2	1		2	3	5	4	7	8	9		11		6							10					
Dec 26	A	Leyton *S*	10000	0-1	1-1	1		2	3	5	4	7		9¹		11		6							8					
Dec 27	H	Leyton *S*	10000	1-1	2-2	1		2	3		4	7		9¹		11	10	6						5	8¹					
Dec 31	A	Plymouth *S*		0-2	0-4	1		2	3	5	4	7		9		11	10	6							8					
Jan 7	H	Southampton *S*	9000	0-0	0-1	1		2	3	5	4	7		9		11	10	6							8					
Jan 14	H	Aston Villa *FAC1*	17415	0-1	1-4	1	5	2	3	4		7	8	9		11¹	10	6												
Jan 21	A	Southend *S*		0-2	0-2	1		2	3	5	4	7				11	10	6							8	9				
Jan 28	H	Coventry *S*		2-0	3-0		5	2	3	6	4	7				11	10¹								8¹	9¹	1			
Feb 4	A	New Brompton *S*		0-1	0-1	1		2	3	6	4	7				11	10								8	9				
Feb 11	H	Millwall *S*		1-2	2-2	1	5	2	3	4		7				11	10	6							8¹	9¹				
Feb 18	A	Q.P.R. *S*		0-1	0-1	1		2	3		4	7	8	9		11	10	6						5						
Mar 4	A	Luton *S*		0-2	1-4	1		2	3		4	7		9			10	6			11¹			5	8					
Mar 11	A	Norwich *S*		0-0	1-1	1			3	5	4	9¹	8			7	10	6			11						2			
Mar 18	H	Northampton *S*		0-0	0-0	1			3	5	4	9	8			7	10	6			11						2			
Mar 25	A	Brighton *S*		0-1	1-2	1			3	5	4	9	7¹			8	10	6			11						2			
Mar 29	H	West Ham *S*	4000	0-0	0-0	1			3	5	4	9	7			8	10	6			11						2			
Apr 1	H	Exeter *S*	3000	0-0	0-0	1			3	5	4	9	7	10	11	8		6									2			
Apr 8	A	Swindon *S*		0-2	1-2	1	5		3		4	7		9				6			11				8		2		10¹	
Apr 14	H	Watford *S*	10000	0-0	0-0	1	5	2		6	4	7		9							11				10		3	8		
Apr 15	H	Bristol Rovers *S*		0-0	1-2	1	5		3		4	7		9				6			11				10		2	8¹		
Apr 17	A	Watford *S*	6000	2-2	2-3	1	5		3		4	7		9²							11				10		2	8		6
Apr 29	H	Brentford *S*		2-1		1	5	2	3		4	7¹		9				6			11				10			8¹		
Southern League Appearances						37	20	29	32	25	38	31	34	12	12	21	34	29	7	7	11	4	3	7	10	1	9	4	1	
Southern League Goalscorers								1			3	9	3			1	6		2	1				3	3		2			
Cup Appearances						3	2	3	3	2	2	2	3	2	1	3	3	3	1											
Cup Goalscorers															1	2														

Southern League Totals   P38 W8 D11 L19 F34 A53 Pts 27 Posn 20th out of 20

Season 1911/12   Southern League Division 2

Date	Venue	Team	Attendance	FA HT	FA FT	Sanderson D.S.	Warner J.	Knight A.E.	Menzies J.	Wardrope A.C.	Reid R.	Dowling M.	Stringfellow F.	Cullen J.	Hunt J.	Jones J.L.	Croft R.	Hogg J.	Duncan A.	Louch L.A.	O'Gara J.	Reeves V.	Pearce T.H.	Hemstock J.	Taylor H.	Rollinson F.
Sept 2	H	Chesham *SL2*	6000	7-0	11-0	1	2	3	4	5	6	7^2	8	9^5		10^4				11						
Sept 4	A	Walsall *SL2*		0-1	0-1	1	2		4	5	6	7	8	9		10	3			11						
Sept 9	A	Treharris *SL2*		1-0	1-2	1	2	3	4	5	6	7			9	10		8		11^1						
Sept 16	H	Aberdare *SL2*	6000	2-0	4-0	1	2^1	3	4	5	6	7	8^1	9^1		10				11^1						
Sept 20	H	Reading *SCC1*		0-0	1-1	1	2		4	5	6	7	8^1	9		10	3			11						
Sept 23	A	Merthyr Town *SL2*		1-1	2-1	1	2	3	4	5	6	7	8^2	10		11			9							
Oct 14	A	Ton Pentre *SL2*		1-0	1-0	1	2	3	4	5	6	7	8	10^1		11			9							
Oct 21	A	Cardiff *SL2*	3500	0-0	0-0	1	2		4	5	6	7	8	10		11			9							
Oct 25	A	Southampton *BFC*	2000	0-2	1-5	1	2		4	5	6	7^1	8	10		11			9							
Nov 4	H	Mardy *SL2*	6000	1-0	2-0	1	2	3	4	5	6	7	8			11			9^2							
Nov 8	A	Reading *SCC1R*		0-0	0-2	1	2		4	5	6	7	8	9		10	3			11						
Nov 11	A	Cwm Albion *SL2*	1000	3-1	6-1	1	2	3	4	5	6^1		8^2	10^1		11			9^2			7				
Nov 18	A	Pontypridd *SL2*		0-2	1-3	1	2		4	5	6		8	10		11^1	3		9		7					
Nov 25	A	Kettering *SL2*		1-0	2-0	1	2	3	4	5	6		8^1	9^1		10				11			7			
Dec 16	H	Cwm Albion *SL2*	5000	2-0	4-1	1	2	3	4	5	6		8			11			9^2	7				10^2		
Dec 25	A	Southend Utd. *SL2*		0-0	0-0	1	2	3	4	5	6	7	8		9	11								10		
Dec 30	H	Merthyr Town *SL2*	9965	1-1	1-1	1	2	p	4	5	6	7	p			11			p					p^1		
Jan 1	H	Walsall *SL2*	5000	0-0	3-0	1	2	3	4	5	6	7	8^1		9^2	11								10		
Jan 13	A	Bristol R. *FAC1*	15000	1-0	2-1	1	2	3	4	5	6	7	8		9^1	11^1								10		
Jan 20	H	Pontypridd *SL2*	11036	1-1	3-1	1	2	3	4	5	6	7^1	8^1		9	11^1								10		
Jan 27	H	Southend Utd. *SL2*	11708	2-0	2-0	1	2	3	4	5	6	7	8^1		9	11								10		
Feb 3	A	Bradford *FAC2*		0-1	0-2	1	2	3	4	5	6	9	8	11		10			7							
Feb 10	A	Aberdare *SL2*		1-1	1-4	1	2	3	4^1	5	6	7	8			11			9					10		
Feb 17	H	Cardiff *SL2*	11000	1-1	3-2	1	2	3	4	5	6	7	8^1			11									9^1	10^1
Mar 9	A	Kettering *SL2*		0-0	2-0	1	2	3	4	5	6	7	8			11									9^2	10
Mar 23	A	Mardy *SL2*		3-2	4-2	1	2	3	4	5	6^1	7^1	8			11^1									9^1	10
Mar 30	A	Chesham *SL2*		2-0	7-0	1	2	3	4	5	6	7	8			11									9^6	10^1
Apr 5	H	Croydon Com. *SL2*	14000	0-0	2-1	1	2	3	4	5	6	7	8			11^1									9^1	10
Apr 6	H	Ton Pentre *SL2*	10901	2-0	3-0	1	2	3	4	5	6	7	8			11									9^3	10
Apr 8	A	Croydon Com. *SL2*		0-0	2-1	1	2	3	4	5	6	7	8			11^1									9^1	10
Apr 13	H	Treharris *SL2*	12000	3-0	5-0	1	2	3	4	5	6	7	8^1			11^1									9^2	10^1
Southern League Appearances						26	26	23	26	26	26	22	25	7	7	23	3	1	7	12	1	1	1	7	8	8
Southern League Goalscorers							1		1		1	4	10	9	2	12				6				3	17	3
Cup Appearances						5	5	2	5	5	5	5	5	3	2	4	3		1	3			1	1		
Cup Goalscorers												1	1			1				1						

Southern League Totals   P26 W19 D 3 L 4 F73 A20 Pts 41 Posn 2nd

Own goal: Southend (Jan 27)

Complete list of POMPEY Managers

From	To	
1898	4/6/1901	Frank J. Brettell
1901/02	1904	Robert Blyth (former player) (d. 7/2/41)
1904/05	1908	Richard Bonney
3/6/1911	14/4/1920	Robert Brown
–/5/1920	14/5/1927	John McCartney (d. 18/1/33)
27/6/1927	1947	John W. Tinn (d. 13/3/71)
1947	1952	J.R. 'Bob' Jackson
23/8/1952	30/4/1958	Eddie Lever (former player)
23/8/1958	8/2/1961	Freddy Cox (d. 2/4/66)
1961	1961(acting)	William Thompson (former player)
1/4/1961	1970	George Smith (d. 2/11/83)
1970	10/5/1973	Ronald Tindall (former player)
10/5/1973	6/9/1974	John Mortimer
1974(10 days)	1974(acting)	Ronald Tindall
13/9/1974	4/5/1977	Ian St. John
4/5/1977	12/5/1979	James William Dickinson (former player) (d. 8/11/82)
12/5/1979	31/3/1982	Frank Burrows
31/3/1982	22/5/1982(acting)	Bobby Campbell (former player)
22/5/1982	11/5/1984	Bobby Campbell
11/5/1984	5/6/1984 (acting)	Alan Ball
5/6/1984		Alan Ball

Complete list of POMPEY Financial Secretaries

From	To	
1899	17/5/1907	Percy G. Whitney (d. 17/5/07)
1907	resigned June 1946	George F. Preston
1947	1950	Daniel J. Clarke
1950	emigrated to Canada 1956	Phillip Harris
1956	1968	Reginald N.A. Mulcock
1968	4/5/1977	James William Dickinson (d. 8/11/82)
12/9/1977		William J.B. Davis

Complete list of POMPEY Chairmen

From	To	
1899	1912	Sir John Brickwood
1912	14/4/1920	George L. Oliver (d. 22/12/34)
24/4/1920	27/8/1924	Rev. Edward Bruce Cornford
10/9/1924	7/8/1934	Robert Blyth (former player and manager) (d. 7/2/41)
7/8/1934	30/6/1937	Alfred E. Hooper
11/8/1937	18/9/1940	William C. Kiln
18/9/1940	10/10/1945	Sydney B. Leverett
10/10/1945	1946	Stephen Cribb (d. 2/2/63)
1946	1949	Richard Vernon Stokes
1949	1951	James Chinneck
1951	1954	Richard Vernon Stokes (d. 16/2/82)
1954	1955	John Privett
1955	1957	Guy Spriggins
1957	1959	John H. Sparshatt
5/5/1959	1966	Dr. J.M. McLachlan (d. 9/3/74)
1966	1973	John Dennis P. Collett
10/5/1973		B. John Deacon

Season 1912/13   Southern League Division 1
Southern Alliance

Date	Venue	Team	Attendance	FA HT	FA FT	Sanderson D.S.	Warner J.	Knight A.E.	Menzies J.	Wardrope A.C.	Reid R.	Dowling M.	Hunt J.	Taylor H.	Rollinson F.	Jones J.L.	Stringfellow F.	Martin G.	Wright H.	Dexter C.	Jackson	Gibson A.	Hamilton F.	Murray T.	Walls J.	Louch L.A.	Bradley W.	Duncan A.	Mouncher S.	Powell H.	Edginton C.	Arnold G.	Asht.
Sept 4	A	Brighton *SL1*	6000	0-1	0-2	1	2	3	4	5	6	7	8	9	10	11																	
Sept 7	H	Merthyr Town *SL1*	11000	0-0	0-0	1	2	3	4	5	6	7		9	10	11	8																
Sept 11	H	Brighton *SL1*	6000	1-0	1-0	1	2	3	4	5	6				10	11	8	9	7¹														
Sept 14	A	C. Palace *SL1*		0-1	0-2	1	2	3	4		6	9			10	11	8	5	7														
Sept 18	H	Croydon Com. *SA*	2000	0-0	0-0	1	2			5				9	6	11	8		7	3	4	10												
Sept 21	H	Plymouth A. *SL1*	14000	0-0	0-0	1	2	3	4	5				9	10	11	8	6	7														
Sept 25	A	Southend *SA*		0-3	0-3	1	2		4		5			9		11			7	3		8									6	10		
Sept 28	A	Southampton *SL1*		0-2	3-2	1	2	3			6			9	10¹	11	8¹	5	7¹														
Oct 2	A	Croydon Com. *SA*		0-1	0-2	1	p									11			7			5											
Oct 5	H	Reading *SL1*	12000	1-0	1-2	1			4		6				10¹	11	8		7	3		5	2	9										
Oct 12	H	Norwich *SL1*		0-0	0-0			3	4		6		8		10	11	9		7			5	2		1								
Oct 16	H	Southampton *PBC*	2000	1-0	2-0			3¹	4		6		8		10	11	9¹		7			5	2		1								
Oct 19	H	Gillingham *SL1*	12000	0-0	2-1		2	3	4		6	8²		9	10	11			7			5			1								
Oct 26	A	Northampton *SL1*		0-0	2-1		2	3	4		6	8		9¹	10¹				7			5			1								
Oct 30	H	Luton *SA*	very fair	2-0	3-0		2		4		6			9	10	11³		8	7	3		5			1								
Nov 2	H	QPR *SL1*	14000	1-1	1-1		2	3	4		6	8		9¹	10	11			7			5			1								
Nov 6	A	Southampton *SA*	2–3000	2-0	3-0	1	2		4		6				10¹	11	8	9²	7	3		5											
Nov 9	A	Brentford *SL1*		0-1	0-1		3				6			9	10		8	4	7			5	2		1	11							
Nov 13	A	Brentford *SA*	1000	1-0	3-1		2					7		9²	10¹		8				4		3	5		1	11						6	
Nov 16	H	Millwall *SL1*	11000	0-1	2-1		2	3	4		6			9¹	10		8¹		7			5			1	11							
Nov 20	H	Southampton *SA*	1500	0-0	2-0		2	3	4		6						8¹	9				10¹	5		1	11	7						
Nov 23	A	Bristol R. *SL1*		0-2	2-2		2	3	4		6			9	10		8¹		7			5			1	11							
Nov 30	H	Swindon *SL1*	12000	1-0	1-2		2	3	4		6			9	10¹		8		7			5			1	11							
Dec 7	A	Stoke *SL1*		0-0	0-2			3	4		6			9	10		8		7			5	2		1	11							
Dec 14	A	Exeter *SL1*		0-1	1-2		2	3	4		6	7			10		8	9¹				5			1	11							
Dec 21	H	West Ham *SL1*		1-0	1-2		2¹	3	4		6	7			10		8	9	11			5			1								
Dec 25	A	Coventry *SL1*		0-0	0-2	1	2	3	4		6	7			10		8	9	11			5											
Dec 28	A	Merthyr Town *SL1*		0-1	0-2	1	2		4		6	7		10		11	8					5	3										
Jan 1	H	Southend *SA*	3000	3-0	4-0	1	2				6	7		10²		11				3		5										4	
Jan 4	H	C. Palace *SL1*	12000	0-0	2-0	1	2	3	4		6	7		10		11						5										4	
Jan 15	H	Brighton *FAC1*	15556	1-0	1-2	1	2	3	4		6	7		10		11						5										4	
Jan 18	A	Plymouth A *SL1*		0-0	0-2	1	2		4		6			10	,,		7	3				5											11
Jan 25	A	Southampton *SL1*	14000	0-0	2-0	1	2¹	3			6			10			8¹	11	7			5										4	
Feb 1	A	Cardiff C. *SA*	3000		1-1	1	2				6			10¹			8	11	7	3		5										4	
Feb 8	A	Reading *SL1*		1-1	1-3	1	2				6			10			8		7	3		11	5									4	
Feb 12	H	Brentford *SA*	fairly good	0-1	0-1		2										8	6	7	3		11	5			1						4	
Feb 15	H	Norwich C. *SL1*		1-0	2-0	1	2	3			6						8		7			5										4	11
Feb 22	A	Gillingham *SL1*		0-1	0-2	1		3			6			9			8		7	2		5										4	
Feb 24	A	Millwall *SA*			0-1	1	2		4		6	7					8	11	3			5									4	
Mar 1	H	Northampton *SL1*	10000	1-0	1-1	1	2	3			6	7					8															4	
Mar 5	H	Millwall *SA*	fairly large	0-1	3-1	1	2				6	7		8¹				3				9										4¹	
Mar 8	A	QPR *SL1*		1-0	1-1	1	2	3			6	7					8					4										9¹	
Mar 12	H	Brighton *SA*			1-4			3				7					8	6				5	4	1						9	
Mar 15	H	Brentford *SL1*		1-0	1-0	1	2	3			6	7					8	7				4										9	
Mar 21	A	Watford *SL1*		0-1	2-1	1	2				6						8²	7	3			4											
Mar 22	A	Millwall *SL1*		0-1	0-2	1	2		4		6			10			8	7	3														
Mar 24	H	Watford *SL1*	12000	0-1	1-1	1	2¹		4		6						8	7	3													9	
Mar 25	A	Luton *SA*	4000		1-2	1	2							p¹																		
Mar 29	H	Bristol R. *SL1*		0-0	2-1	1	2	3			6	9					8	7															
Apr 5	A	Swindon *SL1*		0-2	0-3	1	2	3			6	9					8	7															
Apr 9	H	Coventry *SL1*	5000	1-0	2-1	1	2	3			6	7		9			8					4											
Apr 12	H	Stoke *SL1*		1-0	4-1	1	2	3				7		9³	10		8¹	6				4											
Apr 16	A	Brighton *SA*	3000		0-3	s	s				s	s		s	s							s						s	1			s
Apr 19	H	Exeter C. *SL1*	8628	2-1	2-1	1	2				6	7²		9	10		8			3		4											
Apr 23	H	Cardiff C. *SA*	2000		3-1	1	2				6	7								3	8¹	10	4										
Apr 26	A	West Ham *SL1*		0-1	1-2	1	2	3			6	7		p		p						5											
Southern League Appearances						27	34	29	22	3	37	20	1	20	24	12	31	12	27	8	1	19	5	8	1	11	6					8	2
Southern League Goalscorers								3			4			6	5		7	1	2													1	
Southern Alliance Appearances						9	12	2	5		10	6		6	6	6	8	6	8	9	3	4	8	2	5	1	6	2	1	1	1	6	
Southern Alliance Goalscorers														5	4	3	1	2				1	1								1	
Cup Appearances						1	1		1	2		2	2		1	1	2			1	1				1	1	1		1				
Cup Goalscorers							1										1																

Southern League Totals   P38 W14 D 8 L16 F41 A49 Pts 36 Posn 11th
Southern Alliance Totals   P16 W 7 D 2 L 7 F24 A20 Pts 39

Mounteney A.	Greenwell L.	Batey J.	Young S.	Harwood J.	Galloway T.	Hamilton J.	Scrimgeour D.	Gibson D.
	9							
8	9²							
8¹	9¹							
8¹	9							
8		9						
9								
9								
9¹								
10		9						
10¹	9¹							
10		11						
10	9							
10	9¹	11	5					
10		11¹	5		2			
10		11	5					
10¹		11			2			
10¹		11	5					
10	9	11		5				
9		11	5					
10		11	5					
10¹		11¹	5		4			
10		11	5		4			
10¹		11¹	5					
		11	5					
		s						
		11	5					
			5			9²	11	
		p¹	4					
15	3	3	13	11	3			
6	1	2	3					
6	1	2	2	2	2	1	1	
1	2		1			2		
1	1							
1								

Season 1913/14   Southern League Division 1
Southern Alliance

Date	Venue	Team	Attendance	FA HT	FA FT	Sanderson D.S.	Warner J.	Knight A.E.	Arnold G.	Harwood J.	Reid R.	Hogg J.	Stringfellow F.	James W.	Mounteney A.	Upton T.	Stemp P.	Johnson G.	Dexter C.	Hamilton F.	Walls J.	Abbott S.	Thompson E.	Powell H.	Buddery H.	Shaw F.	Davis	Galloway T.	Heath J.W.	Cummings	Gibson D.	Probert W.	Hall
Sept 3	H	Plymouth A. SL1			0-2	1	2	3		5	6	7	8	9	10	11			4														
Sept 6	A	C. Palace SL1		0-3	1-3	1	2	3	4	5		7	8	9^1	10	11				6													
Sept 8	A	Brentford SA		0-2	1-3				4			7	8	9	10^1	11	2	3					6								1	5		
Sept 13	H	Coventry C. SL1	12000	0-0	0-0	1	2	3	4	5		7	8	9	10					6					11								
Sept 17	H	Southampton SA	3000	2-1	3-1	1	2^1	3		5		7^1			10^1					4	6	8	9		11									
Sept 20	A	Watford SL1		1-0	2-0	1	2	3	6	5		7			10^1					4		8	9^1		11									
Sept 24	A	Southampton SA		0-0	0-1					5	6		8					3		4	7				10			1	9	11	2		
Sept 27	H	Norwich C. SL1		1-0	1-0	1	2	3	6	5		7^1			10					4		8	9		11								
Oct 1	H	Brentford SA	1000	1-0	2-4		2^1		4		6	7	8		10^1					5				9	11			1				3	
Oct 4	A	Gillingham SL1			1-0	1	2	3	6	5		7^1			10	8				4			9		11								
Oct 8	A	Southampton BFC	1000	1-0	1-0	1		3	4		6		8		10^1	7	2			5			9		11								
Oct 11	H	Northampton SL1	6400	1-0	3-0	1	2	3	6	5		7			10	8				4			9^2		11^1								
Oct 15	A	Luton SA		2-2	3-4						6	7^1	8				2	3	5	4				10^2		11		1					
Oct 18	A	Southend Utd. SL1		0-1	2-3	1	2	3	6	5		7^1			10	8				4			9^1		11								
Oct 25	H	Brighton SL1	14000	1-0	1-0	1	2	3	6	5		7			10					4		8	9		11								
Oct 29	H	Luton SA		1-1	1-2		2		4	5	6	7	8	9^1	10			3							11		1						
Nov 1	H	QPR SL1	10694	0-0	1-1		2	3	4	5	6	7	8	9	10^1										11		1						
Nov 8	A	Millwall SL1		2-0	3-1		2		4	5	6	7	8^1		10^1			3						9^1		11		1						
Nov 12	H	Cardiff SA	very small	0-0	2-0						6^1	7	8		10^1		2	3		4				9		11		1						5
Nov 15	H	Exeter C. SL1	12000	2-2	2-2		2		4	5	6	7	8^1		10^1			3						9		11		1						
Nov 22	A	Cardiff C. SL1	15000	2-0	3-1		2^1	3	4	5	6	7	8^1		10^1	9										11		1						
Nov 26	H	Brighton SA	small	0-0	0-1				4				8				2	3					6	7	10	11								5
Nov 29	H	Swindon SL1	20403	0-1	1-1		2	3	4	5	6	7^1	8		10	9									11		1						
Dec 4	A	Newport Co. SA			2-1								p^1											p									p^1
Dec 6	A	Bristol R. SL1	5000	1-1	1-3		2	3	4	5	6	7	8^1		10	9									11		1						
Dec 20	A	West Ham Utd. SL1		2-1	2-3		2	3		5		7		10^2	8	11					4							1						
Dec 25	H	Southampton SL1	14000	1-0	2-0		2	3	6	5		7	8	10	9^2						4					11		1						
Dec 26	A	Southampton SL1	19291	1-3	3-4		2	3	6	5		7^1	8	10^2							4					11		1						
Dec 27	H	C. Palace SL1	16000	0-0	1-1		2	3	6	5		7	8		10^1						4			9		11		1						
Jan 3	A	Coventry C. SL1		1-1	2-2		2	3	6	5		7	8		10^1						4			9		11^1		1						
Jan 10	H	Exeter C. FAC1	19000	0-2	0-4		2	3	6	5		7	8		10						4			9		11		1						
Jan 17	H	Watford SL1		0-0	1-0	1	2	3	6	5			8	10	11						4^1		7	9										
Jan 21	A	Croydon Com. SA		0-0	0-1							6	8	11	10		2	3			4		7					1						5
Jan 24	A	Norwich SL1		0-0	0-0	1		3	6	5			8		10		2				4		7	9		11								
Jan 31	H	Merthyr Town SL1	8000	1-0	5-1			3	6	5					10^2		2				4		7	8^1		11^1		1						
Feb 7	H	Gillingham SL1	6000	0-0	0-0		2		6	5					10			3			4		7	8		11		1						
Feb 11	H	Croydon Com. SA	small	0-0	3-0						6	7	8^1		10		2	3			4	5				11^1		1						
Feb 14	A	Northampton SL1		0-0	0-0		2		6	5		7			10	8		3			4					11		1						
Feb 21	H	Southend Utd. SL1	5117	2-2	4-2		2	3	6	5					10^1						4		7	8^3		11		1						
Feb 25	A	Cardiff C. SA	2000		1-3		2		4		6	7	8		10	11		3				5						1						
Feb 28	A	Brighton SL1		0-1	2-3		2			5				11	10			3			4		7	8				1						
Mar 4	H	Southend Utd. SA			2-0							6		11	10	1	2	3			4		7	8^1									
Mar 11	H	Newport Co. SA	poor	1-0	1-0		2		6						10	1		3			4		7^1	8		11								5
Mar 14	H	Millwall Ath. SL1	6000	1-0	1-0		2	3	6	5				11	10^1						4		7	8				1						
Mar 18	A	Brighton SA		0-3	0-4			3							p		2						s	s				1						
Mar 21	A	Exeter C. SL1		0-1	0-1		2	3	6	5				11	10						4		7	8				1						
Mar 26	A	QPR SL1		0-0	0-1		2	3	6	5				11	10						4		7	8				1						
Mar 28	H	Cardiff C. SL1	12477	0-1	1-1		2	3	6	5			8		10						4		7					1						
Apr 1	A	Southend Utd. SA		0-0	1-3				p						p												1						
Apr 4	A	Swindon SL1		0-3	0-5		2		6	5					10			3			4		7					1						
Apr 10	H	Reading SL1	20000		2-0		2	3	6				8^1		10^1						4	5	7				1						
Apr 11	H	Bristol R. SL1	12000	0-0	1-0		2	3	6				8^1		10	11					4	5	7				1						
Apr 13	H	Reading SL1	13000	0-0	0-0			3	6				8								4	5	7		10		1						
Apr 18	A	Merthyr Town SL1		3-1	3-3		2	3	6				8			11					4	5^1	7		10^1		1						
Apr 22	A	Plymouth A. SL1		0-1	1-2	s	s	s					p^1	s		s	1				s	s	s		s								
Apr 25	H	West Ham Utd. SL1	9000	2-0	5-1		2	3	6			7	8^2		10^2					1	4	5			9^1								

						Sanderson D.S.	Warner J.	Knight A.E.	Arnold G.	Harwood J.	Reid R.	Hogg J.	Stringfellow F.	James W.	Mounteney A.	Upton T.	Stemp P.	Johnson G.	Dexter C.	Hamilton F.	Walls J.	Abbott S.	Thompson E.	Powell H.	Buddery H.	Shaw F.	Davis	Galloway T.	Heath J.W.	Cummings	Gibson D.	Probert W.	Hall
Southern League Appearances						12	34	31	35	32	8	26	21	33	18	9	2	3	6	1	30	5	18	17	3	18		24					
Southern League Goalscorers						1						5	9	16	5	1					1	1		9	2	2							
Southern Alliance Appearances						1	5	2	7	5	7	9	9	7	10	2	2	10	9	1	9	5	6	6	3	8	1	1	9	1	1	2	5
Southern Alliance Goalscorers											1	2	1	4	2						1		1	2	1							1
Cup Appearances						1	1	2	2	1	1	1	2	2	1	2		1			2		1	1		1		1					
Cup Goalscorers													1																				

Southern League Totals   P38 W14 D12 L12 F57 A48 Pts 40 Posn 9th

Turner	Danagher M.	Quinn J.	Matthews H.	Armstrong J.	Dryden W.	Randall A.	Eltringham S.	Gray T.	Turner J.	Gibson A.
	9									
1	9									
		9								
			9							
			9							
			9							
				9^2						
				9						
		9^1								
				9						
				9						
9^1							1			
				9^2						
				9^1	5					
			9							
				9						
	p			s				p		
				9						
				9						
				9^1					11	
	p			p^1		3				
	11		8	9						
	11			9						
				9						
	11			9						
				9^1						
				s						
	11									
	4	1	3	14						1
				6						
1	2	3	1	2	2	1	1	1	1	
1		1		2						

Season 1914/15   Southern League Division 1

Date	Venue	Team	Attendance	HT	FT	Neil J.	Robertson J.	Harwood J.	Tattum B.	Probert W.	Stringfellow F.	Warner J.	Walls J.	Abbott S.	Arnold G.	Thompson E.	Buddery H.	James W.	Metcalfe G.	Potts J.E.	Upton T.	Hogg J.	Robertson W.	Armstrong J.	Hammond	Gray T.	Turner J.	Chesser J.
Sept 2	A	Reading *SL1*			1-1	1		11	3	8^1	2	4	5	6	7	9	10											
Sept 5	H	Watford *SL1*	6423	1-3	2-3	1		11	3	8^1	2	4	5		7	9	10^1	6										
Sept 9	H	Reading *SL1*	small	1-0	1-0	1		11	3	8	2	4	5	6	7	9^1	10											
Sept 12	A	Plymouth A. *SL1*	1500	1-2	2-2	1	10^1	11	3	8^1	2	4	5	6	7	9												
Sept 19	H	West Ham *SL1*	8000	2-0	3-1	1		11	3	8	2	4	5	6	7	9^1	10^2											
Sept 26	A	Norwich C. *SL1*		0-0	0-0	1		11	3	8	2	4	5	6	7	9	10											
Sept 30	A	Croydon Com. *SL1*		1-0	1-0	1		11	3	8	2	4	5	6	7	9	10^1											
Oct 3	H	Gillingham *SL1*	8000	1-0	1-0	1		11		8^1	2	4	5	6	7	9	10		3									
Oct 10	A	Brighton *SL1*	4000	0-0	0-1	1		11	3	8	2	4	5	6	7	9	10											
Oct 17	H	Cardiff C. *SL1*	6887	0-0	0-1	1			3	8		4	5	6	7	9	10			2	11							
Oct 24	A	Exeter C. *SL1*		0-0	1-1	1		5	3	8^1		4		6	7	9	10			2	11							
Oct 31	H	Luton *SL1*	capital	1-0	3-1	1		11	3	8^1		4	5	6	7	9^2	10			2								
Nov 7	A	C. Palace *SL1*		0-0	0-1	1		11	3	8		4	5	6	7	9	10			2								
Nov 14	A	Swindon *SL1*		2-1	3-1	1				8	2	4	5	6	7	9^1	10^2			3			11					
Nov 21	H	Southend Utd. *SL1*	6000	1-0	1-0	1				8	2	4	5	6	7	9	10^1			3			11					
Nov 28	A	QPR *SL1*		2-0	2-1	1				8^2	2	4	5	6	7	9	10			3			11					
Dec 5	H	Millwall *SL1*	6757	0-0	1-1	1				8	2	4	5	6^1	7	9	10			3			11					
Dec 12	A	Bristol R. *SL1*		2-1	3-2	1			3	8^2		4	5	6	7	9^1	10			2				11				
Dec 25	H	Southampton *SL1*	9494	0-0	0-1	s	s			p	s		s	s	p	s				p	p			p			
Dec 26	A	Southampton *SL1*	7000	3-2	3-4	1			3	8^2		4	6		7		10			2		11		9^1				
Jan 2	A	Watford *SL1*	3000	0-0	1-2	1				8		4			7	9^1							11	10				
Jan 9	A	Bradford P.A. *FAC1*	14000	0-0	0-1	1			3	8		4	5	6	7	9	10			2			11					
Jan 16	H	Croydon Com. *SL1*		0-0	1-1	1			3	8		4	5	6	7	9	10^1			2			11					
Jan 23	A	West Ham *SL1*		1-2	3-4	1			3	8^1		4		6	7	9^1	10^1			2			11	5				
Jan 30	H	Plymouth A. *SL1*	5678	2-0	3-1	1		11^1	3	8^1		4	5	6	7	9	10^1			2								
Feb 6	A	Gillingham *SL1*	2000	1-1	1-3	s		11	s	8^1	s	s			7	9				s			10		1			
Feb 13	H	Brighton *SL1*	3099	1-0	2-0	1		11	3	8		4		6	7					2^1			9^1	10				
Feb 20	A	Cardiff C. *SL1*	6000	2-0	2-3	1		11	3	8		4		6	7					2			9^1	10^1				
Feb 27	H	Exeter C. *SL1*	6000	0-0	0-2	1		11		8		4	6		7					2			9				10	3
Mar 6	A	Luton *SL1*		1-0	2-0	1			s	p^1	s		s		s	s	s			p^1	s		s					
Mar 13	H	C. Palace *SL1*	6000	0-0	1-0	1			3	8		4		6		9	10^1			2	7		11					
Mar 20	H	Swindon *SL1*	6000	1-1	1-1	1			3	8		4		6	7	9^1	10			2			11					
Mar 27	A	Southend Utd. *SL1*		1-0	2-0	1			3	8^1		4		6	7	9	10			2	11^1					1		
Apr 2	H	Northampton *SL1*	10220		2-0				3	8		4		6	7^2	9^1	10			2			11			1		
Apr 3	H	QPR *SL1*	5838	1-0	1-1	1			3	8		4		6^1	7	9	10			2			11			1		
Apr 5	A	Northampton *SL1*		0-1	0-1					p													p					
Apr 10	A	Millwall *SL1*		0-1	1-1																						p^1	
Apr 17	H	Bristol R. *SL1*	4121	1-0	3-0	1		5	11	3	8^2			4^1	6	7	9			2							10	
Apr 28	H	Southampton *PC*	1601	2-0	2-0	s		s	s	s		s	s	s	p^1	p^1	s	s		s			s				s	
May 1	H	Norwich C. *SL1*		0-0	0-0	1		5	11	3		4	6	7	9	8				2							10	

						Neil J.	Robertson J.	Harwood J.	Tattum B.	Probert W.	Stringfellow F.	Warner J.	Walls J.	Abbott S.	Arnold G.	Thompson E.	Buddery H.	James W.	Metcalfe G.	Potts J.E.	Upton T.	Hogg J.	Robertson W.	Armstrong J.	Hammond	Gray T.	Turner J.	Chesser J.
Southern League Appearances						31	1	29	20	27	34	13	31	24	12	33	33	29	1	25	8	5	7	5	1	4	6	1
Southern League Goalscorers							1	1		19			2	1		2	10	12		1	1			3			2	
Cup Appearances						1		1	1	1		1		1	1	1	2	2		1	1		1					
Cup Goalscorers																	1	1										

Southern League Totals   P38 W16 D10 L12 F54 A42 Pts 42 Posn 7th

Complete list of POMPEY Directors

From	To	
1898	1912 resigned	John Brickwood
1898	1906 resigned	John Wyatt Peters
1898	1910 resigned	Alfred H. Bone
1898	14/4/1920 resigned	George Lewin Oliver (d. 22/12/34)
1898	1911 resigned	William Wigginton
1899	1900 resigned	Frederick Windrum
1900	1911 resigned	Bernard Murtough
1900	1905 resigned	Richard Bonney
1905	1909 resigned	John Edward Pink
1906	1914 resigned	Henry W. Hume
1906	30/8/1938 resigned	James Poole (d. 27/7/39)
1906	1909 resigned	Harry Dexter Harrison
1909	27/8/1924 resigned	Rev. Edward Bruce Cornford
1909	17/11/1938 resigned	Robert Blyth (d. 7/2/41)
1910	1912 resigned	J.H. Slater
1911	30/6/1937 died	Albert Edward Hooper
1912	Summer 1959 died	Sidney B. Leverett
1913	18/11/1918 died	H.E.D. Hooper
1913	1943 resigned	Henry Pannell
1913	1920 resigned	H. Waterman
1919	25/8/1956 resigned	J. Stephen Cribb (d. 2/2/63)
11/8/1937	4/3/1944 resigned	R.J. Winnicott
11/8/1937	8/5/1950 suspended	Richard Vernon Stokes
9/12/1938	1951 resigned	James Chinneck
1944	1955 resigned	John Privett
1944	1951 resigned	H.J. Hiley Jones
1944	8/5/1950 suspended	Harold S. Wain
1945	1950 resigned	George F. Preston
1950	26/12/1975 resigned	Guy Spriggins
1950		J.H. Sparshatt
1/3/1951	16/2/1982 died	Richard Vernon Stokes
1/3/1951	24/11/1954 died	Harold S. Wain
1952	9/3/1974 died	Dr. I. McLachlan
1955	1977 resigned	J. Dennis P. Collett
1955		A.L. Blake
1958	1982 resigned	W. Wain
1958	26/11/1975 resigned	Arthur R.L. Oliver
1969	28/4/1975 resigned	David J. Sparshatt
1970	22/12/1975 resigned	Edwin W. Reeves
1971	7/2/1976 resigned	F. Peter Faulkner
28/12/1972		Bramwell John Deacon
1972	4/10/1974 resigned	David W. Russell
1974		David K. Deacon
1974	7/5/1975 resigned	John P.N. Brogden
7/2/1976	1976 resigned	Peter Clark
1976		J.R. Parkhouse
6/11/1976		S.W. James Sloan
13/11/1976		Gordon Gauntlett
17/12/1982		Mrs. Joan Deacon

Season 1915/16   South Western Combination

Date	Venue	Team	Attendance	FA HT	FA FT	Gray T.	Potts J.E.	Probert W.	Abbott S.	Harwood J.	Arnold G.	Hogg J.	Caddick J.	Armstrong J.	James W.	Turner J.	Dix J.	Booth	Whittaker F.	Abbott F.	Stevens C.	Little F.	Stringfellow F.	Holmes A.	Gill G.	Miller W.	McKay J.	Smith S. Jr.	Priestley H.	Wardrope A.	Salter R.	Dougherty J.	March
Sept 4	H	Swindon FR	4000	3-0	5-2	1	2	3	4[1]	5	6	7	8[1]	9[1]	10[2]			11															
Sept 11	H	Southampton FR	4000	0-2	2-2	s	s	s		s	s	s		s	p[1]	s	p[1]	s	s	s													
Sept 18	A	Reading FR		1-1	1-2																		p[1]										
Sept 25	H	Bristol C. FR	capital	1-0	4-2	s			s	s	s	s		s	p[1]						p[1]	s	p[2]										
Oct 2	H	Southampton FR		0-0	2-1	1	2	3	4[1]	5	6			7	10					9			8[1]			11							
Oct 9	H	Reading FR	4000	0-2	0-2	1	2	3	4	5	6	7			10					9			8			11							
Oct 16	A	Bristol C. FR		0-2	1-5			p[1]																									
Oct 23	H	Cardiff C. FR	2000	2-2	3-2	2	2	3		5	6			7	10	9[1]			4						1	8[2]	11							
Oct 30	H	Footballers Batt. FR	3000	0-0	0-0	1	2	3	4	5	6			7	10	9							8				11							
Nov 6	A	Luton FR		1-3	1-3									p[1]																			
Nov 13	H	Reading FR		1-0	3-0	s	s		s	s	p[1]	s	s	s	p[1]	p[1]	s										s	s	s				
Nov 20	A	Swindon FR			2-0												p[2]										s						
Nov 27	H	Swindon FR		4-0	6-0	s	s		s	s	s	s		s	p[1]	s			p[1]		p[1]		p[2]				s	s					
Dec 4	A	Reading FR			2-1					p[1]				p[1]																			
Dec 11	H	Luton FR			2-1	s	s		s	s	s			p[1]	p[1]	s			s									s	s			s	
Dec 18	H	Boscombe FR			2-1												p[2]																
Dec 26	H	Southampton FR	2000	0-0	1-1	p								p[1]					p														
Dec 27	A	Southampton FR	good	1-0	1-2	1	2		4	5	6	7		8	10[1]	9											11	3					
Jan 1	H	Swindon FR	large	1-0	2-0	1	2	3	4	5	6	7		9[1]									8[1]										11
Jan 8	A	Newport Co. SWC		1-0	3-1									p[1]																			
Jan 15	H	Portsmouth Dist. FR			8-2	s	s		s	s		p[1]		s	p[2]	p[3]					p[1]		s[1]										
Jan 22	H	Reading FR		2-2	6-3			p[1]				p[1]			p[2]								p[2]										
Jan 29	A	Bristol C. SWC		1-0	1-0																												
Feb 5	H	Southampton FR	3000	2-2	2-2	1	2	3	4	5	6	7[1]		11	9[1]								8										
Feb 12	H	Bristol R. SWC	3000	1-0	3-0		2	3		5	6	7		11[1]	9[2]								8										
Feb 19	H	Newport Co. SWC	2000	1-0	4-0		2		4		6	7		11[1]	10	9[3]											3						
Feb 26	H	Arg.&Suth. Highlanders FR		2-1	3-3																												
Mar 4	H	Bristol C. SWC		2-0	3-0	s	s	s	s	s	s	p[1]		s	s	p[2]							s										
Mar 11	A	Southampton FR		0-3	2-4															p[2]													
Mar 18	A	Bristol R. SWC		1-0	1-2									p[1]																			
Mar 25	H	Cardiff C. SWC		2-0	4-0								p[1]	p[2]																			
Apr 1	A	Swindon SWC			2-1			p[2]																									
Apr 8	H	Southampton FR	good	1-0	7-0	1	2		4	5[1]		7		10[2]									8[3]										
Apr 15	A	Cardiff C. SWC		0-1	2-1									p[1]									p[1]										
Apr 21	H	Southampton SWC	6000	0-1	0-2	1	2	3	9	4	6	7		10									8										
Apr 22	H	Bristol C. FR			2-0									p[2]																			
Apr 24	A	Southampton SWC	5000	0-0	0-3	1	2	9		4		11		10									8				3						
Apr 29	H	Swindon SWC		3-0	6-1								p[1]	p[4]									p[1]										
Friendly Appearances						9	9	7	10	10	9	9	1	9	15	11	2		3	3			12	2	1	1	1	2	1				1
Friendly Goalscorers							4	2	1	4	1	5		15	13	1			1	2			15					2					
South Western Combination Appearances						2	4	3	2	3	5	6		2	7	4							5				2						
South Western Combination Goalscorers								2		1	2	2		7	9								2										

South Western Combination Totals   P12 W9 D0 L3 F29 A11
Friendlies   P26 W15 D5 L6 F70 A41

Salter H.	Porter R.	Priestley F.	Sanderson R.	Starks N.	Carmichael	Jones	Flannigan H.	Middleton F.	Abbott J.	Richardson G.	McGough R.	Lee A.	Wardle A.	Ryman W.	Jones L.	Emerson J.	Rymark W.
10																	
					p^1	p^1											
	s	s	s	s													
						p^1											
							10										
							1	4	10								
							1		8	5							
p^2							p^1										
										s							
							p^1										
									9^1						3	6	
				7			11				5						
												5	6	7			
2				1			2		1						1	1	
2								1	1								
					1	2	2	2	1	2	1	1	1	1	1		
				1	2		1										

Season 1916/17 London Combination

Date	Venue	Team	Attendance	FA HT	FA FT	Middleton F.	Potts E.J.	Probert W.	Abbott S.	Stevens C.	Arnold G.	Stringfellow F.	Turner J.	McBain N.	Collins E.	Upton T.	Wardrope A.	Jones J.M.	Sanderson	Harwood J.	Grey D.	Carr J.	Priestley S.	Pagnum F.	Armstrong J.	Hulme W.	Sanderson D.	Gisborne E.	Shaw F.	Rankin J.	Buddery T.	James W.	N.
Oct 21	H	Arsenal LC	5000	0-0	1-0								p[1]																				
Oct 28	A	Luton LC		1-1	2-2														p[1]										p[1]				
Nov 4	H	Southampton LC	5000	0-1	0-1	1	2	3	8	6				9	10			4	5	7	11												
Nov 11	A	Millwall LC		0-1	0-1		2	3	4	6	8			10		1		5	7	11	9												
Nov 18	A	Watford LC		0-0	0-1		2		4	6	8			10	5	1	7			11	3	9											
Nov 25	H	Fulham LC		1-2	3-4	1	2		4	6				10					5	11[1]	3	9[1]	7	8									
Dec 2	A	Q.P.R. LC		2-1	7-1		3	2	4	8[3]	6									7	11[1]			9[3]	10	1	5						
Dec 9	H	West Ham LC	5000	0-1	1-2		3	2		6	8	10	4						5	11		9	7[1]	1									
Dec 16	A	Tottenham LC		0-0	0-1		3	1	4		6					5		10		11	2		9							7	8			
Dec 23	H	Crystal Palace LC		2-2	2-2		2	3	4	6	10	8[1]	1				9[1]	5		7														11
Dec 25	A	Clapton Orient LC			1-1		2	3	4	6	10						9	5		7											8[1]	11	1
Dec 26	H	Clapton Orient LC	6000	1-0	2-0		2	3	4	6	10[1]						9	5		7												8	11[1]	1

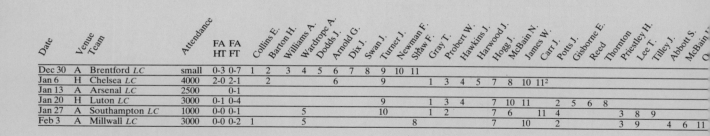

Date	Venue	Team	Attendance	FA HT	FA FT	Collins E.	Barton H.	Williams A.	Wardrope A.	Dodds J.	Arnold G.	Dix J.	Swan J.	Turner J.	Newman F.	Shaw F.	Gray T.	Probert W.	Hawkins J.	Harwood J.	Hogg J.	McBain N.	James W.	Carr J.	Potts J.	Gisborne E.	Reed	Thornton	Priestley H.	Lee T.	Tilley J.	Abbott S.	McBain
Dec 30	A	Brentford LC	small	0-3	0-7	1	2	3	4	5	6	7	8	9	10	11																	
Jan 6	H	Chelsea LC	4000	2-0	2-1	2				6				9			1	3	4	5	7	8	10	11[2]									
Jan 13	A	Arsenal LC	2500		0-1																												
Jan 20	H	Luton LC	3000	0-1	0-4									9			1	3	4		7	10	11	2	5	6	8						
Jan 27	A	Southampton LC	1000	0-0	0-1				5					10			1	2			7	6	11	4					3	8	9		
Feb 3	A	Millwall LC	3000	0-0	0-2	1			5				8				7				10		2						3	9	4	6	11

Date	Venue	Team	Attendance	FA HT	FA FT	Collins E.	Wardrope A.	Hogg J.	McBain N.	James W.	Carr J.	Potts J.	Priestley H.	Stevens L.C.	Simms W.	Lee J.	Gray T.	Probert W.	Mercer J.	Andrews W.	Simms A.	Armstrong J.	Croad J.	Barton J.	Powell P.	Killigan P.	Shaw F.	Simpson J.	Pagnum F.	Harwood J.	Pettifer J.	Turner J.	O'Hara
Feb 10	H	Watford LC		1-0	3-0	1	5	7	6[1]	10	11	2	3	4	8[1]	9[1]																	
Feb 17	H	Tottenham LC	4000	1-1	2-4		7[1]			6	11		3				1	2	4	5		8	9	10[1]									
Feb 24	A	Watford LC		0-6	0-9																												
Mar 3	H	Southampton LC	3000	0-0	1-0	1			11[1]								3	4				9			2	5	6	7	8	10			
Mar 10	A	Clapton Orient LC		1-2	1-6				p[1]																								
Mar 17	H	West Ham LC	4000	1-3	2-5		7	10									1	3			11[2]			2				8	4	5	6	9	

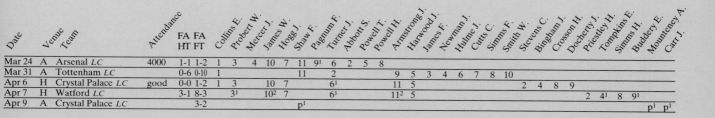

Date	Venue	Team	Attendance	FA HT	FA FT	Collins E.	Probert W.	Mercer J.	James W.	Hogg J.	Shaw F.	Pagnum F.	Turner J.	Abbott S.	Powell T.	Powell H.	Armstrong J.	Harwood J.	James F.	Newman J.	Hulme J.	Cutts C.	Simms F.	Smith W.	Stevens C.	Bingham J.	Crosson H.	Docherty J.	Priestley H.	Tompkins E.	Simms H.	Buddery E.	Mounteney A.	Carr J.
Mar 24	A	Arsenal LC	4000	1-1	1-2	1	3	4	10	7	11	9^1	6	2	5	8																		
Mar 31	A	Tottenham LC		0-6	0-10	1			11					2			9	5	3	4	6	7	8	10										
Apr 6	H	Crystal Palace LC	good	0-0	1-2	1	3		10	7		6^1					11	5								2	4	8	9						
Apr 7	H	Watford LC		3-1	8-3	3^1			10^2	7		6^1					11^2	5												2	4^1	8	9^1	
Apr 9	A	Crystal Palace LC			3-2						p^1																					p^1	p^1	

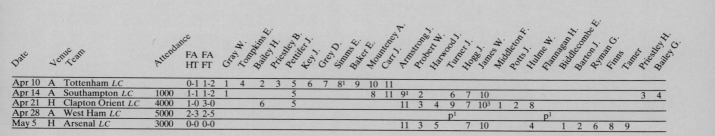

Date	Venue	Team	Attendance	FA HT	FA FT	Gray W.	Tompkins E.	Bailey H.	Priestley B.	Pettifer J.	Key J.	Grey D.	Simms E.	Baker E.	Mounteney A.	Carr J.	Armstrong J.	Probert W.	Harwood J.	Turner J.	Hogg J.	James W.	Middleton F.	Potts J.	Hulme W.	Flannagan H.	Biddlecombe E.	Barton J.	Ryman G.	Finns	Tamer	Priestley H.	Bailey G.
Apr 10	A	Tottenham LC		0-1	1-2	1	4	2	3	5	6	7	8^1	9	10	11																	
Apr 14	A	Southampton LC	1000	1-1	1-2	1				5					8	11	9^1	2		6	7	10										3	4
Apr 21	H	Clapton Orient LC	4000	1-0	3-0			6		5						11	3	4	9	7		10^3	1	2	8								
Apr 28	A	West Ham LC	5000	2-3	2-5												p^1									p^1							
May 5	H	Arsenal LC	3000	0-0	0-0											11	3	5		7	10				4		1	2	6	8	9		

Own goal: Fulham (Nov 25)

London Combination Totals   P34 W9 D4 L21 F50 A84

London Combination Appearances—Middleton F. 3; Potts J.E. 12; Probert W. 20; Abbott S. 12; Stevens C. 2; Arnold G. 11; Stringfellow F. 4; Turner J. 20; McBain N. 11; Collins E. 11; Upton T. 1; Wardrope A. 4; Dix J. 1; Jones J.M. 3; Sanderson 1; Harwood J. 15; Grey D. 5; Carr J. 18; Priestley S. 3; Pagnum F. 7; Armstrong J. 19; Hulme W. 4; Sanderson D. 2; Gisborne E. 2; Shaw F. 9; Rankin J. 1; Buddery T. 2; James W. 18; Neal J. 2; Barton H. 2; Williams A. 1; Dodds J. 1; Swan J. 1; Newman F. 1; Gray T. 5; Hawkins J. 2; Hogg J. 13; Reed 1; Thornton 1; Priestley H. 4; Lee T. 2; Tilley J. 1; McBain H. 1; Quinn J. 1; Stevens L.C. 1; Simms W. 1; Lee J. 1; Mercer J. 3; Andrews W. 2; Simms A. 1; Croad J. 2; Barton J. 3; Powell P. 1; Killigan P. 1; Simpson J. 1; Pettifer J. 4; O'Hara J. 1; Powell T. 1; Powell H. 1; James F. 1; Newman J. 1; Hulme J. 1; Cutts C. 1; Simms F. 1; Smith W. 1; Bingham J. 1; Mounteney A. 3; Buddery E. 1; Tompkins E. 2; Crosson H. 1; Docherty J. 1; Simms H. 1; Gray W. 2; Bailey H. 2; Priestley B. 1; Key J. 1; Simms E. 1; Baker E. 1; Flannagan H. 1; Biddlecombe E. 1; Ryman G. 1; Finns 1; Tamer 1; Bailey G. 1.

London Combination Goals   —Probert W. 1; Stringfellow F. 3; Turner J. 5; McBain N. 2; Jones J.M. 1; Grey D. 1; Carr J. 7; Pagnum F. 2; Armstrong J. 9; Shaw F. 2; Buddery T. 1; James W. 6; Hogg J. 1; Simms W. 1; Lee J. 1; Croad J. 1; Mounteney A. 1; Buddery E. 1; Tompkins E. 1; Simms E. 1; Flannagan H. 1.

Season 1917/18   South Hants War League

Date	Venue	Team	Attendance	FA HT	FA FT	Middleton F.	Probert W.	Rhodes	Arnold G.	Green A.	Ryman G.	Brooks J.	Sims	Croal	Moore	Rothwell	Dunbar	Harwood J.	Goodwin	Spink T.	Hogg J.	Quinn J.	Collins E.	Priestley H.	Scott	Danagher M.	Harvey C.	Dix J.	Mercer A.	Smith S. Jr.	Hughes T.	Armstrong	Ashe
Sept 1	A	Southampton *FR*	3000	1-2	2-3	1	2¹	3	4	5	6	7	8	9¹	10	11																	
Sept 8	H	Southampton *FR*		2-0	4-4	1	3		6						10²	11	2	4	5	7	8¹	9¹											
Sept 15	H	Reading *FR*	fair	2-0	4-1		2¹		4	10¹	6							5		7	11²		1	3		8	9						
Sept 22	H	Swindon *FR*	2000	3-0	6-0		2		4		6							5		7¹	8²		1	3		9	10³	11					
Sept 29	H	Thornycrofts Woolston *FR*	few	2-0	2-2		2		4		6							5		7	8¹		1	3		9	10¹	11					
Oct 6	H	Bristol City *FR*		2-0	4-0		2		9¹		6							5		7			1	3		8	11²	4	10¹				
Oct 13	H	Highlanders *FR*		2-0	3-0	1	2		4		6	8						5		7¹				3		11¹			10¹		9		
Oct 20	H	London Scottish *FR*		3-0	8-0	1	2		4¹									5		7	8¹			3						6¹	9³	10²	11
Oct 27	H	Royal Engineers *FR*		1-0	1-0		2		8		6							4		7			1	3¹		9							
Nov 3	H	Southampton *FR*	1200	0-0	3-0		2		4¹		6							5		7			1	3		8							
Nov 10	A	Thornycrofts Woolston *FR*	1500	1-3	3-3		2		4		6							5		7	8		1	3		10							
Nov 17	H	Royal Flying Corps *FR*	small	1-1	3-1	1	2		4		6							5		8¹	7			3		10							
Nov 24	H	Special School of Flying *FR*	small	1-0	5-0		2		4		6							5		7				3		8							
Dec 1	H	Thornycrofts Woolston *FR*		1-2	4-2		2		4		6							5		7			1	3		8¹							
Dec 8	H	RN Torpedo Depot *FR*	small	2-0	5-0	1	2		4¹		6							5						3		7¹							
Dec 15	H	Royal Garrison Art. *FR*	small	4-1	4-1	1			4		6							5		7	11			3		8¹							
Dec 25	H	Southampton *FR*			1-1																												
Dec 26	A	Southampton *FR*	3000	1-2	3-2		2		4														1	3		8¹							
Jan 5	H	Spec. Sch. of Flying *SHWL*	fair	4-0	9-0	1	2		4¹									5		7	11					8³							
Jan 12	H	Royal Garrison Art. *SHWL*	fair	2-1	2-1	1			4									5			11			3		8							
Jan 19	A	Th'crofts Woolston *SHWL*	large	0-0	3-0		2		4									5		7				3		8¹							
Jan 26	A	RN Torpedo Depot *SHWL*	small	2-0	4-0		2		4¹											7			1	3		8							
Feb 2	A	Spec. Sch. of Flying *SHWL*			4-1																				p¹								
Feb 16	A	Harland & Wolfe *SHWL*	good	0-1	3-1	1	2		4		6													3		10							
Mar 2	H	Royal Garrison Art. *FR*		1-0	4-0	1	2		4¹		6							5		7¹				3		8							
Mar 9	H	Harland & Wolfe *SHWL*	large	0-0	1-0		2		4		6							5		7			1	3		8							
Mar 16	H	Royal Marine Band *FR*		0-0	3-0				p¹																								
Mar 23	H	Th'crofts Woolston *SHWL*	1500	0-0	0-2	1	2		4		6									7				3		8							
Mar 29	H	Southampton *SHWL*	4000	2-1	4-2	1			4		6									7	11			3		8							
Mar 30	A	Cowes *SHWL*			5-0																				p¹								
Apr 1	A	Southampton *SHWL*			4-0				4											7¹	11		1	3									
Apr 6	H	Cowes *SHWL*	fair	6-0	12-0																												
Apr 13	H	RN Torpedo Depot *SHWL*		2-0	4-0					p¹										p¹													
Apr 20	A	Southampton *FR*	1000	1-0	3-2				4											7				3									
Apr 27	H	Rest of the League *SHWL*		2-1	6-5																												
South Hants War League Appearances						5	6		9		5							4		9	4		3	8		9							
South Hants War League Goalscorers							2		1											2	1					5							
Friendly Appearances						9	17	1	19	4	13	2	1	1	2	2	1	16	1	8	15	2	9	17	1	10	4	3	3	1	4	1	1
Friendly Goalscorers							2		6	1				1	2					2	7	3		1		4	5	2	2	1	3	2	

Own goals: Spec. Sch. of Flying (Nov 24) (Jan 5), Southampton (Mar 29)

Jan 19: Pompey's keeper Collins missed the train, McKay in goal!

Stemp F.	Kean F.W.	Crout	Hughes E.	Turner J.	Ashton E.	Green E.	McKay J.	Jameson	Whalley J.	Brooks H.	James W.E.	Wright H.	Emery	Tout	Coles	Howard J.	Shaw F.	Farwood	Hobbs J.	Stringfellow F.	Gill L.	Barton J.	Trapp C.S.	Matthews	Woodford S.	Miller J.	Jewet A.	Hollingsworth H.	Woolworth	Cummins	"Smith"
5	10	11																													
			9^1	10^1	11																										
				9^2		11^1																									
				9^2		11																									
				9^3		11^1	10																								
				9^2		11^1	10																								
				9^2		11	10^1	8																							
				9^2		2	10^1																								
																								p^1							
				9^1	6	10^1																							5	11	7
				9^3	6^1					3	10																				
				9^1	10^1							7	2	6																	
				11	1	10^1							6		9^1																
				9^1	6	10^1									5	11^1															
				p^3																											
				9^2		11^1										5	7	8													
				9	10^2	11																									
				9	10	11^1																									
				p^1																	p^1										
				9			10									5					11										
				9^2			10^1									5					2										
					p^1		p^1			p^2																					
				6			10		8^3							5					2								9		
			p^5		p^1				p^3							p^2															
			p^2				p^1																								
							10		8^2												11	1	9^1	2	5	6					
							p^2		p^2																						
				11	7	9			6	1	1	1	2	1	1	5	1	1	1	1	1	2		1							
				19	4	7	12									1	2	1					2								
1	1	1	1	10	1	8	6	1	2													2	1	1	1	1	1	2	1	1	1
			1	16	5	2	3															1		1	1						

Season 1918/19   South Hants War League

Date	Venue	Team	Attendance	FA HT	FA FT	Collins E.	Probert W.	Priestley H.	Morris A.	Harwood J.	Evans J.	Armstrong J.	Turner J.	McKay J.	Gill L.	Prince J.	Dyer	Green E.	Orsmond R.	Hogg J.	Quinn J.	James W.	Hollings	Green J.	Middleton F.	Arnold G.	Dowling	Porter R.	Harris	Stringfellow F.	Kimpton	Meader	Gill F.
Sept 7	H	Southampton *FR*	2000	1-1	5-2	1	2	3	4	5	7^1	8	9^3	10	11^1								6										
Sept 14	A	Southampton *FR*	small	1-1	1-1	1	2	3			8	9^1	10	11	4			7															
Sept 21	H	Harland & Wolfe *SHWL*	large	2-0	4-0	1	6	2	5^2		9^1	8^1	7					3	4	10	11											
Oct 5	H	Cowes *SHWL*		4-0	7-1						p^2	p^1							p^1	p^2	p^1												
Oct 12	A	Th'crofts Woolston *SHWL*	large	1-1	2-2	1	2	3		5		9^2	10	11				7		8	4	6											
Oct 19	H	Th'crofts Woolston *SHWL*		0-1	2-3		2	3		5		9	10	11				7^1					6	1	4^1	8							
Oct 26	A	Cowes *SHWL*		0-2	1-3																												
Nov 2	H	RAF *FR*	capital	2-0	3-2	1		3				9^2	10^1	11				7					6	5	2	4	8						
Nov 9	A	Harland & Wolfe *SHWL*		4-2	4-3																												
Nov 16	H	RN Depot C. Palace *FR*	splendid	0-4	0-6	1	2	3	6			9	10					7					11	4					5	8		
Nov 23	H	Harland & Wolfe *SHWL*	excellent	1-0	2-0		2	8	4			9	10^2	11				7					6			3							1
Nov 30	H	Canadians *FR*	good	1-1	1-1		2	3	4^1	7		9	8	11									6										1
Dec 7	H	Royal Engineers *FR*	fair	4-0	11-0		2	3	4			9^5	11						7^1				6							8^2			1
Dec 14	H	RAF Roehampton *FR*	fairly large	2-1	4-2		2	3	4			9^4	11						7				10			6				8			1
Dec 21	H	Th'crofts Woolston *FR*	2000	2-0	4-1		2	3	p			9^2	11^1						7											8^1			
Dec 25	H	Southampton *SHWL*	5500	2-0	5-1		2	3	5^1			9	11					7		10^2					4	6				8^2			
Dec 26	A	Southampton *SHWL*	good	2-2	6-3		p^1					p^1							p^1														p^3
Dec 28	H	Cowes *SHWL*		3-0	4-2		2	3	5			11	9^2	10			6	7							4					8^2			
Jan 4	H	5th Cavalry Regt. *FR*	fair	2-0	4-1		2	3	5^1			11	9^2				11	7^1							4					8			1
Jan 11	H	Harland & Wolfe *SHWL*	2500	4-2	4-3		2	3	5			9^2						7		10^1					4	11				8^1			
Jan 18	H	Th'crofts Woolston *FR*	5000	2-0	3-0		2	3				9^3						7												8			
Jan 25	H	No.1 SARB *FR*	3000	1-1	2-2	1	2	3	5			9^1	11					7		10					4	6				8^1			
Feb 1	A	Th'crofts Woolston *SHWL*	fairly large	1-2	3-3		2	3	5			9		1				7		10^1					4					8^2			
Feb 8	H	RMLI Gosport *HVC1*	4000	0-1	3-2	1	2	3	5			9^2						7	10^1						4					8			
Feb 15	H	Th'crofts Woolston *SHWL*	4–5000	4-0	10-2		2	3	5^1			9^5	11					7	10^2											8^2			
Feb 22	H	No.1 SARB *FR*		1-1	3-1		p		p			11	9^2	s				7												8^1			
Feb 29	H	Swindon *FR*	good	3-0	5-0		2	3	5			11^2	9^1	4				7	10^2											8			
Mar 8	A	Harland & Wolfe *SHWL*		0-1	0-2		s	s	s			9						7	s											8			
Mar 15	H	RMA Eastney *HVC2*	fair	1-0	3-0		2	3	5			11	9^1	6				7	10^1							s				8^1			
Mar 22	H	Reading *FR*		2-1	3-1			3				11^1	9^1					7	s											8^1			
Mar 29	A	Harland & Wolfe *HVC SF*		1-2	1-4		2	3	5			11	9	s			s	7	s							4				8^1			
Apr 2	H	RMLI *FR*	2000	1-0	2-0		3		4			9^2		6				7	8														
Apr 5	H	RFA Salisbury Plain *FR*	fairly large	2-0	5-0		2	3	5			9^3	4	6				7	10											8^2			
Apr 9	H	RMA Eastney *FR*	1000	2-0	3-0			3	4			8^1	6					7	10^1														
Apr 12	H	Harland & Wolfe *FR*		2-1	5-1		s	s	s			9^3	8^1	s				7^1	11	10										s			
Apr 18	H	Southampton *SHWL*	8000	1-0	1-1		2	3	5			10	11	6				7^1	9											8			
Apr 19	H	Brighton *FR*	5000	4-0	6-0		2	3	5			9		6				7	10^3											8^3			
Apr 21	A	Southampton *SHWL*	fair	1-4	1-9		2		5			7	9	6					10											8^1			
Apr 26	A	Cowes *SHWL*		1-1	2-1				4										10														
Apr 30	H	RAF Anti Air Brig *FR*	1200	4-0	6-1				4^1			9^2	6^1	11					10^2														
July 26	H	Southampton *FR*	3–4000	2-1	5-3		2		5			9^2							10^1											8^2			

						Collins E.	Probert W.	Priestley H.	Morris A.	Harwood J.	Evans J.	Armstrong J.	Turner J.	McKay J.	Gill L.	Prince J.	Dyer	Green E.	Orsmond R.	Hogg J.	Quinn J.	James W.	Hollings	Green J.	Middleton F.	Arnold G.	Dowling	Porter R.	Harris	Stringfellow F.	Kimpton	Meader	Gill F.
South Hants War League Appearances						2	11	11	12	3		13	11	5	1	2	1	12	3	6	1	5	1	5	1	3				9			2
South Hants War League Goalscorers							1		4			13	5	1				3	5	3	2	1			5	1				3			13
Friendly Appearances						5	16	16	1	15	3	19	15	5	1	1		17	1	8		7		6	3	1		13			1	1	4
Friendly Goalscorers							3	1	11	33	3	1						3	9										13				
Cup Appearances						1	3	3				2	3	1				3	2							1				3			
Cup Goalscorers												3							2											2			

South Hants War League Totals   P17 W10 D3 L4 F58 A39

Feb 1: Pompey goalkeeper did not turn up, so McKay played in goal.

Stent	Thompson R.	Thompson L.	Trapp C.S.	Hollingworth H.	Wright H.	Hamilton A.	Craig C.	Biddlecombe E.	Powell A.	Bundy	Wynne	Wright	Crago	Smith S. Jr.	Page D.E.	Rutledge B.	Timpson S.	Brownlee R.	Garnett	Hanaway	Stevens	Parker	Simms	Smith G.	Floyd R.F.	Riddle A.	McKinnon	Brown T.H.	Cooper J.	Green H.
																													5	6
5																														
	5	10																												
	5	10[3]																												
	5																													
			1																											
			1																											
		10		6																										
	6																													
					11	6																								
					11		6																							
						4	6	1																						
				p					4																					
				6				1																						
				s		s		1																						
		1				4																								
		1	s																											
	s	s				s																								
		10								1	2	5	11																	
		1												11																
										1	2			11	5	9[1]														
	s	s								s				s	5															
		1				4																								
						4										1	11													
						4					3					1	11													
													11[1]																	
																		1	2	3	7	8	5							
	4																			3					1	7	6	11		
1	1		3		1	4	1	2			1			1		1	1													
															1															
4	4	2	3		1		1	1	2	2	1	1	2	2	1	1	1	1	1	2	1	1	1	1	1	1	1	1	1	1
															1															
			1			1	1	1																						

Season 1919/20   Southern League Division 1

Date	Venue	Team	Attendance	FA HT	FA FT	Robson E.	Watson D.	Priestley H.	Thompson E.	Warden A.	Armstrong J.	Chapman G.W.	Buddery H.	Probert W.	Knight A.E.	Arnold G.	Harwood J.	Hunter G.	Hogg J.	Stringfellow F.	Turner J.	James W.	Brown T.H.	Smelt J.W.	Newton T.	Taylor W.	Crutchley	Wilson W.	Taylor E.	Abbott S.	Youtman B.A.	Potts J.	Frampton
Aug 30	A	Southend	5–6000	2-0	2-0	1						2	3	4	5	6	7	8¹	9	10¹	11												
Sept 3	H	Crystal Palace	12000	0-0	0-0	1						2	3	4	5	6	7	8	9	10	11												
Sept 6	H	Norwich City		0-0	3-0	1			10			2	3	4	5	6	7	8²	9¹	11													
Sept 10	A	Crystal Palace		0-1	1-2	1			4		10	2	3		6	7	8¹	9	11														
Sept 13	A	Brentford		1-0	2-0	1		7	9¹		10¹	2	3	4	5	6	8		11														
Sept 20	H	Merthyr Town	12000	3-2	4-2	1		7	9²		10	2	3	4	5	6	8²		11														
Sept 24	H	Brighton		2-0	3-0	1		7	9¹		10¹	2	3	4	5	6	8¹		11														
Sept 27	A	Plymouth A.	13000	0-1	2-1	1		7	9¹		10	2	3		5	4	8	6	11¹														
Oct 4	H	Bristol Rovers	16000	0-0	0-0	1		7	9		10	2	3	4	5		8	6	11														
Oct 8	H	Brighton	10000	0-0	0-0			7	4		9	10	2	3		5	8	6	11		1												
Oct 11	A	Reading		0-1	1-2		3	7	4		9	10¹	2		5	8	6	11		1													
Oct 18	H	Southampton	20000	1-0	5-1	1			4		9²	10	2	3		5	7²	8	6	11¹			1										
Oct 25	A	Luton		0-1	0-2		3		4		9	10	2		5	7	8	6	11		1												
Nov 1	H	Gillingham	10000	3-0	4-0	1			4		9¹	10²	2	3		5	7	8	6	11¹													
Nov 8	H	Swansea T.	11000	0-0	0-0	1		7	9		10	2	3		5	8	6	11				4											
Nov 15	H	Exeter	9–10000	1-0	2-0	1	3	7	9		10	2		4	8¹	6¹	11					5											
Nov 22	A	Cardiff City	16000	1-0	1-0	1		4	10		9	2	3		5	7	8	6	11¹														
Nov 29	H	Q.P.R.	16–17000	2-0	4-2			4	10¹		9	2	3		5	7¹	8	6	11²		1												
Dec 6	A	Swindon		0-0	0-0		3	4	10¹		9	2		5	7	8¹	6¹	11															
Dec 13	H	Millwall	14000	0-1	3-2	1		4	10¹		2	3		5	7	8²	6	11										9					
Dec 25	A	Watford		0-0	1-0	1		7	10		9¹	2	3		5	8	6	11										4					
Dec 26	H	Watford	23791	1-2	1-2	1		7	10		9¹	2	3		5	8	6	11										4					
Dec 27	H	Newport Co.	14000	3-0	3-1	1		4	10¹		9¹	2	3		5	7	8	6	11														
Jan 3	H	Southend	10000	0-1	0-1	1		7	10		9	2	3		5	8	6	11										4					
Jan 10	A	Bradford C. *FACI†*	12000	2-1	2-2	1		4	10		9	2	3		5	7	8¹	6¹	11														
Jan 17	A	Bradford C. *FACI*	30000	0-1	0-2	1			10		9	2	3		5	7	8	6	11									4					
Jan 24	H	Brentford	14000	3-0	3-0	1		4	9		10²	2	3		5	7	8¹	6	11														
Jan 31	A	Merthyr Town	6000	1-0	2-0	1		4	10		9	2	3		5	7	8²	6	11														
Feb 7	H	Plymouth A.	18000+	1-0	1-1	1		4	10		9¹	2	3		5	7	8	6	11														
Feb 14	A	Bristol Rovers	14000	3-0	3-0	1			10		9¹	2	3		5	7	8²	6	11				4										
Feb 21	H	Reading	15000	2-0	2-0	1			10			2	3		5	7	8¹	6	11									9¹	4				
Feb 28	A	Southampton	18000	0-0	0-0	1					10	9	2	3		5	7	8	6	11									4				
Mar 6	H	Luton	13629	1-1	1-1	1					9	2	3		5	7	8	6	10¹									4	11				
Mar 13	A	Gillingham		0-0	0-0	1		4	9		2	3		5	7	8	6	10										11					
Mar 20	H	Swansea T.	16031	2-0	2-0	1		4	10		2	3		5	7¹	8	9¹	6	11									6	11				
Mar 27	A	Exeter		0-0	0-2	1			10		2	3		5	7	8	9	6	11									6	11				
Apr 2	H	Northampton	16245	1-0	6-0	1		4	9²		10¹	2	3		7¹	8	6	11¹										5¹					
Apr 3	H	Cardiff City	24606	0-0	0-0	1		4	9		3	7	8	6	11		10						5	2									
Apr 6	A	Northampton	10000	0-0	1-0	1		4	9		3	5	7	8¹	6	11					10		5	2									
Apr 8	A	Norwich	4000	1-0	1-1	1			11		10	2	3		5	7	8	6	9¹									4					
Apr 10	A	Q.P.R.		1-0	1-1	1					10	2	3		5	8¹	11	9										4					
Apr 17	H	Swindon	18–20000	1-1	4-1	1		4	10²		9	2	3		5	7	8	6²	11														
Apr 24	A	Millwall	25000+	1-0	1-1	1		4	10		9¹	2	3		5	7	8	6	11									11					
May 1	A	Newport Co.	12000	0-1	0-1	1		4	10		9	3		5	7	8	6	11				2						11	2				
May 15	A	Southampton *BFC*	7000	0-0	0-2				4			3		5	7	8	6	9	11		2							9	11	2	12	10	

						Robson E.	Watson D.	Priestley H.	Thompson E.	Warden A.	Armstrong J.	Chapman G.W.	Buddery H.	Probert W.	Knight A.E.	Arnold G.	Harwood J.	Hunter G.	Hogg J.	Stringfellow F.	Turner J.	James W.	Brown T.H.	Smelt J.W.	Newton T.	Taylor W.	Crutchley	Wilson W.	Taylor E.	Abbott S.	Youtman B.A.	Potts J.	Frampton
Southern League Appearances						37	2	2	32	2	34	1	34	42	35	7	40	8	29	42	38	30	5	8	2	1	1	1	2	13	7	3	
Southern League Goalscorers													15	15				5		20	6	7		1	2					1	1		
Cup Appearances						2			2		2		2	3	2		3		3	3	3	2							2	1	1	1*	1
Cup Goalscorers																				1	1												

Southern League Totals   P42 W23 D12 L7 F73 A27 Pts 58 Posn 1st

† abandoned after 63 mins, ground unfit
* appearance as substitute, Probert injured, Frampton appearance as substitute with Saints permission

Season 1920/21   Division 3

Date	Venue	Team	Attendance	FA HT	FA FT	Robson E. R.	Probert W.	Knight A. E.	Buddery H.	Harwood J.	Turner J.	Thompson E.	Stringfellow F.	Armstrong J.	James W.	Youtman B. A.	Newton T.	Frampton H. J.	Cumming J.	Abbott S.	Hogg J. A.	Mackie J.	Reid J.	Beedie W.	Potts J.	Cold D.	Brown J. B.	Martin J.	Smelt J. W.	Watson D.	Lewry W. G.	Cherrett P.	Leavey H. J.	Philpin R.
Aug 28	H	Swansea	20232		3-0	1	2			5	6	7	8¹		10¹				4			9¹	11	3										
Aug 30	A	Luton		0-1	2-2	1	2			5	6	7	8¹		10				4			9¹	11	3										
Sept 4	A	Swansea	14000	0-0	0-0	1	2		9	5	6	7	8				2	11	4			9	11	3										
Sept 8	H	Luton	14000		3-0	1	2	3		5	6	7	8²	9	10¹	11			4																
Sept 11	A	Southampton	18000	0-2	0-2	1	2	3	9	5	6	7	8		10				4			11												
Sept 15	A	Gillingham	8000	1-1	1-1	1	3	4	10		6	7	8¹		11	2	5					9												
Sept 18	H	Southampton	20585	0-1	0-1	1	3	4	10		6	7	8		11	2	5					9												
Sept 25	H	Millwall	16000	0-0	0-0	1	2	3		5	6		8	10	11				4	7		9												
Oct 2	A	Millwall		0-0	0-1	1	2	3		5	6		8		11				4	7	10	9												
Oct 9	A	Northampton		0-0	0-1	1	2	3		5	10	4	8		11			9	6	7													
Oct 16	H	Northampton	15000	1-0	2-0	1	2	3	9	5	6	4	8¹	10	11¹				7															
Oct 23	A	Newport Co		0-1	0-1	1	2	3	9	5	6	4	8	10	11											7							
Oct 30	A	Newport Co	13679	0-1	0-2		2	3		5	6	4	8	10	11	1				9	7												
Nov 6	A	Southend		1-1	1-2	1	2	3	4		5			10	9			6¹	7	8		11												
Nov 13	H	Southend	13729	2-0	3-0	1	2	3			5¹			10	6			4¹	7	8		11	9¹												
Nov 27	H	Gillingham	14718	1-0	2-2	1	2	3			5			10¹	6			4¹	7	8		11	9												
Dec 11	H	Merthyr Town	12719	0-0	0-0	1	2	3			7			10	6			4		8		11	9	5										
Dec 18	H	Swindon Town	11111	0-0	1-1	1	2	3			6	7	8		10			4		11¹			9	5										
Dec 25	A	Watford			2-3	1	2	3	10		6	7	8		11			4	7				9²	5										
Dec 27	H	Watford	25173	1-0	1-0	1	2	3	10		6		8		11			7¹				9	4	5										
Jan 1	A	Swindon Town		1-4	2-5	1	2		10		6		8¹		11			7¹				3	9	4	5									
Jan 8	A	South Shields FAC1	16000	0-1	0-3	1	2		10		6	4	8		11			7				3	9	5										
Jan 15	H	Reading	14160	0-0	2-2	1	2				6¹	4	8¹	10	11			7				3	9	5										
Jan 22	A	Reading	Large	0-1	0-1	1	2	3			4	8	9					6	7			11				5	10						
Feb 5	H	Plymouth	12357	0-1	1-1	1	2	3	9		5	8		6¹	7							11				4		10						
Feb 12	H	Bristol Rov	13966	1-0	1-0	1	2	3			5	8¹		6	7							11				4		10	9					
Feb 19	A	Bristol Rov	12000	1-0	2-2	1	2	3		5		7	8¹		6							11				4		10¹	9					
Feb 21	A	Merthyr Town	12000	1-1	1-2	1	2			5		7	8		6							11	3			4		10	9¹				
Feb 26	H	Brentford	13645	0-0	0-2	1	2	3		5		7	8		6							11				4		10	9				
Mar 5	A	Brentford		2-0	2-1	1	2	3	9	5	6¹	7	8	11¹												4		10					
Mar 12	H	Norwich	12128	0-1	2-1	1	2	3		5	6	7	8									11				4					9²	10	
Mar 19	A	Norwich		1-1	2-2	1	2			5		7	8¹					3				11				4	6					9¹	10	
Mar 25	H	Exeter City	19701	1-1	2-1	1	2	3		5		7	8									11				4	6					9²	10	
Mar 26	A	Crystal Palace	18000		0-3	1	2			5		7						3				11				4	6		8		9		10	
Mar 28	A	Exeter City	10000	0-0	0-0	1	2			5		7	8					3				11				4	6				9		10	
Apr 2	H	Crystal Palace	18353	0-0	0-0	1	2	3		5		7	8									11				4	6				9		10	
Apr 9	A	Brighton		0-1	0-3	1	2	3		5		7	8									11				4	6				9		10	
Apr 13	A	Plymouth	11000	0-1	0-2	1	2		9	5		7	8					3								4	6				10		11	
Apr 16	H	Brighton	13599		0-1	1	2	3	9	5	10¹	7	8¹						4								6¹						11	
Apr 23	A	Grimsby	10000	0-0	3-0	1	2		9¹	5		7	8¹					3								4	6				10¹		11	
Apr 30	A	Grimsby	13697	1-1	2-1	1	2		9¹	5¹		7	8					3								4	6				10		11	
May 2	A	Q.P.R.		0-0	0-0	1	2		9	5			8					3	7							4	6				10		11	
May 7	H	Q.P.R.	14933	0-0	0-0	1	2		9	5		7	8					3								4	6				10		11	
May 11	H	Southampton PBC	6740	0-0	1-0	1	2		9¹		6		8					3				7				4	5				10			11
League Appearances						41	42	28	17	29	22	36	37	13	22	1	1	3	8	23	15	6	7	21	5	7	24	16	1	13	4	7	13	
League Goalscorers									2	1	2	1	13	2	3				1	3	2			2	1		3			1	2	1	5	
FA Cup Appearances						1	1		1		1	1	1		1			1				1		1	1		1							

Total League Division 3   P42 W12 D15 L15 F46 A48 Pts 39 Posn 12th

Season 1921/22   Division 3

Date	Venue	Team	Attendance	FA HT	FA FT	Robson E.R.	Probert W.	Abbott S.W.	Robinson J.W.	Harwood J.	Martin J.	Cringan R.	Stringfellow F.	Cherrett P.	Watson D.	Beedie W.	Newton T.	Cooper C.R.	Knight A.E.	Wilson J.R.	Maitland R.	Turner J.	Blyth R.	Hoten R.V.	Bishop R.	Buddery H.	Brown J.B.	Kennedy J.	Mackie J.	Edwards M.W.	Hancox T.
Aug 27	A	Aberdare		0-0	0-0	1	2	4	5	6	7		8	9	10	11	3														
Aug 31	H	Bristol Rov	15050	1-0	1-0	1	2	4	5		6		8	9¹		11	3						10		7						
Sept 3	H	Aberdare	17318	2-0	2-2	1	2	4			6		8	9¹		11	3		5				10¹		7						
Sept 7	A	Bristol Rov		1-1	1-1	1	2	3	5		6	7		9¹		11			4				10		8						
Sept 10	A	Exeter		0-1	4-1	1	2	3		6¹			8¹			11			4	5			10¹		7				9¹		
Sept 17	H	Exeter	10466	0-0	2-0	1	2	3		6			8¹			11¹			4	5			10		7				9		
Sept 24	A	Millwall		1-0	1-1	1	2	3		5			8¹	9		11			4		6		10		7						
Oct 1	H	Millwall	18757	1-2	2-2	1	2	3	6	5			8	9²		11			4	5			10		7						
Oct 8	A	Gillingham		0-0	2-1	1	2	3		5			8²	9		11			4		6		10		7						
Oct 15	H	Gillingham	16472	2-0	4-1	1	2	3		5			8	9³		11			4		6		10¹		7						
Oct 22	A	Luton		0-1	0-1	1	2	3		5			8	9		11			4		6		10		7						
Oct 29	H	Luton	16004	1-0	1-1	1	2	3		5			8¹	9		11			4		6		10				7				
Nov 5	A	Brentford		1-1	2-2	1	2	3	4	6			8	9		11			5				10¹				7				
Nov 12	H	Brentford	12894	0-0	1-0	1	2	3	4	6			8	9		11			5				10¹		7						
Nov 19	H	Newport Co	13000	3-0	4-3	1	2	3	4	6²			8	9¹		11			5			7¹	10								
Nov 26	A	Newport Co		0-0	0-0	1	2	3	6	5			8	9		11			4			7	10								
Dec 3	A	Plymouth		0-0	0-0	1	2	3		5			8	9		11			4		6	7	10								
Dec 10	H	Plymouth	20500	1-0	3-1	1	2	3		5			8¹	9		11¹			4		6	7	10¹								
Dec 24	A	Merthyr Town		1-0	1-2	1	2	3	6	5			8¹	9		11			4			7	10								
Dec 26	A	Southend			2-1	1	2	3	6	5			8²	9		11			4			7	10								
Dec 27	H	Southend	9465	3-0	6-0	1	2	3	6				8²	9¹	10²	11			4			7¹					5				
Dec 31	A	Swindon		0-0	0-0	1	2	3	6				8	9	10	11			4			7					5				
Jan 7	H	Luton FAC1	22437	0-1	1-1	1		3	s	6			p¹	p	p	p		s	2	s		7					5				
Jan 11	A	Luton FAC1R		0-0	1-2	1		3	6	5			8¹	9		11	2		4			7	10								
Jan 14	H	Swindon	9461	1-0	1-3	1		3	6	5			8¹			11	2		4				10					7		9	
Jan 21	A	Brighton		0-1	0-3	1	2	3	5	6				9	10	11			4									7		8	
Feb 4	A	Watford			3-0	1	2	3		6				9¹		11			4				10²				5	7		8	
Feb 8	H	Brighton	6000	0-0	0-0	1	2	3		6				9		11			4				10				5	7		8	
Feb 11	H	Watford	11414	1-0	2-0	1	2	3		6				9¹		11			4				10¹				5	7		8	
Feb 18	A	Charlton		1-1	2-1	1	2	3		6				9¹		11			4				10				5	7		8¹	
Feb 25	H	Charlton	11942	1-0	1-0	1	2	3		6				9¹		11			4				10				5	7		8	
Mar 4	A	Northampton		0-0	0-0	1	2	3		6				9		11			4				10		7		5			8	
Mar 8	H	Merthyr Town		1-1	2-1	1	2	3		6¹				9		11			4				10	7¹			5			8	
Mar 11	H	Northampton	13411	0-0	1-1	1	2	3		6¹				9		11			4				10	7			5			8	
Mar 18	H	Southampton	26382	0-1	0-2	1	2	3		6				9		11			4				10				5	7			8
Mar 25	A	Southampton		1-1	1-1	1	2	3		6				9¹		11			4				10				5	7		8	
Apr 1	H	QPR	10615	1-0	1-0		2	3		6				9		11	1		4				10				5	7		8¹	
Apr 8	A	QPR		1-1	1-1		2	3		6				9		11	1		4				10				5	7		8¹	
Apr 14	H	Swansea Town	17555	2-0	3-0		2	3	5¹	6				9²		11	1		4				10					7		8	
Apr 15	H	Norwich City	13286	0-1	0-1		2		5	6				9		11	1	3	4				10					7		8	
Apr 17	A	Swansea Town	15000	0-2	2-2		2	6	5	3				9²		11	1		4				10					7		8	
Apr 22	A	Norwich City		0-0	1-2		2	3	6	5				9¹		11	1		4				10					7		8	
Apr 29	H	Reading	10402	1-0	1-0		2	6	5					9	10	11¹	1	3	4									7		8	
May 6	A	Reading		1-1	1-1		2	3	6					9¹	10	11	1		4								5	7		8	
May 8	A	Southampton PC		0-1	1-3		2	5	6					9	10	11	3		4									7		8¹	1

						Robson E.R.	Probert W.	Abbott S.W.	Robinson J.W.	Harwood J.	Martin J.	Cringan R.	Stringfellow F.	Cherrett P.	Watson D.	Beedie W.	Newton T.	Cooper C.R.	Knight A.E.	Wilson J.R.	Maitland R.	Turner J.	Blyth R.	Hoten R.V.	Bishop R.	Buddery H.	Brown J.B.	Kennedy J.	Mackie J.	Edwards M.W.	Hancox T.
League Appearances						34	41	39	9	12	40	1	23	39	6	42	8		6	40	2	7	8	36	11	4	14	20	19	1	
League Goalscorers									1	5			15	24	1	4							2	9	1	1				6	
FA Cup Appearances			incomplete																												
FA Cup Goalscorers													2																		

Total League Division 3   P42 W18 D17 L7 F62 A39 Pts 53 Posn 3rd

Season 1922/23   Division 3

Date	V	Team	Attendance	FA HT	FA FT	Newton T.	Probert W. H.	Abbott S. W.	Wilson J. R.	Shankly J.	Robinson J. W.	Mackie J.	Cherrett P.	Hoten R. V.	Beedie W.	Cooper C. R.	Davies R.	Gilchrist Duncan	Meikle A.	Croft H.	Brown A.	March Z.	Martin J.	Watson D.	Tumelty J.	Strange A.	Quinn C.	Parker T. R.	Haines W.	McPhail D.
Aug 26	H	Bristol Rov	18445	0-0	0-0	1	2	3	4		6		8	9	10	11			7			5								
Aug 28	A	Charlton	8000	1-0	2-0	1	2	3	4		6		8²	9	11				7			5	10							
Sept 2	A	Bristol Rov		0-0	1-0	1	2	3	4		6		8	9¹	11				7			5	10							
Sept 6	H	Charlton	12496	2-0	3-0	1	2	3	4		6		8	9¹	11¹				7	5			10¹							
Sept 9	A	Aberdare		0-0	2-0	1	2	3	4		6		8	9²	11				7	5			10							
Sept 16	H	Aberdare	15180		1-0	1	2	3	4		6		8	9	11				7	5¹			10							
Sept 23	H	Newport Co	14294	1-0	2-0	1	2	3	4		6		8¹	9	11¹				7	5			10							
Sept 30	A	Newport Co		0-0	0-0	1	2	3	4		6		8	9	11				7	5			10							
Oct 7	H	Plymouth A	22261	0-2	1-2	1	2	3	4				8	9	11					7			10	6¹						
Oct 14	A	Plymouth A	20000	0-0	0-2	1	2	3	4				8	9	11					7			10	6						
Oct 21	H	Reading	10986	0-0	1-0	1	2	3				5	8	9¹	11	4			7				10	6						
Oct 28	A	Reading		0-0	0-0	1		3				5	8	9	11	4	2		7				10	6						
Nov 4	A	Bristol City		0-0	1-2	1		3	4			5	8	9	11		2		7				10	6						
Nov 11	H	Bristol City	13790	0-1	1-2	1		3	4			5	8	9	11		2		7				10¹	6						
Nov 18	H	Swansea	11607	0-1	0-3	1	2	3	4			5	8		11				7				10	6						
Nov 25	A	Swansea	12000	0-1	1-2	1	2	3				5	8	9	11¹	4			7				10	6						
Dec 2	H	Millwall	11013	0-0	2-0	1	2	3				5	8¹	9	11	4			7¹				10	6						
Dec 16	H	Luton	10185	1-1	1-2	1		3				5	8¹		11	4	2		7				10	6						
Dec 23	A	Luton	10000	0-0	2-0	1	2	3				5	8		11	4			7				10¹	6			9¹			
Dec 25	A	Brighton	15000	1-2	1-7	1	2	3				5	8		11	4¹			7				10	6			9			
Dec 26	H	Brighton	19603	0-1	1-2	1	2		4				8		11				7				10¹	6		5	9	3		
Dec 30	A	QPR		0-0	1-0	1	2					5	8		11				7				10	6¹		4	9	3		
Jan 1	A	Millwall	Fair	2-1	3-1	1	2					5	8		11				7				10¹	6¹		4	9¹	3		
Jan 6	H	QPR	11851	0-1	1-1	1	2					5	8		11				7				10	6		4	9¹	3		
Jan 13	H	Leeds Utd *FAC1*	26046	0-0	0-0	1	2					5	8	9	11				7				10	6		4		3		
Jan 17	A	Leeds Utd *FACR*	25000	0-1	1-3	1	2					5	8		11				7¹				10	6		4	9	3		
Jan 20	A	Gillingham		1-3	2-4	1	2					5	8		11				7¹				10	6¹		4	9	3		
Jan 27	H	Gillingham	8571	4-1	6-1	1	2					5	8		11				7¹				10	6		4	9⁵	3		
Feb 3	H	Southend	8000	0-0	0-0	1	2					5	8		11				7				10	6		4	9	3		
Feb 10	A	Southend		0-0	0-0	1	2					5	8		11		4		7				10	6			9	3		
Feb 17	H	Merthyr Town	7430	1-1	1-1	1	2					5			11		4		7				10	6			9¹	3		
Feb 24	A	Merthyr Town		0-1	0-3	1	2					5	8		11		4		7				10	6			9	3		
Mar 3	H	Exeter	8640	2-2	3-4	1	2					5	8¹		11				7				10	6		4		3		
Mar 10	A	Exeter		2-0	3-2	1	2	3				5	8¹		11				7				10	6		4	9²			
Mar 17	A	Northampton		0-2	0-3	1	2	3				5	8		11				7				10	6		4	9			
Mar 24	H	Northampton	7790	0-0	0-0	1	2	3				5	8		11				7				10	6		4	9			
Mar 30	H	Swindon	13401	4-0	4-1	1	2	3				5	8¹		11²				7				10	6		4	9¹			
Mar 31	H	Norwich	8972		2-1	1	2	3				5	8		11				7				10	6		4	9²			
Apr 2	A	Swindon		0-2	0-3	1	2					5	8		11				7				10	6		4	9	3		
Apr 7	A	Norwich	6000	2-0	2-0	1	2					5	8¹		11				7¹				10	6			9	3		
Apr 14	A	Brentford		0-1	0-1	1	2					5	8		11				7				10	6			9	3		
Apr 16	H	Southampton *HC*	7592	0-2	1-2	1	2						8		11				7				10	6			9	3	5¹	
Apr 21	H	Brentford	8106	3-0	3-0	1	2						8¹		11¹				7¹				10	6			9	3	5	
Apr 23	A	Southampton *PC*		2-0	2-2	1	2						8¹		11				7				10	6			9¹	3	5	
Apr 28	A	Watford		0-1	3-2		2						8²		11				7				10¹	6		4	9	3	5	1
May 5	H	Watford	8832	1-0	1-0		2						8		11				7				10	6		4	9	3	5¹	1
League Appearances						40	38	34	21	2	17	38	21	3	39	4	21	2	40	5	5	3	39	35	5	13	17	12	6	2
League Goalscorers								1	2				10	9	6	5			1				4	6			9	1	3	
FA Cup Appearances						2	2					2	1		2				2				2	2		2	1	2		
FA Cup Goalscorers																			1											

Total League Division 3S   P42 W19 D8 L15 F58 A52 Pts 46 Posn 7th

Own goal: Bristol City (Nov 4)

Apr 23: Cup was shared!

Season 1923/24   Division 3

Date	Venue	Team	Attendance	HT	FT	Kane A.	Probert W.	Davison J.	Davies Reg	Martin J.	Meikle A.	Mackie J.	Watson D.	Beedie W.	Moore H.	McNab D.	Shankly J.	Haines W.	Dean S.	Parker T.	Strange A.	Gilchrist Duncan.	Quinn C.	McColgan J.	Foxall H.
Aug 25	A	Plymouth		0-1	2-1	1	2	3	4	6	7	8^1	10	11				9^1		5					
Aug 29	H	Newport Co	7353	2-0	5-0	1	2	3	4	6	7	8^1	10^2	11				9^2		5					
Sept 1	H	Plymouth	20540	2-1	2-1	1	2	3	4	6	7	8	10	11				9^2		5					
Sept 6	A	Newport Co		1-2	1-2	1	2	3	4	6^1	7	8	10	11				9		5					
Sept 8	H	Reading	13689	0-1	1-1	1	2	3	4	6	7	8	10	11				9^1		5					
Sept 12	A	Exeter		0-0	0-0	1	2	3	4	6	7		10	11	8	9				5					
Sept 15	A	Reading	8000	1-0	4-1	1	2	3	4	6	7^1	8	10^1	11^1				9^1		5					
Sept 19	A	Southend	6000	0-0	1-0	1	2	3	4	6	7	8	10	11				9^1		5					
Sept 22	H	Luton	11375	2-0	3-0	1	2	3	4	6	7^1	8	10	11				9^2		5					
Sept 29	A	Luton		0-3	1-4	1	2	3	4	6	7	8^1	10	11				9		5					
Oct 6	H	Brighton	12475	0-3	1-3	1	2	3	4	6	7	8	10	11				9^1		5					
Oct 13	A	Brighton		3-0	4-0	1	2	3	4	6^2	7	8	10	11^1				9^1		5					
Oct 20	H	Bristol Rov	Sparse	1-1	1-1	1	2	3	4	6	7	8	10^1	11				9		5					
Oct 27	A	Bristol Rov		0-0	1-0	1	2	3	4	6	7	8	10	11						5	9^1				
Nov 3	H	Brentford	9867	3-0	3-0	1	2	3	4	6^1	7	8^1	10	11						5	9^1				
Nov 10	A	Brentford		1-0	1-1	1	2	3	4	6	7	8^1	10	11						5	9				
Nov 24	H	Southend	8680	1-0	3-0	1		3	4	6	7	8^1	10^1	11				9^1		5		2			
Dec 1	A	L Caledonians *FAC1*	6000	3-0	5-1	1	2				p^2	p^1	10	11				p^2							
Dec 8	H	Exeter City	9764	3-0	4-0	1	2	3	4	6	7	8	10	11^1				9^3							
Dec 15	A	Brentford *FAC2*		0-0	1-1	1	2	3			7							9^1							
Dec 19	H	Brentford *FAC2R* aet	11664	0-0	1-0	1	2	3	4	6^1	7	8	10	11				9		5					
Dec 22	H	Aberdare Ath.	9381	2-0	4-0	1	2			6	7	8	10^1	11		4		9^3		5					
Dec 25	A	Millwall	4761	0-2	0-2	1	2			6	7	8	10	11		4		9		5					
Dec 26	H	Millwall	21292	0-0	0-1	1	2			6	7	8	10	11		4		9		5					
Dec 29	A	Q.P.R.		2-0	2-0	1	2	3		6	7	8^1	10	11		4^1	5	9							
Jan 5	H	Q.P.R.	11085	2-0	7-0	1		3	4	6	7^2	8^1	10	11^2				9^2					2		
Jan 12	H	Newcastle *FAC3*	26422	2-0	2-4	1	2	3	4	6	7	8^1	10	11				9^1		5					
Jan 19	A	Merthyr Town		0-1	2-2	1		3	4		7	8	10^1	11		6		9^1		5			2		
Jan 26	H	Merthyr Town	10366	0-0	1-0	1	2		4	6	7	8	10	11				9^1		5				3	
Feb 9	H	Charlton	8871	0-0	0-0	1	2		4	6	7	8	10	11				9						3	
Feb 16	A	Norwich	8000	0-1	1-3	1	2		4	6	7^1	8	10	11				9						3	5
Feb 23	H	Norwich	10017	1-0	4-0	1	2		4	6	7^1	8	10	11				9^3						3	5
Mar 1	A	Swindon		0-0	0-0	1	2		4	6	7	8	10								9			3	5
Mar 10	A	Charlton		1-1	1-1	1	2		4	6^1	7	8	10	11							9			3	5
Mar 15	H	Watford	11775	1-0	4-0	1	2		4	6	7	8^1	10	11^1							9^2			3	5
Mar 17	A	Aberdare Ath.	6000	0-0	0-0	1	2		4	6	7	8	10	11							9			3	5
Mar 22	A	Watford	5000	0-2	3-2	1	2		4	6^2	7	8	10	11							9^1			3	5
Mar 29	H	Swansea	20091	1-0	3-0	1	2		4	6	7	8^1	10	11							9^2			3	5
Apr 5	A	Swansea	16700	0-0	0-0	1	2		4	6	7	8	10	11							9			3	5
Apr 12	A	Northampton	11704	0-0	1-3	1	2		4	6^1	7	8	10	11							9			3	5
Apr 18	H	Bournem'th & Bos	19960	1-0	3-0	1	2			6^1	7	8	10^1	11				9^1		4				3	5
Apr 19	A	Northampton		2-0	4-0	1	2			6^1	7	8^1	10^2	11				9		4				3	5
Apr 21	A	Bournem'th & Bos		0-0	0-0	1	2			6	7	8	10	11						4	9			3	5
Apr 26	H	Gillingham	13850	1-0	3-0	1	2			6	7	8	10^1	11				9^1		4				3	5
Apr 30	H	Swindon	18000	3-1	4-1	1	2			6^1	7	8	10^1	11				9		4				3	5^2
May 3	A	Gillingham			2-0	1	2		4		7	8	10	11						9^2	6			3	5
May 5	A	Southampton *HC*		2-1	3-2	1	2		4	6	7	8		11				9^2	10^1					3	5
May 7	H	Southampton *PC*	7496	1-0	2-0	1	2		4	6	7	8		11^1					10	9^1				3	5
League Appearances						42	38	25	23	41	42	41	42	41	1	5	1	31	1	30	10	1	4	17	16
League Goalscorers										11	5	12	12	6		1		28		2	7				2
FA Cup Appearances			incomplete																						
FA Cup Goalscorers										1	2	2						4							

Total League Division 3 South   P42 W24 D11 L 7 F87 A30 Pts 59 Posn CHAMPIONS

Season 1924/25   Division 2

Date	Venue	Team	Attendance	FA HT	FA FT	Kane A.	Probert W.	McColgan J.	Davies Reg	Foxall H.	Martin J.	Meikle A.	Mackie J.	Haines W.	Watson D.	Beedie W.	Clifford G.	Davison J.	Foxall A.	Kennedy J.	Dean S.	Cooke G.	Parker T.	Williamson W.	Smith
Aug 30	A	South Shields	10000	0-0	2-0	1	2	3	4	5^1	6	7	8^1	9	10	11									
Sept 6	H	Derby Co.	27063	1-0	1-1	1	2	3	4	5	6	7	8	9	10	11^1									
Sept 13	A	Blackpool	13000	1-0	1-1	1	2	3	4	5	6	7	8	9^1	10	11									
Sept 15	A	Port Vale		1-0	2-0	1	2	3	4	5	6	7^1	8	9^1	10	11									
Sept 20	H	Hull City	20000	1-0	2-0	1	2	3	4	5	6	7	8^1	9	10	11^1									
Sept 27	A	Southampton	19366	0-0	0-0	1	2	3	4	5	6	7	8	9	10	11									
Oct 4	A	Fulham	30000	0-0	0-0	1	2	3	4	5	6	7	8	9	10	11									
Oct 11	H	Wolverhampton	18000	1-1	2-2	1	2	3	4	5	6	7	8^2		10	11								9	
Oct 18	A	Barnsley	10000	2-0	4-1	1	2	3	4	5^1	6^1	7	8^1		10	11								9^1	
Oct 20	A	Bradford City	5000	0-0	0-2	1	2	3	4	5	6	7	8		10	11								9	
Oct 25	H	Chelsea	23000	0-0	0-0	1	2	3	4	5	6	7	8		10	11								9	
Nov 1	A	Stockport Co.		2-0	2-1	1	2	3	4	5	6	7	8		10					9^2	11				
Nov 8	H	Manchester Utd.	25000	0-1	1-1	1	2	3	4	5	6	7	8		10	11^1				9					
Nov 15	A	Leicester		0-2	0-4	1	2	3	4	5	6	7	8		10	11					9				
Nov 22	H	Stoke	16000	0-0	0-0	1		3	4	5	6	7	8		10	11	2				9				
Nov 29	H	Southampton	25000	0-0	1-1	1		3	4	5	6	7	8	9^1	10	11	2								
Dec 6	H	Oldham Ath.	17000	2-1	2-2	1		3	4		6	7	8^1	9	10	11	2				5				
Dec 13	A	Sheffield Wed.		1-2	2-5	1	2	3	4	5	6	7	8^1	9	10^1	11									
Dec 20	H	Clapton O.	10000	0-1	0-2	1	2	3	4	5		7	8	9	10	11					6				
Dec 25	H	Crystal Palace	18000	0-0	0-0	1	2	3	4		6			9	10	11					7	5		8	
Dec 26	A	Crystal Palace	25000	1-0	2-1	1		3	4		6			9^1	10	11	2				7	5		8^1	
Dec 27	H	South Shields	6000	0-0	1-0	1		3	4		6	7^1	8	9				2			5		11	10	
Jan 3	A	Derby Co.	15000	0-4	1-6	1		3	4		6	7	8	9^1		11		2			5			10	
Jan 10	A	Accrington FAC1	10800	2-2	5-2	1		3	4	5	11^1	7^1	8^1	9^2				2			6			10	
Jan 17	H	Blackpool	17000	1-0	1-1	1		3	4	5	11	7	8	9^1				2			6			10	
Jan 24	A	Hull City	9000	0-3	0-5	1				5	6	7	8	9	10	11	3	2	4						
Jan 31	A	Blackburn FAC2	18200	0-0	0-0	1		3	4	5	6	7	8	9	10	11	2								
Feb 4	H	Blackburn FAC2R	24746	0-0	0-0	1		3	4	5	6	7	8	9	10	11	2								
Feb 7	H	Fulham	18000	0-0	3-0	1		3	4	5^1		7	8	9	10^1	11^1	2				6				
Feb 9	†	Blackburn FAC2(2)R	22827	0-1	0-1	1		3	4	5	6	7	8	9	10	11	2								
Feb 12	A	Coventry	2000	1-0	1-2	1		3	4	5	6	7	8		10	11^1	2							9^1	
Feb 14	A	Wolverhampton	20000	2-0	5-0	1		3	4	5	6	7	8	9^3	10^1		2							11^1	
Feb 21	H	Barnsley	15000	0-0	0-0	1		3	4	5	6	7	8	9	10		2							11	
Feb 28	A	Chelsea		1-2	3-2	1		3	4	5		7	8^1	9^1	10^1	11	2				6				
Mar 7	H	Stockport Co.	12000	1-1	1-1	1		3	4	5		7	8	9^1	10	11	2				6				
Mar 14	A	Manchester Utd.	27525	0-2	0-2	1		3	4	5		7	8	9	10	11	2				6				
Mar 21	H	Leicester City	16000	1-1	1-1	1		3	4	5	6	7	8	9	10	11^1	2								
Mar 28	A	Stoke	8000	0-1	1-2	1		3	4	5	6	7	8^1	9	10	11	2								
Mar 30	H	Port Vale		1-0	2-0	1		3	4	5	6	7^1	8	9^1	10	11	2								
Apr 4	H	Coventry City		0-0	1-0	1		3	4	5	6	7	8^1	9	10	11	2								
Apr 10	H	Middlesbrough	20000	2-0	3-1	1		3	4	5	6	7	8^1	9^1	10^1	11	2								
Apr 11	A	Oldham Ath.	8000	1-0	2-0	1		3	4	5	6	7	8	9^1	10^1	11	2								
Apr 13	A	Middlesbrough		0-1	1-1	1		3	4	5	6	7	8	9	10	11^1	2								
Apr 18	H	Sheffield Wed.	15000	1-1	1-1	1			4	5	3	7	8^1	9	10	11	2				6				
Apr 25	A	Clapton O.	10000	0-0	1-1	1		3	4	5	6	7	8^1	9	10	11	2								
May 2	H	Bradford City	18000	4-0	5-0	1		3	4	5	6	7	8^3	9^2	10		2							11	
May 4	H	Southampton HC	7590	2-0	2-0	1		3	4	5	6	7	8^1	9^1	10		2							11	
May 6	A	Southampton PC		1-1	1-1	1			4	5	6^1	7	8		10		2	3						11	9
League Appearances						42	17	40	41	36	40	40	40	33	39	36	22	4	1	2	15	2	1	11	
League Goalscorers										3	2	3	16	17	6	7				2				3	
FA Cup Appearances						4		4	4	4	4	4	4	4	3	3	3	1			1			1	
FA Cup Goalscorers											1	1	1	2											

Total League Div 2   P42 W15 D18 L9 F58 A50 Pts 48 Posn 4th

† at Highbury

Season 1925/26   Division 2

Date	V	Team	Attendance	HT	FT	Kane A.	Clifford G.	McColgan J.	Davies Reg	Foxall H.	Martin J.	Meikle A.	Mackie J.	Haines W.	Watson D.	Beedie W.	McPhail D.	Haywood	Davison J.	Forsyth J.	Moffat W.	Goodwin H.	Merrie A.	Williamson W.	Dean S.	Toner F.	Havelock H.	Cook F.	Bennett
Aug 29	H	Middlesbrough	20000	1-2	1-5	1	2	3	4	5	6	7	8^1	9	10	11													
Aug 31	A	Preston N.E.		2-2	2-3	1	2	3	4	5	6	7	8	9^1	10	11^1													
Sept 5	A	Southampton	18000	2-0	3-1	1	2	3	4	5	6	7	8^1		10	11^1								9^1					
Sept 12	A	Wolverhampton		0-2	1-4	1	2	3	4	5	6^1	7	8		10	11								9					
Sept 19	H	Swansea	11000	0-0	0-0	1	2	3	4	5	6	7	8											9	10	11			
Sept 26	A	Sheffield Wed.		1-2	2-4	1	2	3	4	5	6^1	7	8	9^1	10	11													
Sept 30	H	Preston N.E.	12000	3-0	5-2	1	2	3	4	5^1	6	7^1	8^2	9	10	11^1													
Oct 3	H	Stoke	16000	1-0	2-0	1	2	3	4	5	6	7	8	9	10^1	11^1													
Oct 10	A	Oldham Ath.	10000	1-0	3-1	1	2	3	4	5^1	6	7	8^1	9^1	10	11													
Oct 17	H	Blackpool	16000	1-0	2-0	1	2	3	4			7^1	8	9^1	10	11				5	6								
Oct 24	A	Darlington	7000	0-4	1-7	1	2	3	4	5		7	8	9^1	10	11					6								
Oct 26	A	South Shields	3000	0-3	1-5	1	2	3	4	5		7	8	9	10^1	11					6								
Oct 31	H	Derby Co.	17000	1-1	2-2		2	3	4	5		7	8	9^2	10	11	1				6								
Nov 7	A	Notts Forest		0-2	1-3		2	3	4	5	6	7	8	9^1	10	11	1												
Nov 14	H	Clapton O.	13000	0-0	3-2		2	3	4	5		7^2	8	9	10	11	1				6								
Nov 21	A	Barnsley	1500	1-1	2-2		2	3		5	6	7^1	8	9^1	10		1			4			11						
Nov 28	H	Port Vale	12500	2-0	3-2			3	4	5		7	8^2	9^1	10		1		2		6		11						
Dec 5	A	Bradford City	10000	0-0	1-0			3	4	5		7	8	9^1	10	11	1		2		6								
Dec 7	H	South Shields		2-1	4-2		2	3	4	5		7	8^1		10	11^1	1				6								
Dec 12	H	Hull City	17000	1-1	2-2		2	3	4	5		7	8^1	9^1	10	11	1				6								
Dec 19	A	Chelsea	28500	0-0	0-0		2	3	4	5		7	8	9	10	11	1				6								
Dec 25	A	Stockport Co.	9000	0-1	3-3		2	3	4	5		7	8^2	9^1	10	11	1				6								
Dec 26	H	Stockport Co.	25000	3-0	4-0		2	3	4	5		7	8	9^2	10^2	11	1				6								
Jan 2	A	Middlesbrough	6000	0-1	1-4		2	3	4	5		7	8	9	10	11^1	1				6								
Jan 9	A	Derby Co. *FAC3*	18854	0-0	0-0		2	3	4	5		7	8	9	10	11	1				6								
Jan 13	A	Derby Co. *FAC3R*	25761	0-0	0-1		2	3	4	5		7	8	9	10	11	1				6								
Jan 16	H	Southampton	12000	1-1	1-2		2			5	3	7	8	9^1	10	11	1				6			4					
Jan 18	†	Derby Co. *FAC3(2)R*	11076	0-1	0-2		2	3	4	5		7	8	9	10	11	1				6								
Jan 23	H	Wolverhampton	10000	0-0	3-0		2		4	5	3	7^2	8^1		10		1				6	9	11						
Feb 6	H	Sheffield Wed.	17000	0-1	1-2		2	3	4	5		7	8		10		1				6	9^1	11						
Feb 13	A	Stoke	6000	1-1	1-2		2	3	4	5	11	7	8^1		10		1				6	9							
Feb 20	H	Oldham Ath.	12000	0-1	0-2		2		4	5	3	7	8		10	11	1				6	9							
Feb 27	A	Blackpool		2-1	2-2		2	3	4	5	6	7^1	8	9^1	10		1						11						
Mar 6	H	Darlington	13000	1-0	2-0		2	3	4	5	11^1		8^1	9	10		1				6	7							
Mar 13	A	Derby Co.	16000	0-0	2-0		2	3	4	5	11		8		10^1		1				6	7^1					9		
Mar 18	A	Swansea	15000	0-0	0-1		2	3	4		11		8		10		1			5	6	7					9		
Mar 20	H	Notts Forest	14000	3-0	5-1		2	3	4	5	11		8^1		10		1				6	7					9^4		
Mar 27	A	Clapton O.	10000	0-0	1-1		2	3	4	5	11		8^1		10		1				6	7					9		
Apr 2	H	Fulham	20000	0-0	0-0		2	3	4	5	11		8		10		1				6	7					9		
Apr 3	H	Barnsley	16000	0-1	1-2		2	3	4	5	11		8		10		1				6^1	7					9		
Apr 5	H	Fulham	15000	1-1	3-2		2	3	4	5	11		8		10		1				6	7^1					9^2		
Apr 10	A	Port Vale	6000	0-1	1-1		2	3	4	5	11^1		8		10		1				6	7					9		
Apr 17	H	Bradford City	13000	2-1	3-1		2	3	4	5	11^1		8^1	9^1	10		1				6	7							
Apr 24	A	Hull City	5000	0-0	0-1		2	3	4	5	11		8	9	10		1				6	7							
May 1	H	Chelsea	17000	2-0	4-0		2	3	4	5			8^1	9	10		1				6	7^2						11^1	
May 3	A	Southampton *HC*		3-1	4-2		2	3^1	4	5^1			8^1		10^1		1				6	7					9	11	
May 5	H	Southampton *PC*	3000	3-0	5-1		2	3	4				8	9^3			1		10^1		6	7						11^1	5

						Kane A.	Clifford G.	McColgan J.	Davies Reg	Foxall H.	Martin J.	Meikle A.	Mackie J.	Haines W.	Watson D.	Beedie W.	McPhail D.	Haywood	Davison J.	Forsyth J.	Moffat W.	Goodwin H.	Merrie A.	Williamson W.	Dean S.	Toner F.	Havelock H.	Cook F.	Bennett
League Appearances						12	32	38	40	40	35	30	42	27	41	23	30		2	3	32	12	7	1	3	3	8	1	
League Goalscorers									2	5	8	18	20	5	6						1	3	2				6	1	
FA Cup Appearances							3	3	3	3		3	3	3	3	3	3				3								
FA Cup Goalscorers												1																	

Total League Division 2   P42 W17 D10 L15 F79 A74 Pts 44 Posn 11th

† at Leicester

Season 1926/27   Division 2

Date	Venue	Team	Attendance	FA HT	FA FT	McPhail D.	Clifford G.	McColgan J.	Davies Reg	Foxall H.	Moffat W.	Goodwin H.	Mackie J.	Haines W.	Watson D.	Cook F.	McKenzie M.	Jarvie J.	Meikle A.	Martin J.	Smith E.	Forward F.	Havelock H.
Aug 28	H	Southampton	27896	1-1	3-1	1	2	3	4	5	6	7¹	8	9¹	11	10¹							
Sept 1	A	Manchester City	20000	0-0	0-4	1	2	3	4	5	6	7	8	9	11	10							
Sept 4	A	Oldham	16000	0-0	0-1	1	2	3	4	5	6	7	8	9	11	10							
Sept 11	H	Fulham	12000	2-0	2-0	1	2	3	4	5	6		8	9¹	11	10		7¹					
Sept 18	A	Grimsby	15000	0-0	0-0	1	2	3	4	5	6	7	8	9	10	11							
Sept 25	H	Blackpool	15000	2-0	5-0	1	2	3	4	5	6	7	8¹	9³	10¹	11							
Oct 2	A	Reading	2000	1-1	2-1	1	2	3	4	5	6	7	8¹	9¹	10	11							
Oct 9	H	Swansea	17000	0-0	1-0	1	2	3	4	5	6	7	8	9¹	10	11							
Oct 16	H	Chelsea	18000	1-2	2-3	1	2	3	4	5	6¹	7¹	8	9	10	11							
Oct 23	A	Bradford City	10000	0-1	2-1	1	2	3	4¹	5	6	7	8	9	10¹	11							
Oct 25	A	Darlington	8000	0-0	0-0	1	2	3	4	5	6	7	8	9	10	11							
Oct 30	H	Port Vale	13000	1-0	4-0		2	3	4	5	6	7	8¹	9²	10¹	11	1						
Nov 6	A	Middlesbrough	9000	1-2	3-7		2	3	4	5	6	7	8	9²	10¹	11	1						
Nov 8	A	Darlington		2-0	4-0		2	3	4	5	6	7²	8	9¹	10¹	11	1						
Nov 20	A	Notts Co.	8000	2-1	3-2	1	2	3	4	5	6	7	8¹	9²	10	11							
Nov 24	H	Clapton Orient	7000	1-1	1-1	1	2	3	4	5	6	7	8	9	10	11¹							
Nov 27	H	Wolverhampton	15500	1-0	2-1	1	2	3	4	5	6	7	8	9²	10	11							
Dec 4	A	Hull City		1-2	1-2	1	2	3	4	5	6	7	8	9¹	10	11							
Dec 11	H	South Shields	15000	0-0	1-1	1	2	3	4	5	6	7¹	8	9	10	11							
Dec 18	A	Preston	18000	1-0	2-1	1	2	3	4	5	6	7¹	8	9¹	10	11							
Dec 25	H	Notts Forest	20000	0-0	0-0	1	2	3	4	5	6	7	8	9	10	11							
Dec 27	A	Notts Forest	30000	0-0	0-1	1	2	3	4	5	6	7	8	9	10	11							
Jan 1	H	Manchester City	20000	0-1	2-1	1	2	3	4	5	6	7	8	9¹	10¹	11							
Jan 8	A	Bristol R. FAC3	25000	1-3	3-3	1	2	3	4	5	6	7¹	8	9¹	10¹	11							
Jan 12	H	Bristol R. FAC3R	20963	2-0	4-0	1	2	3¹	4	5	6	7	8¹	9¹	10¹	11							
Jan 15	A	Southampton	19058	1-0	2-0	1	2	3	4	5	6	7	8	9²	10	11							
Jan 22	H	Oldham	16000	3-1	7-2	1	2	3	4	5¹	6	7	8¹	9³	10²	11							
Jan 29	A	Reading FAC4	23283	0-3	1-3	1	2	3	4	5	6	7	8	9¹	10	11							
Feb 5	H	Grimsby	14000	2-1	5-2	1	2		4	5¹	6	7	8²	9¹	10¹	11			3				
Feb 12	A	Blackpool		0-2	0-2	1	2		4	5	6	7	8	9	10	11					3		
Feb 26	A	Swansea	9054	0-1	1-1	1	2		4	5	6		8	9	10¹	11					3	7	
Mar 12	H	Bradford City	15000	0-0	1-0	1	2		4	5	6		8	9¹	10	11					3	7	
Mar 14	A	Fulham		0-0	0-0	1	2	3	4	5	6		8	9	10	11						7	
Mar 19	A	Port Vale	8000	2-1	3-2	1	2		4	5	6		8	9²	10¹	11					3	7	
Mar 26	H	Middlesbrough	25000	0-0	0-1	1	2		4	5	6		8	9	10	11					3	7	
Mar 30	H	Reading	10000	2-0	5-0	1	2		4	5	6		8²	9¹	10¹	11¹					3	7	
Apr 2	A	Clapton Orient	18000	3-2	5-4	1	2		4	5	6		8	9	10	11¹					3	7¹	
Apr 9	H	Notts. Co.	14000	4-1	9-1	1	2		4¹	5	6		8²	9³	10	11²					3	7¹	
Apr 15	H	Barnsley	26000	1-1	1-2	1	2		4	5	6		8	9	10	11¹					3	7	
Apr 16	A	Wolverhampton	15000	1-0	1-0	1	2		4	5	6		8	9		11					3	7	10¹
Apr 18	A	Barnsley	20000	0-2	0-2	1	2		4	5	6		8	9	10	11					3	7	
Apr 23	H	Hull City	18000	2-0	2-0	1	2		4	5	6		8	9¹		11					3	7	10¹
Apr 30	A	South Shields	5000	0-1	0-1	1	2	3	4	5	6		8	9		11						7	10
May 4	A	Chelsea	50000	0-0	0-0	1	2	3	4	5	6		8	9	10	11						7	
May 7	H	Preston	27000	1-1	5-1	1	2	3	4	5	6		8	9⁴	10	11						7¹	
May 9	A	Southampton PC	3000	0-3	1-4	1	2		4		6		8	9¹	10	11					3	7	5
May 11	H	Southampton HC	7000	2-0	5-1	1	2		4	5	6	7¹	8¹	9²	10	11¹					3		

						McPhail D.	Clifford G.	McColgan J.	Davies Reg	Foxall H.	Moffat W.	Goodwin H.	Mackie J.	Haines W.	Watson D.	Cook F.	McKenzie M.	Jarvie J.	Meikle A.	Martin J.	Smith E.	Forward F.	Havelock H.
League Appearances						39	42	29	42	42	42	26	40	42	35	42	4	3	2	1	12	15	3
League Goalscorers									2	2	1	5	12	40	11	6	1			1		3	2
FA Cup Appearances						3	3	3	3	3	3	3	3	3	3	3							
FA Cup Goalscorers								1				1	1	3	2								

Total League Division 2   P42 W23 D8 L11 F87 A49 Pts 54 Posn 2nd

Season 1927/28   Division 1

Date	Venue	Team	Attendance	FA HT	FA FT	McPhail D.	Clifford G.	McColgan J.	Davies Reg	Foxall H.	Moffat W.	Forward F.	Mackie J.	Haines W.	Watson D.	Cook F.	Jarvie J.	Rutherford S.	Haslam G.	Nichol J.	Davey H.	Smith J.	McIlwaine J.	Weddle J.	Irvine R.
Aug 27	A	Sunderland	30000	3-1	3-3	1	2	3	4	5	6	7	8^1	9^1	10	11^1									
Aug 31	H	Aston Villa	32050	1-1	3-1	1	2	3	4	5	6	7^1	8	9	10^1	11^1									
Sept 3	H	Derby Co.	25000	1-2	2-2	1	2	3	4	5	6	7	8	9^1	10	11^1									
Sept 5	A	Aston Villa		1-4	2-7	1	2	3	4	5	6	7	8^1	9^1	10	11									
Sept 10	A	West Ham	25000	2-0	2-4	1	2	3	4	5	6	7	8	9^1	10^1	11									
Sept 17	H	Tottenham H.	30000	2-0	3-0	1	2	3	4	5	6	7^1	8	9^1	10	11^1									
Sept 24	H	Leicester	25000	0-0	2-0	1	2	3	4	5	6	7^1	8	9	10^1	11									
Oct 1	A	Liverpool	35000	0-6	2-8		2	3	4	5	6	7	8^1	9	10	11^1	1								
Oct 8	H	Arsenal	20000	0-2	2-3	1	2	3	4	5	6	7	8	9^1	10	11^1									
Oct 15	A	Burnley	25000	0-2	0-2	1	2	3	4	5	6	7	8	9	10	11									
Oct 22	A	Cardiff	10000	1-1	1-3	1	2	3	4	5	6	7	8	9	10	11^1									
Oct 29	H	Everton	Large	1-1	1-3	1	2	3	4	5^1	6	7	8	9	10			11							
Nov 5	A	Manchester Utd.	6000	0-1	0-2	1	2	3	4	5	6	7	8	9	10	11									
Nov 12	H	Blackburn	20000	0-2	2-2	1	2	3	4		6	7	8	9^2	10	11			5						
Nov 19	A	Bolton		0-1	1-3	1	2	3	4		6	7	8	9^1	10	11			5						
Nov 26	H	Birmingham	19000	1-0	2-2	1	2	3			6	7	8^2	9	10	11			5	4					
Dec 3	A	Middlesbrough	20000	1-4	1-5	1	2	3			6	7	8	9^1	10	11			5	4					
Dec 10	H	Sheffield Wed.	19258	0-0	0-0	1	2	3	4	5	6	7	8		10	11					9				
Dec 17	A	Newcastle		2-1	3-1	1	2	3	4	5	6	7^1	8		10^1	11^1					9				
Dec 24	H	Huddersfield	20000	0-0	2-1	1	2	3	4	5	6	7	8		10^1	11					9^1				
Dec 26	A	Bury		0-2	0-4	1	2	3	4	5	6	7	8		10	11					9				
Dec 27	H	Bury	15000	0-0	1-0	1	2	3	4	5		7	8		10^1	11			6		9				
Jan 2	A	Sheffield Utd.	23000	1-3	1-3	1	2	3	4	5	6	7	8		10	11					9^1				
Jan 7	A	Derby Co.	20000	1-2	2-2	1	2	3	4^1	5	6	7	8	9^1	10	11									
Jan 14	H	West Ham *FAC3*	27691	0-0	0-2	1	2	3	4	5	6	7	8		10	11					9				
Jan 21	H	West Ham	16000	1-0	2-1	1	2	3	4		6	7		9	10	11				5		8^2			
Feb 4	A	Leicester	25000	0-3	2-6	1	2	3	4		6	7		9	10^2	11				5		8			
Feb 11	H	Liverpool	18000	1-0	1-0	1	2	3		5	6	7		9	10^1	11				4		8			
Feb 18	H	Sunderland	20000	1-1	3-5	1	2	3			6	7			10	11				4	9	8^3	5		
Feb 25	H	Burnley	20000	0-0	1-0	1	2	3			6	7			10	11				4		8	5	9^1	
Mar 3	H	Cardiff	26000	1-0	3-0	1	2	3			6	7			10^1	11				4		8^1	5	9^1	
Mar 10	A	Everton		0-0	0-0	1	2	3			6	7			10	11				4		8	5	9	
Mar 17	H	Manchester Utd.	20000	1-0	1-0	1	2	3			6	7				11				4		8	5	9^1	10
Mar 19	A	Tottenham H.	20000	1-0	3-0	1	2	3			6	7				11				4		8^2	5	9^1	10
Mar 28	A	Arsenal		0-0	2-0	1	2	3			6	7			10	11				4		8^1	5	9^1	
Mar 31	H	Bolton	20000	0-0	1-0	1	2	3			6	7			10	11				4		8	5	9^1	
Apr 7	A	Birmingham	30000	0-1	0-2	1	2	3			6	7				11				4		8	5	9	10
Apr 9	H	Sheffield Utd.	28400	1-1	4-1	1	2	3			6	7				11^1				4		8	5	9^2	10^1
Apr 14	H	Middlesbrough	16000	2-1	4-1	1	2	3			6	7^1			10	11				4		8^2	5	9^1	
Apr 21	A	Sheffield Wed.	20000	0-1	0-2	1	2	3			6	7			10	11				4		8	5	9	
Apr 24	A	Blackburn	40000	0-3	0-6	1	2	3			6	7				11				4		8	5	9	10
Apr 28	H	Newcastle	28000	0-0	0-1	1	2	3			6	7				11				4		8	5	9	10
May 5	A	Huddersfield	10000	1-2	1-4	1	2	3			6	7				11^1				4		8	5	9	10
May 7	H	Southampton *HC/PC*		3-0	6-1	1	2	3			6	7			10^1	11				4		8^1	5	9^4	

						McPhail D.	Clifford G.	McColgan J.	Davies Reg	Foxall H.	Moffat W.	Forward F.	Mackie J.	Haines W.	Watson D.	Cook F.	Jarvie J.	Rutherford S.	Haslam G.	Nichol J.	Davey H.	Smith J.	McIlwaine J.	Weddle J.	Irvine R.
League Appearances						41	42	42	24	21	41	42	19	26	35	41	1	1	4	21	7	18	15	14	7
League Goalscorers									1	1		5	5	11	10	10					2	11		9	1
FA Cup Appearances						1	1	1	1	1	1	1	1		1	1					1				

Total League Division 1   P42 W16 D7 L19 F66 A90 Pts 39 Posn 20th

Season 1928/29   Division 1

Date	V	Team	Attendance	FA HT	FA FT	McPhail D.	Clifford G.	McColgan J.	Moffat W.	Nichol J.	Thackeray D.	Forward F.	Smith J.	Weddle J.	Irvine R.	Cook F.	Watson D.	McIlwaine J.	Mackie A.	Bell T.	Lewis Ben	Gilfillan J.	McNeil J.	Easson J.	Latimer J.	Smith W.
Aug 25	H	Huddersfield	33475	0-0	1-0	1	2	3	4	5	6	7	8	9¹	10	11										
Sept 1	A	Everton	50000	0-1	0-4	1	2	3	4	5	6	7	8	9	10	11										
Sept 5	H	Manchester City	26000	1-0	1-0	1	2	3	4	5	6	7	8¹	9	10	11										
Sept 8	H	Arsenal	25000	1-0	2-0	1	2	3		5	6	7	8¹	9	10¹	11	4									
Sept 15	A	Blackburn	15000	0-0	0-4	1	2	3	4	5	6	7	8	9	10	11										
Sept 22	H	Sunderland	20000	3-0	4-0	1	2	3		4	6	7¹	8¹	9	10¹	11¹	5									
Sept 29	A	Derby Co.	20000	0-1	0-1	1	2	3		4	6	7	8	9	10	11	5									
Oct 1	A	Manchester City	20000	0-1	1-2	1	2	3		4	6	7¹	8	9	11	10	5									
Oct 6	H	Sheffield Wed.		1-0	3-2	1	2	3		4	6	7	8	9	11	10³	5									
Oct 13	A	Bolton	12000	2-2	2-4	1	2	3		4	6¹	7	8	9	11¹	10	5									
Oct 20	A	Leicester	25000	0-5	0-10	1	2	3		4	6	7	9	8	11	10	5									
Oct 27	H	Bury	15000	1-1	4-1	1		3		4	6	7¹	8¹	9¹	10¹	11		5	2							
Nov 3	A	Leeds	25000	2-1	2-3	1	2			4	6	7	8	9	10	11¹		5¹		3						
Nov 10	H	Liverpool	20000	0-0	0-1	1			4	5	6	7	8	9	10	11			2	3						
Nov 17	A	West Ham	25000	0-0	1-0	1			4	5	6	7	8¹	9	11	10			2	3						
Nov 24	H	Newcastle	18000	0-0	0-1					4	6	7	8	9	11	10		5	2	3			1			
Dec 1	A	Burnley	20000	0-3	1-4					4	6	7	9	8¹	11	10		5	2	3			1			
Dec 8	H	Cardiff		0-0	0-1					4	6	7	8	9	10	11		5	2	3			1			
Dec 15	A	Sheffield Utd.		0-3	0-3					4	6	7	8	9	11	10		5	2	3			1			
Dec 22	H	Manchester Utd.	10000	2-0	3-0					4	6	7	8²	9	11	10		5	2	3			1			
Dec 25	H	Aston Villa	25000	2-2	3-2				6	4		7	8	9¹	10²	11		5	2	3			1			
Dec 26	A	Aston Villa	60000	1-3	2-3					4	6	7	8		10	11		5	2	3			1	9²		
Dec 29	A	Huddersfield	15000	1-2	1-3					4	6	7	8	9¹	10	11		5	2	3			1			
Jan 5	H	Everton	24000	2-0	3-0					4	6	7¹	8¹	9	10¹	11		5	2	3			1			
Jan 12	H	Charlton *FAC3*	20000+	0-1	2-1			3		4	6	7	8¹		10	11		5	2			1		9¹		
Jan 19	A	Arsenal	25000	0-3	0-4					4	6	7	8	9	10	11		5	2	3		1				
Jan 26	H	Bradford C. *FAC4*	20000	0-0	2-0				4	5	6	7	8		10¹	11			2	3		1		9¹		
Feb 2	A	Sunderland	15000	0-2	0-5				4	5	6	7	8	9	10	11			2	3		1				
Feb 9	H	Derby Co.	16000	0-0	1-5					4	6	7	8	9	10¹	11		5	2	3		1				
Feb 16	A	Chelsea *FAC5*	38474	1-1	1-1			3		4	6	7	8	9¹	10	11		5	2			1				
Feb 20	H	Chelsea *FAC5R*	31966	1-0	1-0			3		4	6	7	8	9¹	10	11		5	2			1				
Feb 23	H	Bolton		2-3	4-4			3		4	6	7	8	9¹	11²	10¹		5	2			1				
Mar 2	H	West Ham *FAC6*	39088	3-0	3-2			3		4	6	7	8¹	9¹	11¹	10		5	2			1				
Mar 4	A	Sheffield Wed.	16000	0-2	1-2			3		4	6		8	9¹	11	10		5	2			1			7	
Mar 9	A	Bury	12000	0-0	0-0			3		4	6	7	8	9	11	10		5	2			1				
Mar 13	H	Blackburn	15000	1-1	2-2			3	4	5	6	7¹	8	9	11	10			2			1				
Mar 16	H	Leeds	15000	0-1	0-2	1		3		4	6	7	8	9	11	10		5	2							
Mar 23	†	Aston Villa *FACSF*	26147	1-0	1-0	1		3		4	6	7	8¹	9	11	10		5	2							
Mar 29	H	Birmingham	25000	2-0	3-1					4	6	7¹	8	9	11	10¹		5	2	3		1				
Mar 30	H	West Ham		3-0	3-0			3		4	6	7	8	9²	11	10		5¹	2			1				
Apr 1	A	Birmingham	20000	0-1	0-1			3	6	4		7	8	9	11	10		5	2			1				
Apr 6	A	Newcastle	30000	0-0	0-0			3		4	6	7	8	9	11	10		5	2			1				
Apr 10	H	Leicester	21000		1-0					4	6	7	8	9¹	11	10		5	2	3		1				
Apr 13	H	Burnley	20000	1-1	3-1			3		4	6	7	8	9	11	10¹		5¹	2			1				
Apr 17	A	Liverpool	15000	0-0	0-0					4	6	7	8	9	11	10		5	2	3		1				
Apr 20	A	Cardiff	10000	0-1	1-1			3		4	6	7	8	9	11¹	10		5	2			1				
Apr 27	‡	Bolton *FAC Final*	92570	0-0	0-2					4	6	7	8	9	11	10		5	2	3		1				
Apr 29	H	Sheffield Utd.	12000	1-1	2-3				4	5	6	7¹	8	9¹	11	10			2	3		1				
May 4	A	Manchester Utd.	18000	3-0	3-0					4	6	7	9	8	11			5	2			1			10	3
May 6	H	Southampton *HC*	2000	0-1	1-2					4	6	7	8¹	9	11			5	2			1			10	3
May 8	A	Southampton *PBC*		1-1	2-3	1				4	6	7	8	9	11			5	2						10²	3
League Appearances						16	14	17	15	40	39	41	38	31	24	42	24	32	31	20	2	24	9	1	1	1
League Goalscorers										1	8	9	8	8	6	6		4				4				
FA Cup Appearances								5	1	7	7	7	7	5	4	7	3	6	7	2		7		2		
FA Cup Goalscorers												3	3	1	1									2		

Total League Division 1   P42 W15 D6 L21 F56 A80 Pts 36 Posn 20th

† at Highbury
‡ at Wembley

Own goals: Blackburn (13 Mar), Burnley (13 Apr)

Season 1929/30   Division 1

Date	Venue	Team	Attendance	FA HT	FA FT	Gilfillan J.	Mackie A.	McColgan J.	Nichol J.	McIlwaine J.	Thackeray D.	Forward F.	Smith J.	Weddle J.	Watson D.	Cook F.	Latimer J.	Irvine R.	McNeil J.	Bell T.	Easson J.	Clifford G.	Kearney R.	Rutherford S.	Smith W.	Ross G.	Hill	Jackson	Methuen	Woolston	Lazenby
Aug 31	H	Sheffield Wed.	30000	0-2	0-4	1	2	3	4	5	6	7	8	9	10	11															
Sept 4	A	Grimsby	Big	1-0	1-1	1	2	3	4	5	6	7	8	9¹	10	11															
Sept 7	A	Burnley			0-4	1	2	3	4	5	6	7	8	9	10	11															
Sept 11	H	Grimsby	10000	0-0	1-1	1	2	3	4	5¹	6			9	10	11	7	8													
Sept 14	H	Sunderland	20000	0-0	1-1	1	2	3	4	5	6				10	11	7	8	9¹												
Sept 21	A	Bolton		0-1	1-2	1	2		4	5	6				10	11	7¹	8	9	3											
Sept 23	A	Leeds	12000	0-1	0-1	1	2		4		6		8	10	11	7			9	3		5									
Sept 28	H	Everton	21000	1-2	1-4	1	2		4	5	6			9	8¹	11	7			3	10										
Oct 5	A	Derby Co.	10000	1-2	2-3	1			4	5	6		8	9	11¹	7				3	10¹	2									
Oct 12	A	Manchester C.	20000	2-2	2-2	1			4	5	6		8	9¹	11	7				3	10¹	2									
Oct 19	H	Manchester Utd.	20000	1-0	3-0	1			4		6	7¹	8¹	9¹		11				3	10	2	5								
Oct 26	A	West Ham	20000	0-0	1-0	1			4		6	7	8	9						3	10	2	5	11¹							
Nov 2	H	Liverpool	19000	2-1	3-3	1			4		6	7	8	9¹		11¹				3	10	2	5								
Nov 9	H	Leicester	20000	2-0	5-0	1			4		6	7²	8¹	9¹		11¹				3	10	2	5								
Nov 16	H	Blackburn	20000	2-0	4-0	1		3		5	6	7	8¹	9¹		11¹					10¹	2	4								
Nov 23	A	Newcastle	15000	0-1	1-4	1		3	4		6	7	8	9		11					10¹	2	5								
Nov 30	H	Sheffield Utd.	15000	1-0	3-1	1	2		4¹		6	7	8¹	9¹		11					10	3	5								
Dec 7	A	Huddersfield	8000	1-1	1-2	1	2		4		6	7	8	9¹		11					10	3	5								
Dec 14	H	Birmingham	18000	1-0	2-1	1	2		4		6	7¹	8	9¹		11					10	3	5								
Dec 21	A	Middlesbrough		0-0	0-2	1	2			5		7	8	9		11					10	3	6		4						
Dec 25	H	Arsenal	28000		0-1	1	2		4		6	7	8	9		11					10	3	5								
Dec 26	A	Arsenal	50000	1-0	2-1	1	2		4		6	7	8¹	9		11					10¹		5		3						
Dec 28	A	Sheffield Wed.	24000	1-0	1-1	1	2		4		6¹	7	8	9		11					10		5		3						
Jan 4	H	Burnley	15000	2-1	7-1	1	2		4		6¹	7¹	8	9³		11¹					10¹		5		3						
Jan 11	H	Preston N.E. FAC3	29000	1-0	2-0	1	2		4		6	7¹	8¹	9		11					10		5		3						
Jan 18	A	Sunderland	20000	1-1	1-1	1	2		4		6	7	8	9		11					10¹		5		3						
Jan 25	H	Brighton FAC4	37522	0-0	0-1	1	2		4		6	7	8	9		11					10		5		3						
Feb 1	A	Everton	30000	0-0	0-1	1	2		4		6	7	8¹								10		5	11	3						
Feb 5	A	Bolton	15000	1-0	3-0	1	2		4		6	7	8¹	9²							10		5		3						
Feb 8	H	Derby Co.		2-0	3-1	1			4		6	7	8	9¹		11¹					10¹	2	5		3						
Feb 22	A	Manchester Utd.	25000	0-2	0-3	1			4		6	7	8	9		11					10	2	5		3						
Feb 26	A	Manchester C.	10000	0-3	2-5	1			4		6¹	7	8	9		11					10¹	2	5		3						
Mar 8	A	Liverpool		0-1	0-2	1	2		4		6	7	8	9		11					10		5		3						
Mar 12	H	West Ham	10000	1-1	3-1	1	2		4		6	7		9²		11	8¹				10		5		3						
Mar 15	H	Leicester		1-0	3-0	1	2		4¹		6	7	8	9¹							10¹		5	11	3						
Mar 22	A	Blackburn	10000	0-0	0-1	1	2		4		6	7	8	9							10		5	11	3						
Mar 29	H	Newcastle	18000	1-0	2-0	1	2		4		6	7	8¹	9		11					10¹		5		3						
Apr 5	A	Sheffield Utd.	20000	2-1	3-2	1	2		4		6¹	7	8	9¹		11					10¹		5		3						
Apr 12	H	Huddersfield	18000	0-0	0-1	1	2		4		6	7	8	9		11					10		5		3						
Apr 18	H	Aston Villa	28000	0-1	1-2	1	2		4		6	7	8	9¹		11					10		5		3						
Apr 19	A	Birmingham		0-0	0-1	1	2		4		6	7	8	9		11					10		5		3						
Apr 21	A	Aston Villa	25000	1-0	1-0	1	2		4		6		8	9		11					10¹		5		3	7					
Apr 26	A	Middlesbrough		0-0	1-1	1	2		4		6		8	9		11					10¹	3	5			7					
May 3	H	Leeds	15000	0-0	0-0	1	2		4		6		8	9		11					10	3	5			7					
May 5	H	Southampton PBC	4240	0-0	0-0	1	2		4		6		8	9		11					10	3	5			7					
May 7	A	Southampton HC			2-0	1	2		4		6												5			7	3	8	9²	10	11
League Appearances						42	31	7	40	10	41	32	36	42	6	38	7	4	3	9	35	18	32	4	22	3					
League Goalscorers									2	1	4	4	8	21	1	6	1	1	1		15		1								
FA Cup Appearances						2	2		2		2	2	2	2		2					2		2		2						
FA Cup Goalscorers												1	1																		

Total League Division 1   P42 W15 D10 L17 F66 A62 Pts 40 Posn 13th

Season 1930/31   Division 1

Date	Venue	Team	Attendance	FA HT	FA FT	Gilfillan J.	Mackie A.	Smith W.	Nichol J.	Kearney R.	Thackeray D.	Forward F.	Smith J.	Weddle J.	Easson J.	Cook F.	Clifford G.	Ross G.	Methuen H.	Allen J.	Salmond R.	Rutherford S.	Robson	Shackleton	Butcher
Aug 30	A	Leeds	12000	1-2	2-2	1	2	3	4	5	6	7	8	9^2	10	11									
Sept 1	A	Blackburn	10000		2-1	1	2	3	4	5	6	7	8^2	9	10	11									
Sept 6	H	Sunderland	24000	1-1	1-1	1	2	3	4	5	6	7	8	9	10^1	11									
Sept 10	A	Blackpool	23000		2-2	1	2	3	4	5	6	7	8	9	10	11^2									
Sept 13	A	Leicester	15000	0-1	1-3	1	2	3	4	5	6	7	8	9	10^1	11									
Sept 17	H	Blackpool	15000	1-1	4-3	1	2	3	4	5	6	7	8	9^3	10	11^1									
Sept 20	H	Birmingham		2-2	2-2	1	2	6	4	5		7	8^1	9^1	10	11		3							
Sept 27	A	Sheffield Utd.		1-1	1-3	1	2	6	4	5		7	8	9^1	10	11		3							
Oct 4	H	Derby Co.	20000	2-0	2-0	1	2	3	4	5	6	7^1	8	9	10^1	11									
Oct 11	A	Manchester City	25000	2-1	3-1	1	2	3	4	5	6	7	8	9^1	10^1	11^1									
Oct 18	A	Grimsby	15000	1-0	3-0	1	2	3	4	5	6	7	8	9^1	10^1	11^1									
Oct 25	H	Manchester Utd.	20000	3-1	4-1	1	2	3	4	5	6	7^1	8	9	10^3	11									
Nov 1	A	Middlesbrough	12000	0-0	1-0	1	2	3	4	5	6	7^1	8	9	10	11									
Nov 8	H	Huddersfield	25000	1-0	2-2	1	2	3	4	5	6	7	8^1	9^1	10	11									
Nov 15	A	Newcastle	23000	4-2	7-4	1	2	3	4	5	6	7	8^2	9^2	10^2	11^1									
Nov 22	H	Liverpool	18000	1-0	4-0	1	2	3	4	5	6	7		9	10^3	11	8^1								
Dec 3	A	Aston Villa	15000	2-1	2-2	1	2	3	4	5	6	7	8	9^1	10^1	11									
Dec 6	H	Sheffield Wed.	30000	0-2	2-4	1	2^1	3	4	5	6^1	7	8	9	10	11									
Dec 13	A	Bolton	10000	1-1	1-3	1	2	3	4	5	6	7	8	9	10^1	11									
Dec 20	H	Chelsea	20000	0-0	1-1	1	2	3	4	5	6	7	8	9^1	10	11									
Dec 25	A	West Ham			3-4	1	2	3	4	5	6	7	8	9^1	10^2	11									
Dec 26	H	West Ham		2-0	2-0	1	2	3	4	5	6	7^1	8	9^1	10	11									
Dec 27	H	Leeds	15000	1-1	1-1	1	2	3	4	5	6	7	8	9^1	10	11									
Jan 3	A	Sunderland	20000	0-0	0-0	1	2	3	4	5	6	7	8	9	10	11									
Jan 10	A	Fulham *FAC3*	27516	0-0	2-0	1	2	3	4	5	6	7^1	8	9	10^1	11									
Jan 17	H	Leicester	18000	1-0	2-1	1	2	3	4	5	6	7^2	8		10	11					9				
Jan 24	A	Brentford *FAC4*	23454	0-0	1-0	1	2	3	4	5	6	7	8^1		10	11					9				
Jan 28	A	Birmingham	5000	1-1	1-2	1	2	3		5	6	7^1	8		10	11			4		9				
Jan 31	H	Sheffield Utd.	18000	1-2	2-3	1	2	3	4	5	6	7	8^1	9	10^1	11									
Feb 7	A	Derby Co.	12000	1-2	1-5	1	2	3		5	6	7	8	9^1	10	11			4						
Feb 14	H	W.B.A. *FAC5*	30891	0-0	0-1	1	2	3	4	5	6	7	8	9	10	11									
Feb 18	H	Manchester City	5000	1-1	1-1	1	2	3	4		6	7	8	9	10^1	11				5					
Feb 21	H	Grimsby	18000		4-3	1	2	3	4		6	7	8^1	9^1	10^2	11				5					
Mar 7	H	Middlesbrough	12000	0-0	1-0	1	2	3	4		6	7	8	9	10	11				5					
Mar 14	A	Huddersfield	10000	0-1	3-1	1	2	3	4		6	7	8	9^1	10^1	11^1				5					
Mar 16	A	Manchester Utd.	5000	1-0	1-0	1	2	3	4		6	7	8	9^1	10	11				5					
Mar 21	H	Newcastle	17000	0-2	1-2	1	2	3	4		6	7	8	9	10^1	11				5					
Mar 28	A	Liverpool	20000		1-3	1	2	3	4		6	7		9	10	11	8^1			5					
Apr 3	H	Arsenal	31000		1-1	1	2	3	4		6	7	8	9	10^1	11				5					
Apr 4	H	Aston Villa	26000	3-0	5-0	1	2	3	4		6^1	7	8^1	9^1	10^2	11				5					
Apr 6	A	Arsenal	45000	0-1	1-1	1	2	3	4		6	7	8^1	9	10	11				5					
Apr 11	A	Sheffield Wed.	15000	1-1	2-2	1	2	3^1	4		6	7	8	9^1	10					5		11			
Apr 18	H	Bolton	14000	1-0	1-0	1	2	3	4		6	7	8	9	10^1	11				5					
Apr 25	A	Chelsea		0-2	0-2	1	2	3	4		6	7	8	9	10	11				5					
May 2	H	Blackburn	15000	2-0	3-0	1	2	3	4		6	7	8	9^1	10^1					5		11^1			
May 4	A	Southampton *PC*			4-0	1	2	3	4		6	7		9^1	10^1		8			5		11^2			
May 6	H	Southampton *HC*	2098	2-1	2-2	1	2		4		6			9^1	10^1		8					11	5	3	7
League Appearances						42	42	42	40	28	40	42	40	40	42	40	2	2	2	14	2	2			
League Goalscorers							1	1			2	6	10	24	29	7	2					1			
FA Cup Appearances						3	3	3	3	3	3	3	3	2	3	3					1				
FA Cup Goalscorers												1	1		1										

Total League Division 1   P42 W18 D13 L11 F84 A67 Pts 49 Posn 4th

Season 1931/32 Division 1

Date	V	Team	Attendance	FA HT	FA FT	Gilfillan J.	Mackie A.	Smith W.	Nichol J.	Allen J.	Thackeray D.	Forward F.	Smith J.	Weddle J.	Easson J.	Cook F.	Rutherford S.	Pateman G.	Hough E.	Maidment T.	Smith A.	Salmond B.	Worrall F.	Bell W.	O'Hare W.	Kennedy W.	Nicol J.C.	Rochford W.
Aug 29	A	Sheffield Utd.	18000	0-0	2-1	1	2	3	4	5	6	7	8	9¹	10¹	11												
Sept 2	H	Everton	20000		0-3	1	2	3	4	5	6		8	9	10	11							7					
Sept 5	H	Blackburn	18000	2-0	2-0	1	2	3	4	5	6	7	8¹	9	10¹	11												
Sept 9	A	Arsenal			3-3	1	2	3	4	5	6¹	7	8¹	9	10¹	11												
Sept 12	A	Bolton	12000		0-4	1	2	3	4	5	6	7	8	9	10	11												
Sept 16	H	Arsenal			0-3	1	2	3	4	5	6	7	8	9	10	11												
Sept 19	A	Derby Co.			1-2	1	2	3	4	5	6	7	8	9¹	10		11											
Sept 26	H	W.B.A.	16000	0-0	0-1	1	2	3	4	5	6	7	8	9	10		11											
Oct 3	A	Birmingham	25000	1-1	1-2	1	2	3	4	5	6	7	8	9	10¹		11											
Oct 10	H	Sunderland	20000	0-0	0-0	1	2	3	4	5	6	7	8		10	11		9										
Oct 17	H	Aston Villa	16000	0-0	0-3	1	2		4	5		7			10	11		9	3	8	6							
Oct 24	A	West Ham	20000	1-1	1-2	1	2	3	4		6	7	8¹	9	10	11						5						
Oct 31	H	Chelsea		1-0	1-0	1	2	3	4	5	6		8	9¹	10	11							7					
Nov 7	A	Grimsby	Poor	1-2	1-3	1	2	3	4	5	6			9	10¹	11				8			7					
Nov 14	H	Huddersfield	18000	3-1	3-2	1	2	3	4	5	6		8	9¹	10¹	11¹							7					
Nov 21	A	Middlesbrough		1-0	1-0	1	2	3	4	5	6		8	9¹	10	11							7					
Nov 28	H	Sheffield Wed.	20000	1-0	2-0	1	2	3	4	5	6		8	9¹	10¹	11							7					
Dec 5	A	Newcastle	20000	0-0	0-0	1	2	3	4	5	6¹		8	9	10	11							7					
Dec 12	H	Liverpool	17000	0-0	2-0	1	2	3	4	5	6		8	9	10²	11							7					
Dec 26	H	Manchester City	32000	2-0	3-2	1	2	3	4	5	6		8	9	10²	11							7					
Jan 1	A	Manchester City	Huge	2-2	3-3	1	2	3	4	5	6		8¹	9	10¹	11							7¹					
Jan 2	H	Sheffield Utd.	15000	0-0	2-1	1	2	3	4	5	6		8	9¹	10¹	11							7					
Jan 9	A	Middlesboro *FAC3*	23000	1-0	1-1	1	2	3	4	5	6		8	9¹	10	11							7					
Jan 13	H	Middlesboro *FAC3R*	24403	2-0	3-0	1	2	3	4	5	6		8	9	10²	11							7¹					
Jan 16	A	Blackburn	10000	2-4	3-5	1	2	3	4	5	6		8	9	10³	11							7					
Jan 23	H	Aston Villa *FAC4*	36956	0-0	1-1	1	2	3	4	5	6¹		8	9	10	11							7					
Jan 27	A	Aston Villa *FAC4R*	55000	0-0	1-0	1	2	3	4	5	6		8	9	10¹	11							7					
Jan 30	H	Derby Co.	17000	1-0	2-0	1	2	3	4	5	6		8	9¹	10¹	11							7					
Feb 4	A	Leicester	6000	1-0	1-2	1	2	3¹		5				9		11				8	4		7	6	10			
Feb 6	A	W.B.A.		0-2	0-3	1	2	3	4	5	6		8	9	10	11							7					
Feb 13	H	Arsenal *FAC5*	38915	0-1	0-2	1	2	3	4	5	6		8	9	10	11							7					
Feb 17	H	Birmingham	9000	1-0	2-1	1	2	3	4	5	6		8	9²	10	11							7					
Feb 20	A	Sunderland	20000	0-1	1-5	1	2	3	4	5	6		8¹	9	10	11							7					
Feb 27	A	Aston Villa	28000	0-0	1-0	1	2	3	4	5	6		8	9	10	11							7¹					
Mar 5	H	West Ham	15000	1-0	3-0	1	2	3	4	5	6		8	9³	10	11							7					
Mar 9	H	Bolton	8000	1-1	3-2	1	2	3	4	5	6		8¹	9¹	10	11¹							7					
Mar 16	A	Chelsea		0-0	0-0	1	2	3	4	5	6			9	10	11					8		7					
Mar 19	H	Grimsby	15000	1-0	2-0	1	2	3	4	5	6		8	9¹	10¹	11							7					
Mar 25	A	Blackpool	20000	1-1	1-1	1	2	3	4	5	6		8	9	10	11							7¹					
Mar 26	A	Huddersfield			0-1	1	2	3	4	5	6		8	9	10	11							7					
Mar 28	H	Blackpool	16000	0-2	2-2	1	2	3	4	5	6		8	9¹	10¹	11							7					
Apr 2	H	Middlesbrough		1-0	2-0	1	2	3	4	5	6		8	9¹	10	11							7¹					
Apr 9	A	Sheffield Wed.	Thin	1-1	1-3	1	2	3	4	5	6		8	9	10	11							7					
Apr 16	H	Newcastle	14000	3-0	6-0	1	2	3	4	5	6		8¹	9¹	10¹	11²							7¹					
Apr 18	A	Southampton *HCC*		0-0	0-1	1	2	3	4	5	6		8		10	11							7				9	
Apr 23	A	Liverpool		2-0	3-1	1	2	3	4	5	6		8	9²	10	11							7¹					
Apr 30	A	Leicester	15000	0-0	0-1	1	2	3	4	5	6		8	9		11							7			10		
May 7	A	Everton	20000	1-0	1-0	1	2	3	4	5	6		8	9	10¹	11							7					
May 9	A	Southampton *HC*	Small	1-1	2-2	1		3	4	5	6		8	9	10¹	11							7¹					2
May 11	H	Southampton *PBC*		2-1	5-1	1	2	3	4	5	6		8	9¹	10²	11¹							7¹					
League Appearances						42	42	42	41	42	39	13	37	40	40	39	3	2	1	3	3	1	29	1	1	1		
League Goalscorers							1				1		7	22	21	4							6					
FA Cup Appearances						5	5	5	5	5	5		5	5	5	5							5					
FA Cup Goalscorers											1			1	3								1					

Total League Division 1   P42 W19 D7 L16 F62 A62 Pts 45 Posn 8th

Season 1932/33   Division 1

Date	Venue	Team	Attendance	FA HT	FA FT	Grilfillan J.	Mackie A.	Smith W.	Nicol J.	Allen J.	Thackeray D.	Worrall F.	Smith J.	Weddle J.	Easson J.	Cook F.	Rutherford S.	McHugh J.	Surtees E.	Friar	Nicol J. C.	Smith A.	Salmond R.	Weekes	McCarthy L.	Jolliffe C.A.	Rochford W.	Welsh R.
Aug 27	H	Huddersfield	20000	1-0	1-0	1	2	3	4	5	6	7	8	9^1	10	11												
Aug 31	H	Chelsea	18000	0-0	2-0	1	2	3	4	5	6	7	8	9^2	10	11												
Sept 3	A	Sheffield Utd.	20000	1-1	3-2	1	2	3	4	5	6	7^1	8	9	10^1	11^1												
Sept 7	A	Chelsea	30000	1-2	4-4	1	2	3	4	5	6	7^1	8	9^1	10^1	11												
Sept 10	H	Wolverhampton	20000	0-0	2-0	1	2	3	4	5^1	6	7	8^1	9	10		11											
Sept 17	A	Newcastle	40000	1-1	1-1	1	2	3	4	5	6	7	8	9	10		11											
Sept 24	H	Aston Villa	30000	1-1	2-4	1	2	3	4	5	6	7^1	8	9	10		11^1											
Oct 1	A	Middlesbrough	8000	1-2	4-5	1	2	3	4	5	6		8	9^1	10^1		11^1			7^1								
Oct 5	H	Soton *HCC SF*	8000	3-0	6-0	1	2	3	4	5	6	7^3	8				11					9^2			10^1			
Oct 8	H	Bolton	17500	0-1	2-1	1	2	3	4	5	6	7^2	8		10		11						9					
Oct 15	A	Liverpool	20000	0-2	3-4	1	2	3	4	5	6	7	8^1		10^1		11					9^1						
Oct 22	H	Blackpool	15000	2-0	2-1	1	2	3	4	5		7	8^1	9^1	10		11							6				
Oct 26	H	Bournm'th *HCC Final*	2000	2-0	5-1	1	2	3	4	5		7^1	8	9^1			11^2							6	10^1			
Oct 29	A	Everton	20000		1-1	1	2	3	4	5	6	7	8^1	9	10		11											
Nov 5	H	WBA	25000	1-0	3-0	1	2	3	4	5	6	7	8	9	10		11^3											
Nov 12	A	Sheffield Wed.	15000	0-1	1-2	1	2	3	4	5	6	7	8	9	10		11											
Nov 19	H	Leeds		2-0	3-3	1	2	3	4	5	6	7^1	8^1	9	10		11^1											
Nov 26	A	Blackburn	12000	2-1	2-3	1	2	3	4	5	6	7	8	9^1	10^1		11											
Dec 3	H	Arsenal		1-0	1-3	1	2	3	4	5	6	7	8	9	10		11^1											
Dec 10	A	Manchester C.	20000	1-3	1-3	1	2	3	4		6	7		10^1	8		11		9		5							
Dec 17	H	Sunderland	14917	0-3	1-3	1	2	3	4	5	6	7	8^1	9	10		11											
Dec 24	A	Birmingham	23000	0-3	0-4	1	2	3	4	5	6	7	8	9	10		11											
Dec 26	H	Leicester	20000	1-1	2-1	1	2	3	4	5	6	7	8	9^1	10		11											
Dec 27	A	Leicester	25000	0-0	1-2		2	3	4	5	6	7	8	9	10		11	1										
Dec 31	A	Huddersfield	12000	2-1	2-2		2	3		5	6	7	4	9^1	10^1		11	1			8							
Jan 7	H	Sheffield Utd.	15000	1-0	1-0		2	3		5	6	7	8	9			11				4	1			10			
Jan 14	A	Grimsby *FAC3*	9200	1-0	2-3		2	3	4	5	6	7	8^1	9			11	1							10^1			
Jan 21	A	Wolverhampton	15000	1-3	2-5	1	2	3	4	5	6	7	8	9			11^2								10			
Jan 28	H	Newcastle	13000	0-0	2-0	1	2	3	4	5	6	7	8	9^1			11								10^1			
Feb 4	A	Aston Villa	25000	0-2	1-4		2	3	4	5	6	7^1		9	10		11	1							8			
Feb 17	H	Middlesbrough	14000	1-0	2-0	1	2	3	4	5	6	7^1	8^1	9	10		11											
Feb 22	A	Bolton	5000	0-2	1-4	1	2^1	3	4	5	6	7	8	9	10		11											
Feb 25	H	Liverpool	5000	1-0	2-1	1	2	3	4	5	6	7	8	9	10		11^2											
Mar 4	A	Blackpool	12000		2-0	1	2	3	4	5	6	7	8	9	10^2		11											
Mar 11	H	Everton	20000	1-1	2-2	1	2	3	4	5	6	7	8	9^2	10		11											
Mar 18	A	WBA	20000	0-2	2-4	1	2	3	4	5	6	7		9^2	10		11								8			
Mar 25	H	Sheffield Wed.	15000	3-0	3-0	1	2	3	4	5	6	7	8	9	10^2		11^1											
Apr 1	A	Leeds	10000	0-0	1-0	1	2	3	4	5	6	7	8	9^1	10		11											
Apr 8	H	Blackburn	14000	1-0	2-0	1	2	3	4	5	6	7^1	8	9^1	10		11											
Apr 14	H	Derby Co.	23000	1-0	2-0	1	2	3	4	5	6	7	8	9^1	10		11^1											
Apr 15	A	Arsenal	45000		0-2	1	2	3	4	5	6	7	8	9	10		11											
Apr 17	A	Derby Co.	12000	0-0	0-2	1	2	3	4	5	6	7	8		10		11								9			
Apr 22	H	Manchester C.	15000	1-1	1-2	1	2	3	4	5	6	7	8	9	10		11^1											
Apr 29	A	Sunderland	3000	2-0	3-0			3	4	5	6	7	8^1	9	10^2		11									1	2	
May 3	H	Southampton *PBC/HC*	2716	3-0	5-0	1	2	3	4	5	6	7^3	8	9^1	10		11											
May 6	H	Birmingham	12000	1-0	1-1		2		4	5	6	7	8	9	10		11									1		3
League Appearances						36	41	41	39	41	41	41	39	39	39	4	38	3	1	1	3	2	1	1	6	2	1	1
League Goalscorers							1			1	1	10	8	20	13	1	14				1	1			1			
FA Cup Appearances							1	1	1	1	1	1	1	1			1	1							1			
FA Cup Goalscorers													1												1			

Total League Division 1   P42 W18 D7 L17 F74 A76 Pts 43 Posn 9th

Own goals: Chelsea (Sept 7), Southampton (May 3)

Season 1933/34   Division 1

Date	Venue	Team	Attendance	FA HT	FA FT	Gilfillan J.	Mackie A.	Smith W.	Nichol J.	Allen J.	Thackeray D.	Worrall F.	Smith J.	Weddle J.	Easson J.	Rutherford S.	Bagley W.	Smith A.	Parker C.	McCarthy L.	Salmond R.	Anderson J.	Williams L.	Mackrell J.	Rochford W.	Wallbanks
Aug 26	A	Newcastle	55000	2-0	2-2	1	2	3	4	5	6	7	8	9^1	10	11^1										
Aug 30	A	Sunderland	22000		2-0	1	2	3	4	5	6	7	8	9	10	11^2										
Sept 2	H	Huddersfield	25000	2-0	3-0	1	2	3	4	5	6	7	8	9^1	10^2	11										
Sept 6	H	Sunderland	23000	0-0	0-0	1	2	3	4	5	6	7	8	9	10	11										
Sept 9	A	Stoke	29500	0-1	1-2	1	2	3	4	5	6	7	8	9^1	10	11										
Sept 16	H	Wolverhampton	21000	1-0	1-1	1	2	3	4	5	6	7	8^1	9	10	11										
Sept 23	A	Sheffield Utd.	14000	1-0	1-0	1	2	3	4	5	6	7	8	9	10	11^1										
Sept 30	H	Aston Villa	30000	2-1	3-2	1	2	3	4	5	6	7^1	8	9^1	10^1	11										
Oct 7	A	Leicester	27000	0-1	1-2	1	2	3	4	5	6	7	8	9	10	11^1										
Oct 14	H	Tottenham H.		0-0	0-1	1	2	3	4		6	7	8	9	10	11				5						
Oct 21	A	Leeds	20000	0-0	0-1	1	2	3	4	5	6	7	8	9		11	10									
Oct 28	H	Derby Co.	18000	0-0	0-1	1	2	3	4	5	6	7	8	9	10^1	11										
Nov 4	A	Arsenal	55000	0-1	1-1	1	2	3	4	5	6	7	8	9		11	10									
Nov 11	H	Birmingham	15000	0-1	0-2	1	2	3	4	5	6	7	8	9	10	11										
Nov 18	A	Sheffield Wed.	Poor	1-0	2-1	1	2	3		5	6	7	8^1	9	10^1	11			4							
Nov 23	H	Soton *HCCSF*		1-0	1-0	1	2	3		5	6	7	8		10	11			4							9^1
Nov 25	H	Manchester C.	12000	2-0	2-0	1	2	3		5	6	7	8^1	9	10	11^1			4							
Dec 2	A	Blackburn	10000	0-1	2-3	1	2	3		5	6	7^1	8	9^1	10	11			4							
Dec 9	H	Everton	15000	0-0	0-0	1	2	3		5	6	7	8	9	10	11			4							
Dec 16	A	Middlesbrough	10000	0-0	0-2	1	2	3	4	5	6	7	8	9	10	11										
Dec 23	H	WBA	16000	1-1	2-2	1	2	3	4	5	6	7	8^1	9	10^1			11								
Dec 25	A	Liverpool	27000		2-2	1	2	3	4^1	5	6	7	8	9^1	10			11								
Dec 26	H	Liverpool	23000	1-0	1-0	1	2	3	4	5	6	7	8	9	10			11^1								
Dec 30	H	Newcastle	15000	1-0	2-0	1	2	3	4	5	6	7	8	9^1	10			11^1								
Jan 6	A	Huddersfield		0-2	0-4	1	2	3	4	5	6	7	8	9	10			11								
Jan 13	A	Man. Utd. *FAC3*	23282	1-0	1-1	1	2	3	4	5	6	7	8	9		11	10^1									
Jan 17		Man. Utd. *FAC3R*	18748	2-0	4-1	1	2	3	4	5	6	7	8^1	9^2			10	11^1								
Jan 20	H	Stoke	17000	2-1	3-1	1	2	3	4	5	6	7	8	9^1	10			11^2								
Jan 27	H	Grimsby *FAC4*	34565	2-0	2-0	1	2	3	4	5	6	7	8^1	9^1	10	11										
Feb 3	H	Sheffield Utd.	14000	0-1	1-1	1	2	3	4	5	6	7^1	8	9		11	10									
Feb 7	A	Wolverhampton		0-1	1-1	1	2	3	4		6	7		9	10					11	5	8^1				
Feb 10	A	Aston Villa		1-0	1-1	1	2	3	4			7^1	8	9					6	11	5	10				
Feb 17	A	Swansea *FAC5*	27920	1-0	1-0	1	2	3	4	5	6	7^1	8	9		11	10									
Feb 21	H	Leicester	10000	0-2	3-5	1		3	4	5	6	7	8^2	9^1	10					11					2	
Feb 24	A	Tottenham H.	25000	0-0	0-0	1	2	3	4	5	6		8	9		11	10					7				
Mar 3	A	Bolton *FAC6*	52181	1-0	3-0	1	2	3	4	5	6	7	8	9^1	10	11^2										
Mar 7	H	Leeds	12000	1-1	2-1	1	2	3	4	5	6	7	8^1	9		11^1	10									
Mar 10	A	Derby	12000	0-0	1-0	1	2	3	4	5	6	7	8	9^1		11	10									
Mar 17	†	Leicester *FACSF*	66544	2-1	4-1	1	2	3	4	5		7	8	9^3	10	11^1			6							
Mar 24	A	Birmingham	12000	0-1	1-3	1	2	3	4	5		7	8	9^1		11	10		6							
Mar 30	H	Chelsea	30000		0-2	1	2	3	4	5		7	8	9	10	11			6							
Mar 31	H	Sheffield Wed.	20000	0-1	0-2	1	2	3	4	5		7	8	9		11	10		6							
Apr 2	A	Chelsea	50000	0-1	0-4	1	2	3	4	5		7	8	9		11	10		6							
Apr 7	A	Manchester C.	35000	0-1	1-2	1	2	3	4	5		7^1	8	9	10	11			6							
Apr 14	H	Blackburn	13351	2-0	2-0	1	2	3	4	5	6	7	8	9^1	10^1	11										
Apr 18	H	Arsenal	28442		1-0	1	2	3	4	5	6	7	8	9^1	10	11										
Apr 21	A	Everton	25000	1-1	1-1	1	2	3	4	5	6	7	8		10	11^1							9			
Apr 28	‡	Man. C. *FAC Final*	93258	1-0	1-2	1	2	3	4	5	6	7	8	9	10	11^1										
Apr 30	H	Middlesbrough	13546	1-1	4-1	1		3	4	5	6	7	8	9^3		11^1	10							2		
May 2	H	Bournem'th *HCC Final*	3267	2-1	8-2	1			4	5	6	7^3	8^2	9^2		11^1	10							3	2	
May 5	A	WBA	10692	0-2	1-2	1		3	4	5	6	7	8	9^1		11	10							2		
May 7	A	Southampton *PBC/HC*	Fair	1-1	4-1	1		3	4	5	6	7^1	8^1	9^1		11^1	10							2		

						Gilfillan J.	Mackie A.	Smith W.	Nichol J.	Allen J.	Thackeray D.	Worrall F.	Smith J.	Weddle J.	Easson J.	Rutherford S.	Bagley W.	Smith A.	Parker C.	McCarthy L.	Salmond R.	Anderson J.	Williams L.	Mackrell J.	Rochford W.	Wallbanks
League Appearances						42	39	42	42	35	35	41	38	41	30	32	14	10	6	4	3	3	1	2	1	
League Goalscorers									1			5	7	17	7	9	2	2				1				
FA Cup Appearances						7	7	7	7	7	6	7	7	7	3	5	4	1	2							
FA Cup Goalscorers												1	2	7		4	1	1								

Total League Division 1   P42 W15 D12 L15 F52 A55 Pts 42 Posn 10th

Own goal: Arsenal (Nov 4)

† at St. Andrews, Birmingham
‡ at Wembley

Season 1934/35   Division 1

Date	Venue	Team	Attendance	FA HT	FA FT	Gilfillan J.	Mackie A.	Smith W.	Smith A.	Salmond R.	Thackeray D.	Worrall F.	Smith J.	Weddle J.	Easson J.	Rutherford S.	Nichol J.	Anderson J.	Clarke	Rochford W.	Bagley W.	Muir	Rowe T.	Parker C.	Mackrell J.	McCarthy L.	Strong G.
Aug 25	H	Arsenal	39710	2-3	3-3	1	2	3		5	6	7^1	8	9	10^1	11^1	4										
Aug 29	A	Middlesbrough	17981		1-1	1	2	3		5	6	7	8	9	10^1	11	4										
Sept 1	A	Grimsby	14552	0-1	0-3	1	2	3		5	6	7	8	9	10	11	4										
Sept 5	H	Middlesbrough	16788		1-0	1	2	3	4	5	6	7	8	9	10	11^1											
Sept 8	A	Liverpool	27980	0-0	1-0	1	2	3	4	5	6	7	8	9	10^1	11											
Sept 15	H	Leeds	17470	0-0	0-0	1	2	3		5	6	7	8	9	10	11	4										
Sept 22	A	WBA	11574	2-2	2-4	1	2	3		5	6	7	8	9	10	11^1	4^1										
Sept 29	H	Sheffield Wed.	17358	1-1	2-1	1	2	3		5	6	7	8	9^1	10	11	4^1										
Oct 6	A	Birmingham	20916	1-1	1-2	1	2	3		5	6	7^1	8	9	10	11	4										
Oct 13	H	Stoke	18065	0-0	0-1	1	2	3		5	6	7	8	9	10	11	4	·									
Oct 17	H	Aldershot *HPC*	1405	1-1	4-2	1		3		5	6	7	8	9^2	10^2	11	4	2									
Oct 24	H	Preston	15110	2-0	4-0	1		3		5	6	7^1	8	9^3	10	11	4	2									
Oct 27	A	Tottenham H.	33461	1-2	1-4	1	2	3		5	6	7	8	9^1	10	11	4										
Nov 3	H	Huddersfield	18636	3-0	5-0	1	2	3		5	6	7		9^3	10	11	4			8^1							
Nov 10	A	Everton	25365	1-2	2-3	1		3		5	6	7		9^1	10	11	4	2		8^1							
Nov 17	H	Derby Co.	19346	2-1	5-1	1	2	3		5	6	7		9^1	10^1	11^2	4^1			8							
Nov 26	A	Aston Villa	16000	1-2	4-5	1	2	3		5	6	7		9^2	10^1	11	4			8^1							
Dec 1	H	Chelsea	18076	1-1	1-1	1	2	3	6	5		7		9	10	11^1	4			8							
Dec 8	A	Wolverhampton	16168	2-1	3-2	1	2	3		5		7^1		9^2	10	11	4	6		8							
Dec 15	H	Sunderland	16348	1-3	2-4	1	2	3		5	6	7		9^1	10	11	4			8^1							
Dec 22	A	Leicester	9010	2-3	3-6	1	2	3		5	6	7		9^1		11	4^1			8	10^1						
Dec 25	A	Blackburn	24560	0-0	0-0	1	2	3			6	7		9		11	4			8	10		5				
Dec 26	H	Blackburn	27199		3-1	1	2	3			6	7^2	8	9^1	10	11	4						5				
Dec 29	A	Arsenal	33901	0-1	1-1	1	2	3		5	6	7	8^1	9	10	11	4										
Jan 5	H	Grimsby	18821	1-0	1-0	1	2	3		5	6	7		9	10	11	4			8							
Jan 12	H	Huddersfield *FAC3*	29307	0-1	1-1	1	2	3		5	6	7^1		9	10	11	4			8							
Jan 16	A	Huddersfield *FAC3R*	55570	2-1	3-2	1	2	3		5	6	7	8	9^2	10^1	11	4										
Jan 19	A	Liverpool	14448	1-0	1-2		2	3		5	6	7			10	11	4	9^1	8			1					
Jan 26	H	Bristol C. *FAC4*	29239	0-0	0-0	1	2	3		5	6	7	8	9	10	11	4										
Jan 30	A	Bristol C. *FAC4R*	42885	0-0	0-2	1	2	3		5	6	7	8	9	10	11	4										
Feb 2	H	WBA	11009	0-0	0-2	1	2	3		5	6	7		9	10	11	4				8						
Feb 9	A	Sheffield Wed.	17396	0-2	0-3	1	2	3		5	6	7		9	10	11	4				8						
Feb 23	A	Stoke	15019	1-1	2-1	1	2	3		5	6	7^1		9^1	10		4				8			11			
Mar 2	A	Leeds	13450	0-1	1-3	1	2	3		5	6	7		9	10		4				8			11^1			
Mar 6	A	Preston	10160	1-0	1-1	1		3		5	6	7		9	10^1		4	2			8			11			
Mar 9	H	Tottenham H.	11687	1-0	1-1	1		3		5	6	7		9	10		4	2			8			11			
Mar 16	A	Huddersfield	14566	0-2	0-2	1		3		5	6	7		9	10		4	2			8			11			
Mar 23	H	Everton	14262	2-1	5-1	1		3		5	6	7^1		9^2	10		4^1	2			8			11^1			
Mar 30	A	Derby Co.	14845	1-0	1-0	1			4	5	6	7		9^1				2			8			11	3	10	
Apr 6	A	Aston Villa	20813	0-0	0-1	1		3		5	6	7		9	10		4	2			8			11			
Apr 10	H	Birmingham	8621	2-1	2-1	1	2	3		5	6	7^1		9^1	10		4				8			11			
Apr 13	A	Chelsea	44787	1-0	1-1	1	2	3		5	6	7^1		9	10		4				8			11			
Apr 19	A	Manchester C.	33477	3-0	4-2	1	2	3		5	6	7^2		9^1	10		4				8^1			11			
Apr 20	A	Wolverhampton	16012	0-1	0-1	1	2	3		5	6	7		9	10		4				8			11			
Apr 22	H	Manchester C.	20510	3-1	4-2			3		5	6	7^1		9^2	10		4	2			8			11^1			1
Apr 27	A	Sunderland	9361	0-1	1-4	1		3		5	6	7		9	10		4	2			8			11^1			
May 4	H	Leicester	12605	1-0	1-1	1		3		5	6	7		9	10		4	2			8			11			
May 6	A	Bournm'th *HPC Final*	6500	0-0	1-0	1		3		5	6	7		9^1	10		4	2			8			11			
May 8	H	Southampton *PC*	2515		1-0	1				5	6	7		9	10	11^1	4	2			8				3		
League Appearances						40	31	41	4	40	40	41	14	39	36	27	39	20	1	11	17	1	2	15	1	1	1
League Goalscorers												14	1	25	7	6	5	7		1				5			
FA Cup Appearances						4	4	4		4	4	4	3	4	4	4	4			1							
FA Cup Goalscorers												1		2	1												

Total League Div 1   P42 W15 D10 L17 F71 A72 Pts 40 Posn 14th

Own goals: Grimsby (Jan 5), Tottenham H. (Mar 9), Leicester (May 4).

Season 1935/36   Division 1

Date	Venue	Team	Attendance	FA HT	FA FT	Gilfillan J.	Rochford W.	Smith W.	Nichol J.	Salmond R.	Thackeray D.	Worrall F.	Bagley W.	Weddle J.	Easson J.	Rutherford S.	Symon J.S.	Smith A.	Anderson J.	Morgan L.	Rowe T.	Brown A.R.	McCarthy L.	Parker C.	Groves A.	Hird T.	Gundry R.	Dalton B.	Pringle A.
Aug 31	A	Middlesbrough		0-1	2-3	1	2	3	4	5	6	7	8	9^{2}	10	11													
Sept 4	H	Everton	23000	2-0	2-0	1	2	3	4	5	6	7	8	9^{2}	10	11													
Sept 7	H	Aston Villa	34000	1-0	3-0	1	2	3	4	5		7	8	9^{2}	10	11^{1}	6												
Sept 11	A	Everton	17000		0-3	1	2	3	4	5		7	8	9	10	11		6											
Sept 14	A	Wolverhampton	25000	0-1	0-2	1	2	3	4	5		7	10	9		11	6		8										
Sept 21	H	Sheffield Wed.	Full	2-2	3-2	1	2	3	4	5	6	7^{2}	8	9^{1}	10	11													
Sept 28	A	Manchester C.		0-0	0-0	1	2	3	4	5		7	8	9	10	11	6												
Oct 5	A	Preston N.E.		1-1	1-1	1	2	3	4	5		7	8	9^{1}	10	11	6												
Oct 12	H	Brentford	24000	1-2	1-3	1	2	3	4	5		7	8	9^{1}	10	11	6												
Oct 19	H	Arsenal	35000	1-1	2-1	1	2	3	4	5		7^{1}	8	9	10^{1}	11	6												
Oct 26	A	Birmingham		0-1	0-4	1		3	4			7	8	9	10	11	6			2	5								
Nov 2	H	Sunderland	23000	2-1	2-2	1	2	3	4	5		7	8	9^{1}	10	11^{1}	6												
Nov 9	H	WBA		0-2	0-2	1		3	4	5		7	10			11	6		8	2		9							
Nov 13	H	Bournm'th *HPC SF*	Poor	0-0	0-1	1		3		5			10			11	6		4	8		9^{1}			7	2			
Nov 16	H	Leeds Utd.	16000	2-1	2-2	1		3	4	5		7	8	10^{1}		11	6		9^{1}	2									
Nov 23	A	Stoke C.		0-0	0-2	1		3	4	5		7		10			6		9	2			8	11					
Nov 30	H	Liverpool	17000	1-1	2-1	1		3	4	5		7		9	10		6^{1}		8	2				11^{1}					
Dec 14	H	Blackburn R.	16000	2-1	3-1	1		3	4	5		7^{1}		9	10		6						8	11^{2}					
Dec 21	A	Grimsby T.		0-1	2-1	1		3		5		7^{1}	8	9			6		4	2			10	11^{1}					
Dec 25	H	Derby Co.			3-0	1	2	3	4	5		7^{1}	8	9^{1}	10^{1}		6							11					
Dec 26	A	Derby Co.			1-1	1		3		5		7^{1}	8	9			6		4	2			10	11					
Dec 28	H	Middlesbrough	22000	0-0	1-0	1	2	3				7		9	10		6		4				8	11^{1}					
Jan 1	A	Bolton W.			0-4	1	2	3				7	8	9			6		4				10	11					
Jan 4	A	Aston Villa	35000	1-2	2-4	1	2	3	4	5		7^{1}	8^{1}	9	10		6							11					
Jan 11	A	Man. City *FAC3*	53340	0-2	1-3	1	2	3	4	5		7^{1}	8	9	10		6							11					
Jan 18	H	Wolverhampton		1-0	1-0	1	2	3	4	5		7	10	9			6^{1}							11	8				
Feb 1	H	Manchester C.	20000	0-0	1-2	1	2	3	4	5		7	10	9			6^{1}							11	8				
Feb 8	H	Preston N.E.	16000	1-1	1-1	1	2	3	4	5		7		9^{1}	10		6							11	8				
Feb 12	A	Sheffield Wed.		0-0	1-0	1	2	3		5		7		9	10		6		4					11^{1}	8				
Feb 22	A	Arsenal	30000	2-1	3-2	1	2			5		7	10	9			6		4	3				11^{1}	8^{2}				
Feb 29	H	WBA	14000	2-1	3-1	1	2	3	4	5		7^{1}		9	10^{1}		6							11	8^{1}				
Mar 7	A	Liverpool		0-0	0-2	1	2	3		5		7		9	10		6		4					11	8				
Mar 14	H	Birmingham	17000	0-1	0-3	1	2	3	4	5		7		9	10		6							11	8				
Mar 21	A	Leeds Utd.		0-1	0-1	1	2	3	4	5		7		9	10		6							11	8				
Mar 25	A	Brentford		1-1	1-3	1		3	4	5		7	10	9			6			2				11^{1}	8				
Mar 28	H	Stoke C.	15000	1-0	2-0	1	2	3	4	5			10	9			6			8^{1}				11	7^{1}				
Apr 4	A	Sunderland		0-2	0-5	1	2	3		5		7	10	9			6		4	8				11					
Apr 10	H	Huddersfield		0-0	0-0	1	2	3	4	5		7	10	9			6			8				11					
Apr 11	H	Chelsea	20000	1-0	2-0	1		3	4	5		7	10^{1}	9			6			2				11	8^{1}				
Apr 14	A	Huddersfield		0-1	1-1	1	2			5		7	10	9^{1}			4			2				11	8		6		
Apr 18	A	Blackburn R.	8000	0-1	1-3	1		3	4	5		7	10	9			6			2				11^{1}	8				
Apr 22	A	Chelsea		0-0	0-1	1		3	4	5		7	10	9						2				11	8				6
Apr 25	H	Grimsby T.	10000	1-2	3-2	1		3	4	5		7	10	9^{2}			6			2				11	8^{1}				
Apr 27	A	Southampton *PC*		1-1	2-1	1		3	4	5		7	10^{1}	9			6			2				11	8				
May 2	H	Bolton W.	15000	1-0	2-1	1		3	4	5		7	10	9^{1}			6								8^{1}			2	11
League Appearances						41	27	41	33	41	3	41	35	39	21	14	36	10	8	15	1	1	7	26	16	1	1	1	2
League Goalscorers												9	3	16	3	2	3		2					9	6	1			
FA Cup Appearances						1	1	1	1	1		1	1	1	1		1							1					
FA Cup Goalscorers												1																	

Total League Div 1   P42 W17 D8 L17 F54 A67 Pts 42 Posn 10th

Own goal: Southampton (Apr 27)

Season 1936/37   Division 1

Date	Venue	Team	Attendance	FA HT	FA FT	Gilfillan J.	Rochford W.	Smith W.	Nichol J.	Salmond R.	Symon J. S.	Worrall F.	Groves A.	Weddle J.	Bagley W.	Parker C.	Easson J.	Morgan L.	Smith A.	McCarthy L.	Rowe T.	Anderson J.	Crawshaw H.	Strong G.	Pringle A.	Beaumont L.	Beattie J.
Aug 29	A	Birmingham	40000	1-1	1-2	1	2	3	4	5	6	7	8	9	10^1	11											
Sept 2	H	Liverpool		2-1	6-2	1	2	3	4	5	6	7^1	8	9^1	10^2	11^2											
Sept 5	H	Middlesbrough	23000	2-0	2-1	1	2	3	4	5	6	7	8	9^1	10^1	11											
Sept 9	A	Liverpool		0-0	0-0	1	2	3	4	5	6	7	8	9		11	10										
Sept 12	A	W.B.A.		0-3	1-3	1	2	3	4	5	6	7^1		9	10	11	8										
Sept 16	A	Leeds Utd.			3-0	1	2	3	4	5	6	7^1	8^1	9	10	11^1											
Sept 19	H	Manchester City	26000	1-0	2-1	1	2	3	4	5	6	7	8	9^1	10	11^1											
Sept 26	A	Sheffield Wed.		0-0	0-0	1	2	3	4	5	6	7		9	10	11	8										
Oct 3	A	Chelsea		0-0	1-1	1	2	3	4	5	6	7		9	10	11	8^1										
Oct 10	H	Stoke C.	22000	1-0	1-0	1		3	4	5		7		9^1	10	11	8	2	6								
Oct 17	H	Manchester Utd.	21000	0-0	2-1	1		3	4	5	6^2	7		9	10	11	8	2									
Oct 24	A	Derby C.	20000	1-1	3-1	1		3		5	6	7^1		9^1	10^1	11		2	4	8							
Oct 31	H	Wolverhampton	19000	0-1	1-1	1	2	3	4		6	7		9	10	11				8^1	5						
Nov 7	A	Sunderland	25000	0-2	2-3	1	2	3	4^1	5	6	7^1		9	10	11				8							
Nov 14	H	Huddersfield	21500	1-0	1-0	1	2	3	4	5	6	7		9	10	11				8^1							
Nov 21	A	Everton	20000	0-1	0-4	1	2	3	4	5	6	7		9	10	11				8							
Nov 28	H	Bolton W.	20000	1-1	1-1	1	2	3		5	6	7		9	10	11^1		4				8					
Dec 5	A	Brentford	38000	0-3	0-4	1	2	3		5	6	7			10	11		4				8	9				
Dec 12	H	Arsenal	33000	0-3	1-5	1	2	3	4	5	6			8	9	10^1	11				7						
Dec 19	A	Preston N. E.		0-0	1-1			3		5	6	7^1	8	9	10	11		2	4				1				
Dec 25	A	Charlton A.		0-0	0-0			3		5	6	7	8	9	10	11		2	4				1				
Dec 26	H	Birmingham	33000	1-0	2-1			3		5	6	7^1	8	9	10	11^1		2	4				1				
Dec 28	H	Charlton A.		0-0	0-1					5	6		8	9	10	11		2	4		3		1		7		
Jan 2	A	Middlesbrough	15000	0-2	2-2			3		5			8	9	10	11^2		2	4				1	6	7		
Jan 9	H	W.B.A.	18000	1-2	5-3	2		3		5	6		8^1	9^1		11^1	10^1		4				1		7^1		
Jan 16	H	Tottenham H. *FAC3*	32665	0-3	0-5	2		3		5	6		8	9		11	10		4				1		7		
Jan 23	A	Manchester City	15000	0-2	1-3			3		5			8	9	10	11		2	4				1	6	7^1		
Feb 3	H	Sheffield Wed.	10000	1-0	1-0			3		5		7	8	9	10	11		2	4				1	6			
Feb 6	H	Chelsea	17000	2-0	4-1			2		5		11		9^1	8	7^2		3	6		10				4^1		
Feb 13	A	Stoke City	15000	2-1	4-2			3		5		7^1		9	10	11		2	4		8^3			1	6		
Feb 20	A	Manchester Utd.	15000	1-0	1-0	1		3		5		7		9^1	10	11		2	4		8				6		
Feb 27	H	Derby C.		1-1	1-2	1		3		5		7		9	10	11		2	4		8				6		
Mar 13	H	Sunderland	22000	1-0	3-2			3		5		7		9^1	10	11		2	4		8^2			1	6		
Mar 17	A	Wolverhampton		1-1	1-1			3		5		7		9	10	11		2	4		8^1			1	6		
Mar 20	A	Huddersfield		1-1	2-1			3		5		7		9	10	11		2	4		8^2			1	6		
Mar 26	A	Grimsby T.			0-1			3		5		7		9	10	11		2	4		8			1	6		
Mar 27	H	Everton	25000	2-1	2-2			3		5		7		9^1	10	11		2	4		8^1			1	6		
Mar 29	H	Grimsby T.	22000	1-0	2-1			3		5					11	10	2	4		8^1			1	6	7	9^1
Apr 3	A	Bolton W.		0-1	0-1			3		5		7		10		11		2	4		8			1	6		9
Apr 10	H	Brentford	20000	0-2	1-3			3		5		7			10	11		2	4		8			1	6^1		9
Apr 17	A	Arsenal	35000	0-1	0-4			3		5		7			11	10		2	4		8			1	6		9
Apr 24	H	Preston N. E.	16000	0-0	0-1			3				7	8		10	11		2	4		5			1	6		9
May 1	A	Leeds Utd.	15000	0-2	1-3			3						9	8	11	10	2	4		5			1	6	7^1	

League appearances						21	17	41	16	39	23	34	16	38	37	42	10	25	27	6	3	16	1	21	18	6	5
League goalscorers								1			2	7	2	11	6	12	2				2		11		2	3	1
FA Cup appearances						1	1		1	1		1	1		1	1		1						1	1		

Total League Div 1   P42 W17 D10 L15 F62 A66 Pts 44 Posn 9th

Own goal: Derby (Feb 27)

Season 1937/38   Division 1

Date	Venue	Team	Attendance	FA HT	FA FT	Strong G.	Rochford W.	Morgan L.	Symon J.S.	Salmond R.	Pringle A.	Worrall F.	Anderson J.	Weddle J.	Bagley W.	Parker C.	Smith A.	Beattie J.	Young	Guthrie J.	Rowe T.	Groves A.	Wharton G.	Jones E.	Easson J.	Walker H.	Hall J.
Aug 28	H	W.B.A.	28000	1-2	2-3	1	2	3	4	5	6	7	8^1	9	10^1	11											
Sept 1	A	Liverpool			2-3	1	2	3	4	5	6	7	8^2	9	10	11											
Sept 4	A	Birmingham	30000	0-2	2-2	1	2	3		5	6	7	8^1	9	10	11^1	4										
Sept 8	H	Liverpool	18000	1-0	1-1	1	2	3		5	6	7^1	8		10	11	4	9									
Sept 11	H	Middlesbrough	22000	0-2	0-2	1	2	3		5		7			10	11	4	9	6	8							
Sept 15	A	Leeds Utd.		1-1	1-3	1	2	3		5		7			10	11	4	9	6	8^1							
Sept 18	A	Stoke City		0-2	1-3	1	2	3	4	5	6	7			10	11^1		9		8							
Sept 25	H	Manchester City	19000	1-0	2-2	1	2	3	4^1		6	7				11		9^1		8	5				10		
Oct 2	H	Chelsea	26000	2-2	2-4	1	2	3	4			7				11		9		8^1	5		6		10		
Oct 9	A	Charlton	34000	1-3	1-5	1	2	3	4			7				11		9^1		8	5		6		10		
Oct 16	A	Arsenal	50000	1-0	1-1	1	3	2	4			7				11		9^1		8	5		6		10		
Oct 23	H	Blackpool	13000	1-0	1-2	1	3	2	4			7				11		9^1		8	5		6		10		
Oct 30	A	Brentford	27000	0-2	0-2	1	3	2	4			7				11		9		8	5		6		10		
Nov 6	H	Leicester	18000	1-0	1-1	1	3	2				7			10	11		9		4	5	8^1	6				
Nov 13	A	Huddersfield	11902	0-2	0-2	1	3	2								11		9		4	5	8	6	7	10		
Nov 20	H	Derby	20000	3-0	4-0	1	3	2				7^1				11^1		9^2		4	5	8	6		10		
Nov 27	A	Wolves		0-1	0-5	1	3	2				7				11		9		4	5	8	6		10		
Dec 4	H	Bolton	15000	1-1	1-1	1	3	2				7				11		9		4	5	8	6		10^1		
Dec 11	A	Sunderland	3000	0-0	2-0	1	3	2				7				11		9^2		4	5	8	6		10		
Dec 18	H	Everton	20000	2-1	3-1	1	3	2				7				11^1		9^2		4	5	8	6		10		
Dec 25	H	Preston	26000	1-2	3-2	1	3	2				7^1				11^2		9		4	5	8	6		10		
Dec 27	A	Preston		1-1	1-1	1	3	2				7				11		9^1		4	5	8	6		10		
Jan 1	A	W.B.A.	15000	1-1	2-1	1	3	2				7^1				11^1		9		4	5	8	6		10		
Jan 8	A	Tranmere *FAC3*	16131	2-1	2-1	1	2	3				7	10			11		9^1		4	5	8^1	6				
Jan 15	H	Birmingham	20000	0-0	1-1	1	3	2				7				11		9^1		4	5	8	6		10		
Jan 22	A	Brentford *FAC4*	36718	1-0	1-2	1	2	3				7				11^1		9		4	5	8	6		10		
Jan 26	A	Middlesbrough	8000	0-0	0-0	1	3	2				7				11		9		4	5	8	6		10		
Jan 29	H	Stoke City	21000	0-0	2-0	1	3	2				7				11^1		9		4	5	8^1	6		10		
Feb 5	A	Manchester City		1-2	1-2	1	3	2				7				11^1		9		4	5	8	6		10		
Feb 12	A	Chelsea		0-3	1-3	1	3	2				7				11		9		4	5	8	6		10^1		
Feb 19	H	Charlton	23000	1-1	2-1	1	3	2				7				11^1		9^1		4	5	8	6		10		
Feb 26	H	Arsenal	43741	0-0	0-0	1	3	2				7	9			11				4	5	8	6		10		
Mar 5	A	Blackpool		0-1	0-2	1	3	2				7	9			11				4	5	8	6		10		
Mar 12	H	Brentford	27000	2-0	4-1	1	3	2				7	9			11^3				4	5	8	6		10^1		
Mar 19	A	Leicester		1-3	3-3	1	3	2				7				11		9^3		4	5	8	6		10		
Mar 30	H	Huddersfield	19000	3-0	3-0	1	3	2				7^1				11		9^1		4	5	8^1	6		10		
Apr 2	A	Derby		0-0	0-1	1	3	2				7				11		9		4	5	8	6		10		
Apr 9	H	Wolves	29000	1-0	1-0	1	3	2				7				11^1		9		4	5	8	6		10		
Apr 15	A	Grimsby		0-0	0-1	1	3	2				7				11		9		4	5	8	6		10		
Apr 16	A	Bolton		0-1	1-1		3	2				7	8^1			11		9		4	5		6		10	1	
Apr 18	H	Grimsby		1-0	3-0		3	2				7				11		9^1		4	5	8	6		10^1	1	
Apr 23	H	Sunderland	27000	0-0	1-0		3	2				7^1				11		9		4	5	8	6		10	1	
Apr 30	A	Everton		1-3	2-5		3	2				7				11^1		9^1		4	5	8	6		10	1	
May 7	H	Leeds	30000	3-0	4-0		3	2				7^1				11		9^2		4	5	8^1	6		10		1

						Strong G.	Rochford W.	Morgan L.	Symon J.S.	Salmond R.	Pringle A.	Worrall F.	Anderson J.	Weddle J.	Bagley W.	Parker C.	Smith A.	Beattie J.	Young	Guthrie J.	Rowe T.	Groves A.	Wharton G.	Jones E.	Easson J.	Walker H.	Hall J.
League appearances						37	42	42	9	7	6	41	6	6	8	42	11	36	2	38	35	34	28	1	26	4	1
League goalscorers									1			7	5		1	15		22		1		4			4		
FA Cup appearances						2	2	2				2	1			2		2		2	2	2	2		1		
FA Cup goalscorers																1		1				1					

Total League Div 1   P42 W13 D12 L17 F62 A68 Pts 38 Posn 19th

Own goals: Chelsea (Oct 2), Grimsby (Apr 18)

Season 1938/39   Division 1

Date	Venue	Team	Attendance	FA HT	FA FT	Walker H.	Morgan L.	Rochford W.	Guthrie J.	Rowe T.	Wharton G.	Worrall F.	Groves A.	Beattie J.	Easson J.	Parker C.	Taylor E.	Bagley W.	Smith A.	Salmond R.	Anderson J.	McAlinden J.	Rookes P.	Barlow H.	Hall J.	Flewin R.
Aug 27	A	Arsenal	60000	0-1	0-2	1	2	3	4	5	6	7	8	9	10	11										
Aug 31	H	Blackpool	26000	0-0	1-0	1	2	3	4	5	6^1	7	8	9	10	11										
Sept 3	H	Bolton	29000	0-1	2-1	1	2	3	4	5	6	7^1	8	9^1		11	10									
Sept 6	A	Grimsby		0-2	1-2	1	2	3	4	5	6	7		9		11	8	10^1								
Sept 10	H	Huddersfield	26000	1-0	4-0	1	2	3	4	5	6	7^1	8^1	9^1		11^1	10									
Sept 17	A	Everton	43913	1-2	1-5	1	2	3		5	6	7	8	9		11	10^1	4								
Sept 24	H	Wolves	26000	1-0	1-0	1	2	3	4	5	6	7	8	9	10^1	11										
Oct 1	A	Aston Villa		0-1	0-2	1	2	3	4	5	6	7	8	9	10	11										
Oct 8	H	Sunderland	25000	1-1	2-1	1	2	3	4	5	6	7^1	8	9	10	11^1										
Oct 15	A	Preston		1-1	2-2	1	2	3	4		6	7	8	9^1	10	11^1				5						
Oct 22	H	Charlton	25000	0-1	0-2	1	2	3	4	5	6	7	8	9	10	11										
Oct 29	A	Leeds Utd.	10000	0-1	2-2	1	2	3	4	5	6	7	8	9^1	10^1	11										
Nov 5	H	Liverpool	23000	0-1	1-1	1	2	3	4	5	6	7	8		10	11					9^1					
Nov 12	A	Leicester		0-1	0-5	1	2	3	4	5	6	7	8		10	11					9					
Nov 19	H	Middlesbrough	22000	1-1	1-1	1	2	3	4	5	6		8	9^1	10	11		7								
Nov 26	A	Birmingham		0-0	0-2	1	2	3	4	5	6	7		9	10	11					8					
Dec 3	H	Manchester Utd.	10000	0-0	0-0	1	2	3	4	5	6	7		9	10	11					8					
Dec 10	A	Stoke		0-1	1-1	1	2	3	4	5	6	7			11^1	8	10				9					
Dec 17	H	Chelsea	22000	1-1	2-1	1	2	3	4	5	6^1	7^1				11	10				9	8				
Dec 24	H	Arsenal	25000	0-0	0-0	1	2	3		5	6	7				11	10	4			9	8				
Dec 27	H	Brentford	32000	0-1	2-2	1	2	3		5	6	7				11	10	4			9^1	8^1				
Dec 31	A	Bolton	12000	0-3	1-5	1	2	3		5	6	7				11	10	4			9^1	8				
Jan 7	H	Lincoln *FAC3*	27432	2-0	4-0	1	2	3	4	5	6	7^1				11^1	10				9^2	8				
Jan 14	A	Huddersfield	6000	0-2	0-3	1	2	3	4	5	6	7				11	8				9	10				
Jan 21	H	W.B.A. *FAC4*	36661	2-0	2-0	1	2	3	4	5	6	7				11	10				9^2	8				
Jan 28	A	Wolves		0-2	0-3	1	2	3	4	5	6	7				11	10				9	8				
Feb 1	H	Everton	18000	0-0	0-1	1	2	3	4	5	6	7				11	10				9	8				
Feb 4	H	Aston Villa	28000	0-0	0-0	1	2		4	5	6	7		9		11	10					8	3			
Feb 11	H	West Ham *FAC5*	47614	0-0	2-0	1	2		4	5	6	7^1				11^1	10				9	8	3			
Feb 18	H	Preston	25000	0-0	0-0	1	2		4	5	6	7				11	10				9	8	3			
Feb 22	A	Brentford		0-1	0-2	1	2		4	5	6	7				11	10				9	8	3			
Feb 25	A	Charlton	8000	1-1	3-3	1	2		4	5		7^1				11			6		9^1	8	3	10^1		
Mar 4	H	Preston *FAC6*	44237	0-0	1-0	1	2	3	4	5	6	7				11	10				9^1	8				
Mar 8	H	Leeds Utd.	15000	2-0	2-0	1	2	3	4	5	6	7^1				11					9	8		10^1		
Mar 11	A	Liverpool		1-2	4-4	1	2	3	4	5	6	7				11^1					9^1	8^1		10^1		
Mar 16	A	Sunderland	8000	0-0	2-0		2	3	4	5	6	7				11					9^1	8^1		10	1	
Mar 18	H	Leicester	24000	0-0	0-1		2	3	4	5	6	7				11					9	8		10	1	
Mar 25	†	Huddersfield *FAC SF*	60053	0-1	2-1	1	2	3	4	5	6	7				11					9^1	8		10^1		
Mar 29	A	Middlesbrough	5000	1-5	2-8	1	2	3^1	4	5	6	7				11					9^1	8		10		
Apr 1	H	Birmingham	22000	0-0	2-0		2	3	4	5	6	7				11					9^1	8^1		10	1	
Apr 7	H	Derby	37000	0-1	1-3		2	3	4	5	6	7				11^1					9	8		10	1	
Apr 8	A	Manchester Utd.	25000	0-1	1-1		2	3	4	5	6	7				11	10				9	8^1			1	
Apr 10	A	Derby	20000	0-0	1-0		2	3	4	5	6	7^1				11	10				9	8			1	
Apr 15	H	Stoke	22000	1-0	2-0		2	3	4	5		7				11^1	10		6		9^1	8			1	
Apr 19	H	Grimsby		1-0	2-1			3	4		6	7				11^1	10				9^1	8	2		1	5
Apr 22	A	Chelsea	3000	0-0	0-1	1	2	3	4	5	6	7				11					9	8		10		
Apr 29	‡	Wolves *FAC Final*	99370	2-0	4-1	1	2	3	4	5	6	7				11^2					9^1	8		10^1		
May 6	A	Blackpool		0-1	1-2	1	2	3	4	5	6	7				11					9	8		10^1		
League Appearances						34	40	39	38	40	38	41	14	17	14	42	4	18	6	1	27	20	5	14	8	1
League Goalscorers							1		2	7	1	5	2	8	1	1					10	4		5		
FA Cup Appearances						6	6	5	6	6		6				6	4				6	6	1	2		
FA Cup Goalscorers												2				4					7	2				

Total League Div 1   P42 W12 D13 L17 F47 A70 Pts 37 Posn 17th

† At Highbury
‡ At Wembley

Season 1939/40 Division 1
Regional League South 'B' and 'C'

Date	Venue	Team	Attendance	FA HT	FA FT	Walker H.	Morgan L.	Rochford W.	Smith A.	Flewin R.	Wharton G.	Worrall F.	McAlinden J.	Anderson J.	Barlow H.	Parker C.	Hutchinson	Candy	Bagley W.	Rowe T.	Bushby T.	Royston	Miller A.	Jackson	Guthrie J.	Bryan	Allen J.	Barnes J.	Gilchrist	Briggs	Jones E.	Summerbee	Mas...
Aug 26	H	Blackburn R.§	23996	0-0	2-1	1	2	3	4		6	7^{1}	8	9^{1}	10	11		5																
Aug 30	A	Derby Co.§	10211	0-2	0-2	1	2	3	4		6	7	8	9	10	11		5																
Sept 2	A	Bolton W.§	12832	1-2	1-2	1	2	3	4		6	7	8	9	10^{1}	11		5																
Oct 21	A	Fulham†	6468	0-0	1-2	1	2		6	5			8	9	10^{1}			11	7	3			4										
Oct 28	H	Brentford†	3396	0-1	3-1	1	2	3	6	5			8	9^{1}	10			11^{2}	7				4										
Nov 4	H	Q.P.R.†	3643	0-0	2-1	1	2	3	6	5			8	9	10			11^{1}	7^{1}				4										
Nov 11	A	Aldershot†	5304	4-2	4-4	1	2	3	6	5			8^{1}	9^{1}	10^{1}			11^{1}	7				4										
Nov 18	H	Bournemouth†	2406	0-3	3-5	1	2	3^{1}	6	5			8	9	10^{1}			11	7^{1}				4										
Nov 25	A	Chelsea†	6127	0-1	0-1	1	2	3	6	5			8	9	10			11	7				4										
Dec 2	H	Southampton†	4518	2-0	4-1	1	2	3	6	5			8^{3}	9	10^{1}			11	7			1	4										
Dec 9	A	Brighton†	3000	1-1	2-1	1	2	3	6	5			8^{1}	9	10		7^{1}	11					4										
Dec 16	A	Reading†	2704	1-1	1-2	1	2	3	6	5			8	9	10^{1}		7	11					4										
Dec 23	H	Fulham†	1964	2-0	3-1	1	2	3	6	5			8^{1}	9	10^{1}		7	11^{1}					4										
Dec 25	A	Brentford†	4811		0-4	1	2	3	6	5			8	9	10^{1}		7	11					4										
Dec 26	A	Q.P.R.†	5188	1-3	2-5	1	2	3	6	5			8	9^{2}	10		7	11					4										
Dec 30	A	Aldershot†	2458	3-0	4-2	1	2	3	6	5			8^{1}	9	10^{2}			11^{1}	7				4										
Jan 6	A	Bournemouth†	5000	0-1	0-5	1	2	3	6	5			8	9	10			11	7				4										
Jan 13	H	Chelsea†	3470	1-1	1-2	1	2	3	6	5			8^{1}	9	10			11					4		7								
Jan 20	A	Southampton†	2499	0-0	0-2	1	2	3	6				8	9	10			11	7				4		5								
Jan 27	H	Brighton†	1718	5-1	5-1	1	2	3	6				8^{1}	9^{2}	10			11^{2}	7				4		5								
Feb 10	A	Fulham‡	3842	1-3	2-3	1	2	3	6				8^{1}		10			11^{1}	7				4		5	9							
Feb 24	A	West Ham‡	1800	1-3	1-4	1	2		6					9	10^{1}			11	7				4		5			3	8				
Mar 2	A	Charlton‡	5033	0-1	1-3	1	2	3	6				8	9^{1}	10			11	7				4		5								
Mar 9	A	Chelsea‡	8091	0-3	1-4	1		3	6	5			8	9	10			11	7^{1}				4	2									
Mar 16	H	Tottenham H.‡	6012	1-0	1-2	1		3	6	5				9	10^{1}			11	7				4	2							8		
Mar 22	A	Brentford‡	9046	1-2	1-3	1			6	5				9	10^{1}			11	7				4	2						3			
Mar 23	H	Southampton‡	5850	1-0	3-1	1			6	5					10^{1}			11	7				4	2							8^{1}		
Mar 25	A	Brentford‡	6463	0-1	1-3	1			6	5				9	10^{1}			7					4	2									
Mar 30	H	Millwall‡	4857	1-1	1-1	1	2	3		5			8		10			11^{1}	4	7					9					6			
Apr 6	H	Fulham‡	5007		0-3	1	2	3	6	5				9	10			11					4		7								
Apr 8	A	Millwall‡	3864	2-0	4-3	1	2	3					8^{2}	9^{1}	10			11	7				4							6			
Apr 13	A	Arsenal‡	6328	1-2	2-3	1	2	3					8	9^{1}	10			11	7				4^{1}							6			
Apr 20	A	W.B.A. LC	12000	0-2	1-3	1	2		6	5		7	10	9^{1}	11								4					3			8		
Apr 24	A	Southampton‡		0-1	0-1	1	2			5			8	9	10			11	7	3			4							6			
Apr 27	H	W.B.A. LC	10000	2-0	3-2	1	2		6	5		7^{1}	10^{1}	9^{1}	11								4					3			8		
May 4	H	Chelsea‡	3688	3-1	3-1	1	2	3		5			10	9^{1}	11^{1}				7				4							6	8^{1}		
May 11	A	Tottenham H.‡	5301	0-2	1-4	1	2	3		5			10	9	4		8						7^{1}							6			
May 13	H	West Ham‡	2405	1-0	1-1	1	2	3		5			10^{1}	9					4											6			
May 25	H	Arsenal‡	3806	1-1	1-1	1	2	3		5			10	9	11				4												8^{1}		
June 1	A	Charlton‡	855	0-2	2-4	1	2	3		5			10																	6			
June 8	A	Reading†	748	1-0	2-2	1	2	3		5			10						4											6			
Appearances (not Div. 1)						37	30	34	24	31	2	2	31	32	33	1	5	28	22	2	7	1	30	2	7	2	1	1	1	13	6		
Goalscorers (not Div. 1)								1				1	8	17	12		1	9	2		3		2		2					3			3

Totals Regional League South 'B' Home P9 W6 D0 L3 F26 A16
Away P9 W1 D2 L6 F11 A26 Home & Away Pts 16 Posn 7th

Totals Regional League South 'C' Home P9 W2 D3 L4 F12 A16
Away P9 W1 D0 L8 F14 A29 Home & Away Pts 9 Posn 10th Last!

† Regional League South 'B'
‡ Regional League South 'C'
§ Division One (Discontinued because of the outbreak of war)
LC League Cup South 'B'

Tann	Saunders	Wattie	Emery	Wilkinson	Cadnam R.	Wilbert G.	Cross	Lovery	Hassell	Harris	Buchanan P.	Colkliffe J.	Layton W.	Mills D.
	8													
6	9^1													
6		11												
	8													
					11									
						11	8			7				
								7	6					
				7^1	8	11				9^1				4
		7^2				11					8	9		
2	3	1	1	1	1	1	3	1	1	2	1	1	1	1
	1		2	1						1				

Season 1940/41   South Regional League
Football League South

Date	Venue	Team	Attendance	FA HT	FA FT	Walker H.	Morgan L.	Rochford W.	Guthrie J.	Hutchinson	Higgins H.	Moffatt	Bagley W.	Wilkes	Walters	Mills D.	Buchanan P.	Flewin R.	Hart	Barlow H.	Parker C.	Summerbee G.	Ferguson	Black A.	Smith C.	Wilkins G.	King	Cavell	Emery	Littlewood	Taylor	Emptage A.	Flack A.
Aug 31	A	Watford†	600	2-1	2-1	1	2	3	4	5	6	7	8¹	9¹	10	11																	
Sept 14	A	Brighton†§	—		2-1	1	2	3	4					9¹		6	8¹	5	7	10	11												
Sept 28	A	Aldershot†	3500	2-2	3-2	1	2	3	4					9²		11	8	5	7	10¹		6											
Oct 5	H	Brighton†	1643	3-0	5-1	1	2	3	4				10	9³				5	7	8¹	11¹	6											
Oct 12	A	Southend†	1500	0-0	0-0	1		3	4		6			9		8		5	7	10	11	2											
Oct 19	H	Aldershot†	3985	0-3	1-3	1	2	3	4					9				5		8	11	6	7	10¹									
Oct 26	A	Tottenham H.†	1360	1-0	2-1	1	2		4				8¹	9				5		10¹	11	6	7		3								
Nov 2	A	Brentford†	1090	1-2	1-3	1	2	3	4				8	9¹				5		10	11	6	7										
Nov 9	H	Bournemouth†	803	2-1	4-2	1	2	3	5					9³		4				10¹		6	7	8				11					
Nov 16	A	Bournemouth†	901	2-1	3-4	1	2	3	4							10		5		10²	11¹	6	7	9									
Nov 23	H	Chelsea†	2324	2-0	4-2	1	2	3	8							4		5		10²	11	6	7							9²			
Nov 30	H	Chelsea†*	2473	2-0	5-0	1	2	3	4					9²				5		10²	11	6	7	8									
Dec 21	H	Brentford†	1814	0-2	2-3	1	2	3	4					9				5		10	11	6		8¹					7¹				
Dec 25	H	Southampton†	1992	0-1	1-2		2	3	4				10					5			11¹	6		9					7	1	8		
Dec 28	H	Charlton†	1833	1-0	3-1		2	3	4				10					5			11	6		8²					7¹	9	1		
Jan 25	A	Bournemouth‡	1142	6-0	10-2	1	2	3	4					9²				5		10⁶	11	6		8					7¹				
Feb 1	H	Watford‡	1821	4-1	7-1		2	3	4¹					9⁵	6			5		10¹	11	5		8					7	1			
Feb 8	H	Southampton‡	2134	1-1	5-2		2	3	4¹					9³				5		10	11¹	6		8					7			1	
Feb 15	A	Chelsea *LWC1*	4284	0-3	1-3		2	3	4					9				5		10	11			8					7¹			1	
Feb 22	A	Chelsea *LWC1*	4632	0-1	1-4		2	3	4					9				5		10	11	6		8					7¹			1	
Mar 1	A	Brighton‡	1800	0-1	0-4		2		4					9				5		10	11	6	3	8					7				
Mar 8	H	Luton‡	2108	6-1	9-2		2		4					9³				5		10¹	11¹	6		8²					7²				
Mar 15	H	Southampton‡	2296	1-0	6-0		2		4									5		10	11²	6¹		8					7				
Mar 22	A	Bournemouth‡	1854	0-2	0-3		2		4									5		10	11	6		8					7				
Mar 29	H	Brighton‡	2149	1-1	3-2		2		4									5		10	11	6¹		8²					7				
Apr 5	H	Fulham†	3099	3-3	3-3	1	2	3	4¹									5		10	11	6		9¹					7				
Apr 12	A	Southend‡	2500	1-0	1-3	1	2	3	4									5			11	6		10					7				
Apr 14	H	Southend‡	2605	0-0	1-2	1	2	3	8									4			11	6		10									
Apr 26	A	Watford‡	2500	0-5	0-6	1	2													10	11	6		8									
May 3	A	Luton‡	1400	1-0	1-2	1	2													10	11	6		8									
May 10	H	Bournemouth‡	1424	2-0	5-0		2											5		10	11			8³									
May 17	H	Aldershot *HCC SF*¶	1948	1-3	10-5		2	3	4									5		10³	11	6		8³									
May 24	A	Cardiff†	2732	0-3	1-4	1	2	3	4									5		10	11	6											
May 31	A	Aldershot†	2513	0-5	2-9	1	2		4									5			11	6		10					7				
June 2	H	Soton *HCC Final*	2466	6-0	8-1	1	2	3	4									5			11	6		10¹					7¹				

						Walker H.	Morgan L.	Rochford W.	Guthrie J.	Hutchinson	Higgins H.	Moffatt	Bagley W.	Wilkes	Walters	Mills D.	Buchanan P.	Flewin R.	Hart	Barlow H.	Parker C.	Summerbee G.	Ferguson	Black A.	Smith C.	Wilkins G.	King	Cavell	Emery	Littlewood	Taylor	Emptage A.	Flack A.
League Appearances						23	29	22	40	2	2	1	6	16	1	7	2	26	4	25	28	28	7	16	2	2	1	2	15	4	1	4	1
League Goalscorers								3	1				1	26		1				18	7	2		12					2	5			
London War Cup Appearances						2	2	2						2		1		2		2	2	1							2			2	2
London War Cup Goalscorers																													2				

Totals South Regional League P31 W16 D2 L13 F92 A71 Posn 9th (out of 34)

Totals Football League South   P13 W7 D0 L6 F48 A29 (these totals are part of Sth R L)

Totals other First Team Games P4 W2 D0 L2 F20 A13

† South Regional League
‡ Football League South
LWC League War Cup
§ only 43 mins played, because of enemy action, result stood
* game played at Fratton Park, by permission
¶ after extra time

Own goal: Bournemouth (Jan 25)

Winch	Burke	Hooper H.	Ward	Wharton G.	Blakeney	Else	Gardener	Rowe T.	Anderson J.	Grace R. A.	Lacey	Walker S.	Allport	McIntosh	Moores
1															
1	3														
1		3	9^3												
		3	9												
		3		9											
					8^1										
						9	8^1								
							7^1	5	9						
			9				7	5		3					
			9^1				7	5			3				
			9^2				7			3	6				
							7^1						1	9^3	
			9				7						8^1		
							8			3			9^2		
							8^2							9^4	
3	1	3	2	1	1	1	8	3	1	1	3	1	2		
		3		1			4							3	

Season 1941/42   London War League

Date	Venue	Team	Attendance	FA HT / FT	Walker H.	Morgan L.	Rochford W.	Guthrie J.	Flewin R.	Summerbee G.	McIntosh	Black A.	Moores	Barlow H.	Parker C.	Aston	Ward	Wharton G.	Platt E.	Harrigan	Griffiths	Worrall F.	Slater	Gregory	Emery	Burke	Ranner	Sykes	Bullock	Court H.	Martin	Rookes P.	Lene
Aug 30	A	West Ham *LWL*	6250	0-1 3-1	1	2	3	4	5	6	7	8^{2}	9	10^{1}	11																		
Sept 6	A	Watford *LWL*	3691	1-0 5-1	1	2	3	4	5	6		8^{2}	9	10^{3}	11								7										
Sept 13	H	Aldershot *LWL*§	6328	0-0 2-2	1	2	3	4	5	6	7	8^{1}	9	10	11^{1}																		
Sept 20	A	Millwall *LWL*	3507	1-0 3-1	1	2	3	4	5	6	7	8^{2}	9^{1}	10	11																		
Sept 27	H	Arsenal *LWL*	15785	0-1 1-5	1	2	3	4^{1}	5	6	7	8	9	10	11																		
Oct 4	A	Q.P.R. *LWL*	2935	1-0 2-0	1	2	3	4	5	6		10^{2}	9		11	7	8																
Oct 11	H	Reading *LWL*	5441	1-0 1-0	1	2	3	4	5			8	9^{1}	10	11	7																	
Oct 18	A	Brighton *LWL*	4250	1-0 1-2	1	2	3	4	5	6	9^{1}	8		10	11	7																	
Oct 25	H	Brentford *LWL*	5806	1-0 2-1	1	2	3^{1}	4	5		7	8		10	11^{1}	9	6																
Nov 1	A	Crystal Palace *LWL*	5493	1-1 1-3	1	2	3	4	5	6	7	8^{1}		10	11	9																	
Nov 8	H	Fulham *LWL*	6324	3-1 5-3	1	2	3	4	5		7	8^{2}		10	11^{1}	9^{2}	6																
Nov 15	H	Tottenham *LWL*	6044	1-0 1-2		2	3	4	5	6		8^{1}		10	11	9		1					7										
Nov 22	A	Cl. Orient *LWL*	2403	2-0 4-0	1	2	3	4	5				9^{1}	10	11	8^{1}	7^{1}	6															
Nov 29	H	Chelsea *LWL*	6469	0-0 2-3	1	2	3	4	5	6		8^{1}	9^{1}	10	11	7																	
Dec 6	H	Charlton *LWL*	4336	5-0 7-2	1	2	3	4	5	6		9^{4}	10^{1}	11							8^{2}	7											
Dec 13	H	West Ham *LWL*	6319	0-0 1-0	1	2	3	4		6			9^{1}	10	11	7					8		5										
Dec 20	H	Watford *LWL*	4633	3-1 7-1	1	2	3	4		6			9^{3}	10^{3}	11	7					8^{1}		5										
Dec 25	A	Aldershot *LWL*	4715	0-2 2-3	1	2	3	6^{1}	5			10			11	9					8					4	7^{1}						
Dec 27	H	Millwall *LWL*	6217	1-1 3-2	1	2	3	5^{1}		6		10^{2}			11	9					8					4	7						
Jan 3	A	Arsenal *LWL*	10160	0-1 1-6	1		3	6	5				9	10^{1}	11	4					8				7	2							
Jan 10	H	Q.P.R. *LWL*	4251	2-0 3-1		2	3	4	5				9^{1}	10	11^{1}	6					8^{1}			1	7								
Jan 17	A	Reading *LWL*	3888	0-4 2-5	1			4	5	6			9^{1}	10^{1}	11	7					8	3											
Jan 24	H	Brighton *LWL*	4190	1-2 5-3	1	2	3	4^{1}	5				9^{2}	10^{1}	11		6				8				7								
Jan 31	A	Brentford *LWL*	3820	3-0 5-2	1	2	3		5	6			9^{2}	10^{2}	11						8^{1}				7			4					
Feb 7	H	Crystal Palace *LWL*	4515	1-0 3-1	1	2	3	4	5	6		10			11						8				7					9^{3}			
Feb 14	A	Fulham *LWL*	4404	2-0 7-2	1	2	3	4	5	6		10^{3}			11^{1}						8^{1}				7^{2}					9			
Feb 21	A	Tottenham *LWL*	4813	0-0 1-1	1	2	3	4	5	6		10			11		9								7^{1}				8				
Feb 28	H	Cl. Orient *LWL*	5010	6-1 16-1	1	2	3	4^{1}	5	6		9^{8}	10^{2}	11^{2}							8^{2}				7^{1}								
Mar 7	H	Chelsea *LWL*	3258	0-2 4-3	1	2	3	4	5	6		9^{2}	10^{1}	11							8				7								
Mar 14	A	Charlton *LWL*	4901	3-1 5-2	1	2	3	4	5	6		9^{2}	7	10^{3}	11	8																	
Mar 21	H	Fulham *LWC*	6215	2-1 9-1	1	2	3	4	5	6			9^{1}	10^{3}	11						8^{3}				7^{2}								
Mar 28	A	Crystal Palace *LWC*	7329	2-0 2-0	1	2	3	4	5				9	10	11			6			8^{1}				7^{1}								
Apr 4	A	Fulham *LWC*	5187	0-1 1-2	1	2	3	4	5				9^{1}	10	11						8				7								
Apr 6	H	Crystal Palace *LWC*	11671	1-1 2-1	1		3	4	5			9^{2}		10	11	7		6			8											2	
Apr 11	H	Chelsea *LWC*	8326	0-0 2-0	1		3	4	5	6		9^{2}	10								8				7							2	11
Apr 18	A	Chelsea *LWC*	7721	0-0 0-0	1		3	4	5			9	10	11				6			8				7							2	
Apr 25	†	Charlton *LWC SF*	19036	1-0 1-0	1		3	4	5			9^{1}	10	11				6			8				7							2	
May 16	H	Aldershot *HCC Final*	4917	2-0 4-4	1	2	3	9^{1}	5	6		10^{2}			11						8^{1}	4			7								
May 30	‡	Brentford *LWC Final*	72000	0-1 0-2	1		3	4	5			9	10	11				6			8				7							2	
London War League Appearances					28	29	29	29	27	22	9	24	12	27	29	4	15	6	1	1	15	1	2	2	7	2	1	1	4	2	1		
London War League Goalscorers						1		5			1	41	5	22	6	1	4				9			1					3	3			
London War Cup Appearances					8	3	8	8	8	3		6	2	8	7		1	5			8				7							5	1
London War Cup Goalscorers												5	2	3							4								3			

Own goals: Clapton Orient (Nov 29), Brighton (Jan 24), Chelsea (Mar 7)

† At Stamford Bridge

‡ At Wembley

§ Abandoned after 77 mins, because of broken goalpost, result stood

Totals London War League	P30 W20 D2 L8 F105 A59 Pts 42 Posn 2nd (out of 16)
Totals London War Cup	P 6 W 4 D1 L 1 F 16 A 4 Pts 9 Posn 1st (out of 4) Plus Semi Final & Final
Semi Final & Final LWC	P 2 W 1 D0 L 1 F 1 A 2

LWL London War League
LWC London War Cup

Most, Fewest, Lowest etc.

Most League Points:	2 per win: 65 – Div 3 1961/2
	3 per win: 91 – Div 3 1982/3
Player with most league goals in a season:	40 – Billy Haines, Div 2 1926/7
Most goals in career with Pompey:	Peter Harris 1944 to 1960, 193 league, 15 cup
Most goals for in a season:	140 – 1899/1900 Southern League
	103 – 1932/3 Div 1
	87 – 1926/7 Div 2
	87 – 1961/2 Div 3
	87 – 1923/4 Div 3 South
	91 – 1979/80 Div 4
Fewest goals for in a season:	37 – 1910/11 Southern League
	65 – 1936/7 Div 1
	56 – 1964/5 Div 2
	41 – 1977/8 Div 3
	57 – 1920/1 Div 3 South
	62 – 1978/9 Div 4
Most goals against in a season:	97 – 1908/9 Southern League
	112 – 1958/9 Div 1
	91 – 1960/1 Div 2
	75 – 1977/8 Div 3
	59 – 1922/3 Div 3 South
	49 – 1979/80 Div 4
Fewest goals against in a season:	32 – 1919/20 Southern League
	48 – 1948/9 Div 1
	54 – 1974/5 Div 2
	42 – 1980/1 Div 3
	40 – 1923/4 Div 3 South
	48 – 1978/9 Div 4
Most successive wins:	12 – 1911/12 Southern League & Friendlies
	7 – 1982/3 Div 3
	6 – 1948/9 Div 1
Most Consecutive Losses:	9 – 1959/60 Div 2
	7 – 1958/9 Div 1
Most Consecutive wins and draws:	26 – 1917/8 Southern League
	13 – 1950/1 Div 1
	17 – 1921/2 Div 3 South
	14 – 1961/2 Div 3
Most home games without a win:	League: 16 – 6/12/58 to 26/9/59
Lowest post-war League attendance:	4688 v. Middlesbrough 16/12/72
Fewest games played in a season:	35 – 1917/18, 1940/1
Most games played in a season:	63 – 1899/1900
Most League appearances for Pompey:	Jimmy Dickinson – 764
Most capped Pompey player:	Jimmy Dickinson – 48 for England
Most wins in a season:	42 – 1899/1900
Fewest wins in a season:	6 – 1958/9
Most drawn games in a season:	22 – 1924/5
Fewest drawn games in a season:	2 – 1940/1
Most losses in a season:	27 – 1958/9
Fewest losses in a season:	2 – 1917/18
Longest run of losing to one club:	Brighton – 15th Jan 1913 to 10th Oct 1914 (8 games)
Longest run of wins over one club:	Swindon – 4th Sept 1915 to 11th Apr 1920 (10 games)
Longest run of drawn games with one club:	Sunderland – 14th Sept 1929 to 10th Oct 1931 (5 games)
Most consecutive drawn games:	5 – 28th Sept 1977 to 15th Oct 1977
	5 – 8th Dec 1979 to 26th Dec 1979
Most consecutive games lost:	9 – 27th Mar 1959 to 25th Apr 1959
	9 – 21st Oct 1975 to 6th Dec 1975
Highest reserve attendance:	1/3/52 – 30,289 v. Charlton
Pompey's Heaviest Player:	Fred Brown (Goal) 14st 11lb
Pompey's Tallest Player:	Andy Gosney (Goal) 6ft 4in
Pompey's Shortest Player:	Ray Wilde (OR) 5ft 2½in
Consecutive Away wins:	8 – 1917 Boxing Day to 20/4/1918
Biggest win:	16–1, 28/2/42 Home Clapton Orient
Biggest defeat:	0–10, 31/3/17 Away Tottenham H.
	0–10, 20/10/28 Away Leicester
Biggest draw:	4–4, numerous
Biggest Cup win:	10–0, 30/9/1899 Home Ryde
Biggest Cup defeat:	0–5, 5/2/1900 Away Blackburn
	0–5, 16/1/37 Away Tottenham H.
Biggest League win:	16–1, 28/2/42 Home Clapton Orient
Biggest League/Milk Cup win:	5–1, 25/9/62 Away Brighton
	5–1, 17/10/62 Home Coventry
Biggest League/Milk Cup defeat:	1–5, 11/9/74 Home Derby Co.
Largest Attendance:	99,370 v. Wolves (FAC Final) 29/4/39
	Home: 51,385 v. Derby Co. (FAC6) 26/2/49
	Away: 67,000 v. Tottenham H. 12/4/52

Season 1942/43   League South

Date	Venue	Team	Attendance	FA HT FT	Tweedy G.	Morgan L.	Rochford W.	Guthrie J.	Flewin R.	Summerbee G.	Bullock	Griffiths	Ward	Black A.	Parker C.	Walker H.	Barlow H.	Wilkes	Swindin G.	Anderson J.	Pond	Westland	Bushby T.	Mackintosh	Fagan J.	Brown W.	Davie	Arnold	Martin	Scrimshaw	Wilson R.	McK.
Aug 29	H	West Ham *LS*	7811	1-2 4-5	1	2	3	4	5	6	7	8	9²	10²	11																	
Sept 5	A	Millwall *LS*	6464	1-0 2-1		2	3	4	5	6	7	8		9²	11	1	10															
Sept 12	A	Chelsea *LS*	8760	1-1 1-2		2	3	4	5	6	7			8	11	1	10	9¹														
Sept 19	H	Aldershot *LS*	7190	2-1 2-1		2	3	4	5	6	7¹	8¹			11	1	10	9														
Sept 26	H	Arsenal *LS*	13033	0-1 2-2		2	3	4	5	6	7¹			8	11¹	1	10	9														
Oct 3	H	Reading *LS*	7432	0-1 2-1		2	3	4	5		7	8¹			11		10¹			1	9	6										
Oct 10	A	Brighton *LS*	1200	0-0 1-2		2	3	4	5		7	8	9		11		10¹			1		6										
Oct 17	H	Crystal Palace *LS*	6374	0-1 2-1		2	3	4	5	6	7	8			11		10					1	9²									
Oct 24	H	Tottenham *LS*	8516	1-0 1-0		2	3	4	5	6	7	8			11		10					1	9¹									
Oct 31	A	Watford *LS*	1971	1-3 2-4		2	3	4	5		7	8			11		10¹		9¹			6										
Nov 7	H	Fulham *LS*	5844	0-0 1-1		2	3	4	5	6		8	7		11		10¹		9													
Nov 14	A	Cl. Orient *LS*	2190	1-1 2-3		2	3	4		6	7¹	8	9¹		11		10							5								
Nov 21	H	Luton *LS*	5504	1-1 4-2		2	3	4	5	6	7²	8			11¹		10¹								1	9						
Nov 28	A	West Ham *LS*	6143	1-1 1-2		2	3	4	5	6	7				11		10¹										9	8				
Dec 5	H	Millwall *LS*	4579	1-0 6-1		2	3	4	5	6	7²	8¹			11	1	10										9²					
Dec 12	H	Chelsea *LS*	7785	2-0 3-0		2	3	4	5	6	7¹	8			11	1	10²										9					
Dec 19	A	Aldershot *LS*	6028	3-2 4-3		2		4	5	6	7²	8¹			11	1	10										9¹	3				
Dec 25	H	Southampton *LS*	10012	0-2 2-3		2	3	4	5			8¹			11	1						6					9		10¹			7
Dec 26	A	Southampton *LS*	18416	1-0 2-0		2	3	4	5			8			11	1	10¹										9¹					6
Jan 2	A	Arsenal *LS*	9788	0-2 0-5		2	3	4	5	6	7	8			11	1	10										9					
Jan 9	A	Reading *LS*	3340	1-2 2-2		2	3	4¹	5	6	7				11¹	1	10					8										
Jan 16	H	Brighton *LS*	5099	1-1 2-1		2	3	8²	5	6	7					1	10															4
Jan 23	A	Crystal Palace *LS*	4355	1-1 2-1		2	3	8	5	6	11¹					1	10¹															4
Jan 30	A	Tottenham *LS*	7146	1-4 2-5		2	3	4	5	6					11	1	10¹					8¹										
Feb 6	H	Watford *LS*	4005	1-2 6-2		2	3	4¹	5	6	7²	8¹			11²	1	10															
Feb 13	A	Fulham *LS*	4837	4-0 6-2		2	3	4	5	6	7⁴				11	1	8															
Feb 20	H	Cl. Orient *LS*	5925	1-0 1-0		2	3	4	5	6	7				11	1	8															
Feb 27	A	Luton *LS*	2050	0-0 1-0		2	3	4	5						11	1	8					6										
Mar 6	H	Aldershot *LSWC*	9472	1-1 2-3		2	3	4	5						11	1	8					6										
Mar 13	A	C. Palace *LSWC*	4763	1-0 1-0		2	3	4	5						11	1	8¹															
Mar 20	A	Fulham *LSWC*	5810	1-1 2-2		2	3	4	5	6	7					1	8¹															
Mar 27	A	Aldershot *LSWC*	6024	2-0 2-1		2	3	4	5	6	7					1	8¹															
Apr 3	H	C. Palace *LSWC*	9137	2-3 3-3		2	3	4	5	6	7²				11¹	1	8															
Apr 10	H	Fulham *LSWC*	7265	0-2 1-3		2	3	4	5		7¹				11	1	8					6										
League South Appearances					1	28	27	28	27	22	23	18	4	4	26	22	25	4	1	3	1	3	7	2	1	1	4	1	4	1	1	3
League Cup South Appearances						6	6	6	6	4	4				4	6	6					2										
League South Goalscorers								4			16	6	3	4	5		10	1			1	2	3				2		3			
League Cup South Goalscorers											3				1		3															

LS League South
LSWC League South War Cup

Totals Football League South   P28 W16 D3 L9 F66 A52 Pts 35 Posn 4th

Totals League Cup South   P6 W2 D2 L2 F11 A12 Pts 6 Posn 3rd out of 5 in group 4

Moores	Crowther	Ross G.	Tomlinson	Pointon	Whitchurch	Buchanan P.	Biggs	Speak
7								
9								
9	11							
9		7						
9		7						
9								
			9^2	10				
			10^1	9				
			10^1	9	7			
			10^1		7	9^1		
			10		7	9		
			10^1			9	11	
			10^1		11	9		
			10			9		
			10			9		
6	1	2	1	3	2	1		
				6		3	6	1
		2	2			1		
				3				

Season 1943/44   League South

Date	V	Team	Att	FA HT	FA FT	Walker H.	Morgan L.	Rochford W.	Guthrie J.	Flewin R.	Summerbee G.	Buchanan P.	Bushby T.	Anderson J.	Barlow H.	Parker C.	Pinkerton	McLeod	Robertson	Wilkes	Tann	Cumner R.	McIntosh H.F.	Quigley E.	Ward	Buckingham V.	Kerr A.	Dickinson J.W.	Sears	Martin	Mills D.	Storey	Cook
Aug 28	H	West Ham *LS*	5735	1-0	2-0	1	2	3	4	5	6	7	8	9^1	10	11^1																	
Sept 4	H	Millwall *LS*	8237	1-2	1-5	1	2	3		5	6	7	8^1	9	10	11	4																
Sept 11	A	Chelsea *LS*	9572	1-2	2-6	1	2	3	8		6	7		9	10^1	11^1		4	5														
Sept 18	A	Arsenal *LS*	12738	0-1	2-1	1	2	3	8		6	7			10	11		4	5	9^2													
Sept 25	H	Q.P.R. *LS*	9025	1-0	1-1	1	2	3^1	8		6	7			10	11		4	5	9													
Oct 2	A	Clapton Orient *LS*	3793	1-0	1-1	1	2	3	8		6				10	11		4			5	7	9^1									
Oct 9	H	Reading *LS*	12483	0-0	1-1	1	2	3	4	5	6	8			10	11						7	9^1									
Oct 16	A	Crystal Palace *LS*	7065	0-0	3-2	1	2		4	5	6				10^2	7		3	11			9	8^1									
Oct 23	A	Charlton *LS*	5178	2-0	5-1	1	2	3	4		6	7			10^3	11		5					8^2	9									
Oct 30	H	Watford *LS*	8189	0-2	2-3	1	2	3^1	4			7	8		10	11		5			6		9^1										
Nov 6	H	Aldershot *LS*	8790	1-0	4-1	1	2	3	4	5	6	8^1			10^2	7						11^1			9							
Nov 13	A	Brentford *LS*	6880	0-1	0-2	1	2	3	4	5	6	8			10	7						11			9							
Nov 20	H	Luton *LS*	6597	2-1	4-2	1	2	3	4	5	6				10	7						11			9^2	8^2						
Nov 27	A	West Ham *LS*	7622	1-2	1-5	1	2	3	4	5	6	8^1				11		10							9				7			
Dec 4	A	Millwall *LS*	4069	1-0	3-1	1	2		4		6	8^1			10	11^1			5			3			9^1				7			
Dec 11	H	Chelsea *LS*	4780	0-1	1-5	1	2	3	4	5	7	8			10	11									9^1				6			
Dec 18	H	Brighton *LS*	4401	1-0	2-3	1	2		4	5	6	7			10	11^2		3								8	9					
Dec 25	A	Southampton *LS*	7314	2-1	3-6	1	2		4	5		8										7^2						6	10	3		9^1
Dec 27	H	Southampton *LS*	12210	2-1	4-2	1	2			5		8^2										11				7^1		6	10	3	4	9^1	
Jan 1	H	Arsenal *LS*	17007	1-0	2-1	1	2	3		5	7	8			10	11								9^2		4		6				
Jan 8	A	Aldershot *LS*	6524	1-2	2-3	1	2			5	3	7	8		10	11										4		6				
Jan 22	H	Clapton Orient *LS*	4745	1-1	2-1	1	2			5	3	7			10	11^1							9	4^1			6	8				
Jan 29	A	Reading *LS*	4603	3-0	4-1	1	2			5	3	7	4		10^1	11										6	8^1				
Feb 5	H	Crystal Palace *LS*	8309	1-0	1-0	1	2			5	4	7	8		10							11				6		3			
Feb 12	H	Charlton *LS*	7862	0-0	4-0	1	2	3		5	7^1	4			10^1	11^1										6					
Feb 19	H	Aldershot *LSC*	8491	0-2	0-2	1	2	3		5		7	4			11										6					
Feb 26	A	Tottenham H. *LSC*	15224	0-0	0-1	1	2	3		5		4			10	11										6	8				
Mar 4	A	Millwall *LSC*	5148	0-3	0-5	1	2	3	8	5	4	6				11										10			7		
Mar 11	A	Aldershot *LSC*	5742	0-0	1-1	1	2	3	4	5						11									8	6	9			
Mar 18	H	Tottenham H. *LSC*	13061	1-1	1-2	1	2	3	4	5	7					11^1									8	6	9			
Mar 25	H	Millwall *LSC*	8065	1-1	1-1	1	2		4	5	3	7													8	6	10			
Apr 1	A	Watford *LS*	2481	1-1	3-1	1		3	4	2	7	6			10^1	11										8^2	5				
Apr 10	A	Q.P.R. *LS*	7492	0-0	1-1	1			4		7				10^1	11									10	8	6		2		
Apr 22	A	Brighton *LS*	4363	1-0	3-0	1			4	2					10^1	7											6				
Apr 29	H	Brentford *LS*	8996	1-2	3-2	1		4^1		3		8			10^1	7	9^1										6		2		
May 6	A	Luton *LS*	2749	1-1	1-1	1			4	3					10	11^1		5									6		2		
League South Appearances						30	25	16	23	17	24	17	18	3	26	27	1	6	7	2	5	9	5	2	9	7	3	13	6	3	1	1	1
League Cup South Appearances						6	6	5	4	5	3	4	3		1	5											3		5	5		1	
League South Goalscorers								2	1		2	6	1		13	10		1				2	1		3	3	6	3	1		3		1	1
League Cup South Goalscorers															1																		

Totals League South   P30 W16 D5 L9 F68 A59 Pts 37 Posn 6th

Totals League Cup South   P 6 W 0 D2 L 4 F 3 A12 Posn 4th out of 4 in Group C

LSC League South Cup
LS League South

Thomas	Whitchurch	Mitchell	Langley	Emptage A.	Lucas D.J.	Stubbings	Black S.	McArdle	Mason	Saunders	Dent
9^1											
9^2											
	9^1										
	9^1	8									
8	9	10									
9			7								
9											
				10^1							
				10							
	9			11^1							
	9										
	9					3	5	11^1			
	9^1					3	5	11^1	8		
							5	11			
	9									7	8
2	6	1				2	3	3	1	1	1
3	2	1	1	2	1						
3	3							2			
			1	1							

Season 1944/45   League South

Date	V	Team	Attendance	FA HT	FA FT	Walker H.	Morgan L.	Rochford W.	Guthrie J.	Flewin R.	Summerbee G.	Bushby T.	Buckingham V.	Anderson J.	Wayman C.	Parker C.	Whitchurch	Emptage A.	McLeod	Kerr A.	Black J.	Forrester	Harris P.	Gardiner	Massie A.	Speed	Jamieson	Dickinson J.W.	Jefferies	Drummond I.	Evans F.J.	Barlow H.	H.
Aug 26	H	Clapton Orient *LS*	9823	3-0	5-1	1	2	3	4	5	6	7	8²	9²	10¹	11																	
Sept 2	H	Brentford *LS*	8955	2-2	2-4	1	2	3	4	5	6		8	9¹	10¹		7	11															
Sept 9	H	Charlton *LS*	12705	3-1	5-1	1	2	3	4	5			10¹	11²	9	8¹	6	7¹															
Sept 16	A	Tottenham *LS*	14167	1-1	1-1	1	2	3	4¹				10	11	9	8	6	7	5														
Sept 23	H	West Ham *LS*	15429	1-2	1-3	1	2		4	5	3		10¹	11	9	8	6	7															
Sept 30	H	Southampton *LS*	13695	1-1	3-1	1	2	3	4	5			10¹	11	9¹	8	6	7¹															
Oct 7	H	Chelsea *LS*	13539	1-0	1-5	1	2	3	4	5			10¹	11	9	8	6	7															
Oct 14	A	Millwall *LS*	4729	0-0	0-0	1	2	3	4		6		8	11	9			10	7	5													
Oct 21	A	Watford *LS*	3752	0-1	0-3	1	2		4	5	6		8	11	9						3	7	10										
Oct 28	H	Aldershot *LS*	10056	1-0	3-0	1	2		4	5	3			11	9	8	6	10¹				7²											
Nov 4	H	Q.P.R. *LS*	10742	2-1	4-1	1	2		4	5	3		9²	11		8	6					7²			10								
Nov 11	H	Reading *LS*	8758	1-1	3-1	1	2		4	5			9²	11		8	6¹				3	7			10								
Nov 18	A	Fulham *LS*	8986	0-0	2-0	1	2		4	5	6		8²	9	11						3	7			10								
Nov 25	H	Brighton *LS*	10511	0-0	0-1	1	2		4	5	3		9	11			6					7			10	8							
Dec 2	A	Clapton Orient *LS*	2587	1-1	1-2	1	2		4	5	6		8		10					3		7¹						9	11				
Dec 9	A	Brentford *LS*	9550	1-4	1-7	1	2	3	4	5			8	9								7						10¹	6	11			
Dec 16	A	Charlton *LS*	2917	0-1	0-1	1	2	3	4	5	6		8	10	11				9			7											
Dec 23	A	Crystal Palace *LS*	7160	0-0	0-1	1	2	3	4	5	6		8	11								7						9	10				
Dec 26	H	Crystal Palace *LS*	13063	3-1	9-1	1	2	3	4				10	11¹								7						9³					5
Dec 30	H	Tottenham *LS*	11507	0-0	0-0	1	2	3	4				10	9	11				6			7											
Jan 6	A	West Ham *LS*	6390	0-3	0-4	1	2	3	4				10	8	9				6			7					11						5
Jan 13	A	Southampton *LS*	11294	3-1	4-2	1	2	3	4	5	6		10	8								7³					11		9¹				
Jan 20	A	Chelsea *LS*	11404	1-0	1-1	1	2	3	4	5	6		10	8¹	11							7							9				
Feb 3	A	Cl. Orient *LSC*	2500	1-0	1-0	1	2	3	4	5	6		8	11					9¹			7											
Feb 10	A	Reading *LSC*	12850	3-0	5-0	1	2	3	4	5	6		8	11¹								7							9³				
Feb 17	H	Arsenal *LSC*	27118	0-1	2-4	1	2	3	4		6		8	9		11¹						7¹									10		
Feb 24	H	Cl. Orient *LSC*	12626	1-1	4-1	1	2	3	4	5	6		8²	9		11²						7											
Mar 3	A	Reading *LSC*	5694	0-0	0-1	1	2	3	4	5	6		8	9		11						7									10		
Mar 10	A	Arsenal *LSC*	13552	2-1	4-2	1	2	3	4		6		8	9		11²						7²	5								10		
Mar 17	H	Watford *LS*	8501	2-2	3-4		2	3	4		6		8	9		11²						7¹	5	10									
Mar 24	A	Aldershot *LS*	4996	1-1	2-1	1	2	3	4	5			8	9		11¹						7¹					6						
Mar 31	A	Q.P.R. *LS*	5000	0-0	0-1	1	2	3					8	10	11							7					6						
Apr 2	H	Millwall *LS*	12733	1-3	2-4	1	2	3					10	11²								7					6						
Apr 14	H	Reading *LS*	4469	0-0	0-1	1		3	4	5			8	11								7					6						
Apr 21	H	Fulham *LS*	7983	0-1	3-1	1	2	3	4	5			8	11¹								7¹					6		10			
Apr 30	A	Brighton *LS*	2941	0-3	0-8	1		3	4	5			8	11								7					6		10			
League South Appearances						29	26	22	27	15	20	13	7	22	7	25	9	10	12	7	3	4	21	1	6	1	1	8	5	2	4	1	2
League Cup South Appearances						6	6	6	6	4	6	5		5		6						2	6							1	3		
League Sth Goalscorers								1			4	8	6	9	1	1	1		3				11		1						4		
League Cup South Goalscorers												2		6					1			3								3		

Totals Football League South   P30 W11 D4 L15 F56 A61 Pts 26 Posn 12th

Totals League South Cup   P6 W4 D0 L2 F16 A8 Posn 2nd

LSC League South Cup
LS League South

Bell	Drake E.	Clements	Dempsey	Gunn	Offord	Halton R.	Grant	Ashmore	Short	Lonnon	Salter	Storey	Crossley	Mackie J.	Monk
6	8⁴			7¹											
		5	8												
				10											
					10¹										
					5										
						10									
								1							
10															
4		5						9							
4									5	8	9				
												9	2	10	
															9¹
													2		9
4	1	2	1	1			1	1	1		1	2	2	1	2
			1	2	1										
		4		1											1
				1											

Season 1945/46   League South

Date	Venue	Team	Attendance	FA HT	FA FT	Walker H.	Morgan L.	Rochford W.	Guthrie J.	Flewin R.	Dickinson J.	Harris P.	Bushby T.	Stott A.	Barlow H.	Parker C.	Bell	Kerr A.	Bell K.	Haddington	Evans F.	Hopkins	Froggatt J.	Worrall F.	Halton R.	Anderson J.	Hudson G.	Foxton J.	Richards S.	Humpston R.	Bowe J.	Wharton C.
Aug 25	A	Millwall LS	13550	0-3	0-4	1	2	3	4	5	6	7			10	11		8	9													
Aug 29	H	Swansea LS	11663	4-0	5-0	1	2	3		5	6	7¹		9³	10	11		4	8¹														
Sept 1	H	Millwall LS	17828	0-1	1-1	1	2	3		5	6	7	8		10	11¹		4			9												
Sept 8	H	Southampton LS	23061	3-0	3-2	1	2	3		5	6	7¹			10	11		4	8¹		9¹												
Sept 12	H	Plymouth A. LS	12595	4-1	6-1	1	2	3		5	6	7¹			10	11²		4	8¹		9²												
Sept 15	A	Southampton LS	18279	0-0	1-3	1	2	3		5		7	8		10			4			9			11¹			6					
Sept 22	A	Derby LS	19362	1-1	1-3	1	2	3	4¹	5			8		10	11					9		7				6					
Sept 29	H	Derby LS	27473	1-0	3-0	1	2	3	4	5		7¹			10	11					9¹				8¹		6					
Oct 6	H	Leicester C. LS	21930	1-0	2-0	1	2	3	4	5		7			10						9¹			11¹	8		6					
Oct 13	A	Leicester C. LS	18646	1-2	2-3	1	2	3	4	5		7			10¹	11					9¹				8		6					
Oct 20	A	Coventry C. LS	13621	0-2	1-3	1	2	3	4	5		7			10	11					9¹				8		6					
Oct 27	H	Coventry C. LS	18602	0-1	1-1	1	2	3	4	5		7			10¹	11									8	6	9					
Nov 3	H	Luton T. LS	17925	0-1	2-1	1	2	3	4	5		7	5		10¹	11					9¹				6		1	8				
Nov 10	A	Luton T. LS	8334	0-1	1-1	1	2	3	4	5		7¹	5		10	11					9				6		8					
Nov 17	A	Aston Villa LS	37391	2-1	2-3	1	2	3	4	5		11¹	5		10¹								7	9			8	6				
Nov 24	H	Aston Villa LS	31519	1-2	2-3	1	2	3	4	5		7	5		10						9²			11		8	6				
Dec 1	H	Arsenal LS	26639	1-0	1-1	1	2	3	4	5	6	7¹									9		11		10	8	5				
Dec 8	A	Arsenal LS	18480	0-1	3-4	1	2	3	4		5	7			10¹						9¹		11¹		6	8					
Dec 15	A	Charlton Ath. LS	23816	0-0	0-2	1	2	3	4			7			10						9		11	5	8			6				
Dec 22	H	Charlton Ath. LS	20627	0-0	0-3	1	2	3	4	5		11			10								9	7			8	6				
Dec 25	H	Fulham LS	11841	0-1	2-2	1	2		4	5					10¹	11					9		7¹	8	3		6					
Dec 26	A	Fulham LS	22324	1-3	2-5	1	2			5		7	4	9¹		11¹					10		8			6					
Dec 29	A	Plymouth A. LS	18444	2-0	3-1	1	2			5		11¹	4	9	10¹						7¹		8	6							
Jan 5	A	Birmingham FAC3	33845	0-1	0-1	1	2		4	5		11		9	10						7		8			6					
Jan 9	H	Birmingham FAC3	23716	0-0	0-0	1	2		4	5	6			10	11					9	7		8								
Jan 12	H	Notts Forest LS	17783	1-2	2-2	1	2		4	5					10	11					9¹	7¹		8		6					
Jan 19	A	Notts Forest LS	11713	0-1	0-3	1	2			5		7			10	11					9			8		6				6	4
Jan 26	A	Newport Co. LS	8211	1-2	2-4	1	2		4			7¹			10	11					9			8¹	5						6
Feb 2	H	Newport Co. LS	10261	0-2	2-3	1	2		4	5		7			10	11¹					9¹			8							6
Feb 9	H	Wolverhampton LS	20268	0-0	0-2	1	2	3		5		7			10	11					9					6					4
Feb 16	A	Wolverhampton LS	27842	0-1	0-4	1	2	3		5		7				11					9					6					4
Feb 23	A	West Ham LS	20154	1-0	1-3	1	2	3		5					10	11					7		9¹		8	6					4
Mar 2	H	West Ham LS	14603	1-0	2-3	1				5		7¹			10¹	11					9					6					4
Mar 9	H	West Brom LS	21282	1-0	3-0	1				5		7			10	11¹					9²					6					4
Mar 16	A	West Brom LS	16146	0-2	0-2	1				5					10	11					9		7			6					4
Mar 30	H	Birmingham LS	24389	1-2	3-4	1				5					10	11					9¹					6					4
Apr 6	H	Tottenham LS	20571	0-1	0-1	1										11					9			10		5			6		
Apr 10	A	Birmingham LS	20000	0-1	0-1	1	2															11			6					4
Apr 13	A	Tottenham LS	23000	0-2	0-2	1				5						11					9					6					4
Apr 19	A	Brentford LS	15830	0-0	2-0	1				5		7				11					9					6					4
Apr 20	H	Chelsea LS	25824	1-0	3-0	1				5		7				11					9					6					4
Apr 22	H	Brentford LS	20173	2-0	2-0	1				5		7				11					9¹					6					4
Apr 27	A	Chelsea LS	23450	0-2	0-3	1				5		7				11								9		6					4
May 4	A	Swansea LS	12796	0-1	0-3	1				5		7				11										6					4

						Walker H.	Morgan L.	Rochford W.	Guthrie J.	Flewin R.	Dickinson J.	Harris P.	Bushby T.	Stott A.	Barlow H.	Parker C.	Bell	Kerr A.	Bell K.	Haddington	Evans F.	Hopkins	Froggatt J.	Worrall F.	Halton R.	Anderson J.	Hudson G.	Foxton J.	Richards S.	Humpston R.	Bowe J.	Wharton C.
League South Appearances						40	30	23	19	30	5	33	8	6	31	32	1	1	6	3	22	4	20	7	21	3	19	1	1	7	6	20
FA Cup Appearances						2	2		2	2		1		1	1	2					1		2		2							1
League South Goalscorers							1			10		4	8	6				3	12		9	3		2							
FA Cup Goalscorers																																

League South Totals   P42 W11 D6 L25 F66 A87 Pts 28 Posn 19th out of 22

LS League South
Note: The FAC games this season were played over 2 legs

Crossley	Rookes P.	Phillips Len	Chisholm	Ferrier H.	Reid D.	Paterson E.	Morby J.	Goodwin	Henderson J.	Edwards S.	Butler E.
3											
3											
3											
3											
3											
	3										
3											
3											
		8									
		8	10								
	2	8		3							
	2			3	8						
	2			3	8						
	2			3	8	7[2]					
	2	8		3	4	7					
3		10			8		5	7	9		
	2	10		3	8	7					
	2	10		3	8[2]						
	2	10		3	8[3]						
	2			3	8					10[1]	
	2	10		3	8						
	2	8		3	9					10	1
5	13	10	1	11	11	3	1	1	1	2	1
2											
					5	2				1	

Season 1946/47   Division 1

Date	Venue	Team	Attendance	FA HT	FA FT	Walker H.	Rookes P.	Ferrier H.	Dickinson J.	Flewin R.	Wharton G.	Harris P.	McAlinden J.	Reid D.	Phillips Len	Froggatt J.	Butler E.	Yeuell J.	Hindmarsh W.	McCoy W.	Foxton J.	Evans F.	Barlow H.	Nutley R.	Parker C.	Scoular J.	Bowler G.
Aug 31	H	Blackburn R.	30962	3-1	3-1	1	2	3	4	5	6	7	8	9^2									10	11			
Sept 4	A	Derby Co.	21797	0-1	0-2	1	2	3	4	5	6	7		8		9							10	11			
Sept 7	A	Bolton	31722	0-0	0-1	1	2	3	4	5	6		10	8		9							7	11			
Sept 11	H	Blackpool	27496	0-0	0-1	1	2	3	4	5	6		10	8		9							7	11			
Sept 14	A	Everton	47909	0-0	0-1	1	2	3	4	5	6		10	8		9							7	11			
Sept 21	H	Huddersfield	30591	2-0	3-1	1	2	3	4	5	6		10	8		9^1							7	11^2			
Sept 23	A	Blackpool	18517	1-2	3-4	1	2		4	5	6		10	8^1		9		3					7^1	11^1			
Sept 28	A	Wolverhampton	40243	0-1	1-3	1	2	3	4	5	6			8^1		9							10	7	11		
Oct 5	H	Sunderland	33502	2-0	4-1		2	3	6	5	4		10^1	8		9^1	1						7^2		11		
Oct 12	A	Aston Villa	44935	0-1	1-1		2	3	6	5			10	8^1		9							7		11	4	
Oct 19	H	Chelsea	36474	0-1	0-2	1		3	6	5			10	8		9		2					7		11		
Oct 26	A	Grimsby	16845	0-2	2-3	1		3	6	5	4^1		10	8^1		9		2					7		11		
Nov 2	H	Leeds	25984	1-1	4-1			3	6	5	4	7^1	10^1	8		9^2	1	2							11		
Nov 9	A	Liverpool	43525	0-1	0-3			3	6	5	4	11	10	8		9	1	2					7				
Nov 16	H	Stoke	37768	0-2	1-3		2	3	6	5	4		10	8^1		9	1						7		11		
Nov 23	A	Middlesbrough	30721	3-3	3-3		2	3	6	5	4		10	8^2		11^1	1					9	7				
Nov 30	H	Charlton	24773	1-0	3-0		2	3	6	5	4		10	8^2		11	1					9	7				
Dec 14	H	Preston N.E.	24702	2-2	4-4		2	3	6	5	4		10	8^1		11^1	1					9	7^2				
Dec 25	A	Arsenal	38000	1-1	1-2		2	3	6	5	4		10^1	8		9	1						7	11			
Dec 26	H	Arsenal	31723	0-1	0-2		2		6	5	4		10	8		9	1	3					7	11			
Dec 28	A	Blackburn R.	24389	0-0	1-0		2	3	6	5				8	10	9^1	1						7	11	4		
Jan 4	H	Bolton	25221	1-0	2-0		2	3	6	5				8^1	10	9	1						7^1	11	4		
Jan 11	A	Doncaster FAC3	25000	2-1	3-2		2	3	6	5				8		7^2	1					9^1	10	11	4		
Jan 18	H	Everton	30002	0-0	2-1		2	3	6	5				8		7	1					9	10^2	11	4		
Jan 25	A	Birmingham FAC4	50000	0-1	0-1		2	3	6	5				8		7	1					9	10	11	4		
Jan 29	A	Huddersfield	4172	1-1	2-1		2	3	6	5				8		7	1					9^2	10	11	4		
Feb 8	A	Sunderland	20500	0-0	0-0		2	3	6	5				8		7	1					9	10	11	4		
Feb 15	H	Aston Villa	26791	1-2	3-2		2	3	6	5				8^1		7^1	1					9	10^1	11	4		
Mar 1	H	Grimsby	27099	2-1	4-1		2	3	6	5				8^2		7^1	1					9	10	11^1	4		
Mar 15	H	Liverpool	30296	0-0	1-2		2	3	6	5				8		7^1	1					9	10	11	4		
Mar 22	A	Stoke	27295	0-0	1-1		2	3	6	5			8	9^1		7	1						10	11	4		
Mar 29	H	Middlesbrough	30502	1-1	3-1		2	3	6	5			8	9^1		7	1						10^2	11	4		
Apr 4	A	Brentford	23712	2-0	3-1		2	3	6	5			8	9^2		7	1						10	11^1	4		
Apr 5	A	Charlton	38000	0-0	0-0		2	3	6	5			8	9		7	1						10	11	4		
Apr 7	H	Brentford	33409	2-0	3-0		2	3	6	5			8^1	9^2		7	1						10	11	4		
Apr 12	H	Sheffield Utd.	31669	0-0	0-0		2	3	6	5			8	9		7	1						10	11	4		
Apr 19	A	Preston N.E.	22530	0-0	1-1		2	3	6				8	9^1		7	1		5				10	11	4		
Apr 26	H	Manchester Utd.	30623	0-0	0-1		2	3	6				8	9		7	1		5				10	11	4		
May 3	H	Wolverhampton	37711	1-0	1-1		2	3					8	9^1		7	1		5				10	11	6	4	
May 10	A	Sheffield Utd.	25000	0-3	1-3		2	3	6				8	9^1		7	1		5				10	11	4		
May 17	A	Manchester Utd.	37614	0-1	0-3		2	3	6				8	9		7	1		5				10	11	4		
May 24	A	Leeds	15000	1-0	1-0		2	3	6				8^1	9		7	1						10	11	4	5	
May 26	A	Chelsea	25000	1-0	3-0		2	3	6				8	9^3		7	1						10	11	4	5	
May 31	H	Derby Co.	20852	1-1	1-2		2	3					8	9^1		7	1					6	10	11	4	5	

League Appearances						11	38	40	40	34	18	4	32	42	2	41	31	1	5	5	1	9	35	9	36	24	4
FA Cup Appearances							2	2	2	2				2		2	2					2	2		2	2	
League Goalscorers											1	1	5	29		10						3	10	1	5		
FA Cup Goalscorers														2								1					

Totals Division 1   P42 W16 D9 L17 F66 A60 Posn 12th
Totals FA Cup   P 2 W 1 D0 L 1 F 3 A 3

Own goals: Blackburn (Aug 31), Charlton (Nov 30)

Season 1947/48   Division 1

Date	Venue	Team	Attendance	FA HT	FA FT	Butler E.	Rookes P.	Ferrier H.	Scoular J.	Flewin R.	Dickinson J.	Froggatt J.	McAlinden J.	Reid D.	Barlow H.	Parker C.	Hindmarsh W.	Harris P.	McCoy W.	Brown T.	Hudson G.	Phillips Len	Clarke I.	Humpston R.	Yeuell J.	Wharton G.	Lunn H.	Bowler G.	Juliussen A.	Drummond I.
Aug 23	H	Burnley	34000	0-1	0-1	1	2	3	4	5	6	7	8	9	10	11														
Aug 25	A	Stoke	25000	0-0	1-2	1	2	3		5	6	9		8	10	11	4	7^1												
Aug 30	A	Huddersfield	25415	1-0	2-0	1	2	3	4	5	6			9^1	10^1	11		7		8										
Sept 3	H	Stoke	30000	1-0	3-0	1	2	3	4	5	6			9^1	10^1	11^1		7		8										
Sept 6	A	Bolton	25000	0-1	0-4	1	2	3	4	5	6			9	10	11		7		8										
Sept 13	H	Liverpool	33000	0-0	1-0	1	2	3	4		6	11		9^1	10			7	5	8										
Sept 17	H	Sheffield Utd.	27000	1-0	6-0	1	2	3	4		6	11^3		9^1	10			7^1	5	8										
Sept 20	A	Middlesbrough	35000	0-1	2-1	1	2	3	4		6	11^1		9	10			7^1	5	8										
Sept 27	H	Charlton	36000	0-1	3-1	1	2	3	4		6	11^1		9	10^1			7^1	5	8										
Oct 4	A	Arsenal	62000	0-0	0-0	1	2	3	4		6			9		11		7	5	8						10				
Oct 11	H	Derby Co.	43000	0-0	0-0	1	2	3	4		6			9	10	11		7	5	8										
Oct 18	A	Blackpool	22000	0-1	0-1	1	2	3	4		6			9	10	11			5	8						7				
Oct 25	A	Blackburn	32620	1-0	1-1	1	2	3	4		6				10	11		7^1	5	8	9									
Nov 1	A	Manchester City	47285	0-1	0-1	1	2	3	4		6	11			10			7	5	8		9								
Nov 8	H	Aston Villa	40000	2-2	2-4	1	2	3^1	4		6	11			10			7	5	8		9^1								
Nov 15	A	Wolverhampton	36000	0-1	1-3	1	2	3	4		6			9	10^1	11		7	5	8										
Nov 22	H	Grimsby	24000	2-0	4-0	1	2	3	4		6	11		9^3	10^1			7	5	8										
Nov 29	A	Sunderland	39000	0-2	1-4	1	2	3	4		6	11		9^1	10			7	5	8										
Dec 6	H	Everton	25000	2-0	3-0	1	2	3	4	5	6	11		9^1	10^1			7^1		8										
Dec 13	A	Chelsea	41096	0-0	0-1	1	2	3	4	5	6	11		9	10			7		8										
Dec 20	A	Burnley	30000	2-2	2-3	1	2	3	4	5	6	11^1		9	10^1			7		8										
Dec 25	†	Manchester Utd.	42776	1-1	2-3	1	2	3	4	5	6	11^1		9	10			7		8^1										
Dec 27	H	Manchester Utd.	28000	1-1	1-3	1	2	3	4	5	6	11		9^1	10			7		8										
Jan 1	A	Sheffield Utd.	22000	1-1	2-1			3	4	5	6	11^1						8				7^1	9	1	2	10				
Jan 3	H	Huddersfield	23000	1-0	3-2		2	3	4	5	6	11						8				7^1	9^2	1		10				
Jan 10	H	Brighton *FAC3*	37646	1-1	4-1	1	2			5	6	11						8^1				7^1	9^1			10^1			4	3
Jan 17	H	Bolton	28978	0-0	2-0	1		3		5	6	11^1						8				7	9		2	10			4	
Jan 24	H	Preston *FAC4*	41798	1-1	1-3	1		3	4	5	6	11						8				7	9		2	10				
Jan 31	A	Liverpool	23097	2-0	3-0	1		3	4	5	6	11						8^2				7	9		2	10^1				
Feb 14	A	Charlton	38000	1-1	2-2	1		3	4	5	6	11^1						8				7	9		2	10				
Mar 6	A	Blackpool	38000	0-1	1-1	1		3	4	5	6	11						8^1				7	9		2	10				
Mar 13	A	Blackburn	27300	0-0	0-1	1		3	4	5	6	11						8				7	10		2				9	
Mar 20	H	Manchester City	29000	0-0	1-0	1		3	4^1	5	6	11						7				8			2	10			9	
Mar 26	H	Preston	34913	1-0	1-0	1		3	4	5	6	11		9^1				7				10	8		2					
Mar 27	A	Aston Villa	45000	0-2	1-2	1		3	4	5	6	11		9				7				10^1	8		2					
Mar 29	A	Preston	30000	1-0	2-1	1		3	4	5	6	11^1		9	10^1			7					8		2					
Apr 3	H	Wolverhampton	29000	0-0	2-0	1		3	4	5	6	11^2		9	10			7					8		2					
Apr 10	A	Grimsby	10000	0-1	0-1	1		3	4	5	6	11		9	10			7					8		2					
Apr 14	A	Middlesbrough	24000	4-0	6-1	1		3	4	5	6	11						8^1				7	10^2		2				9^3	
Apr 17	H	Sunderland	29057	2-2	2-2	1		3	4	5	6	11						8^1				7^1	10		2				9	
Apr 21	H	Arsenal	42000	0-0	0-0	1	2	3	4	5	6	11						8				7	10						9	
Apr 24	A	Everton	30000	1-0	2-0	1	2	3	4	5	6	11						8				7^1	10						9^1	
Apr 28	A	Derby Co.	15859	0-2	1-2	1	2	3	4		6	11						8				7^1	10					5	9	
May 1	H	Chelsea	24000	1-0	2-1	1		3	4	5	6	11						8				7^1	10		2				9^1	
League Appearances						40	41	28	40	28	42	36	1	31	24	15	1	40	13	17	1	13	17	2	15	7	1	2	7	
FA Cup Appearances						2	2		1	2	2	2						2				2	2		1	2			1	1
League Goalscorers								1	1			13		14	10	1		13		1		3	5		1				4	
FA Cup Goalscorers																		1				1	1			1				

Totals Division 1   P42 W19 D7 L16 F68 A50 Pts 45 Posn 8th
Totals FA Cup   P 2 W 1 D 0 L 1 F 5 A 4

† At Maine Road, Manchester

Own goals: Sheffield Utd (Sept 17), Preston (Jan 24)

Season 1948/49   Division 1

Date	Venue	Team	Attendance	FA HT	FA FT	Butler E.	Rookes P.	Ferrier H.	Scoular J.	Flewin R.	Dickinson J.	Harris P.	Reid D.	Froggatt J.	Phillips Len	Barlow H.	Bowler G.	Clarke I.	Yeuell J.	Delapenha L.	Parker C.	Hindmarsh W.	Thompson W.
Aug 21	A	Preston	32000	0-1	2-2	1	2	3	4	5	6	7	8^1	9	10	11^1							
Aug 25	H	Everton	31000	2-0	4-0	1	2	3	4	5	6	7	9	11^2	10	8^2							
Aug 28	H	Burnley	38000	1-0	1-0	1	2	3	4	5	6	7	9	11^1	10	8							
Sept 1	A	Everton	40911	3-0	5-0	1	2	3	4		6	7^1	9^1	11^2	10	8^1		5					
Sept 4	A	Stoke C.	30000	1-0	1-0	1	2	3	4		6	7^1	9	11	10	8		5					
Sept 8	H	Middlesbrough	33000	0-0	1-0	1	2	3	4	5	6	7	9^1	11	10	8							
Sept 11	H	Charlton	39000	1-0	3-1	1	2	3	4	5	6	7	9^3	11	10	8							
Sept 15	A	Middlesbrough	35000	0-1	1-1	1	2	3	4	5	6	7	9	11	10	8^1							
Sept 18	A	Manchester City	46372	0-1	1-1	1	2	3	4	5	6	7	9	11	10	8							
Sept 25	H	Sheffield Utd.	36000	1-0	3-0	1	2	3	4	5	6	7^2	9	11	10^1	8							
Oct 2	H	Newcastle	44000	0-0	1-0	1	2	3	4	5	6	7	9	11	10^1	8							
Oct 9	A	Aston Villa	55000	0-0	1-1	1	2	3	4	5	6	7	9^1	11	10	8							
Oct 16	A	Sunderland	35000	2-0	3-0	1	2	3	4	5	6	7^1	9^1	11	10	8							
Oct 23	A	Wolverhampton	50000	0-2	0-3	1	2	3	4	5	6	7	9	11	10	8							
Oct 30	H	Bolton W.	35000	0-0	0-0	1	2	3	4	5	6	7	9	11		8	10						
Nov 6	A	Liverpool	43665	1-2	1-3	1	2	3	4	5	6	7^1	9	11		8	10						
Nov 13	H	Blackpool	44000	0-1	1-1	1	2	3	4	5	6	7^1	9	11				10		8			
Nov 20	A	Derby Co.	34000	0-0	0-1	1	2	3	4	5	6	7		11		10		9		8			
Nov 27	H	Arsenal	42500	2-0	4-1	1	2	3	4	5	6	7		11^1	10^1	8^1		9^1					
Dec 4	A	Huddersfield	21785	0-0	0-0	1	2	3	4	5	6	7		11	10	8		9					
Dec 11	H	Manchester Utd.	30000	0-1	2-2	1	2	3	4	5	6	7		11^1	10	8		9^1					
Dec 18	H	Preston	26000	2-0	3-1	1	2	3	4	5	6	7^1		11	10^1	8^1		9					
Dec 25	A	Chelsea	42153	0-1	2-1	1	2	3	4	5	6	7^2		11	10	8		9					
Dec 27	H	Chelsea	43000	3-1	5-2	1	2	3	4	5	6	7^2		11	10	8^1		9^1					
Jan 1	A	Burnley	31305	1-1	1-2	1	2	3	4	5	6	7		11	10	8		9					
Jan 8	H	Stockport *FAC3*	33590	3-0	7-0	1	2	3	4	5	6	7^3		11	10^2	8		9^2					
Jan 15	H	Stoke C.	34000	0-0	1-0	1		3	4	5	6	7		11^1	10	8		9	2				
Jan 22	A	Charlton	61475	1-0	1-0	1		3	4	5	6	7		11	10	8		9^1	2				
Jan 29	H	Sheff W. *FAC4*	47188	1-1	2-1	1		3	4	5	6	7^1		11	10^1	8		9	2				
Feb 5	H	Manchester City	34500	0-1	3-1	1		3	4	5	6	7^1		11	10	8		9^2	2				
Feb 12	H	Newport Co. *FAC5§*	48581	1-2	3-2	1		3	4	5	6	7		11^1	10^2	8		9	2				
Feb 19	A	Sheffield Utd.	46000	1-1	1-3	1		3	4	5	6		7^1	10	8			9	2	11			
Feb 26	H	Derby Co. *FAC6*	51385	1-1	2-1	1		3	4	5	6	7		11	10	8		9^2	2				
Mar 5	H	Aston Villa	34000	1-0	3-0	1		3	4	5	6	7		11^1	10^2	8		9	2				
Mar 12	A	Sunderland	57229	3-1	4-1	1		3	4	5	6	7	8^2	9^1	10^1				2	11			
Mar 19	H	Derby Co.	43000	1-0	1-0	1		3	4	5	6	7	8	9	10				2	11			
Mar 26	‡	Leicester *FAC SF*	62000	1-2	1-3	1		3	4	5	6	7^1		11	10	8		9	2				
Apr 2	H	Liverpool	34500	2-0	3-2	1		3	4	5	6	7^1	8	11	10^1			9^1			2		
Apr 6	A	Newcastle	60611	3-0	5-0	1		3	4	5	6	7^2	8	11^3	10			9			2		
Apr 9	A	Blackpool	29000	0-0	0-1	1		3	4	5	6	7	8	11	10			9			2		
Apr 15	H	Birmingham	38000	0-1	3-1	1		3	4	5	6	7	8^2	11	10			9^1			2		
Apr 16	H	Wolverhampton	44000	3-0	5-0	1		3	4	5	6	7	8^2	11	10^1			9^2			2		
Apr 18	A	Birmingham	30000	0-1	0-3	1		3	4	5	6	7	8		10			9^1				11	2
Apr 23	A	Bolton W.	28816	2-0	2-1	1		3	4	5	6	7^1	8	11	10			9^1			2		
Apr 30	H	Huddersfield	36500	1-0	2-0	1		3	4	5		7	8^1	11	10			9^1			2	6	
May 4	A	Arsenal	60000	1-2	2-3	1			4	5	6		8	11	10			9^2			7	2	3
May 7	†	Manchester Utd.	39608	2-2	2-3	1			4		6	7^1	8^1	11	10			9	3		2	5	

						Butler E.	Rookes P.	Ferrier H.	Scoular J.	Flewin R.	Dickinson J.	Harris P.	Reid D.	Froggatt J.	Phillips Len	Barlow H.	Bowler G.	Clarke I.	Yeuell J.	Delapenha L.	Parker C.	Hindmarsh W.	Thompson W.
League Appearances						42	25	40	42	39	41	40	29	41	40	29	2	24	8	2	5	10	3
League Goalscorers												17	17	15	11	8		14					
FA Cup Appearances						5	1	5	5	5	5	5		5	5	5		5	4				
FA Cup Goalscorers												5		1	5			4					

Totals Division 1   P42 W25 D8 L9 F84 A42 Pts 58 Posn 1st Champions
Totals FA Cup   P 5 W 4 D0 L 1 F 15 A 7

† At Maine Road
‡ At Highbury
§ After extra time

Own goals: Chelsea (Dec 27), Burnley (Jan 1)

Season 1949/50   Division 1

Date	Venue	Team	Attendance	FA HT	FA FT	Butler E.	Yeuell J.	Ferrier H.	Scoular J.	Flewin R.	Dickinson J.	Harris P.	Reid D.	Clarke I.	Phillips Len	Froggatt J.	Hindmarsh W.	Delapenha L.	Thompson W.	Pickett R.	Dawson J.	Barlow H.	Parker C.	Spence W.	Stephen J.	Elder J.	Ekner D.	Rookes P.	Higham P.	Bennett R.
Aug 20	A	Newcastle	45000	2-0	3-1	1	2	3	4	5	6	7^1	8	9^1	10^1	11														
Aug 24	H	Manchester City	44297	1-1	1-1	1	2	3	4	5	6	7	8^1	9	10	11														
Aug 27	H	Blackpool	44815	1-1	2-3	1	2	3	4	5	6	7	8	9^1	10^1	11														
Aug 31	A	Manchester City	32631	0-0	0-1	1		3	4	5	6	7	8	9	10	11	2													
Sept 3	A	Middlesbrough	45000	2-1	5-1	1		3	4	5	6	7^3		9^1	10	11^1	2	8												
Sept 5	A	Aston Villa	48000	0-0	0-1	1		3	4	5	6	7		9	10	11	2	8												
Sept 10	H	Everton	36054	2-0	7-0	1		3	4	5	6	7^1	8^3	9^1	10^1	11^1	2													
Sept 17	A	Huddersfield	26222	0-0	1-0	1		3	4	5	6	7	8	9^1	10	11	2													
Sept 24	H	Bolton	35765	1-1	1-1	1	2	3	4	5	6	7	8	9^1	10	11														
Oct 1	H	Wolves	50248	1-0	1-1	1		3	4		6	7	8^1	9	10	11	2		5											
Oct 8	A	Birmingham	38000	3-0	3-0	1		3	4		6	7	8^1	9^2	10	11	2		5											
Oct 15	A	Derby	37340	2-0	3-1	1		3	4			7	8^1	9^1	10	11^1	2		5	6										
Oct 19	†	Wolves FA CS	25000		1-1			3	4			6	7	8^1	9		11	2		5			10							
Oct 22	A	W.B.A.	40000	0-2	0-3	1		3	4			6				9	2		5	8	7	10	11							
Oct 29	H	Manchester Utd.	41098	0-0	0-0	1		3	4			6	7			9	10	11	2		8			5						
Nov 5	A	Chelsea	31650	2-1	4-1	1		3	4			6	7	8	9^2	10	11^2	2					5							
Nov 12	H	Stoke	33257	0-0	0-0	1		3	4			6	7	8	9	10	11	2					5							
Nov 19	A	Burnley	28500	0-1	1-2	1		3	4			6	7	8	9		11	2						10^1	5					
Nov 26	H	Sunderland	36707	2-0	2-2	1		3				6	7^1	8	10^1		11						5		2	4	9			
Dec 3	A	Liverpool	44851	1-1	2-2	1		3	4			6	7^1		9	10	11	2					5				8			
Dec 10	H	Arsenal	39537	0-1	2-1	1		3		5		6	7		9^1	10	11^1	2					4				8			
Dec 17	H	Newcastle	30455	1-0	1-0	1		3		5		6	7		8^1	10	11	2					4				9			
Dec 24	H	Blackpool	27000	1-1	1-2	1		3		5		6	7^1	9	8	10	11	2					4							
Dec 26	A	Charlton	38000	1-0	2-1	1		3	4	5	6	7			8	10^1	11^1	2									9			
Dec 27	H	Charlton	43650	0-0	1-0	1		3	4	5	6	7^1			9	10	11	2	8											
Dec 31	H	Middlesbrough	33364	0-1	1-1	1		3	4	5	6	7			9	10	11^1	2	8											
Jan 7	H	Norwich FAC3	42059	1-0	1-1	1		3	4	5	6	7				10		2	8^1		11									
Jan 12	A	Norwich FAC3R	42624	0-0	2-0	1		3	4	5	6	7	8^2	9	10	11	2													
Jan 14	A	Everton	50421	0-1	2-1	1		3	4	5	6	7^1	8	9	10^1		2								11					
Jan 21	A	Huddersfield	29746	1-0	4-0	1		3	4	5	6	7	8^1	9	10	11^2	2													
Jan 28	H	Grimsby FAC4	39364	2-0	5-0	1		3	4	5	6			8	9^2	10^1	11^2	2				7								
Feb 4	A	Bolton	29284	0-0	0-1	1		3	4	5	6			8	9	10	11	2				7								
Feb 11	A	Man. Utd. FAC5	53688	0-2	3-3	1		3^1	4	5	6	7			8^1	10	9	2				11^1								
Feb 15	H	Man. Utd. FAC5R	49962	1-2	1-3	1		3	4	5	6	7^1			8	10	9	2				11								
Feb 18	A	Wolves	40000	0-1	0-1	1		3^1	4	5	6	7			9	10	11			8						2				
Feb 25	H	Birmingham	28429	0-0	2-0	1		3	4		6	7^2			10			5	8						2		9	11		
Mar 8	A	Derby	17000	1-0	1-2	1		3	4			6	7	9		10	11			5	8^1						2			
Mar 11	H	Burnley	26728	2-0	2-1	1		3	4	5	6	7		9^1	10	11^1	2			8										
Mar 18	A	Sunderland	44591	1-1	1-1	1		3	4	5	6	7	9	10			2			8									11^1
Mar 25	H	Chelsea	28574	3-0	4-0	1		3	4	5	6	7^1	8^3	9		11	2			10									
Apr 1	A	Stoke	27000	0-0	1-0	1		3	4	5	6	7^1	8	9		11	2			10									
Apr 7	H	Fulham	39342	1-0	3-0	1		3	4		6	7	7^2	8	9		11^1	2			10			5						
Apr 8	H	W.B.A.	33903	0-0	0-1	1		3	4		6	7		9	8	11	2			10			5						
Apr 10	A	Fulham	43716	1-0	1-0	1		3	4		6	7		9^1		11	2	8		10			5						
Apr 15	A	Manchester Utd.	44908	0-0	2-0	1		3	4			7	8^1	9	10	11^1	2	6					5						
Apr 22	H	Liverpool	47507	0-0	2-1	1		3	4			6	7	8^1	9	10	11^1	2					5						
May 3	A	Arsenal	65000	0-1	0-2	1		3				6	7	8		10	11	2		4	9		5						
May 6	H	Aston Villa	42295	2-0	5-1	1		3		5	6	7	8^3		10	11	2	9^2					4						

League Appearances						42	4	42	36	24	40	40	27	37	34	39	34	6	9	14	1	2	3	16	1	1	4	3	1	2
FA Cup Appearances						5		5	5	5	5	4	2	5	5	4	5	1		1			3							
Charity Sh. Appearances						1		1	1		1	1	1	1		1	1		1			1								
League Goalscorers							1					16	16	17	5	15				2	1		1						1
FA Cup Goalscorers							1					1	2	3	1	2		1				1							
Charity Sh. Goalscorers														1																

Totals Division 1   P42 W22 D9 L11 F74 A38 Pts 53 Posn 1st Champions
Totals FA Cup   P 5 W 2 D2 L 1 F12 A 7

† At Highbury

Own goal: Huddersfield (Jan 21)

Oct 19: Charity Shield shared

Season 1950/51   Division 1

Date	Venue	Team	Attendance	FA HT	FA FT	Butler E.	Hindmarsh W.	Ferrier H.	Scoular J.	Flewin R.	Dickinson J.	Harris P.	Reid D.	Clarke I.	Phillips Len	Froggatt J.	Stephen J.	Thompson W.	Atyeo J.	Ryder T.	Leather M.	Pickett R.	Parker C.	Bennett R.	Rookes P.	Humpston R.	Reid M.	Spence W.	Earl S.	Gaillard M.	Mundy
Aug 19	H	Middlesbrough	44070	0-0	1-1			3	4	5	6	7	8^1	9		11	2				10					1					
Aug 21	A	Sheffield Wed.	46740	0-0	1-2			3	4	5	6	7	8^1	9		11	2				10					1					
Aug 26	A	Huddersfield	28087	0-1	1-2			3	4	5	6	7	8^1	9	10	11	2									1					
Aug 30	H	Sheffield Wed.	27952	2-1	4-1			3	4	5	6		8		10^2	11^2	2				7					1	9				
Sept 2	H	Newcastle	43244	0-0	0-0			3	4	5	6	7	8		10	11	2									1	9				
Sept 4	H	Burnley	30470	0-0	1-1			3	4	5	6	7	8		10	11	2									1	9^1				
Sept 9	A	W.B.A.	35000	0-2	0-5			3	4	5	6	7	8		10	11	2									1	9				
Sept 16	H	Stoke	33973	2-1	5-1	1		3^1	4	5	6	7	8^3	9^1	10	11	2														
Sept 23	A	Everton	40881	2-0	5-1		2	3	4	5		7^1	8	9^2	10^2	11					1										
Sept 30	H	Fulham	32082	1-0	1-0	1	2	3	4	5	6	7	8	9	10	11															
Oct 7	A	Bolton	34055	0-3	0-4	1	2	3	4			7	8	9	10	11		6										5			
Oct 14	H	Blackpool	47829	0-0	2-0	1	2	3	4	5	6	7	8	9^1	10^1	11															
Oct 21	A	Manchester Utd.	41842	0-0	0-0	1		3	4	5	6	7	8	9	10	11													2		
Oct 28	A	Wolves	40821	0-2	1-4	1		3	4		6	7	8	9^1	10	11												5	2		
Nov 4	A	Tottenham H.	66602	1-2	1-5	1		3	4		6	7	8	9		11				10								5	2		
Nov 11	H	Charlton	32755	2-1	3-3	1		3	4^1		6^1	7	8^1			11	2	5		9	10										
Nov 18	A	Sunderland	46110	0-0	0-0			3			6		8	9			2	5		10		1	4	7	11						
Nov 25	H	Aston Villa	30399	2-0	3-3						6		8^1	9			2	5		10^2		1	4	7	11	3					
Dec 2	A	Derby	23872	0-1	3-2			3	4		6	7	8^1	9^1		11	2	5		10^1		1									
Dec 9	H	Liverpool	29470	0-1	1-3			3	4		6	7	8	9^1			2	5		10		1	11								
Dec 16	A	Middlesbro	30000	1-1	1-3			3	4^1		6	7	8	9	10		2	5		11		1									
Dec 23	H	Huddersfield	22411	0-0	1-0			3	4	5	6	7	8	9	10^1	11	2						1								
Dec 25	H	Chelsea	23547	0-1	1-3			3	4	5	6	7	8	9	10^1	11	2						1								
Dec 26	A	Chelsea	41909	4-0	4-1		2		4	5	6	7^1		9^3	10	11				3	8		1								
Jan 6	A	Luton *FAC3*	21631	0-1	0-2				4	5	6	7		9	10	11	2				8		1	3							
Jan 13	H	W.B.A.	23624	1-2	2-2		2		4	5	6	7		9	10^1						8	1	11	3							
Jan 20	A	Stoke	28000	1-1	2-1			3			6	7	8	9^2	10		2			5	11	1	4								
Feb 3	H	Everton	26271	2-2	6-3			3^1	4		6	7	8^2	9	10^2		2			5			1								11
Feb 10	A	Liverpool	36958	1-0	1-2			3	4		6	7^1	8	9	10		2			5			1								11
Feb 24	H	Bolton	25716	0-1	2-1	1		3	4		6^1	7	8^1		10		2			5			9								11
Mar 3	A	Blackpool	30000	0-0	0-3	1		3	4		6	7	8		10		2			5			9								11
Mar 10	A	Manchester Utd.	34148	0-0	0-0	1		3	4		6	7	8		10		2			5										11	9
Mar 17	H	Wolves	30000	2-2	3-2	1		3	4		6	7	8^1		10		2			5										11	9^2
Mar 23	A	Arsenal	52051	0-0	1-0	1		3	4		6	7	8^1		10		2			5										11	9
Mar 24	H	Tottenham H.	49716	1-1	1-1	1		3	4		6	7	8^1		10		2			5										11	9
Mar 26	A	Arsenal	38189	1-0	1-1	1		3	4		6	7	8		10		2			5										11	9^1
Mar 31	A	Charlton	30000	0-0	1-0	1		3	4		6	7^1			10		2			5						9				11	8
Apr 7	H	Sunderland	30364	0-0	0-0	1		3	4		6		8		10		2			5						7				11	9
Apr 11	A	Newcastle	30000		0-0	1		3	4	5	6		8		10		2									7				11	9
Apr 14	A	Aston Villa	40000	0-1	3-3	1		3	4	5	6		8^1		10^1		2				7		11^1								9
Apr 21	H	Derby	28945	0-0	2-2	1		3	4		6	7	8^1		10		2			5			11								9^1
May 2	A	Fulham	24000	3-1	4-1	1		3	4		6	7	8	9^2			2			5										11^2	10
May 5	H	Burnley	22510	2-1	2-1	1		3	4	5	6	7	8	9			2													11	10^1
League Appearances						22	5	40	38	20	41	36	38	26	30	33	33	10	1	10	13	6	9	3	2	7	5	3	3	14	12
League Goalscorers								2	2	2	5	21	11	11	2					3			1				1			2	5
FA Cup Appearances									1	1	1	1		1	1	1	1				1		1	1							

Totals Division 1   P42 W16 D15 L11 F71 A68 Pts 47 Posn 7th
Totals FA Cup   P 1 W 0 D0 L 1 F 0 A 2

Own goals: Tottenham H. (Nov 4), W.B.A. (Jan 13), Burnley (May 5)

Season 1951/52   Division 1

Date	Venue	Team	Attendance	HT	FT	Butler E.	Stephen J.	Earl S.	Pickett R.	Froggatt J.	Dickinson J.	Harris P.	Mundy A.	Clarke I.	Phillips Len	Gallard M.	Yeuell J.	Reid D.	Gordon J.	Mansell B.	Scoular J.	Ferrier H.	Ryder T.	Henderson J.	Dale G.	Beale J.	Wilson A.	Gunter P.	Thompson W.	Bennett R.	Edwards B.	Dore C.	Flewin R.
Aug 18	A	Liverpool	42770	0-0	2-0	1	2	3	4	5	6	7	8^{1}	9	10^{1}	11																	
Aug 22	H	Blackpool	41825	0-3	1-3	1	2		4	5	6	7	9		10	11^{1}	3		8														
Aug 25	H	Charlton	31420	0-0	1-0	1	2		4	5	6	7			10	11^{1}	3		8	9													
Aug 27	A	Blackpool	30000	0-0	0-0	1	2		8	5	6	7	9		10	11							3	4									
Sept 1	H	Chelsea	23910	0-0	1-0	1	2		8^{1}	5	6	7	9		10	11					4	3											
Sept 5	H	Manchester City	31297	0-0	1-0	1	2		8	5	6	7^{1}	9		10	11					4	3											
Sept 8	A	Huddersfield	25861	1-0	1-0	1	2			5	6	7	9		10	11					4	3		8^{1}									
Sept 15	H	Wolverhampton	30759	0-0	2-3	1	2			5	6	7	9^{1}		10	11					4	3^{1}		8									
Sept 22	A	Sunderland	45389	0-2	1-3	1	2			5	6	7^{1}			10						4	3		8	9		11						
Sept 29	H	Aston Villa	37283	2-0	2-0	1	2			5	6	7			10^{1}			8			4	3		9^{1}	11								
Oct 6	A	Fulham	42000	1-1	3-2	1	2			5	6	7^{1}			10			8^{1}				3		9	11	4							
Oct 13	H	Middlesbrough	33631	2-2	5-4	1	2			5	6	7^{1}			10^{2}			8^{1}			4	3		9^{1}	11								
Oct 20	A	W.B.A.	22000	0-0	0-5	1	2		4	5		7			10			8				3		9	11	6							
Oct 22	A	Southampton *HCC*	22699	1-1	2-2	1	2		4	5				9	10	11		8^{1}				3		7		4^{1}		6					
Oct 27	H	Newcastle	30944	0-0	3-1	1				5	6	7	9		10^{1}	11		8^{2}			4	3						2					
Nov 3	A	Bolton	23133	2-0	3-0	1				5	6	7			10^{2}			8^{1}				3		9		4		2					
Nov 10	H	Stoke	21787	3-1	4-1	1	2			5	6	7^{1}			10	11^{1}		8				3^{1}		9^{1}		4							
Nov 17	A	Manchester Utd.	35914	2-0	3-1	1				5	6	7			10	11^{1}		8				3		9^{1}		4		2					
Nov 24	H	Tottenham H.	46815	1-0	2-0	1	2			5	6	7			10	11		8^{2}			4	3		9									
Dec 1	A	Preston	34000	1-2	2-2	1	2			5	6	7			10	11		8^{2}			4	3		9									
Dec 8	H	Burnley	23643	1-2	2-2	1	2			5	6	7^{1}			10	11		8			4	3^{1}		9									
Dec 15	H	Liverpool	29945	0-2	1-3	1				5	6	7			10	11		8^{1}			4	3		9						2			
Dec 22	A	Charlton	30000	2-0	2-0	1					6	7			10	11		8^{1}			4	3		9^{1}				2	5				
Dec 25	A	Arsenal	52241	0-3	1-4	1					6	7			10	11		8			4^{1}	3		9				2	5				
Dec 26	H	Arsenal	41305	0-1	1-1	1		3		5	6	7			10	11^{1}		8			4			9				2					
Dec 29	A	Chelsea	43389	0-0	1-1	1		3			6	7	9^{1}		10			8			4							2	5	11			
Jan 1	A	Manchester City	49412	1-0	1-0	1		3			6	7	8^{1}	9	10						4							2	5	11			
Jan 5	H	Huddersfield	30048	2-0	3-1	1				5	6	7			10			8^{1}			4	3^{1}		9^{1}				2					
Jan 12	H	Lincoln *FAC3*	41093	2-0	4-0	1				5	6	7	10^{1}	9^{1}		11^{2}		8			4	3						2					
Jan 19	A	Wolverhampton	30000	0-1	1-1	1				5	6	7	10^{1}	9		11		8			4	3						2					
Jan 26	H	Sunderland	33613	0-1	0-2	1				5	6	7	10	9		11		8			4	3						2					
Feb 2	A	Notts Co. *FAC4*	46500	3-1	3-1	1				5	6	7	9^{1}		10	11^{1}		8^{1}			4	3						2					
Feb 9	A	Aston Villa	55000	0-0	0-2	1				5	6	7	9		10	11		8			4	3						2					
Feb 16	H	Fulham	36765	2-0	4-0	1				5	6	7^{2}	8		10^{1}	11					4	3		9^{1}				2					
Feb 23	H	Doncaster *FAC5*	44392	2-0	4-0	1				5	6	7^{1}	8		10^{1}	11^{1}					4	3		9				2					
Mar 1	A	Middlesbrough	30000	1-1	1-2	1				5	6	7			10^{1}	11		8				3		9		4		2					
Mar 8	H	Newcastle *FAC6*	44699	1-1	2-4	1				5	6	7			10	11^{1}		8^{1}			4	3		9				2					
Mar 12	H	W.B.A.	21721	1-1	1-1	1				5	6	7	8^{1}		10	11					4	3		9				2					
Mar 15	A	Newcastle	60000	1-2	3-3	1				5	6	7^{1}			10^{2}	11		8			4	3		9				2					
Mar 22	H	Bolton	31098	0-0	3-0					5	6	7			10	11		8^{1}			4^{1}	3		9^{1}				2				1	
Mar 29	A	Stoke	14000	0-0	0-2					5	6			9	10	11		8			4	3	7					2				1	
Apr 5	H	Manchester Utd.	25522	1-0	1-0		2					7			10			8^{1}				3		9	11	4					6	1	5
Apr 11	H	Derby Co.	36120	2-0	3-1		2		5^{1}		6	7			10			8^{2}				3		9	11	4						1	
Apr 12	A	Tottenham H.	67000	1-3	1-3		2			5	6	7			10^{1}	11		8				3		9		4						1	
Apr 14	A	Derby Co.	21455	0-1	0-1		2			5	6	7	9		10			8				3			11	4						1	
Apr 19	H	Preston	27710	1-0	1-2		2		4	5	6	7			10^{1}	11		8				3		9								1	
Apr 26	A	Burnley	16840	0-0	0-1		2			5	6				10			8			4	3	7	9	11							1	
League Appearances						34	24	5	8	37	40	40	13	11	37	30	2	30	3	3	28	32	5	27	8	9	1	17	5	3	1	8	1
FA Cup Appearances						4				4	4	4	3	1	3	4		3			4	4		2				4					
League Goalscorers										1	1	9	4	2	13	5		16			2	4		8	1								
FA Cup Goalscorers												1	2	1	1	4		2															

Totals Division 1   P42 W20 D8 L14 F68 A58 Pts 48 Posn 4th
Totals FA Cup   P 4 W 3 D0 L 1 F13 A 5

Own goals: Fulham (Oct 6), Manchester Utd. (Nov 17), Doncaster (Feb 23)

Oct 22: Cup shared

Season 1952/53   Division 1

Date	V	Team	Attendance	FA HT / FT	Butler E.	Stephen J.	Thompson W.	Scoular J.	Froggatt J.	Dickinson J.	Harris P.	Gordon J.	Mundy A.	Phillips Len	Gaillard M.	Dore C.	Ferrier H.	Reid D.	Uprichard N.	Beale J.	Pickett R.	Hunt R.	Henderson J.	Dale G.	Flewin R.	Gunter P.	Leather M.	Wilson A.	Reagan M.	Clarke I.	Vause
Aug 23	H	Blackpool	43478	0-1 0-2		2		4	5	6	7	8		10	11	1	3						9								
Aug 27	A	Charlton	25000	1-0 2-2		2		4^1	5	6	7^1	8		10	11	1	3						9								
Aug 30	A	Chelsea	52284	0-2 0-2		2	3	4	5	6	7	8		10	11	1							9								
Sept 3	H	Charlton	25558	1-1 1-1		2	3	4	5	6	7^1	8	9	10	11	1															
Sept 6	H	Manchester Utd.	37278	0-0 2-0	1	2	3	4	5	6	7^1	8^1	9	10	11																
Sept 10	A	Arsenal	40743	0-1 1-3	1	2	3	4	5	6	7	8	9^1	10	11																
Sept 13	A	Liverpool	49771	1-1 1-1	1	2	3	4	5	6	7	8^1	9	10	11																
Sept 17	H	Arsenal	37256	0-2 2-2	1	2	3	4	5^1	6	7	8	9	10^1	11																
Sept 20	A	Bolton	26455	2-0 5-0	1	2	3	4	5	6	7^2	8^1		10^1				9^1					11								
Sept 27	H	Aston Villa	35935	0-1 1-1	1	2	3	4	5	6	7	8^1		10				9					11								
Oct 4	A	Sunderland	45145	0-1 1-1	1	2	3	4			7	8		10				9	6				11	5							
Oct 11	H	Manchester City	33644	0-0 2-1	1	2	3	4	5	6	7^2	8	10					9					11								
Oct 18	A	Stoke	29507	2-1 4-2	1	2	3		5	6	7^2	8^1	10					9^1			4										
Oct 25	H	Preston	31865	1-2 2-5	1	2	3	4	5	6	7^2	8^1	10					9^2					11								
Nov 1	A	Burnley	28273	2-1 2-3	1	2	3	4	5	6	7	8	10					9^1					11^1								
Nov 8	H	Tottenham H.	40867	1-0 1-0			3	4	5	6	7^1	8		10	11			9^1	1					2							
Nov 15	A	Sheffield Wed.	44187	3-1 4-3			3	4	5	6	7^1	8^2		10^1	11			9	1					2							
Nov 22	H	Cardiff	31258	0-1 0-2			3	4	5	6	7	8		10	11			9	1					2	1						
Nov 29	A	Newcastle	41120	0-1 0-1		2		4		6	7	8		10	11		3	9						5	1						
Dec 6	H	W.B.A.	27365	0-2 1-2		2			5	6	7	8		10	11		3	9	1	4^1					1						
Dec 13	A	Middlesbrough	24000	1-1 2-3		2			5	6^1	7	8		10			3			4	11		9^1		1						
Dec 20	A	Blackpool	13562	1-0 2-3		2		8	5^1	6	7^1		9	10			3			4	11				1						
Dec 26	A	Derby Co.	30243	0-2 0-3		2		8	5	6	7			10			3		1	4	9	11									
Dec 27	A	Derby Co.	30000	0-1 2-2				4	11^1	6	7	8^1	9	10			3		1					5					2		
Jan 3	H	Chelsea	30000	1-0 2-0		2		4	5	6	7			10			3	8	1				9^2						11		
Jan 10	H	Burnley *FAC3*	40502	0-0 1-1		2	3	4	5	6	7^1			10	11			8	1				9								
Jan 13	A	Burnley *FAC3R*	39673	0-1 1-3		2	3	4	5	6	7			10	11^1			8	1				9								
Jan 17	A	Manchester Utd.	32341	0-0 0-1				4	5	6	7	8	10						1				9			2		3	11		
Jan 24	H	Liverpool	27045	2-0 3-1		2		4^1	5	6	7^1	8	10				3		1				9^1						11		
Feb 7	H	Bolton	25239	3-0 3-1		2		4	5	6	7^1	8					3^1		1		10		9^1						11		
Feb 18	A	Aston Villa	15000	0-2 0-6		2		4		6	7						3	10	1				9	5					11		
Feb 21	H	Sunderland	29690	2-1 5-2		2				6	7^3		10^1	8			3		1				9^1	11	5						
Feb 28	A	Manchester City	38736	0-0 1-2		2		4	5	6	7^1	10		8			3		1				9	11							
Mar 7	H	Stoke	25370	1-0 1-1		2		4	5	6	7	10^1		8			3		1				9	11							
Mar 14	A	Preston	30000	0-0 0-4		2		4	5	6	7	10		8			3		1				9	11							
Mar 21	H	Burnley	33400	1-1 2-1			3	4	5	6	7	8					10^1		1				11	2							9^1
Mar 28	A	Tottenham H.	38636	1-3 3-3				4	5	6	7^1	8					10		1				11^2					3			9 · 2
Apr 3	H	Wolverhampton	39770	1-0 2-2			3	4	5^1	6	7^1	8					10		1				11								9 · 2
Apr 4	A	Sheffield Wed.	29613	5-0 5-2				4	5	6	7^2			8^1			10		1				9^2	11		2	3				
Apr 6	A	Wolverhampton	25000	0-2 1-4				4	5	6	7^1			8				10	1				11	2		3		9			
Apr 11	A	Cardiff	45000	1-0 1-0				4	11^1	6	7			10	8			5	1				9			3					2
Apr 18	H	Newcastle	27835	1-1 5-1			3	4^1			7			10	8^1			5	1		6		11^1								9^1 · 2
Apr 25	A	W.B.A.	24000	0-0 0-2			3	4	10	6	7			8				1					11		5						9 · 2
May 2	H	Middlesbrough	18765	0-3 1-4			3	4	10	6				8				1					7 · 11^1		5						9 · 2

League Appearances					11	36	13	39	36	40	41	21	22	35	14	6	16	24	20	5	4	2	20	15	5	8	5	6	5	1	6 · 6
League Goalscorers								3	5	1	23	8	3	5			1	7		1			11	2							2
FA Cup Appearances					2	2	2	2	2	1	1			2	2			2	2				2								
FA Cup Goalscorers											1				1															

Totals Division 1   P42 W14 D10 L18 F74 A83 Pts 38 Posn 15th
Totals FA Cup   P 2 W 0 D1 L 1 F2 A 4

Own goals: Sunderland (Oct 4), Newcastle (Apr 18)

Competitions won by Portsmouth Football Club

F.A. Cup: 1939
F.A. Cup Finalists: 1929, 1934
F.A. Cup Semi-finalists: 1949
Western League Champions: 1901, 1902, 1903
Southern League Champions, Division 1: 1902, 1920
Southern League Runners-up, Division 2: 1912
Football League Division 1 Champions: 1948/9, 1949/50
Football League Division 2 Runners-up: 1926/7
Football League Division 3 Champions: 1961/2, 1982/3
Football League Division 3 South Champions: 1923/4
Football League Division 4: 4th position, promoted 1979/80
Hants Charity Cup Winners: 1906, 1907
South Western League Champions: 1916
South Hants War League Champions: 1918
Pickford Cup Winners: 1914, 1915, 1921, 1924, 1926, 1928, 1931, 1932, 1933, 1934, 1935, 1936
Hants Benevolent Cup Winners: 1911
Hospital Cup Winners: 1924, 1925, 1926, 1927, 1929, 1930, 1933, 1934, 1935
Hants Professional Cup Winners: 1935, 1982
Hants Professional Cup Runners-up: 1983
Hants Combination Cup Winners: 1933, 1941
Hampshire Football Association Benevolent Fund Cup: Joint Holders 1909
London Combination Winners: 1936 Pompey Reserves
London Combination Runners-up: 1937/38
London War Cup Runners-up: 1942
Midweek League Champions: 1977, 1983, 1984 Pompey Reserves
Midweek League Cup Winners: 1984 Pompey Reserves
Portsmouth Cup Winners: 1901 Pompey Reserves
1902 Pompey Reserves
1904 Pompey Reserves
Hants League Champions: 1903, 1904, 1939/40 Pompey Reserves
Hants League Southern Division Champions: 1911 Pompey Reserves
Southern Charity Cup Winners: 1903
Southern Charity Cup Runners-up: 1909
South Western Combination Champions: 1916
Southern League Runners-up: 1904, 1905, 1908 (all Division 2) Pompey Reserves
Southern League English Section Runners-up: 1921, Pompey Reserves
Southern League Runners-up: 1st team, 1907
Southern Professional Floodlight Cup Winners: 30/4/1958 beating Reading 2–0
Southern Floodlit Combination Cup Winners: 1957/8.

Season 1953/54   Division 1

Date	Venue	Team	Attendance	FA HT	FA FT	Uprichard N.	Stephen J.	Ferrier H.	Pickett R.	Froggatt J.	Dickinson J.	Harris P.	Phillips Len	Vaughan C.	Reid D.	Henderson J.	Hall K.	Gordon J.	Phillips Lionel	Platt E.	Mansell B.	Gunter P.	Pearson R.	Mundy A.	Gill M.	Dale G.	Wilson A.	Mortimore C.	Dore C.	Rutter C.	Mansell J.	Hunt B.
Aug 19	A	Liverpool	39662	1-1	1-3	1	2	3	4	5	6	7		9	10	11^1		8														
Aug 22	H	Sheffield Utd.	32256	1-2	3-4			3	4	5	6	7^1		9^1	10^1	11	2	8											1			
Aug 25	A	Chelsea	40090	3-3	3-4	1		3	4		6	7^1	10		5	11^1	2	8	9													
Aug 29	A	Huddersfield	22474	1-1	1-5		2	3	4		6	7	10		5	11		8	9^1										1			
Sept 2	H	Chelsea	29571	2-1	3-2				4	11	6	7^2	10		5	9	2	8^1		1	3											
Sept 5	H	Aston Villa	31870	2-0	2-1				4	11^1	6	7^1			5	9		8		1	3	2		10								
Sept 7	A	Blackpool	30914	0-0	1-1						6	7	9^1		5	11		8		1	3	2	4	10								
Sept 12	A	Wolverhampton	36524	2-3	3-4				4		6	7^1	9		5	11		8^1		1	3	2		10								
Sept 16	H	Blackpool	29701	1-3	4-4		2		4	11	6	7^1	9^2		5	10		8^1		1	3				1							
Sept 19	H	Sunderland	39053	2-1	4-1				4	11	6	7	9^1		5	10		8^2		1	3	2										
Sept 26	A	Manchester City	35691	1-0	1-2				4	11	6	7	9		5^1	10		8		1	3	2										
Oct 3	H	Cardiff	31765	0-0	1-1				4	11	6	7	8		9^1			10		1	3	2								5		
Oct 10	A	Burnley	28142	0-1	0-1				6	11		7			9			10		1	3	2	4							5		
Oct 17	H	Charlton	39333	1-0	3-1				4		6	7^2			9			10		8^1	3	2				11				5		
Oct 24	A	Sheffield Wed.	37091	0-2	4-4				4		6	7			9^1			10		8^3	3	2				11				5		
Oct 31	H	Middlesbrough	24432	0-1	0-2				4		6	7	10		9					8	3	2				11				5		
Nov 7	A	Bolton	17439	1-3	1-6				4		6	7^1			10	9				8	3	2				11				5		
Nov 14	H	Preston	30731	0-1	1-3			3	4	5	6	7			10	9				8		2				11^1						
Nov 21	A	Newcastle	48830	0-1	1-1					9	6	7	4		5	11		8		1		2								3	10	
Nov 28	H	Manchester Utd.	29233	1-0	1-1					9^1	6	7	4		5	11		8		1		2								3	10	
Dec 5	A	W.B.A.	30000	1-0	3-2					6	7^1	4	9		5	11		8^2		1		2								3	10	
Dec 12	H	Liverpool	23509	2-1	5-1					6	7^3	4	9^1		5	11		8^1		1		2								3		1
Dec 19	A	Sheffield Utd.	32000	1-1	1-3					6	7	4	9		5	11		8^1		1						2				3		1
Dec 25	A	Tottenham H.	36502	0-1	1-1					6	7^1	4	9		5	11		8		1						2	10			3		
Dec 26	H	Tottenham H.	36777	0-1	1-1					6	7	4	9^1		5	11		8		1		2								3		
Jan 2	H	Huddersfield	27533	2-1	5-2					6	7	4	9^3		5	11^1		8		1						2				3		
Jan 9	H	Charlton *FAC3*	37529	1-3	3-3					6	7	4	9^2		5	11		8^1		1		2								3		
Jan 14	A	Charlton *FAC3R*	31482		3-2					6	7^2	4			9	11		8		1		2								3		
Jan 16	A	Aston Villa	23000	0-0	1-1					6	7^1	4			9	11		8		1						2			5	3		
Jan 23	H	Wolverhampton	35312	1-0	2-0					6^1	7	4			9^1	11		8		1						3			5	2		
Jan 30	H	Scunthorpe *FAC4*	23935	1-0	1-1					6	7^1	4			9	11		8		1						2			5	3		
Feb 3	H	Scunthorpe *FAC4R*	30247		2-2					6	7	4	9		10	11^2		8					1			2				3		
Feb 6	A	Sunderland	45935	1-1	1-3					6	7	4	9			11^1		8					1	10	2			5	3		
Feb 8	†	Scunthorpe *FAC4(2)R*	24540		4-0				11^2	6	7^1	4				9^1		8					1	10	2				3		
Feb 13	A	Manchester City	30135	2-0	4-1				11^2	6	7	4			5	9^2		8					1	10	2				3		
Feb 20	A	Bolton *FAC5*	53883	0-0	0-0				11	6	7	4				9		8			3		1	10	2						
Feb 24	H	Bolton *FAC5R*	45806		1-2				11	6	7	4			5	9		8^1		1				10	2				3		
Feb 27	H	Burnley	24155	0-2	3-2				11	6						9		8^2			4		1		2			5	3		
Mar 3	A	Cardiff	28000	1-2	2-3					6					5^1	9		8			4	7^1	1		2			5	3		
Mar 6	A	Charlton	37508	0-1	1-3					6	7				5	9	2	8			4		1		3						
Mar 20	A	Middlesbrough	20000	1-1	2-2					6	7				5	9^1		8		1		4				11	2			3		
Mar 27	A	Bolton	22866	0-1	3-2					6	7^1				5	9^1		8^1		1		4				11	2			3		
Apr 3	A	Preston	17000	0-1	0-4				6			7	4	9	5			8		1						11	2			3		
Apr 7	H	Sheffield Wed.	15179		2-1					6	7	4			5	9		8^1		1						11^1	2			3		
Apr 10	H	Newcastle	26604	1-0	2-0					6	7	4			5			8		1						11^1	2			3		
Apr 16	A	Arsenal	44948		0-3					6	7	4			5			8		1		9				11	2			3		
Apr 17	A	Manchester Utd.	29663	0-0	0-2					6	7							8			4					11	2		1	5	3	
Apr 19	H	Arsenal	30958		1-1					6	7	4			5	9		8		1						11	2			3		
Apr 24	H	W.B.A	28004	0-0	3-0					6	7^2				5^1	9		8			4					11	2		1	3		
League Appearances						2	5	3	16	16	40	40	23	21	34	34	4	40	4	29	13	24	4	3	6	16	19	1	5	11	23	3
League Goalscorers										4	1	21		12	5	8		18	1			1				3						
FA Cup Appearances									3	7	7	7		2	5	7		7		4		3			3	3	5			1	6	
FA Cup Goalscorers										2		4		2		3		2														

Totals Division 1   P42 W14 D11 L17 F81 A89 Pts 39 Posn 14th

Own goals: Chelsea (Aug 25), Wolverhampton (Sept 12), Sunderland (Sept 19), Newcastle (Nov 21)

†at Highbury

Barnard M.	Flewin R.	Henwood R.	Ames K.	Davies J.
10				
10				
10				
10¹	5			
10				
10				
10				
	5			
	5			
	5			
10¹			7	
10	11			
10¹	11			
10¹				
10				
10				
10				
10¹		9		
10				
10		9		
10¹				
10				
16	2	2	1	
5				
3	4			
1				

Season 1954/55   Division 1

Date	Venue	Team	Attendance	FA HT	FA FT	Uprichard N.	Wilson A.	Mansell J.	Phillips Len	Reid D.	Pickett R.	Davies J.	Gemmell M.	Gordon J.	Barnard M.	Dale G.	Harris P.	Henderson J.	Dickinson J.	Rafferty R.	Rees D.	Platt E.	Gunter P.	McGhee T.	Newman B.	Stephen J.
Aug 21	A	Manchester Utd.	38203	1-0	3-1	1	2	3	4	5	6			8	10	11^1	7	9^1								
Aug 25	H	Huddersfield	35873		4-2	1	2	3	4	5	6			8^1	10^1	11	7^1	9^1								
Aug 28	H	Wolverhampton	40876	0-0	0-0	1	2	3	4	5	6			8	10	11	7	9								
Aug 30	A	Huddersfield	22688		1-2	1	2	3	4	5	6	7	8	9	10	11^1										
Sept 4	A	Aston Villa	27000	0-0	0-1	1	2	3	4	5	6			8	10	11	7	9								
Sept 6	A	Bolton	28009		1-3	1	2	3	4	5	6			8	10^1	11	7	9								
Sept 11	H	Sunderland	33512	1-0	2-2	1	2	3	4	5					10	11^1	7	9^1	6	8						
Sept 15	H	Bolton	24113		1-0	1	2	3	4	5					10	11	7^1	9	6	8						
Sept 18	A	Tottenham H.	37404	1-1	1-1	1	2	3	4	5				8	10	11	7	9	6							
Sept 25	H	Sheffield Wed.	28579	1-0	2-1	1	2	3	4	5				8^1	10	11	7^1	9	6							
Oct 2	A	Preston	32500	0-0	1-1	1	2	3	4	5				8	10^1	11	7	9	6			1				
Oct 9	H	Sheffield Utd.	28121	3-2	6-2	1	2	3	4	5				8^2		11	7^4	9	6		10					
Oct 16	A	Arsenal	44866	0-0	1-0	1	2	3	4					8	10	11	7^1	9	6				5			
Oct 23	H	Leicester	34727	1-1	2-1	1	2	3	4						10	11	7^2	9	6	8			5			
Oct 30	A	Burnley	23772	0-1	0-1	1	2	3	4					8	10	11	7	9	6				5			
Nov 6	H	Everton	32403	2-0	5-0	1		3	4					8^1	10	11^2	7	9^1	6				5	2		
Nov 13	A	Manchester City	24564	2-1	2-1	1		3	4					8^1	10	11	7^1	9	6				5	2		
Nov 20	H	Cardiff	31332	1-1	1-3	1		3	4					8	10	11	7	9^1	6				5	2		
Nov 27	A	Chelsea	40358	1-2	1-4	1		3	4		6			8	10	11	7	9					5	2		
Dec 4	H	W.B.A.	28027	3-0	6-1	1		3	4	5	6			8^1	10^1	11	7^2	9^1						2		
Dec 11	A	Newcastle	23400	0-1	1-2	1		3	4	5	6			8	10	11^1	7	9						2		
Dec 18	H	Manchester Utd.	26019	0-0	0-0	1		3	4	5	6			8	10	11	7	9						2		
Dec 25	A	Blackpool	25004		2-2	1		3	4	5	6			8	10	11^1	7^1	9						2		
Dec 27	H	Blackpool	42896	3-0	3-0	1		3	4	5	6			8^1	10^1	11^1	7	9						2		
Jan 1	A	Wolverhampton	30880	1-2	2-2	1		3	4	5	6			8	10	11	7^1	9						2		
Jan 8	A	Bristol Rov *FAC3*	35921	0-0	1-2	1			4	5	6			8^1	10	11	7	9						2		3
Jan 22	A	Sunderland	38703	0-0	2-2	1		3	4	5				8		11	7^1	9^1	6		10			2		
Feb 5	H	Tottenham H.	27539	0-0	0-3	1		3	4	5				8		11	7	9	6		10			2		
Feb 12	A	Sheffield Wed.	21176	1-1	3-1	1		3	4	5	6			8		11^1	7^1	9^1			10			2		
Feb 19	H	Preston	19830	2-0	2-0	1		3	4	5^1	6			8^1		11	7	9			10			2		
Mar 5	H	Newcastle	26923	2-0	3-1	1		3	4	5				8^1		11^1	7	9^1	6		10			2		
Mar 12	A	Leicester	28262	0-2	0-4	1		3	4	5				8		11	7	9	6		10			2		
Mar 19	H	Burnley	21755	0-0	0-2	1		3	4	5				8	10	11	7	9	6					2		
Mar 26	A	Everton	30087	3-0	3-2	1		3	4	5				8^1	10	11	7^1	9^1	6					2		
Apr 2	H	Manchester City	24286	1-0	1-0	1		3	4	5				8	10		7^1	9	6		11			2		
Apr 8	H	Charlton	32291	2-0	2-0	1		3	4	5				8^1	10		7^1	9	6		11			2		
Apr 9	A	W.B.A.	27000	1-1	1-3	1		3	4	5				8	10		7	9^1	6		11			2		
Apr 11	A	Charlton	21834		2-2	1		3	4	5				8			7	9	6		10			2	11	
Apr 16	H	Chelsea	40230	0-0	0-0	1		3	4	5				8			7	9	6		10			2	11	
Apr 23	A	Cardiff	25000	1-0	1-1	1		3	4	5				8		11	7^1	9	6		10			2		
Apr 27	H	Aston Villa	18794		2-2	1		3	4	5				8^1		11	7	9	6		10^1			2		
Apr 30	H	Arsenal	28156	2-0	2-1	1		3	4	5^1				8		11^1	7	9	6					2	10	
May 2	A	Sheffield Utd	20000		2-5	1		3	4	5				8		11	7^1	9	6		10^1			2		
League Appearances						41	15	42	31	35	24	1	1	38	30	31	41	41	25	11	13	1	11	27	3	
League Goalscorers									4					13	5	10	23	13		3						
FA Cup Appearances						1			1	1	1			1	1	1	1	1						1		1
FA Cup Goalscorers														1												

Totals Division 1   P42 W18 D12 L12 F74 A62 Pts 48 Posn 3rd

Own goals: Manchester Utd (Aug 21), Everton (Nov 6), W.B.A. (Dec 4)

Season 1955/56   Division 1

Date	Venue	Team	Attendance	FA HT	FA FT	Uprichard N.	McGhee T.	Mansell J.	Gunter P.	Reid D.	Dickinson J.	Harris P.	Pickett R.	Henderson J.	Rees D.	Neil P.	Dale G.	Robertson J.	Gordon J.	Barnard M.	Newman B.	Barnett A.	Wilson A.	Rutter C.	Phillips J.	Rafferty R.	Penk H.	Phillips Len	Drinkwater R.	McDonald L.	Cairney J.
Aug 20	A	Huddersfield	21062	0-0	0-1	1	2		3	5	6		4	9		7	11		8		10											
Aug 24	H	Wolverhampton	30419		2-1	1	2	3		5	6	7^1	4	9	10		11		8^1													
Aug 27	H	Blackpool	37072	2-2	3-3	1	2	3		5	6	7^1	4	9^1	10		11^1		8													
Aug 31	A	Wolverhampton	40000		1-3	1	2	3	4	5	6	7	8	9^1	10		11														
Sept 3	A	Chelsea	48273	3-0	5-1	1	2	3	4	5	6	7^2	8	9^1	10^2		11														
Sept 10	H	Bolton	30902	0-0	3-3	1	2	3	4	5	6	7	8	9	10		11^1														
Sept 17	A	Arsenal	48816	0-1	3-1	1	2	3	4	5	6	7^2	8	9	10^1		11														
Sept 24	H	Everton	29980	0-0	1-0	1	2	3	4	5	6	7	8	9	10		11^1														
Oct 1	H	Sunderland	38396	1-1	2-1	1	2	3	4	5		7^1	6	9	10		11		8^1												
Oct 8	A	Newcastle	40380	0-1	1-2	1	2	3	4	5	6	7		9	10^1				8			1								
Oct 15	H	Birmingham	29357	0-4	0-5	1	2	3	4		6	7		9			11	10	8								5			
Oct 22	A	Charlton	15871	0-1	1-6	1		3	4	5		7	6					11^1	8	10	9		2				5			
Oct 24	A	Brentford *FC*		0-0	0-0	1		3	4	5		7		9				11	8	10	6	1							5
Oct 29	H	Tottenham H.	26017	1-0	4-1	1	2	3		5	6	7^1		9^2			11		8^1	10						5			
Nov 5	A	Sheffield Utd.	28000	1-0	3-1	1	2	3	4^1	5	6	7^1		9			11		8^1	10									
Nov 7	H	Brentford *FCR*			1-2		2		4		6			9				11	8^1	10						5	7		1	3
Nov 12	H	Preston	27720	0-1	0-2	1	2	3	4	5	6	7		9			11		8	10									
Nov 19	A	Burnley	20615	0-2	0-3	1	2	3	4	5	6	7		9			11		8	10									
Nov 26	H	Luton	27758	0-0	0-0	1	2	3	4	5	6	7	8	9			11			10									
Dec 3	A	W.B.A.	23000	0-1	0-4	1	2	3	4	5	6	7		9			11		8	10									
Dec 10	H	Manchester Utd.	24594	0-1	3-2	1	2	3		5	6^1	7	4	9			11		8	10^1									
Dec 17	H	Huddersfield	16347	2-0	5-2	1	2	3		5	6	7^1	4	9			11^2		8^1	10^1									
Dec 24	A	Blackpool	24182	1-0	3-2	1	2	3		5	6	7^2	4	9			11		8	10^1									
Dec 26	A	Aston Villa	24000		3-1	1	2	3		5	6	7^1	4	9^1					8	10^1									
Dec 27	A	Aston Villa	31316		2-2	1	2	3		5	6	7^1	4	9					8^1	10									
Dec 31	H	Chelsea	29139	2-3	4-4	1	2	3		5	6	7^2	4	9^2					8	10									
Jan 2	A	Manchester City	43133		1-4	1		3		5	6	7	4	9			11		8	10^1									
Jan 7	H	Grimsby *FAC3*	33564	2-1	3-1	1	2	3^1		5	6	7^1	4^1	9			11		8	10									
Jan 14	A	Bolton	23588	0-1	0-4	1	2	3		5	6	7		9			11		8	10				4					
Jan 21	H	Arsenal	30513	1-1	5-2	1	2	3		5	6	7^2		9			11^1		8	10^1				4					
Jan 28	A	W.B.A. *FAC4*	59448	0-1	0-2	1	2	3		5	6	7	4	9			11		8	10									
Feb 4	A	Everton	36875	2-0	2-0	1	2	3		5	6	7	4	9^1			11		8				10^1						
Feb 11	A	Sunderland	29762	1-3	2-4	1	2	3		5	6	7	4	9^1			11		8				10^1						
Feb 22	H	Newcastle	15800		0-2	1	2	3		5	6	7	4	9			11		8	10									
Feb 25	A	Birmingham	32159	1-1	2-3	1	2	3		5	6	7^1	4	9			11			10				8^1					
Mar 3	H	Burnley	19279	1-0	3-1	1	2	3		5	6	7	4	9^3			11			10				8					
Mar 10	A	Tottenham H.	44314	0-0	1-1	1	2	3		5	6	7	4	9^1			11			10				8					
Mar 17	H	Sheffield Utd.	20168	1-0	1-1	1	2	3		5	6	7		9			11			10			4	8^1					
Mar 24	A	Preston	16716	0-1	1-2	1	2	3	4	5		7		9			11^1		8	10				6					
Mar 30	H	Cardiff	26443		1-1	1	2	3	4			7		9			11		8^1	10				6		5				
Mar 31	H	Charlton	21194	0-0	4-0	1	2	3	4		6	7^1		9^2					8	10^1						5	11			
Apr 2	A	Cardiff	30000		3-2	1	2	3			6	7^1	4	9^1					8	10^1						5	11			
Apr 7	A	Luton	17824	0-1	0-1	1	2	3	4		6	7		9					8	10						5	11			
Apr 14	H	W.B.A.	15626	1-1	1-1	1	2	3	4		6	7^1		9					8	10						5	11			
Apr 21	A	Manchester Utd.	38417	0-1	0-1	1	2	3	4		6	7		9					8	10						5	11			
Apr 28	H	Manchester City	24684	1-2	2-4	1	2	3	4		6	7	8	9^2						10						5	11			
League Appearances						41	40	41	38	19	39	41	25	35	22	9	22	12	21	26	2	1	2	8	3	9	6				
League Goalscorers							3	1	1			23	16	9	3		1		4	5				7		3					
FA Cup Appearances						2	2	2	2	2	2	1	2	2			2		2	2											1
FA Cup Goalscorers								1				1	1																		

Totals Division 1   P42 W16 D9 L17 F78 A85 Pts 41 Posn 12th

Own goals: Manchester Utd (Dec 10), Arsenal (Jan 21)

Season 1956/57 Division 1

Date	Venue	Team	Attendance	FA HT	FA FT	Uprichard N.	McGhee T.	Gunter P.	Pickett R.	Rutter C.	Dickinson J.	Harris P.	Gordon J.	Henderson J.	Barnard M.	Dale G.	Rees D.	Drinkwater R.	Wilson A.	Penk H.	Evans I.	Rafferty R.	Mansell J.	Newman R.	McClellan S.	Phillips J.	Weddle D.	Albury W.	Barnett A.	Clugston J.	Stenhouse A.
Aug 18	A	Newcastle	29000	0-0	1-2	1	2	3	4	5	6	7	8^1	9	10	11															
Aug 22	A	Birmingham	33307	0-2	1-3	1	2	3		5	6	7	8	9^1	10	11									4						
Aug 25	H	Sheffield Wed.	23730	2-0	3-1	1	2	3	4	5	6	7	8^2	9^1	10	11															
Aug 29	H	Birmingham	25685		3-4	1	2	3	4^1	5	6	7^1	8^1	9	10	11															
Sept 1	A	Manchester Utd.	40369	0-2	0-3	1	2	3	4	5	6	7	8	9		11	10														
Sept 5	A	W.B.A.	14570		1-2	1	2	3	4	5	6	7	8	9		11	10^1														
Sept 8	H	Arsenal	30768	1-2	2-3	1	2	3	4	5	6	7^1	8	11	10		9^1														
Sept 15	A	Burnley	29756	1-0	1-1		2	5	4		6	7	8	11	10	9^1		1	3												
Sept 22	H	Preston	29197	2-0	2-2		2	5	4		6	7^1	8	11^1	10	9		1	3												
Sept 29	A	Chelsea	31620	1-1	3-3		2	5	4		6	7	8^1	11^1	10^1	9		1	3												
Oct 6	H	Aston Villa	23613	2-0	5-1		2	5	4		6	7^1	8^2	11^2	10	9		1	3												
Oct 13	A	Wolverhampton	35248	0-4	0-6		2	5	4		6	7	8	11	10	9		1	3												
Oct 20	H	Charlton	20070	1-0	1-0		2	5	4		6	7	9	10				1	3				11^1	8							
Oct 27	A	Sunderland	29700	2-0	3-3		2	5	4		6	7	8^1	10^1			9	1	3				11^1								
Nov 3	H	Tottenham H.	31933	1-1	2-3		2	5	4		6	7	8^1	9	10			1	3				11								
Nov 10	A	Everton	37406	0-1	2-2	1	2	5	4		6	7	8^1	11			9		3						10^1						
Nov 17	H	Blackpool	26466	0-0	0-0	1	2	5	4		6	7	8	11								3			9	10					
Nov 24	A	Manchester City	24364	1-1	1-5	1	2	5	4		6	7		11					3			8			9	10					
Dec 1	H	Bolton	19021	1-0	1-1	1	2	5			6	7	8	11								10^1			3	9	4				
Dec 8	A	Leeds	29600	1-1	1-4	1	2		4	5	6	7^1	8	11									3		9	10					
Dec 15	A	Newcastle	18453	1-0	2-2	1	2	5			6	7	10^1	11									3	8^1	9		4				
Dec 29	H	Manchester Utd.	32147	1-0	1-3	1	2	5			6	7	10	11									3	8	9^1		4				
Jan 5	A	Bury FAC3	13927	1-0	3-1	1	2	5			6	7^2	10	11									3	8^1	9		4				
Jan 12	A	Arsenal	48949	1-1	1-1	1				5		7	8	11					2				3		9^1	10	4			6	
Jan 19	A	Burnley	22138	0-0	1-0	1				5		7	8	11					2				3		9	10^1	4			6	
Jan 26	H	Notts Forest FAC4	36438	1-0	1-3	1				5		7	8	11					2				3		9^1	10	4			6	
Feb 2	A	Preston	23482	1-4	1-7	1	2			5	6	7	8	11									3		9	10	4				
Feb 9	H	Chelsea	22964	0-1	2-2	1	2		6	5		7	8^1	9									11		3	10^1	4				
Feb 18	H	Aston Villa	10000		2-2	1	2		6	5		7^1	8	9^1									11		3	10	4				
Mar 2	A	Charlton	20413	2-1	3-1	1	2		6	5		7^1	8	9									11		3	10^2	4				
Mar 9	H	Leeds	23596	2-3	2-5	1	2	4		5	6	7	8	9									11^1		3		10^1				
Mar 13	H	Luton	28378	2-1	2-2		2		6	5		7	9	11^1					2				3	8		10^1	4		1		
Mar 16	A	Tottenham H.	36050	0-2	0-2		2		6	5		7	9	11									3	8		10	4		1		
Mar 20	A	Luton	14589	0-0	0-1	1	2		6	5		7	9	11									3			10	4	8			
Mar 23	H	Everton	23273	0-0	3-2		2		6	5		7^1	8	9^1									11		3	10^1	4		1		
Mar 30	A	Blackpool	14972	0-4	0-5		2		6	5		7	8	9									11		3	10	4		1		
Apr 6	H	Manchester City	24919	0-0	0-1		2			5	6	7	8	9											3	11	4		1		
Apr 9	A	Sheffield Wed.	19890	1-2	1-3		2			5	6	7	8^1											11	9	10	4	3	1		
Apr 13	A	Bolton	16969	0-1	1-1		2			5	6	7	8										3		11	10	4	9^1	1		
Apr 19	H	Cardiff	31223	1-0	1-0					5	6	7^1	8	11									3	2	9	10	4		1		
Apr 20	H	Wolverhampton	31111	1-0	1-0					5	6	7	8	9									3		11^1	10	4		1		
Apr 22	A	Cardiff	25000	1-0	2-0		2			5	6	7^2	8			9							3		11	10	4		1		
Apr 27	H	W.B.A.	24065	0-0	0-1					5	6	7	8	9			10	2	3						11		4		1		
May 1	H	Sunderland	20613	2-1	3-2		2			5	6		8	9^2					3						11	10^1	4		1		7
League Appearances						22	35	22	26	18	42	39	40	33	12	23	11	8	25	3	1	3	17	8	17	18	17	8	12	1	1
League Goalscorers									1			11	13	11	2	2	3		2				2	1	5	6					
FA Cup Appearances						2	1	1			2	2	2	2				1					2		2	2	2		1		
FA Cup Goalscorers													2												1	1				

Totals Division 1   P42 W10 D13 L19 F62 A92 Pts 33 Posn 19th

Own goals: Tottenham H. (Nov 3), Manchester City (Nov 24), Preston (Feb 2)

Season 1957/58   Division 1

Date	Venue	Team	Attendance	FA HT	FA FT	Barnett A.	Gunter P.	Mansell J.	Phillips J.	Rutter C.	Dickinson J.	Harris P.	Gordon J.	Crawford R.	McClellan S.	Henderson J.	Wilson A.	Barnard M.	Weddle D.	Newman R.	Uprichard N.	Albury W.	Dougan D.	McGhee T.	Stenhouse A.	Osmond C.	Chapman S.	Govan A.	Carter B.	Watts M.
Aug 24	H	Burnley	30137	0-0	0-0	1		3	4	5	6	7	8	9			11	2	10											
Aug 28	H	Tottenham H.	33479	4-0	5-1	1		3	4	5	6	7^{3}	8	9^{2}	10	11	2													
Aug 31	A	Preston	22429	0-1	0-4	1		3	4	5	6	7	8	9	10	11	2													
Sept 4	A	Tottenham H.	36458	3-3	5-3	1	2	3	4	5	6	7^{1}	8^{1}	9	10^{1}	11^{2}														
Sept 7	H	Sheffield Wed.	21149	1-0	3-2	1	2	3^{1}	4	5	6	7	8	9^{1}	10^{1}	11														
Sept 11	A	Newcastle	38640	0-1	0-2	1	2		4	5	6	7	8	9			11	3	10											
Sept 14	A	Manchester City	28789	0-1	1-2	1	2		4	5	6	7^{1}	8	9			11	3	10											
Sept 18	H	Newcastle	32093	2-1	2-2	1		3	4	5	6	7	8		10^{1}	11	2			9^{1}										
Sept 21	H	Notts Forest	33805	1-2	1-4	1		3	4	5	6	7	8		10	11	2			9^{1}										
Sept 28	A	Bolton	13184	0-1	0-1	1	2		4	5	6	7	8		10	11		3		9										
Oct 5	A	W.B.A.	31600	1-1	1-3	1	2		4	5	6	7^{1}	8		10		9	3	11											
Oct 12	H	Leeds	23633	1-1	1-2	1	2		4	5	6	7	8		10	11		3		9^{1}										
Oct 14	H	Charlton *SFCC1*		1-0	4-1		2	10^{2}		5	6	7	8^{2}			11		3			1	4	9							
Oct 19	A	Manchester Utd.	38253	3-0	3-0		2			5	6	7^{1}	8		10^{1}	11^{1}		3			1	4	9							
Oct 26	H	Leicester	25947	1-0	2-0			3^{1}		5	6	7	8^{1}		10	11	2				1	4	9							
Nov 2	A	Aston Villa	27000	1-2	1-2		2			5	6	7	8			11		3			1	4	9		10^{1}					
Nov 9	A	Wolverhampton	38320	0-0	1-1		2			5	6		8		10	11		3			1	4	9^{1}		7					
Nov 16	A	Arsenal	40528	1-2	2-3		2	10^{1}		5	6		8^{1}			11		3			1	4	9		7					
Nov 23	H	Everton	27015	2-1	3-2		2	10^{1}		5	6	7	8^{1}			11		3			1	4	9^{1}							
Nov 25	A	Millwall *SFCC2*	6951	2-1	3-2		2	10^{1}		5	6	7	9^{2}			11		3			1	4	8							
Nov 30	A	Blackpool	14722	1-2	1-2		2	10		5	6^{1}	7	9			11		3			1	4	8							
Dec 7	H	Luton	17782	2-0	5-0		2			5	6	7^{3}	8			11^{2}	10	3			1	4	9							
Dec 14	A	Sunderland	25925	1-1	1-1		2			5	6	7^{1}	8			11	10	3			1	4	9							
Dec 21	A	Burnley	19961	0-0	0-0		2			5	6	7	8^{1}			11	10	3			1	4	9							
Dec 25	A	Chelsea	27036	1-5	4-7		2			5	6	7^{1}	8^{1}			11	10^{1}	3			1	4	9							
Dec 26	H	Chelsea	32236	1-0	3-0		2			5	6	7	8^{1}			11	10^{1}	3			1	4	9							
Dec 28	H	Preston	31735	0-1	0-2		2		4		6	7	8			11	10	3			1		9			5				
Jan 4	H	Aldershot *FAC3*	33171	3-0	5-1					5	6	7	8^{2}			11^{2}	10^{1}	3			1	4	9	2						
Jan 11	A	Sheffield Wed.	21308	0-1	2-4		2			5	6	7^{1}	8^{1}			11	10	3			1	4	9							
Jan 18	H	Manchester City	26254	1-1	2-1		2			5	6	7	8	9^{2}		11		3			1	4	10							
Jan 25	A	Wolverhampton *FAC4*	43522	1-2	1-5		2			5	6	7	8	9^{1}		11		3			1	4	10							
Feb 1	A	Notts Forest	23194	0-1	0-2		2	5	4		6	7	8	9		11	10	3			1									
Feb 8	H	Bolton	21500	1-1	2-2			5	4^{1}		6	7^{1}	8	9		11	10	3			1			2						
Feb 22	A	Leeds	26500	0-1	0-2					5	6	11	9	7			10	3			1	4		2				8		
Mar 8	A	Leicester	30951	1-2	2-2				4	5	6	7	8^{1}			11	10	3			1		9	2						
Mar 15	H	Aston Villa	23164	0-0	1-0				4	5	6	7	8				10	3			1		9	2				11^{1}		
Mar 19	H	W.B.A.	24731	2-1	2-2				4	5	6	7	8^{1}				10	3			1		9^{1}	2				11		
Mar 22	A	Everton	23179	1-0	2-4			3	4	5	6	7^{1}	8				10^{1}				1		9	2				11		
Mar 29	H	Arsenal	25770	4-1	5-4				4	5	6	7^{1}	8				10^{1}	3			1		9^{1}	2				11		
Mar 31	A	Watford *SFCC SF*	4466	1-0	1-0				4	5			8			11	10	3			1		9^{1}	2				7	6	
Apr 4	H	Birmingham	33072	0-1	3-2				4	5	6	7	8				10^{1}	3			1		9^{2}	2				11		
Apr 5	A	Wolverhampton	31259	0-1	0-1				4	5	6	7	8				10	3			1		9	2				11		
Apr 7	A	Birmingham	23380	0-1	1-4				4	5	6	7	8			11^{1}	10	3			1		9	2						
Apr 12	H	Blackpool	25311	0-2	1-2				4	5	6	7	8			11	10	3			1		9^{1}	2						
Apr 16	H	Manchester Utd.	39975	0-2	3-3				4	5	6	7^{1}				11	10	3			1		9^{1}	2				8^{1}		
Apr 19	A	Luton	12932	1-1	1-2			3	4	5		7	8^{1}				10				1		9	2				11	6	
Apr 26	H	Sunderland	22545	0-1	0-2			3	4	5		7	8				10				1		9	2				11	6	
Apr 30	A	Reading *SFCC Final*	14864	0-0	2-0			3	4	5		7	8								1		9^{1}	2				11	6	10^{1}
League Appearances						12	32	11	22	35	42	40	39	16	19	24	36	17	4	10	30	15	26	15	3	1	1	9	3	
League Goalscorers								4				18	13	8	4	3	4						8	1				2		
FA Cup Appearances						2				1	2	2	2	1		2	1				2	2	2	2	1					
FA Cup Goalscorers													2									1	2							

Totals Division 1   P42 W12 D 8 L22 F73 A88 Pts 32 Posn 20th

Own goals: Chelsea (Dec 25), Chelsea (Dec 26)

Season 1958/59   Division 1

Date	Venue	Team	Attendance	FA HT	FA FT	Uprichard N.	McGhee T.	Hayward B.	Phillips J.	Dickinson J.	Casey T.	Harris P.	Gordon J.	Dougan D.	Harris H.	Newman R.	Crawford R.	Rutter C.	Govan A.	Gunter P.	Saunders R.	Cutler B.	Wilson A.	Barnard M.	Carter B.	Chapman S.	Brown F.	Weddle D.	Morrison W.	Howells R.	White J.
Aug 23	H	West Ham	40470	0-1	1-2	1	2	3	4	5	6	7^1	8	9	10	11															
Aug 25	A	Aston Villa	33000	1-1	2-3	1	2	3	4		6	7	8		10	9^1	5	11													
Aug 30	A	Notts Forest	23571	0-2	0-5	1	2	3	4		6	7	8		10	9	5	11													
Sept 3	H	Aston Villa	24209	2-1	5-2	1		3	4	5	6	7^5	8		10	11		2											9		
Sept 6	H	Chelsea	31815	1-1	2-2	1		3	4	5	6	7	8		10^2	11		2		9											
Sept 10	A	W.B.A.	34400	1-0	2-1	1		3	4	5	6	7	8		10^1	11		2		9^1											
Sept 13	A	Blackpool	26035	0-1	1-1	1		3	4	5	6	7^1	8		10	11		2		9											
Sept 17	H	W.B.A.	32972	1-5	2-6	1		3	4	5	6	7^1	8		10^1			2		9	11										
Sept 20	H	Blackburn	28537	0-1	2-1	1			4	5	6	7	8		10			2		9^2	11	3									
Sept 27	A	Newcastle	42280	0-1	0-2	1			4	5	6		8		10			2		9	7	3	11								
Oct 4	H	Tottenham H.	26402	1-1	1-1	1			4	5					10	8		2		9^1	7	3	11	6							
Oct 11	H	Leeds	22564	0-0	2-0	1			4	5	6				10	8^1		2		9	7	3	11								
Oct 18	A	Manchester City	31330	1-2	2-3	1			4	5	6				10	8		2		9	7^1	3	11^1								
Oct 25	H	Luton	24831	2-0	2-2	1			4	5	6				10^1	8		2		9^1	7	3	11								
Nov 1	A	Birmingham	23695	2-1	2-2	1	2		4	5	6		8	9	10^1						7^1	3	11								
Nov 3	H	Luton *SFCC1*	5066	0-2	0-2			3	4	5	6		8		10						7		11		1	2				9
Nov 8	H	Leicester	20262	1-0	4-1	1	2		4	5	6				10^2	8				9^2	7	3	11								
Nov 15	A	Preston	16099	1-1	1-3	1	2	5	4		6				10	8				9^1	7	3	11								
Nov 22	H	Burnley	17320	2-1	4-2	1	2	5	4		6				10^1	8^1				9^2	11	3	7								
Nov 29	A	Bolton	20624	1-2	1-2	1	2	5	4		6				10	8				9^1	11	3	7								
Dec 6	H	Arsenal	33321	0-1	0-1	1	2	5	4		6		8		10				7	9	11	3									
Dec 13	A	Everton	23875	1-2	1-2	1	2	5	4		6				10^1	8				9	11	3	7								
Dec 20	A	West Ham	21500	0-4	0-6	1	2	5	4		6				10	8				9	11	3	7								
Dec 26	H	Wolverhampton	28022	1-1	3-5	1	2	5	4	6^1	7				10	11^1				9^1		3		8							
Dec 27	A	Wolverhampton	41347	0-1	0-7	1	2	5			6			9	10				7		11	3		4							
Jan 3	H	Notts Forest	21390	0-1	0-1		2	5			6	7			10					9		3	11	4	8		1				
Jan 10	H	Swansea *FAC3*	23107	1-1	3-1		2	5	4		7				10	11^1				9^1		3		6	8		1				
Jan 17	A	Chelsea	24356	1-0	2-2		2	5		6	7^1				10	11				9^1		3		4	8		1				
Jan 24	A	Accrington *FAC4*	12590	0-0	0-0		2	5		6	7				10	11				9		3		4	8		1				
Jan 28	H	Accrington *FAC4R*	22407	3-0	4-1		2	5		6	7				10	11^1				9^2		3		4	8^1		1				
Jan 31	H	Blackpool	23138	1-1	1-2		2	5		6	7				10^1	11				9		3		4	8		1				
Feb 7	A	Blackburn	32400	1-0	1-2		2	5		6	7				10^1	8				9	11	3		4			1				
Feb 14	A	Burnley *FAC5*	33055	0-1	0-1			5		6	7				10	8				9	11	3	2	4			1				
Feb 21	A	Tottenham H.	27250	1-1	4-4		2	5		6					10	11^1				9^3	8	3	7	4			1				
Feb 28	A	Leeds	15000	0-1	1-1			5		6	11^1	7			10	8				9		3	2	4			1				
Mar 7	H	Manchester City	19919	2-0	3-4			5		6	11				10^1	8				9^2	7	3	2	4			1				
Mar 11	H	Newcastle	19404	0-2	1-5			5		6	11				10	8				9^1	7	3	2	4			1				
Mar 21	H	Birmingham	18149	0-1	1-1	1		5		6	7				10	11				9		3	2	4							8^1
Mar 27	A	Manchester Utd.	51783	0-3	1-6	1		5		6	7				10	11^1	2			9		3		4							8
Mar 28	A	Leicester	17064	1-2	1-3			5		6	7				10	11^1	2			9		3	1	4							8
Mar 30	H	Manchester Utd.	29359	1-2	1-3			5		6	7^1				10	11	2			9		3	1	4							8
Apr 4	H	Preston	15790	0-2	1-2			5		6	7				10	11	2			9		3	1	4							8^1
Apr 11	A	Burnley	18174	0-0	1-2					6	7				10^1		2			9	11	3	5			1				4	8
Apr 15	A	Everton	12714	1-1	2-3					6	7^2				10		2			9	11	3	5			1				4	8
Apr 18	H	Bolton	14161	0-0	0-1				4		7				10		2			9	11	3	5			1				6	8
Apr 22	A	Luton	11592	0-1	1-3				4		7^1				10		2			9	11	3	5			1				6	8
Apr 25	A	Arsenal	24569	1-3	2-5				4^1		7				10		2			9^1	11	3	5			1				6	8
League Appearances						26	18	28	17	39	24	26	9	7	39	35	2	12	2	26	36	22	24	15	9	3	16	3	3	11	10
League Goalscorers								2	1			13	1		13	5	1			21	2			1							2
FA Cup Appearances							3	4	4		4				4	4				4		1		4	1		4				2
FA Cup Goalscorers															2					3				1							

Totals Division 1   P42 W6 D 9 L27 F64 A112 Pts 21 Posn 22nd Bottom Relegated!

Own goals: Aston Villa (Aug 25), Leeds (Oct 11), Swansea (Jan 10)

Season 1959/60   Division 2

Date	Venue	Team	Attendance	FA HT	FA FT	Beattie R.	Rutter C.	Wilson A.	Phillips J.	Dickinson J.	Howells R.	Harris P.	Campbell J.	Saunders R.	Harris H.	Newman R.	Brown F.	Thomas R.	Hayward B.	Carter B.	Priscott A.	Chapman S.	White J.	Taylor D.	Cutler R.	Gunter P.	Davidson D.	Foley T.	Snowdon B.	Gaddes R.
Aug 22	A	Middlesbrough	26929	0-0	0-0	1	2	3	4	5	6	7	8	9	10	11														
Aug 26	A	Lincoln C.	12273	1-0	2-0	1	2		4	5	6	7	8^1	9	10^1	11								3						
Aug 29	H	Stoke	24627	0-0	2-2	1	2	3	4	5	6	7	8	9^1	10^1	11														
Sept 2	H	Lincoln C.	18827	0-1	1-2	1	2		4	5	6	7	8	9^1	10	11								3						
Sept 5	A	Brighton	29153	1-1	1-3	1	5	2		6	4	7^1	8	9	10	11								3						
Sept 9	H	Aston Villa	19910	1-2	1-2	1	2		4	5	6	7	8	9^1	10	11								3						
Sept 12	H	Swansea	14761	0-1	1-3	1	2	3	4	5	6	7			10^1	8							9	11						
Sept 14	A	Aston Villa	36000	2-3	2-5	1		3	4	5	6	7	8^1	9	10^1	11										2				
Sept 19	A	Bristol R.	20634	0-1	0-2	1		3	4	5	6	7	8	9	10	11										2				
Sept 26	H	Ipswich	16646	0-0	0-2			4	5	6	7			9	10	11	1		5		8					2				
Oct 3	A	Huddersfield	15452	3-2	3-6			4	3	6		7^2	9^1		8	1		5						10	11	2				
Oct 10	A	Derby Co.	17302	0-1	0-1	1		4	3			7	9	10				6					8	11	2			5	
Oct 17	H	Plymouth	20698	1-0	1-0	1		4	3			7	9	10	8^1			6						11	2			5	
Oct 24	A	Liverpool	21075	0-1	1-1	1	4		3			7	9	10	8^1			5	6					11	2				
Oct 27	A	Arsenal *SFC*	4108	0-1	1-2	1	4		3			7	9	10	8			5	6					11^1	2				
Oct 31	H	Charlton	17113	1-2	2-2	1			3	4		7	9	10	8			5	6					11^1	2				
Nov 7	A	Bristol City	21043	0-1	0-2	1			3	4		7	9	10	8			5	6					11^1	2				
Nov 14	H	Scunthorpe	14849	1-0	4-0	1			3	4	7		8^1	10^1				9^1	6					11	2			5	
Nov 21	A	Rotherham	15079	0-0	1-2	1			3	4	7		8	10^1				9	6					11	2			5	
Nov 28	H	Cardiff	14018	1-0	1-1	1			3	4	7		8^1	10				9	6					11	2			5	
Dec 5	A	Hull City	14675	2-1	3-1	1			3	4	7		8^1	10^1				9	6					11^1	2			5	
Dec 12	H	Sheffield Utd.	15326	0-0	0-2	1			3	6	7		8	10				9	4					11	2			5	
Dec 19	H	Middlesbrough	9912	2-1	6-3	1			3				8^2	10^1				9^2	6					11	2		7	5	
Dec 26	A	Leyton Orient	14912	1-1	2-1	1			3	4^1			8^1	10				9	6					11	2		7	5	
Dec 28	H	Leyton Orient	21170	0-0	1-1	1			3	4			8^1	10				9	6					11	2		7	5	
Jan 2	A	Stoke	16653	0-1	0-4	1			3	4			8	10				9	6					11	2		7	5	
Jan 9	A	Sheffield Utd. *FAC3*	19528	0-0	0-3	1			3	4			8	10	7			9	6					11	2			5	
Jan 16	H	Brighton	18223	1-1	1-2	1			3	4			8^1	10				9^1	6					11	2		7	5	
Jan 23	A	Swansea	12000	0-1	1-1	1			3	4			8	10^1				9	6			7		11	2			5	
Feb 6	H	Bristol R.	14136	1-2	4-5	1	5		3	4			8	9^2	10^1	11			6					7^1	2				
Feb 13	A	Ipswich	12502	0-0	1-1	1	5	4	3	6			8	9^1	10	7								11	2				
Feb 20	A	Huddersfield	14062	0-1	0-2	1	5	4	3	6			8	9	10	7								11	2				
Feb 27	H	Derby Co.	30220	2-3	2-3	1	5	3	4				8	9^1	10							6		11	2	7			
Mar 5	A	Plymouth	20558	1-1	1-1	1	7	3	4				8	9	10		2		6					11^1				5	
Mar 12	A	Liverpool	14622	0-1	2-1	1	7^1	3					8	9	10^1		2		6	4				11				5	
Mar 19	A	Cardiff	23000	3-1	4-1	1	7	3					8^1	9^2	10^1		2		6	4				11				5	
Mar 26	H	Bristol City	15697	2-0	2-0	1	7	3					8	9	10^1		2		6	4^1				11				5	
Apr 2	A	Scunthorpe	8675	0-0	0-1	1		3				10	8	11			2		6	4		9		7				5	
Apr 9	H	Rotherham	12981	0-0	2-0	1	2	3					8	10^1	9				6	4				11^1			7	5	
Apr 15	H	Sunderland	20299	0-1	0-2	1	2	7	3				8	9	10				6	4				11				5	
Apr 16	A	Sheffield Utd.	13642	0-0	0-0	1	2		6	3		10			9	7				4			8	11				5	
Apr 18	H	Sunderland	16151	1-1	1-2	1	2		6	3		8		10	9^1	7				4				11				5	
Apr 23	H	Hull City	12205	1-1	1-1	1	2		3	4		8		10^1	9	7				6				11				5	
Apr 30	A	Charlton	11825	0-2	1-6		5		3					10^1		2					7	8	9	11		4	6		1
League Appearances						39	17	13	16	42	29	11	24	38	40	28	2	9	16	24	1	12	5	2	33	38	1	7	13	1
League Goalscorers							1		1	1	5	17	16	6				4		1			5							
FA Cup Appearances						1			1	1			1	1	1				1	1					1	1			1	

Totals Division 2   P42 W10 D12 L20 F59 A77 Pts 32 Posn 20th

Own goals: Middlesbrough (Dec 19), Derby Co. (Feb 27)

Season 1960/61   Division 2

Date	V	Team	Attendance	FA HT	FA FT	Beattie R.	Wilson A.	Williams W.	Gunter P.	Snowdon B.	Dickinson J.	Fraser J.	Campbell J.	Saunders R.	Blackburn K.	Edmunds R.	Howells R.	Cutler R.	Chapman S.	Milkins J.	Rutter C.	Thomas R.	Carter B.	Priscott A.	Newman R.	Harris H.	White J.	Hodgkins J.	Gordon J.	Brown A.
Aug 20	H	Lincoln C.	18959	2-0	3-0	1				5	3		8¹	9²	11	4	7	6	2							10				
Aug 24	A	Luton	17514	0-0	0-1	1				5	3		8	9	11	4	7	6	2							10				
Aug 27	A	Southampton	28841	0-4	1-5	1				5	3	7	10	8		4	11	6	2						9¹					
Aug 31	H	Luton	15176	3-0	3-2	1			4	5	3		9²	10			11	6	2						7	8¹				
Sept 3	A	Huddersfield	15237	2-1	3-3	1			4	5	3		9¹	10¹			11	6	2						7	8¹				
Sept 7	H	Stoke	16497	0-0	1-0	1			4	5	3		9	10¹			11	6			2				7	8				
Sept 10	H	Sunderland	16387	1-0	2-1	1			4	5	3		9²	10			11	6			2				7	8				
Sept 12	A	Stoke	11686	0-1	0-1	1			4	5	3		9	10			11	6			2				7	8				
Sept 17	A	Plymouth	20243	0-2	1-5	1			4	5	3		9	10			11	6			2				7	8				
Sept 20	A	Sheffield Utd.	12602	1-2	1-3	1				5	3		8				11¹	6			2	4			7	10	9			
Sept 24	H	Norwich C.	17946	1-0	3-0	1				5	3		9¹				8¹	4			2	6	7¹	11		10				
Oct 1	A	Charlton	10692	1-3	4-7	1				5	3		9¹				8	4			2	6	7¹	11		10²				
Oct 8	H	Rotherham	7759	0-1	2-2	1				5	3		9				11	4			2	6	7	8²		10				
Oct 15	A	Liverpool	26302	3-1	3-3	1	4			5	3						11	10¹			2	6	7	8			9²			
Oct 29	A	Derby Co.	17595	1-4	2-6	1				5	3		9				11	4¹			2	6	7¹	8		10				
Nov 2	H	Coventry *FLC2*	5523	2-0	2-0	1				5	3		9¹		4		8			1	2	6	7¹	11		10				
Nov 5	H	Leyton Orient	11050	1-1	1-2					5	3		9		4		8¹			1	2	6	7	11		10				
Nov 12	A	Scunthorpe	8335	1-1	1-5				2	5	3		9		4		8¹			1		6	7	11		10				
Nov 19	H	Ipswich	11482	0-0	1-0	1				5	3		10		4		8¹				2			7	11	6				9
Nov 21	H	Manchester City *FLC3*	10386	1-0	2-0	1				5	3		10²		4		8				2			7	11	6				9
Nov 26	A	Brighton	14370	1-0	2-2	1				5	3		10¹		4		8				2			7¹	11	6				9
Dec 10	H	Leeds Utd.	9500	0-0	0-0	1				5	3		8		4		10				2			7	11	6				9
Dec 14	H	Chelsea *FLC4*	13054	0-0	1-0	1				5	3		8		4		10				2			7	11	6				9¹
Dec 17	A	Lincoln C.	6042	1-1	3-2	1				5	3		8¹		4		10				2			7	11¹	6				9¹
Dec 26	A	Swansea	10000	0-3	0-4	1				5			8		4		10				2	3		7	11	6				9
Dec 27	H	Swansea	18789	1-1	1-1	1				5	3		8		4		10				2			7	11	6¹				9
Dec 31	H	Southampton	31059	0-0	1-1	1				5	3				4	11	8¹				2			7	10	6				9
Jan 7	H	Peterboro *FAC3*	27533	0-1	1-2	1	11¹			5	3		10		4		8				2			7		6				9
Jan 14	H	Huddersfield	11243	0-2	1-3	1	6			5	3		8		4		11				2			7		10¹				9
Jan 21	A	Sunderland	31062	1-1	1-4	1		4		5			10	11			8¹				2			7		6				9
Jan 28	H	Middlesbrough	7272	0-1	0-3	1		4		5			10	11			8				2	3		7		6				9
Feb 4	H	Plymouth	9178	0-1	0-2	1	4			5	3		10	11							2	6	7		10	8	9			
Feb 11	A	Norwich C.	30160	1-1	1-3	1				5	3		7¹		4	11	8				2					6				9
Feb 13	A	Rotherham *FLC5*	11918	0-3	0-3	1				5	3		11	10	4		8				2			7		6				9
Feb 18	H	Charlton	12400	0-1	1-1	1	3		4	5	6		11		8						2	9		7		10¹				
Feb 25	A	Rotherham	6172	0-1	0-1	1	3		4	5	6		11		8						2	9		7		10				
Mar 4	H	Liverpool	14301	1-2	2-2	1	3		4	5	6		11	9	8						2	3		7¹		10				
Mar 11	A	Bristol R.	15006	0-0	0-2	1	3		4	5	6		11	9	8						2			7		10				
Mar 18	H	Leeds Utd.	16230	1-1	3-1	1	3			5	4		11¹	9¹							2			7¹		6			8	10
Mar 25	A	Leyton Orient	10181	1-0	1-2	1	3			5	4		11	9¹							2			7		6			8	10
Apr 1	H	Brighton	20993	2-0	4-0	1	3			5	6		7	9²	4	11					2								8¹	10¹
Apr 3	H	Sheffield Utd.	21987	0-1	1-2	1	3			5	6		7	9¹	4	11					2								8	10
Apr 8	A	Ipswich	18457	2-2	2-2	1	3			5	6		7	9	4¹	11¹					2								8	10
Apr 15	H	Scunthorpe	15123	1-0	2-2	1	3			5	6		7	9¹	4	11					2								8	10¹
Apr 19	H	Bristol R.	10793	3-0	3-0	1	3			5	6		7	9¹	4	11					2								8²	10
Apr 22	A	Middlesbrough	9339	0-2	0-3	1	3			5	6		7	9	4	11					2								8	10
Apr 29	H	Derby Co.	9966	2-1	3-2	1	3		2	5	6		7¹	9¹		11	10												8¹	4

						Beattie	Wilson	Williams	Gunter	Snowdon	Dickinson	Fraser	Campbell	Saunders	Blackburn	Edmunds	Howells	Cutler	Chapman	Milkins	Rutter	Thomas	Carter	Priscott	Newman	Harris	White	Hodgkins	Gordon	Brown
League Appearances						40	14	3	29	24	40	1	17	33	10	5	24	26	28	2	24	22	9	30	22	27	12	3	9	9
League Goalscorers													4	20	2		1	3	7						6	7	5	3	4	2
FA Cup Appearances						1	1		1		1		1		1		1				1			1		1				1
FA Cup Goalscorers							1																							
League Cup Appearances						3			4	4	1	3	1		4		4	1	3	1	1			4	3	4	3			
League Cup Goalscorers													3											1		1				

Totals Division 2   P42 W11 D11 L20 F64 A91 Pts 33 Posn 21st Relegated

Season 1961/62   Division 3

Date	Venue	Team	Attendance	FA HT	FA FT	Beattie R.	Rutter C.	Wilson A.	Smith R.	Dickinson J.	Priscott A.	Saunders R.	Middleton H.	Cutler R.	Shearing P.	Gunter P.	Brown A.	Snowdon B.	Harris H.	Campbell J.	Gordon J.	White J.	Blackburn K.	Chapman S.	Campbell R.	Barton A.	Dodson D.
Aug 19	A	Swindon	16153	2-0	3-1	1		3		6	7	9¹	10	11		2	4	5		8²							
Aug 23	H	Southend Utd.	18893	0-0	1-0	1		3		6	7	9	10¹	11		2	4	5		8							
Aug 26	H	Halifax	15322	1-0	1-1	1		3		6		9	10	11		2	4	5		8¹	7						
Aug 28	A	Southend Utd.	12827	0-1	2-2	1		3		6		9	10¹	11¹		2	4	5		8	7						
Sept 2	A	Q.P.R.	12856	0-0	1-0	1		3		6		9¹	10	11		2	4	5		8	7						
Sept 6	H	Lincoln C.	13271	0-0	0-0	1		3		6		9	10	11		2	4	5		8	7						
Sept 9	H	Barnsley	16014	3-0	3-2	1		3		6		9¹	10¹	11¹		2	4	5	7	8							
Sept 13	A	Barrow *FLC1*	3630	1-0	2-0	1		3		6		9¹		11		2	4	5	10	7				8¹			
Sept 16	H	Newport	14006	0-1	2-2	1		3		6		9¹		11		2	4	5	10	7¹				8			
Sept 20	A	Torquay	6119	1-0	2-0	1		3		6		9¹	10			2	4	5	11	7¹				8			
Sept 23	A	Crystal Palace	24586	0-1	2-1	1		3		6		9¹	10	7		2	4	5	11¹					8			
Sept 27	H	Torquay	14546	0-0	2-0	1		3		6		9¹	10¹	7		2	4	5	11					8			
Sept 30	H	Bournemouth	25672	0-0	1-1	1		3		6		9	10	7		2	4	5	11					8¹			
Oct 4	H	Derby Co. *FLC2*	11724	1-0	1-1	1		3		6		9				2	4	5	11	7				8¹	10		
Oct 7	A	Notts Co.	9889	1-2	1-2	1		3		6		9	10	7		2	4	5	11					8¹			
Oct 11	H	Hull City	14107	0-0	2-1	1	5	3		6		9¹	10	7		2	4		11					8			
Oct 14	H	Shrewsbury	16683	2-0	3-1	1	5	3	4			9¹		11		2		6	7	8				10²			
Oct 21	A	Brentford	9600	1-1	2-3	1	5	3	4			9¹			11¹	2		6	7	8				10			
Oct 28	H	Reading	18811	1-0	2-0	1		3		6		9		7	11	2	4	5		8¹				10			
Nov 1	A	Derby Co. *FLC2R*	13981	1-1	4-2	1	2	3		6		9		7⁴	11		4	5		8				10			
Nov 4	A	Crystal P. *FAC1*	30464	0-0	0-3	1		3		6		9²		7	11	2	4	5		8				10			
Nov 11	H	Bradford P.A.	11546	1-0	4-2	1		3		6		9		7	11	2	4	5	10¹	8¹							
Nov 13	A	Sheff. Utd. *FLC3*	6018	0-0	0-1	1		3		6		9		7	11	2	4	5	10	8							
Nov 18	A	Grimsby	6889	0-0	0-1	1	2	3		6				7	11		8	5	10						4		
Dec 2	A	Peterborough	14289	1-0	1-0	1	2	3		6	7			11			4	5		8¹	9	10					
Dec 9	H	Port Vale	11925	0-0	1-0	1	2	3		6	7			11			4	5		8	9¹	10					
Dec 16	H	Swindon	13990	1-0	2-2	1	2	3		6		9¹					4	5	10¹	8						7	11¹
Dec 23	A	Halifax	4122	0-0	1-0	1	2	3		6		9²					4	5		8		10				7	11
Dec 26	H	Northampton	17396	1-1	4-1	1	2	3		6		9					4	5		8¹		10				7¹	11
Jan 6	A	Hull City	6454	0-0	1-0	1	2	3		6		9					4	5			8		10			7¹	11
Jan 13	H	Q.P.R.	8229	3-1	4-1	1	2	3		6		9¹					4²	5			8		10¹			7	11¹
Jan 20	A	Barnsley	5992	2-0	2-2	1	5	3		6		9				2	4				8¹		10			7	11
Jan 27	H	Coventry	13405	2-1	3-2	1	2	3		6		9²					4	5			8¹		10			7	11²
Feb 5	A	Newport Co.	7000	2-0	5-0	1	2	3		6		9¹					4	5			8¹		10			7¹	11¹
Feb 10	H	Crystal Palace	22541	2-1	2-1	1	2	3		6		9					4	5			8		10			7¹	11
Feb 17	A	Bournemouth	22942	0-1	0-2	1	2	3	10	6		9					4	5			8					7	11
Feb 24	H	Notts Co.	14438	0-0	0-0	1	2	3	10	6		9					4	5			8					7	11
Mar 3	A	Shrewsbury	5745	0-0	1-0	1	2	3		6		9¹					4	5			8		10¹			7	11
Mar 6	A	Bristol C.	21802	3-0	4-0	1	2	3		6		9					4	5			8		10¹			7¹	11¹
Mar 10	H	Brentford	15256	3-0	4-0	1	2	3		6		9¹					4¹	5			8		10			7¹	11²
Mar 16	A	Reading	22969	2-0	3-0	1	2	3		6		9¹					4	5			8		10			7²	11
Mar 20	A	Northampton	13622	1-2	2-2	1	2	3		6		9					4	5			8		10¹			7	11
Mar 24	H	Bristol C.	20584	2-0	5-0	1	2	3		6		9¹					4	5			8		10¹			7¹	11²
Mar 31	A	Bradford P.A.	10154	1-1	1-2	1	2	3		6		9					4	5			8		10			7	11
Apr 7	H	Grimsby	19285	0-2	0-2	1	2	3	4	6		9						5			8		10			7	11
Apr 14	A	Coventry	9711	0-1	0-2	1	2	3		6		9					4	5			8		10			7	11
Apr 20	A	Watford	12657	0-0	0-0	1	2	3		6		9					4	5			8		10			7	11
Apr 21	H	Peterborough	21167	0-1	0-3	1	2	3		6		9¹					4	5	10	11	8					7	
Apr 23	H	Watford	18139	2-1	2-1		2	3		6		9²			1		4	5	10	11¹	8					7	
Apr 28	A	Port Vale	6071	0-1	3-2			3	10	6		9			1	2	4	5		11¹	8					7	
May 2	A	Lincoln C.	3316	1-1	2-2			3	10²	6					1	2		5		11	8				4	7	
League Appearances						43	36	39	4	46	4	42	17	20	3	20	44	42	14	9	44	6	20	4	2	25	21
League Goalscorers								2		26	5	3				3		3	4	12	1	5	2			9	10
FA Cup Appearances						1	1			1	1	1		1	1	1	1	1		1				1			
League Cup Appearances						4	2	3		4		3	3	3		3	4	4	3	2	3			3			
League Cup Goalscorers												5									1			1			

Totals Division 3   P46 W27 D11 L8 F87 A47 Pts 65 Posn 1st Champions Promoted

Own goals: Hull City (Oct 11), Bristol City (Mar 24)

Season 1962/63   Division 2

Date	Venue	Team	Attendance	FA HT	FA FT	Shearing P.	Rutter C.	Wilson A.	Brown A.	Snowdon B.	Dickinson J.	Barton A.	Gordon J.	Saunders R.	Smith R.	Dodson D.	Harris H.	McCann A.	Neil P.	Milkins J.	Noakes A.	Gunter P.	Campbell R.	Blackburn K.	Armstrong J.	Lill M.	Yeo B.	Ashworth J.	McClelland J.
Aug 18	H	Walsall	18469	2-1	4-1	1	2	3	4	5	6	7^1	8	9	10	11^3														
Aug 21	A	Grimsby	14588	1-0	1-1	1	2	3	4	5	6	7	8^1	9	10	11														
Aug 25	A	Newcastle	35280	1-0	1-1	1	2	3	4	5	6	7^1	8	9		11	10													
Aug 29	H	Grimsby	19087	2-1	2-1	1	2	3	4	5	6	7	8	9^2	10	11														
Sept 1	H	Derby Co.	21628	0-0	1-0	1	2	3	4	5	6	7	8	9^1				10	11											
Sept 7	A	Middlesbrough	15766	1-2	2-4	1	2	3	4^2	5	6	7	8	9		11		10												
Sept 12	A	Plymouth	22661	1-0	1-2	1	2	3	4	5	6	7^1	8	9		11		10												
Sept 15	H	Huddersfield	18410	1-1	1-1	1	2	3	4	5	6	7	8^1	9		11		10												
Sept 19	A	Plymouth	23544	0-2	0-2	1	2	3	4	5	6	7	8	9		11		10												
Sept 22	A	Cardiff	22560	0-1	2-1	1	2	3	4	5	6	7^1	8	9^1		11		10												
Sept 25	A	Brighton *FLC1*	5550	2-0	5-1					5		7		9^3	10^2	11	6			1	3	2	4	8					
Sept 29	H	Chelsea	22627	0-1	0-2	1		3		5	6	7	8	9		11		10				2							
Oct 6	A	Luton	8156	2-0	3-3	1		3	4^1	5	6	7	8	9^2		11		10				2							
Oct 13	H	Southampton	32407	1-0	1-1			3	4	5	6	7^1	8	9		11		10		1		2							
Oct 17	H	Coventry *FLC2*	8685	4-1	5-1			3		5	6	7	8^1	9^2		11^1	4	10^1		1		2							
Oct 19	A	Scunthorpe	8375	1-0	2-1			3		5	6	7	8^1	9		11	4	10^1		1		2							
Oct 27	H	Bury	16830	2-0	2-1			3		5	6	7^1	8	9		11^1	4	10		1		2							
Nov 3	A	Rotherham	8895	0-0	0-0			3		5	6	7	8	9		11	4	10		1		2							
Nov 10	H	Charlton	19026	0-2	3-3			3		5	6	7	8	9^2		11^1	4	10		1		2							
Nov 14	H	Sunderland *FLC3*	13500	0-0	0-0			3		5	6	7	8	9		11		10		1		2	4						
Nov 17	A	Stoke	21142	1-2	1-3			3		5	6	7	8		9	11		10^1		1		2	4						
Nov 21	A	Sunderland *FLC3R*	14484	1-1	1-2			3		5	6	7	8		9	11		10^1		1		2							
Nov 24	H	Sunderland	15000	0-0	3-1			3		5	6	7^1	8		9^1	11	4^1	10		1		2							
Dec 1	A	Leeds	15519	2-2	3-3			3		5	6	7	8	9^1		11^2		10		1		2	4						
Dec 8	H	Swansea	12410	0-0	0-0			3		5	6	7	8	9		11		10		1		2	4						
Dec 15	A	Walsall	8825	3-1	5-3			3		5	6	7^1	8^1	9		11^2		10		1		2	4						
Dec 22	H	Newcastle	18373	1-0	3-1			3		5	6	7	8^1	9		11^1		10^1		1		2	4						
Dec 26	A	Preston	8742	1-3	2-4			3		5	6	7	8	9^2		11		10		1		2	4						
Jan 26	H	Scunthorpe *FAC3*	12000	0-1	1-1	1		3		5	6	7	8^1	9		11	4	10				2							
Feb 23	H	Luton	12428	2-1	3-1			3		5	6	7	8^1	9^1		11	4	10^1				2			1				
Mar 2	A	Southampton	25463	1-3	2-4			3		5	6	7	8	9^1			4	10				2			1	11			
Mar 7	A	Scunthorpe *FAC3R*	9765	0-0	2-1			3		5	6	7	8	9^2		11	4	10		1		2							
Mar 9	H	Scunthorpe	8493	0-2	1-2			3		5	6	7	8	9			4	10				2			1	11^1			
Mar 13	H	Coventry *FAC4*	11482	1-0	1-1			3		5	6		8	9^1		11	4	10		1		2					7		
Mar 16	A	Coventry *§FAC4R*	25642	0-2	2-2	1				5	3		8	9^1		11	6	10^1				2	4				7		
Mar 19	†	Coventry *FAC4(2)R*	15867	1-2	1-2			3		5	6	7	8	9^1			4	10	11	1		2							
Mar 23	H	Rotherham	11493	1-2	1-2					5	6	7	8	9^1			4	10		1	3	2				11			
Mar 30	A	Charlton	10762	0-0	0-2			3		5	6	7	8	9			4	10		1		2				11			
Apr 2	A	Bury	7616	0-2	0-2				3		6	7		9				10			5	2	4	8	1	11			
Apr 6	H	Stoke	19526	0-1	0-3				5		6	8	7	9				10			3	2	4		1	11			
Apr 13	A	Sunderland	35356	0-1	0-1			3		5	6	7	8	9			4	10				2			1	11			
Apr 15	H	Norwich	13349	0-1	0-2			3		5	6	7	8	9			4	10				2			1	11			
Apr 16	A	Norwich	19131	2-5	3-5			3		5	6	7	8	9^2			4	11^1				2	10		1				
Apr 20	H	Leeds	7773	2-0	3-0			3		5		7^1	8^1	9			4	10^1				2	6		1	11			
Apr 27	A	Swansea	5000	0-0	0-0			3		5		7	8	9			6	10				2	4		1	11			
May 1	H	Preston	8599	1-0	1-2			3		5		7	8	9			6	10				2	4^1		1	11			
May 4	H	Cardiff	10538	0-0	2-0			3		5		7	8	9^1			6^1	10				2	4		1	11			
May 10	A	Derby Co.	10078	0-1	0-4					5		7	8	9			6	10			3	2	4		1	11			
May 13	A	Huddersfield	12854	3-0	3-1					5		11^2	8	9^1			6	10			3	2	4		1	7			
May 18	H	Middlesbrough	11605	0-0	1-1			3				11	8	9			6	10				2	4		1			5	7^1
May 21	A	Chelsea	54558	0-3	0-7			3	6	5		7	8	9				10				2	4		1	11			

						Shearing P.	Rutter C.	Wilson A.	Brown A.	Snowdon B.	Dickinson J.	Barton A.	Gordon J.	Saunders R.	Smith R.	Dodson D.	Harris H.	McCann A.	Neil P.	Milkins J.	Noakes A.	Gunter P.	Campbell R.	Blackburn K.	Armstrong J.	Lill M.	Yeo B.	Ashworth J.	McClelland J.
League Appearances						12	10	36	16	32	42	42	41	40	5	24	25	38	1	14	5	32	13	1	16	15		1	1
League Goalscorers								3				11	7	19	1	10	2	6					1			1			1
FA Cup Appearances						2		4		5	5	3	5	5		4	5	5		1	3	5	1				2		
FA Cup Goalscorers													1	5				1											
League Cup Appearances								3		4	3	4	3	3	2	4	3	3		4	1	4	2	1					
League Cup Goalscorers													1	5	2			1											

† At Tottenham
§ after extra time

Totals Division 2   P42 W13 D11 L18 F63 A79 Pts 37 Posn 16th

Own goals: Coventry (Oct 17), Sunderland (Nov 21), Southampton (Mar 2)

Season 1963/64   Division 2

Date	Venue	Team	Attendance	FA HT	FA FT	Armstrong J.	Gunter P.	Wilson A.	Harris H.	Snowdon B.	Dickinson J.	McClelland J.	Gordon J.	Saunders R.	McCann A.	Barton A.	Noakes A.	Summersby R.	Blackburn K.	Campbell R.	Lunniss R.	Lewis Brian	Lill M.	Radcliffe V.	Milkins J.	Shearing P.
Aug 24	A	Manchester City	21822	2-0	2-0	1	2	3	4	5	6	7	8	9^1	10	11										
Aug 28	A	Sunderland	40300	0-1	0-3	1	2	3	4	5	6	7	8	9	10	11										
Aug 31	H	Swindon T.	21975	0-1	1-4	1	2	3	4	5	6	7	8	9^1	10	11										
Sept 4	H	Sunderland	16518	1-3	2-4	1	2		6		5	7	10	9^1				3	8	11	4					
Sept 7	A	Cardiff	18000	1-0	2-1	1	2		6		5	7	10	9				3	8^1	11^1	4					
Sept 11	A	Leeds	24926	0-1	1-3	1	2		6		5	7	10	9				3	8	11	4					
Sept 14	H	Norwich	13996	1-1	1-1	1	2		6		5	7	10	9		11		3	8	4^1						
Sept 18	H	Leeds	12569	0-0	1-1	1	2				5	7	8	9^1	10					6	3	4	11			
Sept 21	A	Scunthorpe	6670	1-0	1-1	1	2				5	7	8	9^1	10					6	3	4	11			
Sept 25	H	Derby *FLC2*	8750	3-1	3-2	1	2					7	8^1	9	10^1					4^1	3	6	11	5		
Sept 28	H	Southampton	29459	2-0	2-0	1	2				5	7	8	9^1	10					4	3	6^1	11			
Oct 2	A	Newcastle	22100	0-0	0-1	1	2				5	7	8	9	10					4	3	6	11			
Oct 5	H	Rotherham	11452	1-1	2-1	1	2				5	7	8	9^1	10^1					4	3	6	11			
Oct 9	H	Swansea	11753	0-0	0-0	1	2				5	7	8	9	10					4	3	6	11			
Oct 12	A	Middlesbrough	17175	1-2	1-3	1	2				5	7	8	9^1	10					4	3	6	11			
Oct 19	H	Newcastle	14996	4-0	5-2	1	2				5	7^1	8	9^3	10^1					4	3	6	11			
Oct 26	A	Leyton Orient	12705	2-3	6-3	1	2				5	7	8	9^3	10^1					4	3	6	11^2			
Nov 2	H	Derby	15623	1-0	1-1	1	2				5	7	8	9^1	10					4	3	6	11			
Nov 4	A	Wrexham *FLC3*	8016	1-1	5-3		2		6		5	7	8^1	9	10^2					4	3		11^1		1	
Nov 9	A	Plymouth	12150	2-0	4-0	1	2				5	7	8	9^2	10					4	3^1	6	11			
Nov 13	A	Notts. Co. *FLC4*	6132	1-1	2-3	1	2		6		5	7^1	8	9	10					4	3		11^1		1	
Nov 16	A	Charlton	22250	2-1	4-1	1	2^1				5	7	8	9	10	11^1				4	3	6				
Nov 23	A	Grimsby	7732	1-0	3-0		2	3			5	7	8	9^1	10^2					4		6	11			1
Nov 30	H	Preston N.E.	18958	0-2	1-2		2	3	6		5	7	8^1	9	10					4			11			1
Dec 7	A	Huddersfield	8087	0-2	1-1	1	2				5	7	8	9^1	10			3		4		6	11			
Dec 14	H	Manchester City	13206	2-1	2-2	1	2				5	7^1	8^1	9	10			3		4		6	11			
Dec 21	A	Swindon T.	13530	0-0	0-2	1	2				5	7	8	9	10			3		4		6	11			
Dec 28	H	Bury	15715	2-1	3-3	1	2				5	7	8	9^1	10^1			3		4		6	11^1			
Jan 4	A	Stoke *FAC3*	28496	0-2	1-4	1	2				5	7	8	9^1	10					4	3	6	11			
Jan 11	H	Cardiff	12046	1-0	5-0	1	2				5	7^1	8	9^2	10^1					4	3	6	11^1			
Jan 18	A	Norwich	16282	1-1	1-3	1	2				5	7	8	9^1	10					4	3	6	11			
Feb 1	H	Scunthorpe	11944	3-1	3-4	1	2	3	6		5	7^1	10^1	9		11^1	8			4						
Feb 8	A	Southampton	26171	2-1	3-2	1	2	3			5	7		9^1	10^1	11	8			4		6				
Feb 15	A	Rotherham	6502	0-2	2-4		2	3			5	7^1		9^1	10	11	8			4		6			1	
Feb 22	H	Middlesbrough	12081	1-0	1-0		2	3			5	7		9	10	11^1	8			4		6			1	
Feb 29	A	Charlton	18463	0-0	1-0		2	3			5	7^1		9	10	11	8			4		6			1	
Mar 7	A	Leyton Orient	10710	0-2	4-3		2	3			5	7		9^3	10	11	8			4^1		6			1	
Mar 21	H	Plymouth	10374	0-2	1-2		2	3			5	7		9^1	10	11	8			4		6			1	
Mar 30	H	Northampton	13597	1-0	3-0		2	3	6		5	7^1	8^2	9	10	11				4					1	
Mar 31	A	Northampton	10245	0-1	1-2		2	3	6		5	7	8	9^1	10	11				4					1	
Apr 4	H	Grimsby	8207	1-0	2-2		2	3	6		5	7	8	9	10^1	11				4					1	
Apr 11	A	Preston N.E.	15933	0-0	0-0		2	3	6		5	7	8	9	10	11				4					1	
Apr 13	A	Bury	7726	0-1	2-3		2	3	6		5	7	8	9^1	10	11^1				4					1	
Apr 18	H	Huddersfield	10974	0-1	2-1		2	3	6		5	7	8	9^1	10	11^1				4					1	
Apr 21	A	Swansea	9905	1-0	1-1		2	3	6		5	7	8	9^1	10	11				4					1	
Apr 25	A	Derby	7837	0-1	1-3		2	3	6		5	7	8	9	10^{11}					4					1	

						Armstrong J.	Gunter P.	Wilson A.	Harris H.	Snowdon B.	Dickinson J.	McClelland J.	Gordon J.	Saunders R.	McCann A.	Barton A.	Noakes A.	Summersby R.	Blackburn K.	Campbell R.	Lunniss R.	Lewis Brian	Lill M.	Radcliffe V.	Milkins J.	Shearing P.
League Appearances						27	22	28	17	3	42	41	36	42	37	20	8	11	3	30	26	34	20		13	2
League Goalscorers							1					9	7	33	9	6			1	1	1	1	2	4		
FA Cup Appearances						1	1		1		1	1	1	1						1	1	1	1			
FA Cup Goalscorers														1												
League Cup Appearances						2	2		1			2	3	3	3					1	3	3	3	1	1	
League Cup Goalscorers													1	2	3					1			2			

Totals Division 2   P42 W16 D11 L15 F79 A70 Pts 43 Posn 9th

Own goals: Manchester City (Aug 24), Sunderland (Sept 4), Wrexham (Nov 4), Plymouth (Nov 9), Charlton (Nov 16)

Season 1964/65   Division 2

Date	Venue	Team	Attendance	FA HT	FA FT	Milkins J.	Wilson A.	Lunniss R.	Lewis Brian	Dickinson J.	Harris H.	McClelland J.	Portwood C.	Saunders R.	McCann A.	Barton A.	Gordon J.	Dodson D.	Hiron R.	Cordjohn B.	Tindall R.	Radcliffe V.	Armstrong J.	Summersby R.	Lill M.	Barlow L.	Edwards D.
Aug 22	A	Leyton Orient	10181	1-2	2-5	1	2	3	4	5	6	7	8^1	9^1	10		11										
Aug 26	H	Bury	11884	2-0	2-1	1	2	3	4^1	5	6	7^1	8	9	10		11										
Aug 29	H	Charlton	15388	2-2	2-3	1	2	3	4	5	6	7	8	9^2	10		11										
Sept 1	A	Bury	8110	1-1	1-1	1	2	3	4	5	6	7	8		10		11	9									
Sept 5	A	Manchester City	16527	0-1	0-2	1	2	3	4	5	6	7	8		10		11	9									
Sept 12	H	Southampton	25024	0-2	0-3	1	2	3	4	5	6	7			10	8	11	9									
Sept 15	A	Rotherham	14462	0-1	0-1	1	2	3	4	5	6	7	8		10		11	9									
Sept 19	H	Swindon T.	12501	5-0	5-0	1		3	4	5	6	7^2	8^2		10^1		11			2	9						
Sept 22	A	Watford §FLC2	5248	1-2	2-2	1		3	4		6^1	7	8		10	11^1	9			2	5						
Sept 26	A	Derby	13120	0-3	0-4	1		3	4	5	6	7	8		10		11			2	9						
Sept 30	A	Rotherham	11192	1-0	2-0	1		3^1	4	5	6	7	8^1		10		11			2	9						
Oct 3	H	Swansea	12699	1-0	1-0	1		3	4	5	6	7	8		10		11			2	9						
Oct 7	H	Northampton	12262	2-3	3-3	1		3	4	5	6	7	8		10		11^2			2	9						
Oct 10	A	Huddersfield	7511	0-1	1-1	1		3	4	5	6	7	8		10		11^1			2	9						
Oct 12	H	Watford FLC2R	8404	0-0	2-1	1		3	4	5	6	7	8^1		10		11^1			2	9						
Oct 17	H	Coventry	14621	0-2	0-2	1		3	4	5	6	7	8		10		11			2	9						
Oct 20	A	Northampton FLC3	7380	0-2	1-2	1		3	4	5	6	7	8		10		11^1			2	9						
Oct 24	A	Cardiff	7000	0-1	0-1			3		5	6		8			11	10			2	9	1	4		7		
Oct 31	H	Preston N.E.	10549	0-0	1-0	1		3	10^1	5	6		8			11			4	2	9				7		
Nov 7	A	Ipswich	12354	0-4	0-7	1		3	8	5	6				10	11			4	2	9				7		
Nov 14	H	Plymouth	9050	0-0	0-1	1		3	8	5	6				10	11			4	2	9				7		
Nov 21	A	Bolton	12986	0-3	2-3	1	2	3	8	5	6	7^1			10	4	11		9^1								
Nov 28	H	Middlesbrough	10653	1-1	2-1	1	2	3	8^1	5	6	7			10^1	4	11		9								
Dec 5	A	Newcastle	29120	0-2	0-3	1	2	3		5	6	7	8		10	11			4		9						
Dec 12	H	Leyton Orient	8708	1-0	1-1	1	2	3		5	6	7	8		10	11			4		9^1						
Dec 19	A	Charlton	9266	1-2	3-3	1		3		5	6	7^1	8^1		10	11			9	2	4^1						
Dec 26	A	Crystal Palace	18758	1-1	2-4	1		3		5	6	7	8		10^1	11			9^1	2	4						
Dec 28	H	Crystal Palace	15450	1-1	1-1	1		3		5	6	7^1	8		10	11			9	2	4						
Jan 2	H	Manchester City	12500	0-0	1-1	1	2	3		5	6	7	8^1		11	4			9		10						
Jan 9	H	Wolves FAC3	25189	0-0	0-0	1	2	3		5	6	7			11	4			9		10						
Jan 12	A	Wolves FAC3R	28629	0-2	2-3	1		3	8	5	6	7^1			10	11			9^1	2	4						
Jan 16	A	Southampton	23911	1-1	2-2	1		3	8^1	5	6	7				11			9^1	2	4						10
Jan 23	A	Swindon T.	14083	0-0	0-0	1	2	3	8	5	6	7				11			9		4						10
Feb 6	H	Derby	12457	1-1	3-1	1	2	3	8^1	5	6	7^1				11			9^1		4						10
Feb 13	A	Swansea	9037	0-0	0-0	1	2	3	8	5	6	7				11			9		4						10
Feb 20	H	Huddersfield	11435	2-0	3-0	1	2	3	8^1	5	6	7				11^1			9		4					12	10^1
Feb 27	A	Coventry	22181	2-1	2-1	1	2	3	8	5	6	7				11			9^2		4						10
Mar 6	H	Newcastle	19399	1-1	1-2	1	2	3	8^1	5	6	7				11			9		4						10
Mar 13	A	Preston N.E.	12028	1-5	1-6	1		3	8	5	6	7				11			9^1	2	4						10
Mar 20	A	Ipswich	7920	0-1	0-2	1	2	3	8	5	6	7				11			9	3	4						10
Mar 27	A	Plymouth	10405	0-1	1-2	1	2	3	8	5	6	7^1				11			9	3	4						10
Apr 3	H	Bolton	11214	2-0	3-0		2	3	8	5	6	7^2			10^1	11			9		4		1				9
Apr 9	A	Middlesbrough	10533	1-2	1-4		2	3	8	5	6	7			10^1	11			9		4		1				9
Apr 17	H	Cardiff	12975	1-0	1-0		2	3	4	5	6	7	8^1		10	11			9				1				9
Apr 19	H	Norwich	15701	2-0	4-0		2	3	8	5	6^2	7^1			10^1	11			9		4		1				9
Apr 20	A	Norwich	12224	1-2	1-3		2	3	8	5	6	7			10	11			9^1		4		1	5			9
Apr 24	A	Northampton	20660	0-0	1-1		2^1	3		5	6	7	8		10	11			9		4		1				9

						Milkins J.	Wilson A.	Lunniss R.	Lewis Brian	Dickinson J.	Harris H.	McClelland J.	Portwood C.	Saunders R.	McCann A.	Barton A.	Gordon J.	Dodson D.	Hiron R.	Cordjohn B.	Tindall R.	Radcliffe V.	Armstrong J.	Summersby R.	Lill M.	Barlow L.	Edwards D.
League Appearances						35	34	26	38	41	42	38	31	3	31	22	28	9	15	14	26	1	7	1	4		16
League Goalscorers							2		9		2	10	11	3	4	4	1		6		1						2
League Cup Appearances						3	1	2	3	2	3	3	3		3		3	1		3	2	1					
League Cup Goalscorers											1		1				3										
FA Cup Appearances						2	1	2	2	2	2	1	2		2	2			2		2						
FA Cup Goalscorers												1							1								

Totals Division 2   P42 W12 D10 L20 F56 A77 Pts 34 Posn 20th

Own goal: Bury (Sept 1)

§ after extra time

Season 1965/66   Division 2

Date	Venue	Team	Attendance	FA HT	FA FT	Armstrong J.	Wilson A.	Lunniss R.	Gordon J.	Radcliffe V.	Harris H.	Lewis Brian	Portwood C.	Edwards D.	McCann A.	McClelland J.	Hiron R.	Barton A.	Milkins J.	Campbell R.	Tindall R.	Haydock F.	Kellard R.	Gamblin D.
Aug 21	H	Plymouth	15828	1-0	4-1	1	2	3	4	5	6	7^1	8^2	9	10	11^1		12						
Aug 23	A	Preston N.E.	17952	0-1	1-4	1	2	3	4	5	6	7	8^1		10		9	11		12				
Aug 28	A	Southampton	26665	1-1	2-2	1	2	3	4	5*	6^1	7			10	8^1	11	9		12*				
Sept 1	H	Preston N.E.	17630	3-0	4-1		2	3	4		5	7^1	8	9	10^1	11^2		12	1	6				
Sept 4	A	Bolton	11975	0-1	0-2		2	3	4		5	7	8	9	10		12	11	1	6				
Sept 8	A	Crystal Palace	15744	0-3	1-4	1	2	3	6		5	7	8^1		10	11	9	12		4				
Sept 11	H	Ipswich	13759	1-0	1-0		2	3	12		5	4		10	8	7	9^1	11	1	6				
Sept 15	H	Crystal Palace	18026	1-0	1-1		2	12			5	4	8	10		7	9	11	1	6	3			
Sept 18	A	Birmingham	11793	3-1	3-1		2	8			5	4	12	9	10	7		11^1	1	6	3			
Sept 22	A	Oldham *FLC2*	8259	0-1	2-1	1		2	4		5	12	8	9	10^1	7		11		6	3^1			
Sept 25	H	Leyton Orient	10615	1-0	4-1	1	12*			6		5	2	8	10^2	4	7	9^2	11		3			
Oct 9	H	Derby	15999	1-1	1-1		2				6	5	4	11	8	7	9	12	1		3			
Oct 13	A	Cardiff *FLC3*	8603	0-1	0-2		2	12			6	5		10	8	7	9	11	1	4	3			
Oct 16	A	Cardiff	11942	1-0	2-1	1	3^1	2			6	5	8	12	11	7	9^1			4	10			
Oct 23	H	Carlisle	14406	1-0	4-1	1	2				4	5	8^1	12	10^1	11^1	7	9^1		6	3			
Oct 26	A	Middlesbrough	9582	1-1	2-5		2				4	5	8^2	10	9	11	7	12	1	6	3			
Oct 30	A	Coventry	25349	1-0	2-3	1	3				4	5	2	12	9	10	7^1	8	11^1	6				
Nov 6	H	Bristol City	15748	1-2	2-4	1	2				4	5	8	12	10^1	11^1	9	7		6	3			
Nov 13	A	Manchester City	22106	0-2	1-3	1	2				4	5	12	9	10^1	7	8	11		6	3			
Nov 20	H	Rotherham	8657	1-1	1-1						4	5	2	8	9	10	7	12	11	6	3			
Nov 27	A	Wolverhampton	17199	0-6	2-8		3	2			6	5*	7	12*	10	8		9^1	11	1	4			
Dec 4	H	Norwich	8540	0-2	0-3	1	2	3			4		7	8	12	10	11	9		6	5			
Dec 11	A	Bury	5747	0-1	0-1	1	2	3			4		10	8	7	9	11			6	5			
Dec 18	H	Cardiff	8434	1-0	3-1		2				4		6	8	9^2	10^1	7	12	11	1	3	5		
Dec 27	A	Charlton	14958	2-1	2-2		2				4		6	8^1	9	10^1	7	12	11	1	3	5		
Dec 28	H	Charlton	14746	3-1	3-1		2	12			4		6	8	9^1	10^1		11	7	1	3	5		
Jan 1	A	Derby	21557	1-3	1-3	1	2	3			4		6	8	9			7	11		12	10^1	5	
Jan 8	H	Manchester City	17352	2-2	2-2		2	3			4		6	8	9^1			7	11^1	1	12*	10*	5	
Jan 15	A	Carlisle	9636	1-1	1-2		2	3			4		6	8	9^1	10		7	11	1	12	5		
Jan 22	A	Grimsby *FAC3*	10204	0-0	0-0	1	2	3			4		6	8	9	10	7		11			5		
Jan 26	H	Grimsby *FAC3R*	23735	0-1	1-3	1	2	3			4		6	8^1	9	10	7		11			5		
Jan 29	A	Plymouth	13262	0-2	1-3	1	2	3		6	4		10	8^1	9	11	7	12				5		
Feb 5	H	Southampton	25860	1-2	2-5	1	2			6	7^1		8	9	10^1	11	12				3	5		
Feb 19	H	Bolton	11995	1-0	1-0		2			6	7		12	9	10	11	8^1		1		3	5		
Feb 26	A	Ipswich	9107	0-1	0-1		2			6	7		12	9	10	11	8		1		3	5		
Mar 12	H	Birmingham	12367	0-0	0-1		2			6	10		4	12*	9	8	7		1		3	5	11*	
Mar 19	A	Leyton Orient	6429	0-0	0-0		2			6	4		7	10	8		9		1	12	3	5	11	
Mar 25	H	Middlesbrough	10640	3-1	4-1		2			6	8		10	12*	7^2	9^1			1		3	5	11	
Apr 2	A	Bristol City	11689	0-1	0-1		2			6	8			10	7	9			1	12	3	5	11	
Apr 6	H	Huddersfield	13932	2-0	2-1		2			6^1	11		8	10	7	9^1			1	12	3	5		
Apr 9	H	Coventry	19216	1-0	2-0		2			6	8^1		10	11	7^1	9	12		1		3	5		
Apr 11	A	Huddersfield	13932	0-1	0-2	1	2			6	8			10	7	9	12				3	5	11	
Apr 16	A	Rotherham	8184	1-3	3-3		2			4^1	6		12*	8^1	10^1	7^*	9		1		3	5	11	
Apr 23	H	Wolverhampton	20282	1-0	2-0		2			4	6		8	12	10	7	9^1		1		3	5	11^1	
Apr 30	A	Norwich	9912	0-0	3-1		2			4^1	6		7	8^1	10^1		9	12	1		3	5	11	
May 7	H	Bury	13553	2-0	4-0		3			4	6^1		8^1	12	10^1	7^1	9		1			5	11	2

						Armstrong J.	Wilson A.	Lunniss R.	Gordon J.	Radcliffe V.	Harris H.	Lewis Brian	Portwood C.	Edwards D.	McCann A.	McClelland J.	Hiron R.	Barton A.	Milkins J.	Campbell R.	Tindall R.	Haydock F.	Kellard R.	Gamblin D.
League Appearances						16	38	17	40	3	24	41	28	32	38	33	31	18	26	15	30	22	9	1
League Goalscorers							1		2		1	10	8	10	12	10	10	3			1		1	
League Cup Appearances						1	1	1	2		2	1	2	2	2	1	2	1	2	2				
League Cup Goalscorers																1				1				
FA Cup Appearances						2	2	2	2		2		2	2	2	2	2		2					
FA Cup Goalscorers													1											
League Substitute							1					3		1			1			1				

Totals Division 2   P42 W16 D8 L18 F74 A78 Pts 40 Posn 12th

*Substituted

Own goals: Derby Co. (Oct 9), Rotherham (Nov 20), Wolverhampton (Nov 27), Charlton (Dec 28), Middlesbrough (Mar 25)

Season 1966/67   Division 2

Date	Venue	Team	Attendance	HT	FT	Milkins J.	Wilson A.	Tindall R.	Lewis Brian	Haydock F.	Harris H.	McClelland J.	Portwood C.	Hiron R.	McCann A.	Kellard R.	Barton A.	Pack R.	Gordon J.	Edwards D.	Armstrong J.	Radcliffe V.	Pointer R.	Jennings N.	Ley G.
Aug 20	A	Norwich	10306	0-0	0-0	1	2	3	4	5	6	7	8	9	10	11	12								
Aug 24	H	Birmingham	16934	0-2	4-5	1	3	10¹	5	6				9¹	8¹	11	7¹	2	4						
Aug 27	H	Coventry	16297	0-1	0-2	1	3	10	5	6	12*			9	8	11	7*	2	4						
Aug 30	A	Birmingham	23493	0-1	0-3	1	3	10	5	6	7	8				11		2	4	9					
Sept 3	A	Bury	4571	1-1	3-1	1	2	3	10	5	6¹	7	8¹	9	12	11			4¹						
Sept 7	H	Hull City	15710	0-0	0-1	1	2	3	10	5	6	7	8	9		11			4						
Sept 10	H	Preston	11022	1-0	2-0	1	3	4¹	5	6	7			9	10	11¹		2	12	8					
Sept 13	A	Swindon FLC2	7784	0-2	1-4		3	4	5	6	7			9	10	11¹		2		8	1				
Sept 17	A	Rotherham	9593	0-0	1-0	1	3	12		5	6	7	8¹	9		11		2	4	10					
Sept 24	H	Millwall	13534	0-1	0-1	1	3	12		5	6	7	8	9	4	11		2		10					
Sept 28	A	Hull City	35929	0-1	0-2	1	3			5	6	7	8	9		11		2	4	10					
Oct 1	A	Northampton	10364	3-1	4-2	1	3	9²	10*	5	6	7¹	12*	8¹		11		2	4						
Oct 8	A	Wolverhampton	19898	1-2	1-3		3	9	12	5	6	7	8		10¹	11		2	4			1			
Oct 15	H	Ipswich	12042	2-0	4-2	1	12	3	8	5	6	7¹		9	10	11²		2	4¹						
Oct 21	A	Bristol C.	16404	2-3	3-3	1	3	10*		5	6	7		9	8³	11		2	4	12*					
Oct 29	H	Carlisle	11674	0-0	2-1	1	12	3		5	6	7	8	9¹	10¹	11		2	4						
Nov 5	A	Blackburn	10097	2-1	2-2	1	2	3		5	6	7¹	12	9	8	11			4	10¹					
Nov 12	H	Bolton	12665	1-1	2-1	1	3	10		5	6	7		9¹	8¹	11		2	4	12					
Nov 19	A	Charlton	9916	1-0	2-0	1	3	4		5	6	7¹		9¹	8	11		2	12	10					
Nov 26	H	Derby Co.	13868	0-2	0-3	1	3	10		5	6	7		9	8	11		2	4	12					
Dec 3	A	Crystal Palace	15700	0-0	2-0	1	3	4		5	6	7		9¹	10¹	11		2	12	8					
Dec 10	H	Huddersfield	13174	0-1	1-1	1	3	10	5¹	6	7			9	8	11		2*	4	12*					
Dec 17	H	Norwich	12431	0-2	3-3	1	3	2	6	5	10		12	8²	7	11¹			4	9					
Dec 26	H	Plymouth	21116	0-1	2-1	1	3	10¹	5	6	7¹			9	8	11		2	4						
Dec 27	A	Plymouth	20302	0-0	0-0	1	3				6	7		9	8	11		2	4	10	5				
Dec 31	A	Coventry	24981	0-2	1-5	1	3	7			6			9¹	8	11		2	4	10	5				
Jan 7	H	Bury	11467	1-0	1-2		2	3	7		6			9	8¹	11	12		4	10	1	5			
Jan 14	A	Preston	14419	0-1	0-1	1	12	3	7	5	6			9	8	11		2	4	10					
Jan 21	H	Rotherham	15253	1-1	3-2	1	12*	3	6	5	10*			9²	7			2	4	8				11¹	
Jan 28	A	Hull City FAC3	29381	1-0	1-1	1	12	9		5			8	7¹	3			2	4	10	6			11	
Feb 1	H	Hull City §FAC3R	33107	0-0	2-2	1	12	3			6		8	7	10			2¹	4	9¹				11	
Feb 4	A	Millwall	17627	0-1	1-1	1	2	3		5	6		8	7¹					4	10		12	9	11	
Feb 6	†	Hull City FAC3(2)R	18448	1-0	3-1	1	12	3		5	6			9	7²	10		2	4	8¹				11	
Feb 11	H	Northampton	18979	2-0	3-2	1	12	3		5	6¹				7	10		2	4	8¹			9¹	11	
Feb 18	A	Tottenham FAC4	57910	0-0	1-3	1	3	4¹			6				7	10		2	12	8	5		9	11	
Feb 25	H	Wolverhampton	23144	2-0	2-3	1*	12*	3			6		7²	8		10		2	4		5		9	11	
Mar 4	A	Carlisle	11100	1-2	1-5		12	3	5		6				7	11		2	4	10	8	1	5	9¹	
Mar 18	H	Bristol C.	14649	1-1	1-1		3		5		6			8	7	10¹		2	4	12		1	9	11	
Mar 22	A	Cardiff	11855	0-0	0-0		3		5		6			8	7	10		2	4	12		1	9	11	
Mar 25	A	Ipswich	13701	2-1	2-4		12		5		6¹			8	7			2	4	8	1	3	9¹	11	
Mar 27	H	Cardiff	16363	1-1	1-2		3		5		6			8¹	7	10		2	4		12	1	9¹	11	
Apr 1	H	Blackburn	13788	0-0	1-1		3		5		6			8	7	10		2	4		12	1	9¹	11	
Apr 8	A	Bolton	11117	1-0	1-0		3		5		6			8	7	10		2	4¹	12		1	9	11	
Apr 15	H	Charlton	13892	0-0	1-2		3		5		6		12	7		10		2	4¹	8		1	9	11	
Apr 22	A	Derby Co.	11690	0-0	0-0		3		5		6			9	7	12	10	2	4			1	8	11	
Apr 29	H	Crystal Palace	13392	0-1	1-1		3		5	6				9	7	4		2	12	10		1	8	11	
May 6	A	Huddersfield	7149	0-0	1-1		6		5	12				9	7	10		2	4			1	8	11	3

						Milkins J.	Wilson A.	Tindall R.	Lewis Brian	Haydock F.	Harris H.	McClelland J.	Portwood C.	Hiron R.	McCann A.	Kellard R.	Barton A.	Pack R.	Gordon J.	Edwards D.	Armstrong J.	Radcliffe V.	Pointer R.	Jennings N.	Ley G.
League Appearances						29	20	38	21	29	41	17	23	39	24	40	2	35	36	20	13	6	14	14	1
League Substitute							2					1		1	1				2						
League Goalscorers							2	3	1	3	4	5		11	11	5	1		4	2			6	1	
FA Cup Appearances						4	1	4		3	3			3	3	4		4	3	4		2	1	4	
FA Cup Goalscorers								1							3				1	2					
League Cup Appearances							1	1	1	1	1			1	1	1		1			1	1			
League Cup Goalscorers														1											

Totals Division 2   P42 W13 D13 L16 F59 A70 Pts 39 Posn 14th

*Substituted
†At Coventry
§ after extra time

Season 1967/68   Division 2

Date	Venue	Team	Attendance	FA HT	FA FT	Milkins J.	Pack R.	Ley G.	Smith G.	Tindall R.	Harris H.	McClelland J.	Pointer R.	Edwards D.	Kellard R.	Jennings N.	Hiron R.	Portwood C.	McCann A.	Haydock F.	Travers M.	Potter R.	Trebilcock M.
Aug 19	H	Q.P.R.	23261	0-0	1-1	1	2	3	4	5	6	7	8¹	9	10	11	12						
Aug 26	A	Plymouth	16979	0-0	2-1	1	2	3	4	5	6		8		10	11	9¹		7¹		12		
Sept 2	H	Cardiff	17308	2-0	3-1	1	2	3	4¹	5	6		8¹		10	11¹	9		7		12		
Sept 6	H	Preston	21435	1-0	2-1	1	2	3	4	5	6		8²		10	11	9		7		12		
Sept 9	A	Huddersfield	11107	1-1	2-2	1	2	3	4	5	6		8		10	11	9¹	12	7¹				
Sept 13	H	Port Vale *FLC2*	16960	1-1	3-1	1	2	3	4	5	6	12	8		10	11¹	9		7²				
Sept 16	A	Norwich	12493	2-0	3-1	1	2	3	4	5	6		8		10	11³	9		7		12		
Sept 23	H	Rotherham	19734	0-0	1-1	1	2	3	4	5	6		8		10	11	9		7¹	12			
Sept 27	H	Charlton	21860	4-0	4-0	1		3	4	2	6		8¹		10	11²	9		7¹	5	12		
Sept 30	A	Derby Co.	27043	0-0	1-0	1		3	4¹	2	6		8		10	11	9		7	5	12		
Oct 3	A	Charlton	13559	1-1	1-4	1		3	4	2	6		8		10	11	9¹		7	12	5		
Oct 7	H	Carlisle	21864	0-0	2-1	1	2	3	4	5	6	7¹	8		10	11	9¹				12		
Oct 11	A	Darlington *FLC3*	6192	0-0	1-4		2	3	4	5	6		8		10	11	9¹		7		12	1	
Oct 14	A	Birmingham	26243	0-1	2-2		2	3¹	4	5	6	7	8		10	11¹	9		12			1	
Oct 21	H	Bristol City	21278	1-0	2-0	1	2	3	4	5	6		8		10	11¹	9		7		12		
Oct 28	A	Middlesbrough	18180	0-0	0-1	1	2	3	4	5	6		8		10	11	9		7		12		
Nov 4	H	Hull City	17602	1-0	3-0	1	2	3	4	5	6		8		10	11¹	9*		7²		12*		
Nov 11	A	Millwall	16057	1-2	2-3	1	2	3	4	5	6		9		10	7		12	8		11¹		
Nov 18	H	Bolton	21437	2-0	3-0	1	2	3	4	5	6¹		12		10	7	9		8¹		11¹		
Nov 25	A	Blackburn	13081	0-1	2-2	1	2	3¹	4	5	6		8		10	7	9		12		11		
Dec 2	H	Blackpool	35058	1-1	3-1	1	2	3	4	5	6		8¹		10	11*	9	7¹			12¹*		
Dec 9	A	Ipswich	14983	1-0	2-1	1		3	4	2	6		8¹		10		9	12	7¹	5	11		
Dec 16	A	Q.P.R.	20195	0-1	0-2	1	2	3	4	5	6		8		10		9		7	12	11		
Dec 23	H	Plymouth	24163	0-0	0-0	1	2	3	4	5	6		8		10		9		7*	12*	11		
Dec 26	A	Crystal Palace	23122	2-1	2-2	1	2	3	4	5	6		8		10		9		7¹	12	11¹		
Dec 30	H	Crystal Palace	28379	1-1	2-2	1	2	3	4	5	6	7	9		10				8¹	12	11¹		
Jan 6	A	Cardiff	14841	0-3	0-3	1	2	3	4	5	6	7	9		10				8	12	11		
Jan 13	H	Huddersfield	17647	1-0	3-1	1	2	3		5	6		8¹		4		9¹	7	11¹	12	10		
Jan 20	H	Norwich	24028	1-0	3-0	1	2	3	4	5	6		8¹		10¹	11	9		7¹		12		
Jan 27	H	Peterboro *FAC3*	16907	0-0	1-1	1	2	3	4	5	6		8		10	11	9¹		7		12		
Feb 3	A	Rotherham	11888	0-1	1-1	1	2	3	4	5	6		8		10		9		7¹		12		11
Feb 10	H	Derby Co.	26561	2-1	3-2	1	2	3	4	5	6		8¹		10¹		9		7		12		11¹
Feb 17	A	Fulham *FAC4*	39831	0-0	0-0	1	2		4	3	6		8		10		9		7	5	12		11
Feb 21	H	Fulham *FAC4R*	44050	1-0	1-0	1		3	4	2	6		8		10		9		7	5	12		11¹
Feb 23	A	Carlisle	11976	0-1	1-1	1		3	4	2	6		8		10	11	8¹		7	5	12		9
Mar 2	H	Birmingham	27836	0-0	1-2	1	2	3	4		6		8		10	11	12¹*		7	5			9*
Mar 9	H	W.B.A. *FAC5*	42642	0-2	1-2	1	2	3	4	5	6				10	11	9¹		7		12		8
Mar 16	A	Bristol C.	16085	0-1	0-3	1	2	3	4	5	6				10	11	9		7		12		8
Mar 23	H	Middlesbrough	18196	0-0	2-0	1	2	3¹	4	5	6				10	11	9¹		7		12		8
Mar 30	A	Hull City	11490	0-1	1-1	1	2	3	4	8	6				10	11	9		7¹	5	12		
Apr 6	H	Millwall	22938	0-0	0-0	1	2	3	4		6				10	11	9		7	5	12		8
Apr 13	A	Bolton	7673	1-1	2-1	1			2	4	6		3		10	11	9	7¹	8¹	5	12		
Apr 15	H	Aston Villa	26035	0-2	2-2	1			4	2¹	6¹		3		10	11			7	8	5		12
Apr 16	A	Aston Villa	16746	0-0	0-1	1	2	3	4	9	6	7			10				12	5	11		8
Apr 20	H	Blackburn	19943	1-0	2-1	1	2	3	4	5,	6				10	11¹	9	7			12		8
Apr 27	A	Blackpool	17042	0-0	0-2	1		2	3	4	6				10	11	9		7	12	7	5	8
May 4	H	Ipswich	25891	1-2	1-2	1		3	4	2	6		8			11	9		7¹	5	12		10
May 11	A	Preston	9938	0-1	1-3	1	2	3	4		6	12			10	11	9¹		7	5			8

						Milkins J.	Pack R.	Ley G.	Smith G.	Tindall R.	Harris H.	McClelland J.	Pointer R.	Edwards D.	Kellard R.	Jennings N.	Hiron R.	Portwood C.	McCann A.	Haydock F.	Travers M.	Potter R.	Trebilcock M.
League Appearances						41	33	42	41	41	40	5	29	1	42	32	36	12	28	14	11	1	13
League Substitute																		1		1	2		
League Goalscorers								4	2	1	1	1	10		2	10	9	4	14		4		1
FA Cup Appearances						4	3	3	4	4	4		3		4	2	4		4	2	4		3
FA Cup Goalscorers																			2				1
League Cup Appearances						1	2	2	2	2	2		2		2	2	2		2			1	
League Cup Goalscorers																	1	1	2				

Totals Division 2   P42 W18 D13 L11 F68 A55 Pts 49 Posn 5th

*Substituted
Own goals: Bristol City (Oct 21), Millwall (Nov 11), Blackburn (Nov 25), Blackburn (Apr 20)

Season 1968/69   Division 2

Date	Venue	Team	Attendance	FA HT	FA FT	Milkins J.	Youlden T.	Ley G.	Smith G.	Tindall R.	Harris H.	Trebilcock M.	Portwood C.	Pointer R.	Hiron R.	Jennings N.	Travers M.	McCann A.	Pack R.	Haydock F.	Brown W.	Hand E.	Bromley B.	Atkins W.	Potter R.
Aug 10	A	Huddersfield	10885	0-0	0-0	1	2	3	4	5	6	7	8	9	10	11	12								
Aug 13	A	Carlisle	11000	0-0	0-0	1	2	3	4	5	6	7		9	10	11	8	12							
Aug 17	H	Middlesbrough	24273	1-0	3-0	1	2	3	4	5	6	7²		9	10	11	8	12							
Aug 21	H	Blackburn	28989	0-0	0-1	1	2	3	4	5	6	8		9	12	11	10		7						
Aug 24	A	Birmingham	23915	2-3	2-5	1	2	3*	4	5	6	7¹		9¹	10	11	8	12*							
Aug 26	A	Preston	13826	0-0	0-0	1	3		4		6	12		7	9	8	11	10	2	5					
Aug 31	H	Cardiff	21871	0-2	1-3	1	2		4	12	6	8¹		9	10	11*		3	7	5					
Sept 3	A	Coventry FLC2	20840	0-0	0-2	1	3		4	5	6	7			10	11	12		2		9				
Sept 7	A	Charlton	18820	1-0	1-2	1	2		4	3	6	7			8	11	10	12		5	9¹				
Sept 13	H	Bury	18317	0-0	1-2	1	2		4	5	6	12		8	10	11		3	7¹		9				
Sept 21	A	Norwich	18898	1-0	1-0	1	2		4	3	6	9*		12*	8	11	10	7¹		5					
Sept 28	A	Crystal Palace	18998	2-3	3-3	1	3		4	5¹	6¹	12		8	9¹	11	10	7	2						
Oct 5	H	Oxford	888	1-0	3-0	1	3		4*	5	6	12²*		8¹	9	11	10	7	2						
Oct 9	H	Preston	20393	0-1	1-1	1	3	12	4	5	6	7¹		8	9	11	10	4	2						
Oct 12	A	Blackpool	16407	0-0	1-1	1	10	3	5		6	9		7	12	11	8¹	2	4						
Oct 19	A	Derby	22041	0-1	0-1	1	2	3	5		6	7		8	9	11	12	4							
Oct 26	A	Bristol City	16071	1-0	2-2	1	2	3	4	5	6	10		7¹	12*	11	8¹		9*						
Nov 2	H	Sheffield Utd.	18497	2-0	2-1	1		3	4	5	6	7		8¹	9¹	11	10	2		12					
Nov 9	A	Fulham	14601	0-0	2-2	1		3	4		6¹	7*		8¹	9	11	10	12*	2		5				
Nov 16	A	Aston Villa	18154	1-0	2-0	1		3	4		6	7		8	11²		12	2			9	5	10		
Nov 23	A	Hull City	14257	1-0	2-2	1	12	2	4	6¹	3			8	9¹	11		7				5	10		
Nov 30	H	Millwall	21868	1-0	3-0	1		3	4		5	7		10	9²	11¹	12	8				2	6		
Dec 7	A	Bolton	7628	0-0	0-1	1	2	3	4		6			8	9*	11	12*	7				5	10		
Dec 14	H	Blackpool	16961	0-0	1-0	1		3	4		6	12*		8¹		11		7	2		9*	5	10		
Dec 21	A	Derby	22061	1-0	1-2	1		3	4¹		6	8		9		11	12	7	2			5	10		
Dec 28	H	Bristol City	529	1-0	1-1	1	6	3	4			8			11	12	7	2			9¹	5	10		
Jan 4	H	Chesterfield FAC3	22503	0-0	3-0	1		3	4	12	6			9		11²		7¹	2			5	10		
Jan 11	A	Sheffield Utd.	14138	0-1	0-2	1		3	4		6	12		8	9	11		7	2			5	10		
Jan 18	H	Fulham	20520	2-1	3-1	1	12	3			6	8¹		7¹		11¹	4	2			9	5	10		
Jan 25	A	Blackburn FAC4	17551	0-3	0-4			3		4	6	9		10	12*	11*	7	2			5	8			1
Feb 1	A	Aston Villa	31593	0-0	0-2	1				5	6	7		12	11	3	9	4				5	4		
Feb 8	H	Hull City	13960	0-0	1-0	1		3		12	6			7	9¹	11	10	8	2			5	4		
Feb 15	A	Millwall	13446	0-0	0-0	1		3			2	6		8	9	11	10	7	12			5	4		
Feb 22	H	Bolton	16500	1-1	2-2	1		3		12*	6	8		7	9²	11*	10	4	2			5			
Mar 1	H	Huddersfield	16427	1-0	1-2	1		3		12*	6	8		7	9	11*	10	4	2			5	10		
Mar 5	A	Oxford	10827	1-2	1-3	1	12*	3			6*			8	9¹	11	10	7	2			5	4		
Mar 8	A	Middlesbrough	23982	0-0	0-1	1	6	3				8		7	9	11	12	4	2			5	10		
Mar 15	A	Birmingham	15556	1-0	6-3	1	6	3				8		4	9	11		7	2			5	10		
Mar 21	A	Cardiff	21814	2-0	2-2	1	6	3			4	11		8	9	12		7²	2			5	10		
Mar 29	H	Charlton	15642	1-0	4-1	1	6	3			12	10¹		8	9	11¹		7²	2			5	4		
Apr 5	A	Crystal Palace	24263	0-0	1-3	1	6*	3			12*	8		10	9	11¹		7	2			5	4		
Apr 7	A	Blackburn	6432	0-2	1-3	1		3		12	6			8	9	11	2	7			4	5	10		
Apr 9	H	Carlisle	18130	2-1	2-1	1		3			6			4	9²	12	11	2	7			5	10	8	
Apr 12	H	Norwich	16259	2-0	5-2	1		3			6			8	9⁴	11¹	2	7				5	4	10	
Apr 18	A	Bury	3063	2-1	2-3	1		3		5	12			4	9¹	11	2	7				6	10¹	8	

						Milkins J.	Youlden T.	Ley G.	Smith G.	Tindall R.	Harris H.	Trebilcock M.	Portwood C.	Pointer R.	Hiron R.	Jennings N.	Travers M.	McCann A.	Pack R.	Haydock F.	Brown W.	Hand E.	Bromley B.	Atkins W.	Potter R.
League Appearances						42	23	33	23	21	34	28	1	40	33	36	28	33	24	6	7	25	23	3	
League Substitute							1			2	1	2		1			1	1	1						
League Goalscorers								1	2	2	9			7	17	6	1	8			2				
FA Cup Appearances						1		2	1	2	2	2		1	1	2	2	2			2	2		1	
FA Cup Substitute															1										
FA Cup Goalscorers															2	1									
League Cup Appearances						1	1		1	1	1			1	1	1	1		1		1				

Totals Division 2   P42 W12 D14 L16 F58 A58 Pts 38 Posn 15th

*Substituted
Own goals: Middlesbrough (Aug 17), Blackburn (Apr 7)

Season 1969/70   Division 2

Date	Venue	Team	Attendance	HT	FT	Milkins J.	Travers M.	Ley G.	Youlden T.	Hand E.	Harris H.	McCann A.	Pointer R.	Hiron R.	Munks D.	Jennings N.	Turner B.	Atkins W.	Bromley B.	Trebilcock M.	Tindall R.	Potter R.	Widdowson R.	Davidson R.	Storrie J.
Aug 9	A	Blackpool	15844	0-1	1-2	1	2	3	4	5	6*	7	8	9¹	10	11	12*								
Aug 13	A	Brighton *FLC1*	19787	0-0	0-1	1	12	3	2	5	6	7	8	11	4		9	10							
Aug 16	H	Sheffield Utd.	19107	0-3	1-5	1	2		3	5	6	12*	7	9	4			8*	10	11¹					
Aug 19	H	Birmingham	24976	1-0	1-1	1	2	3	6	5		7	8	9	10	11¹	4			12					
Aug 23	A	Oxford	10853	0-0	2-0	1	2	3	6	5		7	8	9¹*	10	11¹	4			12*					
Aug 27	A	Norwich	18383	0-0	0-0	1		3	2	5	6	4	7	9		11		8	10	12					
Aug 30	H	Blackburn	18348	1-0	2-0	1		3	2	5	6	7	4	9	10	11		8¹	12						
Sept 6	A	Leicester	25467	1-2	1-2	1		3	2	5	6	12	7	9	4	11		8¹	10						
Sept 13	H	Q.P.R.	21969	0-1	1-3	1	2	3	6	5	12	7	10	9¹	4	11		8							
Sept 17	H	Hull City	14786	0-3	1-4	1	12*	3	2*	5	6	7¹	8	9	4	11			10						
Sept 20	H	Bolton	10280	0-0	1-0	1	2	3		5	6	7	4	9	12	11¹	8		10						
Sept 27	H	Aston Villa	17884	0-0	0-0	1	2	3		5	6	7	4	9	8	11			10	12					
Oct 4	A	Charlton	12723	2-2	2-2	1	2	3		5¹	6	12	7	9¹	4	11		8	10						
Oct 7	A	Sheffield Utd	16136	0-1	0-5	1	2	3		5	6	12	7	9	4	11		8	10						
Oct 11	H	Bristol City	14890	0-0	0-0	1	2	3		5	6	8	4	9	12	11			10	7					
Oct 18	A	Watford	15657	0-1	0-4	1*		3		5	6	7	4	12*		11		9	10	8	2				
Oct 25	H	Swindon	18623	1-0	3-1		2	3¹		5	6	7	8¹	9¹	4*	11			10	12*		1			
Nov 1	A	Carlisle	9804	2-1	3-3		2	3		5	6	7¹	8	9	4	11¹			10	12		1			
Nov 8	H	Cardiff	17302	1-0	3-0		2	3		5	6	7	8¹	9²	4	11			10	12			1		
Nov 12	H	Birmingham	16508	1-0	1-1		2	3		5	6	7	8	9	4¹	11			10	12			1		
Nov 15	A	Huddersfield	12564	0-2	0-4		2	3		5	6	7	8	9	4	11			10	12			1		
Nov 22	H	Middlesbrough	15621	1-1	2-3		2	3	6			7¹	8	9	4	11¹			10	12	5		1		
Dec 6	H	Preston	11121	1-0	4-0	1		3		5	6	7	8	9²	2	11¹	12		10¹		4				
Dec 8	A	Millwall	10564	0-2	1-3	1		3		5	6	7	8	9	2	11¹			10		4			12	
Dec 13	A	Q.P.R.	11831	0-0	0-2	1	2	3		5	6	7	8	9	4	11			10	12					
Dec 20	H	Leicester	12447	0-1	2-3	1	12	3		5	6	7	10	9	2		4		11²						8
Dec 27	A	Blackburn	13411	2-0	3-0	1		3		5	6	8	4	12*	2	11			10	7²*					9¹
Jan 3	H	Tranmere *FAC3*	18366	1-1	1-2	1	2	3		5	6*		8	12*	4	11¹			10	7					9
Jan 10	H	Bolton	10464	0-1	1-1	1		3		2		7	4	10	6	11¹		8		12	5				9
Jan 17	A	Aston Villa	21148	2-2	5-3	1	2	3		5		7²	4¹	9¹	6*	11			10	12*					8¹
Jan 24	H	Oxford	14116	2-1	2-1	1	12	3	2	5		7	10	9	4	11				6¹					8¹
Jan 31	H	Charlton	14201	2-1	5-1	1	12	3	2	5		7¹	4	9³	6	11			10						8¹
Feb 7	A	Bristol City	13931	0-1	0-3	1		3	12*	2	5*	7	4	9	6	11			10						8
Feb 14	A	Blackpool	13949	0-2	2-3	1	12	3	5	2		7¹	4	9	6	11¹			10						8
Feb 28	H	Carlisle	10952	1-0	4-0	1	12*	3	5	2		7¹		9¹	6	11¹			10*					4	8¹
Mar 3	A	Swindon	19947	1-1	1-3	1	12	3	5	2	6	7		9¹		11			10					4	8
Mar 7	A	Middlesbrough	22498	1-1	1-2	1	12*	3*	5	2	6	7		9		11			10					4	8¹
Mar 14	H	Millwall	12007	0-0	0-1	1		3	5	2	6	7	10	9	4	11				12					8
Mar 21	A	Preston	12461	1-0	2-1	1	12	3	5	2	6	7	8		4	11			10						9²
Mar 25	A	Cardiff	17005	0-1	0-2	1	12	3	5	2	6	7	8	9	4				10						11
Mar 28	H	Huddersfield	17326	1-2	1-3	1		3	5	2	6	7	4	9	12	11			10						8
Apr 1	H	Watford	10900	2-0	3-1	1		3	5	2	6	7¹	8	9	4	12			10						11²
Apr 4	H	Norwich	10750	1-1	1-4	1		3	5	2	6	7¹	4	9	12	11			10						8
Apr 15	A	Hull City	11468	2-1	3-3	1		3	5	2	6	10	8	9³	4	11				12					7
League Appearances						36	24	35	20	42	34	38	39	41	34	36	3	8	32	11	3	2	4	3	18
League Substitute							3	1			1		1		1		1				3				
League Goalscorers								1		1		11	3	18	1	10		2	1	6					10
FA Cup Appearances						1	1	1		1	1	1		1	1	1			1	1					1
FA Cup Substitute														1											
FA Cup Goalscorers																1									
League Cup Appearances						1		1	1	1	1	1	1	1	1		1	1							

Totals Division 2   P42 W13 D9 L20 F66 A80 Pts 35 Posn 17th

*Substituted
Own goals: Blackburn (Aug 30), Carlisle (Nov 1)

Season 1970/71   Division 2

Date	Venue	Team	Attendance	FA HT	FA FT	Milkins J.	Hand E.	Ley G.	Piper N.	Blant C.	Munks D.	McCann A.	Storrie J.	Hiron R.	Bromley B.	Jennings N.	Travers M.	Trebilcock M.	Pointer R.	Youlden T.	Smith F.	Standen J.	Harris H.
Aug 15	A	Norwich	15100	0-0	1-1	1		3	4^1	5	6	7	8	9	10	11	12				2		
Aug 19	H	Plymouth *FLC1*	12826	0-0	2-0	1		3	4	5	6	7^1	8^1	9	10	11				12*	2		
Aug 22	H	Bolton	15703	1-0	4-0	1		3	4	5	6	7^1	8	9^2	10	11^1				12	2		
Aug 29	A	Millwall	8809	0-0	0-0	1		3	4	5	6	7	8	9	10	11				12	2		
Sept 2	H	Orient	15218	0-1	1-1	1		3	4	5	6*	7	8	9^1	10	11			12*		2		
Sept 5	H	Sheffield Wed.	18712	2-0	2-0	1		3	4	5	6	7	8	9^1	10	11^1				12	2		
Sept 9	H	Walsall *FLC2*	15967	1-0	1-0	1		3	4^1	5	6	7	8	9	10	11			12		2		
Sept 12	A	Swindon	14682	0-2	1-2	1		3	4	5	6	7	8^1	9		11			10	12	2		
Sept 19	H	Birmingham	18037	1-0	1-0	1	12	3	4	5	6	7	8	9^1	10	11					2		
Sept 26	A	Leicester	25613	0-1	0-2	1		3	4	5	6*	7	8	9	10	11	12*				2		
Sept 30	H	Sheffield Utd.	16587	0-0	1-5	1		3	4	5	6^1	7	8	9	10	11	12				2		
Oct 3	H	Watford	15712	0-0	5-0	1		3	10^1	5	6	4	7	9		11^1		8^3		12	2		
Oct 7	A	Man. Utd. *FLC3*	32080	0-0	0-1	1		3	10	5	6	4	7	9		11		8	12		2		
Oct 10	A	Middlesbrough	18775	2-1	2-3	1	2	3	10	5	6	4^1	7	9		11^1		12					
Oct 17	H	Norwich	15064	0-2	0-2	1	2	3*	4	5	6	7	8	9	10	11	12*						
Oct 24	A	Q.P.R.	14709	0-0	0-2	1	2	3	4	5	6	7		9	10	11		8	12				
Oct 28	A	Cardiff	18529	0-0	0-1	1	2	3	4	5	6	7	8	9	10	11				12			
Oct 31	H	Blackburn	9936	3-0	4-1	1	2	3	4	5	6	12	8		10	11		9^3	7^1				
Nov 7	A	Charlton	8420	2-0	2-2	1	2	3	4	5	6		8	9	10^1	11^1		7	12				
Nov 14	H	Sunderland	10474	0-1	2-1	1	2	3	4	5	6			9^1	10	11	12	8^1					
Nov 21	A	Luton	16876	1-1	1-2	1	2	3*	4	5	6	7^1		9	10	11	12*	8					
Nov 28	H	Hull City	13360	0-0	2-2	1	2	3	4	5	6	7		9	10	11^2		8	12				
Dec 5	A	Carlisle	7540	0-4	0-6	1	2	3	4*	5	6	7		9	10	11		12*	8				
Dec 12	H	Oxford	11456	1-0	1-0	1	2	3	4	5	6	7		9^1	10	11		8		12			
Dec 19	A	Bolton	5528	1-1	1-1	1	12	3	4	5	6			9	10	11		8	7^1		2		
Jan 2	H	Sheff. Utd. *FAC3*	20556	0-0	2-0	1	4	3	7	5	6			9^1	10	11		8^1	12		3		2
Jan 9	A	Sheffield Utd.	18665	0-1	0-2	1	4	3	7	5	6			9	10	11		8	12		3		2
Jan 16	H	Cardiff	24747	0-2	1-3	1		3	4	5	6	7		9	10	11*		8	12^1*		2		
Jan 23	H	Arsenal *FAC4*	39659	0-1	1-1	1	4	3	7	5	6			9	10	11*		8^1	12*		2		
Jan 30	A	Hull City	19958	0-0	1-0	1	4	3	7	5	6			9^1	10	11	12	8			2		
Feb 1	A	Arsenal *FAC4R*	47865	1-2	2-3	1	4	3^1	7^1	5	6			9	10	11		8	12		2		
Feb 6	H	Carlisle	13219	1-1	1-4	1	4	3	7	5	6			9^1	10	11		8	12*		2*		
Feb 20	H	Luton	13661	0-1	0-1	1	4	3	7	5	6			9	10	11		8*	12*		2		
Feb 27	A	Blackburn	7259	0-1	1-1	1	4	3	7	5	6		9		10	11		8^1	12	5	2		
Mar 6	H	Q.P.R.	10402	0-0	2-0	1	4	3*	7	5^1	6			9^1	10	11		8	12*		2		
Mar 10	H	Bristol City	8676	0-1	1-1	1	4^1		7	5	6			9	10	11	12*	8		3*	2		
Mar 13	A	Sunderland	10827	0-0	0-0	1	4		7	5	6			9	10	11		8	12*	3*	2		
Mar 20	A	Charlton	10294	0-0	2-0	1	4^1		7	5	6			9*	10	11^1		8	12*	3	2		
Mar 24	A	Oxford	7517	1-1	1-1	1	4		7	5	6			9	10	11		8^1	12*	3	2		
Mar 30	A	Sheffield Wed.	14134	0-0	1-3	1*	4		7^1	5	6			9	10	11		8	12*	3	2		
Apr 3	H	Millwall	9668	0-0	0-2		2		4	5	6			9	10	11	12	8	7	3		1	
Apr 9	A	Watford	12826	0-0	0-0		4		7	5	6			9	10	11	12	8		3	2	1	
Apr 10	A	Bristol City	14663	0-1	0-2		4		7	5	6	8		9	10	11			12	3	2	1	
Apr 12	H	Swindon	10987	0-1	0-2		4		7	5	6	12		9	10	11		8		3	2	1	
Apr 17	H	Middlesbrough	8916	1-0	1-1				5	10	6	12		9		7	11	8^1	4	3	2	1	
Apr 24	A	Birmingham	19440	0-1	1-1				5*	10	6			9^1		7	11	8	4	3	2	1	12*
Apr 26	A	Orient	3941	1-0	1-1			3	10		6			9^1		7	11	8	4	5	2	1	12
May 1	H	Leicester	18795	0-2	1-2				5*	7	6			9^1		11	12*	8	4	3	2	1	10

						Milkins J.	Hand E.	Ley G.	Piper N.	Blant C.	Munks D.	McCann A.	Storrie J.	Hiron R.	Bromley B.	Jennings N.	Travers M.	Trebilcock M.	Pointer R.	Youlden T.	Smith F.	Standen J.	Harris H.
League Appearances						34	29	28	42	37	42	18	21	39	33	40	11	19	20	17	23	8	1
League Substitute																	1	4	5	4			1
League Goalscorers							2		3	1	1	3	1	13	1	8			8	4	1		
FA Cup Appearances						3	3	2	3	3	3			3	3	2		3	1	1	3		
FA Cup Substitute																				1			
FA Cup Goalscorers							1	1						1				2					
League Cup Appearances						3		3	3	3	3	3	3	3	2	3		1			3		
League Cup Goalscorers							1					1	1										

Totals Division 2   P42 W10 D14 L18 F46 A61 Pts 34 Posn 16th

*Substituted

Season 1971/72   Division 2

Date	Venue	Team	Attendance	FA HT	FA FT	Milkins J.	Smith F.	Ley G.	Hand E.	Youlden T.	Blant C.	Piper N.	Trebilcock M.	Hiron R.	Reynolds R.	Jennings N.	Collins J.	McCann A.	Storrie J.	Travers M.	Standen J.	Munks D.	Bromley B.	Pointer R.	Wilson W.	Lewis Brian
Aug 14	H	Middlesbrough	15649	1-1	2-1	1	2	3	5	6	12	7		9	8		10	4¹	11¹							
Aug 17	A	Bournemouth *FLC1*	15382	0-0	1-2	1	2	3	5	6		7	12*	9	8		10*	4¹	11							
Aug 21	A	Norwich	13787	1-3	1-3	1	2	3	5	6		7		9	8¹		10*	4	11	12*						
Aug 28	H	Birmingham	14729	1-0	1-0		2	3	4	6	5	7	11¹	9	8		10					1	12			
Sept 1	H	Blackpool	16058	1-2	1-3		2	3	4¹	6	5	7	11	9	8		10					1	12			
Sept 4	A	Sheffield Wed.	13170	1-1	1-1		2	3	4*	6	5	7	11	9¹	8		10					1	12*			
Sept 11	A	Orient	10966	1-1	3-2		2	3	4¹*	6	5	10	11¹	9¹	8		7					1	12*			
Sept 18	A	Hull City	14363	0-0	3-1		2	3	4¹	6	5	7¹	11	9	8		12	10¹								
Sept 25	H	Millwall	15485	1-1	1-1	1	2	3	4	6	5	7	11	9¹	8		10				12					
Oct 2	A	Watford	11633	0-0	0-1	1	2	3	4	6	5	7	11	9	8		10				12					
Oct 9	H	Preston	12749	1-1	1-1	1	2	3	4	6*	5	7	11¹	9	8		10				12*					
Oct 16	A	Middlesbrough	16376	1-2	1-2	1	2	3	4		5	7	11*	9	8¹	12*	10						6			
Oct 20	H	Bristol City	12575	0-0	1-1	1	2	3¹	4	5		7	11	9	8	12	10						6			
Oct 23	H	Fulham	14172	2-0	6-3	1	2¹	3	4¹	5		7	9¹		8¹	11²	10						6	12		
Oct 30	A	Q.P.R.	15934	0-0	1-1	1	2	3	4	5		7¹	9	12	8	11	10						6			
Nov 6	H	Sunderland	14387	2-1	2-2	1	2	3	4	5		7¹	9¹	12	8	11	10						6			
Nov 13	A	Carlisle	7955	0-0	0-1	1	2	3	4	5		7	9	12*	8	11*	10						6			
Nov 20	H	Oxford	10423	0-0	2-0	1	2	3	4	5		7*	9¹	12*	8	11¹	10						6			
Nov 27	A	Luton	9910	2-0	2-3	1	2	3	4	5		7	9	12	8²	11	10					1	6			
Dec 1	A	Cardiff	10268	0-2	2-3	1	2	3	4	5		7	9¹	11¹	8*	12*	10						6			
Dec 4	H	Charlton	10007	0-0	0-0	1	2		5		6	7	9	11*	8	12*	3	10					4			
Dec 11	A	Burnley	11338	1-1	3-1	1	2		5		6	7	9	11	8¹		3	10¹				12	4			
Dec 18	H	Sheffield Wed.	10280	0-0	1-2	1	2	12	5		6	7	9¹	11	8		3	10					4			
Dec 27	A	Swindon	20494	0-1	1-3	1	2	3	5	12	6	4¹	9	11	8	7	10								
Jan 1	H	Hull City	8665	0-0	0-0	1	2	10	5	12	6	4		9	8	7	3	11							
Jan 8	A	Birmingham	22410	2-3	3-6	1	2	10¹	5		6	4	8	9¹		7	3	11¹					12		
Jan 15	A	Boston *FAC3*	11000	0-0	1-0	1	2	10	5		6	4	12	9	8	7¹	3	11							
Jan 22	H	Cardiff	11039	2-0	2-0	1	2	10¹	5		6	7	9¹		8	11	3	12					4			
Jan 29	A	Bristol City	10949	1-1	1-1	1	2	10	5		6	7	9		8	11¹	3	12					4			
Feb 5	H	Swansea *FAC4*	19782	0-0	2-0	1	2	10	5		6	7	9	12	8	11¹	3	4							
Feb 12	A	Fulham	8390	0-1	1-1	1	2	10	5		6	7	9*		8¹	11	3	12*					4			
Feb 19	H	Q.P.R.	15563	0-0	1-0	1	2	10	5		6	7		9	8¹	11*	3		12*				4		
Feb 26	A	Birmingham *FAC5*	43886	1-2	1-3	1	2	11	5		6	7	9*		8¹		3	4	12*	10					
Mar 1	A	Sunderland	8273	0-1	2-3	1	2	10	5		6	7¹		9	8		3	11		12		4¹		
Mar 4	H	Carlisle	9098	0-0	1-0	1	2	10¹	5		6	7		9	8		3	11		12		4		
Mar 11	A	Preston	10575	0-2	0-4	1	2	10	5	6		7	9	11	8		3*					12*	4	
Mar 18	H	Norwich	13902	2-0	2-1	1	2	10	5			7	9	11²	8		3					6	12	4	
Mar 24	A	Orient	9492	1-0	1-2	1	2	10	5	9*		7		11	8¹		3					6	12*	4	
Mar 31	A	Millwall	21919	0-0	0-1	1	2	10	5	12*		7		11	8		3					6	9*	4	
Apr 1	H	Swindon	12157	0-0	1-2	1	2	10	5	12		7	9	11	8		3					6		4	
Apr 3	H	Watford	7909	1-0	2-2	1	2	10	5	12*		7	9*	11¹	8		3					6		4¹	
Apr 8	H	Oxford	6933	2-1	2-2	1	2	11		5	4	7²	9	8		3					6	12	10	
Apr 15	H	Luton	8552	0-2	0-3	1	2	11		5	4	7	9	8		3					6	12	10	
Apr 22	A	Charlton	7351	0-0	1-1	1	2	11	5	12*	6	7	9¹	8		3				4*			10	
Apr 24	A	Blackpool	10507	1-1	2-1	1	2	11	4¹	5	6	7¹	9	8		3						12	10	
Apr 29	H	Burnley	5885	0-1	1-2	1	2	11	5		6	7	9*	8¹		3						12*	4	10

						Milkins J.	Smith F.	Ley G.	Hand E.	Youlden T.	Blant C.	Piper N.	Trebilcock M.	Hiron R.	Reynolds R.	Jennings N.	Collins J.	McCann A.	Storrie J.	Travers M.	Standen J.	Munks D.	Bromley B.	Pointer R.	Wilson W.	Lewis Brian
League Appearances						37	42	39	40	22	27	42	29	33	41	13	24	25	4	5	17		4	17		1
League Substitute									3				2				2	1	1		3	1	3			
League Goalscorers							1	4	5			8	9	9	10	3		4	1					2		
FA Cup Appearances						3	3	3	3		3	3	2	1	3	2	3	3			1					
FA Cup Substitute																			1							
FA Cup Goalscorers																		1	2							
League Cup Appearances						1	1	1	1	1		1		1	1		1	1	1							
League Cup Substitute														1												
League Cup Goalscorers																			1							

Totals Division 2   P42 W12 D13 L17 F59 A68 Pts 37 Posn 16th

*Substituted
Own goals: Burnley (Dec 11), Swansea (Feb 5)

Season 1972/73   Division 2

Date	Venue	Team	Attendance	FA HT	FA FT	Horn G.	Smith F.	Collins J.	Wilson W.	Stephenson A.	Hand E.	Piper N.	Reynolds R.	Price P.	Ley G.	Hiron R.	Munks D.	Lewis Brian	Jennings N.	McCann A.	Milkins J.	Pointer R.	Kellard R.	Foggo K.	Tilsed R.
Aug 12	A	Notts. Forest	13175	0-0	0-0	1	2	3	4	5	6	7	8	9*	10	11	12*								
Aug 16	A	Torquay *FLC1*	5202	0-0	2-1	1	2	3	4	5	6	7	8¹		10	9¹	12	11							
Aug 19	H	Cardiff	14067	0-1	3-1	1	2	3	4	5	6	7¹	8¹		10	9	12	11¹							
Aug 26	A	Millwall	12421	1-0	2-0	1	2	3	4	5	6	7	8		10	9	12	11²							
Aug 30	H	Huddersfield	16419	0-1	1-2	1	2	3	4	5	6	7	8¹	10*		9		11	12*						
Sept 2	H	Burnley	11701	0-1	0-2	1	2	3	10	5	6	7	8	12	9	4	11								
Sept 6	H	Chesterfield *FLC2*	6972	0-0	0-1	1	2	3	4	5	6	7	8		10	9	12	11							
Sept 9	A	Sheffield Wed.	17830	1-1	1-2	1	2	3	4	5	6	7	8		10	9¹		11		12					
Sept 16	H	Preston	6965	0-1	0-1	1	2	3	10*	5	6	7	8		9	4		11	12*						
Sept 23	A	Swindon	9431	1-0	1-1		2	3	5	4	7¹	8	9			12	6	11			1		10		
Sept 27	H	Oxford	7385	1-0	1-0		2	3	5	4	7	8	9			12	6	11			1		10		
Sept 30	H	Brighton	15726	1-0	2-0		2	12	3	5	4	7¹	8¹			9	6	11			1		10		
Oct 7	H	Bristol City	9375	0-1	0-3		2	3	5	4	7	8	12*			9	6	11*			1		10		
Oct 14	A	Hull	9513	0-4	1-5		3	5	4	7	8	9¹		12*			6	11			1		10*		
Oct 18	A	Luton	9813	2-2	2-2	1	2	3	4	5		7	8	9¹		12*	6	11¹*					10		
Oct 21	H	Aston Villa	13524	0-1	0-1	1	2	3	4	5	6	7	8	9			12	11					10		
Oct 28	A	Carlisle	6361	0-0	0-1	1	3	2	5	4	8	10	9	12		6	7	11							
Nov 4	A	Oxford	8714	2-0	3-1	1		3	5	2	4²	8	9			10	6	12	11¹					7	
Nov 11	H	Luton	7571	2-0	2-2	1		3	5	2	4¹	8	9			10	6	12	11¹					7	
Nov 18	A	Fulham	9624	0-0	0-0	1	12	3	2	5	4	8	7			9	6	11						7	
Nov 25	H	Q.P.R.	8460	0-0	0-1	1		3	4	5	2	7	8			9	6	12*	11*				10		
Dec 2	A	Blackpool	8409	0-2	1-3	1	12	3	4	5	2	8				9¹	6	7	11				10		
Dec 9	H	Sunderland	5783	1-1	2-3	1		3	4	5	2	7	8			9	6	12¹*	11¹	10*					
Dec 16	H	Middlesbrough	4688	0-0	0-0	1	2	3	10	5		7	8			9	6*	12*	11						
Dec 23	A	Orient	4466	0-0	1-0	1	2	3	10	5	4*	7	8			9¹	6	12*	11						
Dec 26	H	Swindon	7941	0-0	1-1	1	2	3	5	4		7	8			9¹	6	10¹	11	12					
Dec 29	A	Cardiff	12382	0-0	2-0	1		3	2	5	4¹	10	8			9¹	6	7	11	12					
Jan 6	A	Millwall	10031	0-0	1-1	1		3	2	5	4	7	8¹			9	6	12	11				10		
Jan 13	H	Bristol City *FAC3*	15177	0-0	1-1	1		3	2	5	4	7¹	8			9	6	12	11				10		
Jan 16	A	Bristol City *FAC3R*	16699	0-1	1-4	1	2	3*	4	5		7	8	11		9¹	6	12*					10		
Jan 27	H	Sheffield Wed.	9705	1-0	1-0	1	2	3	5	4		8	9			6	12	11¹					10	7	
Feb 10	A	Preston	6230	2-0	5-0			3	2	5	4	8²	12			9¹	6	11¹			1		10¹	7	
Feb 17	H	Notts. Forest	11151	2-0	2-0			3	2	5	4	8				9¹	6	12	11¹		1		10	7	
Feb 24	A	Middlesbrough	7038	0-3	0-3			3	2	5	4	8					6	12	11		1		10	7	
Mar 3	A	Bristol City	10977	0-2	1-3			3	2	5	4	8				9¹	6	12*	11*		1		10	7	
Mar 10	H	Hull	8139	1-1	2-2	12		3	5	2	4	8¹				9	6		11		1		10¹	7	
Mar 17	A	Aston Villa	18432	0-2	0-2	12*		3	5	2	4	8				9	6		11		1		10	7*	
Mar 20	A	Burnley	13569		0-4			3	5	6	11	8	9			2	12				1	4	10	7	
Mar 24	A	Carlisle	5346	0-0	0-0			3	4	5	6	11	8			9	2		12*				10*	7	1
Mar 31	A	Q.P.R.	14086	0-1	0-5			3	4	5	6	11	8			9	2		12				10	7	1
Apr 7	H	Blackpool	6768	0-0	1-0	12*		3	5	4		10	8			9¹*	6	2	11					7	1
Apr 14	A	Sunderland	31340	0-1	0-2	12		3	5	4		10	8				6	2	11	9				7	1
Apr 20	H	Orient	8954	1-0	1-0	12		3	5	4		8	9				6	2	11				10	7¹	1
Apr 21	H	Fulham	9192	1-2	1-2	12		3	5	4		8	9				6	2	11				10	7	1
Apr 23	A	Brighton	15535		1-1	12		3	5	4		8	9				6	2				11¹	10	7	1
Apr 28	A	Huddersfield	8993	0-1	0-2			3	5	4		8	9				6	2		12*		11*	10	7	1

	Horn G.	Smith F.	Collins J.	Wilson W.	Stephenson A.	Hand E.	Piper N.	Reynolds R.	Price P.	Ley G.	Hiron R.	Munks D.	Lewis Brian	Jennings N.	McCann A.	Milkins J.	Pointer R.	Kellard R.	Foggo K.	Tilsed R.
League Appearances	22	17	26	41	41	39	40	40	10	5	31	33	24	24	14	12	4	15	16	8
League Substitute			2							1		2	1	6	3	1				
League Goalscorers						1	8	5			8		6	6	2		1	2	1	
FA Cup Appearances	2	1	2	2	1	2	2	2	1		2	2						2		
FA Cup Substitute															1					
FA Cup Goalscorers							1				1									
League Cup Appearances	2	2	2	2	2	2	2	2		2	2		1	1						
League Cup Goalscorers								1			1									

Totals Division 2   P42 W12 D11 L19 F42 A59 Pts 35 Posn 17th

*Substituted
Own goals: Oxford (Sept 27), Fulham (Apr 21)

Season 1973/74   Division 2

Date	Venue	Team	Attendance	FA HT	FA FT	Tilsed R.	Roberts P.	Wilson W.	Piper N.	Stephenson A.	Munks D.	Marinello P.	Kellard R.	Davies Ron	Foggo K.	Price P.	Lewis Brian	Reynolds R.	Hand E.	Hiron R.	Milkins J.	Mellows M.	Collins J.	Went P.	Manley M.	Jennings N.	McCann A.	Best D.	Smith P.	Stewart A.	Ellis P.
Aug 25	H	Middlesbrough	19799		0-1	1	2	3	4	5	6	7	8	9	10	11	12														
Aug 28	H	Southend Utd. FLC1	9652	1-0	2-1	1	2	3	4	5	6	7	8	9^1	10		12	11^1													
Sept 1	A	Cardiff	10110	1-0	1-1	1	2	3	4^1	5	6	7	8	9	10		12*	11*													
Sept 8	A	Bolton	13367	0-1	0-2	1	2	3	4	5	6*	7	8	9	10		12*	11													
Sept 11	H	Sunderland	18989	1-1	1-1	1	2	3	4	5		7	8	9			10	12	6	11^1											
Sept 15	A	Luton	11552	1-2	3-3	1	2	3	4	5		7	8^1	9^1			10^1	12	6	11											
Sept 18	A	Carlisle	6843	0-0	2-0		2	3	4	5		7	8	9^1			10	12	6	11^1	1										
Sept 22	H	Notts County	14443	1-1	1-2		2	3	4	5		7	8*	9			10	12*	6	11^1	1										
Sept 29	A	Preston	10640	1-0	1-2		2	3	4	5		7	8	9^1	12*		10*		6	11	1										
Oct 2	H	Carlisle	10796		2-1		2	3	4	5		7	8	9			10		6^2	11	1	12									
Oct 6	H	Oxford	11669	1-0	2-1		2	3	4^1	5		7	8	9^1			10		6	11	1	12									
Oct 9	H	Plymouth FLC2	13202	0-2	0-4		2	3	4	5		7	8	9			10		6	11	1	12									
Oct 13	A	Sheffield Wed.	12690	0-1	2-1		2		4^1	5		7	8	9^1			10*	11	6		1	12*		3							
Oct 20	A	Hull City	6874	1-2	1-4		2		4	5		7	8	9			11	12	6^1		1	10		3							
Oct 27	H	Swindon	11819	3-0	3-1		2		4^2	5		7	8^1	9			11	12	6		1	10		3							
Nov 3	A	Blackpool	6535	0-2	0-5		2		4	5		7*	8	9			11	12*	6		1	10		3							
Nov 10	H	Aston Villa	12678	1-0	2-0		2		4^1	5	6	7	8	9^1			11	12			1	10		3							
Nov 17	A	Fulham	8403	0-1	0-2		2		4	5	6	7	8	9			11*	12*			1	10		3							
Nov 24	H	Crystal Palace	14212	1-2	2-2		2		4	5	6	7	8	9			12				1	10^2	11	3							
Dec 8	H	Bristol City	13178	0-0	1-0		2		4	12		7	8	9^1			10		6		1		11	3			5				
Dec 15	A	W.B.A.	11213	1-1	2-1		2		4^1	12		7	8	9^1			10		6		1		11	3			5				
Dec 22	H	Preston	13957	1-0	3-0		2		4^1			7	8	9^1			10^1	12	6		1		11	3			5				
Dec 26	A	Millwall	9797	1-1	1-1		2		4			7	8	9^1			10	12	6		1		11	3			5				
Dec 29	A	Bolton	13684	0-2	0-4		2		4			7	8	9			10	12	6		1		11	3			5				
Jan 1	H	Cardiff	20062	0-0	1-0		2		4			7	8^1	9			10	12	6		1		11	3			5				
Jan 5	H	Swindon FAC3	16682	1-3	3-3		2		4*			7	8^1	9^1			12*		6		1	10	11	3			5^1				
Jan 9	A	Swindon FAC3R	10021				2		4			7	8^1	9^1			12*		6		1	10	11	3*			5				
Jan 12	H	Luton	18647	0-0	0-0		2		4			7	8	9			12		6		1	10	11	3			5				
Jan 19	A	Middlesbrough	21774	0-0	0-3		2		4			7	8	9			12		6		1	10	11	3			5				
Jan 27	H	Orient FAC4	32838	0-0	0-0		2		4			7	8	9			12		6		1	10	11	3			5				
Jan 29	A	Orient §FAC4R	14879	1-1	1-1		2		4			7	8	9			12		6		1	10	11^1	3			5				
Feb 3	H	W.B.A.	19769	0-0	1-1		2		4^1			7	8	9			12		6		1	10	11	3			5				
Feb 5	†	Orient FAC4(2)R	19595	1-0	2-0		2		4			7	8^1	9^1			12		6		1	10	11	3			5				
Feb 9	A	Notts County	8664	0-1	0-4		2		4			7	8	9			12*		6*		1		11	3			5				
Feb 17	A	Notts For. FAC5	38589	0-0	0-1		2	3	4			7*	8	9			12*		6		1	10	11				5				
Feb 20	H	Sheffield Wed.	8699	1-0	1-1		2	3	4			7	8*	9^1			12*		6		1	10			11		5				
Feb 23	A	Oxford	7765	0-0	0-3	1	2	3	4			7	8	9			12*		6			10	11*				5				
Mar 2	H	Millwall	11004	0-0	0-0		2		4			7	8				12*		6			10		3	11*		5	1			
Mar 5	A	Sunderland	8142	0-0	0-3		2	3	4			7	8	9			12		6			10			11		5	1			
Mar 9	A	Swindon	5364	2-0	2-1		2	10	4			7	8	9					6					3	11*		5	1	12*		
Mar 16	H	Hull City	9838	2-0	3-1		2		10			7^2	8	9^1			4		6				11*	3			5*	1	12*		
Mar 23	A	Aston Villa	15517	1-0	4-1		2		10	5		7	8	9			4^1		6					3	11*			1	12*		
Mar 26	A	Notts Forest	14040	0-1	0-2		2		4			7	8	9					6			10		3*	11			1	12*		
Mar 30	H	Blackpool	9693	0-0	0-0		2	3	10			7	8	9			12		6			11		4			5	1			
Apr 6	A	Crystal Palace	23662	0-0	0-0		2	3	10			7	8	9			4		6				11		12		5	1			
Apr 12	A	Orient	10944	0-0	0-0		2	3	10			7	8	9			4		6				11		12		5	1			
Apr 13	H	Fulham	12054	1-0	3-0		2	3	10^2			7	8	9			4		6						12		5^1	1		11	
Apr 15	A	Orient	11540		1-2		2	3	10			7	8*	9			4		6						12*		5	1		11^1	
Apr 20	A	Bristol City	11143	1-0	2-0		2	3	10	5		7	8	9			4								12			1		11	
Apr 27	H	Notts Forest	11765	0-0	0-2		2	3	10			7	8	9			4								12			1		11	6
League Appearances						6	41	24	41	26	6	39	36	42	13	3	14	11	27	10	23	20	21	21	10	3	7	13		4	1
League Substitute																	3	7	2						3				1		
League Goalscorers									12			3	3	13	1		3	3	3			1					1				
FA Cup Appearances							6	1	5			6	6	6			1	2	1		4	6	6	5			6	5			
FA Cup Substitute																	2	1													
FA Cup Goalscorers													3	2									1				1				
League Cup Appearances						1	2	2	2	2	1	2	2	2	1		1	1	1	1	1										
League Cup Goalscorers														1				1													

Totals Division 2   P42 W14 D12 L16 F45 A62 Pts 40 Posn 15th

† At Crystal Palace
*Substituted
§ after extra time

P. Smith's substitute appearance lasted only 8 minutes

Season 1974/75   Division 2

Date	V	Team	Attendance	FA HT	FA FT	Best D.	Roberts P.	Wilson W.	Hand E.	Stephenson A.	Ellis P.	Piper N.	Reynolds R.	Davies Ron	Mellows M.	Stewart A.	Lewis Brian	Went P.	Marinello P.	Kellard R.	Hiron R.	Foggo K.	Graham G.	Bartlett G.	Manley M.	Cahill P.	Figgins P.	Kane A.
Aug 17	A	Bolton	12776	0-2	0-3	1	2	3	4	5	6	7	8	9	10	11*	12*											
Aug 21	A	Swindon FLC1	4779	0-0	1-0	1	2	3	8	6		4¹		10	9			11	12		5	7						
Aug 24	H	Notts Forest	11340	1-0	2-0	1	2	3	8	6		4		10¹	9			11¹	12*		5	7*						
Aug 28	A	Manchester Utd.	42547	0-1	1-2	1	2	3*	8	6	12*	4		10	9¹			11			5	7						
Aug 31	A	Orient	6861	1-0	1-1	1		3	12	6	2	4		10¹	9			11			5	7	8					
Sept 7	H	W.B.A.	9158	0-3	1-3	1		3	4	6¹	2	10	8		9			11			5*	7	12*					
Sept 11	H	Derby FLC2	13568	0-3	1-5	1	2	3	11	6	12*	4		10	9*						5	7¹	8					
Sept 14	A	Southampton	19361	0-1	1-2	1	2	3	11*	6	12*	4		10	9¹						5	7	8					
Sept 17	A	Notts Forest	9534	2-1	2-1	1		3	5	6	2	4			9²			11	12		7	8	10					
Sept 21	H	Cardiff	9519	0-2	2-2	1	2	3	5	6		4¹	12*		9			11¹			7	8	10*					
Sept 24	H	Oldham	9671	1-0	1-1	1		3		6	2	4		10	9			11	12		5	7	8¹					
Sept 28	A	York City	6177	0-2	0-3	1	12	3		6	2	4		10	9			11			5	8	7					
Oct 5	A	Notts County	8573	0-1	1-1	1		3	8	6	2	4			9¹	12	5	11	10			7						
Oct 12	H	Fulham	12520	0-0	0-0	1		3	10	6	2	4	12		9		5	11				8	7					
Oct 15	H	Manchester Utd.	25608	0-0	0-0	1		3	10	6	2	4			9	12	5	11				8	7					
Oct 19	A	Norwich	20899	0-1	0-2	1	12*	3	10	6	2*	4			9		5	11				8	7					
Oct 26	H	Blackpool	10143	0-0	0-0	1	2	3	10	6		4			9*	12*	5	11				8	7					
Nov 2	H	Bristol City	9590	0-0	0-1	1	2	3	10*	6		4	8		9			11			5	7	12*					
Nov 9	A	Oxford	6402	0-0	0-1	1	2	8	3	6		4			9			11		5	7	10*	12*					
Nov 16	H	Hull City	9045	1-1	1-1	1	2	10	3	6		4¹*	8		9			11			5	7	12*					
Nov 23	A	Aston Villa	16821	0-2	0-2	1	2	10	3	6			8*		9			11	12*		5	7	4					
Nov 30	H	Sheffield Wed.	9786	0-0	1-0	1	2	10	3	6		4			9¹			11		5	7	12*	8*					
Dec 7	A	Sunderland	25926	0-1	1-4	1	2	10	3	6	12	4			9			11¹			5	7	8					
Dec 14	H	Bolton	7612	1-0	2-0	1	2	10	3	6		4			9*			11¹		5	7	8	12¹*					
Dec 21	A	Bristol Rovers	9262	1-0	1-0	1	2	10	3	6		4¹			9			11		5	7	12*	8*					
Dec 26	H	Southampton	19534	0-2	1-2	1	2	10	3	6		4¹			9*			11		5	7	8	12*					
Dec 28	A	Millwall	8116	0-0	0-0	1	2	10	3*	6		4			9			11		5	7	8	12*					
Jan 3	A	Notts Co. FAC3	14723	0-2	1-3	1	2	3		6		4			9*			11	5	7	10	12*	8					
Jan 11	H	Sunderland	14133	0-1	4-2	1	2	3		6		4¹					11	12	8	5¹	7	10¹	9¹					
Jan 18	A	Sheffield Wed.	11032	0-0	2-0	1	2	3	5	6		4						11	8¹	7¹	10	12	9					
Feb 1	H	Oxford	13123	1-0	2-1	1	2*		5	6	3	4						11	8	7	10	12¹*	9¹					
Feb 8	A	Bristol City	13802	1-0	1-3	1	2	3		6		4					11	8*	5	7	10¹	12*	9					
Feb 18	H	Aston Villa	13355	2-3	2-3	1	2*		5		3	4						11¹	12*	7	10	8	9¹			6		
Feb 22	A	Hull	6919	0-0	0-0	1	2		5		3	4						11		7	10	8	9		12	6		
Feb 28	H	Orient	11619	3-0	3-0	1	2		5	12	3	4						11		7	10²	8¹	9			6		
Mar 8	A	Oldham	10303	0-0	0-2	1	2		5	6		4	8					11	12*	3	10	7*	9					
Mar 15	H	York City	9906	1-0	1-0	1	2		5	6		4	8					11	3	7	10¹	12	9					
Mar 22	A	W.B.A.	10017	0-1	1-2	1	2		5	6		4¹	8					11	3	7	10*	12*	9					
Mar 29	A	Bristol Rovers	12261	2-0	3-0	1	2		5	6		4	8					11²	3	7	10¹	12	9					
Mar 31	H	Millwall	14329	0-0	1-0	1	2		5	6		4	8					11	3	7	10	12	9					
Apr 2	A	Cardiff	9892	0-1	0-1	1	2		5			4	8					11	3	7	10*	12*	9			6		
Apr 5	A	Blackpool	6543	0-1	2-2	1	2		5			4	8					11¹	10*	3	12¹*	7	9			6		
Apr 12	H	Notts County	10960	0-0	1-1	1	2		5			4	8					11	12	3¹	7	10	9			6		
Apr 19	A	Fulham	17580	0-1	2-2		2		5			4²						11	10*	3	7	8	9			6	1	12*
Apr 26	H	Norwich	18977	0-1	0-3		2		5		12							11	10	3	7	8	9			6	1	4

						Best D.	Roberts P.	Wilson W.	Hand E.	Stephenson A.	Ellis P.	Piper N.	Reynolds R.	Davies Ron	Mellows M.	Stewart A.	Lewis Brian	Went P.	Marinello P.	Kellard R.	Hiron R.	Foggo K.	Graham G.	Bartlett G.	Manley M.	Cahill P.	Figgins P.	Kane A.
League Appearances						40	31	24	40	31	16	41	23	17	36	10	5	34	38	11	17	18	19		1	7	2	1
League Substitute							1				2		1			4	2			1	1		10				2	1
League Goalscorers								1		5	5	5		8	1	1		2	2	1		6	2			3	1	
FA Cup Appearances						1	1	1	1		1		1	1				1	1		1	1						
FA Cup Substitute																							1					
FA Cup Goalscorers																			1									
League Cup Appearances						2	2	2	2	2		2		2	2			1			2	2	1					
League Cup Substitute											1																	
League Cup Goalscorers												1									1							

Totals Division 2   P42 W12 D13 L17 F44 A54 Pts 37 Posn 17th

*Substituted
Own goal: Millwall (Mar 31)

Season 1975/76   Division 2

Date	Venue	Team	Attendance	HT	FT	Lloyd G.	Roberts P.	Piper N.	Reynolds R.	Went P.	Hand E.	Marinello P.	Kane A.	Graham G.	Foster S.	Mellows M.	Ellis P.	Cahill P.	McLaughlin J.T.	Lawler C.	Kamara C.	Wilson W.	McGuinness R.	Stewart A.	Macken A.	Collard I.	Eames W.	Busby M.	Figgins P.	King J.	Viney K.	Denyer P.	Pullar D.
Aug 16	A	York City	4602	1-1	1-2	1	2	4¹	12*	5	6	7	8*	9		11	3						10										
Aug 20	A	Aldershot FLC1	6274	1-1	1-1	1	2	4		5	6	7	8	9¹	12	11	3						10										
Aug 23	H	Notts Forest	10655	0-1	1-1	1	2	4	12*	5¹	6	7	8	9		11	3						10*										
Aug 26	H	Aldershot FLC1	7049	2-0	2-1	1		4	2¹	5	6	7¹	8	9	10	11	3						12										
Aug 29	A	Orient	5056	1-0	1-0	1	2	3	4	5	6	7	8	9	10	11*	12*																
Sept 6	H	Luton	9835	0-1	0-2	1	2	3	4	5	6	7	8	9	10							11	12										
Sept 9	H	Leicester FLC2	10629	0-0	1-1	1	2	4	8	5	6	7*					3					11			10	12¹*							
Sept 13	A	Carlisle	7316	1-1	1-2	1	2	3	8	5	6	4		9		11									10	12¹*							
Sept 17	A	Leicester †FLC2R	11055	0-0	0-1	1	2	4	8	5	6			9	12*	11	3				7*		10										
Sept 20	H	Oldham	8079	1-1	1-1	1	2	4¹	8	5	6			9	12	11	3				7		10										
Sept 23	H	Chelsea	16144	1-1	1-1	1	2	4	8¹	5	6			9	12*	11	3				7*		10										
Sept 27	A	Southampton	17310	0-1	0-4	1	2	4	8	5	6			9	12*	11	3				7*		10										
Oct 4	H	Sunderland	13098	0-0	0-0	1	2	4	8	5	6	7		9*	12*	11		3					10										
Oct 11	A	Blackpool	8351	0-0	0-0	1	2	4	8	5	6	7*		9		11		3					10		12*								
Oct 18	H	Hull	8155	0-0	1-1	1	2	4¹	8	5	6	7		9		11		3					10		12								
Oct 21	H	Bristol Rovers	9078	0-0	1-2	1	2	4	8	5	6	7¹		9		11		3					10		12								
Oct 25	A	Notts County	9594	0-0	0-2	1	2		8	5	6			9		11		3	4		7		10*		12*								
Nov 1	H	Fulham	11441	0-0	0-1	1	2	4	8	5	6	7		9		11		3					10*		12*								
Nov 4	A	Bolton	18538	1-1	1-4	1	2		8	5	6	7		9		11		3	4		12		10¹										
Nov 8	A	Plymouth	13885	0-0	1-3	1	2	4¹	8	5	6	7		9		11		3			12*		10*										
Nov 15	H	Blackburn	7323	0-0	0-1	1		4	8	5	6	7		9		11		3		2	12*		10*										
Nov 22	A	Hull	4549	0-0	0-1	1		4	8	5		7		9				3		2	12	11	10*										
Nov 29	H	Oxford	8648	0-2	0-2	1		4	8	5		7		9	12*			3		2		11	10*										
Dec 6	A	W.B.A.	15325	0-1	1-3	1		4	8	5		7¹		9				3	12	2		11	10										
Dec 13	H	Notts Forest	11343	0-0	1-0	1		4	8	5				9				3		2	7¹	11	10*		12*								
Dec 20	H	York City	7903	0-1	0-1	1		4*	8	5				9	12*			3		2	7	11	10										
Dec 26	A	Charlton	10736	2-0	3-1	1		4¹	8¹	5				9¹	12			3		2	7	11	10										
Dec 27	H	Bristol City	14315	0-1	0-1	1		4	8	5	12*			9				3		2	7	11*	10										
Jan 3	H	Birmingham FAC3	19414	1-1	1-1	1		4	8	5				9				3		2	7	11¹	10		12								
Jan 6	A	Birmingham FAC3R	26106	1-0	1-0	1		4	8	5	6			9				3			7¹	11	10		12								
Jan 10	H	Carlisle	11430	0-0	1-0	1		4	8	5	12			9				3		2	7	11¹	10										
Jan 17	A	Luton	10464	0-2	1-3	1		4	8¹	5				9				3		2*	7	11	10		12*								
Jan 24	A	Charlton FAC4	26333	0-1	1-1	1		4	8¹	5				9				3		2	7	11	10		12								
Jan 27	H	Charlton FAC4R	31722	0-0	0-3	1		4	8	5				9				3		2	7	11*	10		12*								
Jan 31	A	Bristol Rovers	6133	0-2	0-2	1		4	8	5				9				3		2	7	11	10		12								
Feb 7	H	Bolton	8958	0-1	0-1	1		4	8	5				9				3		2	7	11	10		12								
Feb 14	H	Plymouth	9509	1-0	2-0	1		4*	8	5	6			9				3		2	7¹	11	10¹						12				
Feb 21	A	Blackburn	8067	1-0	3-0	1		4	8²	5				9¹				3		2	7	11	10						6		12		
Feb 25	A	Chelsea	12709	0-2	0-2	1		4	8	5	6	5		9				3		2	7	11	10								12		
Feb 28	H	Notts County	9135	0-1	1-3	1			8	5				9	12*	11		3		2	7*	10¹					4	6					
Mar 6	H	Fulham	6928	0-0	1-0				8¹	5				9		11		3		2	7	10					4	6	1				
Mar 13	H	Blackpool	8394	0-0	2-0				8¹	5		7		9	11*			3		2		10					4	6	1	12*		
Mar 20	A	Oxford	6928	0-0	0-1				8	5		7		9				3*	12*	2		10					4	6	1		11	
Mar 27	H	W.B.A.	10617	0-0	0-1				8	5		7*		9	11			3	12*	2		10					4	6	1			
Apr 6	H	Southampton	24115	0-0	0-1			4	8	5		7		9				3		2		11	10						6	1	12		
Apr 10	A	Oldham	6672	0-3	2-5			6*	8¹	5		7		9				3		2		11	10¹					4		1	12*		
Apr 13	H	Orient	5069	2-0	2-1				8	5		7¹		9*		11		3¹		2			10					4	6	1	12*		
Apr 17	H	Charlton	7992	0-0	2-2			4	8	5		7		9		11²		3*		2			10						6	1	12*		
Apr 20	A	Bristol City	27300	0-1	0-1			3	8	5		7		9	12	11				2			10					4	6	1			
Apr 24	A	Sunderland	40515	0-2	0-2		2		8	5		7*		9		11		3	12*	4			10						6	1			

						Lloyd	Roberts	Piper	Reynolds	Went	Hand	Marinello	Kane	Graham	Foster	Mellows	Ellis	Cahill	McLaughlin	Lawler	Kamara	Wilson	McGuinness	Stewart	Macken	Collard	Eames	Busby	Figgins	King	Viney	Denyer	Pullar
League Appearances						33	33	39	19	29	17	15	5	39	8	39	8	32	5	26	21	18	26		10	1	9	6	9	4	6	5	
League Substitute								3		1	2			3				1	1		2	3	2		1		2		1		2	1	
League Goalscorers							1	11	1	1	1	2		2		2				4	1	3				2		1		1	2	1
FA Cup Appearances						4	4	4	4	4	1			4		4		3		4			4		4								
FA Cup Substitute																								1								
FA Cup Goalscorers							1																	1		1						
League Cup Appearances						4	3	4	3	4	4	3	2	4	1	3	3	1				1	3		1								
League Cup Substitute								1																	1							
League Cup Goalscorers							1		1		1														1							

Totals Division 2   P42 W9 D7 L26 F32 A61 Pts 25 Posn 22nd Last. Relegated!

*Substituted
†After extra time.

Own goal: Orient (Aug 29)

Season 1976/77   Division 3

Date	Venue	Team	Attendance	FA HT	FA FT	Lloyd G.	Roberts P.	Wilson W.	Denyer P.	Ellis P.	Lawler C.	Green C.	Piper N.	Went P.	Graham G.	Pollock M.	Viney K.	Cahill P.	Kamara C.	McGuinness R.	Mellows M.	Figgins P.	Pullar D.	Foster S.	Kemp D.	Gilchrist P.	Eames W.	Bennett P.
Jul 31	A	Oxford *KC*	1868	2-1	2-2	12	10	3	4	2			8[1]	5			11		6		7[1]		1		9				12	
Aug 3	H	Watford *KC*	2690	2-1	4-2	1	2	3		12*		12*	8[2]	5*	10	11		6	4[1]			12		9[1]				7*	
Aug 7	H	Luton *KC*	3300	0-2	0-2	12	2	3		5		12*	8*		10	11		6	4	7*	12*	1		9					
Aug 14	A	C. Palace *FLC1*	12936	1-2	2-2	1	2	3	12[1]	5			8[1]			11		6	4	7	10			9*					
Aug 17	H	C. Palace *FLC1*	9778	0-0	0-1	1	2	3		5			8		10	4		6		7	11*			9				12	
Aug 21	A	Wrexham	4752	0-0	0-2	1	2	3	4	5	6	7*	8	9	10	11	12												
Aug 24	H	Swindon	7898	2-0	2-1	1		3	4[1]	5	2	8	9	10[1]	11	7		6											
Aug 28	H	Chesterfield	8700	0-0	0-1	1		3	4	5	2	8	9	10	11	7		6											
Sept 4	A	Sheffield Wed.	12131	0-1	1-1	1		3	4	5	2	9*		10		8		6	7	12	11[1]								
Sept 11	H	Lincoln City	7865	1-1	1-1	1		3	4	5*	2	9[1]		10		8		6	7	12	11								
Sept 18	A	Gillingham	6736	0-1	1-2	1		3	4	5	2	7		9		11	12	6*	8		10[1]								
Sept 25	H	Reading	11937	0-1	0-2	1		3	4	5	2	7*	12	9		11		6	8		10								
Oct 2	A	Shrewsbury	4782	0-3	1-4		7	3	4	2				9	5	11		6	8		10[1]	1							
Oct 9	H	Walsall	7779	0-0	1-1	4	10	7	5		12	2[1]			9	3		6	8*		11	1							
Oct 15	A	Northampton	4805	0-2	1-3	4	10*	8	5	12	9	2			7	3		6			11[1]	1							
Oct 23	H	Port Vale	7516	1-1	1-1	1			4	5		9	2		10	3		6	8*		11		7	12					
Oct 26	A	Rotherham Utd	4428	2-0	2-2	1			4	5		9[1]*	2		10	3		6	8		11		7[1]	12					
Oct 30	H	Peterborough	8622	0-0	0-0	1			4	5		9	2		10	3		6	8		11		7						
Nov 2	H	Chester	8480	1-0	2-1	1			4	5		9	2[1]		10	3		6	8[1]		11		7						
Nov 6	A	Oxford	6228	1-1	1-2	1			4	5		9*	2		10	3		6			11		7	12					
Nov 13	H	Bury	10252	0-0	1-1	1			4[1]			9	2		10	3		6			11		7	5	8				
Nov 20	A	Aldershot *FAC1*	10213	1-0	1-1	1			4			9	2		10	3		6	8		11[1]		7	5					
Nov 23	H	Aldershot *FAC1R*	15089	1-1	2-1	1			4			9[1]	2		10	3		6	8		11		7	5[1]					
Nov 27	A	Grimsby	3836	0-1	0-1	1			4			9	2		11	3		6	8		10		7*	5	12				
Dec 4	H	Preston N.E.	9243	0-0	0-0	1			4			9	2		11	3*		6	12		10		7	5	8				
Dec 11	H	Minehead *FAC2*	14089	1-0	2-1	1			4				2		11	3		6	8[1]		10		7	5	9[1]				1
Dec 18	A	York City	2058	1-0	4-1	1			4[1]				2		10[2]	3		6	9		11		7	5	8[1]				
Dec 27	H	Brighton	32368	1-0	1-0	1			4				2		10	3		6	9		11		7	5	8[1]				
Jan 1	H	Oxford	15954	0-1	1-1	1			4			12	2		11	3		6	8		10		7*	5	9				
Jan 3	A	Peterborough	5424	0-2	2-4	1			4	12		7	2[1]		10	3		6	9*		11[1]			5	8				
Jan 8	A	Birmingham *FAC3*	31598	0-1	0-1	1			4			12	2,,		11	3		6	9		10	1	7	5	8				
Jan 18	H	Mansfield	10720	1-2	2-2	1			4	6		7	2		10	3			8*		11	1	12	5	9[2]				
Jan 22	H	Wrexham	13505	0-1	0-1	1			4*			12	2		11	3		6	8		10	1	7	5	9				
Jan 28	A	Tranmere	3436	2-0	3-1	1	4						2		10	3[1]		6	9		11		7[1]	5[1]	8				
Feb 5	A	Chesterfield	3959	1-0	2-1	1	4		12				2		10[1]	3		6	8	11			7	5*	9[1]				
Feb 12	H	Sheffield Wed.	14279	0-0	0-3	1			4			12	2		11	3		6	8		10		7*	5	9				
Feb 22	A	Crystal Palace	16483	1-2	1-2	1			4[1]		2		3		10			6	9		11		7	5	8				
Feb 26	H	Gillingham	10102	2-1	3-2	1			4				2[1]		10	3		6	9		11		7	5	8[2]				
Mar 5	H	Reading	7873	0-1	0-2	1			4				2		11	3		6	9		10		7	5	8				
Mar 12	H	Shrewsbury	9904	0-0	2-0	1	4						2		10	3		6	12		11[1]		7	5	8[1]	9*			
Mar 15	A	Lincoln	4648	1-0	1-2	1	4						2		10*	3		6	12		11		7	5	9[1]	8			
Mar 19	A	Walsall	4871	0-0	1-1	1	4						2		10[1]	3		6	12		11		7*	5	9	8			
Mar 26	H	Northampton	9195	0-2	1-2	1	4		12				2		10*	3		6			11		7	5	9[1]	8[1]			
Apr 2	A	Port Vale	2984	0-1	0-1	1	4		10				2		12	3		6			11		7*	5	8	9			
Apr 6	A	Brighton	25451	0-2	0-4	1			4			12	2		10	3*		6	7		11			5	8	9			
Apr 9	H	Crystal Palace	14108	0-0	0-0	1						4	2		10	3		6	9		11			5	8	7			
Apr 11	A	Chester	3309	1-0	1-1	1			·			7	2		10*	3		6	4		12		11	5	8[1]	9			
Apr 16	H	Rotherham	10588	2-1	5-1	1			7[2]			4	2			3		6	8				11	5	9[3]	10			
Apr 19	H	Tranmere	12710	0-1	0-3	1			10			7	2			3*		6	4		12		11	5	8	9			
Apr 23	A	Bury	5211	0-0	0-1	1			10	6		7*	2			3			4		12		11	5	8	9			
Apr 30	A	Grimsby	10155	1-1	1-2	1			4	6	5		2		10	3			8*		11		12		9	7			
May 2	A	Mansfield	10774	0-1	0-2	1			4	2			3		7*			6	8		11		12	5	10	9			
May 7	A	Preston N.E.	5347	0-0	0-0	1	2	3	4			10	7					6	11					5	8	9			
May 14	H	York City	14288	1-1	3-1	1	2	3	5			7[2]	4					6	8		11				9[1]	10			
May 17	A	Swindon	6744	0-3	3-4	1	2	3	5			10	7					6	4[2]		11				8[1]	9			

						Lloyd G.	Roberts P.	Wilson W.	Denyer P.	Ellis P.	Lawler C.	Green C.	Piper N.	Went P.	Graham G.	Pollock M.	Viney K.	Cahill P.	Kamara C.	McGuinness R.	Mellows M.	Figgins P.	Pullar D.	Foster S.	Kemp D.	Gilchrist P.	Eames W.	Bennett P.
League Appearances						41	14	13	38	19	9	26	42	8	3	39	33	42	35	1	37	5	27	28	30	16		
League Substitute								2	1	1	5	1				1	2			4	2	3		3	3	1		
League Goalscorers								6				4	4	1		6	1	1	3		6		2	1	14	1		
FA Cup Appearances						2			4			1	4			4	4	4	4		4	1	4	4	2			1
FA Cup Substitute																					1							
FA Cup Goalscorers												1									1			1	1		
League Cup Appearances						2	2	2		2			2		1	2		2	1	2	2		2					
League Cup Substitute									1																		1
League Cup Goalscorers									1				1														

Totals Division 3   P46 W11 D14 L21 F53 A70 Pts 36 Posn 20th

*Substituted

KC Kent Cup

Own Goal: Grimsby (Apr 30)

Season 1977/78   Division 3

Date	Venue	Team	Attendance	FA HT	FA FT	Middleton S.	Roberts P.	Wilson W.	Ellis P.	Foster S.	Cahill P.	Gilchrist P.	Kemp D.	Green C.	Mellows M.	Pollock M.	Stokes R.	Denyer P.	Piper N.	Barnard L.	Pullar D.	Viney K.	Figgins P.	Knight A.	Hand E.	Ruggeiro J.	Taylor A.	Piper S.	McCaffrey J.	Lathan J.	Garwood C.
Aug 13	H	Newport *FLC1*	7541	1-1	3-1	1	2	3	4	5	6	7	9^2	8^1	10	11															
Aug 16	A	Newport *FLC1*	3200	1-3	2-3	1	2	3	4^1	5	6	9	8	10	11	7^1															
Aug 20	A	Peterborough	6099	0-0	0-0	1	2	3	4	5	6	7	8	9	10	11															
Aug 27	A	Swindon	9396	1-1	1-3	1	2	3	4	5	6	9	8^*	7	11	10^1	12														
Aug 31	H	Leicester *FLC2*	13842	0-0	2-0	1	2	3	4	5	6		8^1	10^1	11	7	9														
Sept 3	H	Chesterfield	11132	2-0	3-0	1	2	3	4	5	6		8^2	7	10	11	9^1														
Sept 10	A	Wrexham	5000	0-2	0-2	1	2	3	5	6		12	8	10^*	11	7	9	4													
Sept 13	H	Colchester	11757	0-0	0-0	1	2	3	4	5	6		8	10	11	7	9														
Sept 17	H	Lincoln	11370	0-1	0-2	1	2^*	3	4	5	6		8	7	10	11	9		12												
Sept 24	A	Exeter	5875	1-0	1-0	1	2	3	5		7	8^1	10		9	6	4	11													
Sept 28	A	Oxford	7769	0-0	0-0	1	2	3	5		9	8	11		10	6	4	7													
Oct 1	H	Sheffield Wed.	12020	2-1	2-2	1	2	3	5^1		7	8^1	10		9	6	4	11													
Oct 4	H	Chester	10465	0-0	0-0	1	2	3	5		9	8	11		10	6	4	7^*	12												
Oct 8	A	Walsall	4764	0-0	1-1	1	2	3	5		9	8^1	11		10	6	4	7													
Oct 15	H	Bury	10861	0-0	1-1	1	2	6	5		7	8^1	11		9	3	4	10													
Oct 22	A	Shrewsbury	3726	0-3	1-6	1	2	3	5		9	8^1	11		10	6	4	7													
Oct 25	H	Swindon *FLC3*	14955	1-0	1-1	1	2	3	5	6		8	11^1		10	9	4	7													
Oct 29	A	Plymouth	6594	0-2	1-3	1	2	3			6	8^1	10			7	9	11	3												
Nov 1	A	Swindon *FLC3R*	9378	1-2	3-4	1	2	3^1		5	6		8		11	9	10^1	4	7^1												
Nov 5	H	Tranmere	8782	2-0	2-5	1	2	3	5^*	6		8^2			11	9	10	4	7	12											
Nov 12	A	Carlisle	3828	0-1	1-3		2	3	5			8	9	11	12	10	6	4^*	7	1											
Nov 15	A	Port Vale	7072	0-1	1-1		6	3	4			8^1		11	10	9	5	2	7	1											
Nov 19	H	Hereford	8077	0-0	2-0		6	3	4			8^1		11	10^1	9	5	2	7	1											
Nov 26	H	Bideford *FAC1*	10312	1-0	3-1		6	3	4			8		11^1	10	9^1	5	2	7^1	1											
Dec 3	A	Preston N.E.	5936	0-1	1-3	5	3	6	12			8^1		10	11	9	4	2	7	1											
Dec 10	H	Rotherham	9466	1-2	3-3		3	4				9^1		11	10^2		6	2	7	1	5	8									
Dec 17	H	Swansea *FAC2*	11863	1-1	2-2		3	4	5			9^2		11	10		8	2	7	1	6										
Dec 20	A	Swansea *FAC2R*	8844	0-1	1-2		3	4	5^1			8	9	11			10	2	7	1	6										
Dec 26	A	Gillingham	9811	0-0	0-0		3		5		9	8		11			10	2	7	1	6	4									
Dec 27	H	Cambridge Utd.	13152	0-2	2-2		3		5		9	8^1		11			10	2	7	1	6	4^1									
Dec 30	A	Tranmere	4677	0-2	0-2		3		5		9	8		11	12	10^*	2		7	1	6	4									
Jan 2	H	Bradford C.	12004	0-0	3-1	10	3		5^1		9^1	8^1		11			2	7		1	6	4									
Jan 7	A	Port Vale	3481	0-2	0-2	10	3	12	5^*		9	8		11			2	7		1	6	4									
Jan 14	H	Peterborough	9569	2-0	2-2	2	3	4			9^1	8		11		10^1	5	7		1	6										
Jan 20	H	Swindon	11647	1-0	1-2	2	3	4			9	8		11	12	10	5	7		1	6^1										
Jan 28	A	Chesterfield	4351	0-2	0-3	2	3	4			8		9	10	11		5	7		1	6										
Feb 4	H	Wrexham	9223	0-1	0-1	2		6			9	8	12	11		10	4	7^*		1	5	3									
Feb 11	A	Lincoln	4100	0-0	0-1	2		6	12	9	8		11			10	4		1	5	3	7									
Feb 25	A	Sheffield Wed.	10241	0-0	0-0	2		5^*		4	9	8		10		6	12		1		3	7	11								
Feb 28	H	Exeter	10260	0-0	1-1	2				5^1	9	8		10		6	4^*	12	1		3	7	11								
Mar 4	H	Walsall	9536	1-1	1-2	2				6	9	8		10		4	12		1		5^*	3	7^1	11							
Mar 7	A	Colchester	3570	0-2	0-4	2				6		8		10		4^*	5	12	9	1		3	7	11							
Mar 11	A	Bury	4700	0-0	0-0	1	2		6		5			10		4^*		9			3	12	11	7	8					
Mar 18	H	Shrewsbury	8575	1-1	1-2	1	2		4		5			10		6^1		7			3		11	8	9^1					
Mar 21	H	Plymouth	11010	0-2	1-5	1	2^*		4		5			10		6		7			3	12^1	11	8	9					
Mar 25	A	Cambridge Utd.	5896	0-0	0-1		2	4	5					6			12	7			3	10	11^*	8	9					
Mar 27	H	Gillingham	8108	1-1	1-1	1	2	4	5					6			12	7			3^*	10	11^1	8	9					
Apr 1	A	Bradford C.	4462	0-0	0-1	1	2	4	5					6				7			3	10	11^*	8	9					
Apr 4	H	Oxford	5825	0-0	0-2	1	2	4	5			12		6				7			3	10	11	8	9					
Apr 8	H	Carlisle	5937	2-1	3-3	1	2^1	4	5^1			11		6				7^1			3	10		8	9					
Apr 15	A	Hereford	3893	2-0	2-0	1	2	4	5			11		6^1			7	12			3	10^*		8	9^1					
Apr 22	H	Preston N.E.	6866	0-0	0-2	1	2	4	5			11		6			7	3			10			8	9					
Apr 26	A	Chester	2837	0-2	0-2	1	2	4	5			11		6			7				3	10		8	9					
Apr 29	A	Rotherham	3718	0-0	1-0		2	4	5			11		6			7		1		3	10		8	9					

						Middleton S.	Roberts P.	Wilson W.	Ellis P.	Foster S.	Cahill P.	Gilchrist P.	Kemp D.	Green C.	Mellows M.	Pollock M.	Stokes R.	Denyer P.	Piper N.	Barnard L.	Pullar D.	Viney K.	Figgins P.	Knight A.	Hand E.	Ruggeiro J.	Taylor A.	Piper S.	McCaffrey J.	Lathan J.	Garwood C.
League Appearances						26	33	36	29	30	14	22	33	8	42	11	23	41	23	8	22	2	19	1	12	6	17	13	11	12	12
League Substitute								1	1	1	1			1	1			3		1		3	3	2	2					2	
League Goalscorers								1		3	1	2	16		4	2	3		1						1	1		1	1		2
FA Cup Appearances							1	3	3	2		3	1	3	2	2	3	2			3		3		2						
FA Cup Goalscorers								1			2		1		1										1						
League Cup Appearances						5	5	5	3	5	5	2	5	3	5	3	3	2	2	1	1										
League Cup Goalscorers								1	1				3	2	1	1			1			1									

Totals Division 3   P46 W7 D17 L22 F41 A75 Pts 31 Posn 24th Last — Relegated!

*Substituted

Own goal: Carlisle (Nov 12)

Season 1978/79   Division 4

Date	Venue	Team	Attendance	HT	FT	Mellor P.	Ellis P.	Viney K.	Denyer P.	Foster S.	Hand E.	Hemmerman J.	Lathan J.	Davey S.	McIlwraith J.	Pullar D.	Garwood C.	Wilson W.	Piper S.	Barnard L.	McCaffrey J.	Showers D.	Milligan L.	Bryant S.	James K.	Roberts T.	Gilchrist P.
Aug 12	H	Swindon *FLC1*	9261	0-0	0-0	1	2	3	4	5	6	7	8	9		11		12	10								
Aug 15	A	Swindon *FLC1*	7343	0-0	2-4	1	2	3	4	5	6	7	8		10	11^1		12									9^1
Aug 19	H	Bradford City	8268	0-1	0-1	1	2	3	4	5	6	7*	8	9	10	11	12										
Aug 22	A	York City	2513	1-1	3-5	1	2	3^1	4	5	6*	7	8	9	10^2	11	12										
Aug 25	A	Hartlepool	3074	0-1	1-1	1		3	4	5		7	8	9^1	10	12	11*	2	6								
Sept 2	H	Crewe	7429	1-0	3-0	1	2	3	4			7^3	8	9		11	12	5	6	10							
Sept 9	A	Rochdale	1479	2-0	2-0	1	2	3	4	12		7	8^1	9^1		11		6*	5	10							
Sept 12	H	Scunthorpe	10965	0-0	0-0	1	2	3	4	5		7	8*	9		11	12		6	10							
Sept 16	H	Port Vale	9937	1-0	2-0	1	2	3	4	5		7	8	9*		11	12^1		6	10^1							
Sept 23	A	Aldershot	8967	1-0	2-0	1	2	3	4	5		7^1	8^1	9		11	12		6	10*							
Sept 26	H	Wigan	13902	0-0	1-0	1	2	3	4	5		7*	8	9^1		11	12		6	10							
Sept 29	A	Bournemouth	10056	1-1	1-3	1	2	3^1*	4	5		7	8	9	10	11	12		6								
Oct 7	H	Hereford	11949	0-0	1-0	1	2	3	4^1	5		7*	8	9		11	10		6		12						
Oct 14	A	Grimsby	5141	0-0	0-1	1	2	3	4	5		7	8	9	10	11		12	6								
Oct 17	A	Doncaster	2480	2-1	3-2	1	2	3	4^1	5		7^2	8	12	10*	11	9		6								
Oct 21	H	Halifax	12365	1-0	3-1	1	2	3	4^1	5		7*	8	12	10	11	9^2		6								
Oct 28	A	Torquay	4769	0-1	1-2	1	2	3	4^1	5		7	8	12	10	11	9*		6								
Nov 4	H	Darlington	11394	1-0	3-0	1	2	3	4^1	5		7^1	8	12		11	9^1		6*	10							
Nov 11	A	Crewe	2294	0-0	0-0	1	2	3	4	5		7	8	6		11	9	12		10							
Nov 18	H	Hartlepool	10717	0-0	3-0	1	2	3	4	5^1	12	7	8^1	6		11*	9^1			10							
Nov 25	H	Northampton *FAC1*	13338	0-0	2-0	1	2	3	4	5	12	7^2	8	6		11	9*			10							
Dec 2	A	Northampton	3592	1-0	2-0	1	2	3	4	5		7^1	8	6	12	11	9^1			10*							
Dec 9	H	Huddersfield	11615	1-0	1-0	1	2	3	4	5		7^1	8	6		11	9	12		10							
Dec 16	H	Reading *FAC2*	17195	0-1	0-1	1	2	3	4	5		7	8	6		11	9*	12		10							
Dec 23	H	Reading	12541	2-0	4-0	1	2	3	4^1	5		7^1	8*	9^1	12	11			6	10^1							
Dec 26	A	Wimbledon	7862	1-2	4-2	1	2	3	4	5		7^1	8	6^1		11				10^1	9^1						
Dec 29	A	Stockport	3795	0-1	2-4	1	2*	3	4	5		7	8	6		11^1	12^1	9		10							
Jan 13	H	Rochdale	11595	0-0	1-1	1	2	3	12	5		7	8	9	4	11			6	10^1							
Feb 3	A	Wigan	8289	0-1	0-2	1	2	3	4	5		7*	10	6	8	11	9						12				
Feb 10	H	Bournemouth	12172	0-0	1-1	1	2	3	12	5^1		7	8	6	10*	11					4	9					
Feb 20	A	Newport Co.	8206	1-1	2-1	1	2	3	4	5		7	8	6^1		11		12	9		10^1						
Feb 24	H	Grimsby	12782	0-2	1-3	1	2	3*	4	5		7^1	8	9		11	12		6		10						
Mar 3	A	Halifax	1741	0-2	0-2	1	2		4	5		7	8	6		11	12	3			10	9*					
Mar 10	H	Torquay	8689	0-0	1-0	1	2	3	4	5		7	9	6	12	8					11	10^1					
Mar 21	A	Port Vale	2738	0-0	0-0	1	2	12	4			7	8	6			9		5			10	3	11*			
Mar 24	H	York City	9353	0-0	1-1	1	2			5		7	8*	6			9		12			10^1	3	11			
Mar 28	A	Bradford City	2410	0-0	0-2	1	2			5		7	8	6			9		12			10	3	11			
Mar 30	A	Barnsley	12928	0-0	1-1	1	2			5		7		6^1		8	9					10	3	11			
Apr 3	A	Scunthorpe	1535	1-0	2-2	1	2		4	5			12	6		7	9^2	8				10	3	11*			
Apr 7	H	Northampton	8066	0-0	1-0	1	2*		4	5			12	6		7	9^1	8				10	3	11			
Apr 13	A	Reading	15054	0-1	0-2	1			4*	5		7	8	6	12		9	2				10	3	11			
Apr 14	H	Wimbledon	11453	0-0	0-0	1	2	3		5*		7	8	6	12		9	4				10		11			
Apr 16	A	Newport Co.	5421	0-1	2-1	1	5	3	2				8	6		7	9^1	12			4^1	10		11			
Apr 21	H	Stockport	8177	1-1	1-1	1	2	3	12	5^1			8	6		7	9*	4				10		11			
Apr 24	H	Doncaster	5869	2-0	4-0	1	5	3	2				8^1	6	12	7	9^3	4*				10		11			
Apr 28	H	Huddersfield	2895	0-1	0-2	1	5	3*	2	12		7	8	6	4		9					10		11			
May 5	H	Barnsley	8761	0-1	0-1	1	5	3	2				9	6	8	11	7	4				10*			12		
May 7	A	Hereford	3707	1-0	1-0	1	5	3					8	6	4		9				7^1	10		11	2	12	
May 11	A	Darlington	1140	0-0	0-2	1	5	3					8	6	4		9				7	10		11	2*	12	
May 15	H	Aldershot	6238	1-1	1-1	1	5	3	12				8	6	4		9^1				7	10		11	2		

						Mellor P.	Ellis P.	Viney K.	Denyer P.	Foster S.	Hand E.	Hemmerman J.	Lathan J.	Davey S.	McIlwraith J.	Pullar D.	Garwood C.	Wilson W.	Piper S.	Barnard L.	McCaffrey J.	Showers D.	Milligan L.	Bryant S.	James K.	Roberts T.	Gilchrist P.
League Appearances						46	44	38	39	35	3	37	43	42	16	35	27	15	14	28		19	7	15	3		
League Substitute							1	2	1	2		2	4	3	3	8	3				1	1			1	1	
League Goalscorers							2	6	2	1		14	4	7		1	15	1		7		2					
FA Cup Appearances						2	2	2	2	2		2	2	2		2	2			2							
FA Cup Substitute											1								1								
FA Cup Goalscorers											2																
League Cup Appearances						2	2	2	2	2	2	2	2	1	1	2			1								1
League Cup Goalscorers																	1										1

Totals Division 4   P46 W20 D12 L14 F62 A48 Pts 52 Posn 7th

*Substituted

Season 1979/80   Division 4

Date	Venue	Team	Attendance	FA HT	FA FT	Mellor P.	McLaughlin J.	Viney K.	Brisley T.	Aizlewood S.	Davey S.	Garwood C.	Laidlaw J.	Showers D.	Bryant S.	Rogers A.	Hemmerman J.	Styles A.	Lathan J.	Ellis P.	James K.	Barnard L.	Ashworth P.	Todd K.	Roberts T.	Knight A.	Purdie I.	Perrin S.	Gregory D.	Garner A.	Brown J.
Aug 11	H	Swindon *FLC1*	9978	1-1	1-1	1	2	3	4	5	6	7*	8	9	10	11^1	12														
Aug 14	A	Swindon *FLC1*	9097	0-0	0-2	1	2	3	4	5	6	7	8	9	10	11	12														
Aug 18	A	Hartlepool	3075	1-0	3-0	1	2^1		4	5	6	7^1		9*	10^1	11	12	3	8												
Aug 21	H	Torquay	11430	2-0	3-0	1	2		4	5	6	7^2	8	9^1	10	11	12	3													
Aug 25	H	Scunthorpe	12234	3-0	6-1	1	2		4^1	5	6	7^2	8^1	9	10	11^2	12	3													
Sept 1	A	Wigan	8198	0-1	2-1	1	2		4^1	5	6	7^1	8	9	10	11		3	12												
Sept 8	H	Stockport	14942	1-0	1-0	1	2		4	5	6	7	8^1	9*	10	11	12	3													
Sept 14	A	Tranmere	3550	1-3	1-4	1	2		4^1	5*	6	7	8		10	11	9	3	12												
Sept 18	H	Bournemouth	15524	2-0	4-0	1			4^2	5	6	7	8		10	11	9^2	3			2	12									
Sept 22	A	Rochdale	2423	0-0	2-1	1	2		4	5	6	7^1	8		10*	11^1	9	3		12											
Sept 29	H	York City	14917	2-1	5-2	1	2		4^1	5^1	6	7^2	8^1		10*	11	9	3		12											
Oct 2	A	Bournemouth	13963	1-0	1-0	1	2		4^1	5		7	8		10	11	9	3		6	12										
Oct 6	H	Darlington	16692	2-2	4-3	1	2		4*	5		7^1	8^1		10	11		3		6				9^2						12		
Oct 10	A	Torquay	5525	0-1	1-2	1	2		4	5		7	8		10	11	9^1	3		6										12	
Oct 13	A	Huddersfield	16540	2-0	3-1	1	2		4	5	12	7	8^2		10	11*	9^1	3		6											
Oct 20	H	Bradford C.	23871	3-0	4-1	1			4	5	6	7^1	8		10	11^1		3		2				9^2						12		
Oct 23	H	Newport Co.	20755	0-1	0-2	1	2			5*	12	7	8		10	11	9	3		6		4									
Oct 26	A	Doncaster	9801	0-1	0-2	1	2		4*			5	7	8	10	11	9	3		6				12							
Nov 3	H	Hartlepool	14295	1-1	2-1	1	2		4^1	5	12	7^1	8		10	11	9*	3		6											
Nov 6	A	Newport Co.	7115	2-2	3-4	1	2		4	5	12	7^{1}*	8		10	11	9^2	3		6											
Nov 10	A	Walsall	7468	0-1	1-1	12	3		4	5	6	7^1	8		10	11	9			2						1					
Nov 17	H	Lincoln	14620	1-0	4-0		3		4	5	6	7^{2}*	8^2		10	11				2		9				1	12				
Nov 24	H	Newport Co. *FAC1*	19459	1-0	1-0		3		4^1	5	6	7	8		10	11	12			2		9*				1					
Dec 1	H	Halifax	14087	1-0	3-1	1		3	4^1	5	6	7^1	8^1		10	11	9			2								12			
Dec 8	A	Peterborough	5371	0-0	0-0			3	4	5	6	7	8		10	11	9			2			1						12		
Dec 18	A	Wimbledon *FAC2*	10850	0-0	0-0			3	4	5	6	7*	8		10	11	9			2			1					12			
Dec 21	H	Port Vale	12022	1-1	2-2			3	4	5	6				10^1	11	9			2			1					12		7^1	
Dec 24	H	Wimbledon *§FAC2R*	17265	2-2	3-3			3	4	5	6*		8^1		10^1	11	9			2			1					12		7^1	
Dec 26	A	Hereford	4514	0-0	0-0	1	2			5			8		10		12	3		6		4						11	9	7	
Dec 29	H	Northampton	15579	4-1	6-1		2	3	4	5^1			8^1		10	11^1	9^2			6						1		12		7^1	
Jan 1	H	Aldershot	23462	0-2	1-3		2	6	4*				8		10	11^1	9	3		5						1		12		7	
Jan 5	A	Wimbledon *FAC2(2)R*	7484	1-0	1-0	1	2	3	4				12	8	10	11	9^1			6								5		7	
Jan 9	A	Middlesbro *FAC3*	31743	0-1	1-1	1	2	3	4^1	5			8		10	11	9			6	12									7	
Jan 12	A	Wigan	15625	1-0	1-1	1	2	3	4^1	5	12		8		10	11*	9			6										7	
Jan 14	A	Middlesbro *FAC3R*	22551	0-1	0-3	1	2	3	4	5			9	8	10	11				6*								12		7	
Jan 26	A	Scunthorpe	2609	0-0	0-1	1		3	4	5		7	8		10	11				2					6			9*		12	
Feb 2	H	Tranmere	12821	0-1	1-1		3*		4	5			8		10	11	9			6	2				12^1					7	
Feb 9	H	Rochdale	12207	0-0	3-0	1	2	3		5			8^2		10		9^1			6		4						11	12	7	
Feb 12	A	Crewe A.	3315	1-0	1-1	1	2	3		5			8^1		10		9			6		4						11	12	7*	
Feb 16	A	York City	2589	0-1	0-1	1		3		5			8		10	11	9*			2		4						12	7		6
Feb 23	H	Huddersfield	19203	2-1	4-1	1			4^1	5			8		10	11	9	3		2								12	7^2		6*
Mar 1	A	Bradford C.	9363	0-0	0-0	1	12		4		6		8			11	9	3		2			5					7			10
Mar 8	H	Doncaster	14382	2-0	2-0	1			4^1	5	6		8^1			11	9	3		2								12	7*		10
Mar 10	A	Stockport	2938	1-0	1-1	1*			4	5	6		8		10	11	9^1	3		2								12	7		
Mar 15	A	Darlington	2287	1-0	1-1	1			4	5	6		8		10	11^1	9	3		2					1			12	7		
Mar 22	H	Walsall	21785	0-1	1-2				4		6		8		10	11	9^1	3		2					1			12	7	5*	
Mar 29	A	Lincoln	4682	0-0	0-1	1			4		6		8		10	11	9	3*		2				12				5	7		
Apr 1	A	Port Vale	3614	1-2	3-2	1	2	3	4		6		8^1		10	11	7			5	12							9^1			
Apr 5	H	Hereford	15457	0-0	0-0	1	2	3	4		6		8		10	11	7*			5								9	12		
Apr 7	A	Aldershot	11989	1-0	2-1	1	2	3	4		6		8^1		10*	11	7			5								9^1	12		
Apr 12	H	Crewe A.	13752	0-1	1-1	1	2		4		6		8		10	11^1	7	3*		5								9	12		
Apr 19	H	Halifax	2950	1-0	2-1	1	2		4		6		8		3	11	7^1			5				12				9^1			10
Apr 26	H	Peterborough	15095	2-0	4-0	1	2		4		6		8		3	11^1	7^1			5								9	12		10
May 3	A	Northampton	10774	1-0	2-0	1	2		4		6^1		8		3		7			5								11^1	9	12	10

						Mellor P.	McLaughlin J.	Viney K.	Brisley T.	Aizlewood S.	Davey S.	Garwood C.	Laidlaw J.	Showers D.	Bryant S.	Rogers A.	Hemmerman J.	Styles A.	Lathan J.	Ellis P.	James K.	Barnard L.	Ashworth P.	Todd K.	Roberts T.	Knight A.	Purdie I.	Perrin S.	Gregory D.	Garner A.	Brown J.
League Appearances						38	29	16	41	34	29	23	45	5	44	42	36	18	1	37	2	4	3	1	1	8	4	10	17	3	5
League Substitute								4	1								2			3	1	1	2	1			1	7	4	
League Goalscorers							1		12	2	1	17	16	1	2	9	13					4	1				1	2	5	
FA Cup Appearances						3	3	6	6	5	3	3	6		6	6	4			6	1				3		1	4		
FA Cup Substitute																				1								3		
FA Cup Goalscorers								3					1		1		1											1		
League Cup Appearances						2	2	2	2	2	2	2	2	2	2	2														
League Cup Substitute																	1													
League Cup Goalscorers																1														

Totals Division 4   P46 W24 D12 L10 F91 A49 Pts 60 Posn 4th Promoted!

*Substituted
§After extra time

Own goals: Huddersfield (Feb 23), Port Vale (Apr 1), Peterborough (2) (Apr 26)

Season 1980/81   Division 3

Date	Venue	Team	Attendance	FA HT	FA FT	Mellor P.	McLaughlin J.	Viney K.	Brisley T.	Aizlewood S.	Garner A.	Gregory D.	Laidlaw J.	Tait M.	Barnard L.	Rogers A.	Showers D.	Bryant S.	Ellis P.	Ayrton N.	Perrin S.	Davey S.	Hemmerman J.	Doyle R.	Rafferty W.	Knight A.	Bartlett K.	Croft S.
Aug 9	A	Plymouth *FLC1*	7036	1-0	1-0	1	2	3	4	5	6	7	8¹	9	10	11	12											
Aug 12	H	Plymouth *FLC1*	11997	1-1	2-1	1	2	3	4	5	6	7¹	8	9	10	11¹	12											
Aug 16	A	Barnsley	10253	1-0	2-1	1	2	3	4	5¹	6	7	8	9		11¹	12	10										
Aug 19	H	Swindon	15810	0-0	1-0	1	2	3	4	5	6	7	8¹	9		11	12	10										
Aug 23	H	Rotherham	14767	1-1	3-1	1	2	3*	4	5	6	7¹	8	9		11	12¹	10¹										
Aug 26	A	Oldham *FLC2*	5251	0-2	2-3	1	2		4	5	6¹	7	8¹	10		11	9	3	12									
Aug 30	A	Blackpool	8352	1-0	2-0	1	2	3	4	5	6	7¹	8	12		11	9¹*	10										
Sept 2	H	Oldham *§FLC2*	18548	1-0	1-0	1	2	3	4	5	6	7	8¹			11	9	10	12									
Sept 6	H	Brentford	16971	0-0	0-2	1	2	3	4*	5	6	7	8			11	9	10	12									
Sept 13	A	Walsall	5738	0-1	0-2	1	2	3	4	5	6	7	8			11	9*	10		12								
Sept 16	H	Charlton	12796	0-0	1-0	1	2	3	4	5	6	7	8¹	12		11		10			9							
Sept 20	A	Hull City	4613	1-1	1-2	1	2	3	4¹	5	6	7	8	12		11		10*			9							
Sept 23	A†	Bristol R. *FLC3*	6982	0-0	0-0	1	2	3	4	5	6	7	8	12		11		10			9							
Sept 27	H	Fulham	16460	0-0	1-0	1	2	3	4	5	6	7¹	8	12		11		10			9							
Sept 30	H	Bristol R. *FLC3R*	18965	1-0	2-0	1	2	3	4	5	6	7¹	8	12		11		10			9¹							
Oct 4	H	Chesterfield	14953	1-0	1-0	1	2	3	4	5	6	7*	8			11¹	12	10			9							
Oct 7	A	Colchester	2702	0-0	0-1	1	2	3	4	5	6	7	8	12		11		10			9							
Oct 11	A	Newport	7003	0-2	1-2	1	2	3	4*	5	6¹	7		8	12	11	9	10										
Oct 18	H	Burnley	13459	3-1	4-2	1	2	3	4	5	6	7¹		8¹	12	11¹	9¹	10										
Oct 21	H	Plymouth	15655	1-1	1-3	1	2	3	4*	5	6¹	7		8	12	11	9	10										
Oct 25	A	Oxford	6217	0-1	2-1	1	2	3		5	6	7¹	12	8	4¹	11	9	10										
Oct 28	A	Liverpool *FLC4*	32021	1-2	1-4	1	2	3			6	7*	12	8	4	11	9	10			5							
Nov 1	H	Carlisle	13913	1-0	2-1	1	2	3			6	7¹	12	8	4	11	9¹	10			5							
Nov 4	H	Colchester	10895	1-1	2-1	1	2	3			6	7²	4	8		11	9	10			5	12						
Nov 8	A	Gillingham	6623	0-0	1-0	1	2	3		5	6	7¹	4	8		11	9	10				12						
Nov 11	A	Swindon	8164	0-0	2-0	1	2	3		5	6	7	4¹	8		11	9¹	10				12						
Nov 15	H	Barnsley	14732	0-1	0-1	1	2	3		5	6	7	4	8		11	9	10				12						
Nov 22	A	Colchester *FAC1*	5387	0-1	0-3	1	2	3		5	6		8	4		11	9	10					7	12				
Nov 29	H	Chester	10515	1-0	2-0	1	2	3		5				8¹	4	11¹		10	6		9	12	7*					
Dec 6	A	Sheffield Utd.	12158	0-0	0-1	1		3		5				8	12	11		10	2		9	6	7*	4				
Dec 20	A	Huddersfield	10869	0-0	0-1	1	2	3		5		7		8*		11		10			12	6		4	9			
Dec 26	H	Reading	17412	0-0	0-0	1	2	3		5		7		8		11		10			12	6		4	9			
Dec 27	A	Millwall	8422	0-0	0-0	1	2	3		5		7		8		11		10			12	6		4	9			
Jan 10	H	Sheffield Utd.	14321	1-0	1-0	1	2	3		5		7¹		8		11		10			9	6	12	4				
Jan 14	A	Exeter	3722	0-1	0-2	1	2	3		5		7		8		11		10*				6	12	4	9			
Jan 24	H	Blackpool	13265	2-0	3-3	1	2	3		5*		12		8¹		11		10	6				7¹	4	9¹			
Jan 27	A	Burnley	6683	1-1	3-1	1	2	3						8¹	12	11		10¹	5			6	7¹	4	9			
Jan 31	A	Rotherham	7588	0-1	0-3	1	2	3		5				8*		11		10	6			12	7	4	9			
Feb 7	H	Walsall	11921	1-0	2-0	1	2*	3		5		12		8¹		11		10	6				7	4¹	9			
Feb 10	H	Exeter	12743	1-0	5-0			3		5		12		8³		11		10¹	2			6	7	4	9¹	1		
Feb 14	A	Brentford	10160	1-2	2-2	1		3		5		12		8		11		10*	2			6*	7	4	9²			
Feb 21	A	Fulham	9921	0-1	0-3			3		5		12		8		11		10	2			6*	7	4	9			
Feb 28	H	Hull City	13596	1-1	2-1	1	2	3		5				8		11		10*	6				7	4¹	9¹		12	
Mar 7	A	Chesterfield	6985	0-1	0-3	1	2	3*		5	6			8		11		10			12		7	4	9			
Mar 14	H	Newport	13208	0-0	0-0	1	2	3		5		7		8	10	11						6	12	4	9			
Mar 21	A	Plymouth	6042	0-1	0-1	1	2	3		5		7		8	10	11*						6	12	4	9			
Mar 29	H	Oxford	12243	1-1	1-1	1	2	3		5		7¹		8	10				6	11*			12	4	9			
Apr 4	A	Carlisle	4429	0-0	0-0	1	2	3			6	7		8	10	11							12	4	9			5
Apr 11	H	Gillingham	9172	0-0	0-0	1	2	3			6	7*		8	10	11								4	9	12		5
Apr 14	A	Charlton	8863	0-0	2-1	1	2			5		7		8	10	11		3				12		4	9¹			6¹
Apr 18	H	Millwall	13115	1-1	2-1	1	2			5		7¹		8	10	11		3				12		4¹	9			6
Apr 20	A	Reading	7061	0-2	1-2	1	2			5		7		8*	10	11		3		12¹				4	9			6
Apr 25	H	Huddersfield	10218	1-1	1-2	1	2			5		7		8	10	11		3				12		4¹	9			6
May 2	A	Chester	2153	0-0	1-0	1	2	12		5		7¹		8	10	11		3				6		4	9			
League Appearances						45	42	41	14	41	23	35	15	36	15	45	12	41	14	1	8	12	12	25	22	1		6
League Substitute											3				2	3		2		1	1	3	2	2			2	
League Goalscorers							1	1		2	13	3	8	1		4	5	3			1		2	4	6			1
FA Cup Appearances						1	1	1		1	1		1	1		1	1	1					1					
League Cup Appearances						7	7	6	6	6	7	7	6	4	3	7	3	5			2	1						
League Cup Substitute													1														
League Cup Goalscorers											1	2	3				1				1							

Totals Division 3   P46 W22 D9 L15 F55 A42 Pts 53 Posn 6th

*Substituted

†at Ashton Gate
§After extra time
Own goal: Liverpool (Oct 28)

Season 1981/82 Division 3

Date	Venue	Team	Attendance	FA HT	FA FT	Knight A.	McLaughlin J.	Viney K.	Kamara C.	Aizlewood S.	Rollings A.	Gregory D.	Doyle R.	Rafferty W.	Berry S.	Rogers A.	Hemmerman J.	Tait M.	Ellis P.	Barnard L.	Cropley A.	Leworthy D.	Crown D.	Garner A.	Bryant S.	Bason B.	Bartlett K.	Sullivan C.	Wimbleton P.	Senior T.	Gosney A.
Aug 29	H	Lincoln	10698	0-0	1-1	1	2	3	4	5	6	7	8*	9¹	10	11	12*														
Sept 2	A	Southend *FLC1*	4087	0-0	0-0	1	2	3	4	5	6	7	8	9	10	11	12														
Sept 5	A	Preston	6112	0-1	0-1	1	2	3	4	5	6*	7	8	9	10	11		12*													
Sept 12	H	Brentford	10364	0-0	2-2	1	2	3	4	5			8	9¹	10*	12*	7¹	11	6												
Sept 16	H	Southend *FLC1*	10019	2-1	4-1	1	2	3	4¹	5			8¹	9¹	10¹	12*	7	11	6*												
Sept 19	A	Southend	4355	0-1	0-2	1	2	3	4	5			8	9	10		7	11	6*	12*											
Sept 23	A	Oxford Utd.	4750	1-0	2-0	1	2	3	4	5			8¹	9¹	10	12	7	11	6												
Sept 26	A	Bristol City	10203	1-0	2-0	1	2	3	4	5			8	9	10¹	12	7	11¹	6												
Sept 29	H	Exeter	10989	2-0	2-0	1	2	3	4	5			8*	9¹	10	12*	7¹	11	6												
Oct 3	A	Chesterfield	6150	1-0	2-2	1	2	3	4*	5			8	9	10	12*	7¹	11¹	6												
Oct 6	A	Q.P.R. *FLC2*	13502	0-1	0-5	1	2	3	4		5		9	12	10		7	11	6												
Oct 10	H	Burnley	9891	0-1	1-2	1	2	3	4	5			8¹*	9		11	7	10	6		12*										
Oct 17	A	Walsall	4408	0-1	1-3	1		3	4	5	6		8	9	12¹*		7	10	2		11*										
Oct 20	A	Gillingham	5546	2-1	2-4	1		3	4	5	6		8	9¹	10¹	11*	12*		7	2											
Oct 24	H	Newport	8787	0-0	0-0	1		3		5	6	11	8	9¹			7	10	2	4		12									
Oct 27	H	Q.P.R. *FLC2*	7677	2-1	2-2	1		3		5	6	12*	8¹	9¹*			7	11	2	4	10										
Oct 31	A	Fulham	7542	0-0	1-1	1		3		5	6		8	9			7¹	11	2	12	10	4									
Nov 3	H	Wimbledon	9063	0-0	1-0	1		3			6	12*	4	9*			7	8	2	10¹		11	5								
Nov 7	A	Plymouth	6275	0-0	0-0	1		3		5	6		8	4	9		7	10	2			11									
Nov 14	H	Carlisle	8858	0-1	1-2	1		3		5	6	10	4			8	11	7¹	2		9				12						
Nov 21	H	Millwall *FAC1*	10113	1-0	1-1	1	2			5	6	4			12	7¹	8	9	10	11	3										
Nov 25	A	Millwall *§FAC1R*	6842	0-2	2-3	1	2			5	6	4			12*	7¹	9¹	8	10*	11	3										
Nov 28	H	Huddersfield	8155	1-1	2-1	1	2			5	6	4			12	7	9	8	10	11	3										
Dec 5	A	Doncaster	5912	0-0	0-0	1	2			5	6	4			12*	7	9	8	10	11*	3										
Dec 22	H	Southampton *HPC*	6649	1-1	2-1	1□	2	16		5	6	4	12*	14*		7¹	9*	15	8*	10	11¹	3								13□	
Dec 26	H	Bristol Rovers	11395	0-0	0-0	1	2	3		5*	6	4	12*			7	9	8	10	11										
Jan 6	H	Reading	4018	1-2	1-2	1	2				6	4	12*			7*	9¹	8		11	5	3	10								
Jan 19	A	Chester	1444	1-1	2-3	1	2			5	6	4¹	12			7¹	9	8		11		3	10								
Jan 23	A	Lincoln	3297	0-0	1-1	1	2			5	6	4	12*			7	9¹	8		11*		3	10								
Jan 30	H	Southend Utd.	7731	0-0	0-0	1				5	6	4	12*			7	9	2	8	11*		3	10								
Feb 6	A	Brentford	5950	1-1	2-2	1	2			5	6¹	4	8			7	9¹			12		11	3	10							
Feb 9	H	Oxford Utd.	7095	1-1	1-1	1	2			5¹	6	4*	8			7	9		12*			11	3	10							
Feb 13	H	Chesterfield	8046	2-1	5-1	1	2			5¹	12*	4	8³				9	7*		11¹	6	3	10								
Feb 20	A	Bristol City	9397	0-0	1-0	1	2			5*			8¹			7	9	4		11	6	3	10	12*							
Feb 23	A	Swindon	4860	0-1	0-2	1	2					9	4	8			12*	5	7	11	6	3	10*								
Feb 27	A	Burnley	7024	0-1	0-3	1	2					9	7	8	11*			10	5	4	12*	6					3				
Mar 6	H	Walsall	7133	1-0	1-0	1	2			5¹		9	7	8			12	10	6	4	11						3				
Mar 9	H	Gillingham	6711	1-0	1-0	1				5*		9	7	8¹			12*	10	2	4	11	6					3				
Mar 13	A	Newport	4209	1-0	1-1	1	2			5	9		8	7				10	6	4	11¹						3	12			
Mar 20	H	Fulham	10712	1-0	1-1	1	2			5			8¹	7*				10	6	4	11						3	12*	9		
Mar 27	H	Plymouth	9551	0-0	1-1	1	2			5			4	8¹	7			10	6		11*						3	12*	9		
Apr 3	A	Carlisle	3919	0-2	0-2	1	2			5*			4	8	7			10	6		11						3	12*	9		
Apr 6	H	Preston N.E.	6712	1-0	1-1	1	2						4	8¹	7		12		6		11	5					3	10	9		
Apr 10	A	Bristol Rovers	4833	1-1	1-1	1	2				9		4	8¹	7			10	6			5					3	11			
Apr 12	H	Reading	8427	2-0	3-0	1	2						4¹	8	10	11		6	7*	5							3	12*	9²		
Apr 17	H	Doncaster	8657	0-0	0-0	1	2			5			4	8	10	11		6			12*						3	7*	9		
Apr 24	A	Huddersfield	5658	0-0	1-0	1	2			6	5		4	8¹	10	11	12*										3	7*	9		
Apr 27	H	Aldershot *HPC Final*	3821	0-0	1-0	1	2			6	5¹		4	8	10	11	7	9	12								3		13		
May 1	H	Chester	6196	0-0	1-0	1	2			6	5		4¹	8¹	10	11	7	9									3	12			
May 5	A	Exeter	2596	1-2	3-3	1*	2			6	5		4	8¹	10	11	7	9²	12*								3				
May 8	A	Millwall	4969	0-1	0-1		2			6	5		4		10	11	7	9	8								3			1	
May 15	H	Swindon	6372	2-0	3-0	1	2			6	5		4		10	11	7³	8									3	9			
May 18	A	Wimbledon	2642	1-1	2-3	1	2			6			4¹	9	10	11	7¹	5				8					3	12			
May 21	H	Millwall	4902	1-0	2-2	1				6			4²	12	10	11	7	5	2		8						3	9			
League Appearances						45	36	24	11	36	19	11	43	35	26	14	29	35	31	16	7		25	10	11	9		18	4	9	1
League Substitute											2			4	1	5	5	1	1	2			2	2				1	4		
League Goalscorers								3	1				8	15	2			11	8				2	2						2	
FA Cup Appearances						2	2			2	2		2	2						2	2		2	2	2	2					
FA Cup Substitute																					1										
FA Cup Goalscorers													2	1																
League Cup Appearances						4	3	4	3	3	3	1	4	4	2	2	3	3	3	1	1										
League Cup Substitute								1																						
League Cup Goalscorers										1			2	2	1															

Totals Division 3   P46 W14 D19 L13 F56 A51 Pts 61 Posn 13th

*Substituted
HPC Hampshire Professional Cup
§after extra time

Season 1982/83   Division 3

Date	V	Team	Attendance	HT	FT	Knight A.	McLaughlin J.	Sullivan C.	Doyle R.	Howe E.	Aizlewood S.	Webb N.	Tait M.	Rafferty W.	Biley A.	Rogers A.	Ellis P.	Thomas D.	Crown D.	Senior T.	Berry S.	Ross T.	Rollings A.	Morgan N.	Dillon K.	Gosney A.	Wood P.	Pearce J.	Davies M.	Ball K.	McNab N.
Aug 28	H	Sheffield Utd.	13361	1-1	4-1	1	2	3	4	5¹	6	7¹	8¹	9*	10¹	11	12*														
Aug 31	A	C. Palace *MCI*	6631	0-0	0-2	1	2	3	4	5	6		8	9	10	11	7*		12*												
Sept 4	A	Walsall	2922	1-0	3-0	1	2	3	4	5	6	7*	8¹	9¹	10¹	12*	11														
Sept 8	A	Exeter City	3146	0-1	1-1	1	2	3	4	5	6		8	9¹	10	12*	7*	11													
Sept 11	H	Wrexham	10867	1-0	3-0	1	2	3	4	5	6		8¹	9	10²	12	7	11													
Sept 14	H	C. Palace *MCI*	10698	1-1	1-1	1	2	3	4	5		8	9	10¹*	7	6	11		12*												
Sept 18	A	Oxford	9918	1-1	1-1	1	2	3	4¹	5	6		8	9	10	12	7	11													
Sept 25	H	Newport Co.	10833	0-0	1-2	1	2	3	4	5	6		8	9	10¹	12*	7	11*													
Sept 28	H	Millwall	7615	0-0	2-0	1	2	3	4	5	6	7	8	9¹	10¹	11	12														
Oct 1	A	Southend Utd.	4589	0-1	0-4	1	2	3	4	5	6	7	8	9	10	11	12														
Oct 9	A	Huddersfield	6243	1-1	1-1	1	2	3	4	5	6	7	8	9	10¹	11		12													
Oct 16	H	Bournemouth	10961	0-0	0-2	1	2	3	4	5	6*	7	8		10	11	9		12*												
Oct 19	A	Wigan	4504	0-0	1-0	1	2	3	4	5		7	8	9	10¹	11	6	12													
Oct 23	H	Preston N.E.	10331	1-1	3-1	1		3	4		5	8	6	9³	10	11	7	12				2									
Oct 30	A	Cardiff C.	7082	0-0	0-1	1		3	4		5	8	6	9	10	11	7	12				2									
Nov 2	H	Lincoln	12529	2-1	4-1	1		3	4	5	6	7	8	9¹	10³	11	12					2									
Nov 6	H	Gillingham	12212	0-0	1-0	1		3	4	5	6	7	8	9	10	11¹	12					2									
Nov 13	A	Bristol R.	9389	0-3	1-5	1		3	4	5	6	7	8	9¹	10	11	12*					2*									
Nov 20	H	Hereford *FAC1*	10005	2-0	4-1	1	2	3	4	5	6	7	8	9²	10²	11	12														
Nov 27	A	Doncaster R.	9474	2-1	2-1	1	2	3	4	5	6¹	7¹	8	9	10	11	12														
Dec 4	A	Bradford C.	4961	0-2	2-2	1	2	3	4	5		7	8	9	10²	11	12			6											
Dec 11	H	Aldershot *FAC2*	13250	1-2	1-3	1	2	3*	4	5		7¹	8	9	10	11			12*	6											
Dec 18	A	Chesterfield	2440	0-0	1-0	1	2	3*	4	5		7	8¹	9	10	11	12*			6											
Dec 27	H	Brentford	14476	1-1	2-1	1	2	3	4	5	6	7	8	9	10	11			12		8¹										
Dec 28	A	Reading	7646	0-0	2-1	1	2	3	4	5	6¹	7		9*	10¹	11	8		12*												
Jan 1	H	Plymouth A.	15856	2-0	2-1	1	2	3	4	5	6*	7¹	8	9	10	11	12*														
Jan 15	A	Sheffield Utd.	12907	0-0	1-2	1		3	4	5	6¹	7	8	9	10	11	12					2									
Jan 18	A	Orient	3961	0-1	1-2	1		3	4	5	6	7	8	9¹	10	11	12*					2*									
Jan 22	H	Oxford	10882	1-0	1-0	1		3	4	5	6	7	8	9¹	10*	11	12*					2									
Jan 29	A	Wrexham	3007	0-0	2-0	1	2	3	4	5	6	7	8	9¹	10¹	11	12														
Feb 1	A	Aldershot *HPC SF*	1132	3-1	4-2	1	2	3	4	5¹	6¹	7	8	9	10¹	11*	12*														
Feb 6	A	Millwall	5621	1-0	2-0	1	2	3	4	5	6	7¹	8¹	9	10	12	11														
Feb 12	H	Exeter	10622	2-0	3-2	1	2	3	4	5¹	6	7	8¹	9	10¹	11	12														
Feb 16	A	Lincoln	6311	1-0	3-0	1	2	3	4	5*	6¹	7	8	9²	10	11	12*														
Feb 22	H	Huddersfield	18615	3-0	3-2	1	2	3	4		6¹	7²	8	9	10	11	12						5								
Feb 26	A	Bournemouth	13406	1-0	2-0	1	2	3	4		6¹	7	8	9	10¹	11	12*						5*								
Mar 1	H	Wigan	16139	0-0	0-0	1	2	3	4			7	8		10	11	6		12*	9*			5								
Mar 5	A	Preston N.E.	5610	0-0	0-0	1		3	4		6	7	8	9	10	11	12					2	5								
Mar 12	A	Cardiff C.	24354	0-0	0-0	1		3	4		6	7	8	9	10	11						2	5								
Mar 19	H	Gillingham	6489	0-0	0-1	1	2	3	4		6	7	8	9*	10	11	12*						5								
Mar 26	H	Bristol R.	17828	1-0	1-0	1	2	3			6	7	4		10¹	11	12						5	9	8						
Apr 1	A	Brentford	12592	0-1	1-1	1	2	3	4		6	7	5		10	11	12							9¹	8						
Apr 2	H	Reading	15327	1-1	2-2	1	2	3			6	7	4		10	11	12						5	9	8²						
Apr 9	H	Bradford C.	12198	0-1	0-1	1		3*	4		6	7	5	9	10	11	12*					2			8						
Apr 16	A	Newport Co.	10419	0-0	3-0	1	2*	3	4		6	7	5	9²	10¹	11	12*								8						
Apr 19	H	Bournm'th *HPC Fin.*	2621	0-0	1-3			3	5	4*	11	8								6°	9¹					1	7	13°	12*	2	10
Apr 23	H	Chesterfield	13003	1-0	4-0	1		3	4		6	7	5	9*	10¹	11¹	12*								8²						
Apr 30	A	Doncaster	2974	1-0	2-0	1	2	3	4		6*	7¹	5	9¹	10	11	12*								8						
May 2	H	Orient	16232	0-0	2-2	1	2	3	4		6	7	5	9¹	10¹*	11	12*								8						
May 7	H	Southend	18356	1-0	2-0	1	2*	3	4		6	7	5	9	10¹	11	12*								8¹						
May 10	H	Walsall	22244	1-0	1-0	1		3	4		6¹	7	5	9	10	11	12					2			8						
May 14	A	Plymouth A.	14173	0-0	1-0	1		3	4		6	7	5	9	10¹	11	12					2			8						
League Appearances						46	32	46	44	27	42	42	44	41	46	40	16	9		2		5	10	3	11						
League Substitute																	2		10	4	1	1		3							
League Goalscorers								1	2		7	8	6	17	23	2	1							1	5						
FA Cup Appearances						2	2	2	2	2	1	2	2	2	2	2				1											
FA Cup Substitute																			1												
FA Cup Goalscorers												1		2	2																
Milk Cup Appearances						2	2	2	2	2	1	1	2	1	2	2	2	1													
Milk Cup Substitute																			2												
Milk Cup Goalscorers														1																	

Totals Division 3   P46 W27 D10 L9 F74 A41 Pts 91 Posn 1st Champions

*Substituted
HPC Hampshire Professional Cup

Own goal: Plymouth (Jan 1)

Season 1983/84   Division 2

Date	Venue	Team	Attendance	FA HT	FA FT	Knight A.	Ellis P.	Sullivan C.	Doyle R.	Tait M.	Money R.	Webb N.	Dillon K.	Hateley M.	Biley A.	Rogers A.	Morgan N.	Gosney A.	Aizlewood S.	Thomas D.	Howe E.	McLaughlin J.	Wood P.	Hindmarch R.	Wimbleton P.	Ball K.	Stanley G.	Waldron M.	Hardyman P.
Aug 27	H	Middlesbrough	17547	0-1	0-1	1	2	3	4	5	6	7	8	9	10	11	12												
Aug 31	A	Hereford *MC1*	4631	1-1	2-3		2	3	4	5	6	7	8^{1}	9^{1}	10	11	12	1											
Sept 3	A	Fulham	10672	1-0	2-0	1	2	12	4	5	3	7	8	9^{1}	10^{1}	11			6										
Sept 6	H	Barnsley	12804	1-0	2-1	1	2	12	4	5	3	7^{1}	8	9^{1}	10	11			6										
Sept 10	H	Manchester City	18852	1-2	1-2	1	2		4	5	3	7	8		10	11		9^{1}	6	12									
Sept 13	H	Hereford *MC1*	8363	2-1	3-1	1	2		4	5	3	7	8		10	11	12		6										
Sept 17	A	Cardiff	9033	0-0	0-0	1	2		4	5	3	7	8		10	11		9			12	6							
Sept 24	H	Shrewsbury	11909	1-1	4-1	1			4	5	3	7	8^{1}	9^{1*}	10^{1}	11	12^{1*}		6			2							
Sept 27	A	Crystal Palace	8486	0-1	1-2	1			4	5	3	7	8	9	10^{1}	11	12		6			2							
Oct 1	A	Newcastle Utd.	25411	0-3	2-4	1			4	5^{1}	3	7	8	9	10^{1}	11^{*}	12^{*}		6			2							
Oct 4	H	Aston Villa *MC2*	18484	1-0	2-2	1			4	5	3	7^{*}	8	9	10	12^{*}	11		6			2							
Oct 8	A	Brighton	17582	1-0	1-0	1	12		4	5	3	7	8	9	10	11^{1}			6			2							
Oct 15	H	Sheffield Wed.	16335	0-0	0-1	1	12		4	5	3	7	8	9	10	11			6			2							
Oct 26	A	Aston Villa *†MC2*	20898	1-0	2-3	1			4	5	3	7	8^{1}	9	10^{1}	11	12^{*}		6^{*}			2							
Oct 29	A	Leeds United	16254	0-1	1-2	1	12	3	4	5		7	8	9	10	11^{1}					6	2							
Nov 1	H	Cambridge Utd.	10852	2-0	5-0	1		3	4	5^{1}		7	8	9^{3}	10	11	12					2			6^{1}				
Nov 5	H	Grimsby	12906	2-0	4-0	1		3	4	5^{1}		7	8	9^{3}	10	11	12^{*}					2^{*}			6				
Nov 12	A	Carlisle	4814	0-0	0-0	1	12^{*}	3	4			7	8	9	10	11^{*}				5		2			6				
Nov 19	A	Blackburn	5512	1-0	1-2	1	12^{*}	3	4			7^{1}	8	9	10	11				5^{*}		2			6				
Nov 26	H	Oldham	11444	0-4	3-4	1		3		5		7^{1}	8	9	10^{1}	11	4					2		12	6^{1}				
Dec 3	A	Huddersfield	8724	0-1	1-2	1	12	3	4	5		7	8	9^{1}	10							2	11		6				
Dec 10	H	Derby	11834	2-0	3-0	1		3	4	5		7	8^{1}	9	10^{1*}		12^{1*}					2	11			6			
Dec 17	A	Swansea	6404	0-1	2-1	1		3		5		7	8^{1}	9^{1}	10		12^{*}					2	11			6	4^{*}		
Dec 26	H	Charlton	15331	2-0	4-0	1	3			5		7^{1}	8	9^{1}	10^{1}		4^{1}				6	2	11				12		
Dec 27	A	Chelsea	25440	2-2	2-2	1	3		4	5		7	8^{1}	9^{1}	10		12^{*}				6	2^{*}	11						
Dec 31	H	Fulham	15649	1-2	1-4	1	2	3	4	5		7	8	9	10						6		11						
Jan 2	A	Shrewsbury	4907	0-1	0-2	1		3	4	5		7	8	9	10		12^{*}		6		11^{*}				2				
Jan 7	H	Grimsby *FAC3*	12707	0-0	2-1	1	2	3	4	5		7	8	9^{1}	10^{*}		12^{1*}		6		11								
Jan 14	A	Middlesbrough	7971	0-0	0-0	1		3	4	5			8					10	6		11^{*}		2	9	12^{*}	7			
Jan 21	H	Cardiff	11938	0-1	1-1	1		3	4	5			8^{1}	9	10	11			6				2		12^{*}	7^{*}			
Jan 28	H	Southampton *FAC4*	36000	0-0	0-1	1		3	4	5		7	8	9	10	11	12		6			2							
Feb 4	H	Newcastle Utd.	18686	0-2	1-4	1		3	4	5		7^{1}	8	9	10				6			2	11		12			
Feb 11	A	Manchester City	23138	1-0	1-2	1		3	4	5		7	8	9	10				6			2	11^{1}		12			
Feb 18	A	Leeds United	13911	2-1	2-3	1		3		5		7	8	9^{1}	10^{1}				6			2	11		12	4		
Feb 25	A	Cambridge Utd.	4359	2-0	3-1	1	12	3		5		7	8	9^{2}	10^{1}	11			6			2				4		
Mar 3	A	Grimsby	8729	2-2	4-3	1		3	4	5		7	8^{2}	9^{1}	10^{1}		12		6							11		
Mar 10	H	Carlisle	10748	0-0	0-0	1		3	4	5		7	8	9	10		12^{*}		6							11^{*}	2	
Mar 17	A	Barnsley	7030	1-0	3-0	1		3	4	5		7^{1}	8	9^{1}	10		12									11	6	
Mar 24	H	Crystal Palace	10237	0-1	0-1	1		3	4	8	7			9	10	11			6^{*}							2		5	12^{*}
Mar 31	H	Brighton	12723	0-1	5-1	1		3	4^{1}		6	7^{1}	8^{1}	9^{1}	10^{1}		12				11					2	5	
Apr 7	A	Sheffield Wed.	20239	0-1	0-2	1		3	4		6	7		9	10						11					2	5	8	12
Apr 14	A	Blackburn	8915	2-0	2-4	1		3	4	8	6	7^{2}		9	10^{*}						11					2	5	12^{*}	
Apr 21	A	Charlton	6328	1-0	1-2	1			4	10	6	7	8^{*}			9^{1}							12^{*}		11	2	5		3
Apr 24	H	Chelsea	18660	0-1	2-2	1		3	4	11	6	7	8^{1}	9	10^{1}							12^{*}				2	5		
Apr 28	A	Oldham	3558	1-1	2-3	1		3	4	11	6	7^{1}		9^{1}	10							12^{*}				8^{*}	5		
May 5	H	Huddersfield	7738	1-0	1-1	1		3	4	6		7	8	9^{1}	10								11			2	5	12	
May 9	A	Derby	10189	0-0	0-2	1		3	4	6		7		9	10								11			2	5	12	8
May 12	H	Swansea	7359	2-0	5-0	1		3	4^{*}	6		7		9^{1}	10^{3}	12^{1*}							11			2	5	8	

						Knight A.	Ellis P.	Sullivan C.	Doyle R.	Tait M.	Money R.	Webb N.	Dillon K.	Hateley M.	Biley A.	Rogers A.	Morgan N.	Gosney A.	Aizlewood S.	Thomas D.	Howe E.	McLaughlin J.	Wood P.	Hindmarch R.	Wimbleton P.	Ball K.	Stanley G.	Waldron M.	Hardyman P.
League Appearances						42	10	30	37	36	16	40	36	38	37	13	16		22	12	8	33	7	2	1	1	11	12	2
League Substitute							2										1	9		2					1	1		1	1
League Goalscorers								1	3			10	9	22	16				9			2	1						
FA Cup Appearances						2	1	2	2	2		2	2	2	2	1			2	1		1							
FA Cup Substitute																		1										
FA Cup Goalscorers														1					1									
Milk Cup Appearances						3	2	1	4	4	4	4	4	4	4		1	1	3			2						
Milk Cup Substitute																		1	1									
Milk Cup Goalscorers												1	3	2	2													

Totals Division 2   P42 W14 D7 L21 F73 A64 Pts 49 Posn 16th

*Substituted
†After extra time

Own goal: Aston Villa (Oct 4)

Appendix 1a

Appearances and Goalscorers for the first twenty seasons, August 1899 to May 1920. Assorted cup games are shown as one total. ONE figure shown in parentheses (0) is a substitute appearance.

Abbreviations:

Am	= Amateur	Sc	= Scotland
En	= England	Wa	= Wales
Ir	= Ireland	Int.	= International

The appearance and goalscoring figures in Appendix 1a are meant purely as a guide, regrettably, the statistics for games played during the 1914–18 war were unavailable and are therefore incomplete.

Players name	Birthplace & date	Date signed	Years played	Int. player	League appearances	Goals	Cup & Fr appearances	Goals	Position	Previous club	Left Pompey	Club joined
F. Abbott			1915–16				3 Fr	2 Fr	RH			
J. Abbott			1915–16		1 SWC				RH			
Shirley Abbott	Alfreton	Summer 1913	1913–20		40 S 5 SA 12 LC 2 SWC	3 S 2 SWC	3 Cup 16 Fr	5 Fr	H/FB	Derby	21.5.23	Q.P.R.
Michael J. Allman	1885	Summer 1907	1907–08		1 S 4 W	2 W	1 Cup 2 Fr	2 Fr	HB	Burslem Port Vale Reading		Plymouth
J. Anderson			1903–04		4 S 4 W		1 Cup 1 Fr		H/FB	W'wich Arsenal		
W. Andrews			1916–17		1 LC				CH			
Archibald			1904–06		1 S 1 W		2 Fr		LB	Royal Navy Depot		
James Armstrong	Blayden	24.12.13	1913–20		42 S 2 SWC 2 SA 16 LC 3 SHWL	18 S 2 SWC 9 LC	4 Cup 21 Fr	20 Fr	CF	Scotswood		Sheffield Wed.
George Arnold	West Hartlepool	28.9.12	1912–20		62 S 5 SWC 13 SA 11 LC 14 SHWL	2 S 1 SWC 1 SA 3 SHWL	3 Cup 40 Fr	7 Fr	F/HB	Southend		
E. Ashton			1912–13		2 SL				OL		Summer 1913 £30	
E. Ashton			1917–18				1 Fr		OL			
J. Ashton			1917–18				1 Fr		OL			
E. Aston			1916–17				1 Fr	1 Fr	OL			
D. Axford			1904–05		4 S 8 W	3 W	1 Cup 1 Fr	1 Fr	CF	Hearts	2.5.05	Hearts
G. Bailey			1916–17		1 LC				RH			
H. Bailey			1916–17		2 LC				RB/LH			
J.R. Bainbridge	1880	Summer 1906	1906–07		25 S 4 W	4 S 1 W	2 Cup 2 Fr	1 Cup	OR	Reading	Summer 1907	Southampton
E. Baker			1916–17		1 LC				CF			
B. Baldwin			1911–12				1 Fr	2 Fr	IL			
Banks			1908–09		5 S 1 W		3 Cup		RH			
George Barnes	Liverpool 1878		1899–1900		8 S 5 SDC	1 S 3 SDC	1 Fr	1 Fr	OL	Darwen Bolton W.	2.5.1900	New Brighton Tower
H. Barton			1916–17		2 LC				RB			
J. Barton			1916–18		3 LC 2 SHWL				RB			
Jasper Batey	1891	5.11.12	1912–13		3 S 2 SA	2 S			CF	Coventry South Shields	8.10.13	Brighton
William E. Beaumont	Aston, Lancs. 1883	–.9.07	1907–10		70 S 15 W	2 S	7 Cup 6 Fr	1 Cup	HB	Swindon	22.10.10 £75	Southampton Died 19.11.11
Frank Bedingfield 'Beddy'	Sunderland 1877	4.5.1900	1900–02		37 S 21 W	28 S 22 W	5 Cup 8 Fr	3 Cup 5 Fr	CF	Aston Villa Q.P.R.	Died 5.11.04	
E. Bell		21.2.11	1910–11		4 S	2 S			IR	Exeter		

Players name	Birthplace & date	Date signed	Years played	Int. player	League appearances	Goals	Cup & Fr appearances	Goals	Position	Previous club	Left Pompey	Club joined
James Bellamy	1885	6.11.07	1907–08		17 S / 5 W	5 S / 1 W	3 Cup / 1 Fr	1 Cup / 2 Fr	OR	Reading / W'wich Arsenal		Motherwell
E. Biddlecombe			1916–19		1 LC / 1 SHWL		1 Cup / 1 Fr		Goal	RNB		
J. Bingham			1916–17		1 LC				RH			
Thomas Birtles	Barnsley 1885	–.9.07	1906–10		80 S / 16 W	10 S / 2 W	6 Cup / 8 Fr	3 FR	OR	Barnsley / Swindon		
Robert Blyth	Glenbuck 1871		1899–1904		97 S / 26 W / 11 SDC	3 S / 1 W / 1 SDC	17 Cup / 14 Fr	1 Cup	WH	Rangers / Dundee / Preston		
William Blyth (Brother of Robert)			1903–05		28 S / 16 W		1 Cup / 4 Fr	1 W	HB			
Victor Bolitho					1 W				OL			
Adam Bowman		5.11.09	1909–10		19 S	9 S	3 Cup / 1 Fr	2 Cup	CF	Brentford	Exchanged for W. McCafferty	
Thomas Bowman			1904–10		85 S / 59 W	3 S / 2 W	11 Cup / 5 Fr		RB	Southampton		Eastleigh Railway
William Bradley	1892	9.3.12	1912–13		11 S / 6 SA		1 Cup		Goal	Jarrow Caledonians	20.4.14 £250	Newcastle
C.E. Brawn	1883		1908–09		1 W		1 Cup / 1 Fr		OR	Wolves / Gainsborough		
H. Brooks			1917–18		1 SHWL				LB			
J. Brooks			1917–18				2 Fr		OR			
Brown			1906–07				1 Fr		OL			
Brown			1919–20				1 Fr		RB			
Alexander 'Sandy' Brown	Glenbuck 1878	Re-signed 1.5.1902	1899–1903	Sc	49 S / 15 W / 8 SDC	39 S / 11 W / 2 SDC	9 Cup / 13 Fr	4 Cup / 10 Fr	CF	Preston / Tottenham H.	2.5.1900 / 2.5.1903	Tottenham H. / Middlesbrough
A.C. Brown			1907–09		9 S				Goal	Southampton / Cowes (Am)	30.11.10	Southampton
John 'Jock' Brown			1899–1900		6 S / 7 SDC	1 S / 3 SDC	1 Fr	1 Fr	CF	Sunderland / Hearts		
Thomas Brown (brother of 'Sandy')		13.11.03	1903–04		3 S / 7 W	2 S / 1 W			CF			
T.H. Brown	Darlington		1919–20		5 S	1 S	2 Fr		OL			
R. Brownlee			1918–19		1 SHWL		1 Fr		OL			
Harold Buckle	Belfast 1882		1906–07	Ir	15 S / 2 W	3 S	2 Cup / 1 Fr	1 Cup / 1 Fr	OL	Cliftonville / Sunderland	Summer 1907	Bristol Rovers
E. Buddery			1916–17		1 LC		1 LC		CF			
Harold Buddery	Sheffield 1892	Summer 1913	1913–20		70 S / 3 SA	27 S / 2 SA	4 Cup / 3 Fr	1 Cup / 1 Fr	CF	Doncaster	21.11.21	Southend Utd.
T. Buddery			1916–17		2 LC		1 LC		IR			
Albert Thorogood Buick	Arbroath	11.5.03	1903–11		227 S / 46 W	7 S	26 Cup / 11 Fr	3 Fr	CH	Arbroath / Hearts		
Bundy			1918–19				2 Fr		Goal	7th Middx. Football Batt.		
Charles Burgess	Montrose	6.5.01	1901–03		42 S / 25 W		7 Cup / 11 Fr		RB	Millwall / Newcastle		
James Burnett			1902–04		13 S / 7 W	9 S / 8 W	3 Cup / 6 Fr	3 Cup / 2 Fr	CF		Summer 1904	Dundee
H. Burnham			1919–20				1 Fr		OL			
Sgt.Mj. J. Caddick	Birmingham –.7.1889		1915–16				1 Fr	1 Fr		Bristol Rov.		
John Cameron	1887	28.10.07			22 S / 8 W		6 Cup / 2 Fr		Goal	Glasgow Rangers		
Duncan Campbell			1904–05		5 S / 8 W		1 Cup		RB/H	Glasgow Rangers		
Carmichael			1915–16		1 SWC		1 SWC					
Pte. J. Carr			1916–17		18 LC	7 LC			OL			

Players name	Birthplace & date	Date signed	Years played	Int. player	League appearances	Goals	Cup & Fr appearances	Goals	Position	Previous club	Left Pompey	Club joined
Arthur Chadwick		9.5.01	1901–04	En	43 S 27 W	9 S 3 W	10 Cup 8 Fr	2 Cup	CH	Burton Swifts Southampton		Northampton
George William Chapman	Elsecar		1919–20		1 S		1 Fr		CF	Barnsley Bradford		
J. Chesser			1914–15		1 S				LB	Stockton		
George W. Churchill			1908–09		4 W		1 Fr		LH		4.9.09	Merthyr Town
H. Clarke 'Nobby'	Walsall 1875		1899–1901		54 S 11 W 11 SDC	13 S 5 W 2 SDC	10 Cup 16 Fr	3 Cup 6 Fr	OL/R	Everton		
Thomas Cleghorn	Leith 1871		1899–1902		60 S 22 W 9 SDC		6 Cup 17 Fr		LH	Blackburn Liverpool		
Frederick Clipstone	Geddington 1892	Summer 1907	1907–10		45 S 10 W		6 Cup 5 Fr		FB	Kettering Thurs. Northampton	Summer 1910	Northampton Died 3.7.20
Cobden			1902–03				1 Fr	1 Fr	IR			
Coles			1917–18		1 SHWL	1 SHWL			CF			
E. Collins			1916–19		11 LC 5 SHWL		1 Cup 16 Fr		Goal			
Frederick William Cook		Summer 1905	1905–08		31 S 13 W		2 Cup 6 Fr		Goal	W.B.A.	Summer 1908	
G. Roger Cooke			1903–05		1 S		1 Fr		LH			
Thomas Cooke			1899–1900		1 SDC		1 Fr		IR			
W. Cookson	Blackpool 1882	Summer 1906	1906–07		2 W		1 Fr		CF	Blackpool Bristol City Wellingboro Brentford		
J. Cooper			1918–19				1 Fr		CH			
W. Cooper		Summer 1907	1907–08		1 W		2 Fr	1 Fr	HB	Barnsley		
Thomas Cope	Bilston 1882	Summer 1909	1909–11		79 S		7 Cup 5 Fr		Goal	Chesterfield		
Thomas Corrin	1880	6.5.01	1901–03		16 S 8 W	4 S	6 Cup 9 Fr	1 Cup 4 Fr	OL	Everton		
Cotton			1899–1900		1 SDC				OR			
Frank Count	Wombwell (Sheffield)	5.12.08	1908–11		10 S 4 W		1 Cup 3 Fr		FB		Summer 1911	Rotherham
Crago			1918–18				1 Fr		OL	S.A.R.B.		
C. Craig			1918–19		1 SHWL		1 Cup		LH			
J. Croad			1916–17		2 LC	1 LC			IL			
R. Croft	Newcastle 1890	Summer 1911	1911–12		3 S		3 Cup 7 Fr		FB	Newcastle		
Croal			1917–18				1 Fr	1 Fr	CF			
H. Crosson			1916–17		1 LC				IR			
Crout			1917–18				1 Fr		OL			
J. Crutchley		29.11.19	1919–20		1 S		1 Fr		CH	Halesowen		
J. Cullen	1889	Summer 1911	1911–12		7 S	9 S	3 Cup 7 Fr	3 Fr	CF	Newcastle		
Cummings			1913–14		1 SA				CF			
Cummins			1917–18				1 Fr		OL			
Daniel Cunliffe	Bolton 1877	Re-signed 2.5.01	1899–1906	En	174 S 70 W 12 SDC	98 S 38 W 9 SDC	28 Cup 22 Fr	12 Cup 21 Fr	I/OR	Oldham Liverpool	2.5.1900 25.12.06	New Brighton Tower New Brompton
C. Cutts			1916–17		1 LC				OR			
Robert Dalrymple	Paisley 1881		1906–07		31 S 4 W	8 S	5 Cup 2 Fr	1 Fr	IR	Hearts Plymouth Rangers	28.1.11	Clapton Orient
M. Danagher			1913–18		2 SA 9 SHWL	1 SA 5 SHWL 10 Fr		4 Fr	FWD			
Darling			1901–02		2 S				Goal			

Players name	Birthplace & date	Date signed	Years played	Int. player	League appearances	Goals	Cup & Fr appearances	Goals	Position	Previous club	Left Pompey	Club joined
Davis			1913–14		1 SA				Goal	Clapton Orient		
Charles Dexter			1912–14		14 S 18 SA				FB	Sheffield Wed.		Brighton
E. Didymus			1904–06		2 W		2 Fr	1 Fr	FWD		4.9.09	Blackpool
Harold 'Digger' Digweed			1899–1909		139 S 38 W 2 SDC	2 S	15 Cup 8 Fr		RH	Plymouth		
Joseph Dix	Geddington 1886	13.4.06	1906–18		92 S 21 W 1 LC	22 S 6 W	16 Cup 13 Fr	2 Cup 8 Fr	IF	Kettering	Summer 1910	Clapton Orient
J. Docherty			1916–17		1 LC				CH			
J. Dodds			1916–17		1 LC				CH			
Wally Dorans			1919–20				2 Fr		LH			
Dowling			1918–19		1 SHWL				IR			
Michael Dowling	Jarrow 1889	Summer 1911	1911–13		42 S 6 SA	8 S	7 Cup 9 Fr	1 Cup	OR	Sheffield Wed.		
W. Dryden		29.1.14	1913–14		14 S 2 SA	6 S 2 SA			CF	Watford		
Dunbar			1917–18				1 Fr		RB			
Dunn			1904–05				1 Fr	3 Fr	CF			
A. Duncan	1891	Summer 1911	1911–13		13 S 2 SA		1 Cup 7 Fr	1 Fr	OL	Cambuslang		
Dyre			1918–19		1 SHWL				LB			
C. Edgington		Summer 1912	1912–13		1 SA				IL	Ripley Ath.		
A.E. Elston	Liverpool 1882		1906–08		19 S 7 W	5 S	3 Cup 4 Fr		OL	Aston Villa		
S. Eltringham			1913–14		1 SA				LB			
J. Emerson			1915–16		1 SWC				LB			
Emery			1917–18		2 SHWL				RB/LH			
J. Evans			1918–19				3 Fr	1 Fr	OR			
Farwood			1917–18		1 SHWL				CH			
Finns			1916–17		1 LC				IR			
H. Flannigan			1915–17		2 SWC 1 LC		1 SWC 2 Fr 1 LC	1 Fr	O/IL			
R.F. Floyd			1918–20				2 Fr		Goal			
William Ford			1904–05		6 S 5 W		3 Cup 1 Fr		OR	Motherwell	28.4.05	West Ham Utd.
Foyle		9.2.06	1905–07		1 W		1 Fr		CF			
H.J. Frampton			1919–20				(1) Cup		RB		Summer 1921	
Freeman			1911–12				1 Fr		OR			
Charles Burgess Fry	Croydon 25.4.1872	–.–.02	1902–03	En	1 S 1 W		1 Cup		FB	Corinthians	Died 7.9.56	
D. Gair			1902–03				3 Fr		LB		3.8.03	Burton Utd.
Thomas Galloway		14.3.13	1912–14		3 S 1 SA		2 Fr		RH	Preston Stockport		
Gardiner			1919–20				1 Fr		IR			
W.G. Garnett			1918–19				1 Fr		Goal	Army Ordnance		
Adam Gibson		26.8.12	1912–14		2 S 4 SA	1 SA			IR/L	Glasgow Rangers	1.6.13	St. Mirren
D. Gibson			1912–14		2 SA				OL			
E.R. Gill			1918–19		2 SHWL		4 Fr		Goal			
G. Gill			1915–16				1 Fr		Goal			
L. Gill			1917–19		6 SHWL	1 SHWL	7 Fr	2 Fr	OL			
Gisborne			1908–09				1 Fr		CH			
Gisborne			1919–20				1 Fr		OR			
E. Gisborne			1916–17		2 LC				CH			

Players name	Birthplace & date	Date signed	Years played	Int. player	League appearances	Goals	Cup & Fr appearances	Goals	Position	Previous club	Left Pompey	Club joined
Alfred Gittins		15.12.10	1910–11		4 S				IF	Aston Villa Fulham		
Alec Glen	Kilsyth 1880	Summer 1907	1907–08		7 S 6 W	1 S 7 W	2 Fr		IF	Southampton Tottenham H. Grimsby Notts Co.		Brentford
T. Goodacre			1916–17				1 Fr		OL			
Goodwin			1917–18				1 Fr		CH			
W. Goss	Nottingham		1900–01		1 S 2 W	1 W	1 Fr		IL	Notts Co.		
T. 'Dolly' Gray		25.9.14	1913–17		4 S 2 SWC 1 SA 5 LC		9 Fr		Goal			
W. Gray			1916–17		2 LC				Goal			
Green			1919–20				1 Fr		OL			
A. Green			1917–18				4 Fr	1 Fr	CH			
A.C. Green			1917–18				1 Fr		LH			
E. Green			1917–19		9 SHWL	4 SHWL	9 Fr	5 Fr	OL			
H. Green			1918–19				1 Fr		LH			
J. Green			1918–19		5 SHWL	2 SHWL	7 Fr		LH			
Leslie Greenwell		9.3.12	1911–13		3 S 1 SA	1 S 2 SA	1 Cup 1 Fr	1 Fr	CF	Seaham Utd.		
Sgt. D. Grey			1916–17		5 LC	1 LC			OR			
Grier		7.4.09	1908–09		2 S				OL	Paisley		
Griffiths			1914–15				1 Fr		IR			
R. W. Guy		Summer 1909	1909–10		3 S		1 Cup 2 Fr	1 Fr	OR	Bradford City Leeds City Hastings	Summer 1910 £25	
Thomas Hakin			1909–10		19 S	7 S	1 Cup 1 Fr	1 Cup	CF/IR	Plymouth Grimsby Mexborough		
Hall			1899–1900		1 SDC				IL			
Alex N. Hall		Summer 1910	1910–11		12 S	3 S	2 Cup 3 Fr	1 Cup 1 Fr	CF	Peterhead Newcastle Dundee		
J. Hall		7.11.13	1913–14		5 SA	1 SA			CH			
David A. Halliday	Portsmouth 1876		1899–1909		3 S 6 W		8 Fr	1 Fr	CH	Ryde		
A. Hamilton			1918–19		4 SHWL		1 Cup 1 Fr		RH			
F. Hamilton	1890	28.9.12	1912–14		20 S 9 SA		1 Cup		CH	Aberdare		
J. Hamilton			1912–13		2 SA				FB			
Hammond			1914–15		1 S				CH			
Hanaway			1918–19				1 Fr		RB			
Sgt. D. Hanna			1899–1900	Ir	1 SDC		1 Fr		RH	Portsmouth RA		
Sgt. Harms			1899–1900		1 S		1 Fr		Goal	Portsmouth RA		
Harris			1918–19				1 Fr		RH			
Harris			1919–20				1 Fr		IL			
George 'Bogey' Harris		7.11.01	1901–06		60 S 32 W		9 Cup 5 Fr		Goal	Grimsby		
Stanley Shute Harris		23.9.05	1905–07	En 6 S Am 2 W	4 S 1 W				IL	Corinthians	Died 4.5.26	
C. Harvey			1917–18				4 Fr	5 Fr	FWD			

Players name	Birthplace & date	Date signed	Years played	Int. player	League appearances	Goals	Cup & Fr appearances	Goals	Position	Previous club	Left Pompey	Club joined
Jack Harwood	Somerstown	1.3.13	1913–20		112 S 3 SWC 7 SA 15 LC 16 SHWL	4 SHWL	5 Cup 46 Fr	5 Fr	CH	Chelsea Southend	24.5.22 Free	Swansea
Gunner J. Hawkins			1916–17		2 LC				RH	RMA		
G. Frederick Haycock	1887	Summer 1909	1909–10		28 S	7 S	2 Cup 3 Fr	1 Cup 1 Fr	IF	Luton Crewe W.B.A.	Summer 1910 £50	
J.W. Heath	Sunderland	24.9.13	1913–14		24 S 9 SA		1 Cup		Goal	Houghton Rovers		
J. Hemstock	Stenton Hill (Notts.)	15.12.11	1911–12		7 S	3 S	1 Cup 4 Fr	1 Fr	IL	Hull		
William Hickleton			1905–07		11 W		3 Fr		R/CH		1.11.07	Northampton
Hill			1899–1900		1 SDC				CH			
Hirst			1904–05		1 W				LH	RMLI		
Joseph Hisbent	Plymouth 1884		1906–08		8 W		6 Fr	2 Fr	H/FB	Aston Villa		Brentford
J. Hobbs			1917–18		1 SHWL				OR			
John Hodge		22.5.02	1902–03		1 W		3 Fr		OR	Celtic		
James Hogg	West Calder	13.5.03	1903–04		26 S 10 W		2 Cup 3 Fr		FB	Hibernian		
J. Hogg	1890	Summer 1911	1911–12		1 S		8 Fr		F/HB	Bentley, Scot.		
James Hogg	Sunderland 1892	Summer 1913	1913–19		60 S 6 SWC 9 SA 13 LC 21 SHWL	10 S 2 SWC 2 SA 1 LC 5 SHWL	7 Cup 42 Fr	14 Fr	OR/L	South Shields	9.11.21	Guildford Utd.
Arthur Holden	Fareham (Hampshire)		1903–06		8 S 12 W	1 W	1 Cup 6 Fr	1 Fr	OL			
Hollings			1918–19		1 SHWL				RH			
H. Hollingsworth			1917–19				5 Fr		C/LH			
A. Holmes			1915–16				2 Fr		OL	Coventry		
Albert E. 'Kelly' Houlker		5.5.02	1902–03	En	23 S 15 W	1 S	4 Cup 6 Fr		HB	Blackburn R.	1.5.03	Southampton
J. Howard			1917–18		5 SHWL	2 SHWL			CH			
Hughes			1919–20				1 Fr		LB			
Hughes		Summer 1905	1905–06		1 W		2 Fr	1 Fr	RH	Liverpool		
E. Hughes			1917–18				1 Fr	1 Fr	CF			
T. Hughes			1917–18				4 Fr	3 Fr	CF			
J. Hulme			1916–17		1 LC				LH			
W. Hulme			1916–17		4 LC				IF			
Jack Hunt		Summer 1910	1910–13		18 S	5 S	2 Cup 7 Fr	6 Fr	IL	Camberley		
George Hunter	Peshawar (India) 1890		1919–20		8 S		1 Fr		HB	Aston Villa Manchester Utd.		
John 'Jock' Hunter			1899–1901		24 S 10 W 8 SDC	2 S 1 W 1 SDC	5 Cup 5 Fr	1 Cup	HB	Troon Preston		
John 'Sailor' Hunter		Summer 1905	1905–07		37 S 21 W	10 S 2 W	5 Cup 4 Fr	2 Cup 5 Fr	IF	W'wich Arsenal 8.5.07		Dundee
Hurley			1905–06				1 Fr		LH			
Robert Jackson			1912–13		3 SA	1 SA			RH	Ripley Ath.		Brentford
Richard W. Jackson	1878	2.5.05	1905–07		2 S 11 W		2 Fr		H/LB	Ripley Ath.		
F. James			1916–17		1 LC				LB			

Players name	Birthplace & date	Date signed	Years played	Int. player	League appearances	Goals	Cup & Fr appearances	Goals	Position	Previous club	Left Pompey	Club joined
William E. James	Stockton 1882	Summer 1913	1913–20		92 S 7 SWC 7 SA 15 LC 7 SHWL	35 S 7 SWC 4 SA 6 LC 3 SHWL	8 Cup 25 Fr	4 Cup 24 Fr	CF	Middlesbrough	21.1.21	West Ham Utd.
Jameson			1917–18				1 Fr		IR			
A. Jewet			1917–18				1 Fr		CH			
George Johnson		Summer 1913	1913–14		3 S 10 SA		1 Cup		FB	Clapton Orient Chelsea		
Jones			1915–16		2 SWC	2 SWC						
Sgt. F. Jones			1916–17				1 Fr		OR			
J. Love Jones	1887	Summer 1911	1911–13	Wa	35 S 6 SA	12 S 3 SA	6 Cup 9 Fr	1 Cup 2 Fr	OL	Middlesbrough		
J.M. Jones			1916–17		3 LC	1 LC			CF			
L. Jones			1915–16		1 SWC				OR			
William Joyce	1877	4.5.1900	1900–01		21 S 10 W	13 S 6 W	1 Cup 8 Fr	11 Fr	CF	Morton Bolton Tottenham Thames Ironw'ks		
F.W. Kean			1917–18				1 Fr		IL			
J. Key			1916–17		1 LC				LH			
P. Killigan			1916–17		1 LC				LH			
Kimber			1904–05				1 Fr	1 Fr	IL			
Kimpton			1918–19				1 Fr		CH			
William 'Sunny Jim' Kirby		4.9.05	1904–11		224 S 41 W	81 S 22 W	27 Cup 13 Fr	8 Cup 6 Fr	CF	Swindon West Ham Utd.		Preston
Arthur Egerton Knight	Godalming 1888	1908	1909–20	En 157 S Am 4 SA			13 Cup 9 Fr	1 Cup	LB			Corinthians Died 10.3.56
Albert J. Knight	Portsmouth 1889		1907–10		1 S 6 W		1 Cup 3 Fr	3 Fr	IR			Reading
Langhorne			1901–02		1 S				LH			
Lee			1914–15				1 Fr		Goal			
A. Lee			1915–16		1 SWC				CH			
Pte. J. Lee			1916–17		1 LC	1 LC			CF			
T. Lee			1916–17		2 LC				FWD	A.S.C.		
William Lee		7.5.04	1904–06		47 S 20 W	18 S 7 W	5 Cup 2 Fr	2 Cup 1 Fr	CF	W.B.A.		New Brompton
Leggatt			1907–08				1 Fr		IL			
John Lewis		4.5.1900	1900–01	Ir	11 S 10 W	5 S 2 W	4 Fr	3 Fr	IR	Bristol Rovers		Brighton
A. Lines			1908–09				1 Fr		LB			
Albert Lockyer			1901–03				1 Cup 3 Fr		IL			
E. Long	1888	28.10.08	1908–11		39 S 5 W	9 S	7 Cup 5 Fr	3 Cup 1 Fr	OL	Trowbridge T.	10.5.11 £50	Bristol Rovers
Lionel A. Louch		23.11.07 Am	1907–13		49 S 1 W 1 SA	22 S	3 Cup 2 Fr	1 Cup 1 Fr	IF	Shepherds Bush		Clapton Orient
Louis			1900–01		1 W				OL			
Zechariah G. March	Chichester		1915–16				1 Fr		OR	Brighton		
Marshall		28.8.07	1907–08				1 Fr		RH	Bittern Guild		
Marshall			1919–20				1 Fr		RH			
A.G. Marshall	Liverpool 1880	22.5.03	1903–04		1 S				FB	Crewe Leicester Fosse Manchester Utd.		
Robert G. Marshall	1876		1899–1904	Sc	136 S 55 W 14 SDC	17 S 11 W 2 SDC	22 Cup 31 Fr	5 Cup 5 Fr	OR	Leith Liverpool	Summer 1904	Brighton

Players name	Birthplace & date	Date signed	Years played	Int. player	League appearances	Goals	Cup & Fr appearances	Goals	Position	Previous club	Left Pompey	Club joined
George Martin		7.9.12	1912–13		12 S 6 SA	1 S 2 SA	1 Cup	1 Cup	HB	Sunderland	Summer 1913 £120	Norwich City
Matthews			1917–18				1 Fr	1 Fr				
H. 'Wobbly' Matthews		20.12.13	1913–14		1 S 1 SA	1 SA			CF	RMA Portsmouth		
William McAuley		3.5.01	1901–02		11 S 9 W	5 S 6 W	2 Cup 1 Fr		IF	Celtic Walsall Sheffield Wed. Aston Villa		
Gunner H. McBain			1916–17		1 LC				LH			
Neil McBain			1916–17		11 LC	2 LC	4 Fr	1 Fr	IL			
William McCafferty	1884	7.2.08	1907–10		45 S 7 W	13 S 4 W	9 Cup 2 Fr	2 Fr	CF/IL	Bathgate Reading Bolton Celtic	5.11.09 Exchanged for A. Bowman	Brentford
Alex McDonald		15.3.02	1901–03		7 S 5 W	7 S	1 Cup 7 Fr	2 Fr	CF	West Ham Utd.		
E. McDonald		7.5.04	1904–09		147 S 48 W	13 S 4 W	21 Cup 6 Fr	2 Cup 2 Fr	LH	Notts Co.		
Thomas McDonald	1887		1908–09		28 S 10 W		5 Cup 1 Fr		Goal	Motherwell		
R. McGough			1915–16		1 SWC				CH	Newcastle Utd.		
Robert McGregor			1914–15				1 Fr		CF	Sheffield Wed.	5.2.15 released from contract to join up	
Peter McIntyre	Glenbuck	1.11.02	1902–03		1 S 3 W		4 Fr		CH	Preston Sheffield Utd.		
E. McIntyre			1909–10		4 S		2 Fr		HB			
Jock McKay			1915–19		20 SHWL	12 SHWL	1 Cup 21 Fr	5 Fr	OL			
McKenzie			1899–1900		1 SDC				IL			
J. McKenzie		8.2.07	1906–07		6 S	1 S			CF	Sunderland Plymouth Third Lanark		
McKinley			1919–20				1 Fr		CF			
McKinnon			1918–19				1 Fr		LH			
Edward McMahon	1885		1908–11		42 S 5 W	2 S 1 W	8 Cup 5 Fr	3 Cup	IR	Cowdenbeath Bathgate	Summer 1911	Brentford
Meader			1918–19				1 Fr		IR			
James 'Jemmy' Menzies	1887	Summer 1911	1911–13		48 S 5 SA	1 S	7 Cup 11 Fr		HB	Albion Rovers	£75	
A. Mercer			1917–18				3 Fr	2 Fr	LH			
J. Mercer			1916–17		3 LC				RH			
G.W. Metcalf			1914–15		1 S				HB	Merthyr		
F. Middleton			1915–19		2 SWC 3 LC 6 SHWL		11 Fr		Goal			
W.L. 'Mickey' Mieczbikowski			1900–02		5 S 2 W	2 S			OL			
J. Miller			1917–18				1 Fr		RB			
W. Miller			1915–16				1 Fr	2 Fr	IR	Brighton		
George Molyneax		Summer 1905	1905–06	En	23 S 13 W		3 Cup 1 Fr		FB	Southampton		Southend
Frank Moore			1899–1900		2 S				OL			
Moore			1917–18				2 Fr	2 Fr	IL			
A. Morris			1918–19				1 Fr		RH			
S. Mouncher			1912–13		1 SA				OR			
Arthur Mounteney	Belgrave, Leics 11.2.83	26.12.12	1912–17		33 S 10 W 6 SA 3 LC	11 S 3 SA 1 LC	2 Cup	1 Cup	IR	Grimsby	Died 1.6.33	

Players name	Birthplace & date	Date signed	Years played	Int. player	League appearances	Goals	Cup & Fr appearances	Goals	Position	Previous club	Left Pompey	Club joined
Thomas 'Paddy' Murray			1903–13		23 S 9 W 2 SA	4 S	2 Cup 1 Fr		FB	Southend	21.2.13 Exchanged for S. Young	Airdrie
J. Neal			1916–17		2 LC				Goal			
J. Neil			1914–15		31 S		1 Cup		Goal			
F. Newman			1916–17		1 LC				IL			
J. Newman			1916–17		1 LC				RH			
Thomas Newton	Wyton-on-Tyne 24.10.19		1919–20		2 S				Goal	Clapton Orient Croydon Comm.		
N. Nicholson			1907–08		1 W				IL			Brentford
Robert Noble	1890		1910–11		31 S	3 S	2 Cup 3 Fr	1 Fr	OR	Rangers Carlisle	Summer 1911	Accrington Stanley
William Nurthen		27.1.11	1910–11		1 S				Goal	Romford	21.8.11	Southend
O'Donnell			1919–20				1 Cup		Goal			
James O'Gara	1888	6.11.11	1911–12		1 S				OR	Dundee Hibernian		
J. 'Patsy' O'Hara		27.1.14 Am.	1916–17		1 LC				CF	Navy		
R. Orsmond			1918–19		1 SHWL				IL			
D. E. Page			1918–19				2 Fr		CH	Croydon Comm.		
F. Pagnum			1916–17		7 LC	2 LC			CF	Liverpool		
Parker			1918–19				1 Fr		OR			
V. Parsons			1905–07		3 W		1 Fr		CF			
Thomas H. Pearce	London	15.12.11	1911–12		1 S		1 Cup 1 Fr		OR		9.9.13 £15	
J. Pettifer			1916–17		4 LC				CH			
George Philip	1880	Summer 1906	1906–08		39 S 11 W		5 Cup 3 Fr		Goal	Hearts		
Jack Platt	Preston 1880		1903–05		8 S 11 W	1 S 4 W	2 Fr	3 Fr	CF/IR	Preston Kettering		
William Porteous			1904–05		13 S 10 W	6 S 1 W	1 Cup 1 Fr		OR	Hearts		
R. Porter			1918–19		3 SHWL		3 Fr		LH			
W. E. Porter		17.3.03	1902–03				1 Fr		IR	Weymouth		
Joseph E. Potts			1914–20		28 S 4 SWC 12 LC	1 S	2 Cup 13 Fr		FB	Hull		
A. Powell			1918–19				1 Fr		RH			
Harold Powell	1889	Summer 1913	1912–14		17 S 7 SA	9 S 1 SA			CF	Rotherham T.		Boscombe
H. Powell			1916–17		1 LC				IR			
P. Powell			1916–17		1 LC				CH			
T. Powell			1916–17		1 LC				CH			
B. Priestley			1916–17		1 LC				LB			
H. Priestley	Portsmouth		1915–20		2 S 2 SWC 5 LC 19 SHWL	1 SHWL	3 Cup 35 Fr	1 Fr	LB		Summer 1922 Free	
S. Priestley			1916–17		3 LC				LB			
Prince			1918–19				1 Fr		RH			
William Probert	Worksop 1893	Summer 1911 Re-signed Summer 1914	1911–20		17 SHWL 69 S 2 SA 3 SWC 20 LC	1 LC	7 Cup 42 Fr	4 Fr	FB	Worksop	7.11.13 Summer 1925	Southend
Pyne			1908–09		2 W				RH/LB			

Players name	Birthplace & date	Date signed	Years played	Int. player	League appearances	Goals	Cup & Fr appearances	Goals	Position	Previous club	Left Pompey	Club joined
Joseph Quinn			1913–19		4 S 3 SA 1 LC 6 SHWL	1 SHWL	3 Fr	3 Fr	OL			
A. Randall	1894	Summer 1913	1913–14		1 SA				HB	Durham		
E. Randall	1882	Summer 1907	1906–08		1 W		7 Fr	15 Fr	CF	Accrington Birmingham Northampton Southampton		
J. Rankin			1916–17		1 LC				IR			
Gunner Reed			1916–17		1 LC				LH			
Vernon Reeves			1910–12		8 S	3 S	2 Fr		IR			
Robert Reid	Scotland	Summer 1911	1911–14		72 S 17 SA	1 S 1 SA	8 Cup 13 Fr	1 Fr	WH			
William Reid	1888		1908–09		32 S 8 W	27 S 8 W	5 Cup 1 Fr	5 Cup 2 Fr	CF	Morton Motherwell	Summer 1910	Glasgow Rangers
Mathew 'Ginger' Reilly	Donnybrook, Dublin 1874	Summer 1899	1899–1904	Ir	138 S 53 W 15 SDC		21 Cup 31 Fr		Goal	Portsmouth RA		Dundee
Rhodes			1917–18				1 Fr		LB			
J. Richardson			1915–16		2 SWC		1 Fr	1 Fr	IF			
Bertie Riddle			1918–20				2 Fr		OR			
J. Robertson			1914–15		1 S	1 S	1 Fr		IR	Paisley– St. Mirren		
W. Robertson			1914–15		7 S		1 Cup 1 Fr	1 Fr	HB			
E. R. 'Ned' Robson	Hexham		1919–20		37 S		2 Cup 3 Fr		Goal	Watford	Summer 1922	Sunderland
Frederick Rollinson			1911–13		32 S 6 SA	8 S 4 SA	4 Fr 1 Cup	4 Fr	IR		8.10.13	Luton
Rothwell			1917–18				2 Fr		OL			
Arthur G. Rule		3.11.02	1903–04		3 S 2 W	2 S 1 W	1 Cup	2 Cup	CF		12.1.05	Ryde
B. Rutledge			1918–19				1 Fr	1 Fr	CF	RMA		
G. Ryman			1916–18		1 LC 5 SHWL	1 SHWL	13 Fr		LH			
W. Ryman			1915–16		1 SWC				LH			
W. Rymark			1915–16		1SWC				LH			
Harold Salter			1903–16		4 S 4 W	2 S	5 Fr 1 Cup	5 Fr	I/OR			New Brompton
Daniel Sanderson (brother of R. Sanderson)	1890	Summer 1911	1911–20		65 S 10 SA 2 LC		7 Cup 11 Fr		Goal	Albion Rovers		
R. Sanderson			1916–17		1 LC				RH			
Scott			1917–18				1 Fr		IR			
D. Scrimgeour	1895	23.4.13	1912–14		1 SA	2 SA	1 Fr	1 Fr	CF	Hibernian		
Corp. Frederick E. Shaw		Summer 1913	1913–18		18 S 8 SA 8 LC 1 SHWL	2 S 1 SA 2 LC 1 SHWL	1 Cup		OL	Hull City		
Jack Shufflebotham	Macclesfield 1888	Summer 1909	1909–11		21 S	2 S	4 Cup 3 Fr		CH	Oldham	Summer 1911 £15	Southport Central
Simms			1918–19				1 Fr		IR			
Sims			1917–18				1 Fr		IR			
A. Simms			1916–17		1 LC				IR			
E. Simms			1916–17		1 LC	1 LC			IR			
F. Simms			1916–17		1 LC	1 LC			IR			
H. Simms			1916–17		1 LC				IR			

Players name	Birthplace & date	Date signed	Years played	Int. player	League appearances	Goals	Cup & Fr appearances	Goals	Position	Previous club	Left Pompey	Club joined
Sgt. W. Simms			1916–17		1 LC	1 LC			IR			
J. Simpson			1916–17		1 LC				IR			
John William Smelt	Rotherham		1919–20		8 S (3 in Goal)	2 S	1 Fr		Goal/ FWD	Rotherham County	Summer 1921	Sheffield Wed.
Smith			1905–06				1 Fr		RH			
"Smith"			1917–18				1 Fr		OR			
F. Smith			1902–03				1 Fr		OL			
G. Smith			1918–19				1 Fr		CH			
Jack Smith		21.10.08	1908–10		6 S 5 W		1 Cup 2 Fr		FB	Blackburn	23.8.10	Reading
Stephen Smith		9.5.01	1901–06	En	136 S 65 W	14 S 4 W	16 Cup 13 Fr	2 Cup 2 Fr	OL	Hednesford Aston Villa		New Brompton
Stephen Smith Jr.			1915–18		1 SHWL	1 SHWL	5 Fr	2 Fr	OL			
William Smith (brother of Stephen Snr.)	Hednesford Staffordshire		1899–1917		233 S 90 W 13 SDC 1 LC	75 S 30 W 5 SDC	33 Cup 38 Fr	10 Cup 27 Fr	IL	Wolverhampton	Summer 1908	Gosport Utd.
F. Harry Sparrow			1909–11		5 S		1 Cup		CF			Croydon Comm.
T. Spink			1917–18				8 Fr	2 Fr	OR			
N. Starks			1915–16		1 SWC				OR			
F. Stemp			1917–18				1 Fr		CH			
Peter Stemp	Portsmouth		1913–14		2 S 2 SA				Goal			
Stent			1918–19		1 SHWL				CH			
Stevens			1918–19				2 Fr		LB			
Stevens			1919–20				1 Fr		LH			
C. Stevens			1916–17		2 LC		3 Fr		CH			
C. Stevens			1919–20				1 Fr		LB			
L. C. Stevens			1916–17		1 LC				RH			
Thomas Worsley Stewart		2.5.05	1905–06		1 W		1 Cup 2 Fr		RB	Sunderland	23.5.07	Clapton Orient
Frank Stringfellow	Sutton	Summer 1911	1911–20		153 S 5 SWC 17 SA 4 LC 10 SHWL	65 S 2 SWC 2 SA 13 SHWL	14 Cup 44 Fr	4 Cup 39 Fr	IR	Sheffield Wed.	24.5.22	Hearts
Harold Stringfellow	Burscough 1877		1899–1904		132 S 52 W 10 SDC	2 S 1 W	19 Cup 20 Fr		CH	Southport Central Everton	Summer 1904	Swindon
Robert Struthers			1899–1901		22 S 11 W 3 SDC		2 Cup 2 Fr		FB	Liverpool Gravesend	22.5.01	Bolton W.
Sturgess			1900–01				1 Fr		LB			
J. Swan			1916–17		1 LC				IR			
Tamer			1916–17		1 LC				CF			
B. Tattum			1914–15		20 S	1 S	1 Fr		OL	Merthyr		
Taylor			1903–05		5 S 1 W				RH			
E. Taylor			1919–20		2 S	1 S	2 Fr	3 Fr	CF			
Harold 'Jimmy' Taylor	1890	12.2.12	1912–13		28 S 6 SA	23 S 5 SA	1 Cup 7 Fr	6 Fr	CF	Barnsley	Summer 1913 returned home illness.	
W. Taylor	Earlstown Lancs		1919–20		1 S				RH			
Ernest Thompson	Rotherham	Summer 1913	1913–20		83 S 6 SA	2 S 1 SA	4 Cup 4 Fr		I/OR	Rotherham South Shields	28.5.21	Sheffield Wed.
Frederick Thompson			1904–05		8 S 10 W		1 Cup 1 Fr		Goal	Luton	4.5.05	Crystal Palace
L. Thompson			1918–19				4 Fr		IL			

Players name	Birthplace & date	Date signed	Years played	Int. player	League appearances	Goals	Cup & Fr appearances	Goals	Position	Previous club	Left Pompey	Club joined
R. Thompson			1918–19		1 SHWL		4 Fr		RH			
A. Thomson	1883		1908–09		1 S				OL	Hearts		
James Hunter Thomson (brother of A. Thomson)	Shetland 1884		1906–11		140 S 12 W	2 S 1 W	18 Cup 6 Fr		FB	Leith Hearts	19.6.11	Coventry
Sgt. Thornton			1916–17		1 LC				IR	R.F.C.		
J. Tilley			1916–17		1 LC				CF			
S. Timpson			1918–19		1 SHWL		1 Fr		Goal			
J. Tomlinson	Chesterfield 1881		1906–07		5 S 5 W		1 Cup 1 Fr		OR	Chesterfield W'wich Arsenal Southampton		
E. Tompkins			1916–17		2 LC	1 LC			RH			
Tout			1917–18		1 SHWL				LH			
C. S. Trapp			1917–19		3 SHWL		1 Cup 3 Fr		Goal	Air Force		
Turner			1913–14		1 SA				Goal			
A.E. Turner		14.10.10	1910–11		11 S				OL	Milton Ath.		
Edward Turner 'Old Hookey'	Skerton Lancs 1877	4.5.1900 Re-signed 23.8.02	1899–1903		42 S 5 W 11 SDC		8 Cup 13 Fr		FB	Everton		Northampton Luton
Harold Turner	Birmingham 1877	Re-signed 2.5.01	1899–1903		32 S 21 W 5 SDC		7 Cup 11 Fr		FB	Portsmouth RA 2.5.1900		New Brighton Tower
Joseph Turner	Leyland 1894	4.1.14	1914–20		44 S 4 SWC 1 SA 20 LC 24 SHWL	8 S 9 SWC 5 LC 32SHWL	46 Fr 6 Cup	72 Fr 4 Cup	IF	Preston		
R. W. Turner			1910–11		34 S	6 S	3 Cup 1 Fr	1 Fr	IL	Leicester Fosse	29.8.11	Leyton
T. 'Solly' Upton		Summer 1913	1913–17		17 S 2 SA 1 LC	2 S	2 Cup 3 Fr		OL	Kettering Tottenham H.		
Roderick Walker			1904–08		109 S 39 W	9 S 3 W	12 Cup 8 Fr		FB	Motherwell	8.5.08	Hearts
James Walls	1892	5.11.12	1912–15		69 S 14 SA	1 S	4 Cup 1 Fr		RH		Summer 1919	Glasgow Rangers
A. Warden	Leyland		1919–20		2 S		1 Fr		RH			
A. Wardle			1915–16		1 SWC				CH			
Alexander C. Wardrope	Stewarton Ayrshire 1886	Summer 1911	1911–17		29 S 4 LC		5 Cup 14 Fr		CH	Airdrie Middlesbrough		
Jack Warner	Preston 1883	Summer 1906	1906–15		227 S 14 W 17 SA	10 S 1 W 2 SA	21 Cup 21 Fr	2 Fr	FB	Preston Southampton	Died –.5.48	
Joseph Warrington		2.5.05	1905–06		13 S 9 W	3 S 1 W	2 Cup 1 Fr		OR	Brentford Derby	25.12.06	New Brompton
David Watson	Bannockburn Cowie		1919–20		2 S		1 Fr		IF	Falkirk Bo'ness		
John Whalley	Bradford		1917–18		6 SHWL	12SHWL	2 Fr	3 Fr	IL	C. Palace		
George Frederick Wheldon	Langley Green Birmingham 1.11.1869		1902–04	En	32 S 18 W	11 S 14 W	5 Cup 8 Fr	4 Cup 6 Fr	IL	Small Heath W.B.A. Aston Villa	Summer 1904	Worcester City Died 14.1.24
F. Whittaker			1915–16				3 Fr	1 Fr	CF			
G. Wiggins		27.8.10	1910–11		1 S				LH			
Thomas Wilkie	Edinburgh 1876		1899–1904		105 S 41 W 12 SDC		20 Cup 22 Fr		LB	Hearts Liverpool		Died 8.1.32 Perth Australia
A. Williams			1916–17		1 LC				LB			
Ernest W. Williams	Ryde	23.12.06 (Am)	1907–11		35 S 3 W	4 S 2 W	1 Fr		OL		3.12.09	Chelsea

Players name	Birthplace & date	Date signed	Years played	Int. player	League appearances	Goals	Cup & Fr appearances	Goals	Position	Previous club	Left Pompey	Club joined
David Wilson	Lochgelly 1883	8.6.07	1907–08		7 S / 7 W	1 S / 1 W	1 Cup / 1 Fr		IL	Gainsboro T. / Hearts / Everton		
William Wilson			1919–20		1 S				RH	Seaham Harbour		
S. Woodford			1917–18		1 SHWL	2 SHWL	1 Fr	1 Fr				
Woolworth			1917–18		1 SHWL				CF			
Thomas Worthington	Preston 1888	Summer 1909	1909–11		34 S		5 Cup / 4 Fr	2 Fr	HB	Lancaster / Preston	Summer 1911	Rotherham
E. Gordon Dundas Wright		23.9.05	1905–06	En	4 S / 1 W				OL	Corinthians		
Horace Wright		7.9.12	1912–19		27 S / 8 SA / 2 SHWL	2 S	2 Cup		OR	Derby Co.	Summer 1913 £35	
Wright			1918–19				1 Fr		CH	Red Coy.		
Wynne			1918–19		1 SHWL		2 Fr		FB	Wanderers		
William Yates	1884	1908	1908–11		107 S / 8 W	2 S / 1 W	16 Cup / 5 Fr	3 Cup	IL	Aston Villa / Brighton / Hearts / Manchester City	19.6.11	Coventry
George Young	Beith, Ayrshire		1903–05		48 S / 25 W		5 Cup / 5 Fr		FB	Glasgow Rangers	2.5.05	W.B.A.
Samuel Young			1912–13	Ir	2 SA / 13 S	1 SA / 3 S			OL			
B. A. Youtman		6.3.20	1919–20		7 S		1 Cup		OL	Thornycrofts		

Appendix 1b

Appearances and Goals for seasons 1920/1 to 1983/4 excluding War time (see Appendix 2). Appearances and Goals for F.A. Cup and F.L./Milk Cup are shown as combined totals. Figures shown in parentheses (0) are substitute appearances.

Abbreviations used:

Am	= Amateur	E	= England
Y.C.	= Youth Club	W	= Wales
B.C.	= Boys Club	NI	= Northern Ireland
G.S.	= Grammar School	S	= Scotland
R	= Re-signed	RI	= Republic of Ireland (Eire)
St.	= Station	Sw	= Sweden
Int.	= International	NZ	= New Zealand

Players Name	Birthplace and Date	Date Signed	Years Played	Int. Player	League Appearances	Goals	Cup Appearances	Goals	Position	Previous Club	Left Pompey	Club Joined
Shirley Abbott	Alfreton	–.8.13	1920–3		96	3	4		H/FB	Derby	21.5.23	Q.P.R.
Stephen Aizlewood	Newport 9.10.52	26.7.79	1979–		176	13	27		CH	Swindon		
William Albury	Portsmouth 10.8.33	8.1.51	1956–8		23		3		WH		3.7.59	Gillingham
James Allen	Poole 1910	19.2.30	1930–4	E	132	1	13		CH	Poole	19.6.34	Aston Villa
Keith Ames	Canford 17.9.33	–.9.50	1953–4		2				CF		–.–.56	
John 'Jock' Anderson	Dundee 8.5.15	–.6.33	1933–9		80	36	6	7	CF	Stobswood	21.6.46	Aldershot
James Armstrong	Blayden	24.12.13	1920–21		13	2			CF	Scotswood		Sheff. Wed.
John Armstrong	Airdrie 5.9.36	8.2.63	1963–7		79		7		Goal	Notts. For.	31.7.67	Southport
John Ashworth	Nottingham 4.7.37	Amateur	1962–3	E Am	1				CH	Wealdstone		
Phillip Ashworth	Burnley 14.4.53	–.9.79	1979–80		3(1)	4	1		CF	Rochdale	–.7.80	Scunthorpe
William Atkins	Bingley 9.5.39	2.4.69	1968–9		11	2	1		IF	Stockport	7.11.69	Halifax
John Atyeo	Dilton 7.2.32	Amateur	1950–1	E	2				IF	Westbury Utd	–.6.51	Bristol City
Neil Ayrton	Lewisham 11.2.62	–.12.79	1980–1		1(1)		(1)		F	Maidstone	6.5.81	Maidstone
William Bagley	Wolverhampton	9.6.33	1933–9		129	12	10	1	IL	Newport Co.	1940–1	

Players Name	Birthplace and Date	Date Signed	Years Played	Int. Player	League Appearances	Goals	Cup Appearances	Goals	Position	Previous Club	Left Pompey	Club Joined
Kevin Ball	Hastings	-.-.82	1983–		1				RB	Coventry		
Herbert Barlow	Kilnhurst 22.7.16	24.2.39	1939–49		104	34	9	2	IL	Wolverhampton W.	-.12.49	Leicester
Leigh Barnard	Worsley 29.10.58	-.8.77	1977–82		71(8)	8	10(1)		Mid		25.3.82	Peterborough
Michael Barnard	Havant 8.7.33	20.8.51	1953–9		116	24	7	2	IL	Gosport Boro.	3.7.59	Chelmsford
Alan Barnett	Croydon 4.11.33	19.9.55	1955–8		25				Goal	Croydon Am.	20.12.58	Grimsby
Gordon Bartlett	London 3.12.55	3.12.73	1974–5		(2)	1			F		-.9.75	Brentford
Kevin Bartlett	Portsmouth 12.10.62	-.11.80	1980–2		(3)				F		23.4.82	Fareham
Anthony Barton	Sutton 8.4.37	-.12.61	1961–7		129(1)	34	14	3	OR	Notts. For.		
Brian Bason	Epsom 3.9.55	5.1.82	1982		9				IL	C. Palace	24.2.82	C. Palace
John Beale	Portsmouth 16.10.30	-.8.48	1951–3		14	1			RH		1954	Guildford C.
Richard Beattie	Glasgow 24.10.36	10.8.59	1959–62		122		10		Goal	Celtic	30.5.62	Peterborough
James Beattie	Montrose	13.2.37	1937–9		58	28	2	1	CF	St. Johnstone	8.5.39	Millwall
Leonard Beaumont	Huddersfield	18.7.36	1936–8		6	3	1		OR	Huddersfield	4.7.38	Notts. For.
William Clark Beedie	Montrose	-.-.20	1920–6		202	30	14		OL	Blantyre Celtic	20.8.26	Oldham
N. Bell	Manchester	1.8.31	1931–2		1				LH	Coventry	14.5.32	
Thomas Bell	Osworth	16.3.28	1928–32				2		LB	Leeds	7.5.30	
Paul Bennett		1974	1976–7				1		Goal			
Ronald Bennett	Hinckley 8.5.27	-.7.48	1949–52		8	1			OL	Wolverhampton W.	-.1.52	C. Palace
Stephen Berry	Liverpool 4.4.63	Sum. 1981	1981–		26(2)	2	2(1)	1	Mid		21.3.84	loan to Aldershot
David Best	Wareham 6.9.43	1.3.74	1974–5		53		3		Goal	Ipswich	-.5.75	Bournemouth
Alan Biley	Leighton Buzzard 26.2.57	25.8.82	1982–		83	39	10	5	F	Everton		
Robert Bishop		20.8.21	1921–2		11	1			OR	Winchburgh	Sum.22	Aberamman
Keith Blackburn	Manchester 17.7.40	-.7.59	1960–4		34	8	3		IF	Bolton (Am)	15.3.64	South Africa
Colin Blant	Rawtenstall 7.10.46	-.4.70	1970–2		64	1	9		CH	Burnley	10.7.72	Rochdale
Robert Blyth	Muirkirk	-.4.21	1921–2		8	2	2		OR		29.5.22	Southampton
Gerry Bowler	Derry 8.6.19	20.8.46	1946–9	NI	8		1		CH	Distillery	19.8.49	Hull City
Terence Brisley	Stepney 4.7.50	23.3.79	1979–81		55	13	14	2	Mid	Charlton	Sum.81	Chelmsford
Brian Bromley	Burnley 20.3.46	7.11.68	1968–72		88(1)	3	9		IF	Bolton W.	-.1.72	Brighton
Arthur Brown	Preston	-.-.22	1922–3		5	1			IF	Lancaster T.	-.-.23	
Ambrose Brown	Burton on Trent	29.6.35	1935–6		1				CF	Chesterfield	12.6.36	Wrexham
Allan D. Brown	Fife 12.10.26	13.3.61	1960–3	S	69	8	5		IF/WH	Luton	11.4.64	Wigan
Frederick Brown	Leyton 6.12.31	25.6.58	1958–60		18		4		Goal	W.B.A.	13.7.60	Poole T.
James K. Brown	Wallyford 3.10.43	-.1.80	1980		5				Mid	Ethneicos (Greece)	-.5.80	Ghent (Belgium)
J.B. Brown	Edinburgh	16.11.20	1920–2		38	1			CH	Bathgate	29.7.22	Edinburgh Leith
Thomas Brown	Cowdenbeath 11.8.24	-.10.46	1947–8		17	1			IF	Worcester City	-.8.49	Watford
William Brown	Dagenham 7.2.43	11.6.68	1968–9		7	2	1		CF	Gillingham	-.7.69	Brentford
Stephen Bryant	Islington 5.9.53	21.3.79	1979–82		111	5	16	1	Mid	Northampton	24.3.82	Northampton
Harold Buddery	Sheffield	Sum. 1913	1920–2		21	3	4		CF	Doncaster	21.11.21	Southend
Martin Busby	Slough 24.3.53	5.2.76	1976		6	1			F	Q.P.R.	-.3.76	Q.P.R.
Ernest Butler	Box 13.5.19	4.5.38	1946–53		222		18		Goal	Bath City	26.9.53	Retired
William Butler	Portsmouth 13.8.28	-.12.47	1947		1						-.6.50	Aldershot
Paul G. Cahill	Liverpool 29.9.55	20.2.75	1975–8		95(2)	2	15		Def	Coventry	15.4.78	California Lasers
James Campbell	St. Pancras 11.4.37	30.6.59	1959–62		50	13	3		I/OR	W.B.A.	-.5.62	Lincoln
Robert Campbell	Liverpool 23.4.37	-.11.61	1961–6		63(1)	2	7	1	RH	Liverpool	-.7.66	Aldershot
Brian Carter	Weymouth 17.11.38	23.1.56	1957–61		45		6		LH	Weymouth	30.6.61	Bristol Rovers
Thomas Casey	Cumber Bangor 11.3.30	7.7.58	1958–9	NI	24	1			WH	Newcastle	16.3.59	Bristol City
Samuel Chapman	Belfast 16.2.38	21.2.58	1958–61		48	10	9	1	IR	Mansfield	-.12.61	Mansfield
Percival Cherrett	Bournemouth	8.3.21	1921–3		67	35	3		CF	Bournemouth	28.8.23	Plymouth
William Clarke	Newport	-.-.34	1934–5		1				LH	Newport	15.5.35	
Ike Clarke	Tipton 9.1.15	6.11.47	1947–53		116	49	11	9	IF	W.B.A.	Sum.53	Manager Yeovil
George 'Ginger' Clifford	New Sawley Derbys.	7.5.24	1924–31		173		7		RB	Sutton Town	22.7.31	Mansfield Town
James Clugston	Belfast 30.10.34	29.1.57	1957		1				IF	Glentoran	3.5.58	
David Coid		16.11.20	1920–1		7	3	1		CF	Armdale	Retnd Scotland injured Sum.21	

Players Name	Birthplace and Date	Date Signed	Years Played	Int. Player	League Appearances	Goals	Cup Appearances	Goals	Position	Previous Club	Left Pompey	Club Joined
Ian Collard	Hetton 31.8.47	−.9.75	1975		1		1		IF	Ipswich	1.10.75	Ipswich
John Collins	Rhymney S. Wales	12.5.71	1971–4		71(3)		13		LB	Tottenham H.	12.8.74	Halifax
Frederick Cook	Aberam	29.4.26	1926–33	W	247	41	21	1	OL	Newport Co.	10.5.33	
George H. Cooke	Clowne Derbys.	29.7.24	1924–5		2				OL	Norwich	Sum.25	Southend
Charles R. Cooper	Belper	−.−.21	1922–3		4				RB	Derby Co.	1.7.23	Q.P.R.
Barry Cordjohn	Oxford 5.9.42	−.7.64	1964–5		14		3		RH	Aldershot	Sum.65	
Raymond Crawford	Portsmouth 13.7.36	13.12.54	1957–8	E	18	9	1	1	CF		−.9.58	Ipswich
Harold Crawshaw	Newton Heath	16.2.35	1936–7		1				CF	Newton Heath Locos	28.8.37	Mansfield
Robert Cringan	Muirkirk	28.5.21	1921–2		1				OR	Parkhead	−.−.22	
Henry Croft	Bolton	−.−.22	1922–3		5				IF	Preston	−.−.23	
Stuart Croft	Ashington 9.8.57	−.3.81	1981		6	1			CH	Hull City	17.6.81	York City
Alex Cropley	Aldershot 16.1.51	−.10.81	1981–2	S	8(2)	2	3		Mid	Toronto Blizzards	Sum.82	Retired
David Crown	Enfield 16.2.58	23.10.81	1981–3		25(3)	2	2		OL	Brentford	29.7.83	Reading
John Cumming		−.−.20	1920–1		8	1			LH	Cowden Heath	Sum.21	Kings Park (Scotland)
Reginald Cutler	Birmingham 17.2.35	17.9.58	1958–62		101	13	5		OL	Bournemouth	−.7.62	Stockport
Gordon Dale	Manton Worksop 28.5.28	27.6.51	1951–7		115	18	4		OL	Chesterfield	25.10.57	Exeter
Brian Dalton	Arundel	−.−.35	1935–6		1				OL	Littlehampton	−.−.36	Reading
Hugh Davey	Belfast	2.12.27	1927–8	NI	7	2	1		CF	Reading	2.5.28	
Stephen Davey	Plymouth 5.9.48	20.6.78	1978–81		82(10)	8	9(1)		Def/For	Hereford	Sum.81	Exeter
Dennis Davidson	Aberdeen 18.5.37	12.5.54	1959–60		1				WH	Torry Rangers	−.−.61	
Roger Davidson	Islington 27.10.48	27.5.69	1969–70		3				RH	Arsenal	15.9.70	Fulham
John R. Davies	Portsmouth 26.9.33	−.5.52	1953–5		2				OR		−.7.55	Scunthorpe
Reginald Davies	Mansfield	21.7.22	1922–8		191	3	15		RH	Sutton Town	2.5.28	
Ronald T. Davies	Holywell 25.5.42	16.4.73	1973–4	W	59	17	10	3	CF	Southampton	28.11.74	Man. Utd.
George 'Joe' Davison	Thornaby on Tees	16.5.23	1923–6		31		5		LB	Middlesbrough	−.−.27	
James Dawson	Stoneyburn 21.12.27	−.6.49	1949–50		1				OR	Leicester	−.9.51	Northampton
Stephen Dearn	Halesowen	−.−.23	1924–6		19	4	1		LH	Aston Villa	Sum.26	Brentford
Lloyd L. Delapenha	West Indies 20.5.27	−.4.48	1948–50		8		1	1	OR	Arsenal	27.4.50	Middlesbrough
Peter Denyer	Chiddingfold 26.11.57	26.11.75	1975–9		122(6)	15	13(1)	2	Def		24.7.79	Northampton
James Dickinson	Alton 24.4.25	8.1.44	1946–65	E	764	9	58	1	LH	Alton Y.C.	24.4.65	Retired
Kevin Dillon	Sunderland 18.12.59	24.3.83	1983–		47	14	6	3	IR	Birmingham		
David Dodson	Gravesend 20.1.40	13.12.61	1961–5		54	20	8	1	OL	Swansea	23.1.65	Aldershot
Charles Dore	Gosport 30.9.28	−.5.50	1951–4		19				Goal	Fleetlands	−.−.54	
Derek Dougan	Belfast 20.1.38	27.8.57	1957–9	NI	33	9	3		CF	Distillery	11.3.59	Blackburn
Robert Doyle	Dumbarton 27.12.53	3.12.80	1980–		159	14	14	1	Mid	Blackpool		
Raymond Drinkwater	Jarrow 18.5.31	3.11.55	1956–7		8				Goal	Guildford	1.3.58	Q.P.R.
Ian Drummond	Brechin 27.8.23	17.5.45	1947–8				1		LB		−.6.49	Bournemouth
William Eames	Emsworth 20.9.57	19.9.75	1975–77		9(3)	1	4(2)	2	F		−.8.78	Brentford
Stanley Earl	Alton 9.7.29	−.11.49	1950–52		8				FB	Alton	−.7.53	Leyton Orient
James Easson	Brechin	−.−.28	1928–39	S	294	103	20	5	IL	Dundee	11.3.39	Fulham
Redfern Edmunds	Newport 10.1.43	−.6.60	1960–61		4				OL		−.7.61	Newport
Moses W. Edwards		5.8.21	1921–22		1				IR	Gosport Ath.	Sum.22	
Brian Edwards	Portsmouth 6.10.30	−.10.48	1951–52		1				FB		−.−.53	
Dennis Edwards	Slough 19.1.37	16.1.65	1965–67	E Am	69(3)	14	9	2	IF	Charlton	15.12.67	Aldershot
James Elder	Perth 5.3.27	27.9.45	1949–50						RH	Jeanfields	−.7.50	Colchester
Peter Ellis	Portsmouth 20.3.56	−.3.74	1974–		226(21)	1	31(2)	1	HB			
Daniel Ekner	Sweden	Amateur	1949–50	Sw	4				IF	Sweden	25.3.50	Sweden
Frederick Evans	Petersfield 20.5.23	27.1.45	1946–47		9	3	1	1	CF		−.7.47	Notts Co.
Ivor Evans	Cardiff 25.10.33	29.9.56	1956–57		1				IR	Guest Keen	−.−.59	Sittingbourne
Harold Ferrier	Raths, Midlothian 20.5.20	26.3.46	1946–54		241	8	14	1	LB	Barnsley	−.−.54	Gloucester
Phillip Figgins	Portsmouth 20.8.55	−.7.73	1974–78		36		4		Goal	Waterlooville	22.4.78	
Reginald Flewin	Portsmouth 28.11.20	29.11.37	1938–53	E	152		15		CH	Ryde Sports	−.−.53	Retired

Players Name	Birthplace and Date	Date Signed	Years Played	Int. Player	League Appearances	Goals	Cup Appearances	Goals	Position	Previous Club	Left Pompey	Club Joined
Kenneth Foggo	Perth 7.11.43	10.1.73	1973–75		46(11)	3	1(1)		Wing	Norwich	–.6.75	Brentford
Terence Foley	Portsmouth 8.2.38	30.4.58	1959–60		7				OR	Ryde Sports	–.7.60	Chesterfield
J. Forsyth	Armadale	–.10.25	1925–26		3				HB	Bathgate	2.5.28	
Frederick Forward	Croydon	19.2.27	1927–32		185	26	13	2	OR	Newport Co.	4.11.33	Hull City
Stephen Foster	Portsmouth 24.9.57	–.10.75	1975–79	E	101(8)	6	18(1)	2	FW/CH	Southampton	26.6.79	Brighton
Arthur Foxall	Hockney, Birmingham	28.5.24	1924–25		1				RH	Watford	Sum.25	Kidderminster Har.
Harold Foxall	Birmingham	14.2.24	1924–28		155	10	11		CH	Merthyr	2.5.28	
Jack 'Gabby' Foxton	Salford 17.6.21	10.5.45	1946–47		1				LH	Bolton	–.9.48	Swindon
H. J. Frampton		–.–.20	1920–21		3				RB		Sum.21	
John W. Fraser	Belfast 15.9.38	–.6.60	1960–61		1				OR	Sunderland	–.–.61	Margate
John Friar	New Main	21.4.32	1932–33		1				OR	Hibernian	–.–.33	
Jack Froggatt	Sheffield 17.11.22	10.9.45	1946–54	E	279	65	13	7	CH/FW		–.3.54	Leicester
Robert Gaddes	Byfleet 27.9.41	–.6.60	1960		1				Goal			
Marcel Gaillard	Charleris, Belgium 15.1.27	–.2.51	1951–53		58	7	5	6	OL	C. Palace	–.–.53	
Derek Gamblin	Havant 7.4.43	Amateur	1965	E Am	1				RB	Sutton Utd.	4.9.65	Sutton Utd.
Alan Garner	Lambeth 2.2.51	14.2.80	1980–82		36	2	8	1	LH	Watford	1.4.82	Barnet
Colin Garwood	Measham 29.6.49	9.3.78	1978–80		62(9)	34	7(1)		F	Colchester	12.2.80	Aldershot
Matthew Gemmell	Glasgow 10.3.31	–.9.51	1953–54		3				IF	Glasgow	8.10.54	Swindon
Duncan Gilchrist	Campbelltown	15.8.22	1922–24		3				OL	Died playing football 9.4.24		
Paul Gilchrist	Dartford 5.1.51	10.3.77	1977–78		38(1)	3	3	1	F	Southampton	2.9.78	Swindon
John 'Jock' Gilfillan	Cowdenbeath 1898	6.12.28	1928–37		330		29		Goal	Hearts	16.6.37	Q.P.R.
Mervyn J. Gill	Exeter 13.4.31	Amateur	1953–54		6		1		Goal		–.4.56	Southampton
Henry B. Goodwin	Glasgow	6.6.25	1925–27		38	8	3	2	OR	Bo'ness	2.12.27	Reading
John Gordon	Portsmouth 11.9.31	24.1.49 R.–.3.61	1951–58 1961–67		445	107	38	11	IR	Hillside Y.C.	–.9.58	Birmingham
Andrew Gosney	Southampton 8.11.63	–.–.82	1982–		1		1		Goal	Southampton		
Alex Govan	Glasgow 16.6.29	17.3.58	1958		11	2			OL	Birmingham	–.9.58	Plymouth
George Graham	Bargeddie 30.11.44	28.11.74	1974–76	S	61	5	9	1	Mid	Manchester Utd.13.11.76		C. Palace
Clive Green	Portsmouth 6.12.59	–.7.76	1976–78		34(6)	4	6(1)	3	F		Spr.1978	Yeovil
David Gregory	Peterborough 6.10.51	3.12.79	1979–82		64(10)	18	12(1)	3	Mid	Bury	2.4.82	Wrexham
Arthur Groves	Killamarsh	1.1.36	1936–39		80	13	3	1	IF	Derby	24.6.39	Stockport
Reginald Gundry	Eastleigh	Amateur	1935–36		1				RB	Dorchester	–.–.37	
Phillip Gunter	Portsmouth 6.1.32	18.8.49	1951–64		319	2	35		RB/CH		–.6.64	Aldershot
James Guthrie	Luncarty 6.6.12	23.8.37	1937–39		76	1	8		RH	Dundee	–.3.46	C. Palace
William W.P. Haines	Warminster	9.12.22	1922–28		165	119	15	9	CF	Frome	17.5.28	Southampton
Dennis Hall	Southwell 24.12.30	–.9.48	1952–54		10				FB	Bilsthorpe	–.8.54	Reading
James Hall	Durham	13.5.36	1937–39		9				Goal	West Stanley	–.–.39	
Eoin Hand	Dublin 30.3.46	14.10.68 R.–.12.77	1968–76 1977–79	RI	275(3)	14	27(1)		CH	Drumcondra	–.3.76	South Africa
Paul Hardyman		15.5.84	1984–		2(1)				Mid	Waterlooville		
Derek 'Harry' Harris	Magor 2.11.33	14.7.58	1958–70		376(2)	48	46	1	IL/LH	Newport Co.	8.10.70	Newport Co.
Peter P. Harris	Southsea 19.12.25	6.10.44	1946–60	E	479	194	29	15	OR	Gosport Boro.	–.–.60	Retired
Jack Harwood	Somerstown	1.3.13	1920–22		41	2	1		CH	Chelsea	24.5.22	Swansea
George Haslam	Turton	9.11.27	1927–28		4				CH	Manchester Utd.16.8.28		
Mark Hateley	Liverpool 17.11.61	28.5.83	1983–		38	22	6	3	CF	Coventry		
Henry Havelock	Hartlepool	11.3.26	1925–27		11	8			CF	Hull	3.11.27	C. Palace
Frank Haydock	Manchester 29.11.40	8.12.65	1965–69		71	1	6		CH	Charlton	1.2.69	Southend
Basil Hayward	Leek 7.4.28	18.7.58	1958–60		44	4	5		CH	Port Vale		
Jeff Hemmerman	Hull 25.2.55	–.7.78	1978–82		114(9)	37	14(4)	5	F	Port Vale	2.7.82	Cardiff
Jackie Henderson	Glasgow 17.1.32	20.1.49	1951–58	S	214	70	12	3	CF	Kirkintilloch Y.C.14.3.58		Wolverhampton W.
Rodney Henwood	Portsmouth 27.11.31	–.5.50	1953–54		1				OL	Kingston B.C.		
Peter Higham	Wigan 8.11.30	Amateur	1949–50		1				CF		–.11.50	Bolton W.
Robert Hindmarch	Stannington 27.4.61	8.12.83	1983		2				CH	Sunderland	5.1.84	Sunderland
William Hindmarsh	Crook 26.12.19	–.4.39	1946–51		55		3		RB	Willington	–.7.51	Swindon

Players Name	Birthplace and Date	Date Signed	Years Played	Int. Player	League Appearances	Goals	Cup Appearances	Goals	Position	Previous Club	Left Pompey	Club Joined
Thomas Hird	Crewe	–.8.35	1935–36		1	1			OR	Hartlepool	28.8.37	Selsey
Raymond Hiron	Gosport 22.7.43	–.5.64	1964–75		323(7)	110	34	7	CF	Fareham	–.5.75	Reading
Jeff Hodgkins	Portsmouth 8.10.42	–.3.60	1960–61		3				CF			
James Hogg	Sunderland	Sum. 1913	1920–21		15	2	1		Wing	South Shields	9.11.21	Guildford Utd.
Graham R. Horn	Westminster 23.8.54	26.2.72	1972–73		22		4		Goal	Arsenal	21.2.73	Luton
Ralph V. Hoten	Pinxton	–.–.21	1921–23		39	9	1		IL	Notts Co.	1.3.23	Luton
Edward Hough	Walsall	7.5.31	1931–32		1				FB	Southampton	–.–.32	
Ernest Howe	Chiswick 15.2.53	4.6.82	1982–		35	4	4		CH	Q.P.R.		
Ronald Howells	Ferndale, Rhonnda 3.8.35	11.3.59	1959–61		64	2	6		RH	Wolverhampton W.	–.6.61	Scunthorpe
George W. Hudson	Havant 26.10.23	–.–.44	1947–48		1				CF		–.9.48	Swindon
Ronald Humpston	Derby 14.12.23	–.–.44	1947–51		9				Goal		–.11.51	Huddersfield
Ralph A. Hunt	Portsmouth 14.8.33	–.8.50	1952–54		5				IL		–.2.54	Bournemouth
Robert Irvine	Lisburn	6.3.23	1928–30	NI	35	10	4	1	IL	Everton	7.5.30	Connahs Quay
Keith A. James	Hillingdon 18.8.61	–.7.79	1979–80		5(1)				FB		–.–.80	Norwich
William E. James	Stockton	Sum. 1913	1920–21		22	3	5		CF	Middlesbrough	21.1.21	West Ham Utd.
John Jarvie	Glasgow	29.10.26	1926–28		4				Goal	Leicester	12.3.28	Southend
Nicholas Jennings	Wellington 18.1.46	–.1.67	1967–73		198(8)	45	20	5	OL	Plymouth	–.11.73	Aldershot
Cyril Jolliffe		Amateur	1932–33		2				Goal	South Hants Nomads	–.–.35	South Hants Nomads
Eric Jones	Birmingham 5.2.15	9.11.37	1937–38		1				OR	Wolverhampton W.	–.–.39	W.B.A.
Albert L. Juliussen	Blyth 20.2.20	11.3.48	1948		7	4			CF	Dundee	4.9.48	Everton
Christopher Kamara	Middlesbrough 25.12.57	–.1.76 R.29.8.81	1976–77 1981		67(6)	7	8	2	F	Royal Navy	10.8.77 23.10.81	Swindon Brentford
Allan Kane	Falkirk 20.1.57	–.3.75	1975–76		6(1)		2		F	Hibernian	–.1.76	Contract Cancelled
Alexander Kane	Aberdeen	6.5.23	1923–26		96		8		Goal	Hearts	15.1.26	West Ham Utd.
Robert Kearney	Ashton in Makerfield	17.5.28	1929–31		60		5		CH	Dundee	24.2.31	Died
Robert Kellard	Southend 1.3.43	4.3.66 R.29.12.72	1966–68 1972–75		153(1)	14	22	4	O/IL	Ipswich C. Palace	3.7.68 2.1.75	Bristol City Hereford
David Michael Kemp	Harrow 20.2.53	10.11.76	1976–78		63(1)	30	10	6	F	C. Palace	9.3.78	Carlisle
James Kennedy	Burraden Colliery	24.10.21	1921–25		22				OR	Bedlington	9.7.25	Reading
William Kennedy		–.3.32	1932		1				IL	Royal Albert	10.5.33	
Jeff King	Fauldhouse 9.11.53	12.3.76	1976		4				Mid	Derby Co.	–.4.76	Derby Co.
Alan E. Knight	Balham 3.7.61	23.2.79	1978–		143		18		Goal			
Arthur Egerton Knight	Godalming 1888	–.–.08	1920–22	E/E Am	34		2		FB		–.–.22	Corinthians
Joseph D. Laidlaw	Wallsend 12.7.50	23.6.79	1979–80		60	19	14	4	F	Doncaster	4.12.80	Hereford
John G. Lathan	Sunderland 12.4.52	9.3.78	1978–79		56(2)	4	4		Mid	Carlisle	24.8.79	Mansfield
John Latimer	Hills of Beath	20.10.28	1928–30		8				OR	Hearts of Beath	7.5.30	
Christopher Lawler	Liverpool 20.10.43	–.10.75	1975–77	E	35(1)		4		Def	Liverpool	–.8.77	Stockport
Maurice Leather	Eastleigh 9.11.29	–.1.50	1950–53		18		1		Goal	Southampton	–.–.53	
Herbert J. Leavey		8.3.21	1921		13				IL	Llanelly		
Benjamin Lewis	Cafor	–.–.28	1928–29		2				Goal	Merthyr Town	17.12.29	Merthyr Town
Brian Lewis	Woking 26.1.43	–.7.63 R.8.4.72	1963–67 1972–75		178(13)	32	15(1)		WH	C. Palace Colchester	–.1.67 –.5.75	Coventry Hastings
David Leworthy	Portsmouth	–.–.81	1981–82		(1)				F		20.4.82	Fareham
William George Lewry		8.2.21	1921		4	1			CF	Gosport Ath.	Sum.21	Boscombe
George Ley	Exeter 7.4.46	1.5.67	1967–72		183(1)	10	20	1	LB	Exeter	22.9.72	Brighton
Michael Lill	Romford 3.8.36	–.2.63	1963–65		39	5	4	2	OL	Wolverhampton W.	Sum.65	Guildford City
Grahame Lloyd	Liverpool 10.1.51	–.5.75	1975–78		73		13		Goal	Motherwell	–.4.78	Contract Cancelled
Henry Lunn	Lurgan 20.3.25	–.7.46	1947		1				OR	Notts Co.	–.7.47	Swindon
Roy Lunniss	London 4.11.39	–.5.36	1963–66		69(1)	1	11		FB	C. Palace	14.2.66	Dismissed
Anthony Macken	Dublin 20.7.50	22.11.75 13.2.76	1975–76 2 Loan spells		10	1			Mid	Derby Co.		Derby Co.
John Alex Mackie	Belfast	Sum. 1928	1928–35	NI	257	2	29		RB	Arsenal	16.3.36	Northampton
James Mackie	Motherwell	1920	1920–28		245	77	16	5	IF	Blantyre Celtic	–.3.28	Southampton

Players Name	Birthplace and Date	Date Signed	Years Played	Int. Player	League Appearances	Goals	Cup Appearances	Goals	Position	Previous Club	Left Pompey	Club Joined
James Mackrell	Longridden	8.8.33	1933–35		3				RB	Motherwell	3.3.37	Norwich
T. Maidment	Sunderland	6.8.31	1931–32		3				IR	Lincoln	Sum.32	
Malcolm Manley	Johnston 1.12.49	–.12.73	1973–75		11		5		WH	Leicester	–.4.76	Contract Cancelled
Barry R. Mansell	Petersfield 8.3.32	–.8.49	1951–54		16				FB	Hillside Y.C.	–.2.54	Reading
Jack Mansell	Sale 22.8.27	21.11.53	1953–58		134	7	7	1	LB	Cardiff	27.2.58	Eastbourne Utd.
Zechariah G. March	Chichester	–.–.22	1922–23		3				OR	Brighton	–.–.23	
Peter Marinello	Edinburgh 20.2.50	7.5.73	1973–75		92(3)	6	18	3	Wing	Arsenal	11.12.75	Motherwell
James Martin	Bo'ness	29.11.20	1920–27		213	27	16	2	LH	Hearts	5.10.27	Aldershot
R. Maitland	Preston	–.–.21	1921–22		2				CH	Boscombe	Sum.22	
James McAlinden	Belfast 27.12.17	15.12.38	1938–47	NI/RI	53	9	6		IR	Belfast Celtic	12.9.47	Stoke City
James McCaffrey	Luton 12.10.51	16.2.78	1978		11(1)	1			OL	Huddersfield	25.1.79	Northampton
Albert McCann	Maidenhead 1.11.41	–.8.62	1962–74		331(6)	83	40	13	IL	Coventry	21.4.74	South Africa
Leonard McCarthy	Caeran	–.–.32	1932–37		24	5	3	1	CF/IL	Thames	1.6.37	Q.P.R.
Syd B. McClellan	Dagenham 11.6.25	1.12.56	1956–58		36	9	2	1	IL	Tottenham H.	–.7.58	Leyton Orient
John B. McClelland	Bradford 5.3.35	–.5.63	1963–68		135(1)	35	14	2	OR	Q.P.R.	–.8.68	Newport Co.
John McColgan	Tollcross Glasgow	7.2.24	1924–30		190		16		LB	Albion Rovers	7.5.30	
Wilfred McCoy	Birmingham 4.3.21	–.8.46	1946–48		18				CH		–.12.48	Northampton
Thomas McGhee	Manchester 10.5.29	11.5.54	1954–59	E Am	135		8		RB	Wealdstone	8.7.59	Reading
Robert McGuinness	Motherwell 29.1.54	–.5.75	1975–77		27(4)	3	9(1)	1	F	Motherwell	7.5.77	Australia
John McHugh	Hamilton	25.11.30	1932–33		3		1		Goal	Dundee Utd.	9.10.37	Watford
John McIlwaine	Irvine	–.–.27	1927–30		57	5	6		CH	Falkirk	20.6.30	Southampton
James McIlwraith	Troon 17.4.54	25.7.78	1978–79		16(3)	2	1		Mid	Bury	27.7.79	Bury
Murdock McKenzie	Ayr	19.7.26	1926–27		4	1			IL	Darlington	Sum.27	
John McLaughlin	Edmonton 29.10.54	3.7.79	1979–		172	1	20		RB	Swindon		
John T. McLaughlin	Liverpool 25.2.52	3.10.75	1975		5				Mid	Liverpool	1.11.75	Liverpool
David McNab	Cleland, Lancs.	1.3.23	1923–24		5				RH	Newark Hill Thistle	14.7.25	Fulham
John McNeil		6.12.28	1928–30		12	5	2	2	CF	Hearts	17.1.30	Reading
Daniel McPhail	Campbelltown	4.1.22	1922–29		128		7		Goal	Campbelltown G.S.	6.8.31	Lincoln
Angus Meikle	Coalburn Lanark	24.5.22	1922–27		154	22	13	4	OR	Hearts	13.6.27	Grimsby
Peter J. Mellor	Prestbury 20.11.47	Sum. 1978	1978–81		129		17		Goal	Fulham	21.12.81	Mutual termination
Michael Mellows	London 14.11.47	–.9.73	1973–78	E Am	174(7)	16	29	4	HB/F	Wycombe W.	6.5.78	
Alexander Merrie	Saltcoats	29.8.25	1925–26		7	2			CF	St Mirren	–.–.26	
Harold Methuen	Derby	9.5.30	1930–31		2		1		CF	Gresley Rovers	1.5.31	
Harold Middleton	Birmingham 18.3.37	–.6.61	1961–62		17	5	5	5	IF	Scunthorpe	–.2.62	Shrewsbury
Stephen Middleton	Portsmouth 28.3.53	–.6.77	1977–78		26		5		Goal	Southampton		
John Milkins	Dagenham 3.1.44	–.5.61	1961–74		334		45		Goal		14.8.74	Oxford Utd.
Laurie Milligan	Liverpool 20.4.58	16.3.79	1979		7				FB	Blackpool	–.4.79	Blackpool
William Moffatt	Bells Hill	–.–.25	1925–29		130	2	8		LH	Bo'ness	7.5.30	Brighton
Richard Money	Lowestoft 13.10.55	22.8.83	1983–		16		4		LB	Luton		
Harold Moore	Halesowen	2.6.23	1923–24		1	1			RH	Halesowen	5.8.24	Kettering
Lewis Morgan	Cowdenbeath 30.4.11	24.8.35	1935–39		122		8		FB	Dundee	9.7.46	Watford
Nicholas Morgan	East Ham 30.10.59	23.3.83	1983–		19(12)	10	1(2)	1	CF	West Ham Utd.		
William Morrison	Croy 10.10.39	5.5.58	1958–60		3				FB	Croy Guild	30.4.60	
Charles F. Mortimore	Gosport 12.4.28	Amateur	1953–54	E Am	1				CF	Aldershot	–.–.55	Aldershot
Robert Muir	St Ninians	31.5.34	1934–35		1				Goal	Rutherglen	21.5.35	Third Lanark
Albert E. Mundy	Gosport 12.5.26	–.1.51	1951–53		50	12	3	2	IF	Gosport	–.11.53	Brighton
David Munks	Sheffield 29.4.47	19.5.69	1969–73		132(5)	2	12		LH	Sheffield Utd.	–.12.73	Swindon
Patrick Neil	Portsmouth 24.10.37	Amateur R.–.5.62	1955–56 1962–63	E Am	10	3	1		OL	Pegasus	1956 4.5.63	Wolverhampton W.
B. Newman					5				OL			
Ronald Newman	Portsmouth 19.1.34	10.1.55	1956–61		103	21	10	4	OL	Woking	4.1.61	Leyton Orient
Thomas Newton	Wyton-on-Tyne	24.10.19	1920–23		49		2		Goal	Clapton Orient	–.–.23	

Players Name	Birthplace and Date	Date Signed	Years Played	Int. Player	League Appearances	Goals	Cup Appearances	Goals	Position	Previous Club	Left Pompey	Club Joined
James Nichol	Glasgow	21.11.27	1927–37		351	9	30		RH	Gillingham	27.5.37	Gillingham
James C. Nicol		21.3.32	1932–33		3	1			CF	Leith Ath.	24.8.33	Aldershot
Alfred G. Noakes	Stratford 14.8.33	–.7.62	1962–64		13		1		LB	C. Palace	2.5.64	
Robert Nutley	Paisley 10.9.16	23.8.46	1946–47		9	1			OR	Hibernian	–.–.47	
William O'Hare	Hamilton	17.6.31	1931–32		1				IL	Dundee	–.–.33	
Colin Osmond	Whitchurch 15.5.37	21.5.54	1957–58		1				LB		23.1.60	
Own Goals					League 74		Cup 8					
Roy J. Pack	Islington 20.4.46	1.7.66	1966–69		92		13	1	RB	Arsenal	Sum.69	Oxford
Clifford H. Parker	Denaby Main 6.11.13	11.12.33	1933–51		241	58	16	6	OL	Doncaster	22.8.53	Pompey Scout
Thomas R. Parker	Bolsover	1.3.23	1923–25		43	1	4		CH	Luton	20.5.25	Wrexham
George E. Pateman	Luton	6.8.31	1931–32		2				CF	Gillingham	Sum.32	
Richard J. Pearson	Cosham 14.6.31	23.5.49	1953–54		4	1			IR	Hillside Y.C.	Sum.55	Guildford
Harold Penk	Wigan 19.7.34	10.9.55	1955–57		9	2			Wing	Wigan	–.6.57	Plymouth
Stephen Perrin	London 13.2.52	23.11.79	1979–81		18(10)	3	4(3)	1	F	Plymouth	13.8.81	Hillingdon Boro.
John Phillips	Portsmouth 4.3.37	–.5.55	1955–60		76				RH		3.7.60	Worcester
Leonard Phillips	Hackney 11.9.22	8.2.46	1946–56	E	245	48	21	7	IL/RH	Hillside Y.C.	15.9.56	Poole
Lionel R. Phillips	Much Dewchurch 13.12.29	–.1.53	1953–54		3	1			CF	Yeovil	–.–.54	Tonbridge
Reginald Pickett	India 6.1.27	24.1.49	1949–57		123	2	4		LH	Weymouth	–.7.57	Ipswich
Norman Piper	North Tawton 8.1.48	–.5.70	1970–78		310(4)	51	42	6	OR	Plymouth	–.3.78	Contract Cancelled
Stephen Piper	Brighton 2.11.53	–.2.78	1978–80		27(2)	2	3		Def	Brighton	27.12.80	Retired
Edward H. Platt	Romford 26.3.21	–.9.53	1953–55		30		3		Goal	Arsenal	–.8.55	Aldershot
Raymond Pointer	Cramlington 10.10.36	–.1.67	1967–73	E	150(4)	31	11(3)		CF	Coventry	27.10.73	Blackpool
Maitland Pollock	Dumfries 3.10.52	6.6.76	1976–78		50(4)	10	11	1	F	Luton	22.4.78	Queen of the South
Clifford Portwood	Salford 17.10.37	–.5.64	1964–68		94(3)	28	8	2	IF	Grimsby	–.10.68	Colchester
Raymond Potter	Beckenham 7.5.36	–.5.67	1967–70		3		2		Goal	W.B.A.	Sum.70	
Peter W. Price	Wrexham 17.8.49	21.6.72	1972–74		13(1)	2	1		F	Peterborough	25.7.74	Peterborough
Alan Pringle	Craghead	–.–.33	1935–38		26	2			LH	West Pelton	22.5.39	Chesterfield
Anthony Priscott	Portsmouth 19.3.41	20.7.59	1959–62		36	6	5	1	OR		–.8.62	Aldershot
William Probert	Worksop	Sum. 1911	1920–25		176		7		FB	Worksop	Sum.25	Fulham
Joseph Potts		14.1.20	1920–21		5		1		FB	Hull	Sum.21	Leeds Utd.
David Pullar	Durham 13.2.59	13.2.77	1975–79		84(9)	4	12	3	F		11.7.79	Exeter
Ian Purdie	Motherwell 7.3.53	2.11.79	1979–80		4(1)	1			OL	Wigan	12.12.80	Australia
C. Joseph Quinn	Kilmarnock	28.10.22	1922–23		21		2		LB		4.1.23	U.S.A.
Vincent Radcliffe	Manchester 9.6.45	–.1.61	1963–67		10		4		CH		–.7.67	Peterborough
Ronald Rafferty	Newcastle 6.5.34	–.7.54	1954–56		23	5			IF	Wycombe W.	–.12.56	Grimsby
William H. Rafferty	Glasgow 30.12.50	11.12.80	1980–84		98(4)	40	9	3	CF	Newcastle	22.2.84	Bournemouth
Michael Reagan	York 12.5.24	31.12.52	1952–54		6				OL	Shrewsbury	–.6.54	Norwich
Derick W. Rees	Swansea 18.2.34	–.5.54	1954–57		47	15			IR		–.5.57	Ipswich
Douglas Reid	Mauchline 3.10.17	6.3.46	1946–56		309	129	14	5	IR	Stockport	–.4.56	Tonbridge
Michael John Reid	Wolverhampton 7.8.27	–.7.50	1950–51		5	1			CF	Bournemouth	12.12.52	Watford
James Reid		–.–.20	1920–21		7	2			CF	Blantyre Celtic	Sum.21	Armdale
Richard J. Reynolds	East Looe 15.2.48	16.6.71	1971–76		134(6)	23	20	4	F	Plymouth	–.5.76	
Phillip Stanley Roberts	Cardiff 24.2.50	12.5.73	1973–78		152(1)	1	26		RB	Bristol Rovers	14.6.78	Hereford
Trevor L. Roberts	Southampton 9.5.61	20.1.79	1979–80		1(2)				CH	Southampton	–.–.80	
John C. Robertson	Aberdeen 15.7.28	–.8.55	1955–57		12	4			IF	Ayr Utd.	–.6.57	York City
John W. Robinson	Grangetown	18.7.21	1921–23		26	2			HB	Middlesbrough	13.6.23	Guildford
E.R. 'Ned' Robson	Hexham	1919	1920–22		75		3		Goal	Watford	Sum.22	Sunderland
William Rochford	Newhouse 23.5.13	–.–.31	1932–39		138	1	9		FB	Cuckfield	–.7.46	Southampton
Alan J. Rogers	Plymouth 6.7.54	26.7.79	1979–84		154(7)	14	26(4)	2	OL	Plymouth	22.3.84	Southend
Andrew Rollings	Portishead 14.12.54	1.8.81	1981–83		29	1	5		CH	Swindon	3.8.83	Various trials
Phillip W. Rookes	Dulverton 23.4.19	29.1.38	1938–51		113		7		FB	Bradford City	–.7.51	Colchester
George Ross	Bonnyrigg	3.2.30	1930–32		5	2			OR	Dundee Utd.	Sum.32	Dundee Utd.

Players Name	Birthplace and Date	Date Signed	Years Played	Int. Player	League Appearances	Goals	Cup Appearances	Goals	Position	Previous Club	Left Pompey	Club Joined
Trevor Ross	Ashton-under-Lyne 16.1.57	22.10.82	1982		5				RB	Everton	–.11.82	Everton
Thomas Rowe	Poole 1913	20.8.34	1934–39		81	8			CH	Poole	25.10.39	
John S. Ruggiero	Stoke 26.11.54	10.12.77	1977		6	1			Mid	Brighton	9.1.78	Brighton
Septimus Rutherford	Percy Main	14.9.27	1927–36		121	33	10	4	OL	Blyth Spartans	–.8.36	Blackburn
Cyril H. Rutter	Leeds 21.2.33	–.7.51	1953–63		171		9		CH	Stockport	5.1.63	Stuttgart
Terence R. Ryder	Norwich 3.6.28	–.10.50	1950–52		15	4	1		IF	Norwich	–.7.52	Swindon
Robert Salmond	Kilmarnock	28.5.30	1930–8		135		6		CH	Dundee North End	11.11.38	Chelsea
Ronald Saunders	Birkenhead 6.11.32	6.9.58	1958–64		234	139	24	17	C/IF	Gillingham	31.8.64	Watford
James Scoular	Livingstone St. 11.1.25	–.–.45	1946–53		247	8	17		RH	Gosport Boro.	–.6.53	Newcastle
Trevor Senior	Stratton 28.11.61	16.12.81	1981–3		11	2	(2)		CF	Dorchester	3.8.83	Reading
John Shankly	Glenbuck	–.–.22	1922–3		3	1			CH	Nittesdale Wand.	Sum.23	
Peter F. Shearing	Uxbridge 26.8.38	1.7.61	1961–4		17		2		Goal	West Ham	–.6.64	Exeter
Derek Showers	Merthyr Tydfil 28.1.53	1.2.79	1979–80	W	36(3)	8	4(2)		CF	Bournemouth	–.12.80	Hereford
John William Smelt	Rotherham	–.–.20	1920–1		1				OR	Rotherham Co.	Sum.21	Sheff. Wed.
Abraham Smith	Mansfield	28.5.30	1931–9		74	2			WH	Mansfield		
Edward Smith	Sunderland	12.2.27	1927		12				LB	Newport Co.	22.6.28	Reading
Frederick Smith	West Sleekburn 15.12.42	5.5.70	1970–3		83	1	13		RB	Burnley	–.9.74	Halifax
George Smith	Newcastle 7.10.45	–.5.67	1967–9		64	3	9		RH	Barrow	22.1.69	Middlesbrough
Jack W. Smith	Whitburn	30.12.27	1927–35	E	260	6	29	8	IR	South Shields	–.–.35	Bournemouth
Paul Smith	Bath	–.6.73	1974		(1)				Mid	Man. City	5.4.75	
Roy Smith	India 19.3.36	–.1.62	1962–3		9	1	2	2	IL	Hereford	16.1.65	Retired
William Smith	Whitburn	–.6.28	1928–37		311	2	24		LB	South Shields	19.7.38	Stockport
Brian Snowdon	Bishop Auckland 1.1.35	7.10.59	1959–64		114		15		CH	Blackpool	–.10.65	Millwall
William J. Spence	Hartlepool 10.1.26	–.3.47	1949–51		19				CH		–.12.51	Q.P.R.
James Standen	Edmonton 30.5.35	2.7.70	1970–2		13				Goal	Millwall	6.5.72	
Gary Stanley	Burton 4.3.54	12.1.84	1984–		11(1)				Mid	Swansea		
Alec Stenhouse	Stirling 1.1.33	21.2.57	1957–8		4	1			OR	Dundee Utd.	–.11.58	Southend
James W. Stephen	Fettercairn 23.8.22	–.11.49	1949–55	S	99		3		FB	Bradford P.A.		
Alan Stephenson	Cheshunt 26.9.44	4.5.72	1972–5		98	1	8		CH	Fulham	–.5.75	South Africa
Andrew C. Stewart	Letchworth 29.10.56	–.7.74	1974–6		14(5)	1	1		F	Pompey apprentice	–.4.76	
Robert W. Stokes	Portsmouth 30.1.51	–.8.77	1977–8		23(1)	2	5	1	F	Southampton	–.3.78	Contract cancelled
James Storrie	Kirkintilloch 31.3.40	–.12.69	1969–72		43	12	5	1	CF	Rotherham	–.3.72	Aldershot
Alfred H. Strange	Marehay 1900	–.12.22	1922–5	E	23	16	1		CF	Ripley	26.11.25	Port Vale
Frank Stringfellow	Sutton	Sum. 1911	1920–2		60	25	3	2	IR	Sheff. Wed.	24.5.22	Hearts
George Strong	Morpeth 7.6.16	16.3.35	1935–8		59		3		Goal	Chesterfield	20.8.38	Gillingham
Arthur 'Archie' Styles	Liverpool 3.9.49	–.7.79	1979–80		28				LB	Peterborough	4.3.82	
Colin Sullivan	Saltash 24.6.51	22.2.82	1982–		94		7		LB	Hereford		
Roy Summersby	Lambeth 19.3.35	–.5.63	1963–5		12	1			IR	C. Palace	–.4.65	
John Surtees	Percy Main 1911	25.6.32	1932–3		1				IR	Middlesbrough	–.–.33	Huddersfield
John Scot Symon	Errol 9.5.11	24.8.35	1935–8		68	6	2		LH	Dundee	30.8.38	Rangers
Michael P. Tait	Wallsend 30.9.56	–.6.80	1980–		150(3)	26	20(2)	1	For/Def	Hull		
Anthony Taylor	Glasgow 6.9.46	–.2.78	1978		17				LB	Bristol Rovers	–.12.78	Northampton
David Taylor	Rochester 17.9.40	3.5.59	1959–60		2				IR	Gillingham	23.1.60	
Eden Taylor	Sheffield	Sum. 1938	1938–9		4	1			IF	Bournemouth	11.5.39	
David Thackeray	Hamilton	Sum. 1928	1928–36		278	9	28	1	LH	Motherwell	1.8.36	Retired injured
David Thomas	Kirkby 5.10.50	2.6.82	1982–	E	21(6)		1(1)		Wing	Middlesbrough		
Rees Thomas	Aberdare 3.1.34	22.7.59	1959–61		32		1		FB	Bournemouth	29.6.61	Aldershot
Ernest Thompson	Rotherham	Sum. 1913	1920–1		36	1	3		I/OR	South Shields	28.5.21	Sheff Wed.
William G. Thompson	Glasgow 10.8.21	19.3.46	1948–53		40	2	1		HB	Carnoustie	28.1.53	Bournemouth
Ronald Tilsed	Weymouth 6.8.52	8.3.73	1973–4		14		1		Goal	Arsenal	28.5.74	Hereford
Ronald Tindall	Streatham 23.9.35	14.9.64	1964–70		159(2)	7	19	2	IF	Reading	–.–.70	Becomes manager
Kenneth Todd	Butterknowle 24.8.57	5.10.79	1979–80		1(2)	1			F	Port Vale	19.3.82	Basingstoke

Players Name	Birthplace and Date	Date Signed	Years Played	Int. Player	League Appearances	Goals	Cup Appearances	Goals	Position	Previous Club	Left Pompey	Club Joined
F. Toner		−.−.25	1925–6		3				OL		1.5.26	To U.S.A.
Michael J. Travers	Blackwater 23.6.42	−.1.67	1967–71		74(11)	5	3		F	Reading	−.7.72	Aldershot
Michael Trebilcock	Gunnislake 29.11.44	31.1.68	1968–72		100(9)	32	12	4	F	Everton	29.6.72	Torquay
J. Tumelty	Shotts	21.7.22	1922–3		5		2		HB	Royal Navy		
Brian A. Turner	East Ham 31.7.49	27.5.69	1969–70	NZ	3(1)				RH	Chelsea	2.1.70	Brentford
Joseph Turner	Leyland 1894	4.1.−	1920–2		29	2	1		HB	Preston	5.10.22	
Norman Uprichard	Moyraverty 20.4.28	8.11.52	1952–9	NI	182		8		Goal	Swindon	7.7.59	Southend
Charles J. Vaughan	Sutton 23.4.21	16.3.53	1953–4	E Am	27	14	1	2	CF	Charlton	−.−.54	Bexleyheath
Keith Brian Viney	Portsmouth 26.10.57	−.10.75	1975–82		160(6)	3	27		LB	Pompey apprentice	17.6.82	Exeter
Malcolm Waldron	Emsworth 6.9.56	6.3.84	1984–		12				Def	Burnley		
G. Harold Walker	Ayrgarth 20.5.16	5.3.38	1938–47		49		6		Goal	Darlington	−.4.47	Notts. For.
David Watson	Cowie	23.12.20	1920–30		275	63	20	2	IF	Bo'ness	7.5.30	
Neil Webb	Reading 30.7.63	11.6.82	1982–		82	18	9	2	OR	Reading		
Derick K. Weddle	Newcastle 27.12.35	8.11.56	1956–9		24	8	4	2	CF	Sunderland	10.7.59	Wisbech Town
John Weddle	Fatfield	30.9.27	1927–38		369	173	28	13	CF	Fatfield Albion	27.8.38	Blackburn
E.C. 'Jessie' Weekes	Wilton	−.8.32	1932–3		1		1		Goal	Salisbury (Am)	15.5.35	Clapton O.
Roderick Ernest Welsh	Newcastle 1912	4.11.32	1932–3		1				LB	Durham City	7.5.35	Port Vale
Paul F. Went	Bromley by Bow 12.10.49	−.12.73	1973–6		92	5	17	1	CH	Fulham	8.10.76	Cardiff
Guy Wharton	Broomhill 5.12.16	9.11.37	1937–48		91	4	10	1	LH	Wolverhampton W.	−.7.48	Darlington
James White	Parkstone 13.6.42	15.6.59	1959–62		33	6	4	1	CF	Bournemouth	−.6.63	Gillingham
Robert J. Widdowson	Loughborough 12.9.41	8.11.69	1969		4				Goal	York City	2.12.69	York City
Leonard Williams	Cefnybedd	−.8.33	1933–4		1				OR	Bournemouth	9.7.34	Aldershot
William T. Williams	Esher 23.8.42	−.6.60	1960–1		3				FB		−.7.61	Q.P.R.
William Williamson	Cowdenbeath	3.10.24	1924–5		12	3	1		CF/IL	Hearts	27.11.25	Hamilton
Alex Wilson	Buckie 29.10.33	3.11.50	1951–67	S	349(4)	4	24	1	FB	Buckie Rovers	20.5.67	
John Robert Wilson	Blyth	23.2.21	1921–3		61		2		RH	Bedlington Utd.	−.−.23	
William Wilson	Seaton Delaval 10.7.46	21.1.72	1972–9		187(6)	5	21(7)	1	FB/HB	Blackburn	28.4.79	Retired
Paul Wimbleton	Portsmouth	20.2.82	1982–		5(5)				Mid	Pompey apprentice		
Paul Wood	Middlesbrough	6.5.81	1983–		7(1)	1			For	Guisborough B.C.		
Frederick Worrall	Warrington 8.9.10	31.10.31	1931–9	E	309	65	26	6	OR	Oldham	6.3.46	Stockport
Brian Yeo	Worthing 12.4.44	−.5.61	1962–3				2		F		−.7.63	Gillingham
Jasper H. Yeuell	Bilston 23.3.25	24.8.46	1946–52		31		5		FB	W.B.A. (Am)	−.8.52	Barnsley
Thomas F. Youlden	London 8.7.49	26.4.68	1969–72		82(8)	1	4(3)		FB	Arsenal	14.7.72	Reading
Archibald Young	Paisley	−.12.34	1937–8		2				CH	Clydebank	11.6.38	Notts Co.
B.A. Youtman		6.3.20	1920–1		1				OL	Thornycrofts	Sum.21	

Appendix 2

Appearances and Goals for Second World War years 26/8/39 – 4/5/46 (inclusive of the three games before suspension of League programme)

Abbreviations used:
E   = England
S   = Scotland
W   = Wales
NI   = Northern Ireland
RI   = Republic of Ireland (Eire)
(W/t) = War time

Players Name	International Player	League Appearances	League Goals	Cup Appearances	Cup Goals	Club loaned from (L) or Club signed from (S)
Jock Anderson		85	25	9	2	
James Allen	E	7	—	—	—	Aston Villa(L)
Allport		—	—	1	—	
John Aston	E	4	1	—	—	Manchester Utd.(L)
Arnold		1	—	—	—	Wolverhampton W.(L)
Arthur Ashmore		1	—	—	—	Worcester City(S)
Herbert Barlow		172	87	26	12	
William Bagley		34	9	—	—	
Thomas Bushby		66	10	11	2	
Bryan		2	—	—	—	
Briggs		1	—	—	—	Wrexham(L)
J. Barnes		1	—	—	—	
Peter Buchanan	E	21	3	7	—	Chelsea(L)
Andrew Black	S	44	57	8	9	Hearts(L)
Richard Burke		3	—	—	—	Blackpool(L)
Blakeney		1	1	—	—	Arsenal(L)
George Bullock		27	20	12	6	Barnsley(L)
W. Brown		1	—	—	—	Queens Park(L)
Biggs		—	—	6	1	Aberdeen(L)
Victor Buckingham		14	7	3	—	Tottenham H.(L)
S. Black		3	—	—	—	Third Lanark(L)
J. Black		3	—	2	1	Third Lanark(L)
Kenneth Bell		11	—	—	—	
John Bowe		7	—	—	—	
Ernest Butler		1	—	—	—	
Wally Barnes	W	1	—	—	—	
Ronald Candy		5	1	—	—	
R. Cadnam		1	—	—	—	
Cross		3	—	—	—	
J. Colkliffe		1	—	—	—	Reading(L)
Cavell		2	2	—	—	
Harold Court		2	3	—	—	Cardiff(L)
Crowther		1	—	—	—	
Reginald Cumner		9	1	—	—	Arsenal(L)
Cook		1	1	—	—	St. Johnstone(L)
Stanley Clements		2	—	—	—	Southampton(L)
John Crossley		7	—	2	—	Cliftonville(S)
Chisholm		1	—	—	—	
John Davie		4	2	—	—	Brighton(L)
James Dickinson	E	26	—	5	—	
Dent		1	—	—	—	
Ian Drummond		2	—	—	—	
Edward Drake	E	1	4	—	—	Arsenal(L)
Dempsey		1	—	—	—	Southampton(L)
Emery		22	8	3	3	
Albert Emptage		14	1	4	1	Manchester City(L)
Else		1	—	—	—	
Frederick Evans		25	14	1	3	
Stanley Edwards		2	—	—	—	
Reginald Flewin	E(W/t)	173	—	32	—	
Ferguson		7	—	—	—	Motherwell(L)
Douglas Flack		1	—	2	—	Fulham(L)
Joseph Fagan		1	—	—	—	Manchester City(L)
James Forrester		4	—	—	—	
Jack Froggatt	E	20	6	1	—	
Jack Foxton		19	—	—	—	
Harold Ferrier		11	—	—	—	
James Guthrie		187	16	33	1	
Gilchrist		1	—	—	—	St. Bernards(L)
Gardener		7	2	2	3	
R.A. Grace		1	—	—	—	
James Griffiths		33	16	9	5	
Frederick Gregory		2	—	1	—	
Gardiner		1	—	—	—	
Gunn		1	1	—	—	
Bernard Grant		—	—	1	—	Third Lanark(L)
Goodwin		1	—	—	—	Worcester City(L)
Harris		2	1	—	—	Southampton(L)
Thomas Hassell		1	—	—	—	Southampton(L)
Frank Hutchinson		3	1	—	—	
Henry Higgins		2	—	—	—	
Archibald Hart		4	—	—	—	Third Lanark(L)
Harold Hooper		3	—	—	—	Sheffield Utd.(L)
Harrigan		1	—	—	—	Scotland(L)
Peter Harris	E	54	21	7	3	
George Hudson		5	—	—	—	
Reginald Halton		3	—	2	1	Bury(L)
Raymond Haddington		3	3	—	—	Bradford(L)
John Hopkins		4	—	—	—	
Ronald Humpston		1	—	—	—	
Jackie Henderson	S	1	—	—	—	Third Lanark(L)
John Jackson	S	1	—	—	—	Chelsea(L)
Ernest Jones		1	—	—	—	
Jamieson		1	—	—	—	
Jefferies		5	—	—	—	Sheffield Utd.(L)
King		1	—	—	—	Bournemouth(L)
Albert Kerr		11	4	—	—	Aston Villa(L)
William Layton		1	—	—	—	Reading(L)
Lovery		1	—	—	—	
L. Littlewood		4	—	—	—	

Players Name	International Player	League Appearances	League Goals	Cup Appearances	Cup Goals	Club loaned from (L) or Club signed from (S)
Lacey		3	—	—	—	Sheffield Wed.(L)
Leney		—	—	1	—	Southampton(L)
Langley		—	—	1	—	Bournemouth(L)
D.J. Lucas		—	—	1	1	
Lonnon		1	—	—	—	Southampton(L)
Lewis Morgan		199	—	30	—	
Alfred Miller		7	3	—	—	Plymouth(L)
James Mason	S	5	3	2	—	Third Lanark(L)
Daniel Mills		12	—	1	—	
William Moffatt		1	—	—	—	
Moores		18	6	3	6	Royal Marines(L)
John R. Martin		1	—	—	—	Aston Villa(L)
Martin		4	3	—	—	Clyde(L)
Martin		3	—	—	—	Brighton(L)
Frank Mitchell	E	1	—	1	—	Birmingham(L)
Alec Massie	S	6	1	—	—	Hearts(L)
James Mackie		1	—	—	—	
Frederick Monk		2	1	—	—	Aldershot(L)
J. Morby		1	—	—	—	Aston Villa(L)
James McAlinden	NI/RI	3	—	—	—	
James McIntosh		11	4	1	3	Preston(L)
H.F. McIntosh		7	6	—	—	Queens Park(L)
T.R. McKillop	S	3	—	—	—	Glasgow Rangers(L)
McLeod		18	2	—	—	Motherwell(L)
McArdle		3	2	—	—	Crewe(L)
Offord		—	—	1	—	Bradford(L)
Clifford Parker		204	55	30	8	
Edward Platt		1	—	—	—	Arsenal(L)
Pond		1	—	—	—	Carlisle(L)
William Pointon		3	2	6	3	Port Vale(L)
Pinkerton		1	—	—	—	Falkirk(L)
Leonard Phillips	E	10	—	—	—	
E. Paterson		3	2	—	—	
Edward Quigley		2	3	—	—	Bury(L)
William Rochford		176	4	30	—	
Robert Royston		2	—	—	—	Plymouth(L)
Thomas Rowe		6	—	—	—	
Ranner		1	—	—	—	Royal Marines(L)
Philip Rookes		13	—	5	—	
George Ross		2	—	—	—	Dundee Utd(L)
Robertson		7	—	—	—	Chester(L)
S. Richards		1	—	—	—	
Duggie Reid		11	5	—	—	
Abraham Smith		27	—	—	—	
George Summerbee		127	—	22	—	Preston(L)
Saunders		3	1	—	—	Brentford(L)
Charles Smith		2	—	—	—	
John Slater		2	—	—	—	Rochdale(L)
Sykes		1	—	—	—	
George Swindin		1	—	—	—	Arsenal(L)
Scrimshaw		1	—	—	—	Middlesbrough(L)
Speak		—	—	1	—	Bolton(L)
Douglas Sears		6	3	5	—	Grimsby(L)
Storey		3	1	1	—	Gateshead(L)
Stubbings		2	—	—	—	
Saunders		1	—	—	—	
Speed		1	—	—	—	
Short		1	—	—	—	
Salter		1	—	—	—	Southampton(L)
Alex Stott		6	4	1	—	
James Scoular	S	20	—	1	—	
Tann		7	—	—	—	Charlton(L)
James G. Taylor		1	—	—	—	Fulham(L)
George Tweedy		1	—	—	—	Grimsby(L)
Reginald Tomlinson		1	2	—	—	Southampton(L)
Robert Thomas		2	3	3	—	Brentford(L)
G. Harold Walker		210	—	32	—	
Frederick Worrall	E	11	3	4	1	
Guy Wharton		16	—	7	—	
Wattie		1	—	—	—	Forfar(L)
Wilkinson		1	1	—	—	Charlton(L)
G. Wilbert		1	—	—	—	Tottenham H.(L)
Wilkes		22	29	2	—	W.B.A.(L)
Walters		1	—	—	—	Watford(L)
George Wilkins		2	—	—	—	Brentford(L)
Winch		3	—	—	—	Basingstoke(L)
Thomas Ward		34	19	1	—	Sheffield Wed.(L)
Steven Walker		1	—	—	—	Sheffield Utd.(L)
D. Westland		3	—	—	—	Stoke(L)
R. Wilson		1	—	—	—	C. Palace(L)
Charles Whitchurch		17	4	2	—	
Charles Wayman		7	6	—	—	Newcastle(L)

Pompey's Cricketers

P.J.W. Atyeo (Wiltshire) 1950–1
H.M. Barnard (Hampshire) 1952–66
J.G. Duffield (Sussex) 1938–47
C.B. Fry (Hampshire/Sussex/England) 1892–1911
S.S. Harris (Surrey/Gloucestershire/Sussex) 1900–06
A.E. Knight (Hampshire) 1913–23
A. Mounteney (Leicestershire) 1911–24
J.S. Symon (Perthshire/Hampshire) 1935–8
J.A. Standen (Worcestershire/Minor Counties) 1965–72
R.A. Tindall (Surrey) 1956–66
G.F. Wheldon (Worcestershire/Carmarthenshire) 1899–1910